Di Guoyong

on

Xingyiquan

邸国勇

形意拳械精解

Available from tgl books
Jiang Rongqiao's Baguazhang
Li Tianji's The Skill of Xingyiquan
Yan Dehua's Bagua Applications
Di Guoyong on Xingyiquan: Volume I, Foundations
Di Guoyong on Xingyiquan: Volume II, Forms and Ideas
Di Guoyong on Xingyiquan: Volume III, Weapons
A Shadow on Fallen Blossoms
Falk's Dictionary of Chinese Martial Arts
Beijing Bittersweet
Shadowboxing in Shanghai

tgl books   www.thewushucentre.ca

Di Guoyong
on
Xingyiquan

The 2020 Set Hard Cover Edition

邸国勇
形意拳械精解
2020 年修订版

translated and edited

by Andrea Mary Falk

霍安娣翻译，主板

Library and Archives Canada Cataloguing in Publication of first editions

Di, Guoyong, 1948- . Di Guoyong on Xingyiquan / translated and edited by Andrea Falk. Includes some text in Chinese. Translation of Xingyiquanxie Jingjie originally published by The People's Publishing House of Sports.

Complete contents: v.1 Five element foundation - - v.2. Form and Theory - - v.3. Weapon and partner play. ISBN 978-0-9687517-6-3 (v.1) ISBN 978-0-9687517-7-0 (v.2) ISBN 978-0-9687517-8-7 (v.3).

1. Hand-to-hand fighting, Oriental. I. Falk, Andrea, 1954- II. Title. III. Title: On xingyiquan.

G V 1 1 1 2 .D 5 2 1 3   2 0 0 5 7 9 6 .8 1 5 '5   C 2 0 0 5 - 9 1 0 9 3 8 - 8

Combination of the three volume soft cover set: Volume I Foundations. Volume II Forms and Ideas. Volume III Weapons.

Translated and edited by Andrea Falk in Beijing, China, and Morin-Heights, QC, Canada.

With thanks for the assistance of Di Guoyong, Beijing, China.

2020 Set edition by Andrea Falk, 2021, Morin-Heights, QC, Canada.

The techniques described in this book are performed by experienced martial artists. The author, translator, and publishers are not responsible for any injury that may occur while trying out these techniques. Please do not apply these techniques on anyone without their consent and cooperation.

TABLE OF CONTENTS

ABOUT THE AUTHOR

Di Guoyong was born in Hebei province in 1948 and moved to Beijing in 1960. He began his wushu life in 1963 with the well-known Zhao Zhong, apprenticing in Shaolinquan and Xingyiquan to improve his poor health. Later he also apprenticed to Wu Binlou to learn Chuojiao Fanzi, and Li Ziming to learn Liang style Baguazhang. His home in Beijing has given him access to the best martial artists throughout his life, until he has become one of those men that he emulated as a youth. He glows with the health and energy that training in the internal martial arts can bring.

Di Guoyong's main emphasis has for years been Xingyiquan. The work that he does for Xingyiquan sounds like the work of many: founding member, first secretary general, and long-term president of the Beijing Xingyi Quan Research Association; national level one wushu judge; member of the official Xingyi forms development committee; organizer of national and international Xingyi and traditional wushu competitions; Xingyi teacher at Beijing University and other colleges; coach of fighting and forms champions; teacher also of students every morning in the park and of many foreign visitors; author of numerous published articles; presenter of a popular instructional video series; and presenter of an instructional Xingyi series shown on Chinese television. His love for and skill in martial arts, and particularly in Xingyiquan, stands out as a player, teacher, presenter, judge, organizer, researcher, and writer.

Di Guoyong never backs down from any question until he has reached "three levels of why" and this book reflects that attitude. He has combined his open and inquisitive mind with his years of experience to present the reader with a complete resource for training and teaching Xingyi.

Di Guoyong loves the written word and he loves to research every aspect of Xingyi through every means possible, whether modern or traditional. He never ceases to explore any avenue to learn more about martial arts theory and practice. This book represents the result of over forty years of his love, hard work, experience, and examination. It explains the whole of Xingyiquan – the shape and the meaning, the unarmed and the weapons, the practical and the theory, the training and the teaching, with his particular emphasis always on whole body power. He has tried to present the whole picture to the reader, to combine the form – *xing* – and the intent – *yi* – of Xingyiquan.

Andrea Falk 霍安娣

Morin Heights, QC, Canada, June 2005

AUTHOR'S PREFACE TO THE ENGLISH EDITION OF THE SET

I have just received Andrea's email that the English translation of my book is almost done, and that she would like a new preface for this edition. The Five Element Foundation is the first volume of a three-volume translation of my original two-volume book "Analysis of Xingyi fist and weapons." Due to the size of the original book, Andrea suggested that the English version come out in three volumes, separating the five element foundation techniques, the empty hand forms, and the weapons, to allow the English books to come out more quickly and reasonably priced, which I agreed was a good idea.

Andrea has trained with me since around the year 2000. From that time she has visited Beijing every year to study Xingyi with me and I have come to know her well. She was a bike racer as a youth, and came to the martial arts as a young adult in the 1970s. She was the first foreigner accepted by the Chinese National Wushu Association in the advanced degree program at the Beijing Institute of Sport. During a six-year relationship with the Institute she studied many wushu styles and weapons. She also was the first foreign woman to train sparring here. Andrea had studied Chinese before coming to China, and her language skills developed considerably during her years in Beijing studying wushu. After her return to Canada she continued to teach, research, and translate to spread Chinese wushu. She not only works continuously to popularize wushu, but she herself continues to train and examine what she has learned.

During the time that she has trained Xingyi with me I have found that, with her solidly built foundation in wushu, she learns quickly and knows how to train hard. She has an intuitive and intelligent grasp of any material. Her high level of Chinese ensures that we have no communication problems. Indeed, I have learned many things from her so that, as they say 'teacher and student improve together.'

Andrea is a most appropriate person to translate Chinese wushu into English. Firstly, her mother tongue is English. Secondly, she has studied, trained, taught, and researched wushu for many years, and understands the approaches of both student and teacher. Thirdly, her Chinese is excellent, especially the specialized vocabulary of wushu. My foreign students tell me that with these three strengths her translations are the best!

Every specialty has its own vocabulary. People outside the wushu circle cannot fully understand its vocabulary. People without training in wushu, without firsthand experience in performance, cannot properly understand and express this knowledge in words. People who do not understand Chinese culture cannot properly translate the theoretical aspects of wushu. To translate wushu writings, you need to understand the movements, the power, the applications, the theories, and the terminology, and be able to transfer this knowledge to English speakers. It is not an easy matter to do, but I believe that Andrea is able to do it, and furthermore, that she does it very well.

As this volume on the five element techniques goes to print, I would like to thank Andrea again for the work that she does on the translations. If readers come to understand and enjoy Xingyi more from reading this volume, and if it encourages them to delve deeper into Xingyi, then this is great for Xingyi, and great for Chinese wushu. I invite readers with questions from the book to simply contact me. I'll do my best to answer your questions. My email is guoyong1948@hotmail.com.

Xingyi is a simple, powerful, and functional style. It completely combines the mind and the body. First you need to learn the movements. Once you are comfortable with them you need to change the emphasis to the intention behind the action. "The quality of your intent determines the quality of your power" is something that I emphasize throughout the book. Every individual has his or her own background, social history, educational level, habits and hobbies that make up their mental environment. You must find your own concepts that suit your national characteristics, customs and languages, to better accept, enjoy, and train the intent behind Xingyi.

The five element techniques are the "mother fists of Xingyi." They are the foundation of the foundation. But you must first "set the posts" for the foundation with *santishi* post standing. This is the first step in training. The quality of your post standing will directly determine the quality of your five element techniques. Xingyi emphasizes the post standing to an extraordinary degree – the classics say, "If you want to learn Xingyi you must stand for three years." In former times you were not allowed to learn the five elements before you had done three to five years of post standing. Times have changed and this is no longer a requirement, but you should remember the importance of its lesson. Every time you train, you must absolutely start each session with post standing.

Xingyi is particularly suited to Westerners. Westerners tend to be big, strong, relatively heavy, and tend to like straightforward movements. Xingyi is a simple, practical style with no wasted movement. It moves like a tank in a practical, straightforward, fearless way. Heavier players look like heavy tanks, while lighter players look like light tanks. I think if Westerners are introduced to Xingyi that they will love it, and that they will take to it and reach a high level of skill.

"The more something is of the people the more it is international." Chinese wushu is like a flowing stream, its source is in China but it belongs to the world. I hope that wushu can bring health to the people of the world, and I hope that Xingyi can help to unite the many peoples of the world.

Di Guoyong 邸国勇

Beijing, China, June 28, 2005

AUTHOR'S PREFACE TO THE CHINESE ORIGINAL OF THE SET

I have tried to present in this book the whole contents of Xingyiquan: history, post standing, the five foundation techniques, the twelve animals, many traditional techniques and forms, and weapons. In my presentation of the traditional forms I have held completely to traditional practices. I have, however, added my own understanding of power and meaning gained over years of training and teaching. I have also included some writings based on my experience and research. I have tried to present more than just how to do the movements, and have described the origins and meanings of the techniques and explained the rhythm, breathing, and whole body power within them. Xingyiquan is characterized by whole body power, and I have tried to describe how to achieve this for each technique through detailed analysis and explanation.

Xingyiquan is not an imitative style, but combines the shape and structure of the images available to us in the world with the power available within the human body and mind. Nowadays in martial arts there is great emphasis on the 'form' and less on the 'meaning.' What type of meaning should we bring to practice, what type of meaning should we use to direct our training? We cannot leave out the meaning in Xingyiquan, because the definition of the style itself is form [*xing*] and meaning [*yi*] together. The ideas that we bring to our practice dictate the power [*jin*] that we will develop. The meaningful concepts that we bring to practice dictate the deep skill [*gongfu*] that we will attain.

The process of writing this book has been one of learning and improving for me, and has helped to deepen my understanding of Xingyiquan. Although the book has now been published I do not feel a lightening of my burden. The development of wushu gives us a great responsibility. The theoretical examination of Xingyi in particular falls far behind our need for knowledge if we wish it to develop further. I heartily wish that fellow martial artists, masters, and readers raise questions and opinions to help me improve and to help Xingyi develop.

There are many people involved in the writing of this book that I would like to thank. The editor of the Chinese edition, Zhao Xinhua, for his painstaking help. Liu Mingliang and Yang Shudong, for the many, many photographs that they took. My martial friend Kang Gewu, and former president of the national wushu association Xu Cai, for their prefaces to the original edition, which they took time out of their busy schedules to write.

Di Guoyong 邸国勇

Beijing, China, 2003

TRANSLATOR'S PREFACE TO THE BOOK SET

I wanted to translate this series of books because it fills in many gaps left by current books on Xingyi available in English. I have, since 2000, come to know Di Guoyong and his Xingyi well enough that I felt well qualified to translate his work with full understanding. The time between the original publication and the translation publication of the first volume was less than two years, and I hope to bring out the following two volumes a year at a time.

Translating this book was a new experience for me, marking the first time that the author was available to help me solve problems. This has been an exciting and fun collaborative writer-translator teacher-student team effort. The first time we met we were finishing each other's sentences, and have continued this way ever since. I have occasionally added things that the author said in class but did not write in the book, without using the device of translator's notes. These additions are what I have seen or heard Di Guoyong do or say while I trained with him or acted as interpreter in his classes.

This English edition is actually an improvement over the original, with all the mistakes taken out and a few things added. I have reorganized and edited some of the original text in a way that is (I hope) more useful to the reader. Most especially I made the introduction from comments made throughout the original, created the chapter on teaching to reduce repetition of comments made throughout the original, and considerably reworked the Appendix on the internal organs and added diagrams to it. I also made the glossary as is usual in my translations.

I would like to thank:

The author, Di Guoyong, for his knowledge of and enthusiasm for wushu, for his patient teaching, and for his help with the translation and easy agreement to my editing.

His daughter, Di Hua, for all her efforts with emailing.

My parents, William Andre and Mary Elliott Falk, for their painstaking proofreading. My students, Haim Behar and James Saper, for their knowledgeable help with Appendix I.

And, always, Xia Bohua and Men Huifeng, for teaching me Xingyiquan way back when.

Please forgive the odd placement of some of the Chinese characters; this is a quirk of the whacked-out computer program I work with. Any other mistakes in the book are mine alone.

Andrea Falk 霍安娣

Victoria, B.C., Canada, July 2005

TRANSLATOR'S PREFACE TO VOLUME II OF THE ENGLISH SET

Volume two of Di Guoyong's three volume translated set contains almost all of the further empty hand techniques and forms from his original two volume set in Chinese. I hope that it is a helpful reference material to students and teachers of Xingyiquan.

I am glad to finally get Volume two done, and thank you for your patience. It took a bit longer to complete than planned because of a delay in getting the photos and the amount of work involved in getting over six hundred photos print ready. For this I apologize. I hope that you do not mind the photos in sweatsuit intermingled with those in the proper uniform. Aside from having no real choice, I feel they give a touch of the reality of playing in the parking lot with Di Guoyong. I felt that these additional photos, mostly for views from the front, improved the book enough to make up for the differences in the photo styles.

I have added more words to the glossary from Volume one and added a movement name list. I have also put it in English order so that it can be used as a companion to the glossary in Volume one.

I would like to thank:

The author, Di Guoyong, for his knowledge of and enthusiasm for Xingyiquan, for his patient teaching, and for his help with the translation and easy agreement to my editing.

My parents, William Andre and Mary Elliott Falk, for their painstaking proofreading yet again.

And, always, Xia Bohua and Men Huifeng, for teaching me Xingyiquan way back when.

I have tried hard to get everything right, but if you find any mistakes they are mine alone.

Andrea Falk 霍安娣

Morin-Heights, Canada, April 2007

In the second edition of volume II, reducing the font size reduced the page count, so I was able to include *Zashichui*, the Mixture of Moves Form. Di Guoyong was quite disappointed that I had not translated it orginally, so I am most happy to oblige him in this second edition. The reasons that I had not originally put *Zashichui* in the book were book size issues and that I had not learned it directly from him.

People have asked about the extra photos, taken in training clothes, whether they were to make up for mistakes or what. They are fill in photos that we took to clarify the actions from another angle, or to add in-between moves. I have the original rolls of film, and there are no mistakes in any of the postures of the hundreds and hundreds of photos taken for the three volume set. The photos are always a joy to look at and work with, even reformating them yet again for this edition.

Andrea Falk 霍安娣

Québec, Canada, May 2019

TRANSLATOR'S PREFACE TO VOLUME III OF THE ENGLISH SET

Volume III of Di Guoyong's three volume translated set (from a two volume original) contains the weapons and the advanced partner form *anshenpao.* I am pleased to have completed this series. Relieved is perhaps more the word, but I am having difficulty coming up with words after this long translation process. I am particularly pleased to have finished the final volume on time to present it at master Di's sixtieth birthday celebration in September 2008.

The font size is smaller and the layout more compact in this third volume to keep the size of the book down. Four weapons, each with five elements, a form, and larger photos, would have made this volume too large to be practical if I had kept the same format as Volumes One and Two. Please understand and forgive the well packed layout.

I took supplemental photos again for this volume to get the front views of the basic postures. The best part of that was when Di Guoyong arrived at our training space with a spear, a staff, a sword and a sabre strapped on his bike and his silk uniform stuffed in the basket.

Some may wonder about the use of the word 'play' in the title. The real work of any style is in the basics and the hand techniques. Once you have mastered the empty hand techniques the ability to do the weapons and partner play is almost instinctive. You still need to train hard to get them right, but they are just too much fun to be 'work.'

The glossary in this volume is specific to the weapons. Volumes one, two, and three together contain a pretty comprehensive overall dictionary for Xingyi.

After hours and hours of photoshopping, I know master Di's postures pixel by pixel, and was constantly amazed how perfect was each and every posture in hundreds and hundreds of photos. I worked from the roll of negatives, so know that he did not take backup photos, it was all one pose – one shot. His descriptions, too, are always clear, concise, and helpful in a practical way, much as is his teaching in person.

The photos in this series are proof of the glowing health and fitness that a life of martial arts training can bring you. Photos and descriptions alone, however, do not give the full flavour of the style or the person. I recommend that you go to Beijing and meet Di Guoyong to get the full impact (no pun intended) of his Xingyi.

I hope that this series contributes to the understanding of Xingyi in the English reading population, and that this population grows in number as martial artists discover the clarity of this particular martial art.

I would like to thank:

The author, Di Guoyong, for his knowledge of and enthusiasm for Xingyi, for his patient teaching, for his help with the translation, and easy agreement to my editing. My parents, William Andre and Mary Elliott Falk, for their painstaking proofreading. And, always, Xia Bohua and Men Huifeng, for teaching me Xingyiquan way back when.

Any mistakes in the book are mine alone.

Andrea Falk 霍安娣

Quebec QC, Canada, June 2008

EDITOR'S PREFACE TO THE 2020 SET EDITION

All three books needed to be redone to enable print-to-order sales, but the original files of the books were lost. As I set up the books again, I went through them to standardise the formatting to make them a more cohesive set. The main changes I made were to move things around. This was in order to even out the sizes of the books as much as possible, because the printer had problems making books of widely different thickness come out with the same look. I tried to do the readjustment in accordance with learning and teaching progressions. I moved the twelve animals to Volume I, to include them as basic techniques to Xingyiquan. I put all the theoretical and teaching discussions, the Protect the Body partner form, and the glossaries to Volume II, making it the next level – learning empty hand forms, more applications, and more thinking about things. Volume III is now specific to the weapons.

I corrected some typographical errors, adjusted some translation, and made some editorial changes while I was doing this work. I had to work on the photos yet again, and one yet again impressed with Di Guoyong's perfection and ease in all the movements and postures. If you already have the books, the original translation was solid, you do not need to buy the new set. This is the final edition of the set, and I really hope there are no remaining errors.

Andrea Falk 霍安娣

Morin-Heights, QC, Canada, January 2021

EDITOR'S PREFACE TO TGL BOOKS 20th ANNIVERSARY HARD COVER EDITIONS

At this 20th anniversary of the establishment of tgl books, I have finally completed the reworking of all the books to be available for print to order. To celebrate, I have made hard cover copies of all the translations – the Li Tianji, Jiang Rongqiao, and Yan Dehua, as well as this set. In setting up the hard cover editions, I of course made a few minor changes, but the translations are all in their final state now. If there are any remaining mistakes, that is just too bad.

To make the hard cover copy of the Di Guoyong books into one volume, I had to adjust the formatting, especially the odd spaces that Word had added, but had already adjusted the translation for the 2020 set edition.

Andrea Falk 霍安娣

Québec, QC, Canada, June 2021

xviii

BACKGROUND

HISTORICAL ORIGINS OF XINGYIQUAN

Tradition has it that Xingyiquan originated with General Yue Fei (1103 - 1142) of the Song Dynasty. Recent research has questioned the truth of this tradition. General Yue Fei is a national hero because of his spirit, character, and nationalism, so it is possible that practitioners of Xingyiquan borrowed his name to gain more recognition for the style.

In recent years scholars have published much research into the origins of Xingyiquan. There are some differences of opinion, but the general consensus is that the Xingyiquan system grew out of Xinyi Liuhequan. That is, that Xingyiquan originated with Li Luoneng (c. 1808-1890) of Hebei province, on the foundation of Xinyi Liuhequan that originated with Ji Longfeng (1602-1680, also known as Ji Jike). Ji Longfeng taught Cao Jiwu (1662-1722), who taught Dai Longbang (c. 1713-1802), who taught Li Luoneng. This has been confirmed by the research of many scholars, most notably Huang Xin'ge, who spent many years on the topic and methodologically examined a huge number of historical documents. It seems quite certain that Ji Longfeng created Xinyi Liuhequan and Li Luoneng in turn created Xingyiquan.

The three main branches of Xingyiquan – 'three streams from the same source' – are commonly categorized by region: Shanxi, Hebei, and Henan provinces. The 'source of the streams' is Xinyi Liuhequan. At present, Henan province still refers to the style as Xinyi Liuhequan, and has essentially kept the original characteristics of Xinyi Liuhequan, most notably the chicken step and ten animals. Shanxi and Hebei provinces refer to the style as Xingyiquan and really represent one branch with only regional and stylistic differences, both coming from Li Luoneng.

By the Qianlong reign period of the Qing dynasty [1736-1796], Xinyi Liuhequan was already an established style with its own techniques and theory in Shanxi and Henan provinces. Li Luoneng studied Xinyi Liuhequan with Dai Longbang for ten years. Li Luoneng had trained in other styles and had a strong foundation in martial arts before studying with Dai, so after ten years of diligent analysis and practical experience he achieved a high level of skill in Xinyi Liuhequan. Li accumulated a great depth of theoretical and practical knowledge over several decades of training, and this gave him a level of mastery that allowed him to refine the style and germinate the idea of creating a new style from Xinyi Liuhequan – that is, to create Xingyiquan. By 1856 his style was spreading by this new name.

- In classical Chinese there is only a small distinction between the meaning of the characters *xin* [心 heart, the emotional mind] and *yi* [意 will, the intentional mind]. So the name *xin-yi* was repetitive – heart also partially means will, and will contains heart in its meaning. Li Luoneng changed only one character *xin* [心 heart] to *xing* [形 form, shape, structure] to make the name *xing-yi* [form and intent] more meaningful.

Although there is a difference of only one character in the names *xin-yi* and *xing-yi*, this was a milestone of reform in martial arts history, and a beautiful new 'martial flower' was created in the 'martial arts garden.' Li Luoneng bravely undertook a systematic reorganization of Xinyi Liuhequan. He established a systematic training method with the *santishi* post standing as the basic training, the five element fists as the foundation, and the twelve animals as the advanced techniques. He based his system on a combination of the ancient Chinese traditional theories of *yinyang* and five elements [metal, water, wood, fire, and earth]; the Daoist life enhancing, training, and refining methods and theories; and martial arts internal refinement training. In this way he developed a three-level martial training (obvious, hidden, and transformed; to 'train essence to transform energy,' 'train energy to transform spirit,' and 'train spirit to transform to emptiness'). These aspects were new, and Xingyiquan towered in the martial world with its systematic approach to training and scientific (for its time) theory. Although the theoretical kernel did not depart from Xinyi Liuhequan, it made a qualitative leap to a higher level. Similarly, the later development of Yiquan on the foundation of Xingyiquan created a new style with its own training methods that emphasized will and spirit.

Of course, the establishment and spread of any style, the improvement of theory and enrichment of the technical system take several generations of work. The Xingyiquan now popular throughout China has evolved in theory and technique as the result of the continued innovation of the 2nd, 3rd, 4th, 5th and 6th generations. With further social advances and developments in scientific understanding, future generations will continue to make Xingyiquan's theory and techniques even more systematic and modern and enrich all of mankind.

The author's lineage in Xingyiquan:

Li Luoneng (c. 1808-1890) 李洛能

Liu Qilan (dates unknown) 刘奇兰

Li Cunyi (1847-1921) 李存义

Shang Yunxiang (1863-1937) 尚云祥

Liu Huafu (dates unknown) 刘华甫

Zhao Zhong (1912-1978) 赵忠

Di Guoyong (1948-) 邸国勇

INTRODUCTION TO THE FIVE ELEMENT FISTS

The five element fists – split, drill, drive [or crush], cannon [or pound], and crosscut – are the basic techniques of Xingyiquan. Because they give rise to all other techniques the classic texts called them Xingyi's 'mother fists.'

The five element fists take their name from the Chinese five element theory – a key component of ancient Chinese philosophy. According to this theory, all phenomena of the world are composed of five basic interacting energies/substances – metal, wood, water, fire, and earth. This ancient scientific method explained the myriad phenomena by correlating them to the relationships between the five elements – how they formed and complemented each other, interconnected, and interacted.

[Translator's note: Metal creates water, water creates wood, wood creates fire, fire creates earth, and earth creates metal. Metal controls wood, wood controls earth, earth controls water, water controls fire, and fire controls metal. [1]]

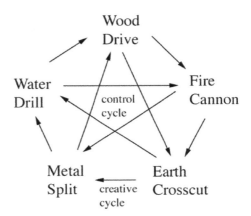

This theory permeated and enormously influenced every aspect of society, so it was natural that the martial artists who developed Xingyiquan should combine the theory of the five elements with martial techniques. Once they simplified their martial techniques and discarded non-functional moves they pared down to five techniques. They then integrated the resulting techniques with their knowledge of body mechanics and Chinese medical theory to explain martial theory and combat methods. They named the resulting techniques the 'five element fists.'

The five element fists are not just five different techniques, five types of applications, and five post standing methods but more importantly, are five methods of generating power and five ways to train the power generation of Xingyi.

• Split (chopping fist) hits mainly forward and down, a vertical downward moving power. [To complete split, the body compresses then lengthens to assist the downward force.]

• Drill (drilling fist) hits mainly forward and up, a vertical upward moving power.

---

[1] Editor's note: There is no explanation or diagram of the cycles in the original book, so I have added this information briefly here. This knowledge is probably assumed. The author does not emphasize the cycles because in actual application different techniques could combine and function equally well. He emphasizes rather the nature of the elements and the techniques, as you will see throughout the book.

[To complete drill, the body settles to assist the upward force.]

- Drive (crushing fist, thrusting punch) hits straight forward, a straight and level power. [To complete drive, the body expands on the straight line.]

- Cannon (pounding fist) drills one hand up to deflect as the other hand punches straight forward, a diagonal power that is effective in all directions. [To complete cannon, the body compresses and expands in a diagonal form.]

- Crosscut (crossing fist) pulls one hand back as the other hand knocks across and forward, a horizontal power that covers all directions from the centre, and it is the key power. [To complete crosscut, the body compresses and expands in a diamond form.]

Each technique hits with whole body power, each shows a complete integrated force. Launched power almost always flows forward, outward, and from the root to the tip of the body. The five techniques form one integrated system, and each one isolates an important power so that you may master it. With mastery you can use the techniques freely and naturally.[2]

---

[2] Editor's note: Note that the author emphasizes action and power flow, which is under-emphasized by some due to Xingyi's tradition of post standing training. For each technique the body needs to generate and balance a distinct power. The body compresses and expands in specific directions to create and launch the power and to counterbalance the forces issued for each technique. This pre-loading is a subtle and functional action – there is no extraneous movement in Xingyi. Compression is often done for the 'defensive' initiation of the action, and release from the compression launches the 'offensive' landing of the action. The author explains this in more detail throughout the book.

POST STANDING

INTRODUCTION TO POST STANDING, *ZHUANG GONG*

Post standing is the foundation of martial arts. Martial arts classics say: "If you desire to learn martial arts you must start with post standing." Xingyiquan is no exception, to the extent that some masters say that to properly learn Xingyi you must stand post for three years.[3] Post standing serves to build a foundation for the skills needed in Xingyiquan and to strengthen the body for its demands.

The first goal is to learn and master the basic body positions for Xingyiquan, such as holding the head up, keeping the chest contained, dropping the shoulders, sinking the elbows, and so on. Once one gains this kinesthetic awareness one gradually develops deep understanding with unremitting practice.

The second goal is to increase leg strength and the strength of the tendons and ligaments surrounding the knees.

The third goal is to master the requirements of all the distinct shapes and body positions. Standing for a long time sets the body into the correct position. The beginner learns to self-correct and gradually builds correct and unchanging positions. This creates a solid foundation for future learning of movements and skills, and the body will naturally hit the correct positions when moving into the stances.

The fourth goal is to regulate the central nervous system and the whole body. Post standing trains the ability to focus and empty the mind of random thoughts, to focus completely on the task at hand. Concentration is on relaxing every part of the body and on regulating the breath. This type of training benefits the circulatory system, improves the metabolism, regulates the qi[4] and blood, and improves the

---

[3] Editor's note: Xingyi is a fast style that hits or throws hard. *Xing* is structure and action – the way the body stands and moves. Standing is done to improve internal power, but also the lines of power, speed and accuracy of the actions, as explained below. Sometimes people underestimate the speed and agility of Xingyi because of its characteristic static training method.

[4] Translator's note: I, along with many translators, have chosen not to translate qi into English. Qi is the energy, life force, or power that circulates throughout the body and keeps us alive. Qi is both energy and the substance that contains this energy, and includes both the life force that you are born with and the life force that you develop through *gong* training. Balanced, flowing, and strong qi causes and shows health, while unbalanced, blocked

immune system, thus aiding one to gain a long healthy life. At the same time, it improves the ability to fight by training a focused combative spirit.

Post standing in Xingyiquan includes primordial post standing, meridian post standing (or *santishi*), descend the dragon post standing, subdue the tiger post standing, and pounding post standing. Each standing method serves a particular goal through different positions and focus. Xingyiquan masters created these post-standing methods through practical training experience over long periods. They are all effective training methods that gradually develop and nourish the deep skills required in Xingyiquan. Each emphasizes a different aspect, but they centre on *santishi*, the kernel of all post training.

The martial arts classics say: "If you train martial arts without training deep skill[5] you will arrive at old age with nothing." Training deep skill means working hard to enhance health and develop fitness in addition to training the basic martial skills. If you train martial arts without making your body strong inside and out, then your body cannot withstand the training. No matter how good your technical abilities they will eventually let you down. This is the integral connection between training and nourishing your body.

TRAINING PROGRESSION FOR POST STANDING

- The first step is to form a correct structure and relaxed body. Each part of the body should be adjusted to the correct position and correct shape. A correct structure is the first requirement, since if the positions are wrong then the *qi* cannot flow. A relaxed body means that every part of the body has released excess tension so it is comfortable and harmonious.

- The second step is to focus the mind. That is to say, discard random thoughts and concentrate until all thoughts blend into one.

- The third step is to breath mindfully. Focus on controlling your breath, so that your breathing pattern becomes slow, even and deep. Mindful breathing permeates to the whole training session. From the opening movement to the closing, at all times the breathing is controlled by the mind. This is one of the most evident characteristics of Xingyiquan.

PRIMORDIAL POST STANDING   húnyuán zhuāng   浑元桩

Introduction to Primordial Post Standing

Primordial refers to the time just before heaven and earth began. [Also translated as mixed essence, 浑元 húnyuán can also be written 混元 hùnyuán.] "The mixed essence means the chaos before things were separated, it is the beginning of the original *qi*." When martial artists brought the term 'primordial' into martial arts terminology they used it in the sense of 'amalgamation of heaven and earth into

---

and/or depleted *qi* causes and shows less than full health.

5 Translator's note: I have translated *gong* as 'deep skill.' *Gong* includes, but it is more than, martial skill, incorporating training to develop basics, fighting, mental and physical health, and strong unimpeded *qi*. Including both internal and external development, *gong* is the result of gradual and continuous training, and its definition implies both the work process and the result of the work.

one,' or 'endless transformations.' Primordial post standing is used to build the foundation for beginners in almost every martial arts style. It serves to enhance the health, strengthen the body, and develop internal power.

The goals during the beginning stage are to collect the spirit and mind, discard random thoughts, regulate breathing, and release excess tension throughout the muscles, tendons, ligaments and interstitial tissues surrounding the joints. The main purpose of primordial post standing at the beginning stage is to clear random thoughts and focus on training. "Cork up your horse's mind, lock up your monkey's heart." The 'horse's mind' means thoughts that shift about like a horse, which never stands still, even when sleeping. The 'monkey's heart' means thoughts that dart around like a monkey, which constantly looks around and grabs at things. Post standing serves to regulate the body and mind to allow the whole body to release its tension. Once the whole body has achieved a relaxed state the *qi* and blood can flow unimpeded and bring health to your body and mind.

The goal during the middle stage is to use the will to lead the energy and clear all channels in the body so that the *qi* flows throughout the entire body. The goal during the higher stage is to nurture your body and your nature, and join together heaven and man. You feel your own body's internal *qi* intermingle with nature's external *qi*.

Description of Primordial Post Standing

ACTION 1: Stand upright and breathe deeply three times. (image 2.1)

ACTION 2: Step the left foot out to the left to shoulder width, with the feet parallel. Place the weight between the feet. Move slowly and synchronize breathing with stepping by inhaling as you lift the foot and exhaling as you place it. (image 2.2)

ACTION 3: Slowly lift the hands forward and up with the palms facing each other, fingers open, and arms naturally bent. When the hands arrive at shoulder height turn them to form a circle in front of the chest with the palms facing the chest, the elbows bent and set down, the shoulders relaxed, the chest contained, and the head slightly pressing up. Imagine you are holding a big ball of air in front of the chest. The elbows must be set down below shoulder height. At this time bend the knees slightly, release the tension around the hip joints and flatten the lower back to lower the body slightly. Look straight ahead. Hold this position, discard all random thoughts and focus on breathing. Breathe through the nose slowly, deeply,

and evenly. The length of standing time is set by your endurance and fitness. (images 2.3 and 2.3 side)

ACTION 4: Close the position by doing the opposite to the opening. First give your mind a signal, tell yourself that you are about to stop, you are about to complete the standing session. Then shift onto the right leg and bring the left foot in beside the right and stand up. As you start to stand up, lower the hands naturally down by the sides of the body, fingers pointing down. Press the head up and look forward. Once you have completed this action breath deeply three times and stand quietly for two or three minutes.

Pointers

o   The three main requirements for primordial post standing are to release excess tension from the body, clear the mind, and regulate the breath. This applies to all post standing, not just primordial post standing. The foundation of post standing is the same as that of most *qigong* training – regulate the body, regulate the mind, and regulate the breath. Relax the body to release the tension from every part of the body so that not a single part of the body holds any stiffness. The key to relaxing is to release the joints, to allow all the joints to hold their natural physiological position. Relaxing the body enables the flow of *qi* and blood throughout the body. Calm the mind to withdraw into yourself and focus on your training, to bring all the activities of the brain to concentrate on one point. During primordial post standing first concentrate on breathing. Regulate the breath to consciously use your breath. Change your normal, natural, unthinking breathing to intentionally regulated breathing that is slow, even, and deep.

o   During primordial post standing the head should be lifted slightly upward and the jaw tucked slightly in to maintain the neck in a straight position. The shoulders should be settled down, the chest held slightly in, the arms slightly bent in front of the body in a circle, the elbow tips pointing down, the wrists slightly bent, the fingers open naturally with the thumbs pointing slightly up, and the palms slightly concave. The lower back should be naturally straightened, the buttocks naturally tucked, the hips relaxed and the knees bent to about 160 degrees. The knees shouldn't be overly bent or straight. It takes up too much energy if they are too bent, making it difficult to control the breathing and to stand for a long time. It the knees are too straight they stiffen. When you stand properly in primordial standing you will feel every part of your body is comfortable and unobstructed.

SANTISHI POST STANDING   sāntǐshì zhuāng   三体势桩

Introduction to *Santishi*

Three bodies [trinity] post standing [三体势桩 sāntǐshì zhuāng] is also popularly called meridian post standing [子午桩 zǐwǔ zhuāng] and three attributes post standing [三才桩 sāncái zhuāng].

'Meridian' and 'three attributes' are traditional cultural references. The meridians – *zi* and *wu* – usually refer to the two-hour periods around midnight and noon. *Zi* is 11:00 to 1:00 around midnight, when *yang* starts to grow, and *wu* is 11:00 to 1:00 around noon, when *yin* starts to grow. The "Golden Elixir Collection" answers the question "What is the meridian line?" with the response:

"The meridian line means the central line of heaven and earth. In the heavens the meridians are the sun and the moon. Among mankind – the Heart and the Kidney. In time – the two-hour periods around midnight and noon. Among the eight trigrams the meridians are *kan* [a central *yang* line with top and bottom *yin* lines] and *li* [a central *yin* line with top and bottom *yang* lines]. And among directions – south and north." The "Discussion of the Three Origins" says that *zi* is the head of *yang* and *wu* is the head of *yin,* so *ziwu* form the heads of the *yinyang* 'fish.' It states; "*Zi* is the head of the six *yangs* and the peak of winter, so around the *zi* time one should sit still and collect one's spirit, release all thoughts, focus on one point, and regulate the breath to accord with the season.... *Wu* is the head of the six *yins* and the peak of summer, so before the *wu* time you should sit quietly and collect the spirit, when the peak of *yang* starts to change to *yin,* then the *yin* energy in the mind will naturally settle."

Three attributes also describes many aspects sought in the stance: 1) three attributes refer to heaven, earth and man. They are the attributes of heaven, the attributes of earth, and the attributes of man. 2) The "Book of Changes" says "Each of the three attributes has two aspects: the way of heaven is to have *yin* and *yang,* the way of earth is to have soft and hard, the way of man is to have benevolence and righteousness. These two aspects of each of the three attributes draw the six lines of the changes that form the trigrams." 3) Chinese medical theory explains the three attributes as the body, spirit and *qi* [internal power or energy and the matter in the body that contains energy]. The "Examination of the Channels" says, "The *qi* houses the spirit and the body houses the *qi.* The spirit gathers in the Heart, the *qi* gathers in the Kidney, and the body gathers in the head. When the body and *qi* intermingle in the spirit, this is the way of the three attributes." 4) The great martial arts master Sun Lutang said; "The three attributes are the head, hands and feet, that is upper, middle and lower." He used the concept of three attributes to describe the relationship between the head, hands, and feet, and extended the meaning to the upper basin [head to solar plexus], middle basin [solar plexus to knees], and lower basin [knees to feet] common in martial arts terminology.

Three bodies post standing, meridian post standing, and three attributes post standing are names for the same stance that emphasize different aspects of the stance. The name 'three bodies' emphasizes the outer structure of the head, hands, and feet, the upper, middle, and lower parts of the body. The name 'meridian' emphasizes the importance of post standing in Xingyiquan, that it is the 'foundation of the foundation.' The name 'three attributes' emphasizes the internal meaning, that it is not just a posture, but even more importantly is a type of training to develop deep ability [*gong*]. The inner meaning of *santishi* post standing is very rich. 'Three bodies' indicates its method and practice, 'three attributes' indicates its theory, and 'meridian' indicates its importance.

Each regional and stylistic branch of Xingyiquan uses the *santishi* post standing as its main post standing method. Each uses essentially the same basic framework, position and requirements for *santishi*, and trains the same functions. There are, of course, differences, since each branch has a different understanding of the classic writings, and each person gains a different understanding through training. This is natural. Great trees never grow quite the same, and leaves are never identical. If one teacher teaches ten apprentices, they will all have different heights, body types, temperaments, characters, preferences and levels of education, so will of course gain different understandings from their training. These ten apprentices cannot possibly be identical.

TRAINING METHOD FOR *SANTISHI*

ACTION 1: Stand upright, looking in the direction to which you will do the stance.

ACTION 2: Gradually lift the hands at either side of the body, arms naturally bent and palms up. Do not extend the arms with force. When the hands reach shoulder height, bend the elbows to bring the palms in to the face, fingers pointing to each other and palms down. (images 2.4A and B)

ACTION 3: Bend the legs to sit down slightly, press the hands down in front of the abdomen and press the head slightly up. (image 2.5)

ACTION 4: Clench fists in front of the belly and turn the fist hearts up. Keep the left fist where it is, and drill the right fist up past the solar plexus then forward to nose height, twisting the ulnar side up. (image 2.6)

ACTION 5: Advance the left foot without moving the right, so that the feet are shin length apart with most of the weight on the right leg. The weight balance is thirty percent on the front and seventy percent on the back. While doing this, drill the left fist from the abdomen up past the solar plexus and forward, fist heart up. When the left fist crosses the right fist, open both hands and rotate them inward [thumb towards palm] to chop forward with the left palm. Keep the left arm slightly bent. The left palm is angled forward and down with the wrist set and the fingers at nose height. While completing the move, pull the right hand back to the abdomen with the palm facing down. Press the head up and look forward. (images

2.7 and 2.7 front)

- This is the left *santishi* stance. To stand right *santishi* post standing, drill out the left fist instead of the right at action 4, then step the right foot forward to chop with the right palm at action 5.

POSITIONAL REQUIREMENTS FOR *SANTISHI*

Santishi is the opening move to start each of the five elements and each form within the Xingyiquan system. Whatever you are practising you will almost always start from left *santishi.*

Santishi can be done at high level, mid level, and low level. For high level, the feet are two foot-lengths apart. For mid level, the feet are two and a half foot-lengths apart. For low level, the feet are three foot-lengths apart.

1. Feet: The feet should be on either side of a straight line – the toes of the lead foot and the heel of the rear foot are to either side of the line. The feet must not be along the same line, and should certainly not be crossing, as this would be unstable. The lead foot is turned slightly inwards at fifteen degrees or less. The rear foot is turned no more than forty-five degrees from the forward line.

2. Legs: The legs are bent such that a plumb bob dropped from the lead knee would not go forward of the heel of the lead foot. The angle formed by the thigh and the shank of the lead leg is about 150 degrees. The rear leg is quite bent, and holds between sixty to seventy percent of the weight. The distance between the feet depends on the degree of bend in the rear leg and the height of the stance. The angle formed by the thigh and shank of the rear leg is 120 to 135 degrees. What is more crucial is that the angle the rear shank forms with the ground is as acute as possible. Considering the biomechanical structure of the lower leg, the ankle can only flex to fifty degrees and approaching this angle assists the thrust from the rear leg. Some books state that a plumb bob dropped from the rear knee should not fall in front of the rear toes, but I feel that this is not logical. This places you too high, with the legs almost straight with almost all of your weight on the rear leg. The rear knee should be in front of the rear foot, with the amount determined by the height of the stance. It will not be far forward in a high stance, and will be more forward in a low stance. The main criteria to determine the optimum angle of the shank are: how to best store thrusting power in the rear leg, how to initiate action quickly, how to get the most distance, how to stand with stability, and how to thrust into the ground strongly. It is as the classics say: "the key is in the thrust of the rear leg." The speed that the body moves forward and the distance that it travels are entirely determined by the thrust of the rear leg. The angle of the rear leg should place the weight between the two legs in the optimum place to allow for stability and forward thrust, about sixty-two degrees towards the rear. That is, not so far forward that the rear thigh goes forward of a vertical line.

3. Hips: the buttocks, the abdomen, and the hip joints bound the hip area. In *santishi* the hips should be angled a bit, about sixty to seventy degrees from the front. This angle helps support the legs to back and front, and helps the upper body to naturally present an angled face to the front. Some people emphasize that the belly should be straight and the upper body angled, but I feel that this does not allow the body to feel at ease. Keeping the belly straight means that your hips face straight forward, but if you then turn your upper body to

present a half-face to the front, then the belly feels uncomfortable and impeded. This position doesn't suit defensive and offensive actions either. The positioning and angle of the hips and legs should give very stable yet agile supporting conditions to the upper body. They should also be comfortable and fit the natural structure of the body.

4. Shoulders: According to the classics, the body position and the angle of the shoulders should be "straight yet appearing angled, angled yet appearing straight." This is a deliberately vague description. Everyone has a different body type and character, and will interpret this saying differently, so this vagueness allows you to find the best angle for yourself through your training. Differences are unavoidable. From my own experience of training and teaching over many years, I have found when standing in *santishi* that the best position is with the upper body and shoulders at forty-five degrees from the front. This position is practical for fighting, as it decreases the frontal surface. It also suits the body's structure and biomechanical action. When you fit with the body's natural structure and biomechanics you can be comfortable, unimpeded, correct, aesthetically pleasing, and improve your health.

5. Hands and forearms: The angle that the left wrist forms with the forearm is 120 to 130 degrees. The wrist sits down slightly, the fingers are slightly bent, the palm concave, the thumb/index finger web spread, the thumb opened, and the index finger lifted. This increases the strength of the muscles in the web of the hand and stabilizes the wrist. Keeping a certain amount of opening in the fingers creates a certain tension in the extensor muscles of the forearm, which in turn gives a certain degree of resistance to strikes. Turning the palm to face downwards twists the distal end of the forearm, crossing the radial and ulnar bones, which increases the work of the involved muscle groups, increasing the strength in the palm. The twist also gives a stabilizing effect to the forearm. If the wrist is too straight then the hand and fingers cannot withstand the strength of a full body strike. If the wrist is pulled back too far then it is stiff and will not move easily, so the hand cannot grab or change positions smoothly. So, for these reasons, the best angle of the forearm to wrist is 120 to 130 degrees.

6. Elbows: the elbow angle is the angle formed by the forearm with the upper arm. The Xingyi classics have this to say on the angle of the elbow; "If it is too bent then you have no reach, if it is too straight then you have insufficient strength." This gives you a rough idea, neither straight nor fully bent. In the early 1980s, as I was teaching Xingyi at Beijing University, I used this phrase when teaching *santishi* – neither straight nor fully bent. A student asked me, "What is the angle?" This left a deep impression on me. From that time on, I have looked at the angle of every joint in the body, examined old photos of Xingyi masters, thought about my experiences in training, measured with a protractor, and sought out the optimum angle for each joint. I found that the optimum angle for the elbow is 150 degrees. Why don't we extend the arm fully in *santishi* or other Xingyi techniques? Don't we have more reach if we extend the arm? First of all, in hitting with the fist or palm in Xingyiquan, we must use its requirements and characteristics, and Xingyi emphasizes the use of whole body power. This degree of extension – neither straight nor bent – enables you to generate and use a great deal of force. Secondly, this degree of extension utilizes a relatively large number of muscles of the arm, stabilizing the elbow

joint. Thirdly, being neither straight nor bent enables the elbow to change quickly, giving more options of actions.

7. Upper arm and shoulders: The angle formed by the upper arms and the shoulder joint is very important to the upper limb unit. The angle should be about sixty to seventy degrees measured from the chest to upper arm. The classics say; "settle the shoulders and sink the elbows." Settle the shoulders means that the shoulder unit should be consciously settled down. Sink the elbows means that the distal ends of the upper arms are always below the shoulder joint. The positioning of the shoulders and elbows are interconnected. If you settle the shoulders correctly then the elbows will naturally drop. If you drop your elbows then your shoulders will naturally settle. There is one more key point. The upper arm should be consciously gathered in, to keep the upper arm as much as possible on a plane with the body. This helps you generate whole body power. Whether post standing or practising you must at all times keep the upper arm rolled and tucked in to the correct position. The thumb and wrist of the rear hand is tightly held to the *dantian*.[6] The elbow of the rear arm should be naturally sunken, so you should pay attention that it does not stick out, so that you maintain an integrated force within the body. The fingers point forward and the palm faces down.

8. Head: "The head should press up and the neck should be upright." You should tuck in the jaw a bit, but be sure not to tighten the neck, otherwise you will reduce the agility of head movements. The reason for pressing the head up is that this reminds you to keep the spine straight, which helps the body to stay centered and straight, and helps breathing. You should look forward, but do not turn the head too much to keep the face facing straight on. You may allow the head to take a 22.5 degree angle from the front and look forward with the eyes.

9. Buttocks: The buttocks should remain naturally tucked in so that the pelvic basin is at a slightly greater angle than normal [do not do a pelvic tilt]. This helps you to settle the *qi* to the *dantian,* to form a bow with the lumbar spine, and to set up the lead foot to step forward.

10. The trunk: The requirement for the upper body is "contain the chest and open the back." These are two sides of the same coin. To achieve a contained chest and opened back, you need to let your shoulders pull slightly forward, relaxing the shoulder blades and the back muscles. While maintaining this position, you must be sure to keep the shoulders set down – never shrug the shoulders. 'Contain the chest and open the back' works together with 'set the shoulders and drop the elbows' to organically connect the whole body. Make sure you do not overdo this action – you should be comfortable. The main reason for relaxing the shoulders and containing the chest is to help the abdomen be solid, that is, to settle the *qi* to the *dantian*. One of the most obvious characteristics of Xingyiquan is that the *qi* is settled to the *dantian*. Keeping the shoulders and chest slightly depressed also helps the upper body's ability to both take a hit

---

[6] Translator's note: One more word that I do not translate, *dantian*, in martial arts refers almost always to the area in the core of the body, the front of which is about three finger widths below the navel. This is the energetic and physical centre of the body, where *qi* is stored, so internal styles emphasize settling the body physically and energetically here.

and to strike. The root of the hand's power is the shoulders, while the root of the body's power is the core area.

LEARNING PROGRESSION FOR *SANTISHI* POST STANDING

Different varieties of Xingyi differ in the exact shape of *santishi*, some being more expansive and some tighter, some with larger stances and some with smaller, some higher, some lower, but this does not matter. Whichever *santishi* you stand, you need to change your intent concerning the power, energy and spirit at each different stage of internal training. Although there will be hardly any change in the external appearance of the stance, at each stage there is a different requirement and a different emphasis for the internal intent, the regulation of breathing, and the leading of the *qi*. Next I will briefly explain the body structure, intent, and breathing for three stages of training *santishi* post standing: the beginning stage, the intermediate stage and the advanced stage

Beginning stage

At the beginning stage you have just started to learn post standing so have only a rudimentary understanding of the requirements. Although you can imitate your teacher's position, yours is not yet correct. With time and more practice, your position will gradually improve. Often you will concentrate on one thing at the expense of another. This is a natural biological reaction, as your brain is overloaded. During this stage you should work on the following three points:

1. First work on getting an upright and correct position, placing each segment of the body at the required angle and position. Go through the checklist given above, from top to bottom, or from bottom to top, checking that each position is exactly as it should be. First get the overall picture of the legs, trunk, arms, and head, then work on the more refined requirements. Pay attention to feeling your body as you correct it, then you will start to understand the requirements of Xingyi, and the requirements for each body part.

2. Second, pay attention to relaxing as you seek to place the body in the correct position, relaxed but not slack. A relaxed body does not use brute force, but, for example, places the leading arm in the right place with just enough force. Concentrate on releasing the tension from each segment of the body. The upper body should be relaxed and the lower body should be solid. A solid lower body means that the legs have a supporting strength. Because the legs are bent to different degrees, the back leg will become more tired. This is normal, as it supports more weight.

3. Third, calm down. 'Entering quiet' means to focus entirely on the post standing, to take all your extraneous thoughts and throw them away. During the beginning stage you should focus entirely on placing your body in the correct posture, on the placement of each angle, on relaxing each body segment, on seeking the kinesthetic awareness throughout your body. Only when you calm your mind can you feel and learn from your body. During the first stage the placement of the body is of primary importance. The structure must be set for the power to develop smoothly. Whether or not the structure is correct has a direct effect on whether or not the power can be smooth. During the first stage breathing should be normal, not emphasized. Once the body is in the correct position and the mind is calm, then you may think of changing your natural breathing pattern to a slower, longer, deeper, and steadier breathing. During

the beginning stage you should constantly adjust your posture, constantly improve it, and seek to copy the perfect model.

Intermediate stage

The requirements during the intermediate stage of *santishi* post standing are:

1. Body structure: take your correct position and seek the finer points within it, deepen your kinesthetic awareness to seek the feelings of power flow and to become comfortable.

2. Thoughts: work on two types of thoughts. One is 'looking inside,' and the other is 'looking outside.' Looking inside serves to make the body healthy. Looking outside serves to develop fighting ability. During the intermediate stage of post standing, you should direct your *qi* with your mind so that it circulates throughout your body. First think of circulating through the conception vessel, traveling up the back, over the head, and down the front of your trunk. Once you can follow the circuit of the conception vessel with your mind then gradually and naturally your *qi* will also follow this path. Then it can go through the small heavenly circuit, flowing through your whole body. Do not seek too hard to do this, the *qi* should be allowed to flow naturally. If you feel the *qi* connect, that is normal, but it is also normal if you do not feel it.

3. Breathing: during the first stage the body has learned the correct position and structure, so during the intermediate stage you do not need to focus so much on this. Now you may pay more attention to the breathing technique. In general, during the intermediate stage, you should use reverse abdominal breathing. That is, raise the diaphragm and bring in the abdomen as you inhale, and lower the diaphragm and round the abdomen as you exhale. Inhale and exhale through the nose. Consciously control the depth, rhythm and rate of your breathing so that it becomes deep, even, and slow. All of this is under the preconditions of a relaxed body and calm mind.

Higher stage

In the beginning stage the *qi* is lead by the mind. In the intermediate stage the *qi* circulates throughout the entire body. Once this has reached a certain level, then you can attain the higher level and can unite the internal and external, connect the form and sprit, become harmonious, and unite heaven and man. This is the stage spoken of in the Xingyi classics, when you 'wash the marrow and transform your power ' and 'train the spirit to return to emptiness.' At this stage, man's consciousness is transformed and man's temperament is changed. He becomes magnanimous, broad minded, and courteous.

All breathing is done through the nose and not the mouth. Inhaling is continuous, long, and deep and permeates the whole body. Exhaling is fine, slight, and almost nonexistent. Inhaling is long, and drawn into every tiny little space, like swallowing breath. Whether inhaling or exhaling, all breath is fine and slight with no sound. This is what the Daoists call "belly breathing." The higher levels in martial arts have many similarities to the higher levels of Daoist and Buddhist practices. The higher level in martial arts is that in which the fist and the Way are as one.

The outer position of *santishi* post standing is no different than in the first two stages, it is just more relaxed and the mind is more quiet, just as Laozi said in the book Dao De Jing: "on arriving at the utmost emptiness, guard the spirit sincere." The heart and mind attain an empty and calm state.

DESCEND THE DRAGON POST STANDING   jiàng lóng zhuāng   降龙桩

Introduction to Descend the Dragon

The name Descend The Dragon post standing is taken from the Daoist technique of 'descending the dragon.' The belief is that when fire rises in your heart you cannot 'fly,' so the technique controls this fire and allows you to build up power in the core of your body. In this technique, the essence and spirit are held in, the water from the Kidneys rises and controls the fire – it lowers, or descends, the 'dragon.' This is the explanation according to *qigong* theory. In Xingyi, 'descend the dragon' also refers to the outer form that the posture takes: the waist and lumbar area twist into a turned bow stance to turn the body around to face backwards, both arms press out with the lead hand bracing and rear hand pressing. This trains the lower back, arms, and legs of the external system, and the heart, mind, and *qi* of the internal system. First train the outer then train the inner, because "the outer trains the muscles, bones and skin, the inner trains the ability to combine everything with one breath." First try to get the body comfortable in the correct position. On this foundation you can then progress to practise the next level within the posture, in which the goal is to focus your thoughts and regulate your breathing.

PRACTISING DESCEND THE DRAGON POST STANDING

ACTION 1: Stand upright, then step the left foot to the side, placing the feet parallel about three foot-lengths apart. While doing this, raise the hands at the sides to shoulder height with the palms up and arms slightly bent. Look forward. (image 2.8)

ACTION 2: Without moving the feet, bend the arms and bring the hands together in front of the face, palms down and fingers pointing to each other. Then rotate the hands to turn the palms out, with the thumbs down, at shoulder height, to brace outward with the arms like holding a ball with the back of the hands. (image 2.9)

2.8   2.9

ACTION 3: Turn the body 180 degrees to the left by pivoting on the left heel to turn the left toes out, and pivoting on the ball of the right foot to turn the right heel out. Bend the left leg to form a left bow stance, and almost fully straighten the right leg, putting almost all the weight onto the left leg. Gradually brace out with both palms. The right palm finishes to the right of the head with the arm bracing round and the elbow slightly higher than the shoulder. The left palm finishes behind the left hip with the palm facing down, the fingers forward, and the arm bracing round. Turn the head around to the left to look at the left hand. This is the left Descend

The Dragon stance. (image 2.10)

ACTION 4: Turn around 180 degrees, pivoting on the feet. Brace out with the palms in front of the chest as you turn. See image 2.9 in action two.

ACTION 5: Turn the body 180 degrees to the right by pivoting on the right heel to turn the right toes out, and pivoting on the ball of the left foot to turn the left heel out. Bend the right leg to form a right bow stance, and almost fully straighten the left leg, putting almost all the weight onto the right leg. Turn the waist to the right. Bring the hands around as the body turns. The left palm finishes to the left of the head with the arm bracing round and the elbow slightly higher than the shoulder. The right palm finishes behind the right hip with the palm facing down, the fingers forward, and the arm bracing round. Turn the head around to the right to look at the right hand. This is the right Descend The Dragon stance. (image 2.11 and 2.11 back)

ACTION 6: The closing is the same for either side. First return to the position described in action two above. Then turn both hands to face the palms in, holding the arms in front of the chest. Then bring in either the left or right foot to stand with the feet together, bringing the hands down in front of the abdomen. Then complete the closing, bringing the hands down.

Pointers

o The opening of Descend The Dragon standing should be done slowly and softly without any hesitation, completed smoothly as one move.

o When settling into the final position pay attention to the position of the hands and arms. The arm/hand above should have a pressing out power, and the arm/hand below should have a pulling and pressing down power. The waist should have a twisting power. Don't use strength or brute force, but relax and maintain the correct position with the chest slightly contained and the head slightly pressing up.

- o When you first start post standing breathe naturally and pay attention to getting the stance settled properly. Once you get the balance and position adjusted then you can gradually increase the length of time that you stand, and alternate sides. If you stand for a long time then you may decrease the distance between the feet to two foot-lengths, taking a higher stance.

- o At first you should concentrate on the position of the body, getting each body segment into the correct placement, going through a checklist from top to bottom, concentrating on relaxing each muscle group. Be sure not to let the body go slack, but relax each muscle group such that each one takes part in maintaining the position so that the *qi* can flow. The waist, especially, must relax. That is, relaxed but not lax, settled but not stiff. The twisting should have elasticity, storing a power with the capability to explode, so that within the relaxation there is a buildup to suddenly shoot power.

USE AND MEANING OF THE DESCEND THE DRAGON STANCE

Since the feet are relatively far apart and the stance is relatively low, the Descend The Dragon stance places high demands on leg strength, so is most suited for younger and stronger players. Older or weaker players may adjust the stance a bit higher, and turn a little less. The main goal of this stance is to strengthen the legs and waist, and the bracing power of the arms, to physically develop more than does the *santishi*. It trains the supporting strength of the legs, the twisting elasticity of the waist, and the bracing up and pressing down power of the arms, developing these relatively quickly.

The twist and lean at the waist is like a dragon bending its body. The upward bracing and downward pressing of the arms is like a dragon stretching its body. The bent front leg and the straight back leg with the sitting body and settled *qi* are like settling into the dragon as you ride it. In all these, use the mind and not strength, at all times focus on 'the intent is tight but the strength is loose' so that gradually your body learns the kinesthetic feeling of each segment, with comfort being the best guide.

In the Descend The Dragon stance, the dragon refers to your mind and spirit. Training regulates the body, mind, and spirit, and thus 'lowers,' or 'descends' the 'dragon.' So, once you have the correct position, the important thing is to regulate the mind and spirit.

SUBDUE THE TIGER POST STANDING   fú hǔ zhuāng   伏虎桩

Introduction to Subdue the Tiger

This stance is also a traditional Xingyi stance used among the people. Descend The Dragon and Subdue The Tiger use Daoist *qigong* terminology. 'Subdue the tiger' means 'the spirit is enclosed and the heart's fire descends and collects as water.' Martial artists of previous generations took this name and gave it to a posture that resembles a crouching tiger, and used the terminology for the internal training that goes with the stance. 'The heart's fire settles down and collects in the Kidney as water' means that the mind settles and allows the *qi* and blood to flow throughout the body. In this stance the legs are in a half horse stance with the empty and solid clearly distinguished, which strengthens the legs. The arms are rounded with a bracing and holding power, which increases the primordial power of the whole body.

TRAINING THE SUBDUE THE TIGER POST STANDING

ACTION ONE: Starting from standing upright, step the left foot forward without moving the right foot, so that the feet are two or three foot-lengths apart with the left foot forward. Lift the hands to embrace in front of the chest with the wrists crossed, the palms in, and the arms bent. Contain the chest and open the back, release tension in the shoulders and drop the elbows, press the head up, tuck in the buttocks and keep the body upright. Look ahead. Straighten the legs with the weight between the feet. (image 2.12)

ACTION TWO: Without moving the feet, bend the knees to sit down with the weight more on the right leg, so that the right leg is more bent than the left, the right thigh parallel to the ground. Shift back to form a sixty/forty stance, that it, a half horse stance. Round the groin area and tuck in the buttocks, press the head up and tuck in the jaw, keep the body upright with a very slight lean forward. As the body sits down, brace the hands out, the left forward and the right back, with the palms facing each other. The left arm is slightly bent above the left knee. The right arm is more bent, with the palm at the right ribs. Brace the elbows out so that the palms have a closing in power. Release the shoulder tension and sink the elbows, contain the chest and stretch the back, settle the *qi* to the *dantian*. Look in front of the left hand. This position is the left subdue the tiger stance. (image 2.13)

ACTION THREE: Stand up, cross the hands in front of the chest, bring the left foot in beside the right foot, then step the right foot forward and do the right subdue the tiger stance. The actions and positions are the same as described above, only on the other side.

Pointers

- Keep the whole body coordinated in the move, so that the arms brace out and the body sits into the stance all at once.

- Use intent rather than strength to put power into the grab with the lead foot, embrace with the hands and brace out with the elbows.

- Keep the whole body coordinated as you step the foot forward and cross the hands, doing everything together.

- The Subdue The Tiger stance helps to strengthen the legs, especially the rear supporting leg. Young and strong players should sit fully into the stance so that the *qi* settles down. Weaker players may sit in a higher stance and gradually settle down as they get accustomed to it.

BREATHING IN THE SUBDUE THE TIGER POST STANDING

1. Put a closing power into the legs as you breathe in, as if you are standing on ice. Roll the hip joints in and close the knees towards the centre of the stance to prevent your feet from sliding out, giving you a closing, pulling in power. At the same time, while breathing in, put an inward, embracing power into the arms.

2. Put a grasping power into the lead foot and drive back into the rear foot as you breathe out. Settle the *qi* into the *dantian* as you breathe out, and sit the body down slightly. These actions are done more with intent, and do not change the outward shape very much. With each breath in and out a rhythmic tautening and releasing of power will develop, releasing when inhaling, tautening when exhaling. This develops a kinesthetic awareness of the muscles throughout the body, so that you can relax without becoming slack, and tauten without becoming tense. Relaxing is the method, tautening is the goal.

3. You need to coordinate the movement of the hands bracing and opening to the back and front with the settling down of the body into the legs. Although the trunk reaches slightly forward, focus on pulling in the buttocks and settling down. Shift the centre of gravity slightly forward and backward with each inhalation and exhalation. The front foot will be training its grasping power with each slight shift forward and backward. When bracing out with the hands, you should feel that you are pulling open a spring, and with each closing in to embrace, you should feel that you are embracing and squeezing a spring. Thinking of this will help you find the whole body power. You should use your imagination, not strength. If you use strength then you will tighten up. If you use your mind then you will remain supple.

POUNDING POST   zá zhuāng   砸桩

Introduction to Pounding Post

The meaning of Pounding Post is that you are pounding your foundation 'post' into the ground to make it even more stable, just as a bridge needs many piles pounded firmly into the ground to make a solid foundation. Making a foundation like this ensures that the bridge will be firm, solid, and lasting.

Pounding Post differs from standard post standing in that stnadard post standing is an unmoving position, and Pounding Post uses movement within a maintained stance. The goals are to master the whole body power of Xingyi and get a feel for Xingyi's requirements more quickly. Standard post standing emphasizes the training of breath. Post pounding trains the connection between breath and power.

Pounding post is not a traditional training method. It is a method that I developed over many years of training and teaching. It serves to augment the standard post standing, and also serves as a stage between static standing and moving training. More importantly, it is a simple application that takes the whole body power developed within the standard post standing, and enables you to train and gain a feeling for launching power. It increases the power in your body within a short time.

Pounding Post With The Lead Foot

ACTION 1: Almost everything is the same as the *santishi*: the distance between the feet, the height of the stance, the position of the trunk (angled but straight, straight but angled), the head pressed up and the buttocks tucked in, the chest contained and the back open. Only the position of the hands and arms differs. For Pounding Post, the lead hand is clenched into a fist and the lead forearm is bent to cross the body with the fist heart facing in, lower than the shoulders. The lead arm is bent ninety to one hundred degrees. The rear hand is placed at the lead wrist, palm on the forearm and fingers up. Relax the shoulders and sink the rear elbow. Look forward. (image 2.14)

Pointers

- o Once you have settled into the preparatory position, take three breaths to settle down into the *dantian*. Relax every muscle not needed to remain standing, paying special attention to releasing the tension in the shoulders and lumbar area

ACTION 2: Shift the centre of gravity back about ten centimetres, lifting the lead foot's heel about three centimetres off the ground, leaving the toes on the ground and bending the knee. Bring the lead forearm and fist in a bit towards the chest, maintaining contact with the other hand. Settle the shoulders and draw them back. Bring the weight back to the rear leg, press the head up, and look forward. Breathe in. This movement is slow, and the breath is long and full. (image 2.15)

ACTION 3: Press into the ground forcefully with the rear foot, so that the centre of gravity moves forward about fifteen centimetres. While doing this, forcefully land the leading foot's heel with a stamping power, landing with a thump. Do not bend the leading knee too much, it should remain springy, so that it snaps back quickly to its original position. As the heel lands, use the power of the lower back to send the shoulders forward, putting power to the forearm and wrist, so that the leading forearm braces out and the rear hand pushes forward. Coordinate your power launch with an exhalation to gain strength. Exhale quickly and forcefully, settling the *qi* to the *dantian*. Bring the power of the whole body through each segment, to culminate and focus in the forearm. At this time the leading elbow is bent about 120 degrees. Press the head up and look straight ahead. (image 2.16)

- • When training the pounding stake, do it about fifty times with the left foot forward, then about fifty times with the right foot forward. The exact number of times you do it depends on your fitness.

Pointers

- The first factor is to coordinate breath with movement. Inhale when storing energy and exhale when launching energy. The second factor is to coordinate the relaxing and tautening of the whole body. Relax tension when storing power, tauten when launching power. Relax as soon as you have completed launching the power. Only by releasing completely, all the way, can you be able to tauten fully and completely, and hit fiercely. The proportion of relaxing to tautening is nine to one. When you relax then your mind tautens, when you tauten then your power can be launched explosively.

- In coordination with the storing and launching of power, the body will have some rise and fall – about one twentieth of the body height. Shift back to load power, and let the body rise slightly. Stomp with a thump, launching power and letting the body drop slightly.

- Once you have set properly into the stance you should press the head up and look into the distance, as if standing on the top of a cliff gazing out, stable as a mountain yourself. As you shift backwards, inhaling and storing energy, it is like an ocean wave drawing back. As you exhale with the power launch, it is like the wave pounding on the shore – with an imposing air, a fierce impulse of power. If you use your imagination in this way as you do the pounding stake exercise it will bring unthought-of results.

- Practise Pounding Post with a progression from light to heavy then back to light, from soft to hard then back to soft. First launch power lightly, softly, and slowly, to regulate the *qi* and the body. Once the *qi* is connecting through the body, the body is comfortable and the power smooth, then launch power more forcefully, to train whole body power. Finally, return to a light and soft practice to regulate the breathing and bring health to the body. Throughout these three phases, maintain correct posture, smooth power, and concentration from beginning to end.

- You must determine your training load according to your strength and conditioning. You must not suddenly put out a lot of power or practise too long because you are feeling good, thus tiring yourself. Post pounding is a method of gaining whole body power quickly, but if you practise it improperly you can develop many problems. If you pound the heel into the ground too hard, or for too long a time, until you become tired, you can cause heel pain. The leading knee takes a lot of stress and impact when pounding, so overtraining can cause problems. The impact of pounding with the foot passes through the whole body, so, although you launch force forward, there can be a slight impact on the head, causing headache or other problems. If you practise according to the above requirements you should not have any problems. Training skill must be done progressively and gradually, it cannot be rushed.

POUNDING POST WITH THE REAR FOOT

ACTION 1: The preparatory stance is the same as described above. (see image 2.14)

ACTION 2: Shift the centre of gravity forward about ten centimetres, without moving the leading foot, lift the rear heel about two to three centimetres without taking the toes off the ground, and lengthen the body upwards slightly. The action of the hands is the same as when doing the lead leg pounding. Pay attention when you bring the leading hand back that you straighten the back a bit and put the chest forward. Prepare slowly and breathe in, looking forward.

ACTION 3: Shift the centre of gravity back and stamp with a thud on the rear heel, supporting yourself on the front leg. Settle the foot forcefully backwards and down. While doing this, forcefully press forward with the leading forearm and wrist, supporting it with the rear hand. Be sure to keep the buttocks tucked down, sit back, round the lower back out, send the shoulders forward, and coordinate the outward breath with the power. Left and right are the same.

Pointers

- The rear foot pounding uses the reaction of the rear foot landing. It quickly transfers up through the waist and shoulders to reach the leading hand, giving an impulse of whole body power.

- The rear foot landing is timed with the power launch to the leading hand.

- Breathe out as you launch power.

THE USE OF THE POUNDING POST

You should practise both lead foot pounding and rear foot pounding, though the lead foot is the main method and the rear foot is the secondary.

You may use this pounding exercise in each of the positions of the five basic techniques to find the power of each one more accurately and quickly, and thus improve your ability. The training is the same as described above, taking the power of the whole body to the leading hand or fist, finding the source of the power and increasing your understanding of the requirements of Xingyiquan. This helps you find the correct postures more quickly and makes the actions more correct.

I have developed this training method after many years of training and teaching, and find that it is a simple means of speeding up the learning process of finding the whole body power.

- You should be comfortable in *santishi* before learning Pounding Post. At least three months of *santishi* post standing is recommended before trying Pounding Post training.

FIVE ELEMENTS

SPLIT   劈拳

INTRODUCTION TO SPLIT, *PI QUAN* (CHOPPING FIST)

Xingyiquan classic texts say "The element that split relates to is metal, its form is like an axe, and the internal organ that it relates to is the Lung."[7] This is the common view of all classic Xingyiquan texts, and is the theory respected by all traditional folk Xingyiquan. "Split relates to metal" means that split corresponds to metal from among the five elements. "Split adopts the form of an axe," means that it splits through objects, copying the action of a metal axe splitting wood. Examining the movements of the hands during split, they really do have the appearance of chopping forward and down while holding an axe – the power is applied from above and descends in an arc towards the front. Therefore, when the old masters said, "split takes its form from an axe," they meant that the action resembled that made while splitting wood with an axe. This is quite descriptive but still vague enough to encourage students to explore and discover the meaning for themselves through training.

There are many methods of doing split. Post standing must be done to start with. Post standing builds the foundation for split – only by doing post standing can one build the strong foundation that will enable one to get a good grasp of split. Variations in footwork include: *fixed stance split, moving stance split, aligned stance split, reverse stance split, advance to split,* and *retreating split.* A variation in handwork is *pull down split.* Variations in bodywork include: *dodging split,* and *split turn around.*

METHODS OF PERFORMING SPLIT

1. STANDARD SPLIT: ALIGNED STANCE SPLIT WITH MOVING STEP

1a Right Split 　　　　　yòu pī quán 　　　右劈拳

Start from left *santishi.* For a description of the *opening move* into *santishi,* see

---

[7] Editor's note: See Part One Chapter One and Part Four Chapter Two for more detail on the correspondences of the five elements.

santishi post standing.

ACTION 1: Clench both hands, pulling the left fist back to meet the right fist at the belly. Hug both elbows into the ribs. Advance the left foot a half-step and immediately bring up the right foot parallel to the ground beside the left ankle. Keep both legs bent with the knees together. Continue on with the left fist – bring it up past the solar plexus then drill forward and up to nose height. Tuck the left elbow in, by twisting the ulnar edge [the little finger side] of the forearm up so that the fist heart is up. Do not move the right fist yet. Press the head up and look at the left fist. (image 3.1)

ACTION 2: Stride the right foot forward and follow in with the left foot a half-step. Keep most of the weight on the left leg to take a *santi* stance with the right foot leading and the left foot back. Drill the right fist up past the solar plexus, towards the left elbow, then along above the left forearm, fist heart up. As the right fist approaches the left fist, unclench both hands and inwardly rotate them, turning the palms down and forward. Pull the left palm down and back to the belly. Chop the right palm forward and down to shoulder height to split, sinking the wrist slightly so the palm faces obliquely forward and down. Keep the arm slightly bent and urge the right shoulder into the strike. Press the head up and look in the direction of the right hand. (images 3.2 and 3.2 top)

3.2 TOP

3.1

3.2

Pointers

- o During the first movement of action one, the left hand should clench gradually as it moves back, and the trunk should move the left shoulder back slightly to draw the hand in. During the second movement of action one, the left fist should drill out at exactly the same time as the left foot advances, so that they work together.

- o The right hand should land its split at exactly the same time that the right foot lands, so that the foot and hand enter together.

- o The left foot should follow in quickly. The length of the stance should be appropriate to its height; the feet should be closer together in a higher stance and farther apart in a lower stance.

- o Split strides forward into a forward and downward strike, so the stance should be slightly shorter than that of *santishi,* and the hand should finish lower than in *santishi* – at shoulder height.

o Split is a complete movement. Perform it slowly when learning, but once comfortable, actions 1 and 2 should be continuous and completed as a single action.

1b Left Split   zuǒ pīquán   左劈拳

ACTION 1: Following from *right split,* advance the right foot a half-step and bring the left foot up to the right ankle with the foot off the ground. Keep both legs bent and the knees together. Clench both hands and pull the right fist back to the belly, then drill it up past the solar plexus and out to nose height, with the ulnar edge twisted up so that the centre of the fist faces up. Keep the right elbow tucked in, the head pressed up, and the eyes on the right fist. (image 3.3)

ACTION 2: Stride the left foot forward and follow the right foot in a half-step, keeping the weight mostly on the right leg. Drill the left fist up past the solar plexus, out past the right elbow and along the top of the forearm, fist heart up. As the left fist approaches the right fist, turn both hands over and open them, and pull the right hand down and back to the belly as the left hand splits forward and down

to shoulder height. The left palm faces obliquely forward and down. Press the head up and look to the direction of the left hand. (images 3.4 and 3.4 front)

1c Split Turn Around   pīquán zhuànshēn   劈拳转身

Starting from the <u>right</u> split as example.

ACTION 1: Clench the right hand and pull it back to the belly. Hook-in the right foot, shift onto the right leg, and turn around 180 degrees to the left to face the direction from which you came. Swivel the left foot to get it pointing straight, so that the legs take a *santi* stance. (image 3.5)

ACTION 2: Advance the left foot a half-step and bring the right foot up beside the left ankle without touching down. Drill the left fist up from the belly past the solar plexus and out to nose height, ulnar edge twisted up. Look at the left fist. (image 3.6)

ACTION 3: Stride the right foot forward and follow in a half-step with the left foot, keeping the weight mostly on the left leg. While doing this, bring the right fist up from the solar plexus to the left elbow then along the top of the forearm to split forward. Press the head up and look forward. This action is the same as *right split.* (image 3.7)

- The action of *split turn around* is the same whether on the right or left side, just transpose the right and left actions.

Pointers

   ○ Pay particular attention while turning that the weight shift of the body stays stable – hook the foot in and turn the body around quickly.

1d Split Closing Move   pīquán shōushì   劈拳收势

On arriving back at the starting point, do a *split turn around* to face the original direction, and continue on until you arrive in a *left split* – that is, continue until the left foot and hand are leading – then perform *closing move*.

ACTION 1: Clench the left hand and cock the fist to press it down at the belly, fist heart down, beside the right fist, which has stayed at the belly, also clenching the fist with the heart down. Do not move the feet, but press the left foot into the ground as the left fist pulls back. Press the head up and look forward. (image 3.8)

ACTION 2: Shift onto the left leg and bring the right foot up beside the left foot, keeping the legs bent to maintain the body at the same height. Keep the fists at the belly. Press the head up slightly and look forward. (image 3.9)

ACTION 3: Unclench the fists and lower the hands, then raise them in a curved route to shoulder height at the sides of the body, arms slightly bent and palms up. Then bend the arms further and bring the hands in to the face, fingers pointing to each other and palms down. Do not change the flexion

of the legs during this action. (images 3.10 A and B)

ACTION 4: Lower the hands past the face, pressing down to the belly, then place them at the sides. Straighten the legs to stand up. Turn the body to face forward, and the closing movement is done. (image 3.11)

Pointers

- o Three actions must occur simultaneously, with full spirit: sink and bring in the left fist, press the left foot into the ground, and press the head up.

- o Circle the hands up then press them down in one continuous action. Press the hands down as you stand up, so that the hands and legs act in unison.

2. FIXED STANCE SPLIT   dìngbù pīquán   定步劈拳

'Fixed stance' means that there is no half-step advance or half-step follow in. There is only one step for each split, and each action finishes in a *santi* stance. The rear hand comes through with the advance of the rear foot, in one single split action. This is a good practice for beginners, before going on to the standard *moving stance split.*

ACTION 1: Start from left *santishi*. Do not move the feet or right fist. Clench both hands and pull the left fist back to the belly, then bring it up past the solar plexus and drill forward and up to nose height. Keep the left elbow tucked in and the ulnar edge turned over. Press the head up and look forward. (image 3.12

ACTION 2: Advance the right foot but do not follow in with the left foot. As the right foot lands and grabs the ground, let the left foot swivel to forty-five degrees to take a *santi* stance with the right foot leading and the left foot back, most of the weight on the left leg. Drill the right fist up past the solar plexus and out to the left elbow, then along above the left forearm, then, as the right fist approaches the left fist, rotate them inward and unclench the hands. Split the right hand forward and down to chest height and bring the left hand back to the belly. Press the head up and look forward. (image 3.13)

- • Carry on in this way, alternating right and left.

Pointers

- o Do not change the height of the stance while changing position. The split must be completed as the foot lands – hands and feet combining with integrated power and timing.

- *Turn around* and *closing move* for *fixed stance split* are similar to those of the *standard split*, see description 1d.

3. REVERSE STANCE SPLIT   àobù pīquán   拗步劈拳

3a Reverse Stance Right Split   àobù yòu pīquán   拗步右劈拳

Start from left *santishi*.

ACTION 1: Withdraw the left foot back to beside the right foot and touch down to shift onto the left leg. Clench fists and pull the left fist back to join the right fist at the belly. (image 3.14)

ACTION 2: Bring the left fist up past the solar plexus then drill forward and up to nose height with the ulnar edge turned up. Step the right foot a half-step forward and follow in with the left foot to nestle it by the right ankle. Press the head up and look forward. (image 3.15)

ACTION 3: Take a big step forward with the left foot and follow in a half-step with the right foot, keeping most weight on the right leg. Bring the right hand past the solar plexus, to the left elbow, then along above the left forearm to unclench and split forward. Pull the left hand back to the belly. The hand movements are identical to those of *standard split* described earlier. Press the head up and look forward. (images 3.16 and 3.16 front)

3b Reverse Stance Left Split   àobù zuǒ pīquán   拗步左劈拳

ACTION 1: Take a half-step forward with the left foot and follow in with the right. Clench the right fist, pull it back to the belly, and then drill it forward and up to nose height, ulnar edge turned over. Look forward. (image 3.17)

ACTION 2: Take a big step forward with the right foot and follow in a half-step with the left. Bring the left fist up past the solar plexus and drill forward above the right forearm. As the left fist approaches the right fist, rotate the fists inward [thumb towards palm] and unclench them, chopping the left hand forward and down and pulling the right back to the belly. (image 3.18)

Pointers

3.18

- o Drill the left fist out as the right foot advances a half-step. Split the right hand forward as the left foot lands forward. The upper and lower body act together.

- o Keep the lumbar and waist area lively and loose. Urge the right shoulder into the *right split*, and urge the left shoulder into the *left split*.

- o The stance should have an appropriate width between the feet for stability – neither on a straight line, nor wider than the shoulders.

4. OLD STYLE SPLIT   lǎoshì pīquán   老式劈拳

This method really is a splitting <u>fist</u>, as it uses fists throughout [although it uses a palm, the name in Chinese of split is 'splitting fist – *piquan*']. One fist pulls back and the other fist strikes out and down to pound. The footwork is the same as the *standard split*, the main difference between them is in the use of fists.

ACTION 1: The actions of the feet and hands are similar to those of the first action of the standard, or moving stance, split, see description 1a.

ACTION 2: Take a big step forward with the right foot and follow in a half-step with the left foot. Bring the right fist up past the solar plexus then drill out along the left forearm. As the fist approaches the left fist, inwardly rotate both forearms slightly so that the fist eyes face up. Pull the left fist back to the belly and split forward and down with the right fist to chest height. Bend the right arm slightly, urge the shoulder forward, settle the elbow, press the head up, and look forward. (image 3.19)

3.19

- • Carry on alternating right and left.

Pointers

- o All points to consider are the same as *standard split,* the only difference being that *standard split* uses the palm and *old style split* uses the fist to strike. When you use the fist to split forward and down this gives a hidden pounding and punching power and intent. It uses the fist and forearm to strike, and is a pounding action forward and down. Just as the fist arrives at the point of contact, use the forward drive of the legs, the settled extension of the shoulder and elbow, and the settling of the wrist forward to create a unified whole body power.

- • *Turn around* and *closing move* for *old style split* are similar to those of *standard split*, see descriptions Split 1c and 1d.

5. DODGING SPLIT   yáoshēn pīquán   摇身劈拳

Dodging split uses body technique and positioning for evasion while the hands still perform the splitting action to counterattack. Start from left *santishi*.

ACTION 1: Clench the left hand to a fist and pull it back to the belly. Withdraw the left foot to beside the right foot and shift back to the right leg. Turn the body a bit to the right. Press the head up and look forward. (image 3.20)

ACTION 2: Advance the left foot a half-step to the forward right with the toes hooked slightly out. Drill the left fist up past the solar plexus, forward and out with the ulnar edge turned up, arm bent, and fist at nose height. Keep the right fist at the belly. Press the head up and look forward. (image 3.21)

- Follow through with a regular splitting strike. The rest of the actions are the same as the *standard split* described above.

Pointers

- o *Dodging split* emphasizes circular footwork. First withdraw the lead foot then step forward.

- o Shift the weight back when the lead foot withdraws. At this time the body should turn away and tuck in with an evasive dodging action.

- o The actions should link together without hesitation.

- *Turn around* and *closing move* for *dodging split* are similar to those of *standard split*, see descriptions 1c and 1d.

6. RETREATING SPLIT   tuìbù pīquán   退步劈拳

Retreating split trains retreating footwork. A characteristic of Xingyiquan's footwork is, "to advance, first advance the lead foot, and when it advances, the other foot must follow in. To retreat, first retreat the rear foot, and when it retreats, the other foot must withdraw." *Retreating split* uses this characteristic footwork – that of first retreating the rear foot then withdrawing the lead foot. Start from left *santishi*.

ACTION 1: Retreat the right foot a half-step and shift back onto the right leg, then withdraw the left foot to touch down beside the right foot. Clench the left fist and pull back to the belly, then drill forward and up past the solar plexus to nose height with the ulnar edge turned up. Press the head up and look forward. (image 3.22)

ACTION 2: Retreat a big step back with the left foot then withdraw the right foot a half-step to take a *santi* stance with the right leading and the left behind. Perform a *standard split* with the right hand and pull the left hand back to the belly. Press the head up and look forward. (image 3.23)

3.22   3.23

- Carry on, alternating right and left.

Pointers

   o When retreating, the toes touch down first, then the rest of the foot. The retreating step needs to be agile, and the withdrawing step must follow smoothly. The backward weight shift should be stable.

   o The first actions must work together – the left fist drills out as the right foot retreats and the left foot withdraws.

   o The second actions must work together – the right hand splits as the left foot retreats and the right foot withdraws.

   o Do not apply hard power when doing the *retreating split*. Keep the movement soft to work on coordination and smoothness.

- *Turn around* and *closing move* for *retreating split* are similar to those of *standard split*, see descriptions Split 1c and 1d.

- Referred to in some classics as *cat washes its face,* the technique *retreating split* is indeed similar, but emphasizes the footwork. The technique *cat washes its face* emphasizes the hand action.

- There is also another type of *retreating split* that is performed thusly – the right hand splits forward as the left foot retreats back. The left foot lands with a thump. This is just a different personal choice in technique. Everyone may choose from a variety of methods according to their experience and preference.

PROBLEMS OFTEN MET IN SPLIT[8]

PROBLEM 1: A beginner often focuses on the route that the hands and fists take in any technique that involves a drilling action [in most techniques the fists drill as they rise] and neglects to keep the elbows snug to the ribs. This causes partial power delivery because whole body power is inhibited.

---

[8] Editor's note: Problems 1 through 7 are common amongst beginners, and must be dealt with as they learn the first technique of splitting palm. If not, the same problems will haunt the students as they learn the next four element techniques, and affect all efforts in Xingyiquan.

CORRECTIONS: The teacher must repeatedly explain the movement requirements and the tracking line of the elbows. The teacher must work physically with the students to help them feel the difference in force between when the elbows are tucked in and when they are not. Do this by leaning into a student's hands or forearms as he holds the different postures. This will help the students to make the correction, to tuck in the elbows and keep them snug to the ribs.

PROBLEM 2: The student allows the body to rise and fall while advancing. He allows his body to come up during the half-step forward, which dissipates power.

CORRECTIONS: The problem arises because not enough attention is paid to the supporting knee. The student is not consciously controlling the height of the stance with the knees. The key lies in controlling the amount of knee flex throughout the action. The student should be sure to bend the supporting leg when advancing into the single leg stance, to keep this stance the same height as the *santishi*. A certain rise and fall cannot be avoided, but it should be limited to five percent of a person's height.

PROBLEM 3: The student's back foot follows in with the heel in a straight line with the lead foot, or even a twisted stance, making the body and stance unstable.

CORRECTIONS: The reason for this problem is incorrect placement of the rear foot as it lands from the follow-in step. As the rear foot lands, the insides of the feet should be on either side of a fist-width line. Any larger lateral distance and the groin area will be open. Any smaller and the stance will be unstable. The base must be just large enough to provide stability. More post standing will make the correct position comfortable and fixed into the body.

PROBLEM 4: The student drags the hip when bringing the back foot in, so that the rear foot lands in a stance that is too open laterally. This causes the groin area to be open.

CORRECTIONS: Weak hip action is usually the result of focusing on the lead foot and hands and forgetting or ignoring the back foot follow-in step. When stepping the back foot up, the teacher must emphasize that the knee brings the foot in. Roll the hip in and align the knee to bring the foot forward. The student must also be careful to place the rear foot at an angle smaller than forty-five degrees to the forward line.

PROBLEM 5: The lead foot slips forward as the student hits, when the back foot comes in.

CORRECTIONS: The main cause of this problem is that the student does not use a 'trampling power' when landing the lead foot – the toes do not grip the ground. When the lead foot lands it should combine a 'stamping downward' power with a 'backward raking' power. The secondary cause is overextension of the lead knee. The knee should always maintain a certain flexion when the lead leg lands, ideally a 150 degree angle between the lower leg and the thigh. The legs should also have an appropriate 'gathering in power' between them. That is, the lead foot should exert a raking force that pulls it back, which will prevent it from sliding forward. The cause of these mistakes is usually taking too big a step forward and keeping too low. Beginners should take an appropriately smaller step forward at first, and keep the stance relatively high. They can gradually lengthen the step as they improve.

PROBLEM 6: The student is unstable or the feet and hands do not arrive simultaneously.

CORRECTIONS: The cause of instability is often either taking too big a step forward or turning the waist too much to punch towards the midline. Focus on punching forward by using a target. Getting the timing of the feet and hands right needs a lot of practice, focusing on the timing.

PROBLEM 7: The buttocks stick out backwards when the student punches forward.

CORRECTIONS: Leaning the trunk forward and sticking the buttocks out is a big error in most styles. Pay attention to pressing the head up as if hitting the sky, and to sitting the buttocks down solid as a rock, "stable as Mount Tai."

PROBLEM 8: The student allows the lead hand to drop or move back towards the body as the rear hand comes through to drill along the forearm. This is a common mistake among beginners.

CORRECTIONS: At all times focus on keeping the lead fist at nose height with the ulnar edge turned over – keep the three tips lined up (lead hand, lead foot, nose). The fist that is drilling out must have a forward and upward drilling power, creating an oblique upward pressing power. Wait until the rear fist approaches the leading fist before both fists unclench and pull down and back. Emphasize that a clenched fist always presses forward, and that an open hand pulls back.

PROBLEM 9: There is no whole body power in the strike; the hand slaps out with the force of the arm alone.

CORRECTIONS: Snapping or slapping with the hand and forearm results in a weak, shallow force instead of the required whole body power of Xingyiquan. Students must pay attention when applying force to maintain the elbow joint at an angle of about 135 degrees. Urge the arm forward from the shoulder and follow through by extending the elbow slightly. In this way the whole body is behind the strike. Focusing on the shoulder and elbow will keep students from slapping out with the hand alone.

POWER GENERATION FOR SPLIT

The hand action of split "rises with a drill and lands with a turn over." There is no straight line movement as the hands rise and fall and the arms extend and return – the hands follow an elliptical route throughout. Each hand rises with a drilling fist and drops with a turning over open hand. We must focus not only on the route of the hands or fists along this elliptical track, but also on the track followed by the elbows, since the hands are pushed out directly from the elbows. The elbows must hug the ribs, whether extending or returning; they must 'adhere to the ribs,' 'slide on the ribs,' or 'rub the ribs.'

How can Xingyi masters knock someone far away with just one splitting palm? I think that first of all, the old masters had deep skills, high technical ability, and used whole body power. In addition to hitting the right spot, applying force at the optimal angle, and applying the optimal timing, the key lies in applying force in a continuous, unbroken manner at the instant of impact. This increases the length of time of the applied force, thus giving the ability to knock someone far away.

Split should be applied with a wavelike power, but this wave must not be too large or obvious. It is more a matter of synchronizing the hands, eyes, body, and feet and adding focus. The power delivery of split is to chop downward and to push forward, with a very slight upward 'lengthening power' in the body to counterbalance the downward action. The application of these three forces at once with a continuous unbroken energy at the instant of impact at the opportune time is what makes split effective. When using split, first apply the downward forward power. This makes the receiver unwittingly apply an upward countering force. 'Borrow his force to augment your own.' Take the receiver's upward opposition and apply an upward force from your lumbar/waist area. This makes it easy to lift his root. Once his root is lost his body is unstable and his power dissipated. A forceful push forward then will propel him a long way off.

- The downward and forward action of split comes from the settling of the elbow.

- The upward lengthening power comes from the upward press of the head and the lengthening of the lumbar area.

- The forward drive comes from the back heel driving into the ground and the body's forward thrust with the shoulder and waist urging into the move; add a drop of the shoulder and an extension of the arm to push and deliver the power.

- The integration of these power applications uses mainly the strength of the legs, lower back and shoulder girdle. The resulting force comes largely from the leg force and body technique. You could say that the legs, lumbar/waist area, and shoulders contribute sixty to seventy percent of the force.

- Concentrate your power and force on the last extension, synchronizing the release of force with an expulsion of breath.

Of course, the key to split is whole body power – the hands and feet arriving smoothly together, the whole body's force as one, the power integrated. When hitting with split, be sure to press the head up. When the hand chops forward and down, hold the idea of lengthening the head slightly upward. This gives greater forward and downward splitting power to the hand.

BREATHING CYCLE FOR SPLIT

You must coordinate positional breathing once you are comfortable with the movement, in order to gain whole body power.

- Inhale as the lead hand clenches and pulls back. Move slowly and focus on keeping an imposing manner.

- Pause your breath as the lead foot advances a half-step and the lead hand drills out.

- Exhale as the rear foot steps forward and the rear hand comes through to split.

PRACTICAL APPLICATIONS FOR SPLIT

The classic texts say, "learn the set way, but there is no set way in application." You need to act according to the actual situation; you cannot just perform actions as if performing a routine form, but must use techniques flexibly. The key to using split is to apply the power specific to the split technique.

The hands protect the centre line when they drill up. The hands should defend the midline at all times no matter whether you are advancing, retreating, or stepping around.

Analyze the utilization of split according to its structure.

- The implication of the lead hand clenching and pulling in, then drilling out, is: the lead hand grabs and pulls down the attacker's hand, grabbing clothes if they are there, otherwise grabbing 'meat.'

- The implication of the forward drill is: hit the attacker's head or defend by jamming, being aware that you can open the hand to change to a hooking pull.

When advancing, advance the whole body, so when the rear hand comes through to chop down it strikes the attacker's head or chest as you advance, using the footwork to shove the body and the hand to split through, seeking to push the attacker away.

Whether or not you can realize these goals depends on hard practice every day, how matched your strength is to your opponent, and your ability to apply the technique with the proper direction, angle, and timing. As long as you are using a technique or power approximating that of split, that is, if you strike forward and down from above using the split power, then whether you strike with open hand, fist, or forearm, it falls into the range of the 'split' technique.

THE POEM ABOUT SPLIT

劈拳似斧性属金，起钻落翻细推寻。拳掌劈落头上顶，手脚齐到方为真。

Split is like chopping with an axe. Its character is that of metal.

Initiate with a drill and land with a turnover, a little force will push an opponent eight feet away.

The head presses up as the fist or hand lands the strike,

The hands and feet arrive together and go direct to the core.

DRILL 钻拳

INTRODUCTION TO DRILL, *ZUAN QUAN* (DRILLING FIST)

Xingyiquan classic texts say: "The element that drill relates to is water; it is like a bolt of lightning, and the internal organ that it relates to is the Kidney." In describing drill as having the form of lightning, previous generations of Xingyiquan masters were alluding to its speed. Drill has the ability to enter in an instant, to enter before an opponent has time to see it or react to it. Drill is like water because it can bubble up continuously and enter into the smallest gap as does water. When drill launches up, it surges up like a bubbling spring out of the ground, or like waves breaking on the shore. "Drill relates to the Kidney" conforms to the correlation of elements to internal organs found in traditional Chinese medical theory. In this correlation between five elements and internal organs, the Kidney relate to water, so to push this reasoning further, drill relates to the

Kidney.[9]

There are many different ways to perform drill, but every region and every style agree on one thing: it drills forward and up from below. This is its common character and wherein lies its key. Variations in footwork for drill include: *aligned stance drill*, *reverse stance drill*, and *retreating drill*. Variations in hand techniques include: *coiling drill* and *pressing drill*. Variations in body techniques include: *dodging drill* and *turn around drill*.

We should first perform the method that is the most representative. As the classics say, "first learn the standard, then refine the variations." By 'standard' they mean the most conventional method, that which uses the standard power, the most common methods and applications. By 'variations' they mean the alternate ways of doing techniques and applications.

METHODS OF PERFORMING DRILL

1. ALIGNED STANCE DRILL (STANDARD DRILL)

shùnbù zuānquán   顺步钻拳

1a Right Drill   yòu zuānquán   右钻拳

Start from left *santishi*.

ACTION 1: First clench the left hand without changing its position relative to the body, and turn the fist heart up. Clench the right hand at the belly. Then advance the left foot a half-step and follow in with the right foot to beside the left ankle without touching down. Turn the left fist over so the fist heart faces down and tuck the thumb in and the wrist down [combine radial flexion of the forearm with dorsiflexion of the wrist]. Bend the left elbow to bring the left fist closer to the chest – one forearm plus a fist away – the fist at shoulder height and the elbow below that. Urge the left shoulder forward into the action, release tension in the shoulders and settle the elbows. Press the head up and look forward. (image 3.24)

ACTION 2: Take a big step forward with the right foot and follow in with the left foot, keeping most weight on the left leg. Drill the right fist up past the solar plexus then along to inside the left fist until it arrives at nose height, ulnar edge twisted up and elbow rolled in. Tuck and press down the left fist and pull it back snug to the belly, fist heart down. Urge the right shoulder into the action and keep an angle of 100 to 120 degrees between the upper arm and forearm. Press the head up and settle the trunk structure slightly

3.24   3.25

---

[9] Editor's note: See Part One Chapter One and Part Four Chapter Two for more detail on the correspondences of the five elements.

[translator's. note: Point the rear knee down and do not allow the leg to collapse, to readjust the trunk structure to settle under the punch.] while lengthening the spine. Look forward. (image 3.25)

1b   Left Drill   zuǒ zuānquán   左钻拳

ACTION 1: Advance the right foot a half-step and follow in with the left foot to beside the right ankle without touching down. Rotate the right fist and bend the elbow to tuck and press down, fist heart down. The fist should be a distance of one forearm plus a fist away from the chest. The fist is at shoulder height and the elbow settled down below that. Press the head up and look forward. (image 3.26)

ACTION 2: Take a big step forward with the left foot and follow in a half-step with the right, keeping most weight on the right leg. Twist the left fist heart up, and drill it up past the solar plexus, forward, and up inside the right fist. The left fist finishes at nose height with the ulnar edge up and the elbow tucked in. Pull the right fist down and back to the belly, fist down and elbow snug to the right ribs. Press the head up and settle the trunk structure down slightly. Look forward past the left fist. (images 3.27 and front and top)

- Carry on practicing *left drill* and *right drill*, the number of repetitions determined by the size of the practice area and your fitness.

Pointers

    o Work the upper and lower limbs together: the leading foot advances a half-step as the leading fist tucks and presses down.

    o Fist and foot must arrive as one, with no time lag. The back foot takes a big step forward as the back fist drills forward.

    o On the first move from *santishi*, do not move the feet while the left hand clenches and turns over. After this, press down as you advance.

1c Drill Turn Around   zuānquán zhuànshēn   钻拳转身

Using _right_ drill as an example.

ACTION 1: Hook the right foot in on the spot and shift onto the right leg, turning the body around to the left to face back in the direction from which you came. After turning around, withdraw the left foot a half-step. Rotate the right fist outward and raise the right elbow over the head. Keep the left fist at the belly. Look forward ['forward' is back in the direction from which you came]. (image 3.28)

ACTION 2: Advance the left foot and follow in with the right to take a _santi_ stance with the left foot leading and the right foot behind. Press and cover forward with

the right forearm and continue down to the belly with the right fist, fist heart down. Drill forward and up to nose height from the belly with the left fist, fist heart and ulnar side twisted up. Press the head up and look forward (image 3.29)

Pointers

o   Lift the right elbow at the same time that you hook-step the right foot in to turn the body around. Hook the foot in as much as possible. The weight shift should be quick and the left foot should withdraw immediately.

o   Three actions must happen together, working as an integrated unit: the left foot advances; the left fist drills out, and the right fist covers and pulls back.

o   The entire _drill turn around_ must be smooth with no hesitation.

1d Drill Closing Move   zuānquán shōushì   钻拳收势

Once you have arrived back at the place and facing the same direction where you did the opening position, continue until you get to a _left drill_. Then you may close the drill practice.

ACTION 1: You are in a _santi_ stance with the left foot leading and the right back, so do not move the feet. Tuck and rotate the left fist inward and press it down to the belly, fist heart down. Press the left foot down into the ground. Press the head up and look forward. (image 3.30)

ACTION 2: Shift forward, bringing the right foot up to the left foot. Keep the legs bent and the knees together to maintain the stance at the same height. Keep the fists at the belly with the elbows snug to the ribs. Press the head up and look forward. (image 3.31)

ACTION 3: Unclench the hands, lower them, and then circle them up at the sides with the arms slightly bent. When they arrive at shoulder height with the palms up and elbows dropped, bring the hands together in front of the face, fingers pointing to each other and palms down. Keep the legs bent. (images 3.32 A and B)

ACTION 4: Press the hands down to the belly then place them at the sides as you straighten up the legs. Turn right to face the front to stand at attention, and *drill closing move* is completed. (image 3.33)

Pointers

o The important points to consider for *drill closing move* are the same as those of *split closing move*, see description Split 1d.

2. REVERSE STANCE DRILL　　àobù zuānquán　　拗步钻拳

The alternative ways of performing drill are just slight changes in footwork or hand technique. Should the leading hand change its technique in a way appropriate and applicable within the drill technique, as long as the rear hand comes through with a drill, then the technique should be seen as drill. Naturally, there will be differences in technique between regions or teachers, so we should look for the similarities. Start from left *santishi*.

2a Reverse Stance Right Drill　　àobù yòu zuānquán　　拗步右钻拳

ACTION 1: Withdraw the left foot to beside the right ankle without touching down (you may touch down if you need to) and shift back to the right leg. Keep the legs bent to maintain the same height as the *santi* stance. Clench the left hand and pull it back to the belly, then bring it up past the solar plexus and drill forward and up to nose height. Keep the left arm bent and twist the ulnar edge up. Clench the right hand and keep it at the belly. Press the head up and look forward past the left fist. (image 3.34)

ACTION 2: Advance the left foot a big step and follow in a half-step with the right, keeping the weight on the right leg. Turn the left fist over to press down, bend the elbow slightly, and press down to the belly, fist heart down. Drill the right fist up past the solar plexus then forward and up to nose height, passing inside the left fist, and rotating out to turn the fist heart and ulnar edge up. Urge the right shoulder forward, press the head up, release tension in the shoulders, drop the buttocks, settle the elbows, and look forward. (images 3.35 and front)

2b Reverse Stance Left Drill   àobù zuǒ zuānquán   拗步左钻拳

ACTION 1: Advance the left foot a half-step and follow in the right foot to by the left ankle. Rotate and tuck the right fist over and to the left to press the forearm down in front, fist heart down. Bend the right arm slightly and keep the fist at shoulder height. Press the head up and look forward past the right fist. (image 3.36)

ACTION 2: Take a big step forward with the right foot and follow in a half-step with the left, keeping the weight back on the left leg. Press the right fist down to the belly, fist heart down, and drill the left fist up past the solar plexus, inside the right fist, forward and up to nose height, ulnar edge twisted up. Urge the left shoulder forward, press the head up, and look forward. (image 3.37)

Pointers

o   The action of the *reverse stance drill* is: advance the left foot, press the right fist down, step the right foot forward, drill the left fist. The hand technique is the same as the *standard drill*, the only difference is the combination of footwork with hand technique. Make sure to synchronize the right and left, upward and downward actions.

o   When you strike with a drill you must keep the lumbar/waist area lively. Increase your force by turning from below to urge the shoulder into the move.

2c Reverse Stance Drill Turn Around   zuānquán zhuànshēn 钻拳转身

From *reverse stance <u>right</u> drill* (image 3.38 A)

ACTION 1: First step the left foot forward, hooked in, and turn the body around 180 degrees to the right, shifting onto the left leg. Withdraw the right foot by the left foot, and then step forward in the new direction. Bring the right fist in to the waist then stab out to the rear [in the returning direction], fist heart turned up. Look at the right fist. (images 3.38 B)

ACTION 2: Take a big step forward with the right foot and follow in a half-step with the left foot. While doing this, cover and press with the right fist and bring it back to the belly, fist heart down. Drill with the left fist to nose height. Look in the direction of the left fist. (images 3.39 A and B)

- *Drill turn around* from *reverse stance <u>left</u> drill* is similar, just transposing right and left.

2d Reverse Stance Drill Closing Move   zuānquán shōushì 钻拳收势

From a *reverse stance <u>right</u> drill*, pull the right fist to the belly and turn the body slightly without moving the feet. From a *reverse stance <u>left</u> drill*, step the left foot forward to take a *santi* stance. Then press the left fist down to the belly. The rest of the closing is the same as the *standard split closing*, see description in Split 1d.

3. DODGING DRILL   yáoshēn zuānquán   摇身钻拳

3a Dodging Right Drill   yáoshēn yòu zuānquán   摇身右钻拳

ACTION 1: Clench both fists and advance the left foot a half-step, bringing the right foot beside the left ankle. Rotate the left fist over to turn the fist heart up. Roll the elbow right and drop, circling down to the left. Then circle up, forward and right, to finish with the fist heart facing down, arm bent, and fist at shoulder height. Bring the right fist up with the fist heart facing out, and circle it up and right around outside the left arm, then lower it to the right waist, fist heart up. Do both hand actions simultaneously. Press the head up and look forward. (images 3.40 and B)

ACTION 2: Take a big step forward with the right foot and follow in a half-step with the left, keeping the weight on the left leg. At this time, tuck and press down with the left fist and bring it back to the belly, fist heart down. Drill the right fist forward and up to nose height, first passing by the solar plexus then inside the left fist. Twist the right arm's ulnar edge up, press the head up and look forward. (image 3.41)

3b Dodging Left Drill   yáoshēn zuǒ zuānquán 摇身左钻拳

ACTION 1: Advance the right foot a half-step and follow in with the left foot to by the right ankle without touching down. Settle the right elbow down and bring the left fist up across the right forearm, then circle it left and down to the left waist, fist heart up. Bring the right fist down and right, then forward and left to tuck in and press down, fist heart down, at shoulder height. Circle both arms simultaneously without interruption. Press the head up and look forward. (images 3.42 A and B)

ACTION 2: Take a big step forward with the left foot and follow in a half-step with the right to take a *santi* stance with the left foot leading and the right foot back. Tuck and press the right fist down to the belly, fist heart down, and drill the left fist forward and up. The action is the same as that described above in *standard drill*. (image 3.43)

Pointers

- o   The key to the *dodging drill* is that the hands work together to circle in opposite directions – up and down, left and right, forward and back. The fists and arms must coordinate with each other and with the body technique. The action of the body is intended to give more power to the hands and arms, so you should practise this until you get it.

    o   Circle the hands as you take the forward half-step, synchronizing the upper and lower limbs. At first make big circles, then once you are comfortable with the action you may gradually decrease the size.

- *Turn around* and *closing move* for the *dodging drill* are similar to those of the *standard drill*, see descriptions in Drill 1c and 1d.

4.   RETREATING DRILL   tuìbù zuānquán   退步钻拳

Start from left *santishi*.

4a   Retreating Right Drill   tuìbù yòu zuānquán   退步右钻拳

ACTION 1: Retreat the right foot a half-step and withdraw the left foot to in front of the right, touching down the toes. Clench the left hand and place the forearm crossways to press down at shoulder height, fist heart down. Keep the right fist in front of the belly and look forward. (image 3.44)

ACTION 2: Retreat the left foot and settle into it with a thump, sitting back onto the left leg without moving the right foot. While doing this, tuck and press the left fist into the belly, fist heart down. Drill the right fist forward and up to nose height, ulnar edge turned up. Press the head up and look forward. (image 3.45)

4b   Retreating Left Drill   tuìbù zuǒ zuānquán   退步左钻拳

ACTION 1: Retreat the left foot a half-step and withdraw the right foot to in front of the left. Cross the right forearm and press down, fist heart down, at shoulder height. Do not move the left fist. Look forward. (image 3.46)

ACTION 2: Retreat the right foot and settle onto it with a thump, sitting back onto the right leg without moving the left foot. Tuck and press down the right fist and pull it back to the belly, fist heart down. Drill the

left fist forward and up to nose height, ulnar edge turned up. Press the head up and look in front of the left fist. (image 3.47)

- Carry on, alternating left and right. The number of repetitions depends on the size of the training ground, training time, and your fitness.

Pointers

o *Retreating drill* is done to train retreating footwork, the hand technique is similar to *standard drill*. To retreat, first retreat the rear foot and then withdraw the leading foot. The retreating step shifts the weight back, giving the impetus of moving back before actually moving the body. Retreat the left foot as you drill the right fist. When the left foot lands the whole foot settles into the ground. Use the reactive force of thumping the left foot to turn the waist and put the shoulder into the right fist's drill. Sit the buttocks down.

o When the leading foot retreats, press the leading fist down as the rear foot withdraws.

4c Retreating Drill Turn Around   tuìbù zhuànshēn   退步转身

There is no *turn around* when practicing the *retreating drill*. When you want to move forward you may perform the *standard advancing drill*.

4d Retreating Drill Closing Move   tuìbù shòushì   退步收势

Closing move of *retreating drill* is similar to that of *standard drill*, see descriptions in Drill 1d.

5. COILING DRILL   chǎnshǒu zuānquán   缠手钻拳

5a Left Coiling Drill   zuǒ chǎnshǒu zuānquán   左缠手钻拳

ACTION 1: Advance the left foot a half-step and bring the right foot beside the left ankle. Turn the left hand to face palm up, then bend the wrist and circle down. Continue the circle up and right, then clench the fist with the fist heart down, the elbow bent, and the fist at shoulder height. Keep the right fist at the belly. Press the head up and look past the left fist. (images 3.48 A and B)

ACTION 2: Step the right foot a big step forward and follow in with the left foot a half-step. Tuck and pull the left fist back to the belly with the fist heart down. Drill

the right fist forward and up to nose height with the ulnar edge turned up. Press the head up and look forward. (image 3.49)

5b Right Coiling Drill   yòu chǎnshǒu zuānquán   右缠手钻拳

ACTION 1: Open the right hand and turn the palm up. Bend the right wrist and wind the hand left and down. Complete the circle right and up and clench the right fist to press left and down, fist heart down, with the forearm crossways and the fist at shoulder height. Keep the left fist at the belly. Advance the right foot a half-step and follow in with the left foot to beside the right without touching down. Press the head up and look at the right fist. (images 3.50 A and B)

ACTION 2: Take a big step forward with the left foot and follow in a half-step with the right. Tuck and press the right fist and pull it back to the belly, fist heart down. Drill the left fist up and forward to nose height, ulnar edge turned up. Press the head up and look forward. (image 3.51)

Pointers

- o The key to *coiling drill* is the coiling, trapping circle of the lead hand. Hook the wrist to trap down and in. Use the shoulder to draw the movement of the elbow, and the elbow to draw the arm and hand in the circular movement. Hide a hooked punch in the forward circle when you clench your fist. The palm traps during the back and down action. The fist punches during the forward and up action.

- o You may make the movement large while training the body technique and finding the power of the waist, shoulder, elbow and hand. When you are comfortable with the movement you may make it smaller to do it faster.

- o Move the hands and feet together. The lead hand coils, hits and presses as the lead foot advances. The back hand drills as the back foot steps through.

- • *Turn around* and *closing move* for *coiling drill* are similar to those of *standard drill*, see descriptions in Drill 1c and 1d.

PROBLEMS OFTEN MET IN DRILL[10]

PROBLEM 1: The student thinks only of the forward drill and forgets the pulling back hand, so that the two hit with unequal force.

CORRECTIONS: Explain the theory clearly, that the drilling out fist and the pulling in fist are paired forces with equal strength, opposite direction, and along the same plane. The classics say, "Swallow and spit with equal strength, hit out with full force and pull in with full force." It helps to have the students hit themselves in the *dantian* with the returning fist.

PROBLEM 2: The student does not turn up the ulnar edge of the drilling fist, or turns it inadequately.

CORRECTIONS: The ulnar edge needs to turn up to apply power. This action keeps the elbow tucked in, and the elbow needs to be tucked in to defend your midline and to attack the opponent's centre line. This position is needed for both the punch and for the hidden elbow technique. When the forearm is externally rotated this brings the little finger side up. This rotation should be neither overdone nor underdone. If the arm is twisted too much then it becomes stiff and the body gets twisted so that the power won't flow smoothly. If it isn't twisted enough then the elbow technique can't be fully used.

PROBLEM 3: The student thinks only of the line of the fist and not the elbow, resulting in a flicking up power.

CORRECTIONS: Pay attention to the requirements of the movement – keep the elbow snug to the ribs when drilling up. The elbow must close in towards the solar plexus and send the fist forward and up, so that both elbow and fist follow a straight line. Twisting the fist over also aids in tucking in the elbow, which will develop the proper elbow line.

PROBLEM 4: The student punches in a curve or follows a crooked line instead of a straight line.

CORRECTIONS: Pay attention to the straight line. Turn the lumbar and waist area, put the shoulder into the attack, and line up the fist with the elbow to send them both out on a straight line forward and up.

PROBLEM 5: The student applies too much force to the punch without proper focus, dissipating power upwards.

CORRECTIONS: First of all, emphasize that drill hits to nose height. Be sure to loosen up and pay particular attention to releasing and settling the shoulders. The instant before the fist arrives at the point of impact, suddenly tighten and apply power. This makes the muscles involved in extension and flexion contract at the same time, stabilizing the joints and increasing the power application.

POWER GENERATION FOR DRILL

The elbows must stay snug to the ribs as the drill strikes forward and up. Actively

---

[10] Editor's note: Review also problems 1 through 7 described in Split.

push the elbow in towards the ribs to start the movement of the fist forward, so that the elbow is fully behind the fist as it goes straight down the midline. The fist must follow a straight line forward and upwards following the midline of the body. The angle between upper arm and forearm should be 120 degrees when the drill is completed. The arm must not be too bent or too straight.

The technique of drill consists of one fist doing a forward and upward torquing uppercut from below as the other fist hooks, presses, and pulls back and down from above. The fists must exert equal power up and down. In biomechanics this is called a couple: two actions of equal force and opposite direction exerted along the same plane. The fist that punches out must have a point of focus, so the fist that pulls in should hit the belly with the same force and focus. This helps to settle the qi to the dantian and to create an explosive whole body force. Hit lightly in early training, then gradually increase the force to develop the ability of the belly to take a hit.

Before drilling out, the fist heart and ulnar edge should twist up to bring the elbow into the ribs. At this time the lumbar and waist area should compress slightly to store power. The elbow should be bent at about a ninety degree angle. Then apply power from the lower trunk area, transfer power to the shoulder, transfer power from the shoulder to the elbow, and transfer power from the elbow to the fist forward. Build a cumulative power from the body core to the shoulder through the elbow and to the fist. The fist continues to twist as it goes forward, like a mechanical drill.

Xingyi's mother fists all use this whole body power instead of segmental power. This whole body power is the most obvious characteristic of Xingyiquan. Xingyiquan's unique positional structure and training methods build this whole body power quickly, better than other styles.

To achieve a strong torquing power all the joints throughout the body need to be adjusted to their optimal state. Since Xingyiquan's power expression is whole body power, you must respect the general principle of "pre-load back to go forward, pre-load right to go left, pre-load left to go right." This is completely in accordance with biomechanical principles.[11] Specifically, this means:

- Urge the left shoulder forward slightly as the left fist circles and presses. This brings the right shoulder slightly back and stores energy in the lower back.

- Then, as the right foot strides forward and the left fist pulls back, urge the right shoulder into the move and turn the waist, sending the right fist forward and up.

- Combine this movement with a settling of qi into the dantian, and, at the last instant of the hit, settle the buttocks down slightly to increase the drilling force

[11] Editor's note: This is not a cocking action that telegraphs your attack, but is rather using an aggressive 'defensive' move to set up the attacking move. This quick and short counter movement pre-loads the muscles and enhances their ability to contract instantly, by using the muscles elasticity added to a well timed contraction, thus simultaneously saving energy, remaining more relaxed, and increasing the resultant force. You need to practice slowly to find the coordination and develop the habit of using this movement, then practice quickly to find the optimal speed and angle. In use it must be done quickly, or else the energy will be absorbed and dissipated.

upward. [translator's note: do not necessarily sit lower, but drive the knee down to settle the body under the punch and direct the force up]

BREATHING CYCLE FOR DRILL

You must coordinate positional breathing once you are comfortable with the movement in order to gain whole body power.

- Inhale as the lead foot advances and the lead hand circles to press.

- Exhale as the rear foot steps through and the rear hand drills forward.

- You may gain more power and remind yourself to breathe with the abdomen by hitting yourself in the belly with the root of the returning fist.

PRACTICAL APPLICATIONS FOR DRILL

The structure of drill shows it to be a close range technique. Drill attacks by stepping in to bring the body tight to the opponent, attacking by entering to destroy his defensive line. If the opponent approaches, drill defends by directly striking. The key to using drill is to enter to get the body close, and the key to entering is to step in. The classics describe this often:

> "To step in and punch, first take the main door.
>
> Stride through the front door to steal your opponent's place, then even an expert will have trouble defending against you.
>
> To connect with a strike first enter the body, when foot and hand arrive together the technique will work."

The entering footwork must 'steal' the main door – it must take over the opponent's groin area, going through into his rear foot. Get the body tight into the opponent's body. The classics say, "Hit your opponent like an embrace, consider your opponent like common grass." Whether or not you can enter in that close also depends on your courage, so you must develop a win at all costs self-confidence.

The main application of drill is an uppercut, equivalent to the uppercut of boxing or Shaolin style. You must fully utilize the strength of the lower back, turn the waist, and urge the shoulder into the strike. The assisting hand responds to the needs of the moment to block down, block up, knock aside, jam, press down or snap up. As long as the power is drilling then it is drill, whether you drill up, drill obliquely, or drill to one side or another. As long as the strike connects it is a good technique, whether the elbow is a little more bent or extended than is ideal. Your principle is to hit the target, to have an effect. Therefore, "understand techniques without being limited by them, cast off the rules without violating them." You should make full use of your own body factors, particular skills and nature, and do what suits you best.

There is an elbow technique hidden in the traditional drill technique. Drill strikes up from below towards the opponent's stomach, jaw, or other upper body part. If the punch misses, you can bend your arm and thrust your elbow to strike his chest. The key is still to step in to get the body very close.

THE POEM ABOUT DRILL

钻拳似电性属水，进步近身功在腿。拧裹钻翻腰肩功，上钻发劲坐臀尾。

Drill is like lightning and its character is that of water.

The ability to enter to get the body close lies in the legs.

Use the power of the lower back and shoulders to twist, wrap, drill and turn.

Settle down the tailbone to launch the drilling up power.

DRIVE, THRUST 崩拳

INTRODUCTION TO DRIVE, *BENG QUAN* (CRUSHING FIST, THRUSTING PUNCH)

Xingyiquan classic texts say, "The element that drive relates to is wood, its form is like an arrow, and the internal organ that it relates to is the Liver." "Drive relates to wood" means that drive corresponds to wood from among the five elements. "Drive is like an arrow" means that it is swift as an arrow, and that its line of attack is as straight and accurate as that taken by an arrow. "Drive relates to the Liver" is derived from the correlation of the five elements with internal organs found in traditional Chinese medical theory. Since the Liver relates to wood in this correlation, and drive also relates to wood, to push this reasoning further, drive relates to the Liver.[12]

The driving punch is simple and functional, and must be fast and straight. It is said, "Value directness and value speed." Value 'straightness,' or 'directness' does not refer to the straightening of the arm, but to the direction and power application of the punch. Value 'speed' means that the punch must be fast. The classics say, "The intent flows throughout the whole body, the movement comes from the footwork, the hands come and go, the posture is like bending a bow." Drive must be as fast as an arrow shot from a bow, and shoot out as continuously.

Traditionally, drive was done pushing off only from the right leg, the left leg leading. The left foot always entered – always one foot advancing and the other foot following in – so the skill could become very deep, the power strong, and the technique always perfect. The Xingyi masters Guo Yunshen and Shang Yunxiang were both famous for this punch. It was said of Guo Yunshen that no one could face his half-step driving punch.

The flavour of drive differs by region and among the traditional branches, with different combinations of footwork with hands, and of power use. This is normal, but there is also a common element, and that is to punch with one extended arm. If this isn't done then it isn't considered a drive.

METHODS OF PERFORMING DRIVE

Traditionally there are many ways of performing drive. Variations in footwork

---

[12] Editor's note: See Part One Chapter One and Part Four Chapter Two for more detail on the correspondences of the five elements.

coordination with hand timing include *rear foot timed drive*, *lead foot timed drive*, *reverse stance (alternating) drive*, and *retreating drive*. A variation in bodywork is *turn around drive*.

1. STANDARD DRIVE: REAR FOOT TIMED DRIVE

hòujiǎo fālì bēngquán   后脚发力崩拳

1a Right [Rear Foot Timed] Drive   yòu bēngquán   右崩拳

Start from left *santishi*.

ACTION 1: Clench both hands. Turn the left fist heart up and lower the fist slightly to solar plexus height with the elbow slightly bent and tucked in. Put the left shoulder slightly forward as the left fist turns. Turn the right fist heart up and lift the fist slightly. Advance the left foot a half-step and settle firmly onto it. Do not move the right foot. Press the head up and look past the left fist. (image 3.52)

ACTION 2: Follow in with the right foot a half-step to behind the left heel, sliding into the landing with a thump. The stance width is about one fist-length, and the weight is mostly on the right leg. Keep the legs bent, the right knee tucked into the hollow of the left knee. Extend the right fist, following the line of the left forearm. As the right fist nears the left fist, turn both fist eyes up. Punch the right fist forward [down the midline] with the fist eye angled slightly down and the elbow bent. Urge the punch forward from the shoulder. Pull the left fist back to the belly, fist heart in, and elbow hugging the ribs. Press the head up, sit the buttocks down and look past the right fist. Punch to solar plexus height. (images 3.53 and front)

1b Left [Rear Foot Timed] Drive   zuǒ bēngquán   左崩拳

ACTION 1: Advance the left foot a half-step without moving the right foot. Turn both fist hearts up. Lift the left fist to chest height[13] and keep the right fist in position. Look past the right fist. (image 3.54)

---

[13] Translator's note: The book simply says to 'chest height' so that is how I have translated it throughout. The fist at the belly, prior to punching, is actually raised about a fist-length above the navel, no lower than solar-plexus height and no higher than chest height.

ACTION 2: Follow-in the right foot a half-step and shift forward, keeping the weight on the right leg. Do not move the left foot as the right foot slides in to land with a thump. Keep the knees bent, the right knee nestled in the hollow of the left knee. The right foot is beside the left heel, turned slightly out, and about a fist-length away. Punch the left fist out along the right forearm to solar plexus height. Keep the left arm slightly bent and angle the punching surface slightly. Pull the right fist back to the belly, fist heart in. Press the head up and settle the buttocks down. Look past the left fist and urge the punch forward from the left shoulder. (image 3.55)

3.54

3.55

Pointers

- o   Rotate the fists as you advance the left foot a half-step.

- o   Punch the right fist as the right foot does the follow-in step. The foot and hand must arrive together.

- o   The left foot's half-step should advance further than your own shin length. Make sure that the stance does not rise or fall.

- o   The right foot should slide in, or rake, to thump, not lift to stamp. These techniques have different power applications. The sliding thump transfers power forward, where you want it, while a stamp transfers power upwards, where it is wasted.

- o   Turn the rear foot less than in it is turned in *santi* stance, so that the tucked-in knee tracks smoothly.

- o   Use equal force in the punching fist and the pulling back fist. Turn the waist and shoulders, urge the shoulders into the punch and sink the elbows, to punch with whole body power.

- o   Urge the left shoulder into the left punch and the right shoulder into the right punch to give power and to keep the fist tracking on the midline. The punching arm's forearm is level and upper arm angled, with the elbow bent 140 to 150 degrees. [The elbow is behind the fist throughout the punch, so it must hug the ribs as it drives the fist out.]

- o   The punching fist should be tightly clenched at the moment of impact to increase its strength. Keep the wrist line (back of the hand to arm) straight.

- o   Be sure not to hook up the fist. This makes it easy to catch, and is a weak punch. Press the fist surface forward slightly with the fist eye angled forward and up, tilting slightly to line the forearm up with the two larger knuckles. Do not overdo the tilt, but keep a comfortable and strong line to the punching surface.

1c Drive Turn Around   bēngquán zhuànshēn   崩拳转身

Drive turn around is traditionally called *leopard cat turns over whilst climbing a tree*. This name comes from the way a leopard cat will, on arriving near the top of a tree, turn over and face down. The name is very expressive of the spirit, intent, and structure of this action.

ACTION 1: Bring the left foot around hooked in outside the right toes, keeping the knees bent. Whichever fist was punching, bring it in to the belly, fist heart in. Shift the weight to the left leg and turn around 180 degrees to the right to face back in the direction from which you came. Press the head up and look forward. (image 3.56)

ACTION 2: Bend the right knee and lift it. Turn out the right foot crossways and do a turned heel kick forward and up to shoulder height. Bend the left leg slightly for stability. Turn the fist hearts up, bring the fists up to the solar plexus, then drill forward. Drill the right fist out on top to nose height and drill the left fist to the right elbow. Tuck both elbows in. Keep the chest closed in, the shoulders settled, the head pressed up, and look at the right fist. (images 3.57 A and B)

ACTION 3: After the kick is completed, stamp the right foot forward and down with the foot turned out. Follow in with the left foot a half-step to bring the thighs together, lowering the body and lifting the left heel to form a high resting stance. Keep the weight between the feet [slightly to the rear, so that the lead foot is able to step forward into the next punch]. Drill the left fist up along the right forearm, and as it reaches the right fist, unclench both hands and turn the palms down. Split the left palm forward and down to waist height. Pull the right palm back to beside the right hip. Press the head up and look past the left hand. (images 3.58 A and B)

Pointers

○ Link up the actions smoothly to hook-step around, pull the lead fist in and turn the body around. Press the

head up while turning, do not lower the head or bend at the waist.

- o Kick and do the double drilling punches at the same time, working the upper and lower body together. Stand firmly on the left leg.

- o Reach forward with the foot to land and turn the foot out to trample. Coordinate the hands and feet so the left hand chops and the right hand pulls back as the right foot lands. Be sure to turn the waist, put the shoulders into the action and press the head up.

- o The whole move should be continuous without a break, completed as one action.

1d   Drive Closing Move (Retreating Drive, Final Closing)

bēngquán shōushì   崩拳收势

The *closing move* is the same for all types of driving punch. After arriving back at the opening place and turning around, complete a *right drive* and then a *retreating drive*. The *retreating drive* that is within the *closing move* may also be practised separately as another variety of drive.[14]

After the *retreating drive*, then do the final *closing move*.

Retreating Drive   tuìbù zuǒ bēngquán   退步左崩拳

ACTION 1: Retreat the right foot a half-step and shift back to the right leg, withdrawing the left foot. Turn the right fist heart up and turn the left fist and bring it up to the chest. Look past the right fist (image 3.59)

ACTION 2: Keep withdrawing the left foot steadily, retreating back a full step and landing the full foot solidly. Shift back onto the left leg and withdraw the right foot a half-step with the foot turned out across the stance. Bring the left fist along the right forearm to punch forward, arm slightly bent, at chest height, fist eye up. Pull the right fist back to the belly. Turn the waist and urge the punch forward from the left shoulder. Keep the thighs tightly together, press the head up, and look past the left fist. (image 3.60)

3.59   3.60

Pointers

- o Retreat the right foot at exactly the same time as you turn the right fist.

---

[14] Editor's note: The *retreating drive* trains the ability to strike forward while seemingly retreating. Much of Xingyi emphasises forward moving techniques, so this technique is vital to having a complete set of skills. The combination of *retreating drive* to *forward drive* – a rebounding attack – within the five elements connected form is also a vital skill.

- o The left foot must land with a thump when it retreats.

- o Three actions happen at once – the left fist punches, the left foot lands, and the right fist pulls back.

- o Exhale to put more power into the action.

Final Closing

ACTION 1: Step the left foot forward without moving the right foot, settling into a *santi* stance. Tuck and press the left fist and pull it back to the belly, fist heart down. Keep the right fist at the belly. Press the left foot into the ground, press the head up, and look forward. (image 3.61)

ACTION 2: Shift onto the left leg and bring the right foot up to the left foot, keeping the legs bent and keeping the body at the same height. Keep the fists at the belly. (image 3.62)

ACTION 3: Lower the hands and unclench them, then lift them at the sides of the body, arms slightly bent, turning them gradually so the palms are up when they reach shoulder height. Bend the elbows to bring the palms together in front of the face, fingers pointing to each other, palms down. Keep the legs bent. (images 3.63 and 3.64)

3.61   3.62

ACTION 4: Press the hands down to the belly then to the sides and straighten the legs. Turn ninety degrees [optional] and stand at attention. (image 3.65)

3.63   3.64   3.65

Pointers

- o Three actions are synchronized together: the left fist tucks, presses, and pulls back in; the left foot presses into the ground; the head presses up. Mental focus must be maintained and shown.

- The hands circle up, come in, and press down in one continuous movement, slowly and evenly. Straighten the legs as the hands press down, as one action.

2. LEAD FOOT TIMED DRIVE qiánjiǎo fālì bēngquán 前脚发力崩拳

Start from left *santishi*.

2a Right Lead Foot Timed Drive   yòu bēngquán   右崩拳

ACTION 1: Clench both fists. Turn the left fist heart up and lower the fist to solar plexus height. Flex and tuck in the left elbow slightly [keeping the fist forward to put pressure into the forearm]. Release tension in the left shoulder and urge it forward slightly. Turn the right fist heart up and lift it slightly. Do not move the feet. Press the head up and look past the left fist. (image 3.66)

ACTION 2: Advance the left foot a half-step and quickly bring the right foot up to land behind the left heel, with a stance width of a fist-length. Keep the weight on the right leg and the knees bent, tuck the right knee into the centre of the stance so that it nestles near the hollow of the left knee. Bring the right fist along the left forearm to punch forward in a straight line. When the right fist approaches the left fist turn both fist eyes up. Tilt the right fist eye slightly forward as well to line up the punching surface on the first two knuckles. Keep the right arm slightly bent

and urge the punch forward from the right shoulder. Pull the left fist back to the belly, fist heart in and elbow snug to the ribs. The right fist is at solar plexus height. Press the head up, settle the buttocks down, and look past the right fist. (image 3.67)

3.66   3.67

2b Left Lead Foot Timed Drive   zuǒ bēngquán   左崩拳

ACTION 1: Turn both fist hearts up and lift the left fist slightly to chest height. Look past the right fist. (image 3.68)

ACTION 2: Advance the left foot a full step and quickly bring the right foot up near the left heel, keeping the weight on the right leg. Keep the legs bent and nestle the right knee into the hollow of the left knee. Follow the line of the right forearm with the left fist to punch forward, fist eye tilted forward and up, elbow slightly bent, and shoulder urging the punch forward. Pull the right fist back to the belly, fist heart inward and elbow hugging the ribs. The left fist punches at solar plexus height. Press the head up, sit down, and look past the left fist. (image 3.69)

3.68

3.69

- Carry on, one step for each punch, punching with the left and right fists without changing the lead foot. The number of repetitions is governed by the size of the training area and your fitness.

Pointers

- o The main difference between the *lead foot timed drive* and the *rear foot timed drive* is the synchronization of the footwork with the punch. The driving punch itself is the same. The *lead foot timed drive* punches as the lead foot lands, and the *rear foot timed drive* punches as the rear foot lands with a thump.

- o The *lead foot timed drive* depends on the thrust from the back leg, so the lead foot must attack forward, the fist leading, the trunk leaning forward slightly, and the back knee pushing down to press the shank down to give good power to drive forward. At the instant of launching the punch, urge the shoulder forward, sink the elbow, and grab the ground with the left foot as it lands. The right foot follows in quickly and lightly.

- o Push the rear knee down as the centre of gravity moves forward to create a small shin-to-ground angle so that the leg thrust directs the force more forward than up. Be careful not to lean forward, but to send the power directly to the centre of the body, then transfer to the fist.

3. REVERSE STANCE DRIVE (ALTERNATING DRIVE)

àobù bēngquán   拗步崩拳

Start in left *santishi*. First do a *rear foot timed right driving punch* as described above. (see images 3.52 and 3.53)

3a Reverse Stance Left Drive   àobù zuǒ bēngquán   拗步左崩拳

ACTION 1: Advance the left foot a half-step and lift the right foot to beside the left ankle. Turn the left fist slightly so the fist heart faces up. Lift the right fist to chest height, fist heart up. Press the head up and look past the right fist. (image 3.70)

ACTION 2: Take a large step angled to the forward right with the right foot and follow in with the left foot a large half-step, so that there is one foot-length between the feet. Keep the weight back on the left leg. Follow the line of the right forearm with the left fist to punch forward in a straight line. Urge the left shoulder forward and bend the left elbow slightly, punching to solar plexus height with the fist eye tilted forward and up. Pull the right fist back to the belly, fist heart in. Press the head up, settle the buttocks down, and look past the left fist. (image 3.71)

3.70   3.71

3b Reverse Stance Right Drive   àobù yòu bēngquán   拗步右崩拳

ACTION 1: Advance the right foot a half-step and lift the left foot to inside the right ankle without touching down. Keep the legs bent and the knees together. Turn the left fist slightly to face the fist heart up. Bring the right fist up to the chest, turning the fist heart up and keeping the elbow snug to the ribs. Press the head up and look past the left fist. (image 3.72)

ACTION 2: Take a large step to the forward left with the left foot and follow in a large half-step with the right foot, keeping the weight back on the right leg. The feet should be about a foot-length apart, the knees bent. Bring the right fist along the left forearm to punch forward in a straight line to solar plexus height, putting the right shoulder forward into the punch and keeping the elbow slightly bent. Angle the right fist eye forward and up. Pull the left fist back to the belly, fist heart in. Press the head up, settle the buttocks down, and look past the right fist. (image 3.73)

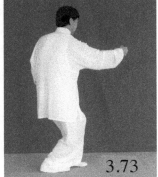

3.72   3.73

- Carry on to left and right.

Pointers

- o The actual punch is still the same as that of the *standard drive*.

- o The *left and right reverse stance drive* is a driving punch that alternates punches by stepping into a reverse stance, changing lead feet each time. The punch should come with the large forward step, hitting as the lead foot lands, that is, the timing is that of a *lead foot timed drive*.

- o The footwork advances in a slight angle to left and right, so pay particular attention that the lead fist stays pointing in the direction to which it will punch. It will then punch straight ahead as the foot comes through. Make sure the body stays stable and does not rise or fall when stepping through.

o For the *reverse stance drive* the action must be tightly coordinated – turn the waist, urge the shoulder into the punch, extend the arm, lead into the fist, drive the lead foot forward and drive hard off the back foot.

PROBLEMS OFTEN MET IN DRIVE[15]

PROBLEM 1: The student's body leans forward and the buttocks stick out. This is an even bigger problem in drive than in the other techniques, due to the shorter stance.

CORRECTIONS: The cause of this is focusing on the forward extension of the arm and moving everything forward into the hit. Correct this by emphasizing pressing the head up and dropping the buttocks like a plumb bob, which will keep the trunk upright.

PROBLEM 2: The student stamps the right foot when doing the *rear foot timed drive*.

CORRECTIONS: Stamping is using force to stamp downward. The *rear foot timed drive* is not a stamp, but is a sliding-in thump, done by rolling in the hip joint and closing the knees to bring the foot forward, shoveling in the right foot to trample forward and down. A shoveling trample has a relatively large forward moving force, which assists transferring power to the punch. A stamp contains only a downward force, which wastes energy.

PROBLEM 3: The student punches with the arms alone, keeping the trunk and shoulders square to the stance. This results in weak spirit and power.

CORRECTIONS: Emphasize using the shoulders to send the punching fist out and pull back the other fist. If the shoulders' power is not used then the body is like a bow without a bowstring – how can it apply its power? The shoulders use the theory of accumulating stretch-tension. Use the lumbar/waist area to draw the shoulders, so that the body technique is played out between the shoulders and body core.

PROBLEM 4: The student loses balance on the hook-step turn around. Three possible reasons for losing balance are: 1) The left foot hooks in too far away from the right foot so that the centre of gravity displaces too far. 2) The head drops down, making the back bend. 3) The left foot hooks in with not enough angle so the body doesn't get turned around.

CORRECTIONS: Firstly, emphasize hooking the foot around to outside the right toes. The hook-step should hook in a lot to make the next movement easier. Secondly, emphasize pressing the head up while turning, and using the spine as an upright pivot line. Thirdly, be sure not to step too far away, just to outside the right toes.

PROBLEM 5: The student loses balance on the landing of *leopard cat turns over whilst climbing a tree*.

CORRECTIONS: The main cause of this is simply lack of mastery of the technique. The thighs do not grip each other tightly enough, the lower back does not turn

---

[15] Editor's note: Review also problems 1 through 7 described in Split.

enough, the left shoulder does not reach far enough into the movement, and/or the right foot does not press out when it lands. Work on each of these problems individually and the student will gradually be able to cope with the whole move.

POWER GENERATION FOR DRIVE

In performing drive, the power is mainly an extension of the arm to punch straight forward while stepping forward or bringing the back foot in, achieving unison of foot and hand, combining the whole body into one hit. How does one hit with a complete power? How does one take the strength of the whole body and transfer power through each segment to build up into the fist surface? This is the goal that we seek in our training. Concentrate on the body technique of countermovement to launch power forward into the punch. Before putting the waist and shoulders into the punch, pull the body back a bit so that it builds up kinetic energy.[16] This action of storing energy [in the body] also increases the line of movement [of the punching shoulder]. When directing the fist forward, send the elbow out from the shoulder, and first bend the elbow ninety degrees, then, when the fist and foot move together, extend the arm to the final point.

The part played by the footwork makes up the majority of the action – the forward reach of the lead foot and the backward thrust of the back foot. This is what the classic saying, "The hands contribute thirty percent and the legs contribute seventy percent to the hit" means. The forward reach and backward thrust of the legs moves the entire body forward as a unit. The forward extension of the fist to punch is built on the forward movement of the body. The power of drive comes from the footwork moving the body forward, turning the lumbar/waist area to urge the shoulder forward, pushing the elbow forward from the shoulder, and finally driving forward into the fist. The power moves from the legs to the arms, increasing cumulatively until it reaches the fist surface.

- Before pushing the body forward be sure to press the back knee down, bringing the shank to an acute angle with the ground to increase the horizontal directional force.

- The driving punch must at all times follow the midline of the body.

  - For the *rear foot timed drive,* you can pretend there is a rope attached to your ankles. Push off with the back foot to forcefully break the rope then step up. Roll in the hip joint and close the knees, bringing the foot in with the knee, and sliding in, not stamping. This type of driving punch is heavy and forceful but not very quick. The *lead foot timed drive* uses a direct charge forward, which is much faster though not quite as strong. You should train both types of drive equally and be able to use either one well.

The kick in the *drive turn around,* or *leopard cat turns over whilst climbing a tree,* is an important skill. Make sure that the upper, middle and lower body segments initiate and land the complete action together.

---

[16] Translator's note: The pre-load is the 'defensive' movement, not an empty or extra action. Be sure to press into the leading fist and forearm. This action of the lead shoulder will pull the body back on the other side.

o° Within the fist drill, the forearms do an additional forward butting power, and the lower back must have lengthening power upward.

o When kicking, tuck the right hip joint back to let the right foot kick up smoothly.

o When the right hand is up and the left hand down, tuck the waist and close in the chest to keep the body centered. Then stomp the right foot, turning it crossways.

o When the left hand chops down it should have a settling power forward and down. The right hand should pull in like a grappling hook.

o When the right foot lands it should have a trampling power forward and down. Use the weight of the body to press forward, chop and trample.

o The head should press up when the hand chops down.

These types of power can be developed gradually with much thought during repeated practice. No matter how clearly someone explains this, you must practise repeatedly and conscientiously to absorb the skill into your body.

Retreating drive is not just an action within the *drive closing move,* it is another variation of the drive technique. It uses whole body power – power coming up from the ground, from the inside to the outside.

o The weight should move back just before the left foot lands on the ground as it retreats, using the entire back surface to hit backwards, and using the buttocks to settle quickly.

o As the centre of gravity passes the right foot, keep moving back so that the body feels like it will fall backwards, then the left foot retreats back to support with force, so that the supporting reactive force reaches to the lower back, transfers to the shoulder, transfers to the elbow, and in turn transfers to the fist.

o The left arm extends forward and the right arm pulls back, the shoulders move forward and back creating a couple.

BREATHING CYCLE FOR DRIVE

You must coordinate positional breathing once you are comfortable with the movement in order to gain whole body power.

• Inhale deeply as you move in between the punches.

• Exhale sharply to punch.

PRACTICAL APPLICATIONS FOR DRIVE

Drive is equivalent to the straight punch of Longfist or the jab of boxing, although with a different power application and timing. Drive is a fast straight-line punch that hits when the feet and body enter into the opponent – the body arrives with the feet, the fist punches when the feet arrive. Because the shortest distance between two points is a straight line, drive is the fastest punch in Xingyi. Looking at the statistics in boxing, the straight jab is used most often and scores the most points, suggesting that a quick, straight, punch is a most useful punch to have in your repertoire.

The traditional drive technique is done as continuous punches, containing defensive moves within the attack and attacking moves within the defense, a fast and furious barrage of punches. The classics describe it well;

> "Enter the body [into the opponent] so that the hand and foot arrive together."

> "The hands are like poisonous arrows, the body is like a bow; it all comes from the drive of the back foot."

> "The hand enters like a rasp and lands like a grappling pole."

> "Strike with purpose, retract with purpose." [both in the intent and the technique – always see what can be done]

The traditional use of drive emphasizes continuous attacking punches, and the key to a continuous attack is the advancing footwork. The 'lead foot half-step advance' is the most effective footwork for this. It is quick, moves the centre of gravity under control, and can change direction easily to react to the opponent.

Other classic sayings point out drive's technique and evoke its fighting spirit, courage, and tactics:

> "Launch like an arrow, land like the wind, chase the wind and the moon without slackening."

> "Initiate like the wind and land like an arrow, don't slow down even after hitting."

> "Don't turn over or drill, one inch is all you need."

> "To step in and launch the punch, first take over the front door."

The target for drive is the head, solar plexus or belly for upper, middle, and lower punches. Do not be content with one hit making contact, but take that opportunity to charge in with more punches, advancing all the time. The classics say,

> "Two fists go back and forth, the technique is like continuous shots."

> "There is no posturing, no blocking, just one strike, and if need be, ten strikes."

- Xingyiquan emphasizes 'hit to break the attack,' it does not 'block and attack.' The block is the attack, the attack is the block.

To put any and all techniques into use you must ignore the set pattern. Do what it needed to break down the opponent's attack and get in. React flexibly.

THE POEM ABOUT DRIVE

崩拳似箭性属木，进步近身全凭步。两手往来连环进，神技妙法在神悟。

Drive is like an arrow and its character is that of wood,

Count on advancing footwork to get the body in close.

Drive the punches in continuously, one after the other,

The secret to skill lies in gaining intuition through experience.

CANNON, POUND 炮拳

INTRODUCTION TO CANNON, *PAO QUAN* (POUNDING FIST)

Xingyiquan classic texts say "The element that cannon relates to is fire; its form is like an artillery cannon, and the internal organ that it relates to is the Heart." Gunpowder exploding in a cannon launches the cannonball out instantaneously towards the enemy. Then the cannonball explodes with unstoppable destructive ferocity. The cannon technique imitates this explosive ferocity. The technique enters fiercely, nothing can stop it, and nothing can block it.

Cannon relates to the fire element because of its explosive nature, and relates to the Heart due to the correlation of the Heart to fire in traditional Chinese medical theory.[17] In learning cannon we must first learn the proper movement and pattern, then, on that foundation, seek its explosive and destructive power. Its combination of quickness with heaviness must be expressed in both the body and the spirit.

Looking at the form [structure and movement] of cannon, one fist drills up then deflects out as the other fist punches forward. Different branches of Xingyiquan perform cannon differently, but all use the drilling deflection combined with the punch. We need to analyze the form and goal of a technique because the goal decides the form that it will use, and form serves the goal. There are a variety of forms that are able to serve and reach a goal. But in this case, the form must meet strict criteria: simple movement, fast, able to change, good for protection, an effective attack when used to enter, an effective defense when used to withdraw, biomechanically sound, and effective in combat. Cannon meets these criteria.

The line of action taken in cannon is a Z line, diagonally left and right as it moves forward to hit with the body angled in a reverse stance.

METHODS OF PERFORMING CANNON

1. STANDARD CANNON

Start from left *santishi*.

1a   **Right Cannon**   yòu pàoquán   右炮拳

ACTION 1: Shift forward without moving the left foot. Then take a big step forward with the right foot. Land firmly on the right foot, keeping the leg bent, and quickly follow in with the left foot to beside the right ankle without touching down. Keep the knees together. While shifting, bring the right hand up along under the left and extend it forward. When the hands meet, step and clench to fists and pull them back to the belly with the fist hearts in. Snug the elbows into the ribs, press the head up, and look forward. (images 3.74 A and B)

---

[17] Editor's note: See Part One Chapter One and Part Four Chapter Two for more detail on the correspondences of the five elements.

ACTION 2: Turn the fists hearts face up, then drill the left fist up past the solar plexus and up by the right side of the face at eyebrow height, keeping the elbow tucked in. Lift the right fist to the solar plexus. Step the left foot a big step forward to the left and follow in a half-step with the right, keeping most weight on

3.74 A   3.74 B

the right leg. Punch the right fist straight out in the forward left direction at solar plexus height with the arm slightly bent. Turn the waist leftward, put the right shoulder forward and bring the left shoulder back. Fix the angle of the left elbow and rotate the left forearm so the fist eye faces the left temple. The left fist is about a fist-length away from the temple, the elbow hangs down, and the forearm is nearly vertical. Press the head up and look past the right fist. (images 3.75 and 3.76, also 3.76 front and top)

3.76 TOP

3.75

3.76 FRONT   3.76

Pointers

- o   In action 1, extend the right hand as the centre of gravity moves forward. Pull the hands back as the right foot advances. Take a long step forward with the right foot and land under control. Bring the left foot in quickly.

- o   Sit down slightly when the left fist drills up, and pull the right shoulder back to both make the drill solid and store energy for the punch. Coordinate the sitting action of the knees with the shoulder action from the waist. Punch with the right fist when the left foot lands, working together with whole body power.

1b   Left Cannon   zuǒ pàoquán   左炮拳

ACTION 1: Advance the left foot a half-step with the foot turned in slightly and follow in with the right foot, lifting it at the ankle. Keep the knees together and the legs bent. While doing this, unclench the hands and lower the left hand to meet the right hand, palms down, and grab and pull forward and down, pulling in to the belly in fists, fist hearts up. Keep the elbows to the ribs, press the head up, and follow the hands with the eyes until they lower, then look to the forward right. (image 3.77)

ACTION 2: Take a big step to the forward right with the right foot and follow in with the left foot a half-step, to finish with the feet about two foot-lengths apart and with most weight on the left leg. Turn the fist hearts up and drill the right fist up the belly to the solar plexus, then up the left side of the face to eyebrow height, keeping the elbow tucked in. Turn the body slightly left and sit down slightly. Lift the left fist to the solar plexus then punch strongly in the forward right direction at chest height, fist eye up. Keep the left arm slightly bent, turn the waist right, put the left shoulder into the punch and bring the right shoulder back. Keep the right elbow angle unchanged and rotate the forearm so that the fist eye faces the temple. The right fist is about a fist-length distance away from the right temple, the elbow dropped, and the forearm near vertical. Press the head up and look to the forward left. (images 3.78 A and B)

Pointers

- o   Advance the right foot as the hands reach forward and down then pull in. Do not stop the fists at the belly, but continue on to drill up.

- o   The punch arrives with the footwork, so hands and feet arrive simultaneously, working together. Take a long advancing step and follow in quickly. The body charges forward, the punch is fierce, and the waist is springy and lively.

- •   Right and left cannon punches are similar, so continue to alternate according to the size of your practice area and your fitness. Make sure to advance in a Z stepping pattern.

1c   Cannon Turn Around   pàoquán zhuànshēn   炮拳转身

Using the *right cannon* as example.

ACTION 1: Settle in a bit after the *right cannon* to prepare for turning around. Hook-in the left foot in front of the right foot, so the feet toe in, taking a character eight [八] stance. Shift onto the left leg and lift the right foot at the left ankle without touching down. Keep the knees together and bent. Turn around to the right to face in the direction from which you came. While doing this, unclench the hands and circle them up at the left, forward, down and in to the belly, clenching as they move. When circling, the right hand is in the lead and the left hand is behind, palms facing down. As the hands come down, the arms bend slightly, fist hearts turn in, elbows hug the ribs, head presses up, and eyes follow the hands. When the fists arrive at the belly, look forward. (image 3.79)

ACTION 2: Take a big step to the forward right with the right foot and follow in a half-step with the left. Keep most weight on the left leg. Turn the fist hearts up then drill the right fist up, following through into a *left cannon.* (images 3.80 A and B)

Pointers

o   The *turn around* is one action, so must be quick and continuous, and the following cannon must hit fiercely.

o   In order for the hook-step to bring the body around and allow a smooth forward step, the foot should hook in sharply and step to the outside of the other foot.

o   The hands must move in coordination with the body turn, and follow a round circle. The waist must be supple, the shoulders lively, and the elbows settled.

o   Press the head up while turning, don't allow it to drop and make the body lean forward. Keep the spine as a vertical pivot line.

1d   Cannon Closing Move   pàoquán shōushì   炮拳收势

Starting from _left_ cannon. (image 3.81)

ACTION 1: Withdraw the right foot to land beside the left foot with the legs together and bent, shifting onto the right leg. Bring the left fist back to the solar plexus and turn slightly left. Bend the right arm to cover with the elbow to the left, the right fist turned and at nose height. Look at the right fist. (image 3.82)

ACTION 2: Step the left foot forward without moving the right foot, taking a *santi* stance with the left leading and the right back. Slide the left hand along the right arm and hit forward with a *left split,* bringing the right hand back to the belly, palm down. Press the head up and look forward. (image 3.83)

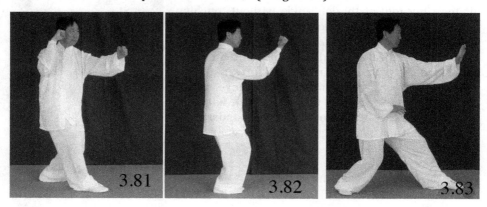

- Continue on to complete the closing as in *standard split closing move*, see description in Split 1d.

Closing starting from <u>*right*</u> *cannon.* (image 3.84)

ACTION 1: Withdraw the left foot to land beside the right foot and shift onto the right leg, putting the legs together and keeping them bent. Bring the right fist back to the solar plexus and turn right. Bend the left arm and do an elbow cover by using the movement of the body; press down with the fist hooked in, fist heart down at shoulder height, forearm crossing the body. Look forward. (image 3.85)

ACTION 2: Without moving the feet, press the left fist down and bring it back to the belly with the fist heart in. Drill the right fist forward and up with the ulnar side turned up, at nose height.

Look at the right fist (image 3.86)

ACTION 3: Step the left foot forward without moving the right foot, to take a *santi* stance. Split the left hand forward, unclench the right fist and pull it back to the belly, palm down. Press the head up and look forward of the left hand. (image 3.87)

- Continue on the complete the closing the same as in *split closing move,* see description in Split 1d.

Pointers

- o In Xingyi the closing moves are always settled and steady. Focus on regulating the breath. The movement may be slowed down, and the spirit must be strong.

- o Turn the waist to bring the fist back and coordinate this with the elbow technique – whether the right elbow covering leftward or the left forearm pressing down and rightward. The action comes from the waist, using it as the axis to bring the arms across.

- o Use the shoulders to bring the arms across, whether the right elbow covering leftward or the left forearm pressing down and rightward. Transfer power from the waist to the shoulders, to the elbows, and finally to the hands.

2. ALIGNED STANCE CANNON   shùnbù pàoquán   顺步炮拳

Start from left *santishi*.

2a   Right Aligned Stance Cannon yòu shùnbù pàoquán   右顺步炮拳

ACTION 1: Clench both hands. Turn the left fist heart up and bring it down and back to press the backfist down at the belly, fist heart up, elbow hugging the ribs. Withdraw the left foot a half-step to just in front of the right toes, touching the toes down. Press the head up and look forward. (image 3.88, before the left fist comes in to the belly)

ACTION 2: Advance the left foot a half-step then take a big step forward with the right foot and follow in with the left a half-step, keeping most weight on the left leg.

Drill the left fist up past the solar plexus, up the right side of the face to the eyebrow, fist heart in, about a forearm distance from the nose. Lift the right fist to the solar plexus and punch forward in a right cannon punch, fist eye up, at chest height, keeping the arm slightly bent and urging the punch forward from the shoulder. Turn the body left and allow the left shoulder to follow it, the left fist turning inward, the fist eye about a fist-length away from the left temple. Keep the left elbow dropped, press the head up, and look past the right fist. (image 3.89)

2b   Left Aligned Stance Cannon   zuǒ shùnbù pàoquán   左顺步炮拳

ACTION 1: Withdraw the right foot a half-step to touch down in front of the left toes. Turn the right fist so the fist heart is up and roll the fist down and back to press the backfist down in front of the belly. Turn the left fist heart up and press the backfist down at the belly past the right elbow. Bend the waist slightly and sit the buttocks down. Press the head up and look forward. (image 3.90)

ACTION 2: Advance the right foot a half-step, take a large step forward with the left foot and follow in a half-step with the right foot, keeping most weight on the right leg. Drill the right fist up past the solar plexus then up to the eyebrows, fist heart in, ulnar side turned. Lift the left fist past the solar plexus and punch out as the left foot steps, fist eye up, arm slightly bent. Put the left shoulder into the punch, punch the left fist to chest height and turn the right fist so the fist eye faces the right temple, about a fist away. Keep the right elbow dropped, press the head up, and look forward. (images 3.91 and front)

- Carry on, alternating right and left.

Pointers

   o Press the backfists down timed with the lead foot withdrawal.

   o Step forward quickly and keep the footwork connected. Punch at the same time as the lead foot lands. Turn the waist to urge the fist forward from the shoulder, synchronizing the upper and lower body.

   o The entire move is done as one action, continuously and smoothly.

2c   Aligned Stance Cannon Turn Around
         shùnbù pàoquán zhuànshēn   顺步炮拳转身

Using the *right aligned stance cannon* as example.

ACTION 1: Hook the right foot in on the spot and step the left foot back in a cross step behind the right leg, turning the body around 180 degrees to the left. (image 3.92 A)

ACTION 2: Pivot the feet on the spot and shift onto the left leg. Turn the right fist heart up and circle it up then forward and press the backfist down at the belly. Turn the left fist heart up and press the backfist down at the belly. Press the head up and look forward, back in the direction from which you came. (image 3.92B)

ACTION 3: Advance the right foot a half-step, take a big step forward with the left foot, and follow in with the right a half-step, keeping most weight on the right leg. Drill the right fist over and punch the left fist forward, in an *advancing aligned stance cannon.* (image 3.93)

- *Aligned stance turn around* is similar starting from the left or the right aligned stance, just transpose left and right directions.

Pointers

- The *turn around* is one move and should be done smoothly without interruption.

- The back cross step and pivot turn are synchronized with the fist circle. The advancing step is synchronized with the punch.

2d Aligned Stance Cannon Closing Move shùnbù pàoquán shōushì　顺步炮拳收势

Once you arrive back at the starting point and have done the turn so that you are facing in the same direction as at the start, continue until you are in a *left aligned stance cannon.* Pull both fists back to the belly, press the head up and look forward. The rest is similar to *split closing move.* (see images 3.8 though 3.11, description Split 1d)

3. DODGING CANNON　　　　yáoshēn pàoquán　　　　摇身炮拳

Start from left *santishi.*

3a　　Dodge, Left Cannon　　yáoshēn zuǒ pàoquán　　摇身左炮拳

ACTION 1: Advance the left foot a half-step and follow in with the right foot to beside the left ankle. Clench both hands and drill the right fist up in front of the left elbow, fist heart turned out. As they come in front of the right shoulder the left fist is in front of the right fist. Without pausing, take the forearms across to the left, right fist in front of the left fist, both in front of the left shoulder. Sink the elbows dropped, release shoulder tension, settle the chest and keep the waist lively. Look in the direction of the fists. (images 3.94 A and B)

ACTION 2: Take a big step to the right front with the right foot and follow in a half-step with the left foot, keeping most weight on the left leg. Drill the right fist up to the right temple and punch out with the left fist in a *left cannon*. Put the left shoulder forward and punch at solar plexus height. The actions are all similar to those of *standard left cannon*. (image 3.95)

3b   **Dodge, Right Cannon**   yáoshēn yòu pàoquán   摇身右炮拳

ACTION 1: Advance the right foot a half-step with the foot hooked slightly inward. Follow in with the left foot to beside the right ankle without touching down. Turn the right fist heart to face out and pull it across leftward to in front of the left shoulder. Turn the right fist heart to face in and roll the forearm towards the left elbow. Turn to the left, with the right fist in front of the body and the left fist behind. Turn the body right and bring the arms across to the right, tucking the elbows, rotating the right forearm inward and the left forearm outward. The left fist is in front of the right fist, which is in front of the right shoulder. Release shoulder tension, sink the elbows, contain the chest, liven up the waist, and look in the direction of the hands. (images 3.96 A and B)

ACTION 2: Take a big step to the forward left with the left foot and follow the right foot in a half-step, keeping most weight on the right leg. Drill the left fist up to

eyebrow height and punch out to chest height with the right fist in a *right cannon.* All particulars are similar to *standard right cannon.* (image 3.97)

- Carry on, alternating right and left.

Pointers

o The half-step advance is synchronized with the elbow crosscut roll. The movement of the hands and arms must be quick and the waist must be supple and lively. The fists rotate in opposite directions at the same time so that the fist hearts face each other. Keep the elbows snug to the heart.

o The punch must come as the foot lands.

3c   Dodging Cannon Turn Around yáoshēn pàoquán zhuànshēn 摇身炮拳转身

Dodging cannon turn around is similar to the *standard cannon turn around*, see description in Cannon 1c.

3d   Dodging Cannon Closing Move yáoshēn pàoquán shōushì   摇身炮拳收势

Dodging cannon closing move is similar to the *standard cannon closing*, see description in Cannon 1d.

4.   REVERSE STANCE CANNON   àobù pàoquán   拗步炮拳

The footwork of *reverse stance cannon* is the same as that of the *standard cannon*, it advances in a Z pattern. The hand technique is the same as the *aligned stance cannon* – the hands turn over and press down, the elbows tuck and draw in, and then they punch out as the foot advances. So the *reverse stance cannon* combines these two techniques.

PROBLEMS OFTEN MET IN CANNON[18]

PROBLEM 1: The student's deflecting arm cuts straight across or blocks up, lacking rolling power.

CORRECTIONS: Focus on keeping the elbow down and first drilling the fist up then turning. Turn from the lower back to draw the shoulder into the action, and then turn the fist to deflect. Be sure to turn the body to deflect rather than cutting across or blocking up. If you block up too high the elbow comes up to leave a big gap, making defense difficult.

PROBLEM 2: The student punches too far to the side on completion of cannon.

CORRECTIONS: The punch should be in the same direction that the lead foot points and aligned with the back heel. The punching fist, elbow, and shoulder are on line with the rear foot. The student should train post standing in the cannon posture to understand the angles and directions of the lines of power.

PROBLEM 3: The student shrugs the back shoulder.

CORRECTIONS: The cause of shrugging is not letting the shoulders loosen up, so

---

[18] Editor's note: Review also problems 1 through 7 described in Split.

during practice the student must keep the shoulders loose and settled.

PROBLEM 4: The student straightens the arms when reaching out to pull in, or even straightens and raises the arms up before pulling down.

CORRECTIONS: Remind the student to maintain a bend in the elbows throughout the movement. Be sure to settle the shoulders, close the lower body, sink the elbows and stretch the back to resist extending with the arms. Give a lot of thought to the proper positioning of each body segment.

PROBLEM 5: The student does not hook in the lead foot during the first half-step forward. Since the line of movement is a Z shape, this causes the foot to be twisted during the push off into the punch. This wastes the strength of the leg, twists the supporting knee, and dissipates power.

CORRECTIONS: Remind the students as they take the first half-step to turn the foot in about twenty degrees when it lands. Then, when it is time to push off, they can put good power into it. The knee will track smoothly so they can push it down to get the best shank angle for a forward drive.

POWER GENERATION FOR CANNON

The classics say; "In the martial way, the postures show visible form and the *qi* or internal strength does not show visible form. The internal power is what moves the postures." 'Postures' mean the structure and form of actions, and 'internal strength' means power (*jin*). Power is shown through the actions, and each different action shows a different type of power. If there is no action then no power is created – actions serve power. The kind of action done creates a corresponding type of power – the power is determined by the action.

1.   In *standard cannon*, when the hands reach out to grab and pull in as you take a big step forward, it is like you are grabbing a big rope and pulling it back. The strong advance of the footwork is like leaping over a wide gully. The movements are done at the same time with an integrated power.

2.   When the hands unclench and reach forward to pull back, the arms should be rounded. When the hands press down, the head should press up. Release shoulder tension, sink the elbows, and close the chest in. Then when the hands press down and pull in, the whole body is tucked in.

3.   When the left fist is deflecting it drills up as the body sits slightly down. The body should turn slightly to the right, the chest close in and the trunk tuck in – these small actions all serve to store power. Pre-load back to launch forward, pre-load right to launch left. Sit down slightly by flexing the right knee and pressing it forward. Turn right by moving the shoulders.

4.   The forward step in cannon must use the drive from the back leg to its full capacity, the back knee must press down to decrease the angle of the shank with the ground. This increases the forward horizontal force and makes the body's centre of gravity move forward rather than up. This is called 'striding forward and driving back' and enables the forward step to be long with great momentum and power.

5.   Turn the lumbar/waist area and urge the punch forward from the shoulder, using the waist to send the shoulder forward, the shoulder to send the

elbow forward, and the elbow to send the fist forward. The shoulder, elbow and fist are all aligned on the same plane. Lengthen the spine when you punch, pressing the head up. The angle of the punching arm of cannon is the same as during the drive punch, but the fist has a very slight upward lifting intent. It is important to settle the elbows and release the shoulders.

During the *aligned stance cannon* the fists turn over and pound. They should have both a pressing down power combined with a rolling back power. Develop this power by simultaneously releasing the shoulders, settling the elbows, sitting down with the buttocks tucked in, tucking in the trunk, and pressing the head up. When the fists drill up the shoulder should reach forward slightly, keeping the chest closed, the back open, and the trunk compressed. When you step forward and punch, the shoulders should turn with force.

The key to *dodging cannon* is taking the arms from side to side. When training this, at first turn quite a lot, then gradually decrease the size of the turn to shoulder width. When turning from side to side, first reach the shoulders forward and spread the back, turn the forearms so that they take the fists across. The power of the whole move comes from the lower back, so the key is to keep the waist loose and lively.

BREATHING CYCLE FOR CANNON

Once you are comfortable with the movement you must coordinate positional breathing in order to gain whole body power.

- Inhale as you take the half-step advance and reach the hands to pull down.

- Contain the breath in the lower body as the fists drill up and the body turns slightly, keeping the lower back relaxed.

- Exhale as you drive forward and land the foot and punch, settling the *qi* to the *dantian*.

PRACTICAL APPLICATIONS FOR CANNON

Combat is the true meaning and essence of the martial arts. In training Xingyi the structure of postures, the power line of actions, and specific characteristics of techniques all serve combative applications.

Cannon contains a defensive action in the attack and an offensive action in the block – it combines both defense and offense in the same moves. As the fist drills up, it protects the midline, then the head. As the fist drills up past the solar plexus, it protects the chest, then, as the waist turns the arm rolls to protect the head. As the waist turns this creates an advantageous condition for the other fist to punch forward.

The target for the punch is the chest, belly, solar plexus, or head, but whether or not you can land the punch depends entirely on your footwork. Do you dare to enter in tight with your footwork? Is your footwork quick? Are your movements coordinated with your footwork? It is not too difficult to achieve good footwork while training on your own, but to perform in a combat situation – using footwork to get in and out successfully while keeping in balance at all times and getting yourself into an advantageous position – is another matter. This ability also reflects a person's psychological qualities and combative will.

The placement and action of the defending arm has strict rules in practice, but in a combat situation you have to see the situation and defend yourself flexibly with a deflection out, a deflection up, a press down, a brush aside or a trap. This is what the classical saying "there is no distinction between defense and attack in postures or timing" means. You must learn a fixed posture, but in use there is no fixed technique.

Any punch or palm technique in Xingyi requires a bent arm, not quite fully extended. This type of requirement cannot be separated from the whole body power of Xingyi. All Xingyi hits use whole body power, the strength of every part of the body culminates in the fist or palm. In action, every part of the body, under a high degree of conscious control, follows the form for the specific technique. Once one part moves, all parts move in coordination. Whole body power is created by gathering and settling, then linking from root to tip; the power initiates in the root, and progressively collects, transferring segment by segment to reach the tip. Active and reactive forces are identical. That is to say, the amount of force you apply to the opponent will be reflected back to you. The arms keep a certain flexion to stabilize and protect the arms from this force. The second reason for the arm flexion is for agility, to be able to adjust a technique easily. If the opponent is knocked back when you strike, then you can still straighten the arm to increase the length of time in contact and drive the opponent even faster and farther away. If the opponent is not moved when you strike then the bent arm allows you to adjust your action quickly in any direction.

- The *aligned stance cannon* uses the sideways positioning of the body when advancing, one hand drills and deflects while the other hand hits the chest, stomach or head, using the extension from the turned body. The key is in the footwork.

- The *dodging cannon* uses both arms to knock aside a double armed attack. The footwork can retreat or enter. But when you attack you always enter, keeping the elbows in to protect your midline, the chest, solar plexus and ribs. Your fists protect your head.

No matter what exactly you do with your hands, if one defends while the other attacks it is within the cannon technique. The main point is not the height or forward placement of the defending arm, or whether it deflects upwards or downwards. The key is to effectively defend and attack simultaneously.

THE POEM ABOUT CANNON

炮拳似炮性属火，进步两手砸带裹。化钻冲打敌身去，欲前先后腰要活。

Cannon is like an artillery cannon and its nature is that of fire,

Enter in and use both hands to pound, draw, and wrap.

Deflect and drill, charge and hit, the opponent will be driven away,

Keep the trunk lively to gather back and recoil forward.

CROSSCUT 横拳

INTRODUCTION TO CROSSCUT, *HENG QUAN* (CROSSING FIST)

Xingyiquan classic texts say "The element that *crosscut* relates to is earth, its form is like a shot, and the internal organ that it relates to is the Spleen, the whole body is round." That crosscut relates to the earth and Spleen is due to the correlation between the five elements and the organs.[19] "Crosscut relates to a shot" should not be understood to mean that it acts like an ammunition shot or pellet, but to mean that it is round like them. It also includes the character's secondary meaning of elasticity.[20] The classics say, "The efficacy of crosscut is that its energy flows smoothly, its shape is round, and its power is harmonious. Only when these three exist together can it be considered a crosscut."

Both the outer structure and the inner power of crosscut are round, even and full. The roundness and fullness of the outer structure helps the *qi* collect and increases the fullness inside. The fullness and collected *qi* inside helps the outer form become fuller, rounder, and more elastic. Internal and external forms support and aid each other. How do you make the outer structure rounded and full? What do you have to do to be considered round and full? When the movement requirements are satisfied, the outer structure is round and full and the whole body – upper and lower, inner and outer – is balanced with no gaps in power, then that is 'round and full.' Not allowing slackening or disconnection of power does not mean to be rigid or to keep the muscles tense. Excess tension in the muscles makes the body awkward, stiff, and uncoordinated. In order for the outer form to be round it is vital that the spirit and energy are full and communicate throughout. Fill the shape with the spirit and control the shape with the will, and a powerful attitude will be shown.

The 'cross' in crosscut has many sayings in the classics; "cross refers to the initial action, aligned refers to the landing," "initiate crossways without seeing the cross, land alongside without seeing the alignment." The term 'crosscut' means a horizontal action, the opposite of a vertical action. Looking at its form, crosscut is a twisting drill that punches forward from a reverse stance with the body turned. Its name would appear not quite appropriate to its action. If it went by its name it should hit side to side horizontally, but why do the classics say that you don't see the cross in the crosscut? Xingyi hand techniques, footwork, positioning and theory are all based on practicality. Hitting is the defense, that is, 'hit to defend,' do not 'defend then hit. ' With this theory underlying all training, of course there is the saying "you don't see the cross in the crosscut." If the 'cross' were emphasized then there would have to be a sideways crossing action. Most of a sideways cross would be for defense, as a sideways block. Crosscut has a defensive action hidden within it, but the emphasis is on the attack. What is emphasized is its goal. During the crosscut the twisting roll of the arm is the 'cross' and the forward drill is the

---

[19] Editor's note: See Part One Chapter One and Part Four Chapter Two for more detail on the correspondences of the five elements.

[20] Translator's note: the character 弹 can be read *dan* as a noun meaning 'pellet, bullet, or shot,' and *tan* as a verb 'to shoot' or an adjective 'elastic.'

hit. The crossing power of crosscut is hidden, so you don't see it in the outer shape.

METHODS OF PERFORMING CROSSCUT

1.   STANDARD CROSSCUT: REVERSE STANCE CROSSCUT

àobù héngquán   拗步横拳

1a   Reverse Stance Right Crosscut   àobù yòu héngquán   拗步右横拳

Start from left *santishi*.

ACTION 1: Do not move the right foot yet. Withdraw the left foot a half-step to touch the toes down in front of the right foot. Clench the left hand and pull it back to the belly, then drill up and forward from the solar plexus to nose height with the ulnar side of the arm and the fist heart twisted up. Clench the right fist as well and lift it to the solar plexus, fist heart down, elbow tucked in to the ribs, and forearm aligned to the front. Press the head up and look ahead. (image 3.98)

ACTION 2: Take a large step forty-five degrees to the forward left with the left foot and follow in a half-step with the right foot, keeping most weight on the right leg. Bring the right fist from the left elbow, fist heart still facing down, and punch forward while turning the forearm so that the fist heart faces up by the time it reaches its full extent (arm slightly bent) at shoulder height. Turn the left fist over and tuck it, pulling back to the belly, fist heart down. Urge the right shoulder forward and bring the left shoulder back. Press the head up and look forward past the right fist. The right punch is straight forward and the stance is angled forty-five degrees. (images 3.99, and front and top

1b   Reverse Stance Left Crosscut   àobù zuǒ héngquán   拗步左横拳

ACTION 1: Advance the left foot a half-step with the toes hooked slightly in, and follow in with the right foot to beside the left ankle. Without moving the right fist, bring the left fist, centre still facing down, up to the solar plexus with the elbow snug to the ribs. Press the head up and look forward past the right fist. (image 3.100)

ACTION 2: Take a large step to the forward right with the right foot and follow in a half-step with the left, keeping the weight mostly on the left leg. Drill the left fist out from the solar plexus, under the right elbow, and straight forward, twisting gradually to turn the ulnar edge and fist heart up. The punch finishes with the front arm slightly bent, the fist at shoulder height, both shoulders settled and

elbows dropped. Turn the right fist over and pull it back to the belly, fist heart down, elbow snug to the ribs. Urge the left shoulder forward, bring the right shoulder back, press the head up, settle the buttocks down and look forward past the left fist. The left punch is straight ahead. (image 3.101)

Pointers

- o In the first action do not pause between pulling the left fist back and drilling it forward. Coordinate this with the withdrawal of the foot.

- o Three actions happen with equal timing and power – step the left foot forward, punch with the right fist, and pull the left fist back. Be sure to turn the waist and put the shoulders into the hit, and to twist, roll, drill and turn the fists. These actions are synchronized in timing and launch the same force.

- o Be sure to keep the fist hearts facing the way they were while initiating the action – while the lead foot advances, the lead fist does not move, and the rear fist rises to prepare.

- o Three actions happen with equal timing and power – the right foot lands, the left fist punches and the right fist pulls back. The hands arrive with the footwork, working together. Be sure to turn the waist and put the shoulders into the action, press the head up and drop the buttocks, the segments of the body moving together to perform a single action.

- • Carry on the *reverse stance crosscut* to right and left as many times as the training area and your fitness allow.

1c   Reverse Stance Crosscut Turn Around

àobù héngquán zhuànshēn　　　拗步横拳转身

Using the *reverse stance right crosscut* as example.

ACTION 1: Step the left foot hooked in outside the right toes and shift back, turning around a full 180 degrees to the right to face in the direction from which you came. Shift onto the left leg and lift the right foot by the left ankle without touching down. Hold the hands in position while taking the steps, so that the arms come firmly around with the body. Look forward past the right fist. Lift the left fist to the solar plexus, fist heart still down. (image 3.102)

ACTION 2: Take a big step to the forward right with the right foot and follow in a half-step with the left foot, keeping the weight on the left leg. While doing this, slide the left fist forward along under the right arm drilling and turning it so the fist heart is up at shoulder height. Turn the right fist and tuck it, pulling it back to the belly with the fist heart down and the elbow on the ribs. Press the head up, lengthen the buttocks down and look forward past the left fist. (image 3.103)

- *Crosscut turn around* is the same on the left side, just transposing directions.

Pointers

   o   To start the turn, hook the foot in as much as possible – to a T stance or tighter.

   o   Stride the right foot out and punch with the left fist in one synchronized action.

1d   Reverse Stance Crosscut Closing Move

àobù héngquán shōushì   拗步横拳收势

Starting from a *reverse stance <u>right</u> crosscut.*

ACTION 1: Withdraw the left foot to beside the right without moving the right foot, and shift back to the right leg. Do not move the left fist; unclench the right hand and turn the palm down. Then clench the right hand and pull it back to the belly, then, without pausing, drill it forward and up again to nose height, fist heart up, ulnar edge twisted up. Press the head up and look forward past the right fist. (image 3.104)

ACTION 2: Advance the left foot without moving the right foot, to take a *santi* stance. Bring the left fist up past the solar plexus then along the right arm, to unclench into a split at chest height. Unclench the right hand and pull it back to the belly. Press the head up and look at the left hand. (image 3.105)

Closing starting from a *reverse stance left crosscut*.

ACTION 1: Withdraw the right foot back to land beside the left foot and shift to the right leg. Bend the left elbow and press down, fist heart down. Then drill the right fist up and forward to nose height, fist heart up, ulnar edge up. Pull the left fist back to the belly, fist heart down. Look at the right fist. (image 3.106)

ACTION 2: Advance the left foot a step without moving the right foot, keeping most weight on the right leg. Unclench the left hand and split while pulling the right hand back to the belly. Press the head up and look past the left hand. (image 3.107)

- *Crosscut closing move* is completed the same as all *closing moves* once you get to the *santishi* stance. See *standard split closing move*, see description in Split 1d. (see images 3.8 to 3.11)

2. ALIGNED STANCE CROSSCUT   shùnbù héngquán   顺步横拳

Start from left *santishi*.

2a   Right Aligned Stance Crosscut   yòu shùnbù héngquán   右顺步横拳

ACTION 1: Advance the left foot a half-step and lift the right foot beside it. Clench the left hand and turn the fist heart up, fist at shoulder height, arm slightly bent. Lift the right fist to the chest, fist heart down. Press the head up and look past the left fist. (image 3.108)

ACTION 2: Take a big step forward with the right foot and follow in the left foot a half-step, keeping most weight on the left leg. Drill the right fist out under the left elbow and along the forearm to shoulder height, turning the fist heart up, keeping the arm slightly bent and putting the shoulder into the punch. Turn the left fist and pull it back to the belly with the fist heart down and elbow snug to the ribs. Turn the waist and urge the shoulders into the hit. Release tension in the shoulders and sink the elbows, press the head up, and look past the right fist. (image 3.109)

2b   Left Aligned Stance Crosscut   yòu shùnbù héngquán   左顺步横拳

ACTION 1: Step the right foot a half-step forward and lift the left foot by the right ankle without touching down. Without moving the right fist, bring the left fist up to the solar plexus, fist heart down. Keep the right shoulder forward and the left shoulder back. Look at the right fist. (image 3.110)

ACTION 2: Take a big step forward with the left foot and follow in with the right foot a half-step, keeping most weight on the right leg. Drill the left fist out under the right elbow and along the forearm to finish at shoulder height with the arm slightly bent, rotating as it goes forward so the fist heart turns up. Rotate the right fist and tuck it back to the belly, fist heart down and elbow snug to the ribs. Urge the left shoulder forward and draw the right shoulder back. Press the head up and look past the left fist. (images 3.111 and front)

3.110   3.111   3.111 FRONT

Pointers

o   When starting from *santishi,* as the left foot advances a half-step, rotate and slightly drop the left fist, without otherwise moving it in relation to the body.

o   The punching fist must hit as the leading foot lands. Coordinate the fists to complete their rotations with the same timing. The key to the timing lies in using the waist and shoulders to do the action.

o   Do not turn the right fist or move it in relation to the body when advancing the right foot a half-step – apply pressure into the arm and fist when advancing the body.

2c   Aligned Stance Crosscut Turn Around

shùnbù héngquán zhuànshēn   顺步横拳转身

ACTION 1: Hook the lead foot in and turn the body around 180 degrees in the direction to which the foot has hooked, to face back in the direction from which you came. Bring in what was the back foot to beside the lead foot. While doing this, let the lead arm come crossways around with the body. Look ahead.

ACTION 2: Step the rear foot through into an *aligned stance crosscut.*

2d   Aligned Stance Crosscut Closing Move

shùnbù héngquán shōushì   顺步横拳收势

You may close when you arrive back at your starting place in a *left aligned stance crosscut* after the *turn around* to face the same direction as the original *santishi*. The closing movement is the same as usual, see description Split 1d.

3. RETREATING CROSSCUT   tuìbù héngquán   退步横拳

This is to practise coordinating a retreating step with a forward punch. When training you can use the *aligned stance crosscut* to advance to the limit of the training area, then use the *retreating crosscut* to go backwards. You can also start the *retreating crosscut* after a *right reverse stance crosscut*.

3a   Retreating Left Crosscut   tuìbù zuǒ héngquán   退步左横拳

ACTION 1: Start with the left foot and right fist leading and the right foot back, in a *reverse stance right crosscut*. Retreat the right foot a half-step and follow by withdrawing the left foot to touch down the toes by the right foot. Keep the legs bent to maintain the same stance height, and keep the legs together. Keep the right fist and arm in the same position and settle the right shoulder forward a bit. Lift the left fist to solar plexus height and keep the fist heart down. Press the head up and look past the right fist. (image 3.112)

ACTION 2: Retreat the left foot diagonally to the left rear and withdraw the right foot, shifting the body back to put most of the weight on the left leg, taking a *santi* stance with the right foot leading and the left foot behind. Do a crosscut with the left fist, coming out from under the right forearm, fist heart up, at shoulder height. Turn the right fist and bring it back to the belly, fist heart down. The basic action of the fists is the same as *standard crosscut*. (image 3.113)

3.112   3.113

3b   Retreating Right Crosscut   tuìbù yòu héngquán   退步右横拳

ACTION 1: Retreat the left foot a half-step and withdraw the right foot back to touch down beside the left foot, shifting back to the left leg and keeping the legs bent to maintain the same stance height. Do not move the left fist and arm, but slightly drop the left shoulder forward. Lift the right fist to solar plexus height with the fist heart down. Press the head up and look past the left fist. (image 3.114)

ACTION 2: Sit back as the right foot retreats to the rear right, so that most weight is on the right leg, then withdraw the left foot a small half-step. Slide the right fist along under the left arm, twisting and drilling forward to shoulder height, fist heart up and arm slightly bent. Rotate the left fist and pull it back to the belly, fist heart down. Put the right shoulder forward into the punch and pull the left shoulder back. Press the head up and look past the right fist. (image 3.115)

Pointers

o The rear foot should take a small step when retreating, and the weight should shift back. The lead fist should not change position relative to the body. The step must be stable, and the other foot should withdraw quickly.

o Be sure to step at a forty-five degree angle when retreating the lead foot. The foot must settle into the ground at the same time that the back fist strikes forward. Turn the waist and urge the strike forward from the shoulders. Press the head up and settle the buttocks down. Release tension in the shoulders and sink the elbows.

o The foot stomps forcibly when landing the diagonal back step, using the backward shift of the weight. The toes should touch down first, then quickly land the whole foot, with a very small time gap. Be careful not to lift the foot too much.

4.   REVERSE STANCE INWARD CROSSCUT

àobù lǐ héngquán   拗步里横拳

The *inward crosscut* is opposite to the *standard crosscut*. The *standard crosscut* uses the outer edge of the forearm to twist, roll, and snap in a forward direction. The *inward crosscut* uses the inside edge of the arm to roll and strike crossways. The power, application, and characteristics all differ.

4a   Right Inward Crosscut   yòu àobù lǐ héngquán   右拗步里横拳

Start from a left *santishi*.

ACTION 1: Shift back and withdraw the left foot to touch down in front of the right toes. Clench the left fst and pull it back to the belly, then, without pausing, drill it up and forward to nose height, fist heart and ulnar edge turned up, elbow tucked in, and shoulder reaching forward into the action. Turn the right fist heart up, lift it by the right nipple, elbow flexed and settled down. Look past the left fist and settle the shoulders. (image 3.116)

ACTION 2: Advance the left foot about twenty-five degrees to the left of straight forward, and follow in with the right foot a half step, keeping most weight on the right leg. Unclench both hands, cross the right hand leftward and forward, rotating out and extending the arm to chest height, palm up, elbow bent, and forearm level. Turn the waist left and put the right shoulder forward and settled down. Rotate the left hand in and pull it back to the belly, elbow hugging the ribs. Press the head up, settle the buttocks down, and look past the right hand. (image 3.117)

4b   Left Inward Crosscut   zuǒ àobù lǐ héngquán   左拗步里横拳

ACTION 1: Advance the left foot a half-step and lift the right foot to the left ankle. Do not move the right hand relative to the body, but settle the shoulder forward a bit and clench the fist. Clench and lift the left fist to the left nipple, fist heart down, elbow bent and dropped. Settle the shoulders down and look at the right fist. (image 3.118)

ACTION 2: Take a big step forward and a bit to the right with the right foot and follow in a half-step with the left, keeping most weight on the left leg. Unclench both hands. Strike the left palm out from the left towards the right and forward, rotating the palm up. Keep the elbow bent and tucked in and the forearm horizontal, to strike with the palm to the right. Rotate the right palm in and pull it back to the belly, palm down, elbow snug to the ribs. Press the head up, turn the waist rightward, put the left shoulder forward and bring the right shoulder back, and look past the left hand. (image 3.119)

- Carry on alternating left and right.

Pointers

- o Pull the left fist back and drill out as the left foot withdraws.

- o Strike with the right hand as the left foot lands.

- o The footwork for the *inward crosscut* is: the lead foot advances a half-step, the back foot takes a big step forward, then the lead foot steps out to a twenty-five degree angle.

o Cut the rear hand across as the rear foot lands. Use the lower back and shoulders and rotate the arm to strike crossways. Use the crossing power of the body, the twist of the forearm, the rotation of the hand plus a forward action. Be sure to keep the lower trunk lively, the shoulders settled and loose, the chest contained, and exhale when you hit. The assisting hand rotates inward and tucks back, or it could also hook and grab to pull back.

- *Turn around* and *closing move* of *inward crosscut* are similar to those of *standard crosscut.* (see images 3.102 to 3.103 for the *turn around*, and 3.104 to 3.107 for the *closing move*)

PROBLEMS OFTEN MET IN CROSSCUT[21]

PROBLEM 1: When the student strikes, the power is just a crossing snap done with the arms.

CORRECTIONS: You must search for the meaning of "you don't see the cross in the crosscut." The crossing action is the block; it is a method, while the forward strike is the attack, the goal. Therefore, the crossing action is not enough, you must also have a forward drilling strike.

PROBLEM 2: The student is unstable when turning around.

CORRECTIONS: Instability may be caused by the lack of mastery of the vertical line of the trunk – lowering the head or leaning the trunk. Or it may be landing the hook-in step in the wrong place or at the wrong angle, making the body move too far off line. So first emphasize keeping the head pressed up and the trunk vertical. Next be sure to hook-in to in front of the toes of the rear foot. The degree of the hook-in should be such that the foot can use power to drive off smoothly, so in general, the more the foot hooks in the better.

PROBLEM 3: When the student strikes he focuses on the lead hand and forgets to coordinate the whole body action with both hands.

CORRECTIONS: Make the student practise repeatedly according to the proper method, making sure he focuses on the coordination of the hands and feet and on the different powers of the lead and rear hands, using the power of shoulders and body.

POWER GENERATION FOR CROSSCUT

Crosscut places particular emphasis on the integration of the strength of the whole body. That is what 'being round' means. There is indeed a 'crossing' action within the crosscut technique. This crossing action is seen in the first half of the action, in the lower back and shoulders, upper arm and forearm action. Since Xingyiquan emphasizes attack and not 'defense then attack,' you should emphasize the final goal of the action.

Every branch of Xingyi uses the *reverse stance crosscut* as the standard and primary crosscut technique. Many classics and teaching materials take it as the primary technique, so we should learn the standard technique first and refine the

---

[21] Editor's note: Review also problems 1 through 7 described in Split.

variations later. If you first build a strong foundation with the *standard crosscut* and develop whole body power it will be relatively easy to learn the variations later.

The legs must have a scissor like force between them in the standard *reverse stance crosscut*. The knees should tuck in slightly and the rear knee should have the sense of stabbing down into the centre of the stance, so the knees have a 'rolling in power' and the legs have a 'closing in' power. It is as if you are standing on ice and want to prevent your legs from slipping out.

The arms have a 'twisting, rolling, drilling, turning' power that is integrated with no slackness. It is as if the hands are twisting a rope – the lead hand rotates inward, turning and rolling to tuck and press down and pull back, and the rear hand rotates outward to twist and roll and drill out. You must pay attention not only to the line of action of the fists, but also to the path taken by the elbows. The lead shoulder draws the elbow back and the elbow protects the heart, pulling the elbow back to the ribs.

When the rear hand hits out the elbow tucks into the solar plexus. Close the chest and shoulders in, settle the shoulders down and send the fist out. The elbows are moved by the shoulders, power is achieved by turning from the lower trunk and putting the shoulders into the strike.

- Crosscut's crossing power is created as the rear fist rolls under the lead elbow and extends, shoved forward by the rear shoulder. The footwork advances at a forty-five degree angle, giving the body a diagonal momentum, while the hand technique hits straight forward, thus creating an angled strike. Overall, the first half of crosscut is crossways, and the second half is a drill forward. The line taken by the fists is curved, and the first half of the arc is large while the second half of the arc is small, almost straight. The crossing power is created during the large initial arc, coming mostly from the shoulders and upper arms. The point of contact is the outer edge of the arm, mostly the upper arm, and secondarily the forearm. The key to the power is in controlling the elbows.

The key to crosscut power is the synchronization of forces coming from the lower back and shoulders to the arms. You must turn the lower trunk and put the shoulders into the action, lengthening the waist and urging the shoulders into the punch, so the power of the whole body reaches the upper limbs.

   o To get the power into the *retreating crosscut* you need to close the chest and lead the *qi*. The key to retreating is to control the weight shift with stable footwork. The power comes from using the stamp as the foot lands to create a rebound force that reaches the whole body, coming from the legs to the lower back and up through the shoulders, through the elbows to the hands.

   o The power of the *reverse stance inward crosscut* is created by the diagonal forward rolling as the front arm rotates and rolls and presses, and the force is applied to the inside edge of the forearm. It has both a diagonal crossing power and a forward power. The power comes from the lower back and shoulders, so the lower back must be relaxed, the shoulders settle then launch, and the power is an instantaneous one inch strike.

- o The *inward crosscut* may also be done with the palms, hitting with the heel of the palm and forearm with the same power. The other hand grabs and pulls back to the belly, the same as the described *inward crosscut*.

It doesn't really matter how many types of crosscut there are, or how they may differ in footwork or movement, they all share the same characteristic whole body force that is also characteristic of all the five basic techniques.

BREATHING CYCLE FOR CROSSCUT

You must coordinate positional breathing once you are comfortable with the movement in order to gain whole body power. The breathing cycle for crosscut is similar to that of cannon.

- Inhale as you take the half-step advance and store power.

- Exhale as you drive forward and land the foot and punch, settling the *qi* to your *dantian*.

PRACTICAL APPLICATIONS FOR CROSSCUT

It isn't really correct to speak of a specific application for crosscut. Crosscut trains a certain type of power, not a specific application. Of course the action contains certain implied attacking and defensive moves, but more importantly, training crosscut develops the ability to use a type of power. This is true for all of the five elemental techniques. Long term training of the five techniques gives us a grasp of the characteristics of Xingyi's power. To use the techniques you need to react according to the situation. When you have achieved a high level with the techniques, then "the technique is born in the heart and goes out the hands."

To examine the form of crosscut; the lead hand turns over, tucks, rolls and draws back, which can be seen as defensive, breaking an opponent's punch down the central line. The other hand simultaneously strikes at the opponent's solar plexus or ribs. The hands hit simultaneously, blocking and hitting together, and adding a charging forward footwork. If the lead hand does not succeed in controlling the opponent's hand then the rear hand can roll in and press down, using the power of crosscut to hit the opponent's chest or head. The hands, legs, and body all enter together, sticking to his body with a lengthwise power. Once you have contacted the opponent with your body you can knock him over with a turn of the lower back, shoulders and arm.

- Although the power application of *aligned stance crosscut* differs from Longfist's 'lean' the practical application is similar. If the opponent hits with a left fist, I use my left hand to roll and pull down his left fist or arm, and enter the right foot behind his left foot. I extend my right arm forward and cross hit right to knock him over. I could also hit his ribs with my right fist.

- The use of *retreat crosscut* is essentially the same hand technique as the standard *crosscut*, but the footwork enables you to apply a crosscut forward while withdrawing your body backward.

- While the *standard crosscut* uses a step to the outside to hit in to the centre from the outside, the *inward crosscut* comes from inside and strikes forward. An inward strike is a block, while a forward strike attacks the chest, solar plexus or ribs.

Crosscut uses a crossways action to break a straight line, it uses defense as its attack. Just as the classics say, "use an attack as the defense and no one can see the defense; use a defense as the attack and no one can see the attack."

Crosscut as a defense defends your midline and as an attack breaks your opponent's centre. It moves at an angle to hit straight, and uses a circuitous route to make a straight line.

THE POEM ABOUT CROSSCUT

横拳似彈性属土，斜身拗步气易鼓。两拳旋拧横破直，五拳之中它为主。

Crosscut is like a round shot and its character is that of the earth,

The body is angled and the footwork is opposing so the energy expands easily.

The fists twist and cross to break a straight attack,

It is the most vital of the five elemental techniques.

FIVE ELEMENT FORMS

FIVE PHASES CONNECTED 五行连环

INTRODUCTION TO THE FIVE PHASES CONNECTED (FIVE ELEMENTS LINKED), *WU XING LIAN HUAN*

The Five Elements Connected form is a widespread and popular short traditional form. It is based on the five foundation techniques of split, drill, drive, cannon, and crosscut. The form is also called Advance And Retreat Connected [or Linked]. Characteristics of the footwork are: there are both advancing and retreating steps, emphasizing advancing; stepping is very quick, has side to side movement, and moves back and forth both lengthways and sideways. Characteristics of the hand techniques are: there are both attacking and defensive moves, emphasizing attacking; the techniques combine soft and hard, are hard without stiffness and soft without slackness; the quick moves are not rushed and the slow moves are not slack. Characteristics of the power are: power is full when launched; settled, stable, thick, and fierce; and is always integrated whole body power, emphasizing hard power.

The form goes back and forth once, it goes out with ten moves, and comes back to the same place with the same ten moves. Practising this form helps you grasp the characteristics and flavour of Xingyi. You should pay attention to performing in a continuous manner, getting the power to flow smoothly, getting a good rhythm and spirit, and showing confidence. Long term practice will develop the nervous system, improve coordination, and improve the fighting spirit. It develops the body, trains self-defense, and helps mould character.

NAMES OF THE MOVEMENTS

0.   Opening Move
1.   Advance Right Drive
2.   Retreat Left Drive
3.   Right Aligned Stance Drive
4.   White Crane Flashes Its Wings
5.   Left Cannon
6.   Wrap
7.   Advance Right Crosscut

8.   Leopard Cat Climbs A Tree

9.   Advance Right Drive

10.   Leopard Cat Turns Over Whilst Climbing A Tree

      (The following moves are a repetition of the first section, in the returning
      direction)

11.   Advance Right Drive

12.   Retreat Left Drive

13.   Right Aligned Stance Drive

14.   White Crane Flashes Its Wings

15.   Left Cannon

16.   Wrap

17.   Advance Right Crosscut

18.   Leopard Cat Climbs A Tree

19.   Advance Right Drive

20.   Leopard Cat Turns Over Whilst Climbing A Tree

      (The following moves are the closing section)

21.   Advance Right Drive

22.   Retreat Left Drive

23.   Closing Move

Description of the Movements

0.   Opening Move   qǐ shì   起势

ACTION 1: Stand upright, facing the direction in which you will go. Place the palms
on the thighs. (image 4.1)

ACTION 2: Lift the hands at the sides, gradually turning them so that they face up
by the time they reach shoulder height. Keep the arms naturally bent and look at
the right hand. (image 4.2)

ACTION 3: Bend the arms to bring the hands past the face, palms down and fingers
pointing to each other. Look ahead. (image 4.3)

ACTION 4: Press the hands down past the chest to the belly, keeping the arms
rounded. Sit down, keeping the knees together. Press the head up and look

forward. (image 4.4)

ACTION 5: Without moving the legs, clench the fists and turn the fist hearts up, keeping the elbows snug to the ribs. Drill the right fist up past the solar plexus then out to nose height, ulnar edge twisted over. Look at the right fist. (image 4.5)

ACTION 6: Step the left foot forward without moving the right foot, to sit into a *santi* stance. Bring the left fist up past the solar plexus and out along the right arm, then unclench and split forward at shoulder height, palm facing the front. Unclench the right hand and pull it back to the belly, palm down. Look at the left hand. (image 4.6)

Pointers

- o When you lift the hands be sure to keep the arms bent and settle the shoulders and elbows down. Lift the arms on the scapular line, slightly ahead of the trunk, to open up the back.

- o Breathe in while lifting the hands. Sit down as you press the hands down. Bend the knees to the height that you will take in *santishi*.

- o Strike the left hand as you place the left foot, working together.

1. Advance Right Drive   jìnbù yòu bēngquán   进步右崩拳

ACTION 1: Clench fists and turn the left fist heart up, tucking in the left elbow. Advance the left foot a half-step and follow in with the right foot to ten centimetres behind the left heel, with the weight on the right leg. Slide the right fist along the left arm to punch forward to solar plexus height, fist surface forward and fist eye up, with the elbow slightly bent. Pull the left fist back to the belly, fist heart in. Press the head up and look at the right fist. (image 4.7)

Pointers

- o Punch with the right fist as the right foot lands, working together with a *rear foot timed drive*.

- As they punch out and pull back, each fist's power 'goes out like a steel rasp and returns like a grappling hook.' Settle the shoulders, tuck in the lower back, urge the right shoulder into the right punch, and turn from the body core. The fists work as a paired couple.

- As the right foot lands it uses the power of the whole foot to strike with an impetus forward and down, landing with a thud. Roll the hip in and use the knee to bring the foot forward, as if someone were pulling your right foot back with a rope. Pretend you are pulling him forward and trying to break the rope. Be sure not to lift the foot to stamp.

- Breathe out to shoot power and settle your *qi* to the *dantian*, so that your whole body works as a unit – upper and lower limbs, inner and outer.

2.   Retreat Left Drive   tuìbù zuǒ bēngquán   退步左崩拳

ACTION 1: Take a half-step back with the right foot and shift weight to the right leg. Turn the right fist over so the fist heart faces up, to press down with the forearm. Look straight ahead. (image 4.8)

ACTION 2: Retreat the left foot a large step backwards and place the whole foot solidly on the ground. Shift your weight mostly onto the left leg and withdraw the

right foot, turning it crossways so that the thighs press tightly together. Slide the left fist along the right forearm to drive forward at solar plexus height. Keep the left arm slightly bent, the fist eye up. Pull the right fist back to the belly. Press the head up and look at the left fist. (image 4.9)

Pointers

- Three actions must happen at once with a complete, integrated power: punch the left fist; land the left foot; pull back the right fist.

- The power of the left fist's punch comes from the weight moving back to the left foot as it lands. The reactive force immediately reaches the lower back and the energy exchange transfers to the shoulder and through the elbow to culminate in the left fist. Co-ordinate the launching power of the lower body turn, shoulder extension, and arm extension, each segment working together to generate power sequentially until the final result reaches the fist surface.

3.   Right Aligned Stance Drive   yòu shùnbù bēngquán   右顺步崩拳

Also called Black Bear Charges Out Of Its Cave   hēixióng chūdòng 黑熊出洞

ACTION 1: Advance the right foot to the forward right and follow-in a half-step with the left, taking a *santi* stance. Turn the left fist over so the fist heart faces up and roll the left elbow inwards slightly. Drive the right fist along the left arm to punch forward with the elbow slightly bent and the fist eye on top, to solar plexus height. Press the head up. Pull the left fist back to the belly with the fist heart inward. Look at the right fist. (image 4.10)

4.10

Pointers

- o Land the right punch timed exactly with the landing of the right foot, that is, the power of a *lead foot timed drive*.

- o Be sure to keep the elbows snug to the ribs when driving out the punch. When the punch is finished, the forearm should be horizontal, with the elbow on line with, though lower than, the shoulder. Be sure to keep the elbow tucked slightly in.

- o At the instant of power launch, land the right foot forward, punch the right fist and pull the left fist back, using the crisp action of turning the lower waist, or body core area and urging the shoulder forward. Co-ordinate this action with an expulsion of breath to create a complete, integrated power. The punch should be strong without being rigid. It should show a spirit capable of pushing mountains into the sea, or surging out ten thousand miles in an instant, with an all-conquering attitude.

4. White Crane Flashes Its Wings   báihè liàngchì   白鹤亮翅

ACTION 1: Withdraw the left foot a half step, half-sitting into a horse stance. Draw the right elbow across the body and stretch the back to bring the left fist underneath. Then lower the right fist to cross the forearms in front of the belly, and finish bracing out to the sides over the knees. Look. towards the right fist. (images 4.11A and B)

4.11A   4.11B

ACTION 2: Without moving the feet, but shifting to the left leg and turning, drill the fists up to head height with the fist hearts facing in and the forearms crossed, left inside the right. Look at the fists. Then shift back into a horse stance and rotate the forearms to turn the fist hearts out and open the arms to brace out to the left and right. Keep the arms slightly bent, fists at head height. Look at the right fist. (images 4.12 A and B)

4.12A   4.12B

ACTION 3: Shift onto the left leg and withdraw the right foot to beside the left foot, landing with a thump. Bring the fists in together at the belly, striking it with some force. Press the head up, settle the *qi* to the *dantian,* and look forward. (image 4.13)

4.13

Pointers

o The actions of *white crane flashes it wings* involve an elbow cover, a low brace, an upward drill, a turning outer brace, a dropping wrap, and a withdrawing embrace at the belly. Be sure to feel the power of each: cover, brace, drill, turn, brace, wrap, and embrace. The whole body must be co-coordinated and the power smoothly integrated without any slackness.

o When the fists drill up, keep the elbows down, the back stretched, and the chest closed. Breathe in while doing this. When the fists turn over, release the shoulders and turn the elbows out. When the forearms brace out and the arms circle down, they should have a wrapping power. Pulling in to the belly should have an embracing power. The fists should hit the belly timed exactly as the right foot lands, settling the *qi* to the *dantian* to assist in generating power.

o Pay particular attention to the leftward and rightward movement of the body. When the fists drill up, the weight should shift more towards the left leg. When the arms brace out, weight should shift more towards the right leg. When the arms wrap, weight should shift more to the left leg.

o When the right foot withdraws it must rub along the ground. Use a wrapping, gathering force in the hips to bring the foot in, as if you are pulling something along with the foot. Land with a thump – be sure not to lift the foot to stamp.

5. Left Cannon   zuǒ pàoquán   左炮拳

ACTION 1: Take a big step to the forward right with the right foot and follow-in a half-step with the left. Drill the right fist up past the solar plexus to nose height. Lift the left fist to the solar plexus to prepare. As the right foot advances, punch the left fist forward at solar plexus height with the arm slightly bent, elbow tucked in, fist eye up and shoulder put forward into the punch. Rotate the right fist at the right temple, elbow down. Look in the direction of the left punch. (image 4.14)

4.14

Pointers

o The left punch and the right foot landing are timed together, so that hand and foot hit as a unit.

o Turn the trunk with a counter-movement a bit leftward as you drill up the right fist. Then when the left fist punches, the whole body generates a power turning to the right, launching from the lumbar/waist area to transfer to the shoulders, which in turn transfer to the elbows, which transfer to the fists. Be sure to make full use of the strength of the lower trunk. Be sure also to keep the right elbow down – don't lift it. Keep the right fist in front of the ears but behind the eyebrows at the temple.

- o When you launch power, urge the shoulder forward from the body core – the lower back urges the shoulder and the shoulder sends the fist out. Settle your *qi* into the *dantian*. In this way, both upper and lower, and inner and outer, work together, and the resulting force is ferocious.

6. Wrap   bāoguǒ shǒu   包裹手

4.15

ACTION 1: Retreat the left foot a half-step, following with the right foot to place it by the left ankle. Pull the left fist back to the belly and turn the torso left. Roll the right elbow in front of the body, so the fist eye faces in. Look at the right fist. (image 4.15)

ACTION 2: Retreat the right foot and shift back to the right leg. Unclench the hands and pull the right hand back and extend the left hand out along the right arm to brace to the left – right palm facing up, and left palm facing down. Withdraw the left foot to beside the right without touching down. Brace the right hand out to the right, palm down, and circle the left hand down, palm up, bringing it back to the belly. Brace with both arms keeping a rounded structure. Look at the right hand. (images 4.16 A and B)

ACTION 3: Advance the left foot and follow in with the right a half-step, taking a *santi* stance. Circle the right hand down to the belly, fingers down and palm forward. Lift the left hand to grab, palm up, and when it gets to in front of the right shoulder, turn the palm over to face down, and brace out to the left and forward. Keep the left arm rounded with the palm at shoulder height. Press the head up. Look at the left hand. (image 4.17)

4.16A

4.16
B

4.17

Pointers

- o The wrapping technique in the connected form is actually the alligator from the twelve animal forms. When you roll the elbow and retreat, focus on drawing in. Draw the body back and shrink in a bit.

- o As the right foot retreats, the right hand knocks and braces out across to the right. As the left foot advances the left hand knocks and braces across to the front. Keep these movement synchronized.

- o The hands should draw two circles, using the waist as the axis. The waist leads the shoulders, the shoulders transfer to the elbows, and the elbows send the hands out. Keep the chest closed in and the arms rounded, the waist lively. The entire movement should be rounded with no sluggishness, the power gentle but not lax. The arms and hands should have a rolling embracing power and a knocking away bracing power. Pay attention that the left and right shifting of body weight is coordinated with the hand actions.

7. Advance Right Crosscut   jìnbù yòu héngquán   进步右横拳

ACTION 1: Clench the hands and turn the left fist over so the fist heart is up, the elbow rolled in to cover the heart. Take a big step to the forward left with the left foot and follow in a half-step with the right foot. With the fist eye down, bring the right fist up past the solar plexus then along under the left arm, gradually drilling it forward until the fist is at shoulder height and the fist eye is up. Keep the right arm slightly bent. Turn the left fist over and pull it back to the belly with the fist eye down. Press the head up. Look at the right fist. (image 4.18)

4.18

Pointers

- o Hit the right fist as the left foot advances. The foot steps diagonally to the forward left and the fist hits straight forward.

- o To launch force to the crosscut, turn the waist to extend the shoulder. The shoulders must first roll in and then open up and release. The fists should have a torqued rolling force – a rolling, drilling, spiraling force. The legs should have a scissoring force, rolling in the hips and closing the knees, settling the buttocks down and pressing the head up. Settle the *qi* to the *dantian*. Keep focused.

8. Leopard Cat Climbs A Tree   límāo shàngshù   狸猫上树

ACTION 1: Unclench the hands and reach forward, palms down, then clench the fists and pull them back to the belly. Advance the left foot straight ahead a half-step and shift forward onto the left leg. Bring both fists up from the belly, past the solar plexus, and drill them forward, the right fist ahead of the left, and the left fist at the right elbow. Both fist hearts slope up and the right fist is at eyebrow height. Look at the right fist. (images 4.19 A, B, and C)

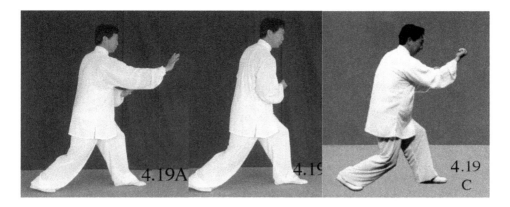

ACTION 2: Lift the right knee, turning the foot out to do a crossways thrust kick forward and up to shoulder height. Keep a forward drilling pressure in the fists. Look ahead of the right foot. (image 4.20)

ACTION 3: After the kick, quickly stomp the right foot forward and down with the foot turned crossways. Follow in a half-step with the left foot, to form a scissors stance. Unclench the hands and turn them over, palms forward. Slide the left hand along the right forearm and chop forward and down, palm down at waist height. Pull the right hand back to beside the right hip, palm down. Look past the left hand. (image 4.21)

Pointers

- o Drill the fists up as the right foot kicks up.

- o Split the left hand down as the right foot lands crossways.

- o The entire movement of *leopard cat climbs a tree* must be continuous, completed as one action.

- o Close the shoulders and chest in and settle the elbows down as the fists drill up, to create an embracing power.

- o Be sure to turn the waist and extend the shoulders into the double split. Time the right hand pulling back with the left hand splitting down.

- o When you kick the right foot be sure to close in the right hip and forcibly lift your knee. This helps give power to the kick. When you land the right foot, use a stamping power as if stomping on a poisonous animal – trying to kill it or prevent it from getting away.

o   In the scissors stance keep a bit more weight on the rear leg so that you are able to smoothly advance the lead foot in the following movement.

9. Advance Right Drive   shàngbù yòu bēngquán   上步右崩拳

ACTION 1: Advance the right foot a half-step then take a big step forward with the left foot and follow in with the right to just behind the left foot – weight on the right leg. Clench fists and do a right driving punch forward from the right waist, following the line of the left arm. The fist eye is up and the punch is at solar plexus height. Pull the left fist back to the belly. Urge the right shoulder into the hit, keeping the right arm slightly bent. Press the head up. Look at the right fist. (image 4.22)

4.22

Pointers

o   Punch with the right fist exactly at the same time as you land the right foot in the follow-in step, in a *rear foot timed drive*.

o   The requirements for the drive punch are the same as usual, but the long forward stride gives it more distance, speed, and power. Put force into both the advancing and pulling back fists. The right leg should thrust the punch forward.

o   Be sure to press the head up to prevent the body from leaning forward.

10. Leopard Cat Turns Over Whilst Climbing a Tree (Drive Turn Around)

límāo dào shàngshù   狸猫倒上树

ACTION 1: Hook-step in the left foot, stepping around so that it hooks in outside the right toes. The more you hook in the better. Bend the knees. Pull the right fist back to the belly. Turn the body around 180 degrees to face back in the direction from which you came. Press the head up. Look forward. (image 4.23)

ACTION 2: Shift onto the left leg and lift the right knee, turning the foot crossways, then kick forward and up to shoulder height. Turn the fists over so the fist hearts are on top, and drill them up past the solar plexus and forward. The right fist is more forward and higher, at nose height, and the left fist is at the right elbow. Look at the right fist. (image 4.24)

ACTION 3: After the kick, stamp the right foot forward and down with the foot turned crossways, and follow-in a half-step with the left foot to form a scissors stance. Unclench the hands and turn them over so the palms face forward. Slide the left hand forward along the

4.23

4.24

right forearm and split down, palm down. Press the head up. Look past the left hand. (image 4.25)

Pointers

4.25

- o During the turn, three actions are done simultaneously: hook-step in the left foot, pull in the right fist, and turn the body around to the right. Press the head up as you turn around. Do not lower the head or bend at the waist.

- o When you hook-in the left foot and turn around be sure to take a good sized hook-in step.

- o Then during the kick, two actions are done simultaneously: drill the fists up and kick the right foot.

- o When you kick the right foot, be sure to turn the foot out and fully extend the leg at the instant you complete the kick. Keep the supporting leg slightly bent to stand firmly. Tuck in the right hip when you kick.

- o When you drill the fists up be sure to keep tightly to the ribs. When you split the hands down, turn the waist, put the shoulders into the action, settle the shoulders and elbows, and put equal force into the forward and backward moving hands. Be sure to press the head up.

- o During the landing, thrust from the left leg to land the right foot forward, being sure to add a stomping force to the crossways landing. Two actions are done simultaneously: split the left hand down and land the right foot. When you form the scissors stance, press the thighs tightly together.

- • That is as far as I need to describe, as it is halfway, and you just continue to repeat the moves for the other half of the form. The following section is a repetition of the first section, going back in a returning direction.

11.	**Step Forward Right Drive**	See move 1.
12.	**Retreat Left Drive**	See move 2.
13.	**Right Aligned Stance Drive**	See move 3.
14.	**White Crane Flashes Its Wings**	See move 4.
15.	**Left Cannon**	See move 5.
16.	**Wrap**	See move 6.
17.	**Advance Right Crosscut**	See move 7.
18.	**Leopard Cat Climbs A Tree**	See move 8.
19.	**Advance Right Drive**	See move 9.
20.	**Leopard Cat Turns Over Whilst Climbing A Tree**	See move 10.
	(Closing section)	
21.	**Advance Right Drive**	See move 1.
22.	**Retreat Left Drive**	See move 2.

23. Closing Move   shōu shì   收势

ACTION 1: Advance the left foot without moving the right foot, to take a *santi* stance. Pull the left fist back to the belly, fist heart down. Press the head up. Look forward. (image 4.26)

ACTION 2: Advance the right foot to place it parallel to the left foot with the knees together. Do not let the body rise yet. Stand firmly on both legs with the knees bent. (image 4.27)

ACTION 3: Unclench the hands and lift them at the sides of the body, palms up and arms naturally bent, not fully extended. When the hands come up to shoulder height, bring them in towards the face, turning the palms down. (images 4.28 A and B)

ACTION 4: Press the hands down in front of the chest and stand up to attention. (image 4.29)

Pointers

o   Do three actions simultaneously: pull the left fist in, press into the left foot, and press the head up.

o   Press the palms down and stand up to finish at exactly the same time so that completion is done throughout the body.

RHYTHM AND POWER GENERATION IN THE FIVE PHASES CONNECTED

One clear measure for judging the quality of a performance and the level to which a player has mastered the movements and skills is the coordination of timing and power in the moves and the rhythm connecting the moves. Every form has its own rhythm to differentiate fast and slow, relaxation and tension, hard and soft. And each movement within the form has its own rhythm. Only after a considerable period of practice with repeated effort and thought can you find the natural patterns and raise your level of artistry. Each person has a different character and understanding, and so brings a different angle to his appreciation of the movements and the form. Add to this that each teacher passes on the form differently, and it is obvious that each person will have a different rhythm for the same form and movements that shows a personal style and character.

Here is a simple analysis of one possible way to deal with the rhythm of fast and slow within the form.

1. At the start it is vital to show stability, so the *opening movement* must not be rushed. You should be slow and steady, purposefully drawing your focus within yourself and regulating your mind and *qi*. Breathe deeply to the *dantian* to settle your spirit and *qi*. At this time get rid of any emotional tension. Although the movement is slow, your spirit should show a fullness that permeates your whole body. Your slow movement and the gathering of spirit should affect a spectator, creating in him a feeling of stability and quietude. You should settle into the *santishi* with a positive shift and raking power in the front foot, putting power through to the lead hand.

2. The combination of three driving punches (*advance drive, retreat drive, aligned drive*) is called 'three arrows shot from a horse,' reminding us that drive is 'wood' and acts like an arrow. These three driving punches must have hard power and be heavy as a mountain – fierce, sonorous and forceful. They should not be rushed, but be done with a fullness of power, showing the dense strength and hard power of Xingyiquan. Each punch should increase in strength, culminating in the final *aligned stance drive*. The spirit should be apparent. The power should be first held back then launch. Breathe in slowly and breathe out sharply. Be sure to make the final launch of power fully connected throughout the body, with a vigorous appearance.

3. *White crane flashes its wings* should be quite rhythmic. The beginning and the middle should be fairly slow, showing the intent leading the movements. The drill, turn, brace and roll should show a full, contained energy. The final embracing movement, when the foot and hand hit simultaneously, should be quick and powerful with full power in the *dantian*. Your whole body should show confidence, your elbows should be tucked into the ribs, your fists should hit your belly. You can do this with an expulsion of sound, using sound to show ferocity and to increase power in the *dantian*.

4. You should have an intention to move forward before the *left cannon*, leaning the body slightly to the forward right to build up power for the sudden launch – incline the whole body by driving the supporting knee down, not by leaning at the waist. Stride forward quickly and punch fiercely with a brave spirit. Stop for an instant after the punch with a stable appearance. The punch should be sudden and very quick. Move quickly and stop absolutely – this is the characteristic of cannon punch.

5. *Wrap*, the alligator form, should be gentle but not lax, with a contained strength, powerful but not stiff. The hands, eyes, body and feet must be coordinated to use the power of the whole body. When the hands circle they should have an unrevealed binding power. The footwork should be light and agile. The waist should be lively and full of elasticity. The speed should be soft and rhythmic, not rushed. Pay attention to the roundness of the movement. The final left hand

brace should cut across a bit more quickly, though, with the foot and hand arriving together.

6. *Advance right crosscut, leopard cat climbs a tree*, and *step forward right drive* should increase in speed and be seamlessly connected. They should show an accumulative increase in power, showing Xingyiquan's characteristic attacking spirit of "chasing the wind and the moon." The movements should not be just fast, but should show a brave appearance with a full spirit – quick but unhurried. When practising, pay attention to the integration of the movements and the changing lines of power through the body to get them smooth and flowing.

7. *Leopard cat turns over whilst climbing a tree* is the turn around for drive. Find the pivot point to turn around, pivoting on the left foot and using your trunk to turn. Step the left foot around to hook-in in front of the right foot so that the weight barely moves between the two feet in order to turn with speed and stability. The whole movement should be of moderate speed, showing quick movements within slowness and calmness within speed – the key is to be stable. Kick the right foot up quickly, and turn the waist to split down with the hands quickly. The eyes should be bright and intimidating.

8. The final *closing move* should be stable and fairly slow, giving a feeling that your intentions have not slackened. Although you have completed the form you still show full power. But you should do this for only a few seconds, and show a settling *qi* to come to a satisfactory conclusion.

• The initial movements in the form show a hard and powerful force, the middle movements show softness and coordination, and the speed in the later movements emphasizes the straight line 'chase the wind and the moon' spirit of Xingyiquan. Throughout the form, the regulation of speed and rhythm should always show Xingyiquan's characteristics and flavour – stressing hard power with softness assisting. You can change the rhythm of the form to suit your own understanding, but it is vital that you not perform at one speed or one unchanging rhythm. If you do that the form will be flat and boring.

ENTANGLING HANDS PARTNER FORM

交手炮

INTRODUCTION TO ENTANGLING HANDS, *JIAO SHOU PAO*

Entangling Hands is the shortest of Xingyi's partner forms. In this form, the stance stays fixed as the hands and arms cross and coil, sticking to each other, entangling the partners arms, so it is called Entangling Hands. Since it contains only split, drive, and cannon it is also called Three Techniques Hit. Traditionally the form is done both as fixed stance and moving stance, but the fixed stance is the more common method.

This form is learned in order to reinforce the understanding of split, drive, and cannon by applying them on a partner. Both partners alternate attack and defense continuously and repetition of the form can help bring mastery of the techniques.

NAMES OF THE MOVEMENTS

1. A: Ready Stance   B: Ready Stance
2. A: Right Drive   B: Left Slap Elbow, Right Driving Punch
3. A: Left Split   B: Left Cannon
4. A: Right Split   B: Right Cannon
5. A: Left Slap Elbow, Right Drive   B: Left Split
6. A: Left Cannon   B: Right Split
7. A: Right Cannon   B: Left Slap Elbow, Right Driving Punch

Description of the movements (fixed stance method)

(A is the author on the left, B is the translator on the right)

1. Ready Stance   yùbèishì   预备势

ACTION 1: Partners A and B stand at attention facing each other about a one and a half arm-lengths away from each other. (image 4.30)

ACTION 2: Both A and B clench their fists and bring them to their waist, fist hearts up. Both step a foot out to the side and sit into horse stances. Partner A steps the right foot out, and B steps the left foot out. The width of the horse stance is three foot-lengths. The partners look at each other. (image 4.31)

2. A: Right Driving Punch   yòu bēngquán   右崩拳

B: Left Slap Elbow, Right Driving Punch

zuǒ pāizhǒu yòu bēngquán   左拍肘右崩拳

ACTION 1: Partner A shifts weight to the left by pressing into the right leg, to form a left transverse stance. As A shifts leftward, he punches the right fist towards B's solar plexus, with the fist eye up and the arm slightly bent. This is a right driving punch. Partner A looks at the right fist. (image 4.32)

ACTION 2: Partner B stays in a horse stance and unclenches the left hand with the palm facing right and the fingers up, to slap A's right arm at the elbow. Partner B allows the left shoulder to come forward slightly. Partner B hits A's right ribs with a right driving punch, allowing the right shoulder to come forward slightly. The fist eye is up and the arm slightly bent. Partner B looks at the right fist. (image 4.33)

Pointers

- ○ When partner A punches to B's solar plexus he should not suddenly strike out, but should have a stable focus.

- ○ The feet can turn a bit as the weight shifts from left to right. When turning left, the left toes can open out and the right heel can push back. When turning right, the right toes can open out and the left heel can push back. The feet turn with the weight shift. Partners A and B are similar in this action.

- ○ Partner B slaps the elbow first, then punches, but the actions are almost simultaneous. Be sure to move the shoulders into the actions.

- ○ When doing partner forms each partner should focus the hits and not try to hit his partner, to avoid unnecessary injury.

3. A: Left Split   zuǒ pīquán   左劈拳

    B: Left Cannon Punch   zuǒ pàoquán   左炮拳

ACTION 1: Partner A unclenches the right hand and turns the palm down to grab B's right wrist to pull it down. Partner A unclenches the left hand and chops toward B's face, palm forward. Partner A shifts weight to the right to form a right transverse stance and looks at B's face. (image 4.34)

ACTION 2: Partner B bends the right elbow to drill the fist up, drilling out inside A's left arm, rolling the right fist so that the fist eye faces the temple. Partner B shifts to the right while doing this, forming a right transverse stance with the right leg bent and the left leg pushing straight, turning the feet on the spot. At this time, B punches the left fist towards A's solar

plexus, the fist eye up and the arm slightly bent, completing the cannon punch. (image 4.35)

Pointers

- o Partner A should pull and strike simultaneously, sending the left shoulder forward.

- o Partner A should just hook onto B's wrist, not grab it, so that B can continue into the next move. In partner forms the partners need to cooperate.

- o When partner B drills the right fist upwards she must roll it and brace out, sticking to A's right arm. The body should have a drilling in power, and should shift to the right to drill and roll, to complete the cannon punch all at once.

4. **A: Right Split**   yòu pīquán   右劈拳

     B: Right Cannon Punch   yòu pàoquán   右炮拳

ACTION 1: Partner A brings the left fist down to the belly, then drills the fist up outside B's left arm. Partner A then coils around B's arm, grabs the wrist, and pulls it down. Partner A unclenches the right hand and chops towards B's face with the palm forward. Partner A shifts leftward, putting most weight on the left leg, in a left transverse stance. (image 4.36)

ACTION 2: Partner B brings the left fist back, bends the elbow and drills up, drilling up inside A's right arm. Partner B shifts leftward and rolls the left fist so the fist eye faces the temple. Partner B bends the left leg and pushes into the right leg, forming a left transverse stance. At this time B punches the right fist towards A's solar plexus. The fist eye is up, the arm slightly bent, and the right shoulder forward. Partner B looks at A. (image 4.37)

Pointers

- o Partner A should bring his left hand down in a circular motion, then circle back up to hook and pull down. He should first turn right then turn left. He should hook and pull quickly, and pull down with a heavy power. He should shift left as he hits with the right hand.

- o When doing partner forms, be sure not to grab and hang on, as this prevents your partner from continuing on with the next move.

5.   A: Left Slap Elbow, Right Driving Punch

zuǒ pāizhǒu yòu bēngquán   左拍肘右崩拳

B: Left Split   zuǒ pīquán   左劈拳

ACTION 1: Partner A unclenches the left hand and slaps B's right elbow rightwards with the fingers up. Partner A urges the left shoulder slightly into the movement and shifts into a horse stance. At this time A punches the right fist to B's right ribs, putting the right shoulder forward into the punch. The fist eye is up and the arm slightly bent. Partner A looks at B. (image 4.38)

ACTION 2: Partner B drops the right hand and unclenches it, sliding it along A's right arm, changing to a grab to pull the arm down and back to the belly. At this time B unclenches the left hand and splits towards A's face. Partner B shifts to the right into a right transverse stance and looks at A. (image 4.39)

Pointers

- o Points to consider for partner A's *slap elbow, drive* are similar to that done by B in move 2.

- o Points to consider for partner B's *left split* are similar to that done by A in move 3.

6. A: Left Cannon Punch   zuǒ pàoquán   左炮拳

   B: Right Split   yòu pīquán   右劈拳

ACTION 1: Partner A bends the right elbow to drill the fist up, drilling up inside B's left arm. Partner A shifts right and rolls the right fist so the fist eye faces the right temple. Partner A shifts into a right transverse stance with the right leg bent and the left leg straight. At this time A punches the left fist to B's solar plexus with a left cannon punch. (image 4.40)

ACTION 2: Partner B brings the left fist back to the belly then drills it out along the outside of A's left arm, unclenching the hand and coiling it to grab A's wrist. Partner B then pulls A's arm down and back. At this time B unclenches the right hand and chops towards A's face with the palm forward. Partner B shifts to the left into a left transverse stance, looking at A. (image 4.41)

7.   A: Right Cannon Punch   yòu pàoquán   右炮拳

B: Left Slap Elbow, Right Driving Punch

zuǒ pāizhǒu yòu bēngquán   左拍肘右崩拳

ACTION 1: Partner A drills the left fist up to the solar plexus, turning the fist heart inward, then, as he drills the fist up to nose height, he shifts weight to the left by pressing into the right leg, to form a left transverse stance. As A shifts leftward, he rotates the left fist so that the fist eye faces the left temple and the elbow drops. At this time A punches the right fist towards B's solar plexus, with the fist eye up and the arm slightly bent. This is a right cannon punch. Partner A looks at his right fist.

ACTION 2: Partner B stays in a horse stance and unclenches the left hand with the palm facing right and the fingers up, to slap A's right arm at the elbow. Partner B allows the left shoulder to come forward slightly. Partner B hits A's right ribs with a right driving punch, allowing the right shoulder to come forward slightly. The fist eye is up and the arm slightly bent. Partner B looks at the right fist.

- Partners A and B continue on exchanging techniques. The number of repetitions is determined by the interest and conditioning of the partners.

- The partners should control their speed, maintaining a speed appropriate to their level of mastery. They should go slowly at first, and hold back their punches. Each should give the other the opportunity to block, cooperating fully with each other, to master the pattern and route of the form and learn the defense and attack applications. Once they are comfortable with the form then they can go quicker and link the actions together more, developing a tight coordination. Never go too quickly, as this causes movement to become rushed and sloppy. The partners must work well together because it is important that the moves be done correctly with good timing.

- When doing partner forms you should have full spirit, and show fierceness.

FIVE PHASES CONTEND 五行炮

INTRODUCTION TO FIVE PHASES CONTEND, *WUXINGPAO*

The Five Phases Contend partner form was created according to the mutual creation and mutual control of the five elements. It is made up of all five basic techniques – split, drill, drive, cannon, and crosscut – and is often called Five Elements Create And Control. One partner performs the five elements as they develop from each other, while the other partner performs the five elements as they control each other. The form practices footwork combined with hand techniques, which makes it more realistic. Partners A and B alternate sides so that they can continue on, making the form long or short, and taking up as much space as they wish.

NAMES OF THE MOVEMENTS

1.   Preparation
2.   A: Advance, Right Drive   B: Withdraw, Left Press Down
3.   A: Advance, Left Drive   B: Step Forward, Right Split
4.   A: Retreat, Right Cannon   B: Right Press Down, Left Drill
5.   A: Retreat, Left Crosscut   B: Advance, Right Drive
6.   A: Withdraw, Left Press Down   B: Advance, Left Drive
7.   A: Step Forward, Right Split   B: Retreat, Right Cannon
8.   A: Right Press Down, Left Drill   B: Retreat, Left Aligned Crosscut

Description of the Movements

(A is in the author on the left, B is the translator on the right.)

1.   Preparation   yùbèishì   预备势

ACTION 1: Partners A and B stand facing each other, about three steps away, looking at each other. They salute each other. (image 4.42)

ACTION 2: Both partners simultaneously sit into *santishi*. (image 4.43)

4.42   4.43

2.   A: Advance, Right Drive   jìnbù yòu bēngquán   进步右本拳

B: Withdraw, Left Press Down   chèbù zuǒ àn   撤步左按

ACTION 1: Partner A steps the left foot forward, bringing the right foot in just behind the left foot, keeping the weight on the right leg. Partner A moves B's left hand aside to the right with the left hand and punches the right fist towards B's solar plexus. (image 4.44)

ACTION 2: Partner B steps the right foot back a small step, shifting back and withdrawing the left foot back in front of the right foot. Partner B presses A's right fist down with the left hand, looking at A's right fist. (image 4.45)

Pointers

o   As partner A punches towards B's solar plexus he should find the proper distancing, as if he could hit B, but he doesn't actually hit.

o   Partner B withdraws her feet quickly, but not too quickly – timed neither too early nor too late. The actions should work well together. She should control well and connect accurately with the left hand pressing down.

3.   A: Advance, Left Drive   jìnbù zuǒ bēngquán   进步左崩拳

B: Step Forward, Right Split   shàngbù yòu pīquán   上步右劈拳

ACTION 1: Partner A steps the left foot a half-step forward, bringing the right foot up. Partner A brings back the right fist and does a driving punch with the left fist towards B's solar plexus. Partner A presses the head up and looks ahead of the left fist. (image 4.46)

ACTION 2: Partner B turns the left foot out on the spot and steps the right foot forward. Partner B drills the left hand out along the outside of A's left arm. Partner B then turns the hand over to grab and pull A's hand down to the belly, chopping towards A's face with the right hand. (image 4.47)

Pointers

o   As partner A advances with the left driving punch he must step the right foot in quickly and extend the left shoulder forward into the punch. His right foot should step in about a foot-length behind his left foot.

o   Partner B must turn her left foot out in the proper place, about a foot-length away from A's left foot. Then B can step her right foot up outside A's left foot. This develops proper footwork. Both sides need to practise to get a feel for the distancing.

o   When partner B drills out and grabs A's arm to pull back, she does not need to hang on, as this is a form, and A needs to be able to continue on.

o   When partner B does the right split she should hold back the hit.

4.   A: Retreat, Right Cannon   tuìbù yòu pàoquán   退步右炮拳

    B: Right Press Down, Left Drill   yòu yā zuǒ zuānquán 右压左钻拳

ACTION 1: Partner A retreats the right foot a step and withdraws the left foot just in front of the right. Partner A bends the left arm to drill up at nose height to break B's split as it comes. Without stopping the left foot, A then advances a step while doing a right cannon punch towards B's solar plexus. Partner A extends the right shoulder into the punch and looks at B. (image 4.48)

ACTION 2: Partner B retreats the right foot back a step and withdraws the left foot a half- step. Partner B rolls the left elbow in across the chest and pulls the right fist in to cover across from the right, down and leftward to break A's right cannon punch. At this time, B advances the left foot a half-step and punches a drilling fist forward and up towards A's jaw. Partner B looks at the left fist and brings A's right fist down towards the belly. (image 4.49)

4.48   4.49

Pointers

o   Partner A needs to perform the retreat, withdraw, and advance quickly and agilely. When retreating he must get the correct foot placement. When doing the right cannon punch, partner A must advance the left foot to the outside of B's right foot, driving it in. Partner A can put his body into the punch a bit. When doing partner forms, the partners should coordinate well together, giving each other space and time to allow each other to break the attacks.

o   Partner B should first retreat the right foot, then withdraw the left foot, then immediately advance, connecting the footwork smoothly. The hands should work together with the footwork – the left elbow rolling across as the right foot retreats, the left drill punching and the right fist drawing back as the left foot advances. She should step her left foot in towards partner A's groin. The drill should be held back.

5.   A: Retreat, Left Crosscut   tuìbù zuǒ héngquán   退步左横拳

   B: Advance, Right Drive   jìnbù yòu bēngquán   进步右崩拳

ACTION 1: Partner A retreats the right foot back a big step then withdraws the left foot a half-step, taking a *santi* stance. Partner A lowers the left fist down the chest to drill and crosscut outside B's left arm, fist heart up, to break B's left drilling punch. Partner A looks at the left fist. (image 4.50)

ACTION 2: Partner B advances the left foot, bringing the right foot in behind the left. Partner B does a right driving punch towards A's left ribs and pulls the left fist back to the belly. Partner B looks in the direction of the right punch. (image 4.51)

Pointers

   o   Partner A does the retreating step into the aligned stance in order to break B's drilling punch. The concept is to dare to use an attacking move as a defense. The left fist must have a crosscutting knocking power. Partner A must move back quickly with stable footwork.

   •   When B advances with the right driving punch she then 'becomes A' and repeats what A just did, while A repeats what B just did.

6.   A: Withdraw, Left Press Down   chèbù zuǒ àn   撤步左按

   B: Advance, Left Drive   jìnbù zuǒ bēngquán   进步左崩拳

ACTION 1: Partner A retreats the right foot a half-step and shifts back, withdrawing the left foot. Partner A presses the left hand down on B's right fist. Partner A turns the body slightly to the right, and looks at the left hand. (image

4.52)

ACTION 2: Partner B advances the left foot and follows up with the right foot. At this time B punches with the left fist towards A's left ribs. Partner B brings the right fist back to the belly, presses the head up, and looks past the left fist. (image 4.53)

7.	**A: Step Forward, Right Split**	shàngbù yòu pīquán	上步右劈拳
	B: Retreat, Right Cannon	tuìbù yòu pàoquán	退步右炮拳

ACTION 1: Partner A turns the left foot out on the spot and advances the right foot. Partner A drills the left hand along the outer edge of B's left arm, then turns the hand to pull back to the belly. Partner A strikes with a right split towards B's face. (image 4.54)

ACTION 2: Partner B retreats the right foot and withdraws the left foot a half-step. Partner B bends the left elbow and drills up to nose height. Without stopping the left foot, B steps to the outside of A's right foot. At this time B does a right cannon punch towards A's solar plexus, looking in the direction of the right fist. (image 4.55)

8.	**A: Right Press Down, Left Drill**	yòu yā zuǒ zuānquán	右压左钻拳
	B: Retreat, Left Aligned Crosscut		
	tuìbù zuǒ shùnbù héngquán	退步左顺步横拳

ACTION 1: Partner A retreats the right foot and withdraws the left foot a half-step. At this time A rolls the left elbow rightward across the chest and brings the right

fist back to press down to the left. Partner A advances the left foot a half-step and does a left drill forward and up towards B's jaw. Partner A pulls the right fist back to the belly and looks towards the left fist. (image 4.56)

ACTION 2: Partner B retreats the right foot a big step then withdraws the left foot a half-step, taking a *santi* stance. At this time B circles the left fist down past the chest, then, without pausing, drills it up and out along the outer edge of A's left arm. B's fist heart is up and the arm bent. Partner B looks towards the fist. (image 4.57)

- Once you have performed to here you have completed a full circuit of the form. The number of repetitions you do depends on your conditioning and the size of the practice area.

- You may do two or three repeats of each person repeating as A and B, or you may switch A and B each time. The partners can agree between them, it doesn't matter.

Closing Move

ACTION 1: Partners A and B touch left arms when they reach an appropriate position, and indicate to each other that they wish to stop. At this time they each retreat the right foot and shift back. They then each withdraw the left foot to beside the right and stand up. While doing this, they unclench the left hand and clench the right fist, holding them out in front of the chest in a salute, looking at each other. (image 4.58)

ACTION 2: Both stand to attention, and the closing is completed.

THE TWELVE ANIMAL MODELS

ONE: DRAGON MODEL 龙形

INTRODUCTION TO THE DRAGON MODEL, *LONG XING*

The Chinese people venerate the dragon. They consider China the homeland of the dragon and themselves the descendants of dragons. The dragon, a mythical animal with horns on its head and scales on its elongated body, can walk, fly, and swim with equal skill. Indeed, it has the ability to 'mount the clouds and ride the mist.'

Xingyiquan is a style that models the actions of animals. The dragon model in Xingyiquan has developed through combining ancient Chinese traditions and writings about the dragon with the form analysis that previous generations of martial artists have done. The present set model has gradually developed over the years to both imitate the dragon's shape and actions and show its character and spirit. The dragon model imitates the great rising and dropping ability of the dragon in the footwork; its ability to close and open, fold in and expand in its handwork; and its ability to bend and extend in its bodywork. But in Xingyiquan it is not enough to just copy the actions and shape of an animal in order to develop correct actions, lines of movement, and combat effectiveness. It is more important to let the mood and spirit of the dragon direct your actions, to meticulously get a feel for the dragon's essence and grandeur. The dragon can fly to the highest and lowest places, it can coil and turn in all directions, it can suddenly jump up to the clouds, and just as suddenly dive down to the lowest gullies. It can travel in and out of the clouds and the seas and can soar even beyond the earth. Only with this image and mood leading your actions can you really express the dragon model. You must train both form and intent. Your intent gives meaning to your form, and your form physically expresses your intent.

METHODS OF PERFORMING THE DRAGON MODEL

1.1   METHOD ONE: STOMPING DRAGON MODEL

tàbù lóngxíng   踏步龙形

Start by settling into *santishi*. [22]

ACTION: Stand to attention and raise the hands at the sides, palms up (image 5.1a).

Then bend the elbows to bring the hands to press down in front of the face (image 5.1b).

Bend the knees to sit down and bring the hands down to the belly, gradually clenching (image 5.2).

Drill the right fist forward (image 5.3).

Step the left foot forward and extend the left hand into a split, pulling the right hand back to the belly to settle into *santishi* (images 5.4 and front).

1.1a   Left Stomping Dragon   zuǒ tàbù lóngxíng   左踏步龙形

ACTION 1: Clench the left fist and pull it back to the belly, withdrawing the left foot to in front of the right foot. (image 5.5)

ACTION 2: Shift back to the right leg and lift the left foot with the foot turned out crossways. Drill the left fist up by the sternum and out to nose height. Lift the right fist to the left elbow and do a crossways kick with the left foot up in front, kicking

---

[22] Editor's Note: See Part One Chapter Two for a more detailed description of *santishi*.

with the heel. Look forward. (images 5.6 and 5.7)

ACTION 3: Land the left foot forward, still turned out, landing firmly on the whole foot. Advance the right foot a half-step, gripping with the ball of the foot and allowing the heel to rise. Squat down so that the right knee is tucked tightly behind the left knee and the buttocks are on the right heel. The left leg is slightly bent and the left foot is turned out and flat on the ground. Slide the right fist forward along the left forearm to chop down, palm down. Pull the left hand back to the left hip. The right hand is in front of the left foot at hip height. Turn the torso leftward and lean forward slightly. Look at the right hand. (images 5.8 and front)

1.1b   Right Stomping Dragon   yòu tàbù lóngxíng   右踏步龙形

ACTION 1: Clench the right hand and pull it back to the belly. As the right hand comes back, raise the stance and advance the left foot a half-step. Drill the right fist up by the sternum then forward to nose height. Look at the right fist. (image 5.9)

ACTION 2: Quickly lift the right knee and kick the foot forward and up with the flat of the foot, foot turned out crossways. Slide the left fist along the right forearm and, when it arrives at the right fist, unclench both hands. Both palms reach forward with the fingers up, the left above and the right below. Kick no lower than the waist and no higher than the head. Keep the supporting leg slightly bent and grab the ground with the toes for stability. (image 5.10)

ACTION 3: After the right kick, drive the right foot forward and down to land firmly on the ground with the foot turned out crossways, and bring the left foot in a half-step, lifting the left heel. Chop the left hand forward and down and pull the right hand back to beside the right hip. Turn the torso rightward, twist the waist and lower the body, reaching the left shoulder into the move and reaching the torso forward slightly. Sit onto the left heel and bring the belly close to the right

thigh. The left hand chops forward of the right foot at hip height, about twenty to thirty centimetres above the ground. Stretch the thumb web and slightly bend all the fingers. Press the head up, keep the neck straight, and look at the left hand. (image 5.11)

Pointers

- o The left fist drills out as the left foot kicks.

- o The right hand chops as the body drops down.

- o The whole rising and dropping action should be done as one movement. There should be no pause in the action, and all segments of the body should rise and fall together.

1.1c   Stomping Dragon Turn Around   tàbù lóngxíng huíshēn   踏步龙形回身

Using the <u>left</u> *dragon* as example.

ACTION 1: Clench the leading hand and pull it back to the belly, standing up. Turn around one-eighty degrees on the spot to face back in the direction that you just came, pivoting on both feet. Drill the fist that you just pulled in up to the sternum and then forward and up to nose height, twisting the ulnar (little finger) side up. Bring the rear fist snug to the lead elbow. (image 5.12)

ACTION 2: Drill the rear fist up along the lead forearm. When it reaches the lead fist, unclench both hands and chop the rear hand forward and down while pulling the lead hand back to the hip. As you split, turn the body and sit down, turning the

lead foot out and raising the rear heel. Press the head up, keep the neck straight, and look at the front hand. (image 5.13)

- The *stomping dragon turn around* is the same on the right side, just turn the other way and transpose right and left actions.

Pointers

- o The *turn around* should be quick and stable. The feet must pivot to turn the body.

- o Three actions happen at once: the rear hand comes through to chop, the lead hand pulls back, and the body drops down.

1.1d   **Stomping Dragon Closing Move**   tàbù lóngxíng shōushì   踏步龙形收势

When you practise Xingyiquan you must always start properly and finish properly, or 'have an opening and a closure.' Finish where you started; always begin with *santishi* and come back to *santishi*; always complete any form by getting back to left *santishi* and finishing properly from there.

- If in a <u>left</u> *stomping dragon* position (left foot and right hand forward):

ACTION 1: Push into the right foot to stand up, clench the left hand and pull it back to the belly, drill the right fist out from the sternum to nose height. Look at the right fist. (image 5.14)

ACTION 2: Step the left foot forward to take a *santi* position. Do a splitting action with the hands to settle into a full *santishi*. Look forward. (image 5.15)

ACTION 3: Without moving the feet, clench the left hand and bring it back to the belly. Press the head up, settle and grab into the front foot. Look forward (image 5.16)

ACTION 4: Shift forward to the left leg and bring the right foot up parallel to the left, with the knees together and bent. Do not move the hands. (image 5.17)

ACTION 5: Unclench the hands and raise them by the sides. When they reach shoulder height, bend the elbows to bring the hands in to the face. Do not move the legs yet. Look at the right hand as you raise the hands, then look forward when the hands come in. (images 5.18 and 5.19)

ACTION 6: Press the hands down in front of the belly and stand up, standing to attention. The form is now completed. (image 5.20)

- If starting from a _right stomping dragon_ position (right foot and left hand forward):

ACTION 1: Push into the right leg to stand up, clench the left fist and pull it back to the belly and clench the right hand, which is also at the belly. The legs are still in the crossed stance. (image 5.21)

ACTION 2: Step the right foot slightly forward and drill the right fist out to nose height. (image 5.22)

ACTION 3: Step the left foot forward into a _santi_ stance. Slide the left fist along the right forearm and settle into a _santishi_. (image 5.23)

- The rest of the _closing move_ is the same as described above in Actions 3 to 6.

1.2   METHOD TWO: LEAPING DRAGON MODEL

yuèbù lóngxíng   跃步龙形

Start from left *santishi*.

1.2a   Left Stomping Dragon   zuǒ tàbù lóngxíng   左踏步龙形

This is the same as the *Left Stomping Dragon* described above. (See images 5.5, 5.6, 5.7, 5.8)

1.2b   Right Leaping Dragon   yòu yuèbù lóngxíng   右跃步龙形

ACTION 1: Step the left foot a half-step forward and push off forcefully to jump up. Drive the right knee up to give impetus to the jump, turning the foot crossways to kick up with the heel. Clench the right hand and pull it back before jumping, then drill it up and forward above the head while jumping. Put the left fist up to the right elbow. Look forward. You should jump with both feet completely up off the ground. (image 5.24)

5.24

ACTION 2: When you land, first land the left foot and squat down, landing the right foot in front with the foot turned out crossways. Land with the legs tightly together, the left knee tucked into the right knee. Chop forward and down with the left hand and pull the right hand back to the right hip, turning the waist and putting the shoulder into the strike. (see image 5.11)

- All the requirements of the stance are the same as those of *stomping dragon* landing, described above.

1.2c   Left Leaping Dragon   zuǒ yuèbù lóngxíng   左跃步龙形

ACTION 1: Clench the left hand and pull it back to the belly. Push back into the left foot to rise, and step forward a half-step with the right foot, then forcefully jump forward and up. Unclench the left hand and drill it by the sternum and up above the head, drilling the right hand to the left elbow. Use the left knee to help drive the power up, doing a crossing kick forward. Press the head up and look forward. (image 5.25)

ACTION 2: When you land, land the right foot first, bending the knee to squat, then land the left foot crossed out. Sit with the right heel off the ground and the legs tight together, the right knee under the back of the left knee. Chop forward and down with the right hand and pull the left hand back to the left hip, both palms down. Turn the waist and extend the shoulder. (see image 5.8)

- All the requirements of the stance are the same as described above in the *stomping dragon*.

5.25

- The number of repetitions depends on personal conditioning and the size of the training area.

Pointers

o To jump, push strongly off the ground with the left foot, drive the right leg up, and drill the right fist up. These actions must be done together.

o The jump should go for both distance and height. The landing must be stable. The chop is done at the same time that the body drops down.

o You may stop for a moment after landing, but you must keep your force and spirit full. Do not take a rest in the squatting posture.

1.2d   Leaping Dragon Turn Around and Closing Move

The *turn around* and *closing move* are the same as those of *stomping dragon* described above.

POWER GENERATION FOR THE DRAGON MODEL

The characteristic of the dragon model is its large rising and dropping action. The body must be springy when rising and tuck in when landing.

In the sitting stance the legs must be pressed tightly together. The rear knee should be tucked in behind, or outside, the lead knee. You must turn your waist and reach with your shoulders to achieve this position. Press the body down on the legs to get power for the strike.

When dropping into the squatting position put power into the hands. This helps the body to gain and hold its position (dropping down from the jump). The lead hand chops forward and the rear hand pulls back forcefully, turning the body and extending the shoulder with a strong exhalation of breath. This coordination helps achieve an explosive power.

Stomping dragon

- The fists drill up as the leg does the crossing heel kick. Keep the body straight and keep the action on the same plane to advance straight forward.

- When doing the crossing heel kick first lift the knee and then thrust into the kick. Press the head up, keep the back straight, and keep the supporting leg slightly bent.

Leaping dragon

- When you jump up from the ground you should press up with your head, reach up with your body, drill up with your arms, and push off strongly from one leg using the other leg to assist the jump. The movement must be coordinated and smooth so that you accelerate throughout to drive the jump up.

- The body technique for the dragon is: when rising, press the head up, straighten the lower back, and expand the belly. When jumping, pull the belly in and close the chest. When landing, turn the waist and put the shoulder into the action. When the landing is completed you should hold the position but the position must remain complete with a fierce attitude and no slackening of power.

Breathing Cycle For The Dragon Model

- Inhale when rising. In *stomping dragon*, inhale when drilling the fists up. In *leaping dragon*, inhale when lifting the body.

- Pause your breath at the peak of the action. In *leaping dragon*, use a lifting breath and pause at the peak of the jump.

- Exhale when landing. In *stomping dragon*, exhale when the foot lands, the hands chop and pull, and the body drops. In *leaping dragon*, exhale when the whole stance lands and launches power.

Practical Applications For The Dragon Model

Looking at the structure of the whole action, the dragon model is a technique that uses the feet and hands at the same time, striking two places at once. The hands drill up the midline to protect the head and chest area. Use them to attack if you advance and to defend if you retreat.

Lifting the knee and kicking with the foot turned out can be understood as a defensive action, kicking an attacker's oncoming kick. It can also be understood as an attacking kick, kicking the opponent's belly or leg, then driving forward to stomp. When you land the leg, keep in mind that you could be sliding and stomping onto your opponent's shin and foot. You should land as described in the classics, "The foot lands with a plan of attack."

One hand grabs and pulls while the other hand chops down, intended for the opponent's chest. This contains many possibilities, as the lead hand could then slice up or hit the groin, and the rear hand could come through with a punch.

The lifted leg can do a heel kick if the opponent is close, and could push off strongly if the opponent is distant, to land and stomp on him.

Training the *leaping dragon* develops the speed and agility needed to rise and drive forward. You can emphasize height or distance. The emphasis is on training the power of the legs and waist.

The Poem About The Dragon

龙形升降缩骨能，踏跃之法在腿功。两手钻翻是起落，伸缩展放意贯通。

The dragon rises and falls with the ability to shrink its bones,

The method of stomping and leaping depends on the skill of the legs.

The technique of rising and dropping depends on the hands drilling as they rise and turning over as they drop,

The intent permeates throughout as the body extends and tucks, expands and releases.

TWO: TIGER MODEL 虎形

INTRODUCTION TO THE TIGER MODEL, *HU XING*

The tiger is a strong and fierce predator, called the king of predators. Xingyiquan's tiger model imitates the tiger's fierceness and skill in pouncing on prey. In training the tiger model, the feet advance right and left in a zigzag pattern. The hands drill when rising and turn over when dropping. The body technique compresses when rising and lengthens when landing. The intent should express the tiger's ferocity. The tiger dominates the mountain regions. It domineers even when still, and when it moves it is like an avalanche. It can jump across gullies and mountain ranges, travelling the mountain regions at will. Its eyes glow like torches, showing the intensity of its spirit. Its power is expressed in its paws. Its cry echoes in the mountains and shakes the forests, terrifying everything that hears it. Its will to kill is strong. The tiger model should express this unapproachable, unbeatable manner and strength. When practising tiger model you should use this imagery to find the tiger's spirit and mood. This will help you to find and express the power within tiger model. When your imagination drives your form, then your form can better express your spirit.

METHODS OF PERFORMING TIGER MODEL

There are six variations of the tiger model: pounce, carry, intercept, trap, brace, and embrace. Each variation develops a specific technique. Although the hand techniques and power application differ, they are all based on the same stance and footwork.

2.1   METHOD ONE: TIGER POUNCES   hǔpū   虎扑

2.1a   Fierce Tiger Jumps over the Ravine   měnghǔ tiào jiàn   猛虎跳涧

Starting from left *santishi*.

ACTION: Take a step forward with the right foot, landing firmly, then quickly lift the left foot to place it beside the right foot without touching the ground. Reach the right hand out along under the left arm. When the right hand reaches the left hand, clench fists and pull both hands back to the belly. Hug the elbows to the ribs, keep the knees together, press the head up, and look forward. (images 5.26, 5.27)

5.26   5.27

2.1b   Tiger Pounces, Left Stance   zuǒbù hǔpū   左步虎扑

ACTION 1: Take a step forward with the left foot and follow in with the right foot a half-step. Drill the fists up past the chest to about six inches away from the jaw. (image 10.28)

ACTION 2: Unclench the hands and turn them over so that the palms face forward. As the left foot lands, extend the arms to pounce to chest height. Keep the arms slightly bent, the thumbs opposing each other, reach the shoulders, drop the elbows, and look forward. (images 5.29 and front)

2.1c   Tiger Pounces, Right Stance   yòubù hǔpū   右步虎扑

ACTION 1: Step the left foot a half-step straight forward and follow in the right foot to beside the left ankle without touching down. Pull the hands down to the belly, clenching them. Look forward. (image 5.30)

ACTION 2: Step the right foot a long step to the forward right and follow in a half-step with the left. Turn the fist hearts up and drill them up to the chest. Turn the hands and unclench them to pounce forward to chest height. The thumb web is rounded, the thumbs face each other, the palm centres face forward, and the fingers point up. Look forward. (images 5.31, 5.32)

2.1d   Tiger Pounces, Left Stance   zuǒbù hǔpū   左步虎扑

ACTION 1: Advance a half-step with the right foot and lift the left foot beside the right ankle without touching down. Pull the hands down and back tight to the belly, clenching fists with the fist hearts in. Look forward. (image 5.33)

ACTION 2: Take a long step to the forward left with the left foot and follow in the right foot a half-step. Drill the fists up past the sternum to in front of the jaw, then unclench them and pounce forward to chest height. Look forward. (image 5.34)

5.33   5.34

- Carry on, doing as many *tiger pounces* left and right as space permits.

Pointers

o   The first long step forward must cover distance and land very firmly. This step must be completed at the same time that the hands pull back.

o   The hands pounce as the leading foot lands – at exactly the same time.

2.1e   Tiger Pounce Turn Around   hǔpū huíshēn   虎扑回身

Using the left *tiger pounces* as example.

ACTION 1: Take a hook-in step with the left foot just in front of the right foot, forming a T stance. Shift to the left leg and turn around to the right, lifting the right foot beside the left ankle. Pull the hands down to the belly and clench them. Press the head up and look around to the new direction. (image 5.35)

ACTION 2: Take a long step to the forward right (in the new direction) and follow in a half-step with the left foot. Unclench the hands and pounce forward as before. (images 5.36, 5.37)

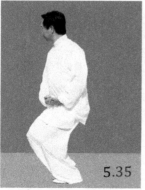

5.35   5.36   5.37

- The action of *tiger pounce turn around* is the same whether on the right or left side, just transpose the right and left actions.

Pointers

○ The turn around must be quick and stable. Be sure to hook-in the foot well.

○ Keep the body straight when turning around. Be sure not to look down, put the head down, or bend at the waist.

2.1f   Tiger Pounce Closing Move   hǔpū shōushì   虎扑收势

Always wait until you get back to your starting point before doing the *closing move.*

• When your *turn around* arrives in *tiger pounces, left stance*:

ACTION 1: Withdraw the left foot to parallel to the right foot without moving the right foot. Pull the hands back to the belly and clench them. Drill the right fist up to the chest and out to nose height. Look forward. (image 5.38)

ACTION 2: Step the left foot forward to take a *santi* stance. Slide the left hand along the right arm to chop forward, and pull the right hand back to the belly. Look forward. (image 5.39)

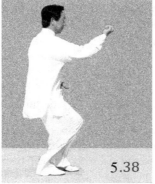

5.38   5.39

• When your turn around arrives in *tiger pounces, right stance*:

ACTION 1: Withdraw the left foot a half-step then withdraw the right foot to beside the left foot and place it firmly. Clench the right fist and pull it back beside the waist, then press down with the left hand and drill the right fist forward and up to nose height. (images 5.40, 5.41)

ACTION 2: Step the left foot forward to take a *santi* stance. Slide the left hand out along the right arm to chop forward. Pull the right hand back to the belly. Look forward. (image 5.42)

5.40   5.41   5.42

- Once to here, complete the closing the same as *santishi* closing, fully described in the dragon model. (see images 5.1.15 to 5.20)

Pointers

- o   The lead foot must withdraw exactly as the hands pull back.

- o   You must express full power when the feet are parallel and the right fist drills out.

- o   The left foot steps into the *santi* stance as the left hand does the split action. These actions must arrive together. All the requirements of the *santishi* are the same as the usual *santishi*.

2.2   TIGER CARRIES   hǔtuō   虎托

Tiger carries does not imitate an action of the tiger at all but is a technique that compensates for a power that would otherwise be lacking if you just practised *tiger pounces*.[23] Both techniques use a power forward and down. Since the hands follow different paths, the power application and combat application are quite different.

Start from left *santishi*.

2.2a   Tiger Carries, Right Stance   yòubù hǔtuō   右步虎托

ACTION 1: Advance the left foot a half-step, then advance the right foot to beside the left ankle. Slide the right hand along under the left arm. When it arrives at the left hand, circle both hands to the sides then wrap them in to the sides of the waist, palms forward, fingers down. Look forward. (images 5.43, 5.44)

ACTION 2: Take a long step to the forward right with the right foot and follow in a half-step with the left foot. Push forward from the waist with both palms, fingers angled down, palms about a fist-length apart at belly height. Urge the shoulders forward, settle the waist down, and look forward. (images 5.45 and front)

---

[23] Translator's note: The English word 'carry' implies a rising meaning, but the *tiger carry* is actually a low technique. 'Carry' is a term for an open palm technique that looks like carrying a tray, but can be applied up, directly forward, or down. When low, the power is like shaking a winnowing basket, so that the rice pops up and the chaff is blown away in the wind.

2.2b   Tiger Carries, Left Stance   zuǒbù hǔtuō   左步虎托

ACTION 1: Advance the right foot a half-step then lift the left foot beside the right ankle. Cross the wrists and drill up with the palms facing in. When the hands arrive at shoulder height rotate them so the palms face out and circle them to the sides then wrap down to beside the waist, palms facing forward and fingers pointing down. Press the head up and look forward. (images 5.46, 5.47)

ACTION 2: Take a long step to the forward left with the left foot and follow in a half-step with the right foot. Push forward to belly height, fingers down, hands a fist-length apart. Look forward. (image 5.48)

Pointers

- o   The hands must complete the circle as the foot advances.

- o   The hands must complete the push as the lead foot lands forward.

2.2c   Tiger Carries Turn Around   hǔtuō huíshēn   虎托回身

Using the left *tiger carries* as example.

ACTION 1: Take a hook-in step with the left foot to in front of the right foot and turn around to the right, shifting onto the left leg. Lift the right foot to beside the left ankle. Bring the hands around with the body, crossing them and drilling up. After you have turned around, circle the hands and bring them down to the sides of the waist. (images 5.49, 5.50)

ACTION 2: Take a long step to the forward right with the right foot and follow in the left foot a half-step. Complete the *tiger carries* to push down to the front to belly height. Look forward. (image 5.51)

- The action of *tiger carries turn around* is the same whether on the right or left side, just transpose the right and left actions.

Pointers

o Do not pause when turning around – move the hands while stepping.

2.2d   Tiger Carries Closing Move   hǔtuō shōushì   虎托收势

From left *tiger carries*:

ACTION 1: Withdraw the left foot to the right foot. Turn the left hand over to press down. Pull the right hand back to the belly. (image 5.52) Clench the right hand, drill up to the sternum and out to nose height, and pull the left hand back to the belly.

ACTION 2: Step the left foot forward without moving the right foot, to take a *santi* stance. Chop the left hand forward and pull the right hand back to the belly. (image 5.53)

From right *tiger carries*:

ACTION 1: Withdraw the right foot to parallel to the left foot, keeping the weight down and the legs bent. Turn the left hand over to cover and press down, and pull the right hand back to the belly, clenching the fist. Then drill the right fist up and out to nose height. Tuck the left hand, clenching it and pressing down to the belly. Look forward. (image 5.54)

ACTION 2: Step the left foot forward without moving the right foot, chop the left hand forward, and pull the right hand back to the belly, to take a *santishi*. Press the head up and look forward. (image 5.55)

- The rest of *closing move* is the same as usual.

Pointers

- Withdraw the left foot, cover with the left hand, and drill the right fist all together. Withdraw the right foot, cover with the left hand, and drill the right fist all together.

2.3 TIGER INTERCEPTS   hǔjié   虎截

Start from left *santishi*.

2.3a   Fierce Tiger Jumps over the Ravine   měnghǔ tiào jiàn   猛虎跳涧

As described above in movement 2a.

2.3b   Tiger Intercepts, Left Stance   zuǒbù hǔjié   左步虎截

ACTION 1: Step the left foot diagonally to the forward left and follow in with the right foot a half-step. Drill the left fist up on the right side and unclench it when it arrives at head height, rotating the palm to face out, fingers up, thumb web stretched as if reaching to grab. Lift the right hand and clench it. (image 5.56)

ACTION 2: Grab and pull the left hand forward and down to the left to the left waist, clenching to a fist. Intercept with the right forearm leftward, fist heart facing in at shoulder height. Keep the elbows settled down, press the head up, and look forward. (images 5.57 and front)

2.3c   Tiger Intercepts, Right Stance   yòubù hǔjié   右步虎截

ACTION 1: Advance the left foot a half-step and lift the right foot to beside the left ankle. Pull the right fist back and drill it up to the left side of the head, then rotate and unclench the hand, stretching it in a grabbing action with the palm facing out. Do not move the left fist. (image 5.58)

ACTION 2: Take a long step diagonally to the forward right with the right foot and follow in a half-step with the left foot. Grab forward and pull back to the right with the right hand, clenching it. Lift the left fist at the left side of the body then intercept across to the right with the forearm vertical. The left fist heart faces in at shoulder height. Keep the elbows settled, press the head up, and look forward. (image 5.59)

5.58   5.59

Pointers

- o The lead foot should take a big step, as large as possible, and the rear foot should follow in quickly and firmly.

- o One hand hooks and pulls as the other hand intercepts and pounds. These actions need to be coordinated to work together. The upper limbs must also work together with the lower limbs.

2.3c   Tiger Intercepts Turn Around and Closing Move

hǔjié huíshēn, shòushì   虎截回身和收势

- The footwork of *tiger intercepts turn around* is the same as that of *tiger pounces turn around*, just change the hand technique to intercept. The action of *tiger intercepts closing move* is the same as that of *tiger pounces closing move.*

2.4   TIGER BRACES   hǔchēng   虎撑

Start from left *santishi*.

2.4a   Fierce Tiger Jumps over the Ravine   měnghǔ tiào jiàn   猛虎跳涧

As described above in move 2.1a.

2.4b   Tiger Braces, Left Stance   zuǒbù hǔchēng   左步虎撑

ACTION: Step the left foot to the forward left and follow in the right foot a half-step. Lift the fists in front of the chest to just above shoulder height. Unclench the hands and turn the palms out, thumbs down. As the left foot lands, brace forward with both palms. Keep the elbows slightly bent, fingers pointing to each other, and thumbs down. Press the head up and look forward. (images 5.60 and front)

2.4c Tiger Braces, Right Stance   yòubù hǔchēng   右步虎撑

ACTION 1: Advance the left foot a half-step and follow in the right foot to beside the left ankle without touching down. Lift the palms slightly, then roll them forward, then curl down to press and draw back to in front of the waist or chest. Press the head up and look forward. (image 5.61)

ACTION 2: Take a long step diagonally to the forward right with the right foot and follow in the left foot a half-step. Lift the hands to the jaw and turn the palms out, shoving forward forcefully. Keep the elbows slightly bent, the thumbs down, and the fingers pointing to each other. Press the head up and look forward. (image 5.62)

Pointers

o While the lead foot advances the half-step, the hands need to complete all the actions of slicing up, rotating, rolling and drawing back.

o As the rear foot comes through to step forward, the hands need to complete the action of bracing and shoving forward. Hands and feet complete their actions simultaneously.

o There is another way of doing *tiger braces* in which the hands first move down, then back, then up, and finally shove forward. Either method is fine.

2.4d Tiger Braces Turn Around and Closing Move

hǔchēng huíshēn, shòushì   虎撑回身和收势

• The footwork of *tiger braces turn around* and *closing move* are the same as that of *tiger pounces turn around* and *closing move*, just change the hand technique to brace instead of pounce.

2.5 TIGER TRAPS   hǔlán   虎拦

Start from left *santishi*.

2.5a   Tiger Traps, Left Stance   zuǒbù hǔlán   左步虎拦

ACTION 1: Take a long step forward with the right foot
and follow in the left foot to the right ankle. Reach the
right hand to meet the left hand, then grab and pull with
both back to the belly. Drill the left fist up to the jaw
then turn the palm forward, fingers up, thumb web
stretched to hook or grab. (image 5.63)

5.63

ACTION 2: Step the left foot diagonally to the forward
left then follow in the right foot a half-step. Turn the
right fist eye up and extend it to the forward left as if to
catch something in the forearm. Then hook and move it
across rightward. The right fist finishes in front of the
right shoulder at nose height with the fist heart in.
Clench the left hand and turn the fist heart out and
knock it horizontally across leftward to in front of the left shoulder. Keep both
elbows settled down and look forward. (images 5.64, 5.65, and 5.65 front)

5.64

5.65

5.65 FRONT

2.5b   Tiger Traps, Right Stance   yòubù hǔlán   右步虎拦

ACTION 1: Advance the left foot a half-step and follow in the right foot to beside
the left ankle. Lower the right fist then drill it up to in front of the mouth, then
unclench it with the palm in, fingers up, and thumb web stretched in a grabbing
shape. As the body moves, lower the left fist to in front of the chest. Look forward.
(image 5.66)

ACTION 2: Take a step diagonally to the forward right with the right foot and
follow in a half-step with the left. Bring the left fist to the right, bend the elbow to
lift up with the forearm, and hook across to the left, finishing with the fist heart in
at nose height in front of the right shoulder. Clench the right hand and turn the fist
heart out, then knock horizontally across to the right to finish in front of the right
shoulder. The forearms are both vertical with the elbows down. Look forward.
(images 5.67, 5.68)

Pointers

- o The right foot steps forward as the hands pull back. Do not stop here, but keep drilling the left fist up to catch.

- o The left foot lands as the forearms check across, working together.

2.5c Tiger Traps Turn Around and Closing Move

hǔlán huíshēn, shòushì   虎拦回身和收势

- The footwork of *tiger traps turn around* is the same as that of *tiger pounces turn around*, just change the hand technique to a trap. The actions of *tiger traps closing move* are the same as that of *tiger pounces closing move*.

2.6   TIGER EMBRACES   hǔbào   虎抱

Start from left *santishi*.

2.6a   Tiger Embraces, Left Stance   zuǒbù hǔbào   左步虎抱

ACTION 1: Take a step forward with the right foot and follow in with the left to beside the right ankle. Reach forward with the right hand, palm down. When it meets the left hand, clench and pull both hands back to the belly. Press the head up and look forward. (image 5.69)

ACTION 2: Take a long step to the forward left with the left foot and follow in the right foot a half-step. Before stepping, raise the hands to cross the wrists in front of the jaw, unclenching and turning them out. Then circle each to the left and right and lower them to the sides, so that when the left foot advances the palms push forward and up in an embracing posture. The palms face each other at chest height. Tuck the elbows in and look forward. (images 5.70, 5.71, and 5.71 front)

2.6b   Tiger Embraces, Right Stance   yòubù hǔbào   右步虎抱

ACTION 1: Advance the left foot a half-step and follow in the right foot to beside the left ankle without touching down. Turn the palms out and cross them in front of the chest. Circle each hand down to either side then open with the palms facing each other. (images 5.72, 5.73)

ACTION 2: Take a long step to the forward right with the right foot and follow in a half-step with the left foot. Push the palms forward and up with the palms facing each other, fingers up, at chest height. Keep the hands shoulder width apart. Look forward. (image 5.74)

Pointers

o   The hands should finish their action as the left foot lands.

o   The whole movement should be done without interruption, smoothly without a break.

2.6c   Tiger Embraces Turn Around and Closing Move

hǔbào huíshēn, shòushì   虎抱回身和收势

• The footwork of *tiger embraces turn around* is the same as that of *tiger pounces turn around*, just change the hand technique to embrace. The actions of *tiger embraces closing move* are the same as those of *tiger pounces closing move*.

PROBLEMS OFTEN MET IN THE TIGER MODEL

Tiger Pounces

PROBLEM 1: The student does not strike as the lead foot lands.

CORRECTIONS: More practice will give the student a feel for this action. While practising, the student must concentrate on landing the technique with the foot landing.

PROBLEM 2: The student does not understand the actions of straightening the lower back and extending the shoulders.

CORRECTIONS: The action of straightening the lower back is to store energy, and the action of extending the shoulders is to release the energy. The lower back should straighten as the fists drill up, sitting the buttocks down. The shoulders should reach forward when the hands pounce forward.

PROBLEM 3: The student straightens the arms when pouncing, or puts the hands too high.

CORRECTIONS: Remind the student to keep the arms rounded when pouncing, urging the shoulders forward and settling the elbows. The heel of the palms should be at chest height, and the fingers should be no higher than the shoulders. Tell the student to think of striking the opponent's chest.

PROBLEM 4: As the student does the half-step forward, pulling the hands back, the hands move along a straight line, or the body rises.

CORRECTIONS: Remind the student to draw a circle with the hands, bending the arms, reaching into the shoulders and keeping the elbows settled, so that the hands come down and then in. Remind the student to press the head up, thinking of doing a head butt.

PROBLEM 5: The student does the move too ferociously, landing without stability, and even sliding forward.

CORRECTIONS: Remind the student to always consciously grip the ground with the landing foot. This will prevent slipping.

Tiger Carries

PROBLEM 1: The student does the carry too high, or straightens the arms.

CORRECTIONS: Remind the student to strike to his own belly height, keeping the arms bent. The hands should be about a foot away from the belly.

PROBLEM 2: The student does the carry with the hands too far apart.

CORRECTIONS: Remind the student that both hands should be able to contact an opponent's body, so are about five to six centimetres apart. Pay attention to keeping the elbows close together, as this will keep the hands close as well.

PROBLEM 3: The student does a slicing up action.

CORRECTIONS: Remind the student of the correct line that the hands should be taking. *Tiger carries* is not a slice or a scoop. The palms should move forward and down with a pushing, 'carrying in the palms' action.

POWER GENERATION FOR THE TIGER MODEL

Tiger Pounces

First of all, you must put the spirit of the tiger into all your actions, so that its ferocity pervades all movement.

The tiger model emphasizes the saying, "The hands drill as they rise and turn over as they land. The hands and feet work together. Straighten the lower back and reach through the shoulders."

Make sure that the elbows hug the ribs as the hands drill to rise, so that the elbows lead the hands up. When the elbows reach the chest, then contain the chest and lengthen the lower back, sitting the buttocks down. This is how the pouncing action pre-loads in order to launch power.

The whole movement is one action, it must continue without hesitation. You must step forward quickly and not stop in the middle. Especially, after the lead foot advances a half-step, the rear foot must come through quickly to take a long step forward. You must not pause in your footwork.

When the hands clench and pull back to the belly, be sure to circle them down and back, do not pull them in a straight line. Keep the thumb web stretched and the palm rounded. Brace out slightly with the elbows and settle the shoulders down. Press the head up and hold a charging forward intent.

When the hands pounce forward, settle the buttocks down and urge the shoulders forward. Fold in the waist and contain the chest. Coordinate your breathing to settle the *qi* to the *dantian* to aid your power release.

When practising repetitive lines, be sure to turn the lead foot in slightly when it advances the half-step. This will help the zigzag line stepping.

Tiger Carries

The carrying action of the hands must come as the lead foot lands.

When you launch power to the hands, press the elbows snug to the ribs in order to send the hands forward with the carrying action. Settle the shoulders down and sit the buttocks down. This settles the torso down. Exhale to assist power output.

When circling the hands in front of the body, the wrists cross as the hands drill up with the palms in. When they reach head height turn the palms forward. Brace out, keeping the arms rounded, and roll down, drawing a circle, roll until the hands reach the sides of the waist, palms out so that they face forward. The elbows should draw back a bit. When the hands drill up, the chest should be contained and the upper back stretched, the lower back flexed and the torso tucked. When the hands lower the head should press up, the lower back should lengthen, the chest should widen, and the shoulders should settle.

The turn around must be quick and stable, turning on the body's pivot point. Be sure to hook the lead foot in to in front of or on the outside of the rear foot.

Tiger Intercepts

Watch your hand shapes as they drill up then hook and pull. Rotate to drill and turn over to pull. The body should pre-load back to assist the forward movement and pre-load right to assist the leftward movement.

When doing the crossing intercept turn the waist and urge the shoulders, settle the elbows, in order to get the power launch from the lower back and shoulders to reach the forearms. The forearms should have a twisting, checking power.

Tiger Braces

The hands may do a rolling circle up and back while the lead foot takes the half-step forward. The hands may move forward and down, then lift to in front of the chest while the lead foot advances a half-step. Either way is fine for *tiger braces*.

When the rear foot comes through to step forward, the hands must complete the pushing and bracing action as the foot lands.

The hands must move in a circular action, whether lifting and rolling forward or reaching forward and pressing down.

When bracing forward the palms must rotate so that they face out. The arms are rounded, the shoulders settled and extended, the chest contained, the abdomen pulled in, and the buttocks settled. Exhale to assist the power release.

Tiger Embraces

All the varieties of the tiger model use the same footwork, only the hand techniques differ. The handwork must always be timed exactly with the footwork. The power output and breathing must be coordinated. This type of power is whole body power.

Tiger embraces has an inward pressing power, there is a closing in as the palms push forward. This combines with a forward checking power. The elbows must urge the elbows forward, keeping a closing in power, so that the palms twist as they check forward.

Tiger Traps

One hand drills then turns to grab and pull while the other hand traps to the back. The forearms use a scissoring checking power.

The lead foot advances while the hands circle forward, down, then drill up and turn to catch. This action should store power, preparing to launch the strike, so the chest closes and the abdomen tucks in.

When the forearms hook and trap, crossing, use the shoulders to close then open, storing then launching power.

BREATHING CYCLE FOR THE TIGER MODEL

You need to coordinate breathing for all movements to assist in storing and launching power.

- Inhale. Generally, inhale when doing the preparatory storing of power, pre-loading, or initiating the movement. Inhale as you advance the lead foot a half-step, pull the fists back and drill up. Inhale as you circle the hands to the sides before the *tiger carries*.

- Exhale. Generally, exhale when launching power, or landing the technique. Exhale as you step the rear foot through a big step, following in with the other foot, and pounce, carry, or strike out.

PRACTICAL APPLICATIONS FOR THE TIGER MODEL

Tiger Pounces

This is like a tiger pouncing on its prey. You can dodge out of the way and then advance to pounce, or you can knock the opponent's attack and get in close to pounce. If going straight in, hit directly on his chest. If going in from the side, hit his shoulders or ribs. You need to get the body in with the footwork, hitting as the foot enters. It is just as the classics say:

> "Your head should barge into the enemy, your torso should press into him, your footwork should chase him, your hands should strike him, your spirit should threaten him, your *qi* should harass him, your power should surpass his."

Tiger pounces is the most important of the tiger techniques and the most dangerous. When done as a single hand technique it is a splitting palm, and as a double handed technique it is *tiger pounces*. The hands protect the torso and head, and both hands attack as the footwork enters.

Tiger Carries: This is a low strike to the opponent's belly. The hands first circle to open out the opponent's hands, then the feet can drive in to allow the strike to the belly, knocking him over. This is a close range attack; you must drive the feet in to get the body close. The head should barge in, the body press in, the feet enter, and the spirit threaten. It is not effective if done at a distance. The key to this attack is to use both hands to open out the opponent's hands, giving you the opening to get your strike in.

Tiger Intercepts: One hand hooks and pulls the opponent's wrist or forearm, while your other fist or forearm strikes it. This is meant to break the opponent's elbow or upper arm so that he cannot continue the attack. The key is that once the hook is made, the intercepting fist must be forceful. In addition, once the interception is done, your action can smoothly change to a drill, a driving punch, a cannon punch, or a crosscut. Your following strike is determined by your preferences and the situation.

Tiger Traps: This knocks and controls the opponent's elbow, using the connected power of your shoulders, one forward and one back, one left and one right. If the opponent strikes at your face with his right fist, you hook his arm with your left hand and pull out, using your right hand to knock his elbow up, knocking it crossways to the right. This will break his elbow. If you don't succeed with this and the opponent is able to continue with a left punch, hook his arm to the right with your right forearm and quickly strike to his face. You must react to the situation and change your techniques to take whatever opportunity presents.

Tiger Braces: This knocks the opponent's arms open to gain an opportunity to strike to the chest with both palms, knocking him away. The key is daring to step in close, using your body for the technique. This is easy to say but hard to do. You need to practise this technique a lot to find the proper way to apply power, and then you need to practise drills with a partner and practise fighting until you can use this technique with spontaneity.

Tiger Embraces: This sticks to the opponent's upper arms, forcing them back as you step forward to strike his chest or ribs with a short forward and inward strike. It looks like you are tying him up in a package. Actually you are pressing into his ribs and using your whole body to shove him away.

- The six methods of doing the tiger model train six types of power and six combat techniques. *Tiger pounces* and *tiger carries* are common, but the other four are seldom seen. The six are called 'tiger model's six matchless techniques.' I have written them out here according to traditional training and my own years of experience, to expand on tiger model's contents and fighting methods.

THE POEM ABOUT THE TIGER

猛虎扑食气势雄，意贯周身卷地风。腰肩之力在臀尾，挺伸两字显其功。

The brave tiger pounces on its prey with a fierce mien,

Its will courses through its entire body like a tornado.

The strength of the back and shoulders comes from the tailbone,

Its skill is expressed in two words: straighten and extend.

THREE: MONKEY MODEL 猴形

INTRODUCTION TO THE MONKEY MODEL, *HOU XING*

The monkey model references monkeys and apes. Although humans resemble monkeys and apes to some extent, we lack their agility. Many animals surpass humans in their natural abilities, which is why Xingyiquan imitates them – to practise certain aspects of these abilities, both for health and combat purposes. The monkey model imitates the monkey's skills at leaping, its overall nimbleness, the strength of its arms, its ability to kick branches, to 'pick and present peaches,' to 'climb up poles' and to 'pull on ropes.'

When you practise the monkey model you should express a monkey's characteristics: quick-wittedness, alertness, bravery, and agility. Its eyes flash like lightning, it spins like the wind, leaps as if flying, and is light as a floating feather. Its scream haunts the mountaintops like the clouds and mist that encircle them. It can go into the deepest gullies and remotest caves. It can compress its body, dodge and tumble. It is capable, energetic, nimble, light and lively – suddenly up, suddenly down, suddenly left, suddenly right, suddenly forward and suddenly back. It can change instantaneously between substantial and insubstantial. It can stare fixedly with rapt attention, or can shift its gaze at will. Its spirit shows in its eyes. It is light and agile, combining hard and soft. When training monkey model, imitate its postures and movements, its spirit and attitude. Don't try to copy 'monkeyness,' but to do what makes the monkey effective. Take your ideas from the form of the monkey, and use these ideas to develop your form. In this way the idea comes from the form, and the form flows from the idea.

METHODS OF PERFORMING THE MONKEY MODEL

There are two main ways to practise the monkey model. One is to four corners, and the other is in a straight line. The techniques are not quite the same but the ideas and mood are the same.

3.1   METHOD ONE: MONKEY MODEL TO FOUR CORNERS

sìjiǎo hóu xíng   四角猴形

3.1a   **Monkey Scratches its Mark (left)**   yuánhóu guà yìn   猿猴挂印

Start from left *santishi*.

ACTION 1: First turn the body thirty degrees to the right and lower the left hand, clenching it and drawing it in to the belly. Withdraw the left foot to beside the right foot. Look at the left hand. (image 5.75)

ACTION 2: Step the left foot in front of the right foot, circling it around and hooking the foot out, turning the body leftward. Drill the left fist up to in front of the jaw, turning it so the fist heart faces out, to hook and knock away in an outward blocking action at shoulder height. Do not move the right hand. Look at the left hand. (image 5.76)

5.75

5.76

3.1b   **Monkey Drops Back on its Haunches**   chèbù hóu dūn   撤步猴蹲

ACTION 1: Shift forward to the left leg and step the right foot in front of the left toes, hooking it in to take a character eight [八] stance. Continue to turn around to the left to face in the direction from which you just came, and shift onto the right foot, withdrawing the left foot behind. Slide the right hand forward on top of the left arm to eye height and pull the left hand back to the left side of the belly. Both palms face down. Look at the right hand. (images 5.77, 5.78)

5.77

5.78

ACTION 2: Withdraw the right foot to in front of the left foot and touch the ball of the foot down, shifting onto the left foot. Squat down to a ninety degree angle of the knees. While doing this, bring the right hand back to the belly and lift the left hand in front of the right shoulder. Keep the elbow set down, the palm down, and the hand at shoulder height. Look to the forward right. The body may lean into the right shoulder a bit. (images 5.79 and 5.79 front)

3.1c   Monkey Pulls at its Leash   hóu dáo shéng   猴才到绳

ACTION 1: Lift the right hand then extend it along above the left arm, circling the left hand down to pull it back to the belly. Then lift the left hand and extend it out on top of the right arm to eye height, while circling and pulling the right hand back to beside the belly. Don't move the feet yet. (image 5.80)

ACTION 2: Advance the right foot a half-step and follow in the left foot. Do a splitting palm with the right hand to shoulder height. Pull the left hand back to the belly. Look past the right hand. (image 5.81)

3.1d   Monkey Scrambles up a Pole   yuánhóu pá gān   猿猴爬竿

ACTION 1: Step the left foot forward and, as soon as it lands, push off to hop forward. Lift the right knee as the left foot pushes off, to help drive the jump forward. As you hop, thread the left hand forward along on top of the right hand to eye height and withdraw the right hand to in front of the chest. The palms are angled downward. Look at the left hand. (image 5.82)

ACTION 2: After the left foot lands, advance the right foot, then follow in a half-step with the left foot. While landing, thread the right hand forward along under the left hand to chest height, fingers up,

palm forward. Pull the left hand back to in front of the belly. Look past the right hand. (image 5.83)

Please refer to images 5.84 a, b, c, d, e, f, g, h (the photo g is taken at slightly different angle from the others, it follows the same line, though) to see the monkey model from the other side.

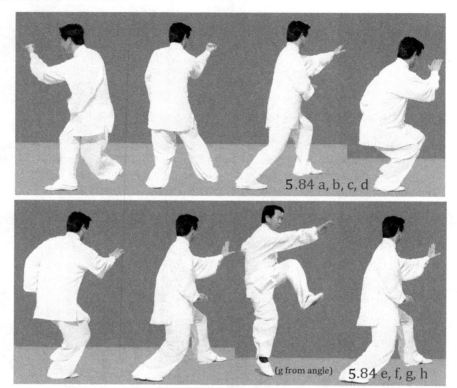

5.84 a, b, c, d

(g from angle)   5.84 e, f, g, h

- The key to the *four-cornered monkey model* method is to use the hook-in step to turn the body around to face the correct direction.

Starting facing south, the first *monkey scratches its mark* turns to face northwest. Advance with *monkey scrambles up a pole* to the northwest.

The second *monkey scratches its mark* turns around one-eighty to face southeast. Be sure to hook-out and hook-in well to get the body turned around to face southeast. Advance with *monkey scrambles up a pole* to the southeast.

The third *monkey scratches its mark* turns to face southwest. Advance with *monkey scrambles up a pole* to the southwest.

Then the fourth *monkey scratches its mark* turns to face northeast.

The last *monkey scratches its mark* turns to face south for the closing.

- The *four-cornered monkey model* depends on getting the *monkey scratches its mark* turning to the correct angles, and this depends on the hook-out and hook-in steps.

- The monkey model alternates left and right sides, and the actions are the same as described, just transposing left and right. There is no limit to how many you do, just wait until you are back at the starting point facing in the starting direction in a left *santishi* to close the form.

Pointers

- o   To start from *santishi*, withdraw the left foot and pull back the left hand together, then do a hook-out step with the left foot and drill and hook the left hand together.

- o   Hook-in the right foot to turn the body around with it. Retreat the left foot a long step, and be quick. Withdraw the right foot quickly as well, and land firmly.

- o   The hand action of *monkey pulls at its leash* must be fast, with the hands and feet working together.

- o   Push off strongly with the hopping leg to cover distance. If pushing off the left leg, drive the right leg forward and thread the left hand forward at the same time, so that the upper and lower actions work together.

- o   As the right foot lands the right hand should strike. The whole action should be continuous without any pause.

3.1e   Monkey Closing Move   shōu shì   收势

ACTION: Once you get back to the starting place in left *santishi*, close as you would normally.

3.2   METHOD TWO: STRAIGHT LINE MONKEY MODEL

zhí tàng hóu xíng   直趟猴形

This method is made up of *present fruit, push a boat, pluck a peach, drop off a branch, kick, sit on haunches,* and *pull a rope*. The actions differ from the *four-cornered monkey model*, but the intent and mood are the same. Start from left *santishi*.

3.2a   White Ape Presents Fruit   bái yuán xiàn guǒ   白猿献果

ACTION: Advance the left foot a half-step and follow in the right foot a half-step. Extend the right hand forward under the left hand, both palms angled down. Draw a small circle with each hand outward and then bring them in front of the chest with the wrists sticking together, palms forward. As the left foot advances, carry with the palms forward and up to jaw height. Look forward. (images 5.85, 5.86)

3.2b   Push a Boat Downstream   shùn shuǐ tuī zhōu   顺水推舟

ACTION 1: Take a step forward with the right foot without moving the left foot, turning the right foot out as it lands. Turn the palms down and pull down and back, the left hand stopping in front of the body and the right hand pulling back to beside the waist. Press the head up and look forward. (image 5.87)

ACTION 2: Step the left foot forward and follow in a half-step with the right foot. Close the elbows together and push forward with the left hand leading and the right hand at the left elbow. Push to chest height with the palms forward and the fingers pointing up. Look forward. (image 5.88)

3.2c   Ape Plucks a Peach   yuánhóu zhāi táo   猿猴摘桃

ACTION: Advance the left foot a half-step and follow in a half-step with the right foot. Do a covering press forward and down with the left hand, palm down and turned crossways. Turn the right hand's thumb web forward and extend it forward above the left hand to neck height with the fingers closed slightly. Keep the arm slightly bent. Look at the right hand and reach with the body forward slightly into the action. (image 5.89)

3.2d   Ape Drops off a Branch   yuánhóu zhuì zhī   猿猴坠枝

ACTION: Step the right foot forward with the foot turned outward crossways, lifting the left heel in place. Turn the right hand palm out, thumb down, and stretch the thumb web to grab and pull back at the right side of the head. Turn the left hand palm up to carry until the left elbow is in front of the chest. Keep a backward drawing action towards the right with both hands. Sit down slightly. Look past the left hand. (image 5.90)

3.2e Ape Kicks a Branch   yuánhóu dēng zhī 猿猴蹬枝

ACTION: Shift forward onto the right leg and lift the left knee to kick forward with the ball of the foot. Kick to chest height and keep the supporting leg slightly bent. Do not move the hands. Look in the direction of the kick. You may also kick with the heel. (image 5.91)

3.2f Monkey Turns and Sits on its Haunches   zhuànshēn hóu dūn 转身猴蹲

ACTION: Bring the left foot back quickly, as soon as it completes the kick, landing hooked in just outside the right foot to turn around two-seventy degrees to the right. Shift onto the left foot. Lift the right foot with the ball of the foot on the ground and sit down slightly. When you turn around, swing the arm to chop with the right hand then pull the hand back to the right side with the palm down. Extend the left hand to reach forward as the body turns around, with the left elbow at the sternum and the palm down. Angle the right shoulder to the front. Look past the left hand. (images 5.92, 5.93)

3.2g Monkey Pulls at its Leash   yuánhóu dáo shéng 猿猴才到绳

ACTION: Advance the right foot a step and follow in the left foot a half-step. Extend the left hand to the front, then do a covering press down and pull it back. Lift the right elbow and thread it forward over the left hand, then hook and pull it back to the belly. Chop the left hand forward to chest height. Press the head up and look forward. (image 5.94)

3.2h   White Ape Presents Fruit   báiyuán xiàn guǒ   白猿献果

ACTION: This is similar to move 3.2a, just transposing right and left.

• Continue on, doing the movements on the other side.

Pointers:

o The hands and feet work together. As the foot advances a half-step the hands need to complete their action. As the right foot steps forward the hands need to complete the action of pulling back. As the left foot steps forward the hands complete the push forward.

o The left hand completes the covering press down as the right hand strikes forward and the feet advance and follow-in.

o *Monkey drops off a branch* and *monkey kicks a branch* are completed as one move with no pause in between.

o To do the turn around, the hook-in step needs to turn well in. Turn the body quickly. Move the hands as the turn is being done.

o All the moves should be linked together smoothly without undue pauses between them.

3.2i   Straight Line Monkey Model Turn Around   hóu xíng zhuànshēn 猴形转身

This is a *monkey turns and sits on its haunches*.

• If the left foot has just kicked, quickly withdraw it and land it hooked-in inside the right foot, turning the body around one-eighty degrees. Then go back with *monkey pulls on its leash.*

• If the right foot has just kicked, quickly withdraw it and land it hooked-in inside the left foot, turning the body around one-eighty degrees. Then go back with *monkey pulls on its leash.*

3.2j   Monkey Model Closing Move   shōu shì   收势

Continue with *straight line monkey model* until you are at your starting place in *monkey pulls at its leash*. If the right foot and hand are forward then move forward to form a left *santishi*, then close the form. If the left foot and hand are forward then simply close the form.

PROBLEMS OFTEN MET IN THE MONKEY MODEL

Monkey to Four Corners

PROBLEM 1: The student goes in the wrong direction.

CORRECTIONS: The key to advancing in the correct direction is to get the feet to hook-out and hook-in to the correct angles.

PROBLEM 2: The student does not coordinate the feet and hands when doing the *monkey drops back and sits on its haunches*.

CORRECTIONS: More practice, reminding the student that when the foot reaches back the hand stretches forward. The move should be light and agile.

PROBLEM 3: The student does not coordinate the hands and feet well during *monkey pulls at its leash*.

CORRECTIONS: Have the student do some hands only practice. For example, left, right, left. Then add the footwork; remind the student that when the right hand reaches forward the right foot steps forward.

PROBLEM 4: During *monkey climbs a pole*, the student doesn't jump very far or doesn't land firmly.

CORRECTIONS: The cause of a short jump is not getting the correct angle at takeoff. Be sure to press the knee of the push-off leg forward and down, bringing the shank to a tight angle to the ground. Move the weight forward and then jump. Use the other knee to forcefully drive forward. Have the student practise just the jump for a while to gain more distance. Bend the knee when landing and grab the ground with the toes to maintain good stability.

Straight Line Monkey

PROBLEM 1: The student makes too big a circle with the hands for *ape presents fruit*.

CORRECTIONS: Remind the student to first cross the wrists. When each hand does its circle, the forearms should move only a little. The fingers circle out, and the circle is only a twenty centimetre diameter.

PROBLEM 2: The student places the hands too far apart for the carry action in the *ape presents fruit*.

CORRECTIONS: Remind the student to keep the wrists close together, no more than ten centimetres apart. The key lies in closing the elbows in. The wrists may touch, but this depends on the flexibility of the student. The movement needs to be natural and strong.

PROBLEM 3: When doing *push the boat*, the student leaves too long a time gap between the pull back and down and the push forward and strike.

CORRECTIONS: Remind the student that the pull down is the power gathering movement in order to launch force forward. When loading back to launch power forward, the action needs to be continuous or else the energy will dissipate.

PROBLEM 4: The student pushes with straight arms or hunches the shoulders when doing *ape plucks fruit*.

CORRECTIONS: Remind the student to keep the elbows bent slightly and to settle the shoulders down. Urge the shoulders forward into the push.

PROBLEM 5: The student lets the hip go forward on the kick, or the supporting leg is unstable.

CORRECTIONS: To do the kick, the student should first lift the knee and then snap the kick from the knee as a snap kick or a thrust kick. If the student grabs the ground with the supporting foot and keeps the knee bent, then he will be more stable.

PROBLEM 6: The student is unstable on the *monkey turns around and sits on its haunches*.

CORRECTIONS: The first thing to check is that the hooking-in foot is placed in the correct position and at the proper angle. In addition, check that the turn around movement is not too forceful, and that the centre of gravity does not move about too much. To be stable on the squat, flex the waist and tuck in the body, lowering the buttocks and flexing the knees. The non-supporting leg's foot should touch the ground in the correct place to help maintain stability.

POWER GENERATION FOR THE MONKEY MODEL

Monkey to Four Corners

- In training the monkey model you should seriously consider what I stated earlier – that you should seek the mood and the actions of the monkey. You should express the monkey's agility and lightness, its ability to spin quickly and leap, the speed and agility of its body and hand actions.

Monkey scratches its mark: For the first move, the lead hand comes back then drills up, and then turns out, all actions done as the lead foot comes in then does the hook-out step. The body technique uses integrated body action with no slackness – pre-load right to go left, pre-load left to go right, and pre-load back to go forward.

Hook-in step, turn around: Use the waist to draw the shoulders around. Withdraw the foot to the rear with a large jump, by shooting back the rear leg and pushing off strongly with the lead foot. Land firmly and squat down. Reach the hand forward as you withdraw the foot.

Monkey pulls at its leash: The hands draw vertical circles continuously in front of the body – one back and the other forward, one up and the other down – so they need to be coordinated. The last palm action is a forward split, and it must land exactly as the foot lands.

Monkey climbs a pole is done with continuous power. The advancing footwork and the hand actions are fast. The hop goes for distance, and the landing is stable. As one leg pushes off, the other leg needs to drive the knee to put more power into the hop. When the hands thread forward, the palms should slide against each other with some friction. They strike to eye height, focusing on the face.

Straight Line Monkey

White ape presents fruit: As the hands circle in front of the body, the movement should be small and the body should tuck in a little by closing the chest. Keep the arms rounded. The movement has a hidden wrapping and bracing power. When the forearms rotate, they lift up as they turn, and this action is done as the foot steps forward. When the hands push and carry up, settle the shoulders and bring the elbows together with a wrapping power. Press into the lower back to urge the shoulders to send the carrying action up.

Push a boat downstream: The hands pull and lead back as the rear foot steps forward. When the foot lands with a stomping action, press the head up to get a charging forward power. The step forward and push uses a closing power in the hands, bringing the elbows together and lengthening the lower back to urge and release power forward. The forward step goes for distance, and the follow-in step needs to be quick.

Monkey picks a peach: The lead hand does a cover and a press down as the rear hand extends forward. The rear shoulder should urge forward into the action and the weight should shift forward. The thumb web reaches forward, with the thumb and fingers hooked as if grabbing someone's neck.

Monkey kicks a branch is also called *monkey moves a branch*. The lead hand turns and draws a small circle, which is a hooking and pulling action as it twists. The rear hand does a lifting carry upwards, so the elbow must stay tucked down. The feet and hands must advance together in order to fully use the power of the waist and shoulders.

To do the kick first lift the knee. Kick with either the ball of the foot or the heel. Keep the supporting leg slightly bent and grab the ground with the foot to stand steadily.

Monkey turns around and sits on its haunches: This turns sideways to the line of action. One leg is bent to ninety degrees and the other touches the ball of the foot on the ground just beside the supporting leg. Flex the lower back and tuck in the torso, close in the chest and shoulder area. When the hand chops towards the back, relax the shoulders and use the shoulders to lead the elbows, the elbows to lead the hand. The key to turning to the correct direction lies in the amount of hook-in that the foot does and the placement of the foot on landing after the kick. If the foot lands hooked-in just inside the supporting foot, then the body turns around to the direction in which you just came. If the foot lands hooked-in outside the supporting foot, then this is a 'big turning' that allows you to continue on in the same direction. The 'big turning' can also be done as a jump, and should be light and agile.

BREATHING CYCLE FOR THE MONKEY MODEL

It is vital to coordinate breathing with the actions. Mastery of correct breathing directly affects the quality of movement.

- Inhale during non power-launch actions.

- Exhale on power launching actions.

- The monkey model uses a number of breathing techniques to complete the actions with power. On turning, lead with the breath. On squatting, settle the breath. On kicking, gather the breath. On pushing off to jump, lift the breath. During a jump, hold the breath. On landing, breathe out.

PRACTICAL APPLICATIONS FOR THE MONKEY MODEL

All of the techniques in the monkey model contain practical applications. These techniques can be practised separately to find how to use your power and to increase your combat effectiveness.

The small circle in *monkey presents fruit* is to release the grip of your opponent so that you can then use both hands to strike upwards into the jaw. The key is to get in close with your whole body.

Push the boat first draws the opponent down and back with both hands so that his oncoming punch loses its target and effectiveness. When the opponent then tries to pull his hand back, time your strike to use this action to push forward with both hands to drive him back. Push between the chest and the belly and step forward, lengthening the spine to launch full power.

Pluck fruit uses one hand to cover and press the opponent's hand down while the other hand grabs his throat. Close the fingers to choke and push forward with a pressing down power.

Drop off a branch uses both hands to hook onto the opponent's arm and pull along with his line of action to one side. The technique is meant to break his arm.

Kick the branch is a kick to the chest or ribs. It works best when combined with the arm controlling technique of *drop off a branch.*

Scratch a mark is a dodging action that hooks with one hand while finding an entrance for the other hand to strike the opponent's face. If there is a chance, then strike. If there isn't, then quickly retreat and try again. So the power is first contained then launched, waiting for an opportunity and adapting. The squat is a defensive move that stores the power, so be sure to use it in that way – to prepare for the attack.

Monkey pulls at its leash alternates both hands to pull down, and then to chop and push forward. Attack by entering the feet with the hands, going for the chest or face.

Climb the pole chases after the opponent. If he is backing up then take the opportunity to advance. Go for his eyes with the hands and for his groin or belly with the feet. Use the hands and feet together, hitting high and low.

- The monkey model often uses a threading action, attacking the eye area. It doesn't use a lot of power, but the speed and agility attacking to the eyes is sufficient to put an opponent off. This creates the opportunity to finish off more strongly with a heavier power.

THE POEM ABOUT THE MONKEY

猴形练灵起纵轻，挂印倒绳爬竿能。摘桃献果蹬枝法，机警敏捷快如风。

The monkey model trains agility for leaping lightly, both high and far,

With the techniques of *scratch your mark, pull a rope,* and *climb a pole.*

The techniques *pluck a peach, present fruit,* and *kick a branch,*

Are all methods of creating opportunities and then taking advantage of them by being as quick as the wind.

FOUR: HORSE MODEL 马形

INTRODUCTION TO THE HORSE MODEL, *MA XING*

The classics say, "The horse has the skill of striking with its hooves. 'Striking with its hooves' means that as the horse gallops, its rear hooves overtake its front hooves. This is what it excels at." When training horse model, you need to push off the rear foot to drive the front foot forward, and then advance the rear foot with force. This footwork is called a gallop. To find the intent and mood of the horse, remember that when one horse takes the lead then all the horses in the herd will take to the gallop. A wild horse gallops forward fearlessly, there is nothing that it won't charge – it 'gallops through the mountain ranges like the wind.' When wild horses fight they kick with their hooves and charge straight in regardless of the consequences. They glare with eyes wide open. So when training horse model, you should express this gallop – charging in for distance – very fast and powerful. Moreover, your hand technique should express the charging in to hit. Your intent and power must be charging and penetrating. The hands and feet arrive together, working together with the power of the whole body.

METHODS OF PERFORMING THE HORSE MODEL

4.1   METHOD ONE: SINGLE HORSE dānmǎ xíng 单马形

4.1a   Single Horse, Right Stance   yòubù dānmǎ xíng 右步单马形

Start from left *santishi*.

ACTION 1: Advance the left foot a half-step and lift the right foot beside the left ankle. Clench the hands and turn the fist hearts up in place. Thread the right fist forward under the left arm. Sink in the chest and settle the elbows. Look forward. (image 5.95)

5.95

ACTION 2: Take a long step forward with the right foot and follow in a half-step with the left foot. When the right fist reaches the left fist, turn both up and in so the fist hearts face down. Bend the elbows so that the right fist is in front of the right shoulder. Step the right foot forward and strike forward with the right fist to chest height. Withdraw the left fist to behind the right elbow. Keep the elbows up, slightly lower than the shoulders. Keep the arms slightly bent. The fist hearts are down, the right fist surface is forward with the wrist slightly cocked. Look past the right fist. (images 5.96, 5.97, and 5.97 front)

5.96

5.97

5.97 FRONT

4.1b   Single Horse, Left Stance   zuǒbù dānmǎ xíng   左步单马形

ACTION 1: Advance the right foot a half-step and lift the left foot to beside the right ankle. Turn the fist hearts up, and bring the elbows in. Thread the left fist forward under the right arm. Sink in the chest and settle the elbows. Look forward. (image 5.98)

ACTION 2: Take a long step forward with the left foot and follow in a half-step with the right foot. When the threading left fist reaches the right fist, turn them up and in so the fist hearts face down in front of the left shoulder. Step the left foot forward and strike forward with the left fist to chest height. Pull the right fist back behind the left elbow, in front of the left shoulder. Keep the arms slightly curved. The left fist surface is forward with the wrist slightly cocked. Look at the left fist. (images 5.99, 5.100)

5.98   5.99   5.100

Pointers

o   As you advance the lead foot you must complete two actions with the hands; threading the rear fist through and also rolling the fists.

o   As the rear foot comes through to charge forward, you must charge forward with the hand strike, hitting with full, integrated power.

o   Keep the elbows tucked in on the midline throughout the whole movement.

4.1c   Single Horse Turn Around   dānmǎ huíshēn shì   单马回身式

ACTION 1: If you are in the _right stance single horse_, with the right foot forward, first take a half-step forward with the right foot, hooked in, and shift to the right leg. Turn around to the left, lifting the left foot by the right ankle. Turn a full one-eighty degrees to face back in the way from which you came. Bring the left fist down to the chest and lift the right fist to nose height with the elbow bent. Both fist hearts face in, hooking and knocking across to the left with the body turn. Look forward. (image 5.101)

5.101

ACTION 2: Step straight forward with the left foot and follow in a half-step with the right. Keep moving the left fist around with the turn, bringing the fist in to in front of the shoulder, fist heart down. Then strike forward to chest height as the left foot steps forward. The right fist finishes just behind the left elbow. Both fist hearts are down, and the elbows are bracing slightly outward with the arms forming arcs. Look at the left fist. (image 5.102)

5.102

- To turn from the _left stance single horse_, just transpose right and left while following the directions.

Pointers:

o When taking the hook-in step to turn around, be sure to take a half-step forward. Hook in the foot as much as possible. The body turns around by using the hooking footwork and turning the waist.

o Turn around quickly and bring the fists and arms around with the body.

4.1d   Single Horse Closing Move   dānmǎ shōushì   单马收势

- From _single horse, left stance._

ACTION 1: Withdraw the left foot a half-step to in front of the right foot. Bend the left wrist to cover and press down, pulling back to the belly. Drill the right fist forward and up to nose height. Look forward.

ACTION 2: Advance the left foot forward without moving the right foot, to take a _santi_ stance. Do a splitting palm with the left hand and pull the right hand back to the belly. Look forward. The rest of the move is the same as _closing move_ from left _santishi_.

- From _single horse, right stance._

ACTION 1: Withdraw the right foot a half-step to beside the left foot and shift onto the right leg. Pull the right fist back to the belly then drill forward and up to nose height. Cover and press down with the left fist, pulling back to the belly. Press the head up and look forward.

ACTION 2: Advance the left foot forward without moving the right foot, to take a _santi_ stance. Do a splitting palm with the left hand and pull the right hand back to the belly. Look forward. The rest of the move is the same as _closing move_ from left _santishi_.

Pointers

o Withdraw the lead foot at exactly the same time as you drill the right fist forward.

o Land the left foot at exactly the same time as you split with the left hand.

4.2   METHOD TWO: DOUBLE HORSE   shuāngmǎ xíng   双马形

Start from left *santishi*.

4.2a   Double Horse, Right Stance   yòubù shuāngmǎ xíng   右步双马形

ACTION 1: Clench the left hand and pull it back to the belly, clenching the right hand as well. Turn the fist hearts up and lift them to the sternum, then drill forward to nose height. Do not hesitate after drilling up, but pound down with the fist hearts up, and lead them back to beside either hip. Advance the left foot a half-step and lift the right foot beside the left ankle. Press the head up and look forward. (images 10.103, 5.104)

5.103

5.104

ACTION 2: Take a long step forward with the right foot and follow in a half-step with the left foot. Bend the elbows to bring the fists up in front of either shoulder, turning the fists so the fist hearts are down, fist surfaces forward, wrists slightly tucked, and elbows raised. Strike forward from in front of the face to chest height. Keep the arms slightly bent, the fists about an inch apart. Press the head up and look forward. (images 5.105, 5.106)

5.105

5.106

4.2b   Double Horse, Left Stance   zuǒbù shuāng mǎ xíng   左步双马形

ACTION 1: Advance the right foot a half-step and lift the left foot beside the right ankle. Turn the fists over so that the fist hearts face up and tuck in the elbows. Circle the fists forward and down to either hip with the fist hearts up. Press the head up and look forward. (images 5.107, 5.108)

ACTION 2: Take a long step forward with the left foot and follow in a half-step with the right foot. Raise the fists from the hips to in front of the shoulders by bending the elbows and turning the fists so that the fist hearts face down and the fist surfaces face forward with the wrists slightly cocked and the elbows out at shoulder height. Strike forward to chest height, keeping the arms slightly bent, the fists about an inch apart. Press the head up and look forward. (images

5.107

5.109, 5.110)

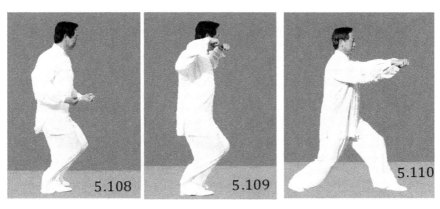

Pointers

- o Pound down with the fists as the lead foot advances.

- o Strike forward with the fists as the foot lands, using whole body power.

4.2c Double Horse Turn Around shuāngmǎ huíshēn shì 双马回身式

Using the *right* double horse as example.

ACTION 1: Hook-in the right foot and turn the body around to the left to face around in the opposite direction. Shift onto the right leg and lift the left foot beside the right ankle. Turn the fists over so the fist hearts face up, and tuck the elbows in. Circle the fists forward and down to beside either hip, fist hearts up. Press the head up and look forward. (image 5.111)

ACTION 2: Step the left foot forward and follow in a half-step with the right foot. Lift the elbows to bring the fists up in front of the shoulders. Turn the fists so that the fist hearts face down, fist surfaces facing forward and wrists cocked. The elbows are raised to about shoulder height. Strike forward with both fists to chest height, keeping the arms slightly bent, and the fists about an inch apart. Press the head up and look forward. (image 5.112)

- • The action of *double horse turn around* is the same whether on the right or left side, just transpose the right and left actions.

Pointers

- o Be sure to hook the lead foot well around. Turn quickly and bring the other foot in quickly to the supporting ankle. The whole movement must be well coordinated.

o   Step forward quickly after turning around. Punch with force, and with whole body integration.

o   Do the whole move as one action without interruption.

4.2d   Double Horse Closing Move   shuāngmǎ xíng shōushì   双马形收势

Using the *left* double horse as example.

ACTION 1: Step the right foot forward to stomp beside the left foot, lifting the left foot to the right ankle and keeping the knees together. First pull the right fist back to the right waist with the fist heart up. Tuck and press the left fist down and drill the right fist forward and up to nose height while pulling the left fist back to the belly. Look at the right fist. (image 5.113)

5.113   5.114

ACTION 2: Advance the left foot a half-step without moving the right foot, to take a *santi* stance. Hit out with a splitting palm with the left hand, the same as the *standard split*. (image 5.114)

•   The closing of *double horse* is the same as that of *single horse*, that is: drill the right fist out, stomp the right foot, then split with the left hand and left foot forward. The only difference is that you are starting out with the right hand in a different place, which makes the movement different. You need to consider this carefully and get a feel for it.

•   There are other versions of *double horse*. In them, the fists perform a double hit the same as described above, but the actions prior to the hit and the stepping differ. Both methods are traditional.

One is to pound down with both fists, drawing back, then turn them over and hit forward. The fists follow a vertical circle down and back.

The other is to turn each fist over independently at either side, completing a horizontal circle, then hit forward.

4.3   METHOD THREE: DODGING HORSE

yáoshēn mǎ xíng   摇身马形

Start from left *santishi*.

4.3a   Dodge to Right (Single) Horse   yáoshēn yòu mǎ xíng   摇身右马形

ACTION 1: Advance the left foot diagonally to the forward left a half-step and lift the right foot to beside the left ankle. Extend the right hand forward with the palm down and fingers forward. When it reaches the left hand, circle both hands forward to the right and pull to beside the right ribs. Press the head up and look in the direction to which you will punch. (images 5.115, 5.116)

ACTION 2: Take a long step forward with the right foot and follow in a half-step with the left foot. Clench fists and lift them in front of the right shoulder, fist hearts down and fist surfaces forward, wrists slightly cocked. Punch forcefully forward and down to chest height. Hit with the left fist behind the right elbow, and keep the right arm slightly bent. Look past the right fist. (image 5.117)

5.115 5.116 5.117

4.3b Dodge to Left (Single) Horse   yáoshēn zuǒ mǎ xíng   摇身左马形

ACTION 1: Advance the right foot a half-step diagonally to the forward right and follow in the left foot to beside the right ankle. Unclench the hands with the palms down. Extend the left hand forward of the right hand and circle both hands leftwards to beside the left ribs. Shift the body a bit to the right front. Look at both hands. (image 5.118)

ACTION 2: Take a long step forward with the left foot and follow in with the right foot a half-step. Clench the hands and lift them in front of the left shoulder, fist hearts down and fist surfaces forward, wrists slightly cocked. Punch the left fist forcefully forward to chest height. Punch with the right fist to behind the left elbow. Keep the left arm slightly bent. Press the head up and look forward. (image 5.119)

5.118 5.119

- Right and left are the same. Continue to repeat according to your fitness and the size of your training area.

Pointers

  o When the lead foot steps out diagonally the body should dodge at a bit of an angle to show a characteristic dodging right and left.

o   When the lead foot steps diagonally the hands hook and pull to the opposite side.

o   The fists punch with the final step, landing at exactly the same time.

4.3c   Dodging Horse Turn Around   yáoshēn mǎ xíng huíshēn   摇身马形回身

Describing with the <u>left</u> *dodging horse* as example.

ACTION 1: Advance the left foot a half-step with the foot hooked in. Turn the body around one-eighty degrees to the right to face back in the direction you just came. Lift the right foot to beside the left foot and shift onto the left leg. As the body turns around, circle the right fist around to the right, keeping it at chest height with the elbow at shoulder height. Bring the left fist around with it, both fist hearts down. Look at the left fist. (image 5.120)

ACTION 2: Take a long step forward with the right foot and follow in a half-step with the left foot. Continue to circle the right fist to bring it just in front of the right shoulder. As the right foot advances, strike out with the right fist to chest height. Hit with the left fist just inside the right elbow. Look past the right fist (image 5.121)

5.120   5.121

• The turn is similar whether turning from right or left position.

Pointers

o   Pointers for *dodging horse turn around* are the same as those for *single horse turn around*.

4.3d   Dodging Horse Closing Move   yáoshēn mǎ xíng shōushì 摇身马形收势

• The action of *dodging horse* closing is the same as that of *single horse* closing.

4.4   METHOD FOUR: REVERSE STANCE HORSE

àobù mǎ xíng   拗步马形

Start from left *santishi*.

4.4a   Reverse Stance Right (Single) Horse   àobù yòu mǎ xíng 拗步右马形

ACTION 1: Take a long step forward with the right foot and lift the left foot beside the right ankle, keeping the knees together. Thread the right hand over the left arm with the palm up, and, when it reaches the left hand, clench both fists. Lift the right hand up and bend the elbow to draw the fist back to in front of the right shoulder, turning the fist heart down. Turn and cock the left fist with the fist heart down in front of the right shoulder. Press the head up and look forward. (image

5.122)

ACTION 2: Take a long step forward with the left foot and follow in the right foot a half-step. Strike forward with the right fist to chest height, fist heart down and wrist slightly cocked, arm slightly bent. The left fist finishes behind the right elbow with the arm rounded and fist heart down. Look past the right fist. (image 5.123)

4.4b   Reverse Stance Left (Single) Horse   àobù zuǒ mǎ xíng   拗步左马形

ACTION 1: Advance the left foot a half-step and lift the right foot beside the left ankle. Unclench the hands and lift them to nose height, drawing them forward and down in a brushing action. As they arrive in front of the left shoulder, clench into fists. Press the head up and look forward. (image 5.124)

ACTION 2: Take a long step forward with the right foot and follow in a half-step with the left. Punch the left fist forward to chest height, punching the right fist to behind the left elbow. Both fist hearts are down and the left wrist is slightly cocked with the arm bent. Press the head up and look forward. (image 5.125)

Pointers

o   The pointers are the same as the standard *single horse*, described above. Only the stance is different.

4.4c   Reverse Stance Horse Turn Around

àobù mǎ xíng huíshēn   拗步马形回身

Starting from *reverse stance __right__ horse*.

ACTION 1: Hook-in the left foot in front of the right toes and turn the body around towards the right to face back in the direction from which you came. Lift the right foot, unclench the hands and brush forward and down toward the left shoulder. Clench the hands, press the head up and look forward. (image 5.126)

ACTION 2: Take a long step forward with the right foot and follow in the left foot a half-step. Punch out

into a *reverse stance left single horse* as described above. (image 5.127)

5.127

- Turning to the left or right is similar, just transpose right and left in the description.

4.4d   Reverse Stance Horse Closing Move   àobù mǎ xíng shōushì 拗步马形收势

- The action of *reverse stance horse closing move* is the same as that of *single horse model closing move*.

PROBLEMS OFTEN MET IN THE HORSE MODEL

PROBLEM 1: The student takes only a small step forward with the rear foot.

CORRECTIONS: Remind the student to charge forward as he brings the rear foot through, thinking of flying forward. When the lead foot takes its half-step forward, press the knee of the rear leg down to minimize the angle of the shank with the ground. This increases the power for the forward drive as it brings the shank as close to horizontal as possible. The student needs to work on leg strength to be able to use this type of power.

PROBLEM 2: The student moves the hands separately from the body when he does the hand circles.

CORRECTIONS: Remind the student that all hand actions work in concert with the body. The actions should be practised slowly at first to search for the feeling and find the coordination between the body and the hands. When the hands draw a vertical circle, the torso should lengthen and tuck slightly, When the hands draw a horizontal circle, the torso should move slightly forward and back. This is the specific way in which the body can assist power output, according to the principles of biomechanics.

PROBLEM 3: The student does not dodge the body when doing *dodging horse*, but simply moves the arms or feet.

CORRECTIONS: Remind the student that the stepping should be diagonal, and that the body should shift immediately to the lead leg. The head should lead the action, and the body should lean slightly forward so that, when the hands do their action, the whole body shows a dodging action.

PROBLEM 4: The student steps to the side when doing the *reverse stance horse*.

CORRECTIONS: Remind the student to step straight forward, both with the lead foot and the rear foot as it strides through. Bring the rear foot in to lightly touch the ankle of the supporting leg, to ensure that the legs do not open up while stepping.

POWER GENERATION FOR THE HORSE MODEL

Single Horse

There are a variety of ways to perform *single horse* – some punch with the lead fist heart up, some punch with the fist tucked to ram straight, and some punch with an upright fist. These differences have come about as each teacher passed on what he learned. Looking at the action of a horse and thinking of imitating the horse's ability, I feel that the true way is to punch straight with the wrist cocked.

The footwork for the horse must cover distance and have good speed, using the rear foot to drive and the front foot to charge. This shows the galloping skill of the horse, its attitude of 'chasing the wind and the moon without relief.'

- When the rear fist threads under the lead arm you should stretch the upper back and close the chest, settling the elbow and tucking the lower back.

- When the fist rises and rolls back you should lengthen the lower back and pull the shoulder back slightly.

- When the fist turns over and punches forward, you should urge the shoulder forward, solidify the body core, and breathe out when you release power. This is done as the lead foot lands, using whole body power.

Double Horse: The double horse is a double pounding, shoving punch. Keep the body square to punch equally with both fists. When the fists turn over to punch down, urge the shoulders forward and drop the elbows, press the head up, and use the elbows to lead the fists down. At this time lengthen the lower back slightly and open the chest slightly, as if barging with the chest. When you lift the fists in front of the face, lift the elbows to shoulder height to store power, then when you turn, tuck, and charge the fists forward, close the chest, urge the shoulders forward, solidify the lower back, and extend the arms. Coordinate this with an expulsion of breath to assist releasing power. Fortifying the body core sets it back – using the kidney area to urge the shoulders, the shoulders to urge the elbows, and the elbows to drive the fists.

Dodging Horse

The footwork of *dodging horse* takes the body to the side by stepping the lead foot to an angle as the body dodges to the angle, then the rear foot comes through to stride straight forward. Be sure when dodging the body to the forward angle to first tuck it back a bit – this is Xingyiquan's characteristic 'dropping back to go forward, loading right to go left.' Use the waist as the fulcrum to lead the shoulders so that the shoulders move the arms. This keeps the whole body connected so that the whole body dodges.

The hand technique of the dodging action is: both hands hook and pull down and back, and then lift and hit forward and down, drawing a large circle. When pulling down and back, be sure to use the power of the waist by settling the shoulders and elbows, so that the shoulders are moved by the lower back, the elbows are moved by the shoulders, and the hands follow the elbows. This is a full, whole body power, and the hands and feet work together.

Reverse Stance Horse

The *reverse stance horse* draws a vertical circle with the hands in front of the body.

The *dodging horse* draws a horizontal circle.

The *single horse* draws a vertical circle up from below.

The *double horse* draws a vertical circle down from above. There is a different double horse that draws a horizontal circle at the sides.

- All variations of horse model have the same essential point: all pound forward. This is the key to horse model, the true meaning of horse model, and what shows the sense of the horse.

- The horse model is a complete action and must be done as one movement without a pause in the middle of the action. It should be completed in one breath. You may pause at the end of the strike.

BREATHING CYCLE FOR THE HORSE MODEL

All the variations of horse model use the same breathing pattern.

- Inhale as the lead foot advances a half-step and the hands circle.

- Exhale to launch your power as the rear foot comes through to stride forward and land, as the hands strike forward.

PRACTICAL APPLICATIONS FOR THE HORSE MODEL

The horse model, whichever one you use, is a charging shove or ram into the opponent, to strike the head, chest, ribs, or whatever opportunity presents. You can strike with one or both fists. The key lies in getting in close to the opponent, to get within his space.

- *Single horse* first hooks any oncoming attack up, then rolls over, tucking and hitting into the chest area. The key is to step through to the opponent's groin area. You may also hook and press the opponent's attack down, then hit.

Speed is essential in the horse model.

- *Double horse* knocks the opponent's arms down with both hands, then moves the body in to shove or strike the chest with both fists. It can also be a double hook to separate the opponent's arms to make a space to strike through to the centre.

- *Dodging horse* steps forward while dodging to the side, dropping the body out of the way, then stepping in to attack the face. You can use it as you like, as long as you drive in hard so that the opponent loses all ability to react.

- *Reverse stance horse* slaps the opponent's hands down and then moves quickly in to strike.

The horse model can also be used as a defensive counter-attack. The forearms can press down on the opponent's arms so that his punch cannot be realized and you can get the strike in. This is an effective technique, but you can't do it unless you have trained deep skills and can fiercely drive in, totally committed.

THE POEM ABOUT THE HORSE

马形练疾击碃功，单双摇拗扬威名。横冲直撞栽拳打，勇猛向前意在冲。

The horse model develops speed and the ability to gallop.

Whether single, double, dodging or reverse, all are famous for their prowess.

Charge across and pound straight in with the fists.

Drive forward bravely, focused only on the charge.

FIVE: ALLIGATOR MODEL 鼉形

INTRODUCTION TO THE ALLIGATOR MODEL, *TUO XING*

The alligator is amphibious but lives mostly in the water. It is very strong and fierce, and an excellent swimmer. Its skill is 'swimming in the water and conquering the waves' and its special ability is 'overturning rivers and seas.' For this reason, the masters chose to imitate its skills. When training alligator model the intent should be that of diving straight through ever-oncoming waves of a river or the sea. If you move quickly then it is like overturning the river or sea, separating the waters. If you move slowly then it like swimming in a slow winding current, following the natural flow of the stream; you go slowly and naturally like resting in your own home. The alligator model can change anytime from up or down, left or right, forward or backward, fast or slow. It always maintains the feeling of swimming in water.

When practising, use the waist as the fulcrum and sweep the arms left and right from it. The footwork goes forward in a zigzag. The hand technique twists, rolls, drills and turns over. The whole body works together and turns naturally. Attack and defense are hidden in the actions, and a short power is hidden in the slow action. Hard and soft intermingle, and the whole form is very natural.

METHODS OF PERFORMING ALLIGATOR MODEL

5.1 STANDARD ALLIGATOR: ADVANCING ALLIGATOR

jìnbù tuó xíng   进步鼉形

5.1a   Advancing Left Alligator   jìnbù tuó xíng zuǒshì   进步鼉形左势

Start from left *santishi*.

ACTION 1: Shift back to the right leg and turn slightly right, pulling the left hand down to in front of the belly and withdrawing the left foot to in front of the right foot. Look at the left hand. (image 5.128)

ACTION 2: Step the left foot forty-five degrees to the forward left and bring the right foot in beside the left ankle without touching down (you may lightly touch the ball of the foot if you need to). Turn the left hand palm up and lift it in front of the chest. Then turn the palm down and brace out to the left at shoulder height. Bring the right hand to the belly, palm up. Brace the left arm in a curve with the palm down and the elbow below the shoulder. Look at the left hand. (images 5.129 and front)

5.1b   Advancing Right Alligator   jìnbù tuó xíng yòushì   进步鼍形右势

ACTION: Take a step to the forward right with the right foot and follow in the left foot to beside the right ankle (you may touch down, but should not). Lift the right

hand from the belly to the chest then turn it palm down to draw it across diagonally to the right to brace out at shoulder height with the elbow slightly below the shoulder. Lower the left hand and turn it palm up in front of the belly. Look at the right hand. (images 5.130 and front)

Pointers

o   Pay attention to the angle when stepping the lead foot forward. You should step in a zigzag pattern and land firmly, following in with the rear foot quickly.

o   The left foot and hand should arrive together, as should the right foot and hand. Use the waist to draw the shoulders across, the shoulders to draw the elbows, and the elbows to draw the hands.

o   The whole action should be coordinated and flow without a break. The arms should work together to draw circles. The bodywork should move forward and back, right and left with the zigzag footwork. The move should have both fast and slow actions within it.

o   You should move softly. You should not release any hard power.

5.1c   Alligator Turn Around   tuó xíng huíshēn   鼍形回身势

The *turn around* is always the same movement, whether starting from left or right side, or from advancing or retreating.

ACTION 1: The stepping foot hooks out as it lands. The other foot steps again and hooks in, pointing to the toes of the lead foot. Turn the body around to face the direction from which you just came. The hands continue to move in relation to the feet – when the left foot lands the left hand braces out, when the right foot lands the right hand braces out. The whole action is the same as usual. (image 5.131)

ACTION 2: When turning from a *retreating alligator*, instead of retreating again, step forward with the foot hooked out. Then step the other foot hooked in outside the foot that just landed and turn the body around. Keep the arms moving with the feet the same as usual. Keep the whole body coordinated and follow the action of the hands with the eyes. (image 5.132)

- Right and left actions are similar.

Pointers

- o Be sure to first hook-out and then hook-in with the feet. Turn quickly and be sure to get turned completely around.

- o Maintain coordination between the body, feet and hands to continue the alligator action as you turn.

5.1d   Alligator Closing Move   tuó xíng shōushì   鼍形收势

When you reach your starting point in <u>left</u> *alligator*.

ACTION 1: Step the right foot straight forward and follow in the left foot to beside the right ankle without touching down. Clench the right hand and drill it up to nose height, turning over the ulnar edge. Bring the left hand back to the belly and clench it. Look at the right hand.

ACTION 2: Step the left foot forward without moving the right foot to sit into a *santi* stance. Perform a splitting palm with the left hand to take a *santishi*, and then finish as usual.

5.2   RETREATING ALLIGATOR   tuìbù tuó xíng   退步鼍形

Starting from left *santishi*.

5.2a   Retreating Right Alligator

   tuìbù tuó xíng yòushì   退步鼍形右势

ACTION: Shift the weight forward then step the right foot diagonally back to the right, and then shift onto the right leg. Lift the left foot beside the right ankle, or touch down if you need to. Turn the right hand palm up and bring it from the belly past the chest to the face and turn it palm down, then brace out to the forward right at shoulder height. Keep the right arm

rounded to brace with the elbow a bit below shoulder height. Lower the left hand to the belly and turn it palm up. Look at the right hand. (images 5.133, 5.134)

5.134

- If starting out from <u>left</u> *alligator*, just directly step the right foot back to the right without first doing a forward shift.

5.2b   Retreating Left Alligator   tuìbù tuó xíng zuǒshì   退步鼍形左势

ACTION: Retreat the left foot to the rear left and shift onto the left leg, lifting the right foot beside the left ankle (or setting it down beside the left foot). Bring the left hand, palm up, past the chest to in front of the face then turn it palm down and draw it horizontally across to the left to brace out at shoulder height. Keep the left arm rounded to brace and keep the elbow lower than the shoulder. Lower the right hand and roll it to turn palm up in front of the belly. Look at the left hand. (images 5.135, 5.136)

5.135

5.136

Pointers

- When retreating, step at bit of an angle. Shift quickly but steadily.

- The hands must move together with the feet in a continuous, unbroken manner.

COMMON PROBLEMS AND CORRECTIONS FOR THE ALLIGATOR MODEL

PROBLEM 1: The student is stiff, not gentle.

CORRECTIONS: Remind the student to use intent instead of brute force. This must not be overdone, however, to the point of slackness. Keep the spirit full and reaching to all parts, but do not use brute strength.

PROBLEM 2: The student does not coordinate the hands with the feet, so that the step arrives before the hands, or the hands push out before the step.

CORRECTIONS: Remind the student to pay attention to the coordination between the hands and feet, and to practise over and over, paying close attention to the exact timing.

PROBLEM 3: The student has a weak, floating power.

CORRECTIONS: The first thing is to practise more. The second is to pay attention to using the body. Remind the student to lead all action from the lower back and body core, so that the waist is the axis. Then the student may connect the power to the shoulders and elbows.

PROBLEM 4: The student only pays attention to the lead hand and leaves the rear hand stiff or powerless.

CORRECTIONS: Once the action of the lead hand is correct, more attention must be paid to the rear hand. The hands must work together for the action to be completed properly. The rear hand should have a closing in power as it comes back to the body, rolling back with power.

PROBLEM 5: The student rises and falls in the steps.

CORRECTIONS: There may be some rise and fall between movements, but not too much. Remind the student to pay attention to the knees and to coordinate the stepping with bending the knees to the correct angle.

PROBLEM 6: The student blocks across with the elbows above shoulder height.

CORRECTIONS: Remind the student that when the elbows are up the shoulders shrug up. When the shoulders shrug then the *qi* cannot settle. So, the elbows must not rise above the shoulders, they must settle slightly below the shoulders.

POWER GENERATION FOR THE ALLIGATOR MODEL

- The alligator model moves back and forth without hesitation. It is rounded without slackness, and turns with agility. The intent and spirit are full and the power is subtle.

- You may practise the *advancing alligator* and *retreating alligator* together, advancing for a while, then retreating.

- The power is subtle, held in the intent. Be sure not to use brute force in the arms. The mind is focused but the body is relaxed. When power is connected to the mind then there will be no gaps, but it will flow continuously like swimming in water. Imagine the alligator swimming to guide your practice.

- Be sure to step to forty-five degrees when doing the advancing or retreating alligator. First land the foot, then bend the knee for stability and grab the ground with the toes. When the rear foot does the follow-in step, bring the knees together and sit down, pressing the head up.

- The hands need to act together – one up, one down; one out, one returning. They alternately rotate inward and outward, knocking across horizontally and rolling back in. Be sure to lead the action of the hands from the elbows, the action of the elbows from the shoulders, and the action of the shoulders from the waist. Be sure also to coordinate the hands with the feet.

- The point of contact of the horizontally blocking arm is the ulnar surface of the forearm and the outer edge of the palm. The arm should form an arc with the chest. Keep the chest contained and keep the elbow below shoulder level. The rear hand should lower with a rolling-in power, keeping the shoulder settled to maintain a closing, relaxed power.

- The centre of gravity needs to move with the footwork, right and left, backwards and forwards. Keep the waist agile and lead its movement with the head. Load right to move left, load left to move right. Practise this carefully and thoughtfully to find the power, keeping the whole body together without any slackening. The action should be gentle and show internal power.

BREATHING CYCLE FOR THE ALLIGATOR MODEL

The alligator model uses natural and unrestricted breathing, light and smooth. The movements are gentle and go along with natural breathing. Breathe with the action, but do not hold your breath or use brute force.

PRACTICAL APPLICATIONS FOR THE ALLIGATOR MODEL

Examining the structure of alligator model, the footwork moves in a zigzag pattern either forward or backward, while the hands circle to either side of the body. The goal of these actions is to dissipate an opponent's attacking force. So, it is mainly an evasive move. The angled stepping, whether forward or backward, avoids the attack of the opponent. The hands are held ready to grab, with the forefinger and thumb open and the other fingers hooked. The main technique is to hook onto the opponent's arm and pull, lead, or knock it across, so that the oncoming punch loses its effectiveness. The power of a pull or lead comes from the shoulders and elbows being well connected. There is a hidden attack in the lower hand, which can come through if opportunity presents. It can strike at will. You may also step forward and use the outer edge of the upper palm to cut at the opponent's neck. You may also step in close to strike with the elbow – remember the classics say that the elbow is also a striking surface.

THE POEM ABOUT THE ALLIGATOR

鼍形意境游水中，两臂拨水在腰功。裹带钻翻加肘打，进退曲折意先行。

The mood in the alligator model is to swim in the water.

The arms push aside the water using the power from the waist.

Wrap and draw, drill and turnover, adding in an elbow to strike.

To advance and retreat, bend and flex, the mind steps first.

SIX: CHICKEN MODEL 鸡形

INTRODUCTION TO THE CHICKEN MODEL, *JI XING*

Chicken model imitates the actions of fighting roosters. It is not a simple imitation, however, but the result of years of development by the masters. Do not seek to copy a rooster, but seek its manner. The primary techniques of chicken model are: *golden rooster stands on one leg, pecks rice, shakes its feathers, heralds the dawn,* and *spreads its wings*. Each regional style of Xingyiquan practises a slightly different chicken model but there is great similarity in these basic techniques. When practising chicken model you should show this type of idea: the chicken is brave, it has the ability to stand on one leg, it can shake fiercely, it has a fighting spirit, and it pecks very accurately. The rooster is a natural fighter, it knows how to get in on an enemy, it is skillful at pecking and biting with its hard beak, it is skillful at grabbing, pouncing, kicking, and stomping with its sharp claws, and it can fly to the sky. It can advance and retreat instantaneously, getting in and out of any opening, alternating feet, and taking every opportunity. It will continue to fight even when its face is covered in blood. It conceals defensive moves in its attack and attacking moves in its defense, so that it attacks and defends at the same time, continuing always to attack with high and low techniques.

METHODS OF PERFORMING CHICKEN MODEL

The Four Techniques of the Rooster is the most common method of practicing chicken model. *Golden rooster stands on one leg* is practised separately. *Golden rooster spreads its wings* and *thrusts a foot* are also practised as a technique. These three methods all show the character of chicken model excellently.

6.1 METHOD ONE: GOLDEN ROOSTER STANDS ON ONE LEG (AS A SEPARATE PRACTICE)   jīnjī dúlì   金鸡独立

6.1a Right Golden Rooster Treads on Snow jīnjī tà xuě yòu shì   金鸡踏雪右势

Start from left *santishi*.

ACTION 1: Advance the left foot a half-step without moving the right foot, and shift forward so that most of your weight in on the left leg. Lift the right heel and bend the right knee. Lift the right hand to the sternum and thread it forward under the left arm with the palm down. Withdraw the left hand, pulling it back to the chest with the palm down. Urge the right shoulder forward slightly and drop the right wrist so that the fingers are at shoulder height. Press the head up and look at the right hand. (images 5.137, 5.138, and 5.138 front)

ACTION 2: Take a step forward with the right foot and quickly follow in the left foot to place it by the right ankle without touching down. Keep the knees together and stand firmly on the right leg with the knee bent. Thread the left hand forward under the right arm with the palm down and fingers forward. Bring the right hand back to in front of the chest and extend the left shoulder. The left hand is at shoulder height with the wrist slightly cocked. Press the head up and look at the left hand. (images 5.139, 5.140, and 5.140 front)

ACTION 3: Advance the left foot a half-step while threading the right hand forward. Advance the right foot a step while threading the left hand forward. This is the same as described in actions 1 and 2.

- Continue on in this manner according to the size of your practice area.

6.1b Left Golden Rooster Treads on Snow   jīnjī tà xuě zuǒ shì   金鸡踏雪左势

Start from right *santishi*.

ACTION 1: Advance the right foot a half-step without moving the left foot. Shift forward and lift the left heel. Thread the left hand forward under the right arm and withdraw the right hand. Both palms are angled downwards. (image 5.141)

ACTION 2: Take a step forward with the left foot and quickly follow in the right foot to by the right ankle without touching down. Stand firmly on the left leg with the knee bent. Thread the right hand forward under the left arm. The action is the same as that described above in *right golden rooster treads on snow*, just transposing right and left. (image 5.142)

Pointers

- Be sure to maintain the same height when moving forward. You must not bounce up and down. The key to this is to control the amount of flex in the knees.

- When the rear foot comes through to take a step you should strive for distance and land with stability. The follow-in step should be agile and quick. The knees should stay together. The stepping should be quick and continuous. The one legged stance should be stable, with a slight pause.

6.1c Golden Rooster Treads on Snow Turn Around

jīnjī tà xuě huíshēn shì　　金鸡踏雪回身

- Using the <u>right</u> *stand on one leg* as example.

ACTION 1: Step the left foot a half-step, landing with the foot hooked in. Hook-in well so that the body can turn around a full one-eighty degrees. Shift to the left leg, lift the right foot to touch down by the left foot, and bend the left knee to stand steadily. Bring the right hand around flat with the body, so that it moves right and then back as the body turns to face in the way from which it came. Circle the left hand also flat across to the right. When the left hand arrives in front of the body, bring the right hand back to in front of the chest. Look at the right hand. (image 5.143)

5.143

ACTION 2: Without moving the feet, thread the right hand forward over the left hand and bring the left hand back to in front of the chest.

ACTION 3: Continue on the same as the advancing *golden rooster treads on snow*.

- *Golden rooster treads on snow* may be done as a one sided practice, doing the right form going one way, and turning and coming back with the left form. It may also be done alternating left and right.

Pointers

  o When the lead foot hooks in to turn, be sure to hook-in as much as you can.

  o Turn the body quickly around. Shift the weight quickly but with stability. Circle the hands with the body turn, so that the whole movement is well coordinated.

6.2 METHOD TWO: FOUR TECHNIQUES OF THE CHICKEN

jīxíng sìbǎ dòngzuò　　鸡形四把动作

Start from left *santishi*.

6.2a Golden Rooster Stands on One Leg jīnjī dúlì　　金鸡独立

ACTION: This is the same as the *golden rooster treads on snow* described above. Do two on the right side.

6.2b Golden Rooster Pecks a Grain of Rice　jīnjī shí mǐ　　金鸡食米

ACTION: Advance the left foot and follow-in the right foot to slide-stomp behind the left heel. Land with a thump. Clench the right hand and punch straight ahead at chest height, fist eye up. Tuck the left hand onto the right wrist. Look at the right fist. (images 5.144, and other side)

5.144

5.144
FROM
OTHER SIDE

6.2c   Golden Rooster Shakes its Feathers   jīnjī dǒu líng   金鸡抖翎

ACTION: Retreat the right foot then withdraw the left foot a bit, to form a half horse stance with the weight more on the right leg. Withdraw the right fist as the right foot steps, bending the elbow and drawing it back to bring the fist up and rightward to just in front of the right temple, turning the fist heart out. The elbow may be slightly raised. Turn the left hand to brace down to the left, palm out at hip height. Look at the left hand. (image 5.145)

5.145

6.2d   Golden Rooster Blocks Up   jīnjī shàng jià   金鸡上架

ACTION 1: Turn the torso ninety degrees by driving the left foot back and pivoting the right foot straight. Keep the same force in both arms. (image 5.146)

ACTION 2: Take a step forward with the left foot. Land firmly and follow in quickly with the right foot, placing it at the left ankle. Squat, keeping the knees together. Unclench the right hand and bring it forward and down to chop finishing at the left hip with the palm out. Thread the left hand past the chest to in front of the right shoulder with the fingers up and palm in. Press the head up and look to the forward right. (image 5.147)

5.146

5.147

6.2e Golden Rooster Heralds the Dawn   jīnjī bào xiǎo   金鸡报晓

ACTION: Take a step forward with the right foot and follow in a half-step with the left foot to take a *santi* stance. As the right foot lands, slice the right hand forward and up to eyebrow height with the wrist cocked. Turn the left hand in and pull down to beside the left hip. The right arm is slightly bent, the shoulders and elbows set down, and the buttocks settled. Press the head up and look past the right hand. (image 5.148)

6.2f Step Forward, Left Split   shàngbù zuǒ pīquán   上步左劈拳

ACTION 1: Withdraw the right foot, pause, then advance it a half-step. Bring the left foot to beside the right foot. When withdrawing, clench the right hand and pull it back to the belly. When advancing, drill the right fist forward and up. Clench the left hand in place at the belly. (image 5.149)

ACTION 2: Take a step forward with the left foot and follow in a half-step with the right foot, keeping most weight on the right leg. Slide the left hand along the right arm to split forward to chest height and pull the right hand back to the belly. Look past the left hand. (image 5.150)

6.2g Stamp, Right Split   zhènjiǎo yòu pīquán   震脚右劈拳

ACTION 1:Withdraw the left foot to beside the right ankle without touching down, by dorsi-flexing the ankle. Clench the left fist and pull it back to the belly, then drill up by the sternum and forward to nose height. The right fist remains at the belly. Look at the left fist. (image 5.151)

ACTION 2: Land the left foot with a thump and lift the right foot. At the same time, slide the right fist forward along the left arm to unclench and chop down at chest height. Pull the left hand back to the belly.

Settle the buttocks down and press the head up. Look past the right hand. This position should be fairly low. (image 5.152)

6.2h   Golden Rooster Pecks a Grain of Rice   jīnjī shí mǐ   金鸡食米

ACTION: Step the right foot forward and follow in with the left foot. Do a driving punch with the left fist and cover the left wrist with the right hand. This is the same as movement 6.2c, just punching with the other fist. (images 5.153 and other side)

5.153

5.153 OTHER SIDE

6.2i   Golden Rooster Shakes its Feathers

6.2j   Golden Rooster Blocks Up

6.2k   Golden Rooster Heralds the Dawn

These three moves are the same as the moves 6.2c, 6.2d, and 6.2e, described above, transposing right and left. Traditionally, the four techniques of chicken model are done on one side, but I feel it is better to balance the body and be able to do the actions on either side.

Pointers:

- The punch in *golden rooster pecks rice* hits timed with the rear foot landing. Be sure to keep the whole body coordinated to punch with full power.

- *Golden rooster shakes its feathers* uses a full, coordinated power. Be careful to accurately place the hands.

- Take a step forward when doing *golden rooster blocks up*, and land with stability. Coordinate the footwork with the hand action.

- Take a step forward for *golden rooster heralds the dawn*, and follow in quickly. The lead hand slices up as the lead foot lands.

6.2l   Chicken Model Closing Move   jī xíng shōushì   鸡形收势

- Do as many repetitions as your training space and fitness allow. Do the closing move when you get back to the starting point.

If you are in a <u>right</u> split then hook in the right foot and pull the right fist back and turn around to the left, drill the right fist forward and advance the left foot to split with the left hand. Then close the same as usual from left *santishi*.

If you are in a <u>left</u> split, then clench the left hand and pull it back, hook-in the left foot, turn around to the left, advance the right foot and drill the right fist out. Then step the left foot forward and split forward with the left hand. Then close the same as usual from left *santishi*.

6.3 CHICKEN MODEL METHOD THREE

Start from left *santishi*.

6.3a Golden Rooster Pecks a Grain of Rice jīnjī shí mǐ 金鸡食米

ACTION: Step the left foot forward a half-step then bring the right foot up with a shovel step, landing with a thump. Clench the right fist and punch forward to chest height with an upright fist. Tuck the left hand on the right wrist. Look at the right fist. (image 5.154)

5.154

6.3b Golden Rooster Spreads its Wings jīnjī zhǎn chì 金鸡展翅

ACTION 1: First withdraw the right foot a half-step and sit back, crossing and drilling the fists up. Turn the fist hearts in, left arm inside the right, and drill up to head height. Then turn and unclench the hands, bracing out to the left and right. (images 5.155, 5.156)

ACTION 2: Withdraw the left foot further to beside the right foot, landing with a thump. While bringing the foot back, continue to circle the hands to the right and left, so that they finish by closing in together at the belly. Press the head up and look forward. (image 5.157)

5.155 5.156 5.157

6.3c Golden Rooster Thrusts a Foot jīnjī dēng jiǎo 金鸡蹬脚

ACTION: Advance the left foot a half-step and stand steadily with the knee slightly bent. Lift the right knee and then the foot, to kick with the ankle dorsi-flexed. Kick to chest height. Put the wrists together and open the palms and fingers to apply a carrying power forward and up to jaw height. Look forward. (image 5.158)

6.3d   Golden Rooster Shakes its Feathers   jīnjī dǒu líng   金鸡抖翎

ACTION: Land the right foot forward with the foot hooked in and follow in the left foot slightly. Turn the body ninety degrees to the left, keeping most weight on the left leg in a half horse stance. Clench the left fist and bring it forward and up. Roll the right hand in to the chest then brace down to the right with the palm facing out, the thumb web down, in front of the right knee. Unclench the left hand, bend the elbow, and pull back above the left temple with the palm out. Look at the right hand. (images 5.159 and from the other side)

6.3e   Step Forward, Left Split   shàngbù zuǒ pīquán   上步左劈拳

ACTION 1: Turn the body ninety degrees rightward to face forward. Withdraw the right foot a half-step, turn the right hand over and pull it back to the belly, clenching it. Keep the left hand at the head. (image 5.160 transitional)

ACTION 2: Advance the right foot a half-step and bring the left foot in without touching down. Cover with the left fist, bringing it forward and down to the belly. Drill the right fist forward and up to nose height. Look at the right fist. (image 5.161)

ACTION 3: Take another step forward with the left foot and follow in a half-step with the right foot. Bring the left hand through to do a split at nose height and pull the right hand back to the belly. Look at the left hand. (image 5.162)

6.3f   Stamp, Right Split   zhènjiǎo yòu pīquán   震脚右劈拳

ACTION 1: Withdraw the left foot to beside the right ankle without touching down, by dorsi-flexing the ankle. Clench the left fist and pull it back to the belly, then drill up by the sternum and forward to nose height. The right fist remains at the belly. Look at the left fist.

ACTION 2: Land the left foot with a thump and lift the right foot. At the same time, slide the right fist forward along the left arm to unclench and chop down at chest height. Pull the left hand back to the belly. Settle the buttocks down and press the head up. Look past the right hand. This position should be fairly low.

- This move is the same as that described in the four techniques of chicken model, move 6.2g.

6.3g   Golden Rooster Pecks a Grain of Rice   jīnjī shí mǐ   金鸡食米

This move is the same as 6.3a, just on the other side. Continue on to do all the moves on the other side.

- This chicken model is practised on both sides, continuing on as space and energy permit. Turn around from a split position, using the normal *split turn around*. The closing is also the same as that of split.

Pointers

- o The action *golden rooster spreads its wings* must be circular – the hands must draw a circle and then come in to the belly timed exactly as the foot comes in.

- o The hands must do the carrying move as the foot stamps.

- o The action *golden rooster shakes its feathers* is not quite the same as that done earlier. That done in the four techniques of chicken model is a retreating move, while this is an advancing move. Land the foot hooked in and keep the body's power integrated.

PROBLEMS OFTEN MET IN THE CHICKEN MODEL

Chicken Stands on One Leg

PROBLEM 1: The student's stance height rises and falls while stepping forward.

CORRECTIONS: Remind the student to pay more attention to the flex in the knees when moving onto the leg to maintain an even height.

PROBLEM 2: The student steps too much to the side, swinging right and left instead of stepping forward.

CORRECTIONS: Remind the student to step straight forward, keeping the footwork within shoulder width at the most.

PROBLEM 3: Some students thread the hands straight forward with no settling power in the palms. Others thread straight through with no lifting power in the wrists.

CORRECTIONS: Remind the student to keep the arms slightly bent when threading forward, about 160 degrees. Remind them to drop into the palms by settling the wrists, using the heel of the palm to strike. Remind them also to lift the wrists first, and then to drop them.

PROBLEM 4: The student is unsteady in the one-legged stance.

CORRECTIONS: Remind the student to keep the knees together and to grab the ground with the toes of the supporting foot. They should also press the head up and tuck the buttocks down, settle the *qi* down and urge the shoulders into the move to aid stability.

Four Chicken Techniques

PROBLEM 1: The student lifts the foot to stamp hard when doing the punch.

CORRECTIONS: As the foot comes in it should strike the ground with a large surface, shoveling or raking in before the stamp. Some people just want to make a big noise, but this does not assist the power output to the fist. The punch is forward, so the foot needs a forward moving action into the thump.

PROBLEM 2: The student has no integrated body power when trying to shake the 'feathers' – the shoulder girdle.

CORRECTIONS: This action needs a lot of repetition. In addition, the final position may be done as a stake standing exercise so that the body knows what position it is seeking when using power and speed. While in the final position, and while gently doing the action, seek out the whole body power and the lines of force, to gradually develop the action and position.

PROBLEM 3: The student stands unsteadily or lifts the raised foot too high when doing the upper block.

CORRECTIONS: Remind the student to sit down slightly into this action, keeping the legs together and pressing the head up while settling the buttocks down. The student should also develop the habit in similar moves of always placing the lifted foot at the ankle of the supporting foot, dorsi-flexing to keep the foot parallel to the ground.

PROBLEM 4: The student just uses arm strength when doing *report the dawn*.

CORRECTIONS: This move should show the body's integrated power. Before releasing power, the body should first gather force, closing in before opening. Be sure that the student moves the shoulders, so that the action of the elbows is launched from the shoulders, that of the hands comes from the upper arms. The elbows should maintain a certain angle as the arm cuts up. The shoulders and hands must work together. This needs to be practised a lot to find the integrated power.

PROBLEM 5: The student does a small action for the stamping split.

CORRECTIONS: The stamp is on the spot, so the hand should drill up higher than usual, lengthening the torso. As the foot lands, the stance should be lower than usual, shrinking the body. This makes the move more difficult and more effective for performance.

Chicken Model Method Three

PROBLEM 1: The student lifts the foot to stamp when doing *golden rooster spreads its wings*.

CORRECTIONS: The student should wait after withdrawing the foot, shifting back after settling. The lead foot should be pulled in by closing the hip and dragging the thigh, to drag the foot in to thump with the heel on the ground.

PROBLEM 2: The student does a straight lifting kick for *golden rooster thrusts a foot*.

CORRECTIONS: This is a heel thrust kick; the knee should be lifted bent, and then thrust straight into the heel with the foot dorsi-flexed.

PROBLEM 3: The student does not coordinate the feet with the hands during *golden rooster spreads its wings*.

CORRECTIONS: The hands drill up as the rear foot withdraws. The hands turn and circle to the sides as the weight shifts back. The hands roll together to the belly as the lead foot withdraws and lands with a thump. The student should practise this repeatedly to develop the coordination.

POWER GENERATION FOR THE CHICKEN MODEL

Chicken Stands on One Leg

When you do the threading palms, first raise the wrists and then drop the wrists and sink into the palms, urging the shoulders forward and settling the elbows to release power. Be sure to sit down and settle into the buttocks, reach the shoulders and thread the palms through with a sinking drop. This is like a chicken reaching its head with each step it takes. Be sure to lift the wrists and then settle them.

This technique develops quick footwork and the ability to stop and go. It must be quick. The steps must cover distance, and the stops must be steady.

Four Chicken Techniques

The punch in *golden rooster pecks a grain of rice* is done by turning the waist and urging the shoulder forward, and is timed as the rear foot does a rubbing step in. After the lead foot has landed firmly, turn the waist and close the hips to bring the rear foot up to land the whole foot with a rubbing action forward and down, making a sound. Be sure not to lift the foot and stamp. Be sure to raise the head and straighten the neck, close the hips and tuck in the buttocks, settle the *qi* to the *dantian*, and release power with an exhalation of breath.

When you step back for *golden rooster shakes its feathers*, the torso should first lead the action. The lead foot pushes off to the rear and the whole body gathers power, then you can suddenly release the power. As the right fist lifts and turns as it pulls to the back, the power is directed through the elbow. As the left hand turns the elbow and rounds the arm, settle the shoulder and brace outward; the power is directed to the heel of the palm. The arm actions must be completed simultaneously with the backward step, and coordinated with an expulsion of breath, so that the power comes from the whole body.

Just before *golden rooster blocks up*, twist the torso. Then take a long step forward and land firmly. The rear foot must follow in quickly, closing the knees in tightly together. The lead hand chops down as the rear hand threads up, so that the hands have a wrapping power between them. Close the shoulders, open the upper back, press the head up, and settle the buttocks down.

Golden rooster reports the dawn is actually a scoop. The power of an upward scoop is in the shoulders. Land the lead foot, scoop one hand forward and up, and lower the other hand all as one action – there must be no mistiming. *Golden rooster reports the dawn* can be either a scooping shoulder strike or a scooping punch. The scooping shoulder strike is applied through the shoulder and upper arm. The scooping shoulder strike is an angled pressing power done once the footwork gets you in close enough. The scooping punch is applied to the heel of the lead hand. For the scooping punch, you need to sit into the hips and lengthen the spine, relax and extend the shoulder, and urge the upper arm forward to release power. The power differs, as does the application and use.

For *step forward, split*, to help take a long and stable step forward, withdraw the lead foot slightly and then advance a half-step. Pull the lead hand back as you withdraw the lead foot, so that foot and hand act together. Drill the lead hand forward as you advance the lead foot a half-step. Then step forward as the rear hand chops forward.

Golden rooster drinks water is a splitting palm combined with a stamp. The lead hand should clench and pull back as the lead foot withdraws. The fist drills up as the knee lifts. The knee should lift to hip height. Lengthen the spine slightly and rise to lend power to the drilling up fist. Settle the torso down, stomp the foot, pull back, chop the rear hand out, and lift the other foot all at once. All actions are done at once with total coordination and whole body power.

Chicken Model Method Three

Golden rooster spreads its wings uses a twisting, drilling power as the fists cross and drill upward. It uses a bracing power in both arms with the chest contained and the arms rounded as the fists turn over and draw a circle. When the hands gather in front of the abdomen, the arms should have an inward and downward wrapping, embracing power, with the elbows hugged tightly to the ribs. The hands should gather in as the foot withdraws, so that feet and hands are coordinated. When the elbows hug the ribs the fists can strike the belly to help sink the *qi* to the *dantian*.

Golden rooster thrusts a foot must be fast – the foot must lift to kick as soon as the other foot steps a half-step forward. The kicking leg must move quickly and the supporting leg should be slightly bent with the toes gripping the ground for stability. To kick, first lift the knee with the foot pulled back to present the heel, and then thrust forcefully forward, straightening the knee. Both palms lift up, keeping the elbows closed in, lengthening the spine and releasing the shoulders to extend the arms. The kick must come at the same time that the palms lift.

Golden rooster shakes its feathers comes immediately after the kick, starting to thrust forward strongly from the supporting leg to send the kicking leg forward to land. The landing foot stomps into the ground, so you need to twist the torso and hook in the foot. When the hands open out to brace upper and lower, left and right, they must complete the action as the foot lands. The hands must first gather power, and then open out, the left hand in front and the right hand behind. Contain the chest, close the shoulders, twist the hands, turn the elbows over, twist the waist, stomp the foot and brace up and down with the palms. The focus is in the lower hand. The power should be full and the technique use whole body power.

BREATHING CYCLE FOR THE CHICKEN MODEL

- Take a small breath in during *golden rooster stands on one leg*. After each power move relax immediately to assist in breathing in. Inhale also during each action that opens up the chest (this principle applies to all such actions in Xingyiquan). For example, breathe in as you circle the arms out to the sides during *golden rooster spreads its wings*.

- Exhale on all the power moves to assist in launching power.

PRACTICAL APPLICATIONS FOR THE CHICKEN MODEL

- In Xingyiquan, all power release moves are effective strikes. The chicken model has many power release moves, and so has many applications.

Golden rooster stands on one leg uses fast footwork to enter quickly to take over the centre of the opponent, threading the hands into his face in order to throw him into confusion. The palms can then drop to strike his chest.

Golden rooster pecks a grain of rice uses the lead hand to hook and press the opponent's fist, entering in with the footwork to punch with the rear fist to his solar plexus.

Golden rooster shakes its feathers can strike with an entry step or a retreating step. One hand blocks up to pull back as the other hand tucks in to strike as the waist turns to enter the body sideways.

- The key lies in the footwork. The lead foot must get in tight to the opponent's body so that you can reach his hip or belly.

Golden rooster blocks up is an entry step with a chopping lean. One hand is down and one is above the shoulder, turn the body sideways and get the feet in with a T step, first gathering and then releasing power.

Golden rooster heralds the dawn is a scoop, that is, a strike that lifts forward and up from below.

Golden rooster spreads its wings is a retreating defensive move. The hands brace up out to the sides then drop and roll in. The upward brace deals with a high attack, and the low roll-in deals with a low attack.

Golden rooster thrusts a foot is a kick to the opponent's chest with a simultaneous lifting strike with both hands to his jaw. It strikes low and high, feinting high while striking low. The main technique is the kick.

The Poem About The Chicken

金鸡踏雪独立能，抖翎发威身劲整。展翅蹬脚上下取，食米报晓上架行。

Golden rooster treads on snow shows the ability to stand on one leg.

Shake the feathers emits all the body's enormous power.

Spread wings and *thrust a foot* deal with high and low.

Peck a grain of rice, *report the dawn*, and *block up* all move forward.

SEVEN: SWALLOW MODEL 燕形

Introduction To The Swallow Model, *Yan Xing*

Swallow model is the most agile of Xingyiquan's animal models, and develops nimbleness and quickness. Swallow model combines martial techniques with the agility that the swallow shows when it swoops over the water, flies straight up to the sky, or wheels over in flight.

One should understand these images when doing swallow model: to do *swallow pierces the sky,* the body lengthens, the hands turn as if they were wings, turning suddenly up to dive down. The image of *swallow skims the water* is dropping down to the water, scooping some up in flight, then rising. The drop stance needs to squat fully down and the lead hand protects you as the rear hand comes from below to rise into a groin strike. As the legs push off to rise, you strike the opponent's torso. Your movements must rise and fall, rising like flying high on wings, and dropping like hiding under the ground. You must leap forward, stand on one leg, slice the palm, punch quickly and with agility, and your strikes must be solid and firm. You should leap for distance and land lightly but firmly, seeking a combination of nimbleness with stability, a power in lightness, combining hard and soft and combining form and spirit as one.

Each branch of Xingyiquan does swallow model slightly differently, and each has its own characteristics. Almost all Xingyiquan books describe *swallow swoops over the water*. Some are done higher and some lower, according to how each teacher taught. Sometimes the name is the same for different movements, and sometimes the movements are the same for different names. Here I will introduce two versions of swallow model that contain some of the main methods.

Methods Of Performing The Swallow Model

7.1   SWALLOW MODEL METHOD ONE

Start from left *santishi*.

7.1a   **Swallow Pierces the Sky**   yànzǐ zuāntiān   燕子钻天

ACTION 1: Rotate both palms to face up and thread the right hand forward under the left arm, shifting forward. As the right hand approaches the left hand, extend the right hand up. Bend the left elbow and turn the palm down to press down past the chest. Thread the right hand up past the head and shift back to the right leg, then bring the right hand back and down to shoulder height. Look at the right hand. Slice the left hand down and forward, and look at the left hand. (images 5.163, 5.164

5.163

ACTION 2: Advance the left foot a half-step and push off to jump. Take a long step forward with the right foot and land firmly, keeping the left knee up in a right one legged stance. Lower the right hand by the waist then thread it forward and up under the left arm, turning the palm up when the hand passes head height. Bend the left elbow and turn the hand over to stab down in front of the groin with the little finger on the outside. Lift the left knee to waist height. Look forward. (images 5.165, 5.166)

5.164

5.165

5.166

7.1b   Swallow Skims the Water   yànzǐ chāo shuǐ   燕子抄水

ACTION 1: Turn ninety degrees to the right and bend the right knee to a full squat, extending the left foot to the left to form a left drop stance. Thread the left hand forward along the inside of the left leg, rolling the arm under to turn the palm up, until it is at the left foot. Brace back with the right hand, palm out and arm rounded. Look at the left hand. (images 5.167a, 5.167b and 5.167b front)

5.167
FRONT

5.167 a

b

7.1c   Step Forward, Slice to the Groin   shàngbù liāo yīn zhǎng   上步撩阴掌

ACTION 1: Thread the left hand forward and shift forward, bending the left knee to support with the left leg, rising slightly. (image 5.168)

ACTION 2: Take a step forward with the right foot, turning the foot out crossways. Do not move the left foot, and sit into a resting stance.

Slice the right hand forward to strike with the palm forward at waist height. Tuck the left hand onto the right wrist and raise the body slightly, lifting the left heel. Look at the right hand. (image 5.169)

5.168

5.169

7.1d   Left Low Punch   zuǒ xià bēngquán   左下崩拳

ACTION: Take a long step forward with the left foot and follow in with the right foot. Clench both fists and tuck in the left elbow. Slide the left fist along the right arm to punch forward and down with the fist heart down, at belly height. Pull the right fist back to the belly with the fist heart up. Look in the direction of the left punch and press the head up. (image 5.170)

5.170

7.1e   Step Forward, Right Split   shàngbù yòu pīquán   上步右劈拳

ACTION 1: Advance the left foot a half-step and follow in with the right foot to beside the left ankle without touching down. Pull the left fist back to the belly, then bring it up to the sternum and drill forward to nose height, twisting the ulnar edge upwards. (image 5.171)

ACTION 2: Take a long step forward with the right foot and follow in a half step with the left foot. Bring the right hand along the left arm to chop forward to shoulder height and pull the left hand back to the belly. Press the head up and look forward. (image 5.172)

5.171

5.172

7.1f   Swallow Turn Around   yàn xíng huíshēn   燕形回身

- The *swallow model turn around* is the same as that of split, adding another split to change sides. First do a split, and then continue on to the next move.

Pointers

- o During *pierce the sky* the hands must not stop. The right hand threads up as you jump, and the entire action is done all as one move.

- o During *skim the water* you must squat fully into the drop stance. The arms should form a straight line. Be sure to slide the left hand along the leg. Do not stop between *pierce the sky* and *skim the water*, but perform them as one move.

- o During *step forward, slice to the groin* bring the right hand through with the right foot. Tuck the legs tightly together. Reach the right hand forward as you strike.

- o Punch with the left fist as the left foot lands its forward step.

7.2   SWALLOW MODEL METHOD TWO

Start from left *santishi*.

7.2a   Swallow Pierces the Sky   yànzǐ zuāntiān   燕子钻天

- This is the same as described above in 7.1a

7.2b   Swallow Skims the Water   yànzǐ chāo shuǐ   燕子抄水

- This is the same as described above in 7.1b.

7.2c   Swallow Spreads its Wings   yànzǐ zhǎn chì   燕子展翅

ACTION 1: Thread the left hand towards the left foot and shift forward to the left foot, bending the left knee and rising slightly. Come through with the head, keeping the left hand extended at waist height and extending the right hand to the rear. Look at the left hand. (image 5.173)

ACTION 2: Bend the right elbow and bring the hand to the waist, then thread up and forward under the left arm with the palm up. Bend the left elbow and rotate the palm so that it faces in in front of the chest. The palms are crossed in front of the chest with the elbows down. (image 5.174)

ACTION 3: Take a long step forward with the right foot, landing firmly and bending the knee to a half squat. Follow up the left foot to beside the right ankle without touching down. Keep the knees together and dorsi-flex the left ankle. Separate the arms to left and right, the

5.173

5.174

elbows slightly bent, the palms upright (left forward and right back), the palms both open and with the fingers up, at shoulder height. Look at the left hand. (image 5.175)

5.175

7.2d   Advance, Right Driving Punch   jìnbù yòu bēngquán   进步右崩拳

ACTION 1: Take a long step forward with the left foot and follow in a half-step with the right. As the right foot comes in to the left heel, half-squat on both legs. Clench the right fist and bring it in to the waist, then punch forward with the fist eye up. Tuck the left palm inward to touch the right wrist. Punch to chest height. Press the head up and look at the right fist. (image 5.176)

5.176

7.2e   Step Forward, Right Split   shàngbù yòu pīquán   上步右劈拳

ACTION 1: Pull both hands back to the belly and advance the left foot a half-step. Drill the left fist up by the sternum and forward to nose height with the ulnar side twisted up. Follow in with the right foot without touching down. Look at the left fist. (image 5.177)

ACTION 2: Take a long step forward with the right foot and follow in a half-step with the left to take a *santi* stance with the right foot forward. Slide the right fist along the left arm, unclench the hands, and chop the right hand forward at shoulder height while pulling the left hand back to the belly, both palms down. Press the head up and look past the right hand. (image 5.178)

5.177

5.178

- Continue on to repeat moves 7.2a, b, c, d, and e on the other side.

7.2f   Swallow Turn Around and Closing Move

- The *turn around* and *closing move* are the same as for the first method of swallow model.

Pointers

o *Swallow spreads its wings* is made up of three actions, but they should be continuous. Take a long step forward with the right foot, landing solidly and at the same time as the hands complete their action.

o The hands and feet arrive together in *advance right driving punch*, the same as in *rooster pecks a grain of rice*.

o The feet and hands arrive together in *step forward right split*, using whole body power.

PROBLEMS OFTEN MET IN THE SWALLOW MODEL

PROBLEM 1: The student is uncoordinated when doing *swallow pierces the sky*.

CORRECTIONS: Tell the student to pay attention when the rear hand starts to thread forward, that the lead hand should start to draw back with a covering action. As the rear hand threads up, the lead hand should thread down. As the rear hand drops back, the lead hand should slice forward. Overall, the hands move at the same time and follow the rule: one forward and one back, one up and one down. Repeating these actions in this way many times will bring coordination

PROBLEM 2: The student's drop stance is too high and unstable when doing *swallow skims the water*.

CORRECTIONS: The higher the stance, the more difficult it is to keep stable, as the centre of gravity is high. The cause of a high stance is that the supporting leg is not squatting fully down – the body should be completely down and the other leg should extend out along the ground. This should be the same as Longfist style's *drop stance thread palm*. If the student is not flexible enough to do this, then he should do more hip and ankle flexibility training.

PROBLEM 3: As the student threads his hand forward in *swallow skims the water* he does not butt forward with the head, but simply comes straight up.

CORRECTIONS: Although this is not considered a huge error, it shows a low quality of movement. You should express the ability of the swallow to drop down, scoop water and then rise. This should be a unique action. The drop stance should go all the way down, then the hand should thread forward and the head should lead into the action before rising.

PROBLEM 4: The student does not smoothly connect *swallow pierces the sky* with *swallow skims the water*, leaving a big gap between the two actions.

CORRECTIONS: When first teaching, one must break down the movements, showing each one separately to make the requirements clear and explain all the details. But once the movements have been learned, you must remind the student to connect them. The action and power flow must be smooth and coordinated.

PROBLEM 5: The student does not connect the hand opening with the foot landing in *swallow spreads its wings*.

CORRECTIONS: Make sure the student prepares the hands by crossing them before stepping – the right hand outside the left. Then step forward and separate the hands to front and back as the foot lands. Have the student do the action slowly to gain the coordination, and only add speed once the movement is comfortable.

PROBLEM 6: The student keeps his torso too erect in *slice to the groin*, or places the hand too high.

CORRECTIONS: Remind the student to lean the torso forward slightly into the *slice to the groin*. The strike up should be done with a slightly bent arm, and the right shoulder should settle down, so that the hand reaches forward as the left foot steps out. The body should settle down and the palm should strike up to waist height. Remind the student to practise to coordinate the actions of the footwork, hand and shoulder.

PROBLEM 7: When doing the *low driving punch* the student cuts down instead of punching.

CORRECTIONS: Remind the student to pay attention to the action and placement of the elbows. When punching, the elbows should roll in so that when the body issues power it is applied through the shoulders, so that one hand goes forward as the other goes back, one up and one down.

POWER GENERATION FOR THE SWALLOW MODEL

The actions of *swallow pierces the sky* and *swallow skims the water* must be done continuously without a break in power. To keep the power smooth, do not stop in mid-movement.

Swallow pierces the sky emphasizes the forward-backward shifting of the body. As the rear hand threads forward so does the centre of gravity. When the hand threads up and then pulls back, the centre of gravity shifts back. Use the waist to draw the shoulder, and the shoulder to draw the elbows, turning while moving. The hands need to coordinate: the right hand goes up as the left hand goes down; the right hand goes back and the left hand goes forward; the right hand goes forward as the left hand goes back. Use the power of the body core, use the shoulders to draw the arms into coordinated movement, so that the whole body works as one.

The movement *swallow pierces the sky* must use the forward movement of the body, as the body moves forward past the lead foot, putting the rear hand forward and up; only then push off the lead foot and take a long step forward with the rear foot. Push off strongly with the rear foot to take everything forward, as long and high as possible. If you are practising *swallow pierces the sky* as a single technique, as the rear foot lands you should stand steady on one leg. Lift the other knee in front of the chest and slice up with the rear hand, stabbing the lead hand down with both arms slightly bent. This one-legged stance is the actual *swallow pierces the sky*. If you are combining *swallow pierces the sky* with *swallow skims the water*, then bring the rear foot up and forward to aid the drive forward, and when landing, turn the foot out and bend the knee to squat. First lift the other knee, then drop down and extend the leg along the ground with the foot hooked in.

Swallow scoops water is a drop stance as the hand threads forward, so you should drop as low as possible. You must squat fully on the supporting leg with the shank tight to the thigh, the belly on the thigh, and the buttocks sitting down as much as possible. Turn the foot out to forty-five degrees with the knee on line with it. Hook the other foot in and extend it out as close to the ground as possible, keeping the whole foot on the ground. When doing *swallow scoops water*, be sure to first tuck the shoulder under to be able to twist the arm and extend it along the leg. The rear hand slices up towards the rear. The key to the move lies in drilling the head forward to butt towards the extended foot, pushing into the rear leg to move the centre of gravity forward. Once the lead elbow has gone past the extended foot, then bend the knee and rise, twisting and threading the lead hand. Settle the shoulder and drop the elbow to put power into the arm twist.

Step forward slice to the groin is a relatively low posture. The rear hand comes through to slice as the rear foot steps through with the foot crossways. Get power into the slice by turning the waist, rolling the torso, and reaching with the arm. The legs cross with the thighs tucked tightly together, and the torso leans forward slightly.

- Do not hesitate between *swallow pierces the sky*, *skim the water*, and *slice to groin*. Complete the three actions as one move, with one continuous power flow.

The *low driving punch* can also be called *planting punch*. There are three actions involved – step and land the foot, punch forward and down, and pull the other hand back to the abdomen. These must be completed together, with one explosive move and breath. When launching power to the punch, be sure to drop one shoulder forward and down, and to pull the other up and back, to put power into the fists. Pay special attention to the lead elbow, keep it rolled in, so that the power is contained and complete.

Both types of swallow model share the moves *swallow pierces the sky* and *swallow skims the water*, but the rest of the actions are not the same. One strikes to the groin then punches down, the other spread the wings and then punches straight. Each has its own application and its own nature.

During *swallow spreads its wings*, as the rear foot steps through, it should take a long step and land firmly. The centre of gravity should move forward past the lead foot, and, as the rear foot thrusts forward, push strongly off the lead foot. In this way the step can cover a lot of distance. When stepping forward, be sure not to push the body upwards – the feet must drive straight forward. Land solidly on one leg with the knee bent and the toes grabbing the ground. Bring the rear foot up quickly to place the knees tightly together. Press the head up and tuck the buttocks in. As the arms open to the front and rear, they must finish the action as the rear foot comes through to land. Close the chest when the rear hand threads forward and slices up and the lead hand rotates and covers in. Open the chest, urge the shoulders into the action, and firm the abdomen when the arms 'spread the wings.'

Advance driving punch is also called *golden rooster pecks a grain of rice*. It is a rear foot timed punch. Combine the rear foot landing and the punch with an exhalation of breath. Be sure to bring the rear hand to the belly before punching.

BREATHING CYCLE FOR THE SWALLOW MODEL

The general rule for breathing is: Each power release action uses an exhalation to help with the power output. Each opening-up action uses an inhalation. Each closing-in action uses an exhalation.

- Inhale when moving forward and up in *swallow pierces the sky*. Use a lifting breath to help you to rise.

- Exhale when dropping down in *swallow skims the water*. Use a settling breath, not a sharp power launching exhalation.

Your ability to breathe smoothly in coordination with your actions directly affects your quality of movement. When first learning new actions and when practising slowly, you need to concentrate on the actions to get them perfect, so just breathe naturally. Once the actions are done correctly then they will influence how you breathe, and you will gradually come to breathe correctly in coordination with your actions. These principles and the progression should be applied to all Xingyiquan training.

PRACTICAL APPLICATIONS FOR THE SWALLOW MODEL

- Swallow model develops flexibility and agility, especially the ability to rise and drop quickly.

In *swallow pierces the sky*, the rear hand that threads forward and slices up to pull back can be an upward block turning to a grab. If you cannot grab, then just knock away and use the lead hand to strike the opponent's chest or face. Move your body back to dodge. Move your body forward to strike. The techniques themselves can be freely used as you see necessary.

In *swallow skims the water,* you must drop down into a full drop stance for training, but in using it you don't usually need to drop so far, just enough to bring the body down, to turn it sideways to facilitate entering. Use the power in the upper arms with a hidden threading cut up into the opponent's groin or belly.

In *swallow pierces the sky*, one leg pushes off as you drive the other leg up to assist the jump for height and distance. To use this technique in combat, kick forward with this leg as the hand threads forward.

In *step forward to strike the groin*, the lead hand takes care of the opponent's hands by scooping up, knocking aside, pressing down, or hooking, so that the rear hand can come through to strike the groin. When using the technique, get the body in tight and use the lead hand to shut down the opponent and protect your head. This technique needs to be fast, to get in before the opponent can react. You can step in the rear foot or the lead foot, but you must stay low.

Advance low punch strikes the opponent's belly. Aim through to behind his body, thinking of going right through him.

Swallow spreads its wings brings the rear hand through to slice up, stepping the foot in quickly and striking with the lead hand. Aim for the opponent's chest or face. Be sure to turn the body sideways as you enter. *Advance punch* is a strike to the solar plexus.

THE POEM ABOUT THE SWALLOW

钻天抄水一气成，撩打招法不容情。缩起长落身法意，劲顺意领气子通。

Pierce the sky and *scoop water* in one breath,

The groin strike is then not easy to fathom.

The body technique is to tuck in as you rise, lengthen as you land;

The power is smooth and the intent leads, so the *qi* naturally connects.

EIGHT: SPARROW HAWK MODEL 鹞形

INTRODUCTION TO THE SPARROW HAWK MODEL, *YAO XING*

The sparrow hawk is one of the fiercest and quickest of the birds of prey. All acccipiters are small but make up for their size with their agility and fierceness.[24] In Xingyiquan, we copy the sparrow hawk's skill at folding its body and wings to thread through the trees, its bravery at flying up to the heavens, its skill at wheeling over, its might at spreading its wings, and its ferocity at grasping prey.

Sparrow hawk model is practised advancing on a straight line, turning the body to attack, wheeling the body to use surprise to get in low while appearing to go high, and tucking the body to advance and strike. The body technique is to tuck and rise, to hide and drop – rising and falling, drilling and wheeling to left and right as if flying. The hand technique should be crisp and tight. The footwork should advance quickly and follow in immediately.

When practicing sparrow hawk model you should show this type of intent: flying up and down, wheeling left and right, tucking to enter straight in like an arrow. Turn the body sideways as if passing through the trees. Punch like a bullet, pierce the sky fiercely, wheel over lightly as if flying. The whole body must be fully coordinated with no slackness. When 'spreading the wings' you must first roll in and then spread, the roll in conceals the body, rolling the power and the intent inward so that you can launch wide open with whole body power. Upper and lower, inner and outer are all united as one. When grabbing prey you should be fierce and powerful. In sum, sparrow hawk model should show a connected spirit, an agile and full power, fierce and quick hand techniques, and a fully coordinated body technique.

METHODS OF PERFORMING THE SPARROW HAWK MODEL

There are two main methods of performing sparrow hawk model. One combines *sparrow hawk tucks in its body, enters the woods, pierces the sky,* and *wheels over.* The second combines *sparrow hawk folds its wings, enters the woods, grabs a sparrow, spreads its wings,* and *wheels over.* There are many similar actions in each

---

[24] Translator's note: Accipiters, or bird hawks, include a number of small hawks that fly through woods after small birds such as sparrows. It is usual, though not perhaps totally accurate, in Xingyiquan to translate *yaozi* as sparrow hawk.

method, though each emphasizes a different aspect. You should practise each on both sides to develop complete skill.

8.1   SPARROW HAWK MODEL METHOD ONE

Start from left *santishi*.

8.1a   Sparrow Hawk Folds its Wings   yàozǐ shù shēn   鷂子束身

ACTION: Clench both fists and bring the right fist up from the belly to the sternum, taking a long step forward with the right foot. Lift the left foot by the right ankle without touching down, keeping the knees together. While doing this, punch the right fist forward and down to belly height, fist eye forward, stabbing out over the left arm. Pull the left fist back towards the belly with the fist heart in. Look forward and press the head up. (image 5.179)

5.179

8.1b   Sparrow Hawk Enters the Woods   yàozǐ rù lín   鷂子入林

ACTION: Take a long step forward with the left foot and follow in a half-step with the right foot. Bend the right elbow to drill the fist up to eyebrow height and lift the left fist to the sternum. Punch the left fist forward at chest height, fist eye up, as

the left foot lands. Rotate the right forearm and drop the elbow, pulling the right fist back to the temple with the fist heart forward about a fist width away from the right temple. Look past the left fist. (images 5.180 and front)

5.180   5.180 FRONT

8.1c   Sparrow Hawk Pierces the Sky   yàozǐ zuān tiān   鷂子钻天

ACTION 1: Advance the left foot a half-step and follow in the right foot to beside the left without touching down. Drop the right fist to the right waist with the fist heart up. Rotate the left fist then cock it with the fist heart down, tucking the forearm across the body. Look forward. (image 5.181)

ACTION 2: Take a long step forward with the right foot and follow in the left foot a half-step. Drill the right fist forward and out from inside the left wrist, finishing at nose height with the fist heart in and ulnar edge up. Cock the left fist down to press and pull back to the belly, fist heart down. Press the head up and look at the right fist. (image 5.182)

5.181

5.182

8.1d   Sparrow Hawk Wheels Over   yàozǐ fān shēn   鹞子翻身

ACTION 1: Hook the right foot in and turn around one-eighty degrees to the left to face back in the way from which you came. Lift the right elbow and bring the right arm past the right ear, crossing the forearm over the head as you turn around to the left. Press the right forearm past the head to cover forward and down with the fist hear down. Keep the left fist at the belly. (image 5.183)

ACTION 2: Complete the right fist cover down to the belly without moving the feet. Shift the weight forward onto the left foot as you drill the left fist up by the sternum then forward along inside the right wrist to drill up to nose height, fist heart in. Look at the left fist. (image 5.184)

5.183

5.184

ACTION 3: Bring the right forearm across the body, lifting it up to the head outside the left fist. Bend the left elbow to bring the fist back to the chest. Turn the body rightward and shift back to the right leg. Pull the right fist back as the body turns, and circle it down to the right waist with the fist heart up. Bend the right knee to squat fully down, and extend the left leg out into a drop stance. Slide the left fist along the left leg, turning it so the fist eye faces down as it extends – the left fist should go past the left foot. Watch the left fist as it drills up, watch the right fist as it lifts crossways and back, then turn the head quickly to watch the left fist again as it extends forward with the drop stance. (images 5.185, 5.186)

5.185

5.186

8.1e　　Sparrow Hawk Folds its Wings　　　yàozǐ shù shēn　　鹞子束身

ACTION 1: Extend the left fist along the left leg and shift forward onto the left leg, bending the knee and rising slightly. Take a long step forward with the right foot and quickly bring the left foot up to the right ankle without touching down. Bring the right fist past the chest to punch forward and down, fist eye forward at belly height, crossing over outside the left fist. Bring the left fist back towards the belly. Look in front of the right punch and press the head up. Keep the arms tight to the ribs. (image 5.187)

5.187

- Repeat the moves again, continuing on as described above.

Pointers

- o　Be sure to take a long step forward with the right foot when doing *sparrow hawk folds its wings*. Land firmly, and close the hands together.

- o　*Sparrow hawk pierces the sky* is a right drilling punch, so the main points are the same as described in the chapter on drill.

- o　The actions in the sparrow hawk model are an integrated unit, so you must practise them as a continuous whole. The entire body must be coordinated. Pay attention to the shifts in weight.

- To practise the other side of the sparrow hawk model, after *sparrow hawk pierces the sky*, take another step forward and do a *left aligned step drill*. Then carry on with *sparrow hawk wheels over*, *folds its wings*, *enters the woods*, and *pierces the sky* on the other side.

8.1f　　Sparrow Hawk Closing Move　　　yào xíng shōushì　　鹞形收势

Once you get back to your starting place, complete *sparrow hawk folds its wings* and *sparrow hawk enters the woods*. Then cock the left fist to press and pull back to the belly. From there you can complete the form the same as from *santishi*.

8.2　SPARROW HAWK MODEL METHOD TWO

Start from left *santishi*.

8.2a　　Sparrow Hawk Folds its Wings　　　yàozǐ shù shēn　　鹞子束身

The same as described above in 8.1a.

8.2b　　Sparrow Hawk Enters the Woods　　　yàozǐ rù lín　　鹞子入林

The same as described above in 8.1b.

8.2c　　Sparrow Hawk Grasps a Sparrow　　　yàozǐ zhuō què　　鹞子捉雀

ACTION 1: Advance the left foot a half-step and unclench the hands. Turn the left palm up and turn the right palm outward. Circle the left hand up, right, and back to beside the right waist, palm down. Circle the right hand back and down, also beside the right waist, palm up. Look at the left hand. (image 5.188)

ACTION 2: Step the right foot forward, hooked out in a cross step. Block with the left arm forward and up to shoulder height, forearm across the body. Thread the right hand forward to chest height as the right foot steps forward, turning the palm up. Look at the right hand. (image 5.189)

ACTION 3: Step the left foot forward and follow in a half-step with the right foot to take a *santi* stance. Lift the right hand to eyebrow height, turning the palm down. Slide the left hand along the right forearm to chop forward and down at waist height. Pull the right hand back to beside the right waist. Look at the left hand and press the head up. (image 5.190)

8.2d　Sparrow Hawk Spreads its Wings　　yàozǐ zhǎnchì　　鹞子展翅

ACTION 1: Step the left foot forward a half-step with the foot hooked out. Lift the right foot to the left ankle without touching down. Clench the hands and pull the left fist back to the belly, then drill the left fist up by the sternum to eyebrow height. Flex and lift the right elbow, keeping it dropped, to lift the right fist up to eyebrow height, circling forward and to the left. The fists end up crossed in front of the chest with the fist hearts in, the left fist inside the right fist. The body is turned ninety degrees to the left. Look at the right fist. (images 5.191 and 5.191 other side)

ACTION 2: Take a long step to the forward right with the right foot, landing it across the line of the form, and bringing the left foot in slightly, to sit into a horse stance. Unclench the hands and turn the palms down to brace out strongly at waist height to the left and right. The arms are curved and the power goes to the heel of the palms. Press the head up and focus forward. Look at the right hand. (images 5.192 and 5.192 other side)

8.2e   Sparrow Hawk Pierces the Sky   yàozǐ zuān tiān   鹞子钻天

ACTION 1: Withdraw the right foot a little then take a step forward, bringing the left foot up to the right ankle without touching down. Clench the fists and bring the left fist back to the belly. Bring the right fist back the belly then drill it up by the sternum and forward to nose height. Look at the right fist. (image 5.193)

ACTION 2: Take a step forward with the left foot and follow in a half-step with the right foot. Turn the right fist heart down and across the body to tuck and press down with the forearm, pulling it back to the belly with the fist heart in. Drill the left fist by the sternum and forward to nose height with the ulnar side turned up. Look at the left fist. (image 5.194)

8.2f   Sparrow Hawk Wheels Over   yàozǐ fān shēn   鹞子翻身

- This is the same as described in 8.1d, the only difference is that this time it turns around to the right. This way you get to practise in both directions.

8.2g   Sparrow Hawk Turn Around and Closing Move

zhuàn shēn, shòu shì   转身和收势

- The *turn around* and *closing move* of the second method of the sparrow hawk model are the same as that of the first method.

Pointers

- ○ *Sparrow hawk folds its wings* and *sparrow hawk enters the woods* should be done as one action with no hesitation.

○ *Sparrow hawk grasps its prey* is described as three actions, but must be done as one.

○ During *sparrow hawk spreads its wings*, the right elbow cover must arrive as the left foot lands, applying one whole body power.

PROBLEMS OFTEN MET IN THE SPARROW HAWK MODEL

PROBLEM 1: In *sparrow hawk enters the woods*, during the action of lifting the right elbow and bringing in the right foot, the student turns the foot out too much, causing the knee to be turned out.

CORRECTIONS: Tell the student to keep the elbow in, so that the right fist first drills up, rotating fully, so that the body turns sideways for the punch. When the student brings in the right foot, remind him to use the knee to bring the foot in, keeping the knee tucked inward. This will prevent the problem of leaving the hip back, which allows the knee to arrive turned out, and the foot to turn across the stance.

PROBLEM 2: The student does not have whole body power during *sparrow hawk wheels over*, moving the hands and body independently, and showing a clear lack of internal power

CORRECTIONS: This problem can only be solved by practice. During repetitions, the student must pay attention to the power flow, looking for it in the line of the movements, and trying to get a feel for it. Practice of any movement must be done with this principle: first learn the movements correctly; train hard once they are well known. When thought is added to hard training then skill will evolve. [25]

PROBLEM 3: The student has power in the lead hand but not in the rear hand during *sparrow hawk spreads its wings*. Also, the hands and feet do not work together.

CORRECTIONS: Hand and foot coordination will come naturally with much thoughtful practice. The student must also pay attention to finding equal power in the hands. As the classics say, "when the lead hand strikes, the power launches from the rear hand." This is the only way to use whole body power, which is an even, heavy power.

PROBLEM 4: The student is unstable during *sparrow hawk wheels over*.

CORRECTIONS: Usually the cause of instability is shifting the weight back and forth too much and too forcefully. The student should pay attention to the hook-in step, making the foot placement slightly ahead. In this way, the body technique can move smoothly into the turn.

POWER GENERATION FOR THE SPARROW HAWK MODEL

First Sparrow Hawk Method

Sparrow Hawk Folds its wings, Sparrow Hawk Enters the Woods

---

[25] Translator's note (verbal instruction from author): In this action, pretend you are holding a spear and twisting it from the hand holding the grip to send power to the hand holding the middle of the spear in front. This helps you find the power transfer through the body core.

- These moves should be done as one action, with no hesitation between them.

During *sparrow hawk folds its wings* the right stabbing punch must hit simultaneously with the right foot landing. To have power, the head presses up, the right shoulder urges forward slightly, the shoulders and elbows settle, the shoulders close in, the chest closes, the abdomen settles firmly, the buttocks drop, and the upper arms adhere tightly to the ribs.

Sparrow hawk enters the woods is an *aligned stance cannon fist*. The lead punch should arrive with the landing of the lead foot, so that the power is complete. To have an effective block, the blocking arm must drill up with the elbow tucked down, and then the body moves in sideways so that the block is a deflection – you must not turn the forearm sideways by lifting the elbow, which turns the action into a straight upper block. To get the correct power, rotate the right forearm, keeping the elbow down.

Sparrow Hawk Pierces the Sky

The fist must drill up as the foot lands. To have correct drilling power and protect the midline, the ulnar edge must twist upward.

To move from the *sparrow hawk enters the woods* into *sparrow hawk pierces the sky*, first bring the right fist down from beside the temple, pulling the right arm slightly back. This creates an inward and downward rolling power in the right forearm, rolling as it pulls back. Once it arrives at the waist, then it is ready to drill forward. As the fist drills forward, urge the fist from the elbow, the elbow from the shoulder, and the shoulder from the lower back, lengthening the lower back in order to send the shoulder forward. To use whole body power, you must be sure to first turn the left fist up and turn back, then bring the forearm across and hook and cover while pulling back. This ensures that both fists are moving from the power of the shoulders and elbows, and working together.

Sparrow Hawk Wheels Over

Moving the weight back and forth must come by using the waist as a fulcrum, so that the whole body remains coordinated. When the torso turns left and the weight shifts leftward to send the left drill out, the torso needs to reach forward slightly. When the weight shifts back and the torso turns right, transfer power from the waist to the shoulders, from the shoulders to the elbows, and from the elbows to the hands, so that the right forearm first slices upward, then the elbow pulls back. Bend the left arm to lift the elbow, stabbing the fist down to slide along the leg as it twists, being sure to keep the shoulders closed. Use a twisting power to circle the right fist down to the waist. The shoulder needs to open, close, and settle.

During the drop stance the weight should be completely on the right leg, which is fully bent to a full squat. The left fist slides down and forward along the top of the left leg, and must go past the left foot. Press the head forward into the movement, moving the centre of gravity forward. The left shoulder should open out and settle down so that the left fist can rotate fully with the fist eye up. Settle the elbow and bend it slightly, so that the left arm has a forward and upward scooping power as it moves forward with a twisting, drilling power.

- Older players do not need to sit right down into the drop stance, but the same power should be maintained in the hands. As the body turns the power should lengthen. The waist and shoulder action is key, so that the arms move together with the waist and the power is complete without slackness, soft but not loose, with a hidden power and no stiffness.

Moving from *sparrow hawk wheels over* to *sparrow hawk folds its wings,* the power should be smooth so that the movement is coordinated.

Second Sparrow Hawk method

Sparrow Hawk Grabs a Sparrow, Sparrow Hawk Spreads its Wings

- Although the two sparrow hawk forms differ in techniques, they should both show the spirit of the sparrow hawk.

The hands must circle into *sparrow hawk grabs a sparrow,* transfering power from the waist to the shoulders, from the shoulders to the elbows, and from the elbows to the hands. The rear foot should step through as the lead hand braces and the rear hand threads forward. The lead hand should have a bracing power forward and up with an upward and outward blocking power. Keep the arm bent so that the forearm and outer edge of the palm have power. As the rear hand stabs forward it needs a twisting, rolling, drilling power, and as it chops forward and down it first circles up a half circle so that it turns, drops, tucks, and pulls back with the forward step.

The action of *sparrow hawk spreads its wings* first closes down then opens out, which means that the power first gathers then launches. To roll in, close the chest and open the upper back, releasing tension in the shoulders and settling the elbows, closing in without telegraphing your intent. When bracing out, be sure to first turn the elbows up, then spread the chest and firm the abdomen, release the shoulders and brace outward with equal power in the right and left hands. The power is completed as you settle into the stance, with equal placement and power right and left, up and down.

BREATHING CYCLE FOR THE SPARROW HAWK MODEL

In general, inhale during transitional actions and exhale for the final power launch of each movement.

- Inhale during *sparrow hawk tucks its wings* and exhale during *sparrow hawk enters the woods.*

- Inhale in the initial action of *sparrow hawk pierces the sky* and exhale for the final action.

- Inhale in the dropping action of *sparrow hawk wheels over* and exhale for the rising action. Settle the breath into the belly to launch power.

- Inhale during the initial actions of *sparrow hawk grasps its prey* and exhale for the final grab.

- Inhale during the initial action of *sparrow hawk spreads its wings* and exhale for the final action.

PRACTICAL APPLICATIONS FOR THE SPARROW HAWK MODEL

- Practice and power application in forms differ considerably as to how you might apply the techniques. You can't expect to apply a move without changing it, and must be ready to react to anything that the opponent does. Forms are a means of practising techniques but do not expect to use the techniques in the theoretical 'model method' that you have practised.

Sparrow hawk tucks its wings and *sparrow hawk enters the woods* are one technique – an *aligned stance cannon punch* that uses a turned body to enter. The lead hand deflects so that the rear hand can get in to punch. The footwork should drive directly into the opponent's groin, hitting as you enter.

Sparrow hawk pierces the sky is a drilling punch to the nose. You need to get inside the opponent's defenses to strike upwards, so must step in to get the body close. The drill hides an elbow strike.

Sparrow hawk wheels over is either a way to hit as you turn around, or a feint up and strike down. You don't need to drop all the way down, because a large movement is slow and you must move quickly to be effective. "The only thing that cannot be beaten is speed." The cover and drill is a feint, and the lower strike is the real strike. You can step forward or back, depending on what is needed.

Sparrow hawk grasps its prey is a double handed aligned stance pull that changes into an entry with a push and stab. This softens the opponent and then you charge in for a strike to the chest.

Sparrow hawk spreads its wings uses one forearm to knock aside and the other arm to cover and roll down to make the opponent lose effectiveness. As your hands drop down and forward they can get in to strike the opponent's belly. You can also use the rear forearm to cover the opponent's arm and slide along it to strike crossways to his neck or throat. One is a low strike, and one is a crosscut to the throat; use what would work as the opportunity presents.

THE POEM ABOUT THE SPARROW HAWK

鹞子入林侧身攻，翻身顾后逞其能。展翅捉雀形贯意，劲力浑厚体均衡。

Sparrow hawk enters the woods attacks with the body turned sideways.

Wheel the body deals with things behind it, flaunting its great ability.

Spread the wings and *grasp the sparrow* have full intent throughout,

The power is dense and the body is balanced.

NINE: SNAKE MODEL 蛇形

INTRODUCTION TO THE SNAKE MODEL, *SHE XING*

The snake is a reptile that, although it has no legs, is known for its speed, agility, instantaneous reaction time, and whole body liveliness. Xingyiquan masters of old examined the movements and spirit of the snake to create the snake form. They created the rich, expansive, and beautiful techniques of the snake form by imitating its imposing look of a snake when it holds itself erect, its ferocity when it spits its tongue, its litheness at slithering through the grass, and its ability to coil around. We should show the skills and attitude of the snake when we practise: the litheness of a snake's body, its ability to bend and lengthen, its ability to encircle and coil, its softness and hardness, its overall ease of movement. If you hit its head then its tail will react, if you hit its tail then its head will react, if you hit its body then its tail and head will react together.

METHODS OF PERFORMING THE SNAKE MODEL

There are two traditional ways of performing the snake model. One is comprised of three movements: *white snake spits its tongue, white snake coils its body,* and *white snake slithers through the grass.* The other emphasizes the scooping lift. Both use Xingyiquan's zigzag stepping pattern, as if following the line of a slithering snake.

9.1   METHOD ONE OF THE SNAKE MODEL

Start from left *santishi.*

9.1a   White Snake Spits its Tongue[26]   báishé tù xìn   白蛇吐信

ACTION: Withdraw the left foot a half-step and lower the left hand to the belly. (no photo) Advance the left foot a half-step to the right with the foot turned out, shifting forward. Thread the left hand up to the sternum and forward to eye height, palm up. Do not move the right hand yet. Look at the left hand. (image 5.195)

5.195

9.1b   White Snake Coils its Body   báishé chán shēn   白蛇缠身

ACTION 1: Turn the left hand over, palm down, and circle it down and back to behind the left hip. Circle the right hand right and up to above the head. Keep both elbows bent. Rise, turning slightly leftward. Look at the left hand. (image 5.196)

ACTION 2: Stab the right hand directly down to outside the left hip, palm out. Thread the left hand in front of the right shoulder, palm up, tucking the left elbow into the chest. Twist the waist leftward and squat down into a resting stance, lifting the right heel. Look at the right hand at first, and as you sit down, look to the forward right. Press the head up. Sit onto the right heel. (image 5.197)

---

[26] Translator's note: in movement names, a snake's forked tongue is sometimes written 芯, but it is usually written 信. The two are pronounced the same, and neither really mean a forked tongue. The character 信 is more common.

9.1c   White Snake Slithers through the Grass   báishé bō cǎo   白蛇拨草

ACTION 1: Advance the left foot a half-step and take a long step to the forward

right with the right foot, following in with the left foot a half-step. Slice the right hand rightwards and upwards to waist height with the thumb web up and the fingers forward. Pull the left hand back to the left hip, palm down. Sit the torso down, settling the weight between the feet. Look at the right hand. (images 5.198 and front)

9.1d   White Snake Spits its Tongue   báishé tù xìn   白蛇吐信

ACTION: Sit back onto the left leg and withdraw the right foot a half-step. Bring the right hand back to the belly without pausing. Advance the right foot a half-step to the forward left with the foot turned out, shifting forward. Thread the right hand up by the sternum and forward to eye height. Do not move the left hand yet. Look at the right hand. (image 5.199)

- Continue on to left and right with the same action, alternating sides.

Pointers

    o   As the left foot advances it should circle and turn out. The left hand should pull back and then thread up to coordinate with the footwork.

    o   Twist the body and sit in coordination with the right palm stab down.

    o   Step the right foot forward to coordinate with the right scooping slice.

9.1e   Snake Turn Around   shé xíng huíshēn   蛇形回身

ACTION 1: If you finish on the <u>right</u> side *white snake slithers through the grass*, then stand up, swinging the left hand forward and up (fingers forward, little finger side up) until the hands form a line on either side of the body. Pivot around a full one-eighty degrees on the feet. Look forward. (image 5.200)

ACTION 2: The arms have swung so that they form a straight line with the right up and the left down. Twist the body and sit down into a resting stance, stabbing the right hand down outside the left hip, palm out, and circling the left hand up to the right shoulder, palm up. First watch the right hand as the hands move, then look to the forward left as soon as you sit down. (images 5.201, 5.202)

- The *snake form turn around* is simply *white snake coils its body*, done while pivoting. Left and right sides are similar, just transposing right and left.

9.1f   Snake Closing Move   shé xíng shōushì   蛇形收势

Continue on until you arrive where you started.

- From a <u>left</u> side *white snake slithers through the grass* stance:

Bring the left foot back beside the right foot. Cover and press down the left hand to the belly. Then lift both hands up, bring them together and turn them down, pressing down. Stand up and close.

- From a <u>right</u> side *white snake slithers through the grass* stance:

Bring the right foot back. Cover and press down the right hand to the belly. Then lift both hands up, bring them together and turn them down, pressing down. Stand up and close.

9.2   SECOND METHOD OF THE SNAKE MODEL

Start from left *santishi*.

9.2a   Snake on Right Side   shé xíng yòu shì   蛇形右势

ACTION 1: Advance the left foot a half-step, shift to the left leg, and bring the right foot in to touch the toes down, with the knee bent and the heel off the ground. Stab the right hand down from the belly to the left, palm out, fingers down, back of the hand adhering to the left hip. Bend the left elbow and bring the left hand to in front of the right shoulder, palm in, fingers forward. Look past the right shoulder. (image 5.203)

ACTION 2: Take a long step to the forward right with the right foot and follow in a half-step with the left foot, putting most weight on the left leg. Clench both fists and slice the right fist to the right and up to waist height, fist eye up. Pull the left fist back to beside the left hip. Drop the torso and lean forward slightly. Look at the right fist. (image 5.204)

5.203

5.204

9.2b   Snake on Left Side   shé xíng zuǒ shì   蛇形左势

ACTION 1: Advance the right foot a half-step and shift onto the right leg, bringing the left foot in to touch the ball on the ground, heel up and knee bent so that the left heel is behind the right foot. Unclench the hands and stab the left hand down by the right hip, palm out and fingers down. Bend the right elbow and close the arm so that the hand is in front of the left shoulder, palm in, fingers up. Look in front of the left shoulder. (image 5.205)

ACTION 2: Take a long diagonal step to the forward left with the left foot and follow in a half-step with the right foot, putting most weight on the right leg. Clench the hands and slice the left fist left and up to waist height, fist eye up. Pull the right fist back to outside the right hip. Drop the body and lean forward. Look at the left fist. (image 5.206)

5.205

5.206

Pointers

- Advance the left foot and stab the right hand down simultaneously. Pay attention to twisting the waist and closing the shoulders.

- Step the right foot forward and slice the right hand up with fully connected power. The same goes for the other side.

9.2c   Snake Turn Around   shé xíng huí shēn   蛇形回身

- If you arrive at the end of the space on the <u>left</u> side *white snake slithers through the grass,*

ACTION 1: Hook-in step the left foot to outside the right foot so that the body turns around to the right two-seventy degrees. Lift the right foot, touching the toes down and shifting onto the left leg. Unclench the hands and stab the right hand down by the left hip. As the body turns around, bend the left elbow to hold the hand in front of the right shoulder.

ACTION 2: Advance the right foot diagonally and slice the right fist up.

- Turning from the <u>right</u> side is the same, just transposing left and right.

PROBLEMS OFTEN MET IN THE SNAKE MODEL

Method One of Snake Model

PROBLEM 1: The student does not thread the hand up during *white snake spits its tongue*, but simply takes the hand across then carries on.

CORRECTIONS: Reinforce the correct movement pattern from the beginning. The hand must first thread through with the ulnar side turned over as much as possible. Then, to continue on, the hand will rotate palm down, and only then continue on to *coil around*.

PROBLEM 2: The student is unstable in the squatting position of *white snake coils its body*.

CORRECTIONS: There are three main causes of loss of balance. A: The centre of gravity is not under control. B: the lead foot is not turned out enough in the resting stance. C: the torso leans forward too far. Watch for these tendencies in the student. Remind the student to lift the head up to maintain a centered torso.

The head is the 'leader of the six *yangs*,' that is to say, if the head is upright then the torso will be straight. Pressing the head up will place the torso on the correct line and keep it centered, thus keeping the weight under control.

For the resting stance, remind the student to turn the lead foot out and keep it flat on the ground to gain stability. In this stance the buttocks should sit all the way down, the waist should be bent, the chest contained, and the upper back tight, but the head should always press upwards.

PROBLEM 3: The student slices the arm up too high during *white snake slithers through the grass*.

CORRECTIONS: The arm must come through no higher than the waist and no lower than the knee. The scooping slice is a strike to the groin.

PROBLEM 4: The student straightens his arm during *slither through the grass*.

CORRECTIONS: Have the student maintain a settled shoulder and elbow, which will help to maintain a bent elbow.

Method Two of Snake Model

PROBLEM 1: The student remains too straight during the step forward, stab down and thread up action.

CORRECTIONS: The student must experiment with what are the characteristics of the snake form. He must use the body, setting the shoulder into the direction that the scooping slice will be done, closing the shoulders and twisting the waist.

PROBLEM 2: The student straightens the arm during the scooping slice.

CORRECTIONS: The classics say, "too straight gives less force, too bent gives less reach." A certain angle is needed in the elbow to put force into the slice, so the shoulder should be extended and the elbow settled.

PROBLEM 3: The student drags the hip when doing the follow-in step.

CORRECTIONS: Leaving the hip behind during the step is a common error in Xingyiquan footwork. Usually it is caused by the rear foot turning out, which in turn turns out the knee. This prevents you from closing the groin, and makes the next driving step difficult to do, so it must be corrected. When practising footwork, have the student first bring the knee forward and only then complete the follow-in step with the foot. Pay attention that the foot is turned at less than a forty-five degree angle, so that the knee tracks straight. Only in this position can the leg push off strongly into the ground, and can the groin remain closed.

POWER GENERATION FOR THE SNAKE MODEL

Method One of Snake Model

- Although there are three actions, there is only one technique. There should be no obvious break between the actions, especially between *spitting the tongue* and *coiling the body*.

White snake spits its tongue: The left hand should thread up as the left foot lands, turned out. The left hand should pull back as the left foot withdraws. Hands and feet always work together. Pay attention to keep the fingers together as the left hand threads up, turning into the ulnar edge to roll the elbow in.

White snake coils its body: As the arms open and swing up, press the head up and rise in the torso. Then as the hands thread and stab, gathering in, squat down fully into the legs. The body technique is to first rise and open, and then drop and fold in. When you open you must open fully, and when you fold in you should shut down completely. When moving, pay attention that the right hand has a rolling in power as it drops into the stab – the palm should have a twisting power, twisting into the stab. The left hand should have a twisting, rolling, drilling power as it threads up. The shoulders and abdomen should close in and the torso bend, closing the chest, so that the whole body tucks and twists as you squat and stab with the hands.

White snake slithers through the grass: The right hand must complete the scooping slice as the right foot lands. Sit the torso down slightly to launch power, dropping into the buttocks, by tucking in the rear knee and stabbing it down. The shoulders move up and down, so coordinate the power launch through the shoulders, combining this with an exhalation to help gain more power. You must practise to find how to coordinate the shoulder and buttocks actions.

White snake coils its body is the preparatory action and *white snake slithers through the grass* is the launching action. You should try to find this power of shooting a spring in your practice. When coiling, you want to coil the spring tightly, pressing it down to store power. When going through the grass you want to suddenly shoot the spring out. You shoot out using all directions – forward and backward, left and right, inside and outside. This is a high quality power launch, using whole body power.

During the *snake turn around,* be sure to first rise, pivot on both feet, and then drop and stab. Raise the body high and drop tightly.

Method Two of Snake Model

- This method of doing snake is appropriate for older players, as it uses a fairly high, less difficult stance.

The hands and feet must be coordinated – as the lead foot advances one hand stabs down and the other threads up. The stabbing down hand gets its power from the turning of the waist, closing of the shoulders, rotating of the arm, and rolling in of the hip. The hand that threads up gets its power from a rolling in of the arm with a drill. The arms should be tightly held in front of the chest, so you need to contain the chest, tighten the upper back, press the head up, relax tension in the hips, and sit into the buttocks.

The slice must come as the foot lands. The rear foot must come through nearby the lead foot as it advances. The power is the same as *white snake slithers through the grass* explained above, the only difference is the use of the fist instead of the palm.

The *turn around* for this snake method is different from the first, so be sure to take a good hook-in step, hooking well in. When turning, press the head up. The rotation should be around the spine, and must be quick, so be sure not to move around too much. Keep the whole body coordinated.

- Keep the elbows appropriately bent during the stabbing and slicing actions. Never over-straighten the arms.

- The vital element of the snake model is the advancing scooping slice. You must find how to use the power from the body by sitting down into the action in order to have a strong shoveling, lifting, slicing action into the arm.

BREATHING CYCLE FOR THE SNAKE MODEL

First, work on the correct line of action of the hands and feet. Get every part of the technique correct and coordinate the hands and feet, without worrying about the breathing. Concentrate on the biomechanical action. Once the action is smooth, then you can concentrate on the power flow and the whole body power. Exhalation can then help you get more power into the strike.

- Inhale in rising actions and opening actions.

- Exhale in dropping actions and closing-in actions. Exhale sharply in power launching actions. Work carefully to coordinate the breathing closely with the actions of the snake form.

PRACTICAL APPLICATIONS FOR THE SNAKE MODEL

White snake spits its tongue is a threading strike to the face, and hides a hooking grab. If the opponent blocks with his hands, then you can turn over to hook onto his hand. If he doesn't block, then you thread directly to his eyes. This is not a heavy hit, but a quick stab to the eyes can throw him off and give your following attack a better chance at getting in.

White snake coils its body is a small, compact movement when used, although it is practised as a large movement. Draw a large circle with the hands in practice, but tighten this down to really use it. Dodge the head out of the way and hook onto the opponent's hand with your lead hand. You may also get in a shoulder strike during this action.

White snake slithers through the grass is a scooping throw, or a slice to the groin. One hand can block up and then pull down. When you step in you can shove with the shoulder or you can strike into the groin with your arm or hand. The key is to drive the footwork to enter through the opponent's main door.

- Although there are a variety of ways to perform snake form, almost all finish with the scooping strike. Each variation gives you a different application. You must learn to react and change techniques according to the situation, so the main thing you are practising is the way to use power throughout your body, so that you can use your power when and as you need.

Do not practice as if the technique is set in stone. If you train empty movements then your training is dead; if you train the power within the forms then your training is lively.

THE POEM ABOUT THE SNAKE

蛇形身法贵屈伸，头闪肩撞藏在心。进步攫挑腰膀力，周身内外劲衡均。

The body technique of the snake is to flex and extend.

Dodge the head and hide the technique of a shoulder shove.

Enter with the footwork to shovel and scoop, using the strength of the back into the arm,

Using an even balance of inner and outer power throughout the whole body.

TEN: WEDGE-TAILED HAWK MODEL

鸟台 形

INTRODUCTION TO THE WEDGE-TAILED HAWK MODEL, *TAI XING*

The classics say, "tai bird[27] has a direct nature, it has the ability to raise its tail

---

[27] Author's note: The character for 'tai' is sometimes written with a bird radical and sometimes with a fish radical. Both are pronounced 'tai.' Although they are pronounced the same, the meaning of the character is changed considerably with the different radicals, as one flies and the other swims. Within Xingyiquan, though, however the character is written, the form is performed much the same way. [Translator's. note: many typesets lack the bird radical character, so this is why it is often typed incorrectly. I had to put together two

straight up, it flies straight up then drops straight down onto its prey. Its innate skill is to lift its tail and fly up past the clouds, and then it can drop straight to grab its prey with its talons. So we copy its form to rise and fall like lightening, to use the tail, to change like the wind. Outwardly it is fierce, inwardly it is soft. It has an indescribable skill."

The action of the wedge-tailed hawk model[28] is to cross the hands in front of the body, open them to the sides, and then strike forward simultaneously. It emphasizes bringing the power from the tailbone, getting the power of the whole body into the arms. It uses Xingyiquan's zigzag stepping pattern, and the strike is forward and down.

METHOD OF PERFORMING THE WEDGE-TAILED HAWK MODEL

10   STANDARD WEDGE-TAILED HAWK MODEL   tāi xíng 鸟台 形

Start from left *santishi*.

10a   Wedge-tailed Hawk, Left   tāi xíng zuǒ shì   鸟台 形左势

ACTION 1: Advance the left foot a half-step and clench the fists, pulling the left fist back to the belly. Turn both fist hearts inward and keep them tight to the belly. Press the head up and look forward. (image 5.207)

ACTION 2: Take a long step forward with the right foot and follow in with the left foot to inside the right ankle without touching down. Drill the fists up to eyebrow height, fist hearts in, crossing the forearms in front of the chest, left inside the right. Turn the fists, open out to right and left, and circle back down to the sides of the body, fist hearts up. Press the head up and look straight ahead to the forward left. (images 5.208, 5.209, 5.210)

characters to make the bird radical character as it is not in the computer program.]
[28] Translator's note: This is also translated as 'Chinese ostrich,' 'phoenix,' and 'mythical tai bird' but I prefer wedge-tailed hawk, as this hawk does exactly this action with its talons, wings, and tail to catch rabbits, which are about the same size as it.

ACTION 3: Take a long step with the left foot to the forward left and follow in a half-step with the right foot, keeping most weight on the right leg. Punch both fists to the lower front at belly height, fist hearts up. Keep the arms slightly bent, and the fists about a fist-width apart. Press the head up and look past the fists. (images 5.211 and front)

5.211

5.211 FRONT

10b   **Wedge-tailed Hawk, Right**   tāi xíng yòu shì   鸟台 形右势

ACTION 1: Advance the left foot a half-step and bring the right foot up to the left ankle without touching down, keeping the toes up. Cross the fists and drill up with fist hearts in, right fist outside the left fist. Drill up to eyebrow height and then open to either side. Circle around and down to the sides, turning the fist hearts up. Press the head up and look to the forward right. (images 5.212, 5.213)

ACTION 2: Take a long step with the right foot to the forward right and follow in a half-step with the left foot, keeping the weight on the left leg. Punch to the forward right with the fist hearts up. Keep the arms slightly bent and the fists about a fist-width apart. Press the head up, settle the shoulders, and look past the fists. (image 5.214)

5.212   5.213   5.214

10c   **Wedge-tailed Hawk, Left**   tāi xíng zuǒ shì   鸟台 形左势

- This is the same as the *wedge-tailed hawk, right* described above in 10b, just transposing left and right.

Pointers:

- Complete the circle of the fists down to the sides as the lead foot advances.
- Complete the punch as the rear foot steps through and lands, so that the punch arrives with the foot.

10d   Wedge-tailed Hawk Turn Around   tāi xíng huí shēn   鸟台 形回身

If starting from *wedge-tailed hawk, left*:

ACTION 1: Step the left foot around to the outside of the right foot, hooking in, turning the body around two-seventy degrees to the right and sitting onto the left leg, lifting the right foot to the left ankle without touching down. Cross the fists and drill up, fist hearts in. On drilling up to eyebrow height, open them and circle down to the sides, fists hearts up. Press the head up and look to the forward right. (image 5.215)

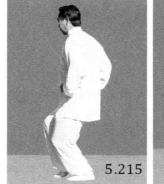

ACTION 2: Step the right foot to the forward right and follow in a half-step with the left, keeping the weight on the left leg. Punch forward and down to belly height with both fists, fist hearts up. The fists are fist-width apart. Press the head up and look past the fists. (image 5.216)

10e   Wedge-tailed Hawk Closing Move   tāi xíng shōushì   鸟台 形收势

Continue until you reach your starting point and turn around.

ACTION 1: If you are in a *left side wedge-tailed hawk*, turn the body forty-five degrees to the right and bring the right fist back to the belly. As the body turns, circle the left fist up and rightward, to cover and press down with the forearm across, fist heart down. Bring the left foot in beside the right foot, drill the right fist up and forward and press and pull the left fist back to the belly. Press the head up and look forward.

ACTION 2: Step the left foot straight forward without moving the right foot. Do a split with the left hand to settle into left *santishi*. Then close the same as usual from *santishi*.

- If you are in a *right side wedge-tailed hawk*, bring the right foot in and cover with the left forearm, drilling up with the right fist. Then step the left foot forward and split with the left hand to settle into left *santishi*, closing as usual.

PROBLEMS OFTEN MET IN THE WEDGE-TAILED HAWK MODEL

PROBLEM 1: The student shrugs his shoulders when drilling up and circling.

> CORRECTIONS: Always be careful to keep the shoulders and elbows settled. Shrugging the shoulders not only breaks the basic positional requirements of most martial arts, it also causes problems of *qi* flow. The *qi* floats in the chest, causing the body to be light and the legs to be unsteady. The way to solve this problem is to concentrate on releasing tension in the shoulder muscles and settling them down, tautening the upper back muscles, while always maintaining a straight and upright head. The student must learn to feel the release in the shoulder joints and the settling down.

PROBLEM 2: The student circles the hands in front of the body instead of bringing them back to the waist before punching forward. This gives a short distance for the punch, and can cause the punch to turn into a poke.

CORRECTIONS: The student must correct the line drawn by the fists, to take them out and down to either side of the waist. He should pay attention to opening the elbows and drawing them back slightly. Then, for the punch, forcefully squeeze the elbows into the ribs and shove them forward, sending the fists forward in a strong punch.

PROBLEM 3: The student leaves too much distance between the fists in the punch.

CORRECTIONS: If the fists are too far apart then they could miss the target, and the power will not be compact. The student must practice getting a fist width – about ten centimetres – between the fists.

POWER GENERATION FOR THE WEDGE-TAILED HAWK MODEL

As the fists rise and cross they need to have drilling power. As the fists reach head height they turn out. At this point the torso should settle, the chest close, and the upper back stretch. When the fists circle to the sides the arms should have a bracing out power. The arms are rounded with slightly bent elbows. When the fists are lowered to the sides, the torso should lengthen slightly and the arms should have a rolling-in power. The fists must draw vertical circles at the sides, and at each instant during the circle there must be a full power; there must be no slackening off at any time.

The footwork to practise the form is a zigzag pattern. There should be no pause halfway through the stepping action.

The fists circle to the sides as the lead foot takes a half-step forward. The fists punch as the rear foot comes through to land.

As the fists circle and drop and the arms roll in, the head should press forward and up and the waist should straighten slightly. The shoulders should open, the chest should expand, and the abdomen should become firm. At this point the torso may rise slightly.

The punch comes as the foot lands. The fists should be tightly clenched with the fist hearts aligned flat. Press the head up, settle the shoulders down, and sit into the buttocks. The fists must continue to twist, as the punch depends on the arms squeezing the elbows into the ribs to send the fists forward. Exhale to launch power to send the fists out; the elbows follow, and the shoulders urge forward. Grab the ground with the foot as it lands.

To turn around the hook-in step needs to hook well in, the body needs to get around quickly and remain stable.

BREATHING CYCLE FOR THE WEDGE-TAILED HAWK MODEL

- Inhale as the arms circle around. Take a long breath in.

- Exhale to punch. Use a short and powerful breath out.

PRACTICAL APPLICATIONS FOR THE WEDGE-TAILED HAWK MODEL

The drill up and circle is a defensive move. You can stick to the opponent's arm and roll through to enter. You should draw a large circle in practice, but when really using it, a small circle is more effective.

The double punch is to between the waist and belly. This is a short punch, thrown when the body is in close, so you need to step in through the 'main door.' If you can get the body in close then you can get the punch in, landing the punch as the foot lands.

- The main technique of the wedge-tailed hawk form is to get in close with the body. The main attacking action is the double punch just below the waist with the fist hearts up. You can hit with one or both fists, and you can hit to the floating ribs.

THE POEM ABOUT THE WEDGE-TAILED HAWK

展翅升空上下飞，双拳直捣纵步追。拳势贯在均衡劲，四梢相齐显其威。

Spread the wings and soar in the sky, flying up and down.

Double fists strike straight, chasing with a direct step.

The value of the technique is in its even balanced power.

Its might lies in the four tips working together.

ELEVEN: EAGLE MODEL 鹰形

INTRODUCTION TO THE EAGLE MODEL, *YING XING*

The eagle, a bird of prey with a hooked beak, a short neck, and feathery feet with long talons, has a fierce nature. Xingyiquan's eagle form borrows its skill at grasping prey, so the hand shape is called an eagle claw. When practising you should feel the eagle soaring in the wilderness, circling slowly with open wings, then suddenly spotting its prey, tucking the wings and dropping, grabbing it in its talons and then taking it to its beak. There is nothing the prey can do to escape this ferocity. The eagle form is traditionally also called 'eagle clutching.' The most important aspect is to drop into the grab with the head up and the eyes spirited like an eagle.

METHODS OF PERFORMING THE EAGLE MODEL

The eagle grab is done either in a reverse stance [opposite hand and foot forward] or an aligned stance [same hand and foot forward]. The hand technique and power application is the same, only the footwork differs.

11.1 METHOD ONE: REVERSE STANCE EAGLE

àobù yīng xíng   拗步鹰形

Start from left *santishi*.

11.1a   Eagle in Left Reverse Stance   zuǒ àobù yīng xíng   左拗步鹰形

ACTION 1: Clench the left fist and pull it back to the belly. Clench the right hand at the belly. Withdraw the left foot to in front of the right foot and shift onto the right leg. Drill the left fist up by the sternum and forward to nose height, twisting the ulnar edge over. Press the head up and look past the left fist. (image 5.217)

ACTION 2: Take a long diagonal step to the forward left with the left foot and follow in a half-step with the right foot, shifting forward to place the weight between the legs. Drill the right fist up by the sternum then along inside of the left forearm. Once the fists cross then unclench them, turning the palms down. Pull the left hand back to the belly and chop the right hand forward to waist height. The direction of the strike is aligned along a line drawn midway between the feet. Press the head up, settle the shoulders and elbows, and look at the right hand. (images 5.218 and 5.218 front)

5.217

5.218

5.218 FRONT

11.1b   Eagle in Right Reverse Stance   yòu àobù yīng xíng   右拗步鹰形

ACTION 1: Advance the left foot a half-step and lift the right foot inside the left ankle. Clench the right hand and pull it back to the belly, then drill it up by the sternum and forward to nose height, twisting the ulnar edge up. Look past the right fist. (image 5.219)

ACTION 2: Take a long diagonal step with the right foot to the forward right and follow in the left foot a half-step, shifting the weight forward to between the legs. Bend the left knee and press it down. Drill the left fist up by the sternum then along inside the right forearm until the fists cross. Then unclench the hands and turn the palms down. Pull the right hand back to the belly and split forward and down with the left hand to waist height. Release tension in the shoulders and settle the elbows. Keep the left arm slightly bent. Press the head up and look at the left hand. (image 5.220)

5.219

5.220

11.1c   Eagle in Left Reverse Stance   zuǒ àobù yīng xíng   左拗步鹰形

ACTION 1: Advance the right foot a half-step and lift the left foot inside the right foot. Clench the left hand and pull it back to the belly, then drill it up by the sternum and up to nose height, turning the ulnar edge up. Look at the left fist.

ACTION 2: Take a long step to the forward left with the left foot and follow in a half-step with the right foot, shifting the weight forward between the legs. Drill the right fist up by the sternum then along the left forearm, and when the fists cross, unclench them both and turn the palms down. Pull the left hand back to the belly and split forward and down to waist height with the right hand. Settle the shoulders and elbows, keep the right arm slightly bent, press the head up, and look at the right hand.

Pointers

- o   Pull the left fist back and drill forward timed exactly with the withdrawal of the left foot.

- o   Land the left foot and the right hand split at exactly the same time. Be sure to press the head up as you look down, turning only the eyes down.

- o   Right and left sides are the same action, just transposing right and left.

11.1d   Eagle Turn Around   yīng xíng huíshēn   鹰形回身

Starting with the *right reverse stance eagle grab* (right foot and left hand forward).

ACTION 1: Hook-in the right foot in front of the left foot, shifting onto the right leg. Lift the left foot and turn around to the left to face back in the way from which you came. Clench the left hand and pull it back to the belly, then drill it up by the sternum and forward to nose height, twisting the ulnar edge up. Do not move the right fist. (image 5.221)

ACTION 2: Step the left foot diagonally to the forward left and follow in a half-step with the right foot. Open the right hand and slide it along the left forearm to split forward and down to waist height. Look at the right hand. (image 5.222)

5.221

5.222

- •   Turning in the other direction is the same, just transposing right and left.

Pointers

- o   You must hook-step in and turn around quickly. Be sure to maintain stability as you lift the other foot to ankle height.

- o   The split in the turn around is the same as the normal eagle grabbing.

11.1e   Eagle Closing Move   yīng xíng shōushì   鷹形收势

Once you get back to the starting point, turn around to face in the same direction as the opening position.

- From _left_ reverse stance eagle grab

ACTION 1: Withdraw the left foot to beside the right foot. Clench the right fist and pull it back to the belly then drill it up to nose height, ulnar edge twisted up. Look at the right fist.

ACTION 2: Advance the left foot a half-step directly forward and split forward with the left hand to settle into a left _santishi_. Close as usual from _santishi_.

- From _right_ reverse stance eagle grab

ACTION 1: Withdraw the right foot to beside the left foot and shift to the right leg. Clench the left fist and pull it back to the belly. Clench the right fist and drill it up by the sternum, then forward to nose height, twisting the ulnar edge up. Look at the right fist.

ACTION 2: Advance the left foot a half-step directly forward without moving the right foot, to settle into a left _santishi_. Split the left hand forward and pull the right hand back to the belly. Press the head up and look straight ahead. Close as usual from _santishi_.

11.2   SECOND METHOD: ALIGNED STANCE EAGLE

shùnbù yīng xíng   顺步鹰形

Start from left _santishi_.

11.2a   Eagle in Right Aligned Stance   yòu shùnbù yīng xíng   右顺步鹰形

ACTION 1: First withdraw the left foot a bit, then advance it a half-step, following in with the right foot to inside the left ankle. Clench the left fist and pull it back to the belly, then drill it up by the sternum and forward to nose height, ulnar edge twisted up. Look at the left hand. (image 5.223)

ACTION 2: Take a long step forward with the right foot and follow in a half-step with the left foot. Drill the right fist up by the sternum then forward along the left forearm. When the fists cross, unclench the hand and turn the palms down, splitting forcefully out with the right hand at waist height and pulling the left hand back to the belly. Press the head up, release through the shoulders and settle the elbows. Look at the right hand. (image 5.224)

5.223

5.224

11.2b   Eagle in Left Aligned Stance   zuǒ shùnbù yīng xíng   左顺步鹰形

ACTION 1: First withdraw the right foot a bit then advance a half-step, following in with the left foot just inside the right ankle. Clench the right hand and pull it back to the belly, then drill it up by the sternum and forward to nose height, ulnar edge twisted up. Look at the right fist. (image 5.225)

ACTION 2: Take a long step forward with the left foot and follow in a half-step with the right foot. Drill the left fist up by the sternum then forward along the right forearm. When the fists cross, unclench the hands and turn the palms down. Split forcefully out with the left hand at waist height and pull the right hand back to the belly. Press the head up, release through the shoulders and settle the elbows. Look at the left hand. (image 5.226)

Pointers

- ○ All the pointers are the same as the *reverse stance eagle*. Only the footwork differs.

11.2c   Aligned Stance Eagle Turn Around and Closing

shùnbù yīng xíng zhuànshēn hé shōushì   顺步鹰形转身和收势

- The turn around is the same as the turn of split, only the splitting action is lower than in split, and the hands are held in an eagle claw shape.

- Closing is the same as that of split.

PROBLEMS OFTEN MET IN THE EAGLE MODEL

PROBLEM 1: The student does not use the eagle claw.

CORRECTIONS: Some people do not use the eagle claw, and there is nothing wrong with this. The eagle claw does, however, better bring out the spirit of the eagle.

PROBLEM 2: The student does not have a strong scissoring action in the legs in *reverse stance eagle*.

CORRECTIONS: The student must bring in the foot from the hip. First land the lead foot, then bring in the rear foot a half step by rolling the hip, closing the knee, and bringing in the foot. The head must be pressed up and the buttocks must sit down, so that there is a raking power between the feet. The rear foot pushes through the heel. With these actions there will be a good scissoring strength between the legs.

PROBLEM 3: The student does not have a whole body power in the landing of the split.

CORRECTIONS: The first thing is to have the student understand what whole body power is. When using power, each segment throughout the whole body must be integrated to a high degree, using the mind. The student must practise each movement such that once one segment moves there is nothing in the body that does not move in total integrated coordination. Use this method: first collect the *qi* and settle down, then move from the root to the tips, sequentially connecting and transferring power. In this way the student can gradually collect his dispersed power to make it whole, and eventually reach the goal of emitting power into the tips.

PROBLEM 4: The student drops his head and bends at the waist to look at the lead hand that is at waist height.

CORRECTIONS: Dropping the head and bending over at the waist is a major error in most martial art styles. The student must press up into the head in the final position and keep the spine of the upper back straight, sitting into the buttocks. As the hand chops down the head presses up to counterbalance. Never let the student bend the back or stick out the buttocks.

POWER GENERATION FOR THE EAGLE MODEL

The hand shape differs from the usual hand shapes in that it is held in an eagle claw. The thumb web is stretched open, the thumb opening strongly, and the other fingers are separated slightly. The last and middle joints of the fingers are bent. The palm is concave, and the wrist sits slightly.

The lead hand grabs and pulls back as the lead foot withdraws slightly. Then the lead foot advances a half-step as the lead hand drills forward. Both hands must split downward as the foot lands.

• The footwork of the *reverse stance eagle* advances in a zigzag pattern, and that of the *aligned stance eagle* advances in a straight line.

Once the hand has clenched and pulled back it should not hesitate, but drill directly up. The foot should also not hesitate once it withdraws, but should immediately advance. The lower back should straighten and the torso should lengthen as the fist drills up. Then when the hands drop down to the chest, the abdomen should close and the torso should press forward slightly, dropping the lead shoulder and lifting the rear shoulder slightly. The elbows should settle down and stay bent so that the palms can press down. The wrist should be slightly cocked, the fingers bent, and the palm held concave.

The head must maintain a vertical line by pressing up while the eyes look down. The legs must have a scissoring power with the knees closing in, the rear knee driving down, the rear heel slightly off the ground. Twist the waist, roll in the hips, close the knees, and coordinate this with the splitting action of the hands to launch power.

• Although *reverse stance eagle* advances in a zigzag pattern, the hands draw a straight line with an imaginary line down the midline of the feet.

• To get the turn of *aligned stance eagle* the foot must hook in considerably. The body must turn around quickly, and the foot must hook in as the fist drills forward. Help maintain body stability by pressing up into the head.

BREATHING CYCLE FOR THE EAGLE MODEL

Always practise with a clear rhythm, distinguishing between action and stillness, and do not rush the movements. Follow your breathing pattern to do each move one at a time, keeping the body balanced and keeping your power full, so that breathing is smooth.

- Inhale as the fist drills up.

- Exhale as the hands split down.

PRACTICAL APPLICATIONS FOR THE EAGLE MODEL

The eagle model has two alternate foot placements for the same technique – either reverse stance or aligned stance. The aligned stance can move in from outside or inside. The key in either case is to get the body in close, as that is the only way to take the opponent out.

- The drill up can take care of an attack, so can be thought of as the defensive move, but it can also be used as an attack.

- Always protect your midline; take charge of the midline; rush the midline.

Xingyiquan classics say, "never send out a fist without results, never bring it back without taking an opportunity." After you've drilled up then you can open the hand for a grab, pull, hook, or controlling technique. If you can grab clothes then grab clothes, otherwise grab the 'meat.' Once you've controlled the opponent's arm then enter and press him down, striking his chest or belly with the other hand.

Drilling both fists up as the lead foot enters both defends the centre and shoves into the opponent. Get the body in tight to shove, hitting with the entire torso, taking over the main door, always attacking the midline. The main door is the space between the opponent's feet, the midline is the opponent's centre, and is the part of the opponent's body that you want to hurt.

THE POEM ABOUT THE EAGLE

鹰形练时爪似钩，起钻落翻拗顺走。拧腰裹胯坐臀力，精神气力功为首。

When training eagle model the hands should be like hooks.

Drill as they rise and turn as they land; stepping either into reverse stance or aligned stance.

Twist the waist and roll in the hips, sitting the buttocks down to get strength.

Deep skill lies in the spirit, *qi*, and strength.

TWELVE: BEAR MODEL 熊形

INTRODUCTION TO THE BEAR MODEL, *XIONG XING*

The bear is a ferocious animal. It appears slow in nature but is unyielding. It has the strength of shaking the body and shoulders, the ability to stand erect right up into the neck, and a natural stance with a lively lower back and relaxed shoulders. So Xingyiquan uses this shape and intent in the techniques. The intent behind your moves is to react like a bear. The bear lives in the wilds, it ambles along slowly with relaxed and soft shoulder girdle and back. It gathers its food in a leisurely way, calmly and peaceably. But, should it meet an attack, it is quick to anger, and shakes its whole body, spreads its forelegs and stands straight up, raises its head and slaps with its paws. It charges forward and doesn't relent until its enemy is dead.

The Xingyiquan classics talk of 'chicken legs, dragon body, bear arms, and tiger head.' This describes the key to the position and function of each body segment. Chicken legs describes the how to stand on one leg and move quickly. Dragon body describes how to use the waist effectively by flexing and extending. Bear arms describes how to relax and settle the shoulder girdle. Tiger head describes how to have a fierce spirit, putting fear into the opponent.

You must pay attention in bear model to charge in with the footwork to get the body in, pressing up the head with a straight neck. The hands guard and shield the centre, completely controlling the centre.

METHOD OF PERFORMING THE BEAR MODEL

Start from left *santishi*.

12a   Black Bear Leaves its Den   hēixióng chūdòng   黑熊出洞

ACTION: Advance the left foot a half-step with the toes hooked in slightly, and follow in the right foot a half-step with ball of the foot on the ground, the heel slightly raised. Bend the right knee, shift the weight forward mostly onto the left leg, and lean forward slightly. Clench both fists and press the left forearm across the body to cover and take the fist down to the belly, fist heart down. Drill the right fist up by the sternum and out inside the left fist, ulnar edge turned out, fist at nose height. Press the head up, tuck the jaw in, and look at the right fist. (images 5.227 and front)

5.227

5.227 FRONT

12b   Old Bear Shoves from its Shoulder   lǎoxióng zhuàng bǎng   老熊撞膀

ACTION: Advance the left foot a half-step and step the right foot forward a long step, following in with the left foot. Shift forward so most weight is on the right leg. Bend the right elbow to bring the right fist to the left chest, fist heart down. Slice forward and up to block with the left forearm outside the right arm, unclenching and taking the hand to the left shoulder, the left palm supporting the right fist surface. As the right foot lands, lift the right elbow and strike forward with the tip. Press the hands together and use the right elbow and Shoulder to butt forward. Look past the right elbow. (image 5.228)

12c   Black Bear Leaves its Den   hēixióng chūdòng   黑熊出洞

ACTION: Advance the right foot a half-step with the foot hooked in slightly. Follow in a half-step with left foot, touching the ball of the foot down with the heel raised. Bend the left knee downward, shift forward onto the right leg and lean slightly forward. Bring the right forearm across the body, fist heart down, to cover and press down, pulling the fist back to the belly. Drill the left fist out from in front of the chest, forward and up inside the right forearm to nose height, fist heart in, ulnar edge turned up. Press the head up, tuck the chin in, and look at the left fist. (image 5.229)

12d   Old Bear Shoves from its Shoulder   lǎoxióng zhuàng bǎng   老熊撞膀

ACTION: Advance the right foot a half-step and step the left foot forward a long step, following in a half-step with the right foot. Shift the weight forward to the left leg. Drill the right fist up outside the left forearm to slice up to nose height, then pull it back in front of the right chest, unclenching. Bend the left elbow and bring the fist back in front of the chest. Lift the left elbow and bring it on line. Press the right palm into the left fist surface, and press the hands together to strike with the left elbow as the left foot steps forward. Shift forward to butt with the left arm. Look past the left elbow. (image 5.230)

• Continue on alternating right and left sides as many times as you have space and energy to do.

Pointers

   o   Be sure to shift forward as you advance the left foot, and to drill the right fist through as you step.

- o The forward step of the right foot should be long and quick, and land as the right elbow butts forward.

- o The entire sequence must link together smoothly.

12e   Bear Turn Around   xióng xíng huíshēn shì   熊形回身势

From the <u>left</u> side *old bear shoves from its shoulder*.

ACTION 1: Step the right foot forward, hooking in outside the left foot and shifting onto the right leg. Turn the body around to the left to face the way in which you came. Lift the left foot to inside the right ankle without touching down. As you turn around, turn the right palm up and thread up, stab the left fist down to the left; press the head up, and look at the right hand. After you have turned, look at the left fist. (image 5.231)

ACTION 2: Take a long step straight forward with the left foot, hooking the toes in. Follow in a half-step with the right foot, landing on the ball with the heel lifted and the knee bent. Shift the weight forward towards the left leg and lean forward slightly. Lift the left fist as the body turns, to cross the forearm and press down, fist heart down, pulling it back to the belly, fist heart on the belly. After the right hand drills up, as the body turns, clench the fist and bring it down to the right waist, then, as the left foot steps forward, drill the right fist forward and up inside the left arm, to nose height, fist heart in, ulnar edge turned up. Press the head up and look at the right fist. (image 5.232)

5.231   5.232

- The *turn around* from the right side is similar, just transposing right and left.

Pointers

- o You must take a good hook-in step and get around quickly. It is the rear foot that comes forward to do the hook-in step.

- o As you do the hook-in step thread both hands – one threading the forearm and one stabbing back, keeping the whole body coordinated.

12f   Bear Closing Move   xióng xíng shōushì   熊形收势

- On arriving at the starting place and turning around into the <u>left</u> side *old bear shoves from its shoulder*.

ACTION 1: Step the right foot forward and stamp it just beside the left foot. Quickly lift the left foot, no higher than the right ankle. Backfist forward and up with the left fist to nose height, then, without stopping, turn the fist over, hook and pull back to the belly, fist heart down. Lower the right hand, clinching it and drill up by the sternum then forward to nose height, ulnar edge twisted up. Press the head up and look at the right fist.

ACTION 2: Step the left foot forward without moving the right foot, slide the left hand along the right forearm and split to shoulder height with the palm down, pulling the right hand back to the belly, to settle into a *santishi*. Press the head up and look at the left hand.

- On arriving at the starting place and turning into the <u>right</u> side *old bear shoves from its shoulder*.

ACTION: Step the left foot forward without moving the right foot, to sit into a *santi* stance. Circle the right fist up and forward, with the peak of the fist forward and fist heart in. Slide the left hand along the right forearm to split forward at shoulder height, and unclench the right hand, turning it in and pulling it back to the belly. Press the head up and look at the left hand.

- Complete the *closing move* the same as usual from left *santishi*.

PROBLEMS OFTEN MET IN THE BEAR MODEL

PROBLEM 1: The student does not straighten the neck properly, tilting the head up to look forward instead.

CORRECTIONS: Remind the student to tuck the chin in and think of butting forward and up with the head. The proper body position will also help – the chest contained and the upper back stretched, the torso leaning forward slightly. The eyes must look up at the fist without tilting the head up. The head should be slightly dropped while the eyes are raised to look forward.

PROBLEM 2: The student bends the elbow too much or straightens it too much during *black bear leaves its den*.

CORRECTIONS: The student should bend the elbow to about ninety to one hundred degrees as he drills up. The angle should be more acute than that of a normal *drilling punch*.

PROBLEM 3: The student does too small a movement into the elbow strike of *old bear shoves from its shoulder*, resulting in a stiff shove.

CORRECTIONS: This results from not giving enough consideration to the body technique of gathering and releasing, which is dependant on an easy moving shoulder girdle. After the rear fist drill up it pulls back to butt the elbow forward. At this time the waist must be supple and the shoulder must turn back slightly. After that, you can step forward and butt with the elbow. In this way the elbow strike can be strong because it uses the full power of a shoulder strike.

POWER GENERATION FOR THE BEAR MODEL

- The key to power in all the actions of the bear model is to press the head forward and up while pressing the torso slightly forward. The classics say, "The bear has the strength of holding its neck straight, the power of cutting across its shoulder girdle, and the ferocity of charging out of its den." The body technique should show the strength of straightening the neck and the ferocity of a wild animal protecting its den.

During *black bear leaves its den,* three actions must be done simultaneously to have full power: the lead foot advances, the lead fist covers and presses, and the rear fist drills out. The head must press forward and up and the body must charge forward, pushing strongly off the rear foot. As the fist drills up the shoulder must first pull back slightly and then close in forward. This small shoulder movement must be coordinated with a turning of the waist and closing of the chest. The upper arm must adhere tightly to the ribs so that as the fist drills out the shoulder moves forward with a butting, shoving power. Butt simultaneously with four parts: the shoulder, elbow, fist, and head.

During *black bear leaves its den,* the lead foot should be turned in slightly as it advances. This rolls the knee in slightly. The rear foot should lift the heel, stabbing the rear knee down. The buttocks should be tucked in and the hips rolled in as well, so there is a closing power between the knees.

Old bear shoves from its shoulder is not a shoulder or an upper arm shove, but is an elbow strike. The elbow should strike as the rear foot lands forward. Since an elbow strike is a short range technique the weight must shift forward. This shift must not be overdone, however, but should be held within the forward third of the stance. To butt with the elbow, the shoulder should first close then open, showing an intention to shove with the shoulder. First lift the elbow and then – as the rear hand assists the front fist, giving a combined force from the hands – lengthen the spine, extend the shoulder, and step into the hit so that the elbow can strike strongly forward.

BREATHING CYCLE FOR THE BEAR MODEL

- Inhale during all gathering movement.

- Exhale during all advancing power launching movements – while drilling up and while butting with the elbow.

In general, use the technique of a long inhale and a short exhale to help store and release power and develop whole body power.

PRACTICAL APPLICATIONS FOR THE BEAR MODEL

- The bear model uses a strong charging attitude and power. It charges in to strike with the shoulder or elbow, so the body should lean a bit into the action to help. Since the head then is slightly forward, be sure to protect the head with both hands.

Black bear leaves its den uses the lead hand to press down and knock aside an opponent's punch. You can then advance and get in a drilling punch to the opponent's chest, jaw, or nose. Be sure to charge into the opponent's groin or past his feet, getting the body in as closely as possible. This technique will not work if you do not get the body in.

The butt uses the rear hand to block up or pull away the opponent's arm, then you can advance and strike with the elbow to the chest or ribs. The key is quick footwork, getting the body in close very quickly.

Once you have got in close for the elbow strike, there is a hidden backfist. You can quickly snap out a backfist to the opponent's face. The backfist isn't a strong hit but it can throw him off and allow you another opportunity to continue your attack.

THE POEM ABOUT THE BEAR

熊形出洞守护能，竖项钻打欺身用。排手冲步顶肘去，得机得势定输赢。

The bear charges out of its den with the ability to protect.

It straightens its neck, drills a hit, and intimidates.

It slaps and charges in to strike with its elbows.

It takes advantage of every opportunity so will certainly win.

THIRTEEN: EAGLE AND BEAR COMBINED

鹰熊合演

INTRODUCTION TO THE EAGLE AND BEAR COMBINED, *YING XIONG HE YAN*

The eagle and bear models each traditionally have their own individual practice, and, although there are differences between methods, they are basically very similar. The *eagle and bear combined* is another widespread traditional method of practice. The animals are combined this way because the pair rhymes with *yingxiong* – hero – which expresses the spirit of the practice. The essence of eagle is the grasping, and that of bear is the uprightness, so combining them combines their strengths.

METHOD OF PERFORMING THE EAGLE AND BEAR COMBINED

Start from left *santishi*.

13a   **Left Reverse Stance Eagle**   zuǒ àobù yīng xíng   左拗步鹰形

ACTION: This is the same as the *left reverse stance eagle* described above in the eagle model.

13b   **Black Bear Leaves its Den**   hēixióng chūdòng   黑熊出洞

ACTION: Clench the right hand and pull it back to the belly. Advance the left foot a half-step straight forward, the foot hooked in slightly, and follow in a bit with the right foot, raising the heel and bending the knee. Drill the right fist up by the sternum and forward to nose height, fist heart in, ulnar edge up. Lean forward slightly, press the head up, and look at the right fist.

13c   **Right Reverse Stance Eagle**   yòu àobù yīng xíng   右拗步鹰形

ACTION: This is the same as the *right reverse stance eagle* described above.

13d   **Black Bear Leaves its Den**   hēixióng chūdòng   黑熊出洞

ACTION: This is the same as move 13b described above, just transposing right and left.

Pointers

- o All the movement requirements and the use of power are the same as eagle model and bear model when practised separately. It is just the transitions that differ, so you need to concentrate on understanding the transitional actions.

- o The lead foot should advance as the rear fist comes through to drill forward.

13e   Eagle and Bear Turn Around   yīng xióng héliàn huíshēn   鹰熊合练回身

Turn around when you arrive at eagle grabs. The description is given starting from the _left reverse stance eagle._

ACTION 1: Lift the left foot and hook-out step directly forward. Step the right foot forward, hooking in just in front of the left toes, shifting onto the right leg. Lift the left foot to by the right ankle. Bring the right hand around with the body turn, circling left, up, right, and down, to finish at the waist. While the right hand draws its circle, circle the left hand down, left and up to nose height, then cover across the body with the left forearm at shoulder height. Look at the right hand as it circles, then when it pulls back to the waist, turn the head to look at the left hand. (image 5.233)

ACTION 2: Take a step forward with the left foot and follow in a bit with the right foot, lifting the heel and bending the knee. Finish the left forearm cover and pull the fist back to the belly. Drill the right fist up by the sternum and forward to nose height, ulnar edge turned up. Press the head forward and up, tuck in the chin, and look past the right fist. (image 5.234)

5.233

5.234

- Turning the other way is similar, just transposing left and right.

13f   Eagle and Bear Closing Move   yīng xióng héliàn shōushì   收势

- This is the same as _eagle closing move._

POWER GENERATION FOR THE EAGLE AND BEAR COMBINED

The key to connecting _eagle grasp_ to _black bear leaves its den_ is the driving forward foot. The foot charges straight forward with the foot turned in slightly and the weight shifts forward. As the hand pulls back to the belly the head should press up, the shoulders settle down, and the waist lengthen. When the fist drills forward the waist should turn, the chest close in, so that the fist leads, the elbow follows, and the shoulder urges forward. Keep focused on the shoulder girdle/upper arm and elbow, so that the drilling fist is backed up by a butting power from the shoulder.

- The *turn around* changes from *eagle grabs* to *black bear leaves its den*, so be sure to first do a hook-out and then a hook-in step. The hands need to draw their own circles in a coordinated way, balancing the up/down and left/right, so that the power is evenly expressed.

PRACTICAL APPLICATIONS FOR THE EAGLE AND BEAR COMBINED

See the explanations in the sections on the eagle model and the bear model.

THE POEM ABOUT THE EAGLE AND BEAR

鹰熊斗智，取法为拳。阴阳暗合，形意之源。

The eagle and bear fight wisely.

Their techniques were taken to make a fighting style

In which *Yin* and *Yang* secretly combine.

This is the source of Xingyi.

SOLO BAREHAND FORMS

THE EIGHT MOVES 八势

INTRODUCTION TO THE EIGHT MOVES, *BA SHI*

The Eight Moves is another short traditional form, usually learned after the Five Elements Connected. Similar to the Five Elements Connected, there are seventeen movements in one direction, and then the movements repeat on the way back. It contains the five elements, the sparrow-hawk, chicken and horse from the twelve animals, and some additional moves such as *dragon and tiger play together*, *white crane flashes its wings*, and *wheel around and pound*.

Why is it called The Eight Moves? You could say because it adds three animals to the five elements. But if you look at it from a structural point of view, in terms of power flow, there are eight key combinations. The first is *sparrow hawk folds its wings* and *sparrow hawk enters the woods*; the second is the *single horse*; the third is the *retreating crosscut, golden rooster drinks water*, and *golden rooster pecks a grain of rice*; the fourth is *retreat and restrain* and *aligned stance pounding punch*; the fifth is *left crosscut, dragon and tiger play together*, and *aligned stance punch*; the sixth is *withdraw elbow cover, aligned stance pounding punch*, and *white crane flashes its wings*; the seventh is *wheel around and pound*; and the eighth is *sparrow hawk pierces the sky* and *sparrow hawk wheels over*. The name makes sense in terms of the overall construction, the flow of power, and the applications contained in the form.

The footwork of The Eight Moves has a distinctive characteristic. When you use a withdrawing step to change the stance, the weight shift must be quick. *Retreat and restrain*, in particular, shifts back to the left foot so that the right foot is able to step forward quickly. Also, when withdrawing the foot for the elbow cover after *aligned stance left punch,* as soon as the left foot withdraws, the weight shifts to the left leg so that the right foot can step forward quickly and easily. The shifting between the feet helps you to initiate an attack.

The rhythm of the form is focussed on the power launch of the eight key combinations. At each point of power launch, first store power and then launch it. Power must be full, stable, and complete. Pay attention to the bodywork, always storing power before launching: pre-load back to launch forward, pre-load right to launch left. The power launch should be hard and ferocious, and the spirit should be powerful.

NAMES OF THE MOVEMENTS

1. Opening Move (left *santishi*)
2. Sparrow Hawk Folds Its Wings
3. Sparrow Hawk Enters The Woods
4. Reverse Stance Right Horse
5. Retreating Left Crosscut
6. Right Splitting Strike
7. Golden Rooster Drinks Water
8. Golden Rooster Pecks A Grain Of Rice
9. Retreat And Restrain
10. Right Aligned Stance Cannon, or Pounding Punch
11. Advance Left Crosscut
12. Dragon And Tiger Play Together
13. Left Aligned Stance Drive, or Crushing punch
14. Right Aligned Stance Cannon, or Pounding Punch
15. White Crane Flashes Its Wings
16. Wheel Around And Pound
17. Sparrow Hawk Pierces The Sky
18. Sparrow Hawk Wheels Over
     (The following moves are a repetition back in the returning direction)
19. Sparrow Hawk Folds Its Wings
20. Sparrow Hawk Enters The Woods
21. Reverse Stance Right Horse
22. Retreating Left Crosscut
23. Right Splitting Strike
24. Golden Rooster Drinks Water
25. Golden Rooster Pecks A Grain Of Rice
26. Retreat And Restrain
27. Right Aligned Stance Cannon, or Pounding Punch
28. Advance Left Crosscut
29. Dragon And Tiger Play Together
30. Left Aligned Stance Drive, or Crushing Punch
31. Right Aligned Stance Cannon, or Pounding Punch
32. White Crane Flashes Its Wings
33. Wheel Around And Pound
34. Sparrow Hawk Pierces The Sky
35. Sparrow Hawk Wheels Over
     (The following moves are the closing section)
36. Sparrow Hawk Folds Its Wings

37.   Sparrow Hawk Enters the Woods

38.   Turn Around With A Left Elbow Strike

39.   Right Aligned Stance Crosscut

40.   Three Basins Touch The Ground

41.   Retreat With A Left Splitting Strike

42.   Closing Move

Description of the Movements

1.   Opening Move (left *santishi*)   qǐ shì   起势

Start with *santishi*. Move into *santishi* as usual. (image 1.1)

See also Chapter Two for more detailed text and images on *santishi*.

2.   Sparrow Hawk Folds Its Wings   yàozǐ shùshēn   鹞子束身

ACTION: Shift forward onto the left leg and take a long step forward with the right foot, landing firmly with the knee slightly bent and the foot grabbing the ground. Bring the left foot to the right ankle without touching down. Clench both fists, pulling the left fist back to the belly and punching the right fist forward and down. The right fist finishes outside the left fist at belly height, fist surface down. Press the head up and look at the right fist. (image 1.2)

Pointers

o   The right foot and fist arrive simultaneously.

o   Take a long step forward, land firmly, and bring the left foot up quickly.

o   Keep the elbows protecting the ribs and keep the fists protecting the midline, like a sparrow hawk tucking in its wings and body.

3.   Sparrow Hawk Enters The Woods   yàozǐ rùlín   鹞子入林

ACTION: Advance the left foot a long step and follow in a half-step with the right foot to take a *santi* stance. Bend the right elbow to drill the fist up to eye height, fist heart in. Turn the trunk ninety degrees rightward. Punch the left fist out past the sternum, finishing at solar plexus height with the arm slightly bent and the fist eye up. Bring the right fist to the right temple, turning the fist heart forward as the body turns rightward, keeping the elbow down. Press the head up and look past the left fist. (image 1.3)

1.3

Pointers

- o The left punch should arrive simultaneously with the left foot.

- o Release the shoulders and drop the elbows, reaching forward into the left shoulder. Turn the waist and send the fist forward from the shoulder.

- o Be especially careful to keep the right elbow down.

4.   Reverse Stance Right Horse   àobù yòu mǎxíng   拗步右马形

ACTION: Advance the left foot a half-step and follow in the right foot, rubbing into the ground just behind the left heel. Bring the right fist from the head to strike forward to chest height with the wrist slightly hooked in and the fist heart down. Hook the left fist and press down, then pull back to in front of the right shoulder. Both arms are slightly bent. Press the head up and look past the right fist. (image 1.4)

1.4

Pointers

- o The right punch arrives simultaneously as the right foot rubs into the ground, so that the power is united.

- o First draw a small circle with the right fist and then punch forward, first pulling it back to send it forward. The right elbow is slightly higher than the shoulder and the arm is rounded. Be sure to reach forward with the shoulder, open the upper back and close the chest to issue power.

5.   Retreating Left Crosscut   tuìbù zuǒ héngquán   退步左横拳

ACTION 1: Withdraw the right foot a half-step and cut the right elbow in, rotating the fist heart up. Lower the left fist to the chest, turning the fist heart down. Look past the right fist. (image 1.5)

ACTION 2: Bring the left foot past the right foot then back to the left rear, landing with a thump and shifting the weight evenly between the feet. Slide the left fist along under the right arm to drill forward to a crosscut strike at shoulder height, fist heart turning up. Tuck the right fist over and press down, pulling back to

1.5

1.6

the waist. Press the head up and look past the left fist. (image 1.6)

Pointers

- o The right fist should complete the elbow cover as the right foot withdraws. The left fist should complete the crosscut as the left foot lands.

- o Be sure to first do a small pre-load forward with the body, to give power to the backward movement.

6.	**Right Splitting Strike**	yòu pīquán	右劈拳

ACTION: Advance the right foot a half-step straight forward and follow in with the left foot a half-step. Bring the right fist to the sternum, along the left arm, and then unclench the hand and split forward to chest height. Unclench the left hand and pull it back to the belly. Press the head up and look forward. (image 1.7)

Pointers

- o The right hand should complete the split as the right foot lands. Reach the right shoulder forward, keeping it released and the elbow down. Exhale and settle the *qi* to the *dantian* to put power into the strike.

7.	**Golden Rooster Drinks Water**	jīnjī zhuó shuǐ	金鸡啄水

ACTION 1: Withdraw the right foot to in front of the left foot, lifting the knee with the foot hooked up at the belly of the calf. Stand firmly on the left leg, keeping the knee bent. Clench the right hand and bring the fist back to the belly, then drill it up by the sternum and mouth to eyebrow height. Clench the left hand and lift it to the chest. Look at the right fist. (image 1.8)

ACTION 2: Land the right foot with a thump and lift the left foot at the right ankle. Bend the right leg to lower the body. Drill the left fist up along the right arm, then unclench it and split forward and down to chest height. Unclench the right hand and pull it down to the right hip, palm down. Press the head up and look forward. (image 1.9)

Pointers

- o Coordinate the hands with the action of the right foot. Complete both the pull back and the drill up with the right hand as the right foot withdraws. Split down with the left hand as the right foot lands with a thump.

    o   The right foot should thump with a settled, powerful feeling. The lower back should be firm, with the buttocks tucked in, and the head pressed up. Release the tension in the shoulders to reach forward, and settle the elbows. The whole body must be stable.

8.   **Golden Rooster Pecks A Grain Of Rice**   jīnjī shí mǐ   金鸡食米

ACTION: Advance the left foot a long step and follow in the right foot with a rubbing step to land with a thump just at the left heel. Clench the right fist to punch forward to chest height. Set the left hand on the right wrist. Press the head up and look past the right fist. (image 1.10)

1.10

Pointers

    o   The left foot must take a long step forward. The right punch hits as the right foot lands.

9.   **Retreat And Restrain**   tuìbù lēiquán   退步勒拳

ACTION 1: Retreat the right foot a half-step. Place the left palm over the right fist and circle the hands, keeping them connected. Circle and turn the right fist over, first turning underneath the left hand and finishing above it, fist heart up. The left hand finishes palm up. Look at the right fist. (image 1.11)

ACTION 2: Withdraw the left foot to land beside the right foot, immediately shifting onto the left leg. Pull the hands back forcefully into the belly. Press the head up and look forward. (image 1.12)

Pointers

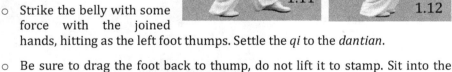

1.11

1.12

    o   Strike the belly with some force with the joined hands, hitting as the left foot thumps. Settle the *qi* to the *dantian*.

    o   Be sure to drag the foot back to thump, do not lift it to stamp. Sit into the buttocks, draw in the hips, pull the leg, and thump with the foot.

10.   **Right Aligned Stance Cannon, or Pounding Punch**

     yòu shùnbù pàoquán   右顺步炮拳

ACTION: Take a long step forward with the right foot and follow in a half-step with the left foot. Clench the left fist and drill it up by the sternum to the mouth, then drill it forward and up to nose height. Lift the right fist to the chest, then, as the right foot steps forward and the body turns leftward, punch it forward to chest height, fist eye up. Turn the left fist and pull it back so the fist eye faces the left temple. Keep the left elbow down. Look past the right fist. (image 1.13)

1.13

Pointers

- o The right punch arrives as the right foot lands. Be sure to reach the right shoulder forward.

- o Drill and turn the left fist, do not block directly up. Use the turn of the body and the right shoulder to deflect with the left arm.

**11.		Advance Left Crosscut**			jìnbù zuǒ héngquán		进步左横拳

ACTION: Advance the right foot a half-step and follow in a half-step with the left foot, keeping most weight on the left leg. Lower the left fist to the chest then slide it forward under the right forearm, drilling and turning the fist heart up to complete a crosscut strike. Tuck, press down, and pull the right fist back to the belly. The left fist finishes at shoulder height with the left shoulder reaching forward. Press the head up and look past the left fist. (image 1.14)

1.14

Pointers

- o Use body technique to get power into the crosscut. First pull slightly back, then send the fist down and forward. Pay attention in every technique to use the principle of pre-loading the body prior to launching force.

- o The left crosscut should arrive as the right foot lands, and the legs should have a scissoring power between them. Tuck in the left knee, stabbing it down into the stance. Twist the waist and reach forward into the shoulder, tucking in the buttocks and pressing the head up. This creates a lengthening feeling, with power stretching up and down.

**12.		Dragon And Tiger Play Together**

		lóng hǔ xiāngjiāo		龙虎相交

ACTION: Advance the right foot a half-step and settle solidly onto the right leg. Then lift the left knee and kick forcefully forward with the heel to waist height. Punch the right fist straight forward to chest height with the fist eye up and the arm slightly bent. Pull the left fist back to the left side. Keep the right knee slightly bent. Press the head up and look forward. (image 1.15)

1.15

Pointers

- Be sure to punch and kick quickly, and at exactly the same time. Stand firmly on the right leg. The kicking knee extends fully with the foot pulled back to drive into the heel.

- Keep the trunk straight, be careful not to lean backwards, forwards or sideways.

- Pull the left fist back as the right fist punches, so that the action and force is complete and together.

13.   Left Aligned Stance Drive, or Crushing Punch

zuǒ shùnbù bēngquán   左顺步崩拳

ACTION: After completing the kick, land the left foot forward and follow in a half-step with the right foot, putting most weight on the right leg. Punch straight forward with the left fist to chest height, arm slightly bent and fist eye up. Pull the right fist back to the belly. Press the head up and look forward. (image 1.16)

Pointers

- Three actions are done as one: punch with the left fist, pull the right fist back, and land the left foot. Be sure to coordinate the left and right, up and down, and forward and backward forces.

14. Right Aligned Stance Cannon, or Pounding Punch

yòu shùnbù pàoquán   右顺步炮拳

ACTION 1: Withdraw the left foot to inside the right foot and land it, shifting immediately onto the left leg. Bend the left arm and do an elbow over in front of the chest turning the torso slightly rightward, then drill the left fist up to nose height. Do not move the right fist yet. (image 1.17)

ACTION 2: Take a long step forward with the right foot and follow in a half-step with the left foot. Turn the torso leftward and extend the right shoulder forward to punch the right fist forward with the fist eye up. Rotate the left fist and bring it back to the left temple, fist eye facing the temple and elbow hanging down. Press the head up and look past the right fist. (image 1.18)

Pointers

- o First tuck the left elbow in and then drill up with the left fist, combining the actions smoothly.

- o Do the elbow cover as the left foot withdraws. Punch the right fist as the right foot steps forward.

- o Be sure to shift immediately onto the left leg after the left foot withdraws. This is the only way that you can step the right foot forward smoothly and quickly.

15.   White Crane Flashes Its Wings   báihè liàngchì   白鹤亮翅

ACTION 1: Withdraw the left foot a half-step and sit into a horse stance. Lower the fists in front of the body to cross in front of the belly, then brace out. Then drill up to head height with the fist hearts in. Look at the right fist. (images 1.19, 1.20)

ACTION 2: Without moving the feet, rotate the fists so the fist hearts are out, and circle them to brace out to the sides, arms slightly bent. Look at the right fist. (image 1.21)

ACTION 3: Shift back to the left leg and withdraw the right foot to land with a thump beside the left foot. Bring the fists back to the belly, pulling in forcefully to strike the belly. Press the head up, settle the *qi* to the *dantian*, and look forward. (image 1.22)

Pointers

- o Sit down as the hands lower and then drill up. After the fists drill up to head height, rotate them to brace out to the sides. When circling them down, keep a wrapping power in the arms. When they pull back to the belly, keep a holding power.

- o The weight shifts first left, then right, and then left again. Pull the fists in to hit the belly as the right foot lands. Settle the *qi* to the *dantian* to help launch power forcefully.

    ○ The right foot should land with a thump, not a stamp. This is a raking and settling type of power that unites the whole body.

16.   Wheel Around And Pound   fānshēn pào   翻身炮

ACTION: Push off with both legs and turn one-eighty degrees rightward around in the air. Separate the feet in the air and land in a half-horse stance or a *santi* stance with the left foot forward. Drill the right fist up and bring it to the right temple as the body turns, fist eye in and elbow set down. Punch straight forward to chest height with the left fist, fist eye up. Keep the left arm slightly bent. Press the head up and look past the left fist. (images 1.23, 1.24)

Pointers

    ○ Push off and land equally with both legs at the same time. There must be no timing difference between them. Land with an opening power between the feet, pressing forward and back. That is, the rear foot presses forward and the lead foot presses back.

    ○ Complete the pounding punch simultaneously with the landing.

17.   Sparrow Hawk Pierces The Sky   yàozǐ zuān tiān   鹞子钻天

ACTION 1: Advance the left foot a half-step and follow in the right foot to the left ankle without touching down. Turn the left fist over to tuck in and press down with the fist heart down and the elbow slightly bent. Lower the right fist to the right side. Look at the left fist. (image 1.25)

ACTION 2: Take a long step forward with the right foot and follow in a half-step with the left foot. Drill the right fist up and forward to nose height, ulnar edge rotated up. Pull the left fist back to the belly. Press the head up and look forward. (image 1.26)

Pointers

    ○ Land the right drilling punch as the right foot lands. Exhale to put power into the punch.

18.   Sparrow Hawk Wheels Over   yàozǐ fānshēn   鷂子翻身

ACTION 1: Pivot the feet in place, turning around one-eighty leftward to face back along the line of the form. Rotate the thumb side of the right fist in and lift the elbow then, as the body turns, bring the fist forward and press down with the fist heart down. Drill the left fist up through the right arm to nose height, fist heart in.

At this point the weight is on the left leg and the right fist is pressing down in front of the belly. Look at the left fist. (images 1.27, 1.28)

ACTION 2: Lift the right fist with the forearm crossways, passing outside the left arm, to block up above the head. Press the left fist down and settle the elbow, pulling back to in front of the chest. Shift back onto the right leg.

Pull the right fist back to in front of the right shoulder. Lift the left elbow and rotate the thumb side in so that the fist eye is on the body, and slide it along the left ribs to stab down at the hip. Look at the left fist. (image 1.29)

ACTION 3: Squat down on the right leg and extend the left leg, to sit into a pouncing stance. Slide the left fist forward along the outside of the left leg, gradually turning the fist eye up. Pull the right fist back to beside the waist. Move the trunk forward as the left fist extends. Look at the left fist. (image 1.30)

Pointers

o   The leftward, rightward, and leftward rotation of the trunk must come from the waist, keeping the whole body together. The right fist covers and presses down as the left fist drills up. The right elbow blocks up as the left elbow settles and pulls in. The right fist pulls back as the left elbow lifts and the left fist lowers to stab forward.

o   Be sure to use the shoulders, rolling one closed and opening the other. Transfer power from the waist to the shoulders, from the shoulders to the elbows, and from the elbows to the hands.

o   The whole movement is done without a pause, as one coordinated action that moves upward and downward, leftward and rightward. Keep the spirit focussed and the power soft but not slack. The power in this move is hidden, not hard.

19.   Sparrow Hawk Folds Its Wings   yàozǐ shùshēn   鷂子束身

ACTION: Extend the left fist forward and shift forward onto the left leg, keeping the knee bent. Take a long step forward with the right foot and land with stability. Bring the left foot to the right ankle without touching down, pressing the legs together. Lift the right fist to the sternum then punch forward and down to groin height. Pull the left fist back to the belly. The arms are crossed, the right fist outside the left arm. The right fist eye is forward and the left fist heart is in. Press the head up and look forward. (image 1.31)

1.31

- The following moves, 20 to 37, are a repetition of the moves 3 through 19, and then move 3 again.

- In this way, all the moves repeat going back in the returning direction. The first section of the form goes out, and the second section comes back.

- Move 35 turns around again. Moves 36 and 37 repeat moves 2 and 3, in the original direction of the form.

- Moves 38 to 42 are the closing combination.

20.   Sparrow Hawk Enters The Woods

This movement is the same as move 3, going back in the returning direction. (image 1.32)

1.32

21.	**Reverse Stance Right Horse**	See move 4.
22.	**Retreating Left Crosscut**	See move 5.
23.	**Right Splitting Strike**	See move 6.
24.	**Golden Rooster Drinks Water**	See move 7.
25.	**Golden Rooster Pecks A Grain Of Rice**	See move 8.
26	**Retreat And Restrain**	See move 9.
27.	**Right Aligned Stance Cannon, or Pounding Punch**	See move 10.
28.	**Advance Left Crosscut**	See move 11.

29.	**Dragon And Tiger Play Together**	See move 12.
30.	**Left Aligned Stance Drive, or Crushing Punch**	See move 13.
31.	**Right Aligned Stance Cannon, or Pounding Punch**	See move 14.
32.	**White Crane Flashes Its Wings**	See move 15.
33.	**Wheel Around And Pound**	See move 16.
34.	**Sparrow Hawk Pierces The Sky**	See move 17.
35.	**Sparrow Hawk Wheels Over**	See move 18.

36.   Sparrow Hawk Folds Its Wings   See moves 2 and 19, going once again in the original direction.

37.   Sparrow Hawk Enters the Woods

This is the same as move 3, going once again in the same direction as at the beginning. (image 1.33)

38.   Turn Around With A Left Elbow Strike   huíshēn zuǒ dǐngzhǒu 回身左顶肘

ACTION: Retreat the left foot back and turn the body around one-eighty degrees to the left, pivoting on both feet. Pull the left fist back, bend the elbow to butt to the rear at shoulder height. The left fist finishes in front of the left shoulder, fist heart down. Lower the right fist in front of the left chest, fist heart down. Press the head up and look at the left elbow. Keep the body weight evenly between the feet. (image 1.34)

Pointers

- o Butt with the left elbow as the left foot lands and the body turns around. The point of focus is the tip of the elbow. Relax and reach forward with the shoulder.

39.   Right Aligned Stance Crosscut   yòu shùnbù héngquán   右顺步横拳

ACTION: Take a long step forward with the right foot and follow in a bit with the left foot. Do a crosscut with the right fist, hitting forward from under the left elbow, finishing fist heart up at shoulder height. Pull the left fist back to the belly. Press the head up and look at the right fist. (image 1.35)

1.35

Pointers

○ Complete the right crosscut as the right foot lands. First withdraw the trunk a bit, then strike. Settle the right shoulder down with a wrapping power. Twist and drill the right fist to complete a crosscut punch.

40.   Three Basins Touch The Ground   sānpán luòdì   三盘落地

ACTION: Bring the right fist leftward to cover with the elbow, unclenching the hand and circling it to outside the left shoulder. Follow the movement of the right hand with the eyes. Step the left foot behind the right foot, landing with the ball of the foot and turning the right foot across to take a scissors stance with the weight evenly distributed between the legs. Unclench the hands and brace out to both sides with the arms rounded and the palms down at hip height, thumb webs in. Release tension in the shoulders, press the head up, and look at the left hand. (images 1.36, 1.37)

1.36

1.37

Pointers

○ Gather power as the right elbow circles and covers, wrapping in the elbows and closing the chest. Launch power equally to both sides as the left foot steps back and the arms brace out.

41.   Retreat With A Left Splitting Strike   tuìbù zuǒ pīquán   退步左劈拳

ACTION 1: Retreat the right foot a step and shift onto the right leg, withdrawing the left foot to in front of the right foot. Clench both fists and drill the right fist up by the sternum and forward to nose height, ulnar edge twisted up. Pull the left fist back to the belly. Look at the right fist. (image 1.38)

1.38

ACTION 2: Advance the left foot a half-step without moving the right foot, to take a *santi* stance. Bring the left fist up to the sternum then out along the right arm, unclenching and splitting forward to chest height. Unclench the right hand and pull it back to the belly, palm down. Press the head up and look past the left hand. (image 1.39)

1.39

Pointers

- o Drill the right fist forward as the right foot retreats. Split the left hand forward as the left foot advances.

42.   Closing Move   shōu shì   收势

- The closing is the same as usual from *santishi*.

THE TWELVE GREAT PUNCHES 十二洪捶

INTRODUCTION TO THE TWELVE GREAT PUNCHES, *SHI'ER HONG CHUI*

The Twelve Great Punches is another traditional Xingyiquan form, and most branches of Xingyiquan have a version of it. Short but varied, with characteristic Xingyiquan movements, it is widely popular. It is a typical traditional form, containing the five elements and four of the twelve animals – sparrow hawk, tiger, snake, and chicken. And as is also typical, there is a repetition of movements out and back, with an additional repetition of movements combined with a closing combination. A characteristic of this form is that it starts with four *aligned stance crosscuts* to four directions, repeats them at the turn around, and then repeats them again at the end – for a total of twelve *aligned stance crosscuts*. This is why the form is often called the Twelve Crossing Punches[29] instead of the Twelve Great Punches.

NAMES OF THE MOVEMENTS

1.   Opening Move

2.   Left Drive, or Crushing Fist

3.   Right Aligned Stance Crosscut

4.   Turn Around With A Right Aligned Stance Crosscut

5.   Turn Around With A Right Elbow Strike

6.   Left Aligned Stance Crosscut

7.   Turn Around With A Left Aligned Stance Crosscut

---

[29] Translator's note: The sounds are similar enough for oral transmission to have confused the two. Twelve crossing punches form is shí èr héng chuí 十二横捶. Twelve great punches form is shí èr hóng chuí 十二洪捶.

8.   Turn Around, Withdraw With A Drive, or Crushing Punch

9.   Advance With A Right Drive, or Crushing Punch

10.   Retreat With A Left Drive, or Crushing Punch

11.   Right Aligned Stance Drive, or Crushing Punch

12.   White Crane Flashes Its Wings

13.   Left Cannon, or Pounding Punch

14.   Retreat And Restrain

15.   Sparrow Hawk Enters The Woods

16.   Step Forward, Tiger Carries

17.   Step Forward, Tiger Braces

18.   White Snake Spits Its Tongue

19.   White Snake Coils Its Body

20.   White Snake Slithers Through The Grass

21.   Thump, Golden Rooster Blocks Up

22.   Golden Rooster Heralds The Dawn

23.   Step Forward, Right Drill

24.   Sparrow Hawk Wheels Over

25.   Sparrow Hawk Folds Its Wings

26.   Sparrow Hawk Enters The Woods

27.   Right Aligned Stance Crosscut
      (the following moves are repetition back in the returning direction)

28.   Turn Around With A Right Aligned Stance Crosscut

29.   Turn Around With A Right Elbow Strike

30.   Left Aligned Stance Crosscut

31.   Turn Around With A Left Aligned Stance Crosscut

32.   Turn Around, Withdraw With A Drive, or Crushing Punch

33.   Advance With A Right Drive, or Crushing Punch

34.   Retreat With A Left Drive, or Crushing Punch

35.   Right Aligned Stance Drive, or Crushing Punch

36.   White Crane Flashes Its Wings

37.   Left Cannon, or Pounding Punch

38.   Retreat And Restrain

39.   Sparrow Hawk Enters The Woods

40.   Step Forward, Tiger Carries

41.   Step Forward, Tiger Braces

42.   White Snake Spits Its Tongue

43.   White Snake Coils Its Body

44.   White Snake Slithers Through The Grass

45.   Thump, Golden Rooster Blocks Up

46. Golden Rooster Heralds The Dawn

47. Step Forward, Right Drill

48. Sparrow Hawk Wheels Over

49. Sparrow Hawk Folds Its Wings

50. Sparrow Hawk Enters The Woods

51. Right Aligned Stance Crosscut

(the following moves are the closing section)

52. Turn Around With A Right Aligned Stance Crosscut

53. Turn Around With A Right Elbow Strike

54. Left Aligned Stance Crosscut

55. Turn Around With A Left Aligned Stance Crosscut

56. Turn Around, Withdraw With A Drive, or Crushing Punch

57. Advance With A Right Drive, or Crushing Punch

58. Retreat With A Left Drive, or Crushing Punch

59. Closing Move

Description of the Movements

1.   Opening Move   qǐ shì   起势

ACTION 1: Stand to attention with the feet together, facing ninety degrees to the line on which you will travel. Press the head up, keep the shoulders settled down, and let the arms hang naturally at the sides with the fingers together. Look straight ahead. Without moving the feet, gradually lift the hands at the sides to shoulder height, palms up and arms naturally bent. Look at the right hand. (image 1.40)

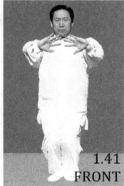

1.40

1.41
FRONT

ACTION 2: Bend the elbows so that the hands point to each other in front of the face, palms down. Lower the hands to shoulder height and turn the palms out, thumbs down, pushing forward at shoulder height. Sit down. Brace the arms out rounded, press the head up and look past the hands. (image 1.41, photo taken from the front)

Pointers

o   Turn the palms and push forward as you sit down. This action is soft and coordinated.

o   Keep the arms rounded as you push forward, settling the chest, releasing the shoulders, tautening the upper back slightly, pressing the head up, and focussing your attention.

2.   Left Drive, or Crushing Fist   zuǒ bēngquán   左崩拳

ACTION 1: Clench the hands and lower them to the waist, with the fist eyes up and fist hearts on the belly. Keep the elbows tight to the ribs. Turn the trunk slightly to the right and look forward. (image 1.42)

ACTION 2: Advance the left foot and follow in the right foot a half-step into a stance shorter than a *santi* stance. Punch the left fist forward to chest height with the fist eye up and the arm slightly bent. Keep the right fist at the waist. Press the head up and look at the left fist. (image 1.43)

Pointers

- When you lower the hands, circle the right hand in an arc.

- The left punch arrives as the left foot lands.

- Bring the right fist in to the waist as the left fist punches. Use the power of the lower back to send the left shoulder forward. Be sure to use body technique to set up the punch. Pre-load back to launch power forward into the punch.

3.   Right Aligned Stance Crosscut   yòu shùnbù héngquán   右顺步横拳

ACTION 1: Advance the left foot a half-step forward and follow in the right foot to inside the left ankle. Rotate the left fist heart up, tucking in the elbow slightly. Rotate the right fist heart down and thread it from the right side towards the left side. Look at the left fist. (image 1.44)

ACTION 2: Step the right foot a long diagonal step to the forward right and follow in the left foot a half-step, keeping most weight on the left leg. Slide the right fist along under the left arm to do a crosscut forward, turning the fist heart up at shoulder height. Rotate the left fist and pull it back to the belly, fist heart down. Press the head up and look past the right fist. (image 1.45)

Pointers

- Hit with the right crosscut as the right foot lands, coordinating the upper and lower segments of the body. Hit as the foot lands, breathing out to launch a fully integrated power.

○ Twist both fists to perform the crosscut. The left fist rotates the thumb side inward to tuck in and the right fist rotates the little finger side inward to drill out. The hands work together with equal and opposite power.

4.   Turn Around With A Right Aligned Stance Crosscut

huíshēn yòu shùnbù héngquán   回身右顺步横拳

ACTION 1: Hook-in step the right foot in front of the left toes, turning the body one-eighty degrees around to the left and shifting onto the right leg. Bend the right elbow and bring the fist to the waist, fist heart down. Stab the left fist to the rear, fist eye down. Look at the left fist. (image 1.46)

ACTION 2: Advance the left foot a half-step forward, shift the weight to the left leg and bring the right foot in to the left foot without touching down. As the body turns around, rotate the left arm to twist the fist heart up at shoulder height. (image 1.47)

ACTION 3: Take a long step forward with the right foot and follow in the left foot a half-step, to sit into a *santi* stance. Slide the right fist forward under the left arm then perform a crosscut, twisting the fist heart up at shoulder height. Tuck the left fist in, twisting the fist heart down, and pull it back to the belly. Press the head up and look at the right fist. (image 1.48)

Pointers

○ Complete the *turn around crosscut* as one continuous action, with no break in the movement or power flow.

○ The key to the movement is the turn, and the order of the actions for a smooth turn is: bend the right elbow and stab out the left fist as you hook-in the right foot; then turn around to the left, twisting the left arm and taking a half step with the left foot; only after that is completed should you step forward with the right foot and complete the right crosscut. Be sure to twist both fists by rotating the arms and the shoulders so that the power of the whole body is integrated.

5.   Turn Around With A Right Elbow Strike

huíshēn yòu dǐngzhǒu   回身右顶肘

ACTION: Step the right foot behind and pivot the left foot in place, turning the body ninety degrees around to the right, to finish in a half horse stance with most weight on the left leg. Rotate the thumb side of the right fist in, to tuck in at the chest with the fist heart down, and butt to the right with the elbow at shoulder height. Bring the left fist out under the right elbow to finish at the right ribs with

the fist heart down. Press the head up and look past the
right elbow. (image 1.49)

1.49

Pointers

- o Complete three actions as one unified movement:
     retreat the right foot, turn the body around to
     the right, and butt to the rear with the right
     elbow. Hit with the elbow as the right foot lands.

- o The left fist is hidden under the right elbow. This
     is a hidden strike and also protects the right ribs.
     An alternate name for this movement is *See the
     Punch Under the Elbow*.

6.   Left Aligned Stance Crosscut   zuǒ shùnbù héngquán   左顺步横拳

1.50

ACTION 1: Take a long step diagonally to the forward
left with the left foot and follow in a half-step with the
right foot. Rotate the left fist and hit forward with a
crosscut, fist heart turning up at shoulder height, arm
slightly bent. Pull the right fist back to the belly,
turning the fist heart down. Release tension in the
shoulders, settle the elbows down, press the head up,
and look at the left fist. (image 1.50)

Pointers

- o Hit simultaneously with the foot and fist,
     completing the left crosscut as the left foot
     lands.

- o Get power into the crosscut by turning from the lower back and reaching
     the shoulder forward, urging from the waist to the shoulder, from the
     shoulder to the elbow, and from the elbow to the fist. Rotate each segment
     as it moves forward, twisting and drilling into the crosscut.

7.   Turn Around With A Left Aligned Stance Crosscut

huíshēn zuǒ shùnbù héngquán   回身左顺步横拳

ACTION 1: Hook-in the left foot and pivot the right foot to turn the body around
one-eighty degrees to the right, shifting onto the left leg. Bend the left elbow to
bring the fist into the chest,
then the waist, fist heart
down. Bend the right elbow
to stab the fist out to the rear,
fist eye down. Shift onto the
right leg and bring the left
foot beside the right foot
without touching down. As
the body turns around,
rotate the right arm so that
the fist heart is up, at
shoulder height. Look at the

1.51

1.52

right fist. (images 1.51, 1.52)

ACTION 2: Take a long step forward with the left foot and follow in a half-step with the right foot, putting most weight on the right leg. Slide the left fist forward under the right arm to hit with a crosscut to shoulder height, ulnar edge twisted up to turn the fist heart up. Rotate and tuck the right fist down, pulling back to the belly, fist heart down and elbow tucking into the ribs. Press the head up and look at the left fist. (image 1.53)

Pointers

- This is the same as move 4, only on the opposite side.

8. Turn Around, Withdraw With A Drive, or Crushing Punch

zhuànshēn chèbù bēngquán   转身撤步崩拳

ACTION 1: Hook-in the left foot slightly to the right. Bend the left elbow and lift it, bringing the left fist to in front of the chest, then lowering it to the waist, twisting the fist heart up. Stab the right fist out from the right ribs towards the rear to chest height, rotating the thumb side inward to twist the fist heart up. At this point the weight is on the left leg. Look at the right fist. (image 1.54)

ACTION 2: Turn the body around ninety degrees to the right to face the right fist. Retreat the right foot behind the body and shift onto the right leg. Rotate the little finger side of the right fist in to turn the fist heart up and bend the elbow slightly, keeping the fist at chest height. Withdraw the left foot a half-step to in front of the right foot. Look at the right fist. (image 1.55)

ACTION 3: Advance the left foot a half-step and follow in the right foot slightly, with most weight on the right leg. Punch the left fist forward to chest height, elbow slightly bent and fist eye up. Pull the right fist back to the belly. Press the head up and look at the left fist. (image 1.56)

Pointers

- Complete the whole movement as one action.

- o Use the shoulders to coordinate and put power into the equal and opposite movement of the fists as the left fist comes in and the right fist stabs out. Tuck the right shoulder in to roll the arm in to stab to the rear. After the body has turned around, rotate the right fist, opening the right shoulder and settling into it to put power into the rotation of the arm. Both shoulders must stay settled and released so that the whole body power is integrated.

- o Punch with the left fist as the left foot lands.

9. Advance With A Right Drive, or Crushing Punch

jìnbù yòu bēngquán   进步右崩拳

ACTION: Advance the left foot and follow in the right foot to behind the left heel, landing with a thump and putting the weight on the right leg. Punch the right fist forward to chest height with the elbow slightly bent and the fist eye up. Pull the left fist back to the belly with the fist heart in. Press the head up and look at the right fist. (image 1.57)

Pointers

- o Three actions must happen simultaneously with integrated power: the right fist punches, the left fist pulls back, and the right foot lands.

- o The right foot follow-in step is done by rolling in the hips and closing in the knees. This brings the foot in. The foot must rake in with power, which makes a heavy thumping sound. Breathe out to put power into the move.

10. Retreat With A Left Drive, or Crushing Punch

tuìbù zuǒ bēngquán   退步左崩拳

ACTION: First retreat the right foot a half-step and shift back. Then retreat the left foot a step and place the whole foot on the ground, putting most weight on the left leg, withdrawing the right foot slightly and turning it out. Turn the trunk slightly rightward, press the thighs together, and bend the knees to sit into a scissors stance. Pull the right fist back to the right side, fist heart up. Punch the left fist forward to chest height, fist eye up. Press the head up and look at the left fist. (image 1.58)

Pointers

- o The left foot should land with a thump, raking into the ground as it retreats. Achieve the thump by coordinating the power: shift the weight back, lean the body to the rear, hit suddenly with the leg, and grasp the ground with the foot.

- o Three actions happen together: land the left foot, punch the left fist, and pull back the right fist. Put the power of the lower back and shoulder into the punch.

11. Right Aligned Stance Drive, or Crushing Punch

yòu shùnbù bēngquán　　右顺步崩拳

ACTION: Advance the right foot and follow in the left foot a half-step, putting most weight on the left leg. Pull the left fist back to the belly, fist heart in. Punch the right fist forward to solar plexus height, elbow slightly bent and fist eye up. Press the head up and look at the right fist. (image 1.59)

Pointers

1.59

○ Punch as the right foot lands, with exact timing. Put power into the punch by using the waist and shoulder and exhaling.

12. White Crane Flashes Its Wings　　báihè liàngchì　　白鹤亮翅

ACTION 1: Withdraw the left foot a half-step and sit into a horse stance. Bend the right elbow and rotate the thumb side of the fist out to circle across past the face to do an elbow cover leftward. Then lower the fists in front of the body to cross in front of the belly, and then brace out just above the knees, fist eyes down. Keep the arms rounded and look at the right fist. (image 1.60)

1.60

ACTION 2: Shift towards the left leg. Drill both fists up to eyebrow height, crossing the wrists with the fist hearts in. The left fist is inside the right. Look at the right fist. (image 1.61)

ACTION 3: Rotate the fists so the fist hearts are out, and circle them to brace out to the sides, arms slightly bent. Shift back to the left leg and withdraw the right foot to land with a thump just beside the left foot. Circle the fists down to the belly. Press the head up, settle the *qi* to the *dantian*, and look forward. (images 1.62 and 1.63)

1.61
1.62
1.63

Pointers

- o The whole movement must be continuous without a break, but with a certain rhythm. Move slowly and then speed up when launching power. The movement must not use brute force, nor should it be rushed. The whole body should be coordinated, not slack, and the power should be integrated.

- o Close the shoulders and chest as the right elbow covers across. Open the chest and abdomen when the arms brace out to the sides. When the fists rise and cross, use a drilling power. When they rotate and circle above the head, use a bracing power. When they circle down, use a wrapping power in the arms. When they pull back to the belly, use a holding power.

- o The right foot should press into the ground as it withdraws. It should land with a thump. This is a settling type of power that unites the whole body, so be sure to strike the belly with the fists and settle the *qi* to the *dantian*.

- o Pay attention to the weight shifts. Shift left as the fists drill up. Shift right as the fists brace up. Shift left again as the fists pull in to hit the belly.

13.   Left Cannon, or Pounding Punch   zuǒ pàoquán   左炮拳

ACTION: Take a long step diagonally to the forward right with the right foot and follow in a half-step with the left foot, putting most weight on the left leg. Drill the right fist up past the sternum to nose height, about twenty centimetres from the left side of the head, twisting the ulnar edge up. Bring the left fist to the sternum, then, as the right foot steps, punch forward to solar plexus height. The left punch finishes with the elbow slightly bent and rolled in, and the fist eye up. Take the right fist rightward with the turn of the body, rotating the fist eye to face the right temple. Keep the right elbow down, press the head up, and look at the left fist. (image 1.64)

1.64

Pointers

- o Punch as the right foot lands. The feet and hands must work together, arriving at the same time.

- o Use power from the lower back and shoulders for the punch. Get the waist behind the shoulder, the shoulder behind the elbow, and the elbow behind the fist. Keep the left elbow tucked in to the ribs.

- o Take the right fist across with the body, rotating as it goes, so that it drills and turns, deflecting rather than blocking. Keep the elbow down; it must not be lifted.

14.   Retreat And Restrain   tuìbù lēiquán   退步勒拳

ACTION 1: Retreat the left foot a half-step and shift back, turning slightly leftward. Roll the right elbow leftward, bringing the fist down to just below shoulder height. Unclench the left hand and place it on the right wrist. Circle the right fist down and in, then up and forward, keeping the left hand on the wrist. Finish the circle with the right fist heart in, arms slightly bent. Look at the right fist. (image 1.65)

ACTION 2: Withdraw the right foot to land with a thump beside the left foot, bending the right leg and lifting the left foot beside the right ankle. Pull the hands back into the belly, pressing the elbows into the ribs. Settle the shoulders, press the head up, exhale, and look forward. (image 1.66)

Pointers

- o Strike the belly as the right foot thumps, hitting with the right fist. Breath out and settle the *qi* to the *dantian* to assist the power launch.

- o When circling the right fist, pay attention to keeping the shoulders settled and the upper back stretched taut, especially when the hands are up. Extend the fist forward to pre-load for the backward grappling/binding action.

15.   Sparrow Hawk Enters The Woods   yàozǐ rùlín   鷂子入林

ACTION: Take a long step forward with the left foot and follow in a half-step with the right foot, keeping most weight on the right leg. Clench the right fist and drill it up by the sternum to nose height then rotate it so that the fist eye faces the temple as the body turns rightward. Keep the right elbow down. Punch the left fist forward to solar plexus height, elbow slightly bent, fist eye up. Look at the left fist. (image 1.67)

Pointers

- o The left punch arrives as the left foot lands.

- o Be sure to keep the left elbow tucked in during the punch. The punch must follow a straight line.

- o Use the turn of the body and the shoulder to get power into the punch. The body turns sideways, like a sparrow hawk flying in between two trees.

- o Drill and turn the right fist to deflect, do not block directly up. Be sure to keep the elbow down.

16.   Step Forward, Tiger Carries   shàngbù hǔtuō   上步虎托

ACTION 1: Advance the left foot a half-step, then advance the right foot to beside the left ankle. Lower the right fist then unclench both hands and slide the right hand forward under the left arm. When it arrives to cross with the left hand, drill both hands up to head height, then circle them to the sides and lower them to the sides, palms forward, fingers down. Look forward. (images 1.68 and 1.69)

ACTION 2: Take a long step forward with the right foot and follow in a half-step with the left foot, keeping most weight on the left leg to take a *santi* stance. Push forward and down from the waist with both palms, palms forward, fingers angled down, palms about five centimetres apart at belly height. Press the head up and look past the hands. (image 1.70)

Pointers

o *Tiger carries* is a technique from the tiger model. The hands must arrive as the right foot lands. They push something away with a forward and downward force.

o Keep the arms rounded and bracing out when circling the hands. Use a wrapping power when bringing in the hands.

o Tuck the elbows in to the ribs just before doing the 'carry,' to send the hands forward. Settle the shoulders down and close the elbows in, settling down into the buttocks and bracing the upper back rearwards. Coordinate these actions with a breath out and a settling of *qi* into the *dantian* to launch power. Complete the whole movement as one action without a pause.

17.   Step Forward, Tiger Braces   shàngbù hǔchēng   上步虎撑

ACTION 1: Advance the right foot a half-step and follow in the left foot without touching down. Cross the wrists, left above the right, palms up. Slice forward and up, and when the hands arrive at nose height, turn the hands over and bend the elbows, so that the hands arrive at chest height, palms out. Look forward. (image 1.71)

ACTION 2: Take a long step forward with the left foot and follow in the right foot a half-step. Extend the arms to brace forward with both palms to chest height. Keep the elbows slightly bent, fingers pointing to each other, and thumbs down. Press the head up and look past the hands. (image 1.72)

Pointers

- o The hands must brace forward as the left foot lands, combining the powers together.

- o Empty the chest, open the upper back, and extend the shoulders forward when slicing up with the hands. Straighten the lower back and lift the elbows when turning the palms over. Bow the lower back, shrink in the body, sit back, and extend the arms when bracing forward with the hands. All these actions help to gain maximum power for the brace.

18.   White Snake Spits Its Tongue   báishé tùxìn   白蛇吐信

ACTION: Advance the left foot a half-step and then take a step forward with the right foot without moving the left, and keeping the weight on the left leg. Swing the left hand forward while turning the wrist, to hook in and press down. Pull the right hand back to the waist then rotate it and thread it from inside the left hand up to eye level with the palm up. Hook in and press down with the left hand under the right elbow, palm down. Look past the right hand. (image 1.73)

1.73

Pointers

- o Thread the right hand through as the right foot steps forward, as one integrated action. Do not overextend the right arm.

19.   White Snake Coils Its Body   báishé chánshēn   白蛇缠身

ACTION 1: Step the left foot forward, turning it out and settling the weight between the legs. Swing the left hand up outside the right arm, then circle it forward and down back to the left hip. Circle the right hand back and up to above the head, palm up and thumb web forward. Brace out slightly with the right arm. Lengthen the body. Look forward. (image 1.74)

ACTION 2: Turn the waist leftward and squat down into a resting stance, lifting the right heel. Stab the right hand directly down outside the left hip, palm out. Thread the left hand in front of the right shoulder, palm up. Tuck the elbows into each other, left forearm outside the right. Look past the left hand. (image 1.75)

1.74

1.75

Pointers

o   Three actions must be done as one: squat and turn the trunk, stab the right hand down, and thread the left hand up. When circling the arms, they should remain rounded and coordinated with the action of the trunk.

o   The downward stabbing hand should have a twisting, wrapping power. The upward threading hand should have a drilling, turning, holding power.

o   The body first opens up and then closes in. The resting stance should be stable. Close in the shoulders, tighten the abdomen, bend the waist, close the chest and stretch the upper back taut.

20.   White Snake Slithers Through The Grass   báishé bō cǎo   白蛇拨草

ACTION: Take a large step forward with the right foot, following in with the left foot a half-step, keeping the weight on the left leg in a *santi* stance. Scoop the right hand forward and up to waist height with the arm bent, the thumb web up, and the fingers forward. Pull the left hand back to the left hip, palm down. Sit the torso down, release the shoulders and settle the elbows. Look at the right hand. (image 1.76)

1.76

Pointers

o   The right arm must scoop forward as the right foot lands. Be sure to settle the trunk down and tuck the buttocks in, rising slightly with the lower back. The shoulders act together, one up and one down. Keep the right elbow settled down. You need to work carefully to find this type of power application.

o   *Snake spits its tongue, snake coils its body*, and *snake slithers through the grass* are completed as one movement. Be careful about the changing direction of the eyes and point of focus. *Snake spits its tongue* should be quick, *snake coils its body* should bring the body in very tight and small, and *snake slithers through the grass* should be fierce.

21.   Thump, Golden Rooster Blocks Up   zhènjiǎo jīnjī shàngjià   震脚金鸡上架

ACTION 1: Shift onto the left leg and withdraw the right foot to inside the left ankle without touching down. Bring the right hand down the left side, then swing the arm forward and up, and finally chop forward and down to the right hip, palm down. Pull the left hand back, then swing it up to in front of the head, thumb web forward. The palms face obliquely up. Look at the left hand (image 1.77)

1.77

ACTION 2: Land the right foot with a thump, squatting and lifting the left foot to the right ankle without touching down. Press the knees together. Twist and stab the left hand down outside the right hip with the fingers down and palm out. Thread the right hand forward and to in front of the left shoulder. Turn the body to bring the left shoulder forward. Press the head up and look past the left shoulder. (image 1.78)

Pointers

1.78

- o Three actions happen as one: stamp the right foot, stab the left hand down, and thread the right hand up.

- o The arms first draw a circle, working together. Be sure to keep the arms rounded, bracing out.

- o Turn the body when the left hand stabs down. The hand leads, the elbow follows, and the shoulder urges on the action. Close in the chest and shoulders. The arms and elbows cross with a holding power in front of the chest, and serve to protect the chest and ribs.

22.   Golden Rooster Heralds The Dawn   jīnjī bàoxiào   金鸡报晓

ACTION: Take a long step forward with the left foot and follow in a half-step with the right foot. Scoop the left hand forward and up with the arm bent, the wrist cocked so that the fingers point up and the palm faces forward. Pull the right hand down to the belly, palm down. Press the head up and look past the left hand. (image 1.79)

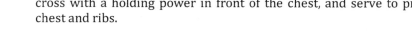

Pointers

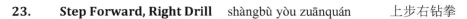
1.79

- o Hit with the left arm as the left foot lands.

- o Before the scoop, press the left elbow tightly to the left ribs and bring the left hand from the left hip to the front, settling down the left shoulder. Then lengthen the trunk, open the chest, reach with the shoulder, extend the arm, and settle the elbow down to put a scooping, digging power into the arm. Exhale to add power. In this way you combine the whole body as one unit, so that upper and lower, inner and outer work together in the strike.

23.   Step Forward, Right Drill   shàngbù yòu zuānquán   上步右钻拳

ACTION 1: Advance the left foot a half-step and follow in the right foot to beside the left ankle. Clench the left hand and rotate it, cocking the wrist to hook in at shoulder height with the fist heart down. Bend the elbow just below shoulder level to press down with the forearm across the body. Press the head up and look at the left fist. (image 1.80)

ACTION 2: Take a long step forward with the right foot and follow in the left foot a half-step. Clench the right hand and drill the fist forward and out, from inside the left wrist, to nose height with the ulnar edge up. Pull the left fist down to the belly, fist heart down. Press the head up and look past the right fist. (image 1.81)

1.80

Pointers

- o Press down with the left forearm as the left foot advances. Drill forward with the right fist as the right foot steps forward. Always coordinate the hands with the feet.

- o When drilling, sit down into the stance, lengthen the lower back, push forward into the shoulder, and send the elbow forward to the fist. Be sure always to use the whole body behind the punch.

- o Use equal and opposite force into the fists, one up and one down.

24.   Sparrow Hawk Wheels Over   yàozǐ fānshēn   鹞子翻身

ACTION 1: Pivot on both feet to turn around one-eighty to the left to face back in the way from which you came. Lift the right elbow and bring the right arm past the

right ear, crossing the forearm over the head as you turn around to the left. As the body gets turned around, press the right forearm past the head to cover forward and down to chest height with the fist heart down. Drill the left fist from inside the right fist, up and forward to nose height, fist heart in. Shift the weight forward onto the left leg. Look past the left fist. (images 1.82, 1.83)

ACTION 2: Do not shift the weight yet. Slide the right fist outside the left forearm to block across the body with the forearm, lifting it above the head, fist heart out. Bend the left elbow to bring the fist back to the chest. Then turn the body rightward and shift back to the right leg. Pull the right fist back as the body turns, and circle it down to the right shoulder. Rotate the left fist and lift the elbow so that the fist eye is in, and slide it out along the left ribs to the left hip. Look at the left fist. (image 1.84)

ACTION 3: Turn the right foot out, bend the right knee to squat fully down, and extend the left leg out, foot hooked in, to take a drop stance. Shift forward and thread the left fist along the left leg, rotating the fist so the fist eye faces up as it reaches forward. Shift forward with the movement of the fist, leading forward with the head. The left fist finishes about ten centimetres ahead of the foot. Pull the right fist back, rolling it down to the waist, fist eye up. Look at the left fist. (image 1.85)

Pointers

○ The movement must be completed without a break in the action, as one coordinated whole. The power comes from lengthening the body, which is a soft, hidden power that is very lively.

○ Coordinate the hands together: the right fist covers and presses down as the left fist drills out; the right fist blocks up as the left fist pulls back. This movement is quick and takes a lot of coordination to get the upward and downward actions to work together.

○ Use the centre of the body to coordinate the backward and forward weight shifts. Turn slightly rightward when shifting back. Coordinate the weight shift with the actions of the hands.

○ Pay attention to the action of the shoulders. Close the left shoulder in and roll it inward when sliding the left fist along the ribs and leg. Draw the right shoulder back to draw the torso back when pulling the right fist back. Twist and roll in the shoulder when lowering the right fist. Rotate and use the shoulder to lead the elbow when rotating the left fist.

○ You may also do the wheel around without dropping fully into the drop stance, if you are unable to do so. You must use the same power, though, and the same coordination. The only difference is the height of the stance.

25.   Sparrow Hawk Folds Its Wings   yàozǐ shùshēn   鹞子束身

ACTION: Extend the left fist along the left leg and shift forward onto the left leg, bending the knee and rising. Then take a long step forward with the right foot and quickly bring the left foot up to the right ankle. Keep the legs together and stand firmly. Lower the left fist to groin height and turn the fist heart in. Punch the right fist forward and down, fist eye forward at belly height. The right fist is outside the the left fist. Keep the arms tight to the ribs. Press the head up and look past the right punch. (image 1.86)

Pointers

○ Coordinate the right foot's forward step with the right fist's punch. Be careful to keep the elbows pressing into the ribs and to keep the shoulders closed in. Lead forward into the right shoulder a bit, extending the shoulder and sinking the elbow. Contain the chest and keep the abdomen solid.

26.   Sparrow Hawk Enters The Woods yàozǐ rùlín 鹞子入林

ACTION: Take a long step forward with the left foot
and follow in a half-step with the right foot. Bend the
right elbow to drill the fist up to nose height. Lift the
left fist to the sternum, then punch it forward at nose
height, elbow slightly bent and fist eye up. Rotate the
right forearm and drop the elbow, pulling the right
fist back to face the right temple. Press the head up
and look past the left fist. (image 1.87)

Pointers

   o   Punch with the left fist as the left foot lands.
       Turn the waist and extend into the shoulder,
       coordinating with the step to launch power.
       Pay particular attention to sinking the right elbow.

27.   Right Aligned Stance Crosscut   yòu shùnbù héngquán 右顺步横拳

ACTION 1: Advance the left foot a half-step and follow in the right foot to the left
ankle without touching down. Rotate the left fist heart up and lower the right fist
to stab through from the left armpit, fist heart down. Close the shoulders in,
contain the chest and tauten the upper back. Look at the left fist. (image 1.88)

ACTION 2: Step the right
foot diagonally to the
forward right and follow in
the left foot a half-step,
keeping most weight on
the left leg. Punch the right
fist out to shoulder height
in a crosscut, fist heart up.
Tuck the left fist down and
pull it back to the belly, fist
heart down. Press the
head up and look past the
right fist. (image 1.89)

Pointers

   o   Move 27 is the same as move 3.

   •   The following moves, 28 through 51, are the same as moves 4 through 34,
       repeating them on the way back. The first section of the form goes out, and the
       second section of the form comes back to the starting place, where there is
       another turn around. There is then another repeat, of moves 4 through 10, for a
       closing combination.

28.   Turn Around With a Right Aligned Stance Crosscut   See move 4.

29.   Turn Around With a Right Elbow Strike   See move 5.

30.   Left Aligned Stance Crosscut   See move 6.

31.   Turn Around With a Left Aligned Stance Crosscut   See move 7.

32.	**Turn Around, Withdraw With a Drive**	See move 8.
33.	**Advance With a Right Drive**	See move 9.
34.	**Retreat With a Left Drive**	See move 10.
35.	**Right Aligned Stance Drive**	See move 11.
36.	**White Crane Flashes Its Wings**	See move 12.
37.	**Left Cannon, or Pounding Punch**	See move 13.
38.	**Retreat and Restrain**	See move 14.
39.	**Sparrow Hawk Enters the Woods**	See move 15.
40.	**Step Forward, Tiger Carries**	See move 16.
41.	**Step Forward, Tiger Braces**	See move 17.
42.	**White Snake Spits Its Tongue**	See move 18.
43.	**White Snake Coils Its Body**	See move 19.
44.	**White Snake Slithers Through the Grass**	See move 20.
45.	**Thump, Golden Rooster Blocks Up**	See move 21.
46.	**Golden Rooster Heralds the Dawn**	See move 22.
47.	**Step Forward, Right Drill**	See move 23.
48.	**Sparrow Hawk Wheels Over**	See move 24.
49.	**Sparrow Hawk Folds Its Wings**	See move 25.
50.	**Sparrow Hawk Enters the Woods**	See move 26.
51.	**Right Aligned Stance Crosscut**	See move 27.
	(the following moves are the closing section)	
52.	**Turn Around With a Right Aligned Stance Crosscut**	See move 4.
53.	**Turn Around With a Right Elbow Strike**	See move 5.
54.	**Left Aligned Stance Crosscut**	See move 6.
55.	**Turn Around With a Left Aligned Stance Crosscut**	See move 7.
56.	**Turn Around, Withdraw With a Drive**	See move 8.
57.	**Advance With a Right Drive**	See move 9.
58.	**Retreat With a Left Drive**	See move 10.
59.	**Closing Move** shòu shì 收势	

ACTION 1: Advance the left foot without moving the right foot to sit into a *santi* stance. Turn over and tuck in the left fist then pull it back to the belly, fist heart in. Do not move the right fist. Press the head up and look forward. (image 1.90)

ACTION 2: Bring the right foot up to the left foot, bringing the knees together while keeping them bent. Unclench the hands and circle them up at the sides, palms up. (images 1.91, 1.92)

ACTION 3: Once the hands get to shoulder height, bring the hands to the front, palms down and thumbs in. Press the head up and look forward. Press the hands down in front of the belly and stand up to attention, letting the hands hang down to the sides. Look forward. (image 1.93)

Pointers

- o   Pull the left fist in as the left foot steps forward.

- o   Press the hands down as you stand up.

- o   The whole move is continuous and stable, with full spirit and attention, as strong as a mountain.

THE XINGYI COMPOSITE FORM 形意综合拳

INTRODUCTION TO THE XINGYI COMPOSITE FORM, *XINGYI ZONGHE QUAN*

This form is composed based on the five elements and the twelve animal models, with some of the eight skills – fifty one movements in four sections. The animal models are represented by tiger, horse, chicken, swallow, monkey, snake, and sparrow hawk, while intercept and pass from the eight skills show up in short combinations. There are also a couple of moves from the traditional Mixture of Moves form – *wind sways the lotus leaves* and *push the shutter to gaze at the moon* – and a move from the Five Elements Connected – *white crane flashes its wings*. This makes for an interesting, varied, and aesthetically pleasing performance form. There are also some good combative combinations such as *stroke hook to ear*, *double intercept and punch*, and *passing pull and drill*, which increase the form's practicality. This is an excellent form that shows well Xingyiquan's style and characteristics.

It has a pleasing and balanced choreography, interesting and varied techniques, well connected combinations, and smooth transitions and changes in power application.

NAMES OF THE MOVEMENTS

1. Opening Move (left *santishi*)
2. Left Splitting Punch
3. Advance With a Right Drive, or Crushing Punch
4. Retreat With a Left Drive, or Crushing Punch
5. Right Aligned Stance Drive, or Crushing Punch
6. Stroke, Hook to Ear
7. White Ape Presents Fruit
8. Retreat and Ride the Tiger
9. Left Bear
10. Right Crosscut
11. Step Forward, Eagle Grasps
12. Turn Around With a Tiger Carry
13. Double Interception
14. Right Aligned Stance Drive, or Crushing Punch
15. White Crane Flashes Its Wings
16. Left Cannon, or Pounding Punch
17. Lead Left and Plant a Punch Right
18. Right Stroke and Drag Back
19. Reverse Stance Drilling Punch
20. Lead Right and Plant a Punch Left
21. Left Stroke and Drag Back
22. Reverse Stance Drilling Punch
23. Sparrow Hawk Pierces The Sky
24. Sparrow Hawk Wheels Over
25. Sparrow Hawk Folds Its Wings
26. Sparrow Hawk Enters the Woods
27. Double Horse
28. Retreating Left Crosscut
29. Right Splitting Punch
30. Golden Rooster Drinks Water
31. Golden Rooster Pecks a Grain Of Rice
32. Tiger Pounces
33. Tiger Carries
34. Double Interception
35. Right Aligned Stance Drive, or Crushing Punch
36. Wind Sways The Lotus Leaves

37. Turn Around With a Snake Coiling Its Body

38. White Snake Slithers Through the Grass

39. Monkey Scratches Its Mark

40. Monkey Drops Back On Its Haunches

41. Monkey Pulls At Its Leash

42. Golden Rooster Stands On One Leg

43. Golden Rooster Thrusts a Foot

44. Swallow Skims the Water

45. Step Forward and Slice to the Groin

46. Step Forward and Plant In a Punch

47. Right Drilling Punch

48. Advance With a Tamping Hand

49. Push The Shutter To Gaze at the Moon

50. Left Splitting Punch

51. Closing Move

Description of the Movements

1.   Opening Move   qǐ shì   起势

ACTION: Stand to attention. Gradually lift the hands at the sides to shoulder height, palms up. Bend the elbows so that the hands point to each other in front of the face, palms down. Then press the hands down to the belly, bending the legs to sit with the knees together. Press the head up. Look at the right hand when lifting, then look forward. (images 1.94, 1.95, 1.96)

2.   Left Splitting Punch *santishi*)

zuǒ pīquán   左劈拳

ACTION 1: Turn the torso ninety degrees leftward. Clench the right fist and drill it up by the sternum, mouth, then forward to nose height, twisting the ulnar edge of the forearm up. Look past the right fist. (image 1.97)

ACTION 2: Advance the left foot without moving the right foot, settling into a *santi* stance biased toward the right leg. Bring the left fist up by the sternum and drill forward by sliding along the right forearm, then un-clench it and split forward and down to chest height. Pull the right hand back to the belly, palm down. Press the head up and look at the left hand. (image 1.98)

Pointers

- o Land with the left foot and left hand at the same time. Be sure to move both hands along the midline of the body.

3. Advance With a Right Drive, or Crushing Punch

jìnbù yòu bēngquán   进步右崩拳

ACTION: Advance the left foot a step and follow in the right foot to just at the left heel, keeping most weight on the right leg. Clench both hands, and punch the right fist straight forward with the elbow slightly bent and the fist eye up. Pull the left fist back to the belly. Reach the right shoulder slightly forward. Press the head up and look past the right fist. (image 1.99)

Pointers

- o The right fist lands as the right foot comes in. The right foot should shovel in with a thump, not lift up to stamp. The foot action is like raking forward.

- o After the left foot lands, when the right foot is following in, pretend that there is a rope pulling the right foot back. Pull forcefully with the right leg as if trying to break the rope.

4. Retreat With a Left Drive, or Crushing Punch

tuìbù zuǒ bēngquán   退步左崩拳

ACTION: Withdraw the right foot a half-step and shift weight to the right leg. Turn the right fist heart up. Retreat the left foot a step backwards and shift your weight mostly onto the left leg. Withdraw the right foot slightly, turning it crossways so that the thighs press tightly together. Pull the right fist back to the waist. Punch the left fist directly forward at chest height, fist eye up. Reach the left shoulder forward into the punch. Press the head up and look past the left fist. (image 1.100)

Pointers

- o Three actions must happen at once with a complete, integrated power: punch the left fist; land the left foot; pull back the right fist.

- o Reach the left shoulder forward and pull the right shoulder back, using both shoulders to put power into the punch.

5.   Right Aligned Stance Drive, or Crushing Punch

yòu shùnbù bēngquán   右顺步崩拳

ACTION 1: Advance the right foot a half-step forward and follow in a half-step with the left, keeping most weight on the left leg to take a *santi* stance. Drive the right fist to punch directly forward to chest height with the elbow slightly bent, the fist eye up and fist surface forward. Pull the left fist back to the belly. Reach the right shoulder forward. Press the head up and look past the right fist. (image 1.101)

Pointers

- o Land the right punch timed exactly as the right foot lands.

- o The punch is driven forward from the legs, but also from the shoulders. Push forward and pull back with the shoulders.

6.   Stroke, Hook to Ear   lǔshǒu guàn ér   将手贯耳

ACTION 1: Advance the right foot forward and follow in the left foot to inside the right ankle. Unclench the left hand and slide it forward under the right arm with the back of the hand on the right arm, fingers up, and thumb web stretched. Pull the right fist back to in front of the right shoulder. Look past the left hand. (image 1.102)

ACTION 2: Take a long step forward with the left foot and follow in a half-step with the right foot, keeping most weight on the right leg. Do a sweeping hook punch with the right fist to hook forward to ear height with the arm slightly bent, finishing with the elbow above the shoulders, fist eye down. Extend the left hand to accept the right fist into the palm. Look at the right fist. (image 1.103)

Pointers

- o Swing the right fist rightward and then forward in a hooking punch, in one action. The punch lands as the left foot lands.

o   The left hand slides forward to catch the opponent and control him so that you can step forward and punch his ear.

7.   **White Ape Presents Fruit**   báiyuán xiàn guǒ   白猿献果

ACTION 1: Advance the left foot a half-step with the toes hooked in and follow in the right foot to beside the left ankle without touching down. Turn the torso ninety degrees rightward. Keep the right fist in the left palm and rotate it with a circular action, so that both palms turn up and the right fist finishes nestled in the left palm. Then unclench the right hand and pull the hands back and down to the belly,

1.104   1.105

hitting with some force. Breathe out, press the head up, and keep the elbows snug to the ribs. (image 1.104)

ACTION 2: Step the right foot forward and follow in a half-step with the left foot, keeping most weight on the left leg. Strike forward and up to mouth height with the heels of the hands together, stretching the fingers forward and up. Look past the hands. (image 1.105)

Pointers

o   This is a carrying action with both hands, and it must land as the right foot lands. Keep the elbows as close together as you can and keep the shoulders settled down.

o   When the hands pull back to the belly, hit the belly equally with both, settling the *qi* to the *dantian*.

o   Be sure to make the change of direction.

8.   **Retreat and Ride the Tiger**   tuìbù kuà hǔ   退步跨虎

ACTION 1: Retreat the left foot a half-step and withdraw the right foot to beside the left foot, keeping most weight on the left leg. Cross the hands and lower them in front of the body, left inside the right. Turn the right palm to face in and the left palm to face out. (image 1.106)

ACTION 2: Retreat the right foot a long step to the right and withdraw the left foot

1.106   1.107

slightly to sit into a horse stance with the weight biased a bit towards the right leg. Pull the right hand back above and to the right of the head, bracing out with the elbow. Bring the left hand past the chest then brace with a rounded arm down to the left, palm down, thumb web inwards. Look at the left hand. This stance is quite low, the right thigh should be parallel to the ground. (image 1.107)

Pointers

- o The hands should exert equal and opposite forces, the right hand upward and back and the left hand forward and down.

- o Pay attention to the weight shift. Be sure to complete the hand actions as the foot lands. The whole body should be balanced, with power applied evenly in all directions. The movement should be fierce, with full and focussed spirit.

9.   Left Bear   zuǒ xióngxíng   左熊形

ACTION 1: Advance the left foot a half-step and follow in with the right foot, turning the torso left. Clench the left fist and bring it back to the waist, first lifting it and then blocking across to the left as it comes in. Bring the right forearm across over the head, fist heart down, to cover and press down in front. Look to the forward left. (image 1.108)

ACTION 2: Take a long step forward with the right foot and follow in a half-step

with left foot, touching the ball of the foot down with the heel raised. Shift forward onto the right leg. Continue to cover and press down with the right fist all the way to the belly, fist heart in. Drill the left fist out past the sternum, forward and up to nose height, ulnar edge turned up. Butt forward with the head, tuck the chin in, and look past the left fist. (image 1.109)

1.108 1.109

Pointers

- o Block and trap with the left fist as the body turns leftward and the left foot advances.

- o Drill the left fist up and cover down with the right fist as the right foot steps forward.

- o The bear model contains a head butt, so be sure to tuck in the chin and shift the body forward.

10.   Right Crosscut   yòu héngquán   右横拳

ACTION 1: Advance the right foot a half-step and follow in with the left foot a half-step to beside the right foot without touching down. Lower the left hand, extending it out at shoulder height with the fist heart up. Lift the right fist to the chest, fist heart down. Look past the left fist. (image 1.110)

1.110

ACTION 2: Take a long step to the forward left with the left foot and follow in a half-step with the right foot, keeping most weight on the right leg. Turn the left fist over and tuck it in, pulling back to the belly, fist heart down. Slide the right fist under the left forearm, fist heart still facing down, and punch forward while turning the forearm so that the fist heart faces up by the time it reaches its full extent at shoulder height. Press the head up and look forward. (image 1.111)

1.111

Pointers

○ Hit with the right fist as the left foot lands.

○ Turn the waist and extend the shoulder forward into the crosscut hit. Press the head up, sit the buttocks down, and apply a scissoring power between the legs. Tuck the right knee in and stab it down, closing the hips and knees. The fists and arms act as if twisting a rope, using the fully connected body.

11.   Step Forward, Eagle Grasps   shàngbù yīngzhuō   上步鹰捉

ACTION 1: Advance the left foot a half-step and lift the right foot inside the left ankle. Drill the right fist up to head height. Lift the left fist to the right elbow, fist heart up. Release the shoulders and close the elbows. (image 1.112)

ACTION 2: Take a long step forward with the right foot and follow in the left foot a half-step. Drill the left fist out along the right forearm until the fists cross, then unclench the hands and turn the palms down. Pull the right hand back to the belly and split the left hand forward and down to waist height. Press the head up and look down at the left hand. (image 1.113)

1.112

1.113

Pointers

○ For the correct angle in the final position: draw a line between the two feet, then draw a perpendicular line out from the middle of that line, and place the hand there. The hand will be in front of the left side of the body.

○ The left hand splits down as the right hand pulls and the right foot lands.

○ Be sure to tuck the buttocks in, press the head up, keep the trunk vertical, and settle the shoulders and elbows. Curve the fingers into eagle claw form.

12.   Turn Around With a Tiger Carry   zhuànshēn hǔtuō 转身虎托

ACTION 1: Take a half-step with the right foot, hooked out, then hook-in step the left foot in front of the right toes and shift onto the left leg, turning the body around rightward one-eighty degrees to face back in the way you came. Bring the hands up as the body turns, swinging the left hand and lifting the right hand to cross in front of the body, left hand above the right. Circle the hands up and out to either side, then in to the sides, palms forward and fingers down. Press the head up and look forward. (images 1.114, 1.115)

ACTION 2: Step the right foot diagonally to the forward right and follow in the left foot a half-step. Push the hands forward and down to belly height. Finish with the hands fist-width apart, palms forward, and fingers down. Press the head up and look past the hands. (image 3.116)

Pointers

- o Take well turned hook-out and hook-in steps to turn the body around quickly. Round the lower back when circling the hands. Hit with the hands as the right foot lands.

- o When doing the carrying action downwards, press the head up, settle the shoulders, set the lower back, and tuck in the buttocks. Coordinate these actions with an exhalation to assist in launching power.

13.   Double Interception   shuāng jiéshǒu   双截手

ACTION 1: Without moving the feet, clench the hands and take them across to the left with a blocking transverse interception. The right forearm is vertical, fist heart in at nose height in front of the left fist. The left fist is in front of the face. Look forward. (image 1.117)

ACTION 2: Withdraw the right foot a half-step and touch the toes down. Intercept across to the right with both forearms. The left arm is in front with the fist heart in and forearm vertical. The right fist is at the left elbow. Look forward. (image 1.118)

Pointers

- o Use the waist to draw the arms left and right to intercept. Transfer power from the waist to the shoulders, from the shoulders to the elbows, and from the elbows to the hands. Be sure to rotate the fists as the arms cut across. When intercepting leftward, the right fist rotates externally [thumb turning away from the palm] and the left fist rotates internally [thumb turning into the palm]. When intercepting rightward, the left fist rotates externally and the right fist rotates internally.

- o Withdraw the right foot slightly when intercepting rightward. The left and right interceptions must be done smoothly and continuously without a break in the action or power.

14.   Right Aligned Stance Drive   yòu shùnbù bēngquán   右顺步崩拳

ACTION: Advance the right foot and follow in the left foot slightly. Lower the right fist to the side then punch straight forward to chest height with the elbow slightly bent and the fist eye up. Pull the left fist back to the belly. Press the head up and look at the right fist. (image 1.119)

Pointers

- o The pointers are the same as move 5 described above.

15.   White Crane Flashes Its Wings   báihè liàngchì   白鹤亮翅

ACTION 1: Withdraw the left foot a half step, sitting into a horse stance. Lower the right fist to cross the forearms in front of the belly, then brace out to the sides over the knees. Without moving the feet, drill the fists up to head height with the fist hearts facing in and the wrists crossed, left inside the right. (images 1.120, 1.121)

ACTION 2: Rotate the forearms to turn the fist hearts out and open the arms to brace out to the left and right, keeping the arms slightly bent. Pull the right foot back beside the left foot, landing with a thump. While doing this, bring the fists in together at the belly. Press the head up, settle the *qi* to the *dantian*, and look forward. (images 1.122, 1.123)

1.122

1.123

Pointers

- The actions of *white crane flashes it wings* involve an upward drill, a turning outer brace, a dropping wrap, and a withdrawing embrace at the belly. Be sure to feel the power of each: drill, rotate, brace, wrap, and embrace. The whole body must be co-coordinated, quick but not rushed, and the power smoothly integrated without any slackness.

- Pay particular attention to the leftward and rightward shifting of the body. When the fists drill up, the weight should shift more towards the left leg. When the arms brace out, weight should shift more towards the right leg. When the arms wrap, weight should shift more to the left leg.

- The fists should hit the belly timed exactly as the right foot lands, settling the *qi* to the *dantian* to assist in exerting power. When the right foot withdraws it must rub along the ground. Land with a thump, do not to lift the foot to stamp.

16.   Left Cannon, or Pounding Punch zuǒ pàoquán   左炮拳

ACTION: Take a long step to the forward right with the right foot and follow-in a half-step with the left. Drill the right fist up by the sternum to nose height. Lift the left fist to the sternum then punch forward as the right foot advances. Punch the left fist to solar plexus height with the arm slightly bent, elbow tucked in, and fist eye up. Rotate the right fist internally (thumb side turning towards the palm) at the right temple, elbow down. Look past the left punch. (image 1.124)

1.124

Pointers

- The left punch and the right foot landing are timed together, so that hand and foot hit as a unit.

- Turn your waist to put your shoulder into the punch, so that the lower back pushes the shoulder to send the elbow and thus the left fist out.

- Be sure to keep the right elbow down – don't lift it. Keep the right fist at the right temple.

- Be sure to turn the body to achieve the punch.

17.   Lead Left and Plant a Punch Right   zuǒ lǐng yòu zāi 左领右栽

ACTION: Step the left foot forward without moving the right foot, dodging the torso to the left and shifting onto the left leg. Internally rotate the left fist (thumb side turns towards the palm) and pull it up across the body as the body turns left, doing a drawing, leading action, to finish with an upward block above the head. Punch the right hand straight down to groin height, fist eye in, fist surface down, and arm slightly bent. Lower the torso. Look forward. (image 1.125)

1.125

Pointers

- Complete the action of both hands as the left foot lands.

- The left hand's action is completed as the body dodges to the left, so that it leads across to the left. Bring the right shoulder forward, close in the right knee and roll in the right hip to plant the right fist straight down.

18.   Right Stroke And Drag Back   yòu lǔ dài   右捋带

ACTION: Step the right foot forward, hooked out, lifting the left heel in place. Unclench the hands and bring the right hand forward and up to slice up to the shoulder with the palm forward and the thumb web down. Turn the left palm up with the fingers forward, and extend it forward and up to lift up at shoulder height. Finish with the left hand forward and the right hand back and higher. Turn the body slightly rightward. Look past the left hand. (image 1.126)

1.126

Pointers

- Complete the action of the hands as the right foot lands.

- The hands should first extend forward, and then follow the rightward turning of the body to draw across to the right. Bend the left elbow. The right hand finishes in front of the head. Be sure to use the waist to draw the hands across.

19.   Reverse Stance Drilling Punch

àobù zuān dǎ   拗步钻打

ACTION: Take a long step forward with the left foot and follow in a half-step with the right foot. Tuck the left hand in and turn it palm down to press down, then clench it and hook to the left, bringing it up by the left shoulder with the fist eye down, bending the elbow above the shoulder. Lower the right hand to the waist and clench it, then drill forward and up to nose height, ulnar edge twisted up. Press the head up and

1.127

look forward. (image 1.127)

Pointers

o   Land the right punch as the left foot lands.

o   The left hand draws a circle, first pressing down, then hooking to the left, then drawing up. Use the waist to draw the hands with a heavy power, and use a shaking power at the end. Put power from the lower back into the right drilling punch. Coordinate the shoulders so that the power from the waist moves smoothly through them.

20.   Lead Right and Plant a Punch Left   yòu lǐng zuǒ zāi   右领左栽

•   This move is the same as move 17, just transposing right and left. (image 1.128)

21.   Left Stroke and Drag Back   zuǒ lǔ dài   左捋带

•   This is the same as move 18, just transposing right and left. (image 1.129)

22.   Reverse Stance Drilling Punch   àobù zuān dǎ   拗步钻打

•   This is the same as move 19, just transposing right and left. (image 1.130)

23.   Sparrow Hawk Pierces the Sky   yàozĭ zuān tiān   鹞子钻天

ACTION: Rotate the left fist, cock it, and press down with the fist heart down, tucking the forearm across the body. Lower the right fist to the right waist. Advance the right foot a half-step and follow in the left foot a half-step. Drill the right fist forward and up from the sternum, finishing at nose height with ulnar edge up. Pull the left fist back to the belly. Press the head up and look forward. (image 1.131)

Pointers

- o Land the right punch as the right foot lands. The fist is at nose height and the elbow is tucked into the chest, which gives the arm a bend of about one-twenty degrees.

24.   Sparrow Hawk Wheels Over   yàozĭ fānshēn   鹞子翻身

ACTION 1: Pivot on the feet to turn around one-eighty degrees to the left to face back in the way from which you came. Lift the right elbow and bring the right arm

past the right ear, crossing the forearm over the head as you turn around to the left. Press the right forearm past the head to cover forward and down with the fist heart down. Shift the weight onto the left foot, and complete the right fist cover down to the chest. Drill the left fist up and forward to nose height, fist heart in. Look at the left fist. (images 1.132, 1.133)

ACTION 2: Bring the right forearm across the body, lifting it up to block above the head. Settle the left elbow to bring the fist back to the chest. Shift back to the right leg. Pull the right fist back in front of the right shoulder as the body turns. Lift the left elbow and slide the fist along the left ribs to stab down at the hip with the fist eye down. Look at the left fist. (image 1.134)

ACTION 3: Bend the right knee to squat fully down with most weight on the right leg, and extend the left leg out into a drop stance. Slide the left fist forward along the left leg and pull the

right fist back down to the waist. Once the left fist passes the left foot, turn the fist eye up. Look at the left fist. Move the body forward as the left fist moves forward. (image 1.135)

Pointers

o *Sparrow hawk wheels over* emphasizes body technique. It trains the power use in the trunk and the ability to use the waist as the fulcrum, transferring smoothly through the shoulders and arms. The action is soft and smooth without being slack. It should show a hidden power, so should not be done with hard power.

o Be sure to shift the body back and forth, and to lead with the head, drawing the action from the waist. After the right fist has covered and the left fist has drilled out, raise the right fist with the arm across the body, and then draw it back. Use the elbow to draw the fist back. Use a wrapping, twisting power to bring the right fist in to the waist, circling it with a settled power in the shoulder.

o Lift the elbow to hug the left fist to the ribs. Be sure to first lift the elbow and then close the shoulder to stab the fist down. Once the left fist has gone past the left foot, lead forward into the head and shift forward. At this point, gradually rotate and settle the left shoulder and settle and bend the elbow to turn the fist over. This action hides a scooping technique.

25.   Sparrow Hawk Folds Its Wings   yàozǐ shùshēn   鹞子束身

ACTION: Shift forward onto the left leg, bending the knee and rising. Take a large step forward with the right foot and quickly bring the left foot up to the right ankle without touching down. Bring the left fist back towards the belly. Bring the right fist by the sternum to punch forward and down, fist eye forward at groin height, crossing over outside the left fist. Finish with the left fist inside, fist heart in and the right fist outside, fist eye forward. Press the head up and look at the right fist. (image 1.136)

1.136

Pointers

o Land the right punch as the right foot lands. You must stand firmly on the right leg.

o Close the shoulders in and hug the elbows to the ribs, closing in the chest and abdomen and tucking in the buttocks. Reach the right shoulder forward slightly into the punch.

26.   Sparrow Hawk Enters the Woods   yàozǐ rùlín   鹞子入林

ACTION: Take a large step forward with the left foot and follow in a half-step with the right foot. Drill the right fist up to nose height. As the foot steps forward, rotate the right forearm and drop the elbow, pulling the right fist back to the temple with the fist heart in. Lift the left fist past the sternum then punch it forward at chest height, fist eye up, elbow bent. Press the head up and look at the left fist. (image 1.137)

Pointers

1.137

- o Punch the left fist as the left foot lands, so that hands and feet work together.

- o Be sure not to block directly up with the right arm. It must drill and then rotate with the elbow held down.

- o Use the forward step, the rotation of the body, and the extention of the shoulder to put power into the punch. Keep the shoulders settled down, and turn the body almost sideways to the line.

27. Double Horse   shuāng mǎxíng   双马形

ACTION 1: Step the right foot forward and lift the left foot to the right ankle. Turn the right fist over so that the fist heart faces up and roll in the forearm, pounding down with the knuckles forward. After the right fist crosses the left arm, pound down with both fists, fist hearts up. Press the head up and look forward. Raise the fists from the hips to in front of the shoulders by bending the elbows and turning the fists so that the fist hearts face down and the fist surfaces face forward with the wrists slightly cocked and the elbows out at shoulder height. (images 1.138, 1.139)

ACTION 2: Take a large step forward with the left foot and follow in a half-step with the right foot. Strike forward to chest height, keeping the arms slightly bent, the fists about a fist width apart. Press the head up and look forward. (image 1.140)

1.138

1.139

1.140

Pointers

- o Settle the shoulders and elbows to pound down with the fists. Use the shoulders and elbows to draw the fists back. Press the head up and lengthen the lower back, straightening the chest a bit, to give a feeling of shoving with the chest.

- o Strike forward with the fists as the left foot lands, using whole body power.

- o Close the chest, urge the shoulders forward, extend the arms, and round the lower back to do the double strike. Rounding the lower back tucks in the abdomen to push the lower back to the rear, so that the back urges the shoulders forward. The power then transfers from the shoulders to the elbows and from the elbow to the fists, consequetively and segmentally increasing in force to the fist surface.

28.   Retreating Left Crosscut   tuìbù zuǒ héngquán   退步左横拳

ACTION 1: Withdraw the right foot a half-step and cut the right forearm in with an elbow cover, rotating the fist heart up. Lower the left fist to the belly, turning the fist heart down. Look past the right fist. (image 1.141)

ACTION 2: Bring the left foot past the right foot then back to the left rear, landing with a thump and shifting the weight back more onto the left leg. Slide the left fist along under the right arm to drill forward to shoulder height, fist heart turning up. Tuck the right fist over and press down, pulling back to the belly. Press the head up and look past the left fist. (image 1.142)

1.141

1.142

Pointers

- o   Turn over the right fist with the elbow cover as the right foot withdraws. Perform a small body movement at this time, pre-loading forward in preparation for the backward movement.

- o   Land the left punch as the left foot lands.

29.   Right Splitting Punch   yòu pīquán   右劈拳

ACTION: Advance the right foot a half-step straight forward and follow in with the left foot a half-step. Bring the right fist to the sternum, along the left arm, and then unclench the hand and split forward to chest height. Unclench the left hand and pull it back to the belly. Press the head up and look past the right hand. (image 1.143)

Pointers

- o   The right hand should complete the split as the right foot lands. Reach the right shoulder forward, keeping it released and the elbow down. Press the head up to lift the trunk

1.143

slightly. Exhale and settle the *qi* to the *dantian* to put power into the strike.

30.   Golden Rooster Drinks Water   jīnjī zhuó shuǐ   金鸡啄水

ACTION 1: Withdraw the right foot to in front of the left foot, lifting the knee with the foot hooked up at the belly of the calf. Stand firmly on the left leg, keeping the knee bent. Clench the right hand and bring the fist back to the belly, then drill it up by the sternum and mouth and forward to nose height, ulnar edge twisted up. Clench the left hand and lift it to the the right elbow. Look at the right fist. (image 1.144)

ACTION 2: Land the right foot with a thump and lift the left foot at the right ankle. Bend the right leg to lower the body. Drill the left fist up along the right arm to head height, then unclench it and split forward and down to chest height. Unclench the right hand and pull it down to the right hip, palm down. Press the head up and look forward. (image 1.145)

1.144   1.145

Pointers

- ○ Complete both the pull back and the drill up with the right hand as the right foot withdraws. Split down with the left hand as the right foot lands with a thump.

- ○ Reach the shoulder forward and settle the elbow for the left split. The right foot should thump with a settled, powerful feeling – settle the whole foot on the ground, bend the knee, straighten the lower back, tuck in the buttocks, and press up the head. The foot should make a firm, solid sound as it lands.

31.   Golden Rooster Pecks a Grain of Rice   jīnjī shí mǐ   金鸡食米

ACTION: Advance the left foot a long step and follow in the right foot with a raking action to thump just at the left heel. Clench the right fist to punch forward to chest height. Set the left hand on the right wrist. Press the head up and look past the right fist. (image 1.146)

1.146

Pointers

- ○ The left foot's step must be both long and quick. The right punch hits as the right foot lands. Reach the shoulder forward into the punch.

32.   Tiger Pounces   hǔ pū   虎扑

ACTION 1: Retreat the right foot and withdraw the left foot a half-step, shifting onto the right leg. Unclench both hands to reach forward, then clench both hands and pull back to in front of the chest. Look forward. (image 1.147)

ACTION 2: Advance the left foot and follow in with the right foot a half-step. Drill the fists up past the chest to the jaw. As the left foot lands, extend the arms to pounce to chest height. Unclench the hands and turn them over so that the palms face forward as they pounce. Keep the arms slightly bent, palms about a fist-width apart. Reach the shoulders, drop the elbows, press the head up and look forward. (image 1.148)

1.147 1.148

Pointers

o One main characteristic of Xingyiquan's footwork is, 'when the lead foot advances then the rear foot must follow in, when the rear foot retreats then the lead foot must withdraw.' The right foot must retreat and the left foot withdraw as the hands reach forward and pull back.

o The hands must complete the pounce as the left foot lands. Practise the use of the lower back and shoulders to put power into the pounce.

33.   Tiger Carries   hǔ tuō   虎托

ACTION 1: Advance the left foot a half-step, hooked in, then advance the right foot to beside the left ankle. Cross the hands, then circle them to the sides, and then wrap them in to the sides of the waist, palms forward, fingers down. Press the head up and look to the forward right. (image 1.149)

ACTION 2: Take a long step to the forward right with the right foot and follow in a half-step with the left foot. Push forward from the waist with both palms, fingers angled down, palms about a fist-length apart at belly height. Urge the shoulders forward, settle the waist down, press the head up, and look past the hands. (image 1.150)

1.149 1.150

Pointers

o Circle the hands out and then in to the sides as the left foot advances. Brace out to the sides with the arms rounded, the chest closed in and the upper back opened taut, bending the waist and shrinking the torso.

o When bringing the hands in, they should have a wrapping, drawing power. Press the head up, lengthen the lower back, settle the shoulders, and tuck in the elbows.

o When the hands push forward in the carrying action, they must land as the right foot lands. Tuck the elbows tightly into the ribs to send the hands forward. Settle the shoulders, tuck in the bottocks and close the elbows together. The torso should drop slightly. Coordinate these actions with a breath out.

34.   Double Interception   shuāng jiéshǒu   双截手

This move is the same as move 13. (images 1.151, 1.152)

35.   Right Aligned Stance Drive   yòu shùnbù bēngquán   右顺步崩拳

This is the same as move 14. (image 1.153)

36.   Wind Sways The Lotus Leaves   fēng bǎi héyè   风摆荷叶

ACTION 1: Turn the body leftward and take a half-step to the left with the left foot. Lower the right hand, then unclench and circle both hands down, to the left, and then up. Look at the right hand. (image 1.154)

ACTION 2: Take a front crossover step with the right foot across the left foot further towards the left side, into a cross stance with the weight between the feet. Circle the hands up, rightward and back, turning the trunk around to the right. Finish with the right hand at shoulder height and the left hand in front of the right shoulder, both palms facing the rear right. Look at the right hand. (image 1.155)

• Perform two or three *wind sways the lotus leaves* without a pause between them.

Pointers

- o The hands draw a vertical circle in front of the body, so the body needs to turn. The hands arrive to the rear as the right foot lands in the cross step.

- o The waist must turn around to face the rear. Settle the shoulders and elbows down so that the final movement of the 'swing' has power – do not just circle the the arms loosely.

37. Turn Around With a Snake Coiling Its Body

zhuànshēn shé chánshēn   转身蛇缠身

ACTION 1: Lower both hands to slice them leftward and upward. Pivot on the feet to turn the body around leftward one-eighty degrees. Swing the left hand leftward from above the head to chop down to the left hip. Lift the right hand to the right of the head. Follow the movement of the left hand with the eyes. (image 1.156)

ACTION 2: Continue to turn the body leftward another ninety degrees and sit down into a resting stance. Bend the right elbow to bring the right hand down past the face to stab outside the left hip, palm out. Thread the left hand up from the left hip to the right shoulder in a circling motion, palm up. Look past the left hand. (image 1.157)

1.156   1.157

Pointers

- o The hands perform the circling chop and the threading stab as you turn and sit into the resting stance. The whole movement must be done in one action with no pausing.

- o The body should rise when the hands do the circling chop. When the hands perform the threading stab they should externally rotate (thumb side turns away from the palm). In the resting stance the body should be tucked in tightly.

38.   White Snake Slithers Through the Grass

báishé bō cǎo   白蛇拨草

ACTION: Take a long step forward with the right foot and follow in a half-step with the left foot, keeping in a low stance with most weight on the left leg. Slice the right hand forward and up from the left hip to waist height with the elbow bent, fingers forward and thumb up. Pull the left hand palm down and back to the left hip. Sit down into the buttocks. Look at the right hand. (image 1.158)

1.158

Pointers

- o Complete the right arm slice as the right foot lands. To launch power into the right arm, sit into the buttocks, tuck in the hips, lengthen the lower back, settle the shoulders, and drop the elbows. Use both shoulders to get power.

39.   Monkey Scratches Its Mark   yuánhóu guà yìn   猿猴挂印

ACTION 1: Turn the body slightly to the left and withdraw the right foot to beside the left foot. Lower the right hand, clenching it and drawing it in to the belly. Then step the right foot a half-step to the forward right, circling it around and hooking the foot out, turning the body rightward. Drill the right fist up to in front of the jaw, turning it so the fist heart faces in, to hook and knock away in an outward blocking action at shoulder height. Look at the right hand. (image 1.159)

ACTION 2: Shift forward to the right leg and step the left foot in front of the right toes, hooking it in to take a character eight [八] stance. Continue to turn around to the right. Lift the left hand to the right elbow and continue to rotate the right fist. Look at the right hand. (image 1.160)

Pointers

- o The right foot must draw a circle when it withdraws and then steps out again, so that it both does a hook-out step and lands hooked out. After the right fist drills up it may unclench as the body turns around, turning into a hooking grab. The hook-out and hook-in steps bring the body around a full one-eighty degrees.

- o The whole movement must be coordinated between the footwork, the body work, and the hands.

40.   Monkey Drops Back On Its Haunches   tuìbù hóu dūn   退步猴蹲

ACTION 1: Shift onto the left foot, and retreat the right foot a long step behind. Slide the left hand forward on top of the right arm to eye height and pull the right hand back to the left side of the belly. Both palms face down. Look at the left hand. (image 1.161)

ACTION 2: Withdraw the left foot to in front of the right foot and touch the ball of the foot down, shifting onto the right foot. Squat down until the thigh is parallel to the ground. Bring the left hand back to the left hip. Lift the right hand in front

of the right shoulder then reach it out in front of the left shoulder, palm down. Look past the left shoulder. The torso should turn rightward when squatting, to bring the left shoulder forward. (image 1.162)

Pointers

o When the right foot retreats you may also push off with the left leg to jump back onto the right leg, landing firmly. When the left foot withdraws it must come in quickly and touch down lightly.

o The left hand thread forward as the right foot withdraws. The squatting position should be low.

41.   Monkey Pulls At Its Leash   yuánhóu dáo shéng   猿猴才到绳

ACTION 1: Rise, drawing a vertical circle in front of the body with both hands. Extend the right hand while pulling back the left hand. Then lift the left hand while pulling the right hand back. The hands each draw one circle. Look forward. (images 1.163, 1.164)

ACTION 2: Advance the left foot a half-step and follow in the left foot. Slide the left hand out from the right shoulder in a splitting palm to chest height, palm forward. Pull the left hand back to the belly. Press the head up and look past the left hand. (image 1.165)

1.163   1.164   1.165

Pointers

o The hand action must be quick and lively. The left hand splits as the left foot advances, hitting sharply together.

42.   Golden Rooster Stands On One Leg

jīnjī dúlì   金鸡独立

ACTION 1: Advance the left foot a half-step without moving the right foot. Shift forward so that most of your weight in on the left leg, bending the left knee and lifting the right heel. Lift the right hand to the sternum and thread it forward under the left arm with the palm down. Withdraw the left hand, pulling it back to the chest with the palm down. Urge the right shoulder forward, bend the elbow,

1.166

and drop the wrist so that the palm is forward and fingers are pointing up at shoulder height. Press the head up and look at the right hand. (image 1.166)

ACTION 2: Take a long step forward with the right foot and quickly follow in the left foot to place it by the right ankle without touching down. Keep the knees together and stand firmly on the right leg with the knee bent. Thread the left hand forward under the right arm and cock the wrist with the fingers at shoulder height. Bring the right hand back to in front of the chest. Reach into the left shoulder. Press the head up and look forward. (image 1.167)

- Perform *golden rooster stands on one leg* twice.

Pointers

- o The step must be long and land with stability. The follow-in step must be quick. When the hands thread forward, first lift the wrists and then sit them down with a settling of the shoulder, to settle into the palms.

43.   Golden Rooster Thrusts a Foot   jīnjī dēngjiǎo   金鸡蹬脚

ACTION 1: Advance the left foot a half-step and shift forward onto the left leg. Thread the right hand out under the left arm, extending it to the left wrist. Once the wrists cross, turn the palms forward and circle them around each other, comng back to the chest with the wrists together, palms up. Look forward. (image 1.168)

ACTION 2: Lift the right knee and then the foot, to thrust kick to chest height with the ankle dorsi-flexed. Bend the left leg slightly to keep balance. Keep the wrists together and apply a carrying power forward and up to jaw height. Look forward. (image 1.169)

Pointers

- o Bend the arms while circling the hands. Stretch the upper back taut and close the chest.

- o Carry with the hands at the same time as you kick. When carrying, lenthen the lower back, release the shoulders, extend the arms, and close the elbows together.

- o Keep the hip tucked in when kicking. Do not release the hip forward.

44.   Swallow Skims the Water   yànzǐ chāo shuǐ   燕子抄水

ACTION 1: Do not land the right foot after the kick, just bend the knee and bring the foot in to the left ankle. Turn the torso ninety degrees to the right and thread the hands up with the wrists still together. Press the head up and look at the hands. (image 1.170)

ACTION 2: Land the right foot, turned out, and bend the right knee to a full squat, extending the left foot to the left to take a left drop stance. Keep the weight on the right leg, but keep the left foot solid on the ground. Slide both hands down along the body, turning the backs of the palms to touch the body. When they arrive at the waist, rotate the palms up and extend them to either side. Thread the left hand forward along the outside of the left leg, until it is in front of the left foot. Extend the right hand back, palm up. Look at the left hand. (image 1.171)

Pointers

- ○ Thread the hands up as the left foot pushes off the ground.

- ○ Stab the hands down as you drop into the drop stance. The whole movement must be smooth and coordinated.

45.   Step Forward and Slice To the Groin   shàngbù liāoyīnzhǎng 上步撩阴掌

ACTION: Continue to thread the left hand forward and shift forward, bending the left knee to support with the left leg, rising slightly. Take a long step forward with the right foot, turning the foot out crossways and crossing the legs to sit into a resting stance. Slice the right hand forward to strike forcefully with the palm forward at waist height. Tuck the left hand onto the right wrist. Lean the body slightly so that the right shoulder is down and the left shoulder is higher. Look at the right hand. (image 1.172, and from the other side)

Pointers

- ○ Slice up with the right hand as the right foot lands. Turn the waist, roll the body under, and reach with the arm, keeping it bent, to slice up. Squeeze the thighs together.

46.　　Step Forward and Plant In a Punch　shàngbù zāidǎ　上步栽打

ACTION: Take a large step forward with the left foot and follow in with the right foot. Clench both fists and slide the left fist along under the right arm to punch forward and down with the fist heart down, at belly height. Pull the right fist back to the belly with the fist heart up. Press the head up and look at left punch. (image 1.173)

Pointers

- Punch with the left fist as the left foot lands, so that the power is integrated.

- To get power into the left punch, be sure to press up into the head, roll the elbow in and pull back forcefully with the right fist. The fists must have equal and opposite power. Be sure to launch power from both shoulders.

47.　　Right Drilling Punch　　yòu zuānquán　　右钻拳

ACTION 1: First withdraw the left foot a half-step and pull the left fist back to the belly. Then advance the left foot a half-step and drill the left up past the sternum then forward to nose height. Look at the left fist. (image 1.174)

ACTION 2: Take a large step forward with the right foot and follow in a half step with the left foot. Tuck the left forearm to press down across the body. Drill the right hand forward and up to nose height, twisting the ulnar edge up, and pull the left fist back to the belly. Press the head up and look forward. (image 1.175)

Pointers

- Drill the left fist forward as the left foot advances a half-step.

- Drill the right fist forward as the right foot lands forward.

48.　　Advance With a Tamping Hand　　jìnbù tāzhǎng　　进步踏掌

ACTION 1: Withdraw the right foot a half-step and touch the ball of the foot down, shifting onto the left leg. Unclench the hands. Slide the left hand up along the outside of the right arm, palm out, to block up at eyebrow height with the forearm across the body. Bend the right elbow to bring the fist to the chest. Look forward. (image 1.176)

ACTION 2: Advance the right foot with the toes hooked in, following in the left foot and turning the torso ninety degrees leftward to land into a horse stance with the weight evenly distributed between the legs. Rotate the right palm out, thumb down, and push forcefully to chest height at the right. Brace up and pull leftward with the left hand, stopping above the head to the left. Look at the right hand. (images 1.177, 1.178)

Pointers

    o   The whole movement must be coordinated together – push the right hand, step the right foot, turn the body, brace and pull the left hand, and breathe out.

    o   Keep the right arm rounded to brace strongly.

49.   Push the Shutter To Gaze At the Moon   tuīchuāng wàngyuè   推窗望月

ACTION 1: Lower both hands, swinging them leftward, upward, then rightward. Shift to the left leg and step the right foot across in front of the left foot with the foot turned out. Turn the body ninety degrees rightward. Look at the left hand. (image 1.179)

ACTION 2: Step the left foot forward without moving the right foot and keeping most weight on the right leg, to sit into a half-horse stance. Swing the hands downward, leftward, and upward. Turn the left palm out with the fingers down and the arm rounded, stopping at eyebrow height at the left of the body. Push forcefully to the left at chest height with the right hand, palm facing left, fingers up, and arm rounded. Press the head up and look past the right hand. (image 1.180)

Pointers

    o   Swing the arms as the right foot steps forward. Block up with the left arm and push with the right hand as the left foot steps forward. Settle the *qi* to the *dantian*.

50. **Left Splitting Punch** zuǒ pīquán 左劈拳

ACTION 1: Advance the right foot a half-step towards the left foot. Clench both hands and pull the right fist back to the belly, then drill it up and out to nose height. Pull the left fist back to the belly. Keep the head pressed up, and look at the right fist. (image 1.181)

ACTION 2: Advance the left foot a half-step wtihout moving the right foot, to sit into a *santi* stance. Drill the left fist along the top of the right forearm, then split forcefully forward to chest height. Pull the right hand down and back to the belly, palm down. Press the head up and look forward. (image 1.182)

51. **Closing Move** shōu shì 收势

ACTION 1: Without moving the feet, clench the left hand and pull it back to the belly. Then shift forward and bring the right foot up beside the left foot, keeping the knees bent. (images 1.183, 1.184)

ACTION 2: Unclench the hands and lift them at the sides, then bend the elbows to bring the hands together at the front. Look at the right hand as it comes up, then look forward. (images 1.185, 1.186)

ACTION 3: Press the hands down in front of the belly and stand up to attention, letting the hands hang down to the sides. Look forward. The form is now completed. (image 1.187)

THE MIXTURE OF MOVES 杂势捶

INTRODUCTION TO THE MIXTURE OF MOVES, *ZASHICHUI*

Zashichui is a classic form, also called Combined Shapes, and Integrated Form[30]. It is the longest traditional form of Xingyiquan. It is a relatively advanced level mixed form, meant to be learned after one has studied the five element techniques, the Five Elements Connected, the Eight Moves, and the twelve animals. It holds an important place among the traditional forms of Xingyiquan.

Zashichui does not contain all of the twelve animals, in fact, there are just a few. It contains some moves that are seldom seen: *cat washes its face, black dragon pours water, spread one wing, three basins land on the ground, push the shutter to gaze at the moon, lazy dragon lies in the road, dragon and tiger play together.* This form has a rich content, a good variety of moves, and smooth connections and power flow bewtween the moves. The move *cat washes its face*, however, occurs a great many times.

In some areas *Zashichui* is called the Floodgate Hits [闸势捶 zhá shì chuí] or the Pounding Hits [砸势捶 zá shì chuí]. This is due to dialect pronunciations of the first character.

NAMES OF THE MOVEMENTS

1.   Opening Move (left *santishi*)
2.   Sparrow Hawk Folds its Wings
3.   Sparrow Hawk Enters the Woods
4.   Retreating Chopping Strike (Cat Washes its Face), twice
5.   Black Dragon Pours Water
6.   Stretch Out One Wing
7.   Advance Left Crushing Punch (Hybernating Dragon Appears)
8.   Right Aligned Stance Crushing Punch (Black Tiger Leaves its Den)
9.   White Crane Flashes its Wings
10.   Left Cannon, Pounding Punch
11.   Spread Both Wings
12.   Sparrow Hawk Enters the Woods
13.   Retreating Chopping Strike (Cat Washes its Face), twice
14.   Swallow Skims the Water
15.   Swallow Spreads its Wings
16.   Advancing Right Crushing Punch
17.   Retreating Left Crushing Punch

---

[30] Translator's note: The name doesn't translate well, and could also be translated as the Mixture of Hits. It is best to just call it *Zashichui*.

18.   Right Aligned Stance Crushing Punch

19.   Spread Both Wings

20.   Sparrow Hawk Enters the Woods

21.   Retreating Chopping Strike (Cat Washes its Face), twice

22.   Black Dragon Pours Water

23.   Golden Rooster Pecks a Grain of Rice

24.   Reverse Stance Eagle Grasp

25.   Push the Shutter to Gaze at the Moon

26.   Three Basins Land on the Ground

27.   Lazy Dragon Lies in the Road

28.   Black Dragon Roils the River (Aligned Stance Left Crossing Punch)

29.   Advancing Right Crushing Punch

30.   Dragon and Tiger Fight Together

31.   Right Aligned Stance Crushing Punch

32.   White Crane Flashes its Wings

33.   Left Cannon, Pounding Punch

34.   Spread Both Wings

35.   Sparrow Hawk Enters the Woods

36.   Retreating Chopping Strike (Cat Washes its Face), twice

37.   Black Dragon Pours Water

38.   Stretch Out One Wing

39.   Left Crushing Punch

40.   Right Aligned Stance Crushing Punch

41.   Wind Sways the Lotus Leaves (three times)

42.   Advancing Left Crushing Punch

43.   Sparrow Hawk Pierces the Sky

44.   Sparrow Hawk Wheels Over

45.   Sparrow Hawk Folds its Wings

46.   Sparrow Hawk Folds Enters the Woods

47.   Closing Move

Description of the Movements

1.   Opening Move (left *santishi*)

qǐ shì   起势

Move to *santishi* the same as usual. Stand to attention, facing forty-five degrees to the direction of travel of the form. Gradually lift the hands at the sides to shoulder height, palms up, looking at the right hand. Bend the elbows to bring the hands in palms down, in front of the face, then press down to the belly, bending the legs

1.188

to sit and turning the head to look forward. Clench both fists and roll the fist hearts up. Drill the right fist up and forward to nose height, twisting the little finger side up, looking at the right fist. Drill the left fist up and forward, sliding along above the right forearm. Advance the left foot, settling into a *santi* stance, unclenching the hands and rolling them palm down, splitting the left hand forward and down to chest height and pulling the right hand back to the belly. Press the head up and look past the left hand. (image 1.188)

See also Chapter Two for detailed description and images of *santishi*.

Pointers

- o Relax the whole body during the opening move, and concentrate.

- o Settle down into the legs as the hands press down.

- o Land the left foot and the left hand simultaneously.

2.   Sparrow Hawk Folds its Wings   yàozǐ shù shēn   鷂子束身

ACTION: Without moving the left foot, shift forward and take a long step forward with the right foot, lifting and dorsi-flexing the left foot by the right ankle without touching down. Bend the right leg slightly to stand firmly, and press the legs together. At the same time, clench both hands to fists, pull the left fist in to the belly with the fist heart in, and drill the right fist up past the sternum then forward to punch downward to solar plexus height with the fist eye forward. The right fist is outside the left fist, the elbows are tight to the ribs, the head presses up, and the eyes look forward. (image 1.189)

1.189

Pointers

- o Step the right foot a long step forward and land firmly. Lift the left foot quickly, and pay attention to keeping the legs together.

- o The left fist must pull back and the right fist must punch forward and down at exactly the moment that the right foot steps forward. Pay attention to keeping the elbows in and the shoulders settled.

3.   Sparrow Hawk Enters the Woods   yàozǐ rù lín   鷂子入林

ACTION: Take a long step forward with the left foot and follow in a half step with the right foot, keeping most weight on the right leg. At the same time, bend the right elbow to drill the right fist up to eyebrow height. Lift the left fist to the sternum then extend a punch to solar plexus height as the left foot steps forward. The left fist eye is on top, the elbow slightly bent, and the shoulder is extended forward. Rotate the right forearm to turn it out, keeping the elbow dropped, and bringing the fist to the right temple with the fist eye facing the temple. Release the shoulders and settle the elbows, press the head up.

1.190

Look past the left fist. (image 1.190)

Pointers

○ The left punch must arrive at the same time as the left foot. Turn the waist and extend the shoulder into the punch, so that the body aligns sideways to the punch. Pay attention to keeping the right elbow down – do not allow it to rise. The right forearm should deflect with a rotation.

○ *Sparrow hawk folds its wings* and *sparrow hawk enters the woods* should be fully connected. There should be no hesitation between them, they are completed as one move.

4.   Retreating Chopping Strike (Cat Washes its Face)

tuìbù pī quán (māo xī liǎn)   退步劈拳（猫洗脸）

ACTION 1 Retreat the left foot and shift back, withdrawing the right foot a half step. At the same time, open the hands. Cover inward with the left hand, pulling down and in to the left side, turning the body slightly left. Cover with the right hand, tucking in the elbow and pressing the forearm at the right of the head, palm in, and about a foot away from the face. The right fingers should be no higher than the nose, and the elbow at solar plexus height. Contain the chest and tuck in the belly. Look forward. (image 1.191)

ACTION 2: Retreat the right foot one step and withdraw the left foot a half step, shifting back and turning the body right. At the same time, cover with the right elbow and pull the hand in and down to the right side, palm in. Bend the left elbow and bring the hand first up and leftward, then across to cover to the right. The left hand is about a foot in front of the face, with the palm in, the elbow at solar plexus height. Contain the chest and tuck in the belly. Look forward. (image 1.192)

1.191   1.192

Repeat Actions 1 and 2.

Pointers

○ This move is repeated twice. The repetitions should flow together smoothly, and the wrapping cover of the hands should allow no gaps. Retreat the left foot with the right elbow cover, and retreat the right foot with the left elbow cover, coordinating well together.

○ The hands must continue to move throughout the *cat washes its face* actions, rotating the forearms externally while tucking in the elbows. The actions wrap downwards, using the waist to lead the shoulders, the shoulders to lead the elbows, and the retreating steps to turn the body sideways. In the form, the retreating steps should be quick and short. It is alright to just step back once, if your hands are quicker than your feet. Try to make the move quick, connected, and smooth.

5.   Black Dragon Pours Water   wūlóng dàoshuǐ   乌龙倒水

ACTION 1: Without moving the feet, lower the right hand to circle it right, to the rear, then swing up over the head, palm forward. Tuck the left elbow in and lower the hand to in front of the belly. Look forward. (image 1.193)

ACTION 2: Press down with the right hand to in front of the belly, clenching the fist, fist heart in. Clench the left fist and drill it up past the sternum, then lift the elbow to do a framing block up with the forearm above the head, fist rotated so the fist heart faces out. Sit down slightly. Look forward. (image 1.194)

Pointers

- o   Do not hesitate between actions one and two.

- o   The hands switch places up and down, so must be coordinated. Pay attention when drilling the left fist up to the framing block that the body has a forward intention. Brace up with the left elbow.

6.   Stretch Out One Wing   dān zhǎn chì   单展翅

ACTION 1: Rotate the left fist to press down with the forearm across, pulling the fist in to the belly, fist heart in. Bring the right fist up past the sternum to drill up past the inside of the left arm to nose height. Then rotate the right fist inwards to turn the fist heart out, for a framing block above the head. Sit back slightly and lengthen the spine. Look forward. (image 1.195)

ACTION 2: Retreat the left foot then withdraw the right foot to in front of the left, sitting on the left leg. Rotate the right fist externally and tuck in the right elbow to turn the right fist heart up, bringing the forearm forward, then down to in front of the belly. The right fist lands into the left hand. Keep the right elbow tight to the ribs. Press the head up. Look forward. (image 1.196)

Pointers

- o   Drill the right fist up then cross for the framing block with a bracing power upwards. Be sure to shift the body back slightly and lengthen it.

o Swing the right fist into the left hand at exactly the same time that the left foot lands in its retreat. As the right fist pounds down, rotate the fist and tuck in the elbow, extend the right shoulder forward slightly, sit the buttocks, gather the belly, contain the chest, release the shoulders, and settle the elbows. All this gives a good power launch for the downward pound. The downward pound should also have a backward pulling, settling, power.

7.   Advance Left Crushing Punch (Hybernating Dragon Shows Itself)

jìnbù zuǒ bēngquán, (zhélóng chūxiàn)   进步左崩拳(蛰龙出现)

ACTION: Advance the right foot and follow up the left foot a half step, keeping most weight on the left leg. At the same time, clench the left fist and punch directly forward with a crushing punch, fist eye up, elbow slightly bent. The right fist stays at the belly. Put the left shoulder forward into the punch. Look forward. (image 1.197)

Pointers

o Land the left punch as the right foot lands. Foot and hand must arrive together. Put the shoulder forward to drive the punch, keeping the shoulders settled and the elbows down. Press the head up.

8.   Right Aligned stance Crushing Punch (Black Tiger Leaves its Den)

yòu shùnbù bēngquán, (hēihǔ chūdòng)   右顺步崩拳 （黑虎出洞）

ACTION: Advance the right foot and follow up the left foot a half step, keeping the weight mostly on the left leg. At the same time, punch the right fist forward with a crushing punch to solar plexus height, fist eye up, elbow slightly bent, shoulder forward. Pull the left fist back to the belly. Press the head up. Look past the right fist. (image 1.198)

Pointers

o The right foot lands, the right fist punches, and the left fist pulls back, all coordinated to arrive simultaneously. The upper and lower body work together so that the hands and feet arrive together. Turn the waist and extend the shoulder for the punch. The right and left fists must have equal power, one spitting and one swallowing. Punch with full power and gather in with full power.

9.   White Crane Flashes its Wings báihè liàngchì   白鹤亮翅

ACTION 1: Retreat the left foot a half step and turn in the right foot, setting down into a horse stance. Lower the right fist down to the belly so that the fists cross in front of the belly with the fist hearts inward. Then drill them up, right fist on the outside of the left, both fists drilling up to head height. Look at the right fist. (image 1.199)

ACTION 2: Without moving the feet, rotate the forearms to turn the fist hearts out then circle them outwards, each going to its own side. The arms brace outwards at shoulder height, slightly bent. Look at the right fist. (image 1.200)

ACTION 3: Sit back onto the left leg, withdrawing the right foot to beside the left foot, landing with a thump. Continue to circle the fists so that they come down, rotating them so the fist hearts face in, gathering them in front of the belly. Hit the belly with some force, sticking the elbows to the ribs, pressing up the head, and settling the *qi* to the *dantian*. Look forward. (image 1.201)

Pointers

o The three actions must continue smoothly without pause, coordinating the whole body and having a full body power.

o Pay attention when circling the fists that they have the powers of drilling, rolling over, bracing, wrapping, and hugging. When they go upwards they drill. When they rotate inwards they roll. When they open to the sides they brace. When they lower and rotate they wrap. When they pound into the belly they hug. Pay attention to the opening and closing of the chest and shoulders, to the release and tightening of the upper back, and to the settling of the elbows.

o The fists pound into the belly at the same time as the right foot thumps, fully coordinated. Settle the *qi* to the *dantian* to assist power output. When the right foot gathers in it must move along the ground, moving from the wrapping in of the waist and hips and the pulling in of the knee. Imagine you are pulling something in with your foot. The final trample of the foot should make a sound, but make sure you are not lifting to purposefully stamp the ground.

o Pay attention to the back and forth shifting of the body. Shift to the left leg when the fists drill up. Shift to the right leg when the fists brace outwards. Shift back to the left leg when the fists wrap and hug inwards.

10.   Left Cannon, Pounding Punch   zuǒ pàoquán   左炮拳

ACTION: Take a long step to the forward right with the right foot and follow in a half step with the left foot, keeping most weight on the left leg. At the same time, drill the right fist up past the chest to nose height and lift the left fist to the sternum. As the right foot steps, punch the left fist forward to solar plexus height, fist eye up, keeping the elbow slightly bent. Release through the shoulders and settle the elbows. Rotate the right fist and brace out with the elbow dropped, the fist eye by the right temple, fist heart forward. As the left shoulder pushes forward the right shoulder follows along. Tuck in the chin and press the head up. Look at the left fist. (image 1.202)

1.202

Pointers

o   The left punch must arrive as the right foot lands – foot and hand working together. Pay attention to the power of the turn of the waist and shoulders. When you drill the right fist up, be sure to keep the elbow down – do not lift it.

11.   Spread Both Wings   shuāng zhǎn chì   双展翅

ACTION 1: Retreat the left foot without moving the right foot. Bring both fists in front of the head, crossing them with the fist hearts in, right fist on the outside of the left. Look forward past the fists. (image 1.203)

ACTION 2: Shift to the left leg and withdraw the right foot to beside the left ankle, then stomp, putting the weight onto the right leg. Rotate the fists inwards and brace them out to their respective sides. Then rotate the fists outwards to turn the fist hearts up, and hug them down and in to the belly. Press the head up and settle the *qi* to the *dantian*. Look forward. (image 1.204)

1.203

1.204

Pointers

o   The fists drill up as the left foot retreats, with a wrapping power. The fists pound into the belly as the right foot stomps.

o   The drill, roll, brace, wrap, and hug of the fists use an internal rotation and external rotation that combines with the containing of the chest, the settling of the elbows, and the gathering of the belly to pound downwards. Settle the *qi* to the *dantian* when the fists hit the belly.

12.   Sparrow Hawk Enters the Woods   yàozǐ rùlín   鹞子入林

ACTION: Take a long step forwards with the left foot and follow up the right foot a half step. Drill the right fist up past the chest to nose height. Lift the left fist to under the right elbow then punch forward as the left foot steps forward. Punch to sternum height with the arm slightly bent, the fist eye on top. Rotate the right fist outwards to turn the fist heart out, and place the fist eye near the right temple, keeping the elbow dropped. Put the left shoulder forward into the punch. Look past the left fist. (image 1.205)

1.205

Pointers

o   The pointers are the same as move 3.

13.   Retreating Chopping Strike (Cat Washes its Face), twice

tuìbù pī quán (māo xī liǎn)   退步劈拳（猫洗脸）

•   This is the same as move 4. Repeat twice. (see images 1.191, 1.192)

14.   Swallow Skims the Water   yànzǐ chāo shuǐ   燕子抄水

ACTION 1: Complete the previous move with the left foot forward and the left hand up. Pull the right hand back, then lift it above the head, then press forward and down with the palm down. Lower the left hand and clench it, then drill it up past the sternum and forward to nose height, fist heart in. Press the right hand down at the side of the waist. Shift forward to the left leg. Look past the left fist. (image 1.206)

ACTION 2: Slice the right hand up in front of the outside of the left forearm and bend the left elbow to stab the left fist down. Continue to circle the right hand back. Open the left hand and slice it forward and up. Shift back. Look at the right hand. (images 1.207, 1.208)

1.206   1.207   1.208

ACTION 3: Advance the left foot a half step then push off to jump, lifting the right knee to step forward, landing with the foot turned out and the left knee raised in a right one legged stance. The body is turned slightly to the right. Slice the right hand forward and up above the head, extending the arm. Bend the left arm and stab down, placing the back of the hand by the left ribs. Look forward to the left. (image 1.209)

ACTION 4: Squat fully on the right leg and dig the left foot forward, extending the leg with the foot tucked in, into a left drop stance. Thread the left hand down and forward along the left leg with the palm turned back, little finger up. Swing the right hand up behind with the arm rounded. Look past the left hand. (image 1.210)

1.209

1.210

Pointers

o The hands work together in opposite directions, one up the other down, one forward the other back, one left the other right. This must be done in coordination with the body.

o Push off with the left leg, swinging the right leg forward and threading the right hand up at the same time. When the right leg sits into the drop stance, the the left hand slides along the left leg.

o The jump must go for both height and distance. Lift the *qi* to help this. The drop stance must be low. Settle the *qi* as you squat and thread out the hand.

o The move should be light and agile, with good coordination between the feet and hands. The actions should be connected and without pause, completed in one breath. Pay attention when threading the left hand along the leg that the head presses forward. As the left hand passes the left foot, shift forward. As the left elbow passes the left foot, bend the leg and move forward and up. You need to train waist strength and leg basics to be able to do this move well.

15.   Swallow Spreads its Wings   yànzǐ zhǎnchì   燕子展翅

ACTION 1: Shift forward to the left leg, bending the knee to rise. Being the left shoulder forward, threading the left hand forward, extending it so it rises to shoulder height, palm to the right. Extend the right hand back. Press the head up. Look past the left hand. (image 1.211)

ACTION 2: Shift forward without stepping. Bend the left elbow to being the hand in to the chest, palm in. Lower the right hand behind, then slice it forward and up along under the left arm, then bend the elbow to bring the hand in front of the

1.211

chest. The hands are now crossed in front of the chest, elbows down, palms in. Turn the body slightly to the right. Look forward. (image 1.212)

ACTION 3: Take a long step forward with the right foot, bending the right leg to stand steady. Follow in the left foot to the right ankle without touching down, keeping the knees together. Rotate both hands to turn the palm out and separate the arms forward and back, bending the elbows. The hands finish with upright sideways palms at shoulder height, the left in front and the right behind, palms facing right. Look at the left palm. (image 1.213)

Pointers

o The move must be done smoothly and well coordinated between upper and lower limbs, with equal attention given to right and left, completed in one breath.

o Take a long step forward and land firmly. Complete the opening of the arms as the foot lands.

16.   Advancing Right Crushing Punch   jìnbù yòu bēng quán   进步右崩拳

ACTION: Step the left foot forward and follow up with the right foot to behind the left, weight on the right leg. Clench both hands and bring the right fist in to the waist, then punch it forward with a crushing punch to solar plexus height. Pull the left fist back to the left side. Press the head up. Look past the right fist. (image 1.214)

Pointers

o Bring the right foot in with a raking action, timing the punch with it.

o Whenever doing the crushing punch, one must try hard to accomplish its requirements that 'the hands never leave the heart, the elbows never leave the ribs, go in and out like in and out of a hole.'

17.   Retreating Left Crushing Punch   tuìbù zuǒ bēng quán   退步左崩拳

ACTION: Retreat the right foot a half step and shift back. Retreat the left foot to the rear, landing with the whole foot. The right foot shifts a bit to allow this, turning out across the stance. Turn the body right, aligning the left shoulder forward. The stance is a scissors stance, with both legs slightly bent. Pull the right fist back to the right side and punch the left fist forward to solar plexus height with a crushing punch. Press the head up. Look past the left fist. (image 1.215)

1.215

Pointers

- o The left punch arrives as the left foot lands behind. The left foot should stomp when it lands.

- o The waist and shoulders should work together to send the left fist out and the right fist back.

18.   Right Aligned stance Crushing Punch

yòu shùnbù bēng quán   右顺步崩拳

ACTION: Advance the right foot and follow up a half step with the left foot, to take a right trinity stance. Pull the left fist back to the left side and punch the right fist forward with a crushing punch to solar plexus height. Press the head up. Look at the right fist. (see image 1.198)

Pointers

- o The right punch arrives as the right foot lands. Turn the waist and send the shoulder into the punch. Settle the shoulders, drop the elbows, and breathe out to punch.

19.   Spread Both Wings

This is the same as move 11. (see images 1.203, 1.204)

20.   Sparrow Hawk Enters the Wood

This is the same as move 12. (see image 1.205)

21.   Retreating Chopping Strike (Cat Washes its Face), twice

This is the same as move 4. (see images 1.191, 1.192)

22.   Black Dragon Pours Water

This is the same as move 5. (see images 1.193, 1.194)

23.   Golden Rooster Pecks a Grain of Rice   jīnjī shímǐ   金鸡食米

ACTION 1: Advance the left foot and shift forward without moving the right foot. Bring the left fist from the head to stab forward and down at the belly. Bring the right fist forward and up to scoop outside the left arm, then pull it back to the right to the right side. Open the left hand and extend it forward to solar plexus height, fingers up, palm to the left. Look past the left hand. (image 1.216)

ACTION 2: Bring the right foot in behind the left foot, landing with a thump, shifting to the right leg. Punch the right fist forward with a crushing punch to solar plexus height. Tuck the left hand onto the right wrist. Press the head up. Look at the right fist. (image 1.217)

1.216   1.217

Pointers

- The right punch comes as the right foot digs into the ground, completing the action as one

- Pull the right fist back as the left hand extends, using the shoulders to coordinate the action. Shift and use body technique to open and close – pre-load back to move forward, and pre-load left to move right.

24.   Reverse Stance Eagle Grasp   àobù yīng zhuō   拗步鹰捉

ACTION 1: Shift forward and step the right foot forward, bending the legs. Pull both hands back to the belly, clench the left hand, and drill them up and forward. Rotate the left fist so the little finger is turned up at nose height. Tuck in the chin and press the head up. Look at the left fist. (image 1.218)

ACTION 2: Take a long step to the forward left with the left foot then follow up a half step with the right foot, keeping most weight on the right leg. Drill the right fist up then forward and up along the left arm. As the fists cross, rotate them and open to eagle claws. Chop the right hand forward and down to waist height. Pull the left hand back to in front of the belly. Press the head up. Look down past the right hand. (image 1.219)

1.218   1.219

Pointers

- Drill the left fist out as the right foot steps forward. Chop the right hand down as the left foot steps forward.

- The eagle claw hand shape is: the fingertips are slightly tucked in, the palm is rounded, and the wrist is settled. Pay attention to releasing the shoulders and settling the elbows, and pressing the head up and tucking the buttocks under, when hitting out with the eagle grab. The legs have a scissoring power. Do not turn the head down to look down, but just look down with the eyes. This is a characteristic of the eagle claw.

25. **Push the Shutter to Gaze at the Moon** tuīchuāng wàngyuè 推窗望月

ACTION 1: Retreat the right foot a half step and withdraw the left foot to in front of the right foot. Circle the left hand from the belly forward and up, then back to by the left shoulder, palm up. Turn the right hand outward to bring the thumb side down, then circle down, forward, up, and back to by the right shoulder, palm down. Look at the left hand. Turn the body leftward. (image 1.220)

ACTION 2: Advance the left foot a long step and follow up a half step with the right foot, landing it turned out to sit into a half horse stance. At the same time, bring the left hand around down, forward, and up, finishing with the palm forward, thumb down, bracing with the arm in a framing high block at eye height. Push the right hand forward at solar plexus height with the fingers up. Tuck in the chin. The right hand is in front of the left ribs. Look past the right hand. (image 1.221)

1.220 1.221

Pointers

- o Circle the hands forward, up and back as the feet retreat and withdraw. Block and push as the left foot advances. The left brace and the right push must work together.

- o Pay attention to the bodywork for the move. When the hands move forward the body moves slightly back. When the hands move up the body sits slightly down. When the hands move back the body moves forward. When the hands push forward the body tucks to press up. The body sits down slightly and the head pushes up.

26. **Three Basins on the Ground** sānpán luòdì 三盘落地

ACTION 1: Withdraw the left foot to by the right ankle without touching down, not moving the right foot. Lower the right hand to the left ribs. Rotate the left hand out to turn the palm in, and settle the elbow to do an elbow cover to the right, lowering it to in front of the right shoulder. The arms are now crossed in front of the body. Look to the left. (image 1.222)

ACTION 2: Take a sideways bridging step with the left foot to the left and follow in slightly with the right foot, sitting into a horse stance. At the same time, brace the hands out

1.222 1.223

to each direction, keeping the arms rounded. The hands brace out on opposite sides at hip height, palms down. Look at the left hand. (image 1.223)

Pointers

o Tuck the left hand in as the left foot withdraws, wrapping the elbow. Brace the hands out as the left foot advances.

o To do the rolling tuck of the left hand and elbow, close the shoulders, contain the chest, and tauten the upper back to store power. To brace out with the hands you need to open the chest, solidify the abdomen, release the waist, sit into the hip joints, settle the shoulders, brace the elbows, and set the wrists. Coordinate this power output with a breath out. The whole body has well balanced power and structure to front and back, left and right.

27.   Lazy Dragon Lies in the Road   lǎnlóng wòdào   懒龙卧道

ACTION 1: Shift forward to the left leg and clench the fists. Pull the left fist back to the right side, fist heart down. Rotate the right fist to fist heart up. and pull it back to the right ribs. Look to the forward left. (image 1.224)

ACTION 2: Lift the right knee, turning the foot out, then step forward with the foot turned out, sitting into a resting stance. At the same time, stab the right fist forward and down, out past the ribs and chest, to hip height. Look at the right fist. (image 1.225)

1.224

1.225

Pointers

o Coordinate the lifting of the right knee, step and sit into the resting stance with the stabbing down of the right fist.

o When stabbing down, contain the chest, close the shoulders, tauten the upper back, and settle and release the shoulders. The left shoulder should angle to the front.

**28. Black Dragon Overturns the Waves
(Aligned Stance Left Crossing Punch)**

wūlóng fānjiāng (shùnbù zuǒ héngquán)

乌龙翻江 （顺步左横拳）

ACTION: Take a long step straight forward with the left foot and follow in the right foot, keeping most weight on the right leg. At the same time, lift and roll over the right fist, pulling it back to the right waist, fist heart down. Rotate the left fist to turn the fist heart up, and do a crossing punch out

1.226

from under the right arm, to shoulder height. Press the head up. Look forward past the left fist. (image 1.226)

Pointers

- o   Complete the left crossing punch as the left foot lands. Twist the fists to complete both actions together with a complete power.

29.   Advancing Right Crushing Punch

This is the same as move 16. (see image 1.214)

30.   Dragon and Tiger Play Together lóng hǔ xiāngjiāo   龙虎相交

ACTION: Advance the left foot a half step and shift to the left leg, standing firmly with the leg slightly bent. Lift the right leg to do a strong heel kick forward, pulling the toes back to kick with the heel to waist height. At the same time, pull the right fist back to the right side of the waist and punch the left fist forward with a crushing punch to solar plexus height, fist eye up. Look forward past the left fist. (image 1.227)

1.227

Pointers

- o   Coordinate upper and lower limbs so that the left fist punches, the right fist pulls back, and the right leg completes the heel kick with full, connected power.

- o   Turn the waist to put the shoulder into the punch. Tuck in the belly to kick, first lifting the knee, then extending into the heel. Pay attention to standing firmly on the left leg.

31.   Right Aligned stance Crushing Punch   yòu shùnbù bēngquán 右顺步崩拳

ACTION: After the kick, land the right foot forward and down, and advance the left foot a half step to take a right trinity stance. Pull the left fist back and punch out the right fist with a crushing punch to solar plexus height, the arm slightly bent. Press the head up. Look at the right fist. (image 1.228)

1.228

Pointers

- o   The pointers are the same as move 8, just, because of the landing from the kick, the right foot has more trampling power.

The following moves, 32 through 36, then 37 through 40, repeat combinations already done, those of moves 9 through 13, and 5 through 8.

32.	**White Crane Flashes its Wings**	See move 9.
33.	**Left Cannon, Pounding Punch**	See move 10.
34.	**Spread Both Wings**	See move 11.
35.	**Sparrow Hawk Enters the Woods**	See move 12.
36.	**Retreating Chopping Strike (Cat Washes its Face), twice**	See move 13.
37.	**Black Dragon Pours Water**	See move 5.
38.	**Stretch Out One Wing**	See move 6.
39.	**Left Crushing Punch (Hybernating Dragon Shows Itself)**	See move 7.
40.	**Right Aligned Stance Crushing Punch (Black Tiger Leaves its Den)**	

See move 8.

41.   Wind Sways the Lotus Leaves (three times)   fēng bǎi hēyè   风摆荷叶

ACTION 1: Turn around one-eighty degrees to the left to move back in the direction from which you came. Advance the left foot a half step to the forward left, without moving the right foot. Open both hands, and lower the right hand past the belly, so that both hands circle down to the left, then up, fingers up, palms facing each other. The left hand is in front of the right hand, both at shoulder height. Look at the right hand. (image 1.229 and from behind)

1.229
FROM
BEHIND

ACTION 2: Step the right foot across to the front, turned out, so that the legs are crossed with the weight between them. Circle the hands from the left up, and back to the right, to lower. The hands now are upright at shoulder height, facing towards the rear right, with the arms slightly bent. Turn the body to the right. Look at the right hand. (image 1.230 and from behind)

1.230

1.230
FROM
BEHIND

Pointers

o   The hands swing to the front as the left foot advances, and swing to the rear as the right foot steps across.

 o Both actions are repeated three times. The movement is soft and well coordinated the first and second times, then hit with power the third time. Pay attention to turning the waist well around to the rear right and swinging the arms with well settled shoulders and elbows. The right foot should cut across forcefully so that the whole move is stable with power – it must not become floating.

42. Advancing Left Crushing Punch jìnbù zuǒ bēngquán 进步左崩拳

ACTION: Advance the left foot to the front and follow in the right foot slightly, keeping most weight on the right leg. Clench both hands and pull the right fist back to the right side of the waist. Bring the left fist down to in front of the chest, then, as the waist turns left, punch forward to solar plexus height. The arm is slightly bent and the fist eye is up. Press the head up. Look past the left fist. (image 1.231)

1.231

Pointers

 o Pay attention to first turn the body, and then step forward and punch.

43. Sparrow Hawk Pierces the Sky yàozǐ zuāntiān 鹞子钻天

ACTION 1: Advance the left foot a half step and follow in the right foot to the left ankle without touching down. Rotate the left fist to turn the fist heart down, tucking the arm to press down across in front of the chest. Look at the left fist. (image 1.232)

ACTION 2: Step the right foot forward and follow in the left foot a half step, keeping most weight on the left leg. At the same time, drill the right fist up past the sternum and forward. Roll the little finger side of the fist up to punch to nose height. Tuck the left fist down, pulling back to the belly, fist heart in. Tuck the chin in and press the head up. Look forward past the right fist. (image 1.233)

1.232 1.233

Pointers

 o Bend the left arm to tuck and press down as the left foot advances, arriving together. Drill the right fist out as the right foot steps forward, also arriving together

 o Settle the body slightly down when the right fist drills up. Twist the waist and put the shoulder into the punch, keeping the shoulders settled and elbows dropped. Breathe out to exert power, and settle the *qi* to the *dantian*.

44.   **Sparrow Hawk Wheels Over**   yàozǐ fānshēn   鹞子翻身

ACTION 1: Pivot both feet on the spot, turning one-eighty degrees to face back in the direction from which you came. Lift the right elbow to bring the arm over the head as the body turns leftward, going forward, then covering down, fist heart down, to chest height. Drill the left fist up past the sternum and forward to nose height, twisting the little finger side up. Shift to the left leg. Look at the left fist. (image 1.234)

1.234

ACTION 2: Do a framing block up with the right arm, elbow across. Bend the left elbow and bring it back to the chest. Shift back to the right leg. Internally rotate the right fist and pull it back to the right side of the head. At the same time, internally rotate the left fist and lift the elbow, turning the fist eye in, then stab out along the left ribs towards the left hip. Look at the left fist. (image 1.235)

ACTION 3: Bend the right leg to squat down, and extend the left leg out to the left in a drop stance. Thread the left fist out along on top of the left leg and pull the right fist back to the right side of the waist, externally rotating it. Extend the left fist past the left foot. Look at the left fist. (image 1.236)

1.235   1.236

Pointers

o   This move is done smoothly, all actions joining together without pause, completed in one breath. This move emphasizes bodywork. It takes expert body power, using the waist as the hub, and loosening the waist and shoulders, so that the entire body works together without slackening. The power is soft but not slack, hidden inside, not hard or stiff.

o   Pay attention to shifting the weight back and forth, leading from the head and pressing from the waist.

o   The fists and arms must work together as one. The left fist threads out inside the right arm, and the right arm blocks up along outside the left arm. When the right fist pulls back, use the elbow to draw it back, then use a wrapping, twisting power to lower the fist. Pay attention to the shoulders, keep them slightly closed, roll them out, and release and settle them, coordinating with the arms and fists to twist and rotate.

45.   Sparrow Hawk Folds its Wings   yàozǐ shù shēn   鹞子束身

ACTION: Shift forward to the left leg and bend the left knee, moving forward and up, threading the left fist forward. Take a long step forward with the right foot and follow up the left foot to inside the right ankle without touching down, keeping the legs together. Tuck and press down with the left fist and pull it back to in front of the belly. Lift the right fist from the right side up to the sternum, then punch forwards and down to groin height. The right fist is rotated so the fist eye is forward. Press the head up. Look forward. (image 1.237)

Pointers

- o   Pointers are the same as for move 2.

46.   Sparrow Hawk Enters the Woods   yàozǐ rùlín   鹞子入林

This is the same as move 3. (image 1.238)

47.   Closing Move   shōu shì   收势

ACTION 1: Without moving the feet, lower the right fist to the belly and tuck and pull the left fist to the belly. both fist hearts face in. Press the left foot into the ground. Press the heaad up and tuck in the chin. Look forward. (image 1.239)

ACTION 2: Bring the right foot back beside the left foot, keeping the knees bent so that the height of the stance does not change. Unclench the hands and lift them at the sides to shoulder height, palms up, arms slightly bent. Then bend the elbows to bring the hands together at the front at shoulder height, fingers pointing to each other, palms down. Look at the right hand. (image 1.240)

ACTION 3: Press the hands down in front of the belly and stand up to attention, letting the hands hang down to the sides. Look forward. (image 1.241)

1.240

1.241

Pointers

- ○ Press into the left foot and press the head up as the left fist tucks and pulls in. Bring the right foot in as the hands move together.

- ○ Stand up gradually as the hands push down, so that the actions of each are completed at the same time.

- ○ The *closing move* is completed without a pause. Pay attention that the spirit remains full, the manner remains dignified, and that the entire movement is completed without slackening.

THE EIGHT SKILLS 八字功

INTRODUCTION TO THE EIGHT SKILLS, *BAZIGONG*

The Eight Skills are an important component of the Xingyiquan system. They are the functional techniques of traditional Xingyiquan, that is, training them improves your ability to apply your power – they are combat effective. The classics say, "the Xingyiquan system is composed of the five elemental techniques and the twelve animal models for training the body, and the other techniques for practicality. The functional techniques are learned in order to be used. The path of learning must develop both the body and train combative applications. Mastery of both is mastery of the system."

The Eight Skills are spread, intercept, wrap, bridge, scoop, butt, pass, and guide. Each skill is practised as a short sequence of actions that have a specific method, power application, and combative application. Each skill can be trained on its own or within the eight skills form. Training the Eight Skills enhances the movement vocabulary of the five elemental techniques and the twelve animals – bringing additional power applications through each segment of the body, and the ability to issue power to many directions and angles.

The Eight Skills were not taught lightly to outsiders of the Xingyiquan system, so they are not widespread. The set of Eight Skills presented here was developed in 1919 by the Baoding Military School, and written up in 'The records of the Wushu Research Society,' but the book only roughly describes the movements with simple diagrams. I studied this old book for many years and asked many elder masters about the skills, and gradually worked out the actions and their requirements. I describe them here thoroughly, and have added many images and created poems as memory aids. I present these so that readers can learn and understand the Eight Skills.

ONE: THE SKILL OF SPREADING 展字功

INTRODUCTION TO SPREAD, *ZHAN*

The classics say, "Spread means to stretch or open out, that is, to open out the hands and feet." Spread means to open up, expand, stretch out, or unfold. Among the eight skills, the Skill Of Spreading gives the imagery of an expansive, opened posture, spreading the feet and hands, turning the body sideways to enter and strike.[31]

The short sequence for training the Skill Of Spreading is: *opening move, right step forward tiger carries, right spread, step forward left splitting fist, left spread,* and *step forward right splitting fist.*

1a Opening Move (left *santishi*) qǐ shì 起势

Description:

ACTION 1: Stand to attention, facing forty-five degrees to the line on which you will travel. You may also start facing directly in the way you will travel, with the right foot turned out to almost forty-five degrees. (image 2.1)

ACTION 2: Without moving the feet, gradually lift the hands at the sides to shoulder height, palms up and arms naturally bent. Look at the right hand. (image 2.2)

ACTION 3: Bend the elbows so that the hands point to each other in front of the face, palms down. Then press the hands down to the belly, bending the legs to sit with the knees together. Press the head up and look forward to the left. (image 2.3)

ACTION 4: Clench the fists at the belly and turn the fist hearts up. Keep the left fist at the belly and drill the right fist up by the sternum then forward to nose height. Twist the ulnar edge of the right forearm up. Look at the right fist. (image 2.4)

ACTION 5: Advance the left foot without moving the right foot. The stance length should be the length of your own shin. The left leg is slightly bent and the right leg

---

[31] Author's note: Some classics write 'break' [折 zhé] instead of 'spread' [展 zhǎn]. This sounds similar, but means something quite different. Break means to snap something by hacking or by knocking with the forearm. It is something similar to a splitting fist, so the movement structure, actions, and application would not be the same as spreading.

more bent, with more weight on the right leg.[32] Bring the left fist up by the sternum and out to the right elbow, drilling forward by sliding along the right forearm, fist heart up. When the left fist arrives at the right fist, unclench both hands and turn the palms down. Split the left hand forward and down with the arm slightly bent and the wrist cocked, fingers at shoulder height. Pull the right hand back to the belly, palm down. Press the head up and look past the left hand. (image 2.5)

Pointers

- o Press the hands down as you sit – complete all actions together.

- o Time the left hand split to finish as the left foot lands.

- o The spirit of the opening move must be full and shown in the eyes.

1b   Right Step Forward, Tiger Carries   yòu shàngbù hǔtuō   右上步虎托

ACTION 1: Advance the left foot a half-step and follow in the right foot beside the left ankle without touching down. Keep the knees together to take a one-legged stance with the left leg bent. Thread the right hand forward, palm down, under the left forearm. Once the wrists cross, circle the hands out to the sides, palms angled forward. Complete the circles by bringing the hands back to the waist, palms forward and fingers down. Press the head up and look forward. (images 2.6, 2.7)

ACTION 2: Take a long step forward with the right foot and follow in a half-step with the left foot to take a *santi* stance with the right foot forward. Do a carrying technique with the palms, to push forward and down with the palms forward and the fingers down. The hands should be a fist width apart at belly height. Look past the hands. (image 2.8)

---

[32] Author's note: The proper weight distribution of a *santi* stance is between seventy-thirty and sixty-forty. The 'sweet spot' is 0.618 weighted on the rear leg.

Pointers

- Circle the hands while advancing the left foot.

- You must apply an integrated power by completing the carrying action of the hands as the right foot lands.

1c   Spread, Right Side   yòu zhǎnshì   右展势

ACTION 1: Retreat the left foot a half-step and withdraw the right foot to just in front of the left, shifting the weight mostly onto the left leg. Clench the hands with the fist hearts up. Drill the left fist up to nose height outside the right forearm. Bend the right elbow to do a hooking cover leftward in front of the body, also with the fist at nose height. Finish with both fist hearts face in and a gathering, embracing power in the elbows. Look past the fists, facing in the direction of the technique. (image 2.9)

ACTION 2: Advance the right foot a long step and hook-in the foot as it lands. Follow in the left foot a half-step, turning the foot out as it lands. Turn the body ninety degrees and sit down with more weight on the left leg to take a half horse stance, with the right leg leading. Pull the left fist up and back to the left temple, rotating the fist and bending the elbow so that the fist eye is down and the arm braces out. Rotate the right fist and lift the elbow so that the fist eye is down with the elbow at shoulder height. Turn the body as you step forward and punch forward to sternum height with the right fist, completing the punch with the arm slightly bent and the fist eye down. Look at the right fist. (image 2.10 and images from the other side and from the front)

Pointers

- Complete three actions together: retreat the left foot, drill the left fist up, and cover leftward with the right fist.

- Complete the planting punch as the right foot lands. Sit well down into a half horse stance.

1d   **Step Forward, Left Split**   shàngbù zuǒ pīquán   上步左劈拳

ACTION 1: Withdraw the right foot a half-step and shift back, turning the torso slightly right. Pull the left fist down the left side to the waist, fist heart up and elbow hugging the ribs. Rotate the right fist out toward the thumb side and pull it back to the belly, fist heart up. Press the head up and look forward. (image 2.11)

ACTION 2: Advance the right foot a half-step and follow in the left foot beside the right without touching down. Drill the right fist up to the sternum and forward to nose height with the ulnar edge turned up. Do not move the left fist yet. Press the head up and look past the right fist. (image 2.12)

ACTION 3: Take a long step forward with the left foot and follow in a half-step with the right foot, keeping most weight on the right leg. Bring the left fist by the sternum then out along the right forearm, then unclench it and split forward. Unclench the right hand, turn it over, and pull it back to the belly, palm down. The split is done to sternum height. Press the head up and look forward. (image 2.13)

Pointers

○   These three actions are done as one movement – it is a stepping forward split.

○   The actions should be done without pause and the hands and feet must be tightly coordinated: Pull the right fist back as the right foot withdraws; Drill the right fist up as the right foot advances; Split with the left hand as the left foot steps forward.

1e   **Spread, Left Side**   zuǒ zhǎnshì   左展势

ACTION 1: Retreat the right foot a half-step and continue by withdrawing the left foot a half-step, keeping most weight on the right leg. Clench both fists. Rotate the left fist so the fist centre is up and bend the elbow to cover rightward to the body's midline. Turn the right fist heart up and slide it forward outside the left forearm to drill up to nose height. Then bend the left elbow and bring it in, turning both fist hearts in and closing in with the elbows. Look forward. (image 2.14)

ACTION 2: Advance the left foot a long step and land with it hooked in. Follow up the right foot with a half-step advance, turning it out. Turn the body ninety degrees rightward and sit down into a half horse stance. Rotate the right fist and pull it up and back to the right side of the head, fist eye down, bending the elbow to brace outward. Roll the left fist down so the fist eye is down, and lift the elbow to shoulder height. As the left foot steps forward and the body turns, plant the left

fist forward to sternum height. Complete the punch with the left arm slightly bent and the fist eye down. Look at the left fist. (image 2.15)

1f   Step Forward, Right Split   shàngbù yǒu pīquán 上步右劈拳

ACTION 1: Turn the torso slightly to the left and withdraw the left foot a half-step. Rotate the right fist and pull it down the side to the waist with the fist heart up and the elbow snug to the ribs. Rotate the left fist and pull it back to the belly, fist heart up. Look forward. (image 2.16)

ACTION 2: Advance the left foot a half-step and follow in the right foot beside the left without touching down, keeping the knees together. Drill the left fist forward and up to nose height, twisting the ulnar edge up. Press the head up and look forward. (image 2.17)

ACTION 3: Take a long step forward with the right foot and follow in a half-step with the left foot. Bring the right fist by the sternum, along the left forearm, and then unclench it and split forward to sternum height. Unclench the left hand and pull it back to the belly. Press the head up and look past the right hand. (image 2.18)

- Continue on, alternating the left and right *skill of spreading* without the opening moves.

1g   Turn Around for the Skill of Spreading

zhǎnzìgōng zhuànshēn   展字功转身

You may perform a *split turn around* or a *tiger carry turn around*, but more usually the *tiger carries*. For more detail on *split turn around*, see Volume I.

- If the <u>left</u> foot is forward, to turn with *tiger carries*:

ACTION 1: Hook-in step the left foot in front of the right toes and shift onto the left leg, turning the body around rightward two-seventy degrees to face back in the way you came. Lift the right foot at the left ankle without touching down. Turn the unclenched hands palm out, crossing them in front of the body, then circle them up, out to either side, then in to the side of the torso with the palms forward and fingers down. Press the head up and look forward. (image 2.19)

ACTION 2: Step the right foot diagonally to the forward right and follow in the left foot a half-step. Push the hands forward and down to belly height. Finish with the hands fist-width apart, palms forward, fingers down, elbows bent and close together. Sit the torso down, press the head up, and look forward. (image 2.20)

- If the <u>right</u> foot is forward, to turn with *tiger carries:*

ACTION 1: Hook-in the right foot toward the left toes to turn the body around one-eighty to the left, facing back in the way you came. Shift onto the right leg and lift the left foot by the right foot without touching down. Bend the knees and keep them together to stand firmly on the right leg. Cross the forearms in front of the chest with the palms out, left hand inside the right hand. Circle the hands up and out to the left and right then bring them back to the sides, palm forward, fingers down. Press the head up and look forward. (images 2.21, 2.22)

ACTION 2: Take a long step diagonally to the forward left with the left foot and follow in the right foot a half-step, keeping most weight on the right leg. Do a low carrying action to belly height with the hands. Finish about fist width apart, palms facing forward, fingers down. Look forward. (image 2.23)

2.23

Pointers

- o Circle the hands as you step around. Be sure to take a good hook-in step so that the turn around is quick.

- o Complete the *tiger carries* as the foot lands forward, so that the hands and feet work together.

1h   Closing Move for the Skill of Spreading

zhǎnzìgōng shōushì   展字功收势

Continue on until you are at your starting point facing in the same direction that you did the *opening move*.

- To start the closing from *tiger carries* in <u>left</u> stance:

ACTION 1: Withdraw the left foot to inside the right foot. Clench the right hand and pull it back to the belly. Turn the left hand over and cover, pressing down with the palm down at shoulder height with the elbow bent. Drill the right fist up by the sternum and forward to nose height, ulnar edge turned up. At the same time, press down and pull the left hand back to the belly, clenching it. Press the head up and look forward. (image 2.24)

ACTION 2: Step the left foot forward without moving the right foot to sit into a santi stance. Drill the left fist out from the sternum to the right elbow and forward until the fists cross. Then unclench the hands and split forward with the left hand while pulling the right hand back to the belly, palms facing down. Press the head up and look forward. (image 2.25)

2.24

2.25

- From a *tiger carries* with the <u>right</u> foot forward:

ACTION 1: Withdraw the right foot to inside the left foot. Land the right foot firmly and shift onto the right leg, lifting the left foot a bit and keeping the knees together. Turn the left hand over and cover, pressing down with the palm down at shoulder height with the elbow bent. Pull the right hand back to the belly, clenching it, then drill the right fist up by the sternum and forward to nose height, ulnar edge turned up. At the same time, press down and pull the left hand back to the belly, clenching it. Press the head up and look forward. (images 2.26, 2.27)

ACTION 2: Step the left foot forward without moving the right foot, to sit into a *santi* stance. Perform a splitting action, splitting forward with the left hand while pulling the right hand back to the belly. Press the head up and look forward. (image 2.28)

- When you arrive in *santishi* then close as you would normally.

Pointers

- o Drill the right fist up and cover with the left forearm as the lead foot withdraws. Be sure to move all together and to sit back to the right leg.

- o Split forward with the left hand as the left foot advances into the *santi* stance. Step an appropriate distance so that the right foot does not need to move, so that you can keep your spirit full and settled.

POWER GENERATION FOR THE SKILL OF SPREADING

The short sequence for the Skill Of Spreading is comprised of a spread technique combined with a split done to both sides. Looking at the structure of the spread technique, it is a planting punch with the body turned sideways. Its power launch is long range with considerable strength. Its long range comes from adding a shoulder width to the length of the arm. Its strength comes from combining a forward step, a body turn and an arm extension to deliver the planting punch.

The final spread position aligns the feet and the body in one plane. Prior to spreading, the lead arm covers in and the rear fist drills up so that the elbows close together in front of the chest. The elbows should use a bracing out power, closing the chest and stretching the upper back to gather energy.

When the feet retreat and withdraw and the fists drill up, the body should rise slightly and shift back to gather energy. Just prior to the planting punch, the shoulder of the punching side should draw back to gather power for the punch.

Launch power forward and down for the planting punch. It should finish between belly and chest height. The lead foot should land with a trampling power. At the instant of launching the punch, the body should have a crossways shoving power in the same direction as the punch. The fist and arm use a drilling power that rolls, tucks, twists, and rotates. Turn the waist and extend the shoulder into the punch to turn the body sideways to complete the punch.

Use the rear hand to give more power to the lead hand by pulling the rear fist back by the head, twisting as it goes, and bracing back with the elbow. The entire strike is fully connected, as the body core leads the shoulders, the shoulders urge the elbows, and the elbows urge the fists forward. The power flows smoothly between each segment. Exhale to complete the whole body connection in the power launch.

The key to getting power when connecting the spread to the split is, as you withdraw the foot, bring the fist back by turning and pulling it from the shoulder and elbow. Bring the shoulder back and stretch it out, then settle it down. Close the elbow in and then settle it down. In this way the shoulders draw the elbows and the elbows draw the fists into the rotation, pulling it back to the belly as the foot withdraws. Then you can roll the fist over and step forward into the split.

- When first learning do not try too hard to get whole body power. First get a feel for the line of action. Concentrate on getting the main actions, hand placement, body shape and footwork smooth. Once the movement is correct then you can get comfortable with it. You can work on whole body power once you have a comfortable foundation. Correct and perfect your technique continually in your practice.

PRACTICAL APPLICATIONS FOR THE SKILL OF SPREADING

The kernel of the Skill Of Spreading's short sequence is the right and left spread techniques. Analysing this spread position, it is a turned planting punch. The whole sequence contains both attack and defense. The retreat and withdrawal of the feet together with the rolling and closing of the elbows closes off any attack, tightly protecting the chest and head area. A quick advance and turn to plant the punch goes for the opponent's chest, belly, or floating ribs. The key lies in entering the lead foot through into the opponent's groin area.

- The spread technique can be either a counter attack that flows from a defensive move or a direct attack, using the theory of 'you do what you want and I'll do what I want.' In Xingyiquan, we often go for a direct hit without bothering to block. If your opponent attacks to your head, you turn sideways and attack his head. Because you have added the length of the shoulder to your extended arm, if you both punch at the same time your punch will land while your opponent's will fall short.

- When counter attacking, retreat the rear foot. When directly attacking, step the rear foot forward.

Duck the head back, protect the chest with the elbows, and protect the head with the fists. The rear fist can drill up in a scooping upper block, or can hook and pull back. The lead fist takes its opportunity to strike forward.

- Of course, in combat you cannot count on one technique finishing the job. The classics say, "once you start, do ten techniques." Attack continuously until you win. As you continue on from the spread to the split, the lead hand does a backfist punch or a drilling punch, and then you step further forward into the split. This is just a simple analysis of the technique; in a combative situation you need to adjust to whatever comes.

THE POEM ABOUT THE SKILL OF SPREADING

展势侧身劲力雄，一展一劈练其功。掩肘上钻胸前抱，拧腰栽打贯腹胸。

The spread position with the body turned has great strength,

Train this skill with a spread and a split.

Cover with the elbows and drill up to hug in front of the chest,

Twist the waist and plant a punch through the belly or chest.

TWO: THE SKILL OF INTERCEPTING

截字功

INTRODUCTION TO INTERCEPT, *JIE*

The classics say, "intercept means to cut out, to cut off the opponent's attack." The action of intercepting is to obstruct and break with a cutting action, and so combines breaking, checking, cutting off, and trapping. The Skill Of Intercepting is thus a trapping cut of the opponent's arm. It can be performed as a single arm or a double arm technique. Intercept's power application is a short, quick hit. It is done just before the opponent's attack is completed, trapping with a hard force vertically across his attack, trapping and checking to attack quickly. Intercept can be seen as simply a defensive move, but since it is able to break the opponent's arm it can finish a fight.

Within the sequence you can either perform intercept alone or you can combine it with a trundle. Trundle means to push or shove straight forward with both hands. You should first learn the standard way, and then work on the alternate ways. Then when you need to use it you will be able to react spontaneously. Beginners should train hard and carefully seek to understand through practice.

The short sequence for the Skill Of Intercepting is *opening move, right step forward tiger carries, intercept,* and *advance and trundle.*

2a   Opening Move (left *santishi*)   qǐ shì   起势

Start with *santishi* as described movement 1a above.

2b   Right Step Forward, Tiger Carries   yòu shàngbù hǔtuō   右上步虎托

This is the same as described above in 1b.

2c   Intercept, Left Side   zuǒ jiéshì   左截势

ACTION: Retreat the left foot a half-step and shift back towards the left leg. Withdraw the right foot a half-step. Clench the left fist and drill it up towards the forward right. Unclench it and rotate it into a hooking position, then pull in an arc to the left, bending the arm in front of the left chest. Clench the right fist and draw it back by the right waist, then without stopping, bend the elbow and lift it, taking

it forward and rolling it
to cut across to the left,
just to the left of the
midline. Then rotate the
right arm ulnar edge up.
The right fist is at nose
height with the elbow
bent about one hundred
degrees. Turn leftward,
twisting the waist, sitting
the torso, and settling the
shoulders and elbows.
Press the head up and
look past the right fist. (image 2.29)

Pointers

- o Hook with the right hand as the left foot retreats.

- o Cut across with the right forearm and elbow as the right foot withdraws.

- o Compress the torso slightly as you intercept with the elbow.

- o Turn the waist and close the shoulders to put power into the elbow as it cuts across to intercept.

2d   Advance and Trundle   jìnbù gǔnshǒu   进步滚手

ACTION: Advance the right foot a long step and follow in a half-step with the left foot to take a *santi* stance with the right foot forward and left back. Unclench the right hand and rotate the thumb outward, settling the elbow down and extending the arm to push forward at sternum height, finishing with the arm slightly bent. Place the left hand at the right forearm, palm forward. Put equal power into both hands and close in the elbows. Contain the chest, lengthen the spine, release the shoulders, settle the elbows, and press the head up. Look forward. (image 2.30)

Pointers

- o Take a long step with the right foot and follow in quickly with the left. Make sure the weight shift is quick and stable.

- o Complete the double push as the right foot lands, with an integrated power.

2e   Intercept, Right Side   yòu jiéshì   右截势

ACTION: Advance the left foot a half-step and shift slightly forward. Lift the left heel slightly and place the weight between the legs. Clench the right fist and pull it down, then drill it forward and up in front of the left side of the body. Unclench it and rotate the thumb inward to hook with the hand, pulling across in front and to the right in an arc towards the right chest with the arm bent and the palm facing down. Clench the left fist and lift the elbow, then cut the elbow across towards the right to just right of the midline. Rotate the left fist into the ulnar edge. The fist is at nose height and the elbow is at sternum height. The left elbow is bent about one hundred degrees. Turn the body a bit to the right. Twist the waist, sit into the torso, settle the shoulders and elbows, and lift the head up. Look past the left fist.

(images 2.31 and 2.31 front)

Pointers

- o This is the same intercept technique, but to the right. Be sure to use the power from the body core.

- o When intercepting, gather the power in the body core and contain the chest. Tighten the fists when cutting across with the forearms.

- o Complete the trundle and intercept as one action, keeping the movement connected and quick.

2f   Step Forward and Trundle   shàngbù gǔnshǒu   上步滚手

ACTION: Take a long step forward with the left foot and follow in a half-step with the right foot. Keep most weight on the right leg. Unclench the left hand and turn it forward, settling the elbow and extending the arm to push forward, finishing with the arm slightly bent and the hand at the sternum. Push forward with the right hand at the same time, just behind the left wrist, palm also facing forward. Apply force equally into the hands, both elbows held in. Contain the chest, lengthen the spine, release the shoulders, steel the elbows, and press the head up. Look forward. Breathe out to assist the power launch. (image 2.32)

- • Carry on alternating left and right as long as the practice area and your fitness allow.

Pointers

- o Advance the right foot a good distance and use the combined force of the step and both hands to push. Unite the power of the whole body to arrive all at the same time.

- o Perform the intercept to the right as the right foot advances a half-step.

- o Do not stop between intercept and trundle, but complete them as one move. Think of them as one move.

2g   Turn Around for the Skill of Intercepting jiézìgòng zhuànshēn 截字功转身

Turn around with a *tiger carries*, as described in movement 1g, then continue on repeating the combination sequence.

2h   Closing Move for the Skill of Intercepting   jiézìgòng shōushì截字功收势

Continue until you are back at your starting place facing in the same direction as you started, then perform a left split as described above in movement 1h. Then close as you would normally from *santishi*.

POWER GENERATION FOR THE SKILL OF INTERCEPTING

The main application in the sequence of the Skill Of Intercepting is the hand hook and elbow cover to break, and then the entry to trundle and push away. If you retreat you must be agile, and if you advance or step forward you must be quick.

Turn the body slightly to get power into the elbow interception, so that one hand hooks and pulls while the other hand cuts across. Use the ulnar side of the forearm for the crossing elbow-cover. Twist your waist, reach the shoulder into the move, settle the elbows down and turn the wrists, twisting to get the cutting power. You need to get the full use out of both elbows, with a settled power, quick and short. Launch an instantaneous power that is hard and fierce but settled.

When you step forward for the trundle and push, take a long step in to charge the body forward. To trundle up the opponent, the lead hand rolls, hooks, and grabs, applying a rolling pressure down, and the rear hand closes in and releases. To do the action of the lead hand, first contain the chest, settle the elbows, flex the waist, and use the body's power to roll and press – close the elbows. Then push forward with both hands simultaneously. When releasing power, lengthen the spine, extend the arms, release the shoulders forward, and charge in with the footwork, driving the body forward to shove. Compress the torso as the hands rise, lengthen the torso as they land. Step forward quickly, get the hands in quickly. Breathe out to launch power. Press the head up. Focus on sending the opponent away a good distance.

- The above has described the single-handed intercept. There is also a double-handed intercept. The double-handed intercept is similar to *tiger intercepts*. The skill of intercept has many variations, such as upper intercept, lower intercept, left intercept, and right intercept. They are just variations on the same power, changing directions, placements, and angles to train the skill in a variety of ways.

PRACTICAL APPLICATIONS FOR THE SKILL OF INTERCEPTING

Intercept is mainly a retreating defense to block the opponent's hands. The trundle then shoves him away.

- The classics say "straight, use intercept; crossways, use jam." This simply means that when the opponent comes at me with a straight technique, then intercept is effective. If the opponent comes at me with a crossing or swinging punch then a jam is effective. That is, jam him at the root of the arm to prevent him from throwing the punch.

When using intercept you must master the timing and wait for the right moment. It works when the opponent has thrown the punch but it has not yet landed – neither earlier nor later will work. If you block too early then he can easily pull his punch away and you will miss him altogether. If you block too late then his punch will land. You must time it just right, and hit the right spot, after his punch has entered your space.

- Another important concept is "far, intercept the middle segment; near, intercept the tip." This means that if you are at a bit of a distance when you intercept, then you should go for the opponent's elbow. If you are close, then intercept his hand, wrist, or forearm.

Intercept is a defensive move, but your goal is to attack. After the intercept you must immediately step in to get your body close, and trundle. The lead hand changes immediately to push, using both hands to shove at the same time. Use an explosive power if you want to injure the opponent. Use a longer power to just throw him down or away.

- When actually using the technique you must adapt to the situation. Techniques come from the heart out to the hands. To really use any technique you must practise hard and get combative experience.

THE POEM ABOUT THE SKILL OF INTERCEPTING

截法意在敌肘手，单双进退随意走。远找中节近截梢，打人全凭后手有。

Focus on the opponent's elbow or hands to intercept,

Use whatever works – advance or retreat, one hand or two.

When at a distance attack the middle segment, when close block the tip.

Hitting the opponent depends entirely on the rear hand making contact.

THREE: THE SKILL OF WRAPPING 裹字功

INTRODUCTION TO WRAP, *GUO*

The classics say, "Wrap means to enclose. You wrap up your opponent so that he loses effectiveness. The body rotates with soft strength. It uses the secret of softness to beat hardness." Wrap means to coil around, to encircle. The character contains both wrapping and coiling meaning.[33]

The short sequence for the Skill Of Wrapping is *opening, right step forward tiger carries, double wrap* (to left and right), and *step forward double shove*.

3a   Opening Move (left *santishi*)   qǐ shì   起势

Start with *santishi* as described above in move 1a.

3b   Right Step Forward Tiger Carries   yòu shàngbù hǔ tuō   右上步虎托

See the description and images in move 1b.

3c   Double Wrap to Left and Right zuǒ yòu shuāng guǒshǒu 左右双裹手

ACTION 1: Move the body forward slightly, retreat the left foot, and shift onto the left leg. Withdraw the right foot to beside the left without touching down. Bend the

---

[33] Author's note: Some writings and teachers refer to this technique as 果，which sounds the same, but simply means fruit. Combined with other characters it has a variety of meanings, but none of them apply to martial arts techniques. 裹 is the correct character.

knees, keeping them together, and stand firmly on the left leg. Extend the left hand to the left, forward, and up, palm facing right, fingers up. Once it reaches forward, circle it horizontally rightward across to in front of the right shoulder. Keep the right hand at the right side. Move the torso slightly leftward. Look forward. (image 2.33)

ACTION 2: Step the right foot diagonally forward and follow in the left foot to beside the right without touching down. Shift onto the right leg, bending the knees to stand firmly on the right leg with the knees together. Extend the right hand to the right, forward and up with the palm facing left and fingers up. After it reaches forward, circle it flat across to in front of the left shoulder. At this time the arms are crossed as if holding something, the left inside the right, both palms turned in, about twenty centimetres in front of the chest. Settle the shoulders, drop the elbows, contain the chest, and stretch the upper back. Look forward. (image 2.34)

2.33   2.34

Pointers

- o Roll the left hand rightward as the left foot retreats, so that both move together.

- o Roll the right hand leftward as the right foot steps forward, both moving simultaneously.

- o Wrapping to the right and left is a soft, continuous movement. Be sure to turn the body sideways as the arms pass across.

3d   Step Forward, Double Shove shàngbù shuāng zhuàng zhǎng 上步双撞掌

ACTION: Take a long step forward with the left foot and follow in the right foot a half-step, keeping most weight back on the right leg. Roll the hands over in front of the chest to face the palms out, thumbs down, then as the left foot steps forward, push forward. Push with the arms curved, the fingers pointing to each other, and the palms out at shoulder height. Release the shoulders forward, press the head up, and look forward. (images 2.35 and 2.35 front)

2.35   2.35
                              FRONT

Pointers

- o Complete the pushing shove as the left foot lands.

- o As the hands do the pushing shove, rotate the arms inward so that they maintain a bracing curve.

- o The *double wrap* and *double shove* should be done as one action, with no break between them.

3e   Double Wrap   shuāng guǒshǒu   双裹手

ACTION 1: Retreat the right foot a half-step and shift to the right leg, withdrawing the left foot to beside the right without touching down. Keep the knees bent and together, and stand firmly on the right leg. Lower the right hand then bring it forward and left, circling it horizontally across to in front of the left shoulder. Circle with the palm facing left and the fingers up, and then turn the palm in. Lower the left hand to the left side. Move the torso to the right and turn the body sideways to the right a bit. Look forward. (image 2.36)

ACTION 2: Take a long step diagonally forward with the left foot and follow in the right foot to inside the left without touching down. Bend the knees and keep them together to stand firmly on one leg. Extend the left hand forward and up, and then circle it across to the right to in front of the right shoulder, palm right and fingers up. Shift to the left leg and turn the torso slightly sideways leftward. Cross the forearms in front of the chest, hands about twenty centimetres from the chest, right hand inside the left hand, palms facing in. Contain the chest and make the upper back taut. Look forward. (images 2.37, 2.38)

3f   Step Forward, Double Shove   shàngbù shuāng zhuàng zhǎng 上步双撞掌

ACTION 1: Take a long step forward with the right foot and follow in the left foot a half-step, keeping most weight on the left leg. Rotate the forearms in front of the chest to turn the palms out and thumbs down. As the left foot steps forward, extend the arms to push forcefully forward. Complete the push with the arms curved to brace, the fingers facing each other, and the palms forward at shoulder height. Release the shoulder forward, press the head up, and look past the hands. (image 2.39)

- Continue on, alternating right and left techniques, as many times as you wish.

3g Turn Around for the Skill of Wrapping guǒ zìgōng huíshēnshì 裹字功回身势

Turn around from the *double shove* with a *tiger carries*, as described above in move 1g.

- *Turn around* is the same on either side, just transpose right and left.

3h   Closing Move for the Skill of Wrapping   guǒ zìgōng shōushì 裹字功收势

You may do the closing once you get back to where you started, facing the same direction. Close as described above in move 1h.

POWER GENERATION FOR THE SKILL OF WRAPPING

The double wrapping action is actually an inward circle, wrap, and draw with both hands. The hands must first go forward, then go out to the opposite side, and finally circle back. Wrap combines an inward checking power with a drawing back power. It also hides a transverse checking power applied inwards.

Keep the bodywork soft, going along with the forward and backward stepping. When advancing to the left and right, the torso moves left and right. Lead from the head, that is, when wrapping rightward with the left hand, move the head slightly to the left, and when wrapping leftward with the right hand, move the head slightly to the right. The actions of the hands and arms must be a coordinated twisting rotation – left and right, forward and back, up and down. This action must be coordinated with the torso – as the hands move forward the torso moves slightly back. When the hands go left the torso goes right. When the hands draw back the torso moves forward. In this way, the hands and body are coordinated according to the rules of biomechanics, which bring out the internal power of the movement.

When wrapping inward, transfer power from the waist and shoulders to the elbows, and from the elbows to the hands. Empty the chest and stretch the upper back. When crossing the arms in front of the chest, cover in with the elbows with a hidden inflating energy. Sit the torso down slightly and set backward slightly to store energy to prepare for a forward launch of power.

- The whole movement should be soft and well coordinated. Seek the action's power and coordination according to the rule of 'pre-load right to go left, pre-load back to go forward.' When your movements can express this principle and use it well, then you can find the proper power.

- The step forward double-handed shove is the power launch portion of the sequence, and continues smoothly from the wrapping move. Just before launching power, gather the torso, bend the knees, settle the buttocks down, empty the chest and gather the lower back. Press the knees down and forward to prepare for a good push off. When you cross the arms in front of the chest, relax the shoulders, and brace the elbows forward slightly in an embracing posture.

When launching power, charge the whole body forward by pushing off the rear foot to drive the lead foot forward. Turn the palms and forcefully extend the arms to push or shove forward. Close the elbows in by using the shoulder girdle, and urge the hands forward from the elbows. Exhale to gain power when launching. Push forward by pressing the head up, lengthening the spine, releasing the shoulders, and extending the arms. Pretend you are using your whole body to push a heavy object away from you.

- When practising the Skill Of Wrapping, focus on soft power for the wrapping portion, and on hard power for the pushing portion.

PRACTICAL APPLICATIONS FOR THE SKILL OF WRAPPING

From its action, you can see that wrap is a defensive move. It covers inward, controlling the outside of the opponent's elbows. Together with the footwork that retreats and dodges, it avoids an opponent's attack, going along with his line of attack to guide him to one side. Grab if you can, if not, then slap aside.

If the opponent punches towards your head with his right fist, you quickly extend your left hand forward and cover his arm, continuing it along his rightward direction. Dodge your head to the left and step either back or to the side. If the opponent punches with the left fist, then quickly use your right hand to cover and follow his leftward force, dodging your head to the right and stepping right. After the wrapping technique, then quickly step forward and attack.

Defense is just the means to an end, which is to attack.

The two-handed shove attacks the opponent's chest. When using it, charge in with your footwork, drive hard from your body, and launch your power into your hands. To be most effective use an explosive force focusing on a point a foot behind the opponent's back. The ideal time to apply the shove is when you have covered your opponent's elbows, tying him up with crossed arms. Then you can step in and shove him away. This ideal situation is not so easy to achieve, though. In a real combat situation you are not always going to be dealing with a simple situation, so you need to be flexible to deal with whatever happens. You need to train hard in your daily exercises, and practise applications often to gain experience. Once your skill is natural to you then you can use techniques freely and control your opponent. The key to this is the deep skills that you gain from training.

THE POEM ABOUT THE SKILL OF WRAPPING

裹手掩肘技法严，顺势进退头微闪。以柔克刚身法妙，上步撞掌意推山。

Wrapping with the hands and covering with the elbows is deadly,

Enter or retreat along the line of the oncoming action, ducking the head slightly.

With skillful body technique, softness conquers hardness,

Step forward and shove as if you are pushing a mountain.

FOUR: THE SKILL OF BRIDGING 跨字功

INTRODUCTION TO BRIDGE, *KUA*

The classics say, "Bridge is like bestriding a horse. It takes the position of lifting the hip."[34] The character 'kua' also means to ford a stream, or to jump over. 'Kua' contains the meaning of taking a big stride to span a distance, and also implies lifting a foot to take a big stride. It implies a horse stance, as the movement is like bestriding a horse. It also has the idea of pushing off the rear foot to jump forward.[35]

The short sequence for the Skill Of Bridging is: *opening move, right step forward tiger carries, retreat close the shoulders, step forward and bridge, stamp and drill,* and *aligned stance driving punch.*

4a   **Opening Move**   qǐ shì   起势

As described in move 1a.

4b   **Right Step Forward, Tiger Carries**   yòu shàngbù hǔ tuō   右上步虎托

As described in move 1b.

4c   **Left Retreat Close the Shoulders (T Stance Stab Down)**

        zuǒ tuìbù héjiān (dīngbù xiàchāzhǎng)   左退步合肩（丁步下插掌）

ACTION 1: Retreat the left foot without moving the right foot, shifting the weight to between the feet. Rotate the left hand thumb inwards to turn the palm forward

---

[34] Translator's note: 'Bestriding' is possibly a better translation than bridging, but is an awkward word in English. Bridging has close to the same meaning, and contains the meaning of fording. I have used stride and hurdle previously, but do not like either of those translations. The final position resembles a bridge, and I like the combination of movement and structure: taking a bridging step to finish with a strong bridge-like structure.

[35] Author's note: Some classics write 'kua' with the muscle or hand radical instead of the foot radical. These characters are pronounced the same but differ in meaning – each refer to different parts of the body and describe different basic actions. 'Kua' with the hand radical means to hook with the upper arm to carry something against the body, or to carry over the shoulder. 'Kua' with the muscle radical means the hip. The technique strikes the waist or hip, so this name reminds you to attack with the hip or towards the hip. Most martial arts skills have been passed on through verbal transmissions, and with the diverse accents in China and various different understandings of techniques and characters, it is no wonder that there is some diversity in the names. I have examined many old classics and photographs and decided that the best way to write this technique is with the foot radical, as it describes the technique the best.

and lift it up, then circle it forward with the arm bent. Then pull it down and back to beside the left hip, palm down. Internaly rotate the right hand (thumb turns in towards the palm) to lift the arm with the elbow bent, palm up to the right of the head. Rise slightly and look at the left hand. (image 2.40)

ACTION 2: Shift back to the left foot and withdraw the right foot to inside the left foot, touching the ball of the foot down. Stand on the left leg with the knees bent and together. Sit the torso down slightly. Bring the left hand up and cover with the elbow to the right shoulder, placing the hand in front of the right shoulder with the fingers up. Rotate the right hand fingers down and palm to the rear, bend the elbow and stab down past the left hip. Turn the torso leftward to bring the right shoulder forward. Look forward. (image 2.41)

Pointers

- o Coordinate the actions of the feet and hands. Retreat the rear foot, withdraw the lead foot, and position the hands. Be sure to close the lead shoulder in, that is, tuck the right shoulder across towards the left. Stab the lead hand down as the torso closes down and you squat on the rear leg.

- o Retreat and withdraw the feet quickly and sit back quickly. The final squat position must be stable. The movement must be completed without a pause.

4d   Step Forward Left Bridge   shàngbù zuǒ kuàshì   上步左跨势

ACTION 1: Step the right foot straight forward, landing with the foot turned outward. Turn the right hand so the thumb web is down and the palm forward and slice forward and up in a curving manner to shoulder height. Lower the left hand and bring it back to beside the left waist, palm forward, fingers down, elbow tight to the ribs. Look at the right hand. (image 2.42)

ACTION 2: Take a long step to the front with the left foot, landing with the foot turned slightly inward. Follow-in the right foot a bit, landing it turned crossways, sitting down into a half-horse stance with the torso turned ninety degrees. Slice the right hand up, clenching it in front of the head, the pulling it back to the right above the head with the fist eye down. Extend the left arm to push forward from the left side to hip height, elbow slightly bent, palm forward, fingers down. Look past the left hand. (images 2.43 and 2.43 front)

2.43

2.43 FRONT

Pointers

- o The bridging step is done in two steps. Advance the lead foot a half step as the hand slices up. Take a long step forward with the lead foot and follow-in the rear foot quickly as you push one hand forward and pull the other hand back.

- o Be sure to turn the torso as you push forward. The push should be on line with the plane of the torso. Sit down into a half-horse stance.

4e   Stamp, Right Drill   zhènjiǎo yòu zuānquán   震脚右钻拳

ACTION 1: Advance the left foot a half-step and shift forward onto the left leg. Turn the left palm and hook it to press down, palm down at shoulder height. Lower the right fist and pull it back to beside the waist, fist heart up. Look at the left hand. (image 2.44)

ACTION 2: Follow in the right foot to land with a thump beside the left foot, immediately lifting the left foot by the right ankle. Drill the right fist forward and up to nose height with the ulnar edge turned up. Cover and press down with the left hand, pulling it back to the belly and clenching it, fist heart down. Press the head up and look past the right fist. (image 2.45)

2.44

2.45

Pointers

- o Drill the right fist up as the right foot stamps. Three actions occur together: the right stamp, the right fist drill, and the left hand pull back.

- o Be sure to do a shoveling thump. Do not lift the foot to stamp down.

4f   Left Aligned Stance Driving Punch   zuǒ shùnbù bēngquán 左顺步崩拳

ACTION: Advance the left foot a long step and follow in the right foot a half-step, keeping most weight on the right leg. Turn the right fist to tuck and press down, then pull it back to the belly, fist heart in. Punch the left fist forward to sternum height with the elbow slightly bent. Reach the left shoulder slightly forward. Press the head up and look forward. (image 2.46)

Pointers

2.46

- o The entire move must be well integrated, using whole body power.

- o Three actions are completed at once: advance the left foot, punch the left fist, and pull the right fist to the belly.

4g   Right Retreat, Close the Shoulders   yòu tuìbù héjiān 右退步合肩

ACTION 1: Retreat the right foot without moving the left foot, and shift the weight to balance between the feet. Unclench the hands and circle the right hand up, forward and then down to pull back to beside the right hip, palm down. Bend the left arm and lift it up at the left of the head, palm obliquely up, fingers back. Raise the torso slightly. Look at the right hand as it moves, then as it pulls back to the hip, look forward. (image 2.47)

ACTION 2: Shift back onto the right leg and withdraw the left foot to beside the right foot, touching the ball of the foot down. Bend the knees to squat to lower the torso, keeping the knees together. Thread the right hand up and do an elbow cover

by the left shoulder, palm and fingers up just in front of the left shoulder. Bend the left elbow and turn the hand fingers down, stabbing down past the right ribs with the palm back at the right hip. Turn right to bring the left shoulder forward. Look forward. (image 2.48)

2.47

2.48

Pointers

- o This is the same as move 4c, just transposing right and left.

4h   Step Forward Right Bridge   shàngbù yòu kuàshì   上步右跨势

ACTION 1: Advance the left foot a half-step, landing with the foot turned out. Turn the left hand so that the thumb web is down and the palm is forward, and then circle it forward and up to slice forward to shoulder height. Lower the right hand to beside the right hip, palm forward, fingers down, elbow tight to the ribs. Look at the left hand. (image 2.49)

ACTION 2: Take a long step forward with the right foot, landing with the foot turned slightly in, and following in a half-step with the left foot, turned crossways. Sit down with the body turned leftward ninety degrees, into a half-horse stance. Continue the slice with the left hand, circling up to in front of the head, and clenching. Then pull it back to above the left side of the head, fist eye down. As the right foot steps forward, push the right hand forward to hip height. Keep the elbow slightly bent; the palm faces forward and the fingers are down. Look past the right hand. (image 2.50)

Pointers

○ This is the same as move 4d, just transposing right and left.

4i   Stamp, Left Drill   zhènjiǎo zuǒ zuānquán   震脚左钻拳

ACTION 1: Advance the left foot a short half-step and shift forward without moving the right foot. Turn the right palm down and tuck and press down. Lower the left fist and pull it back beside the left waist, fist heart up. Look at the right hand. (image 2.51)

ACTION 2: Follow in the left foot to land by the right foot with a thump, lifting the right foot by the left ankle. Drill the left fist forward and up to nose height, twisting the ulnar edge up. Cover and press the right hand down, pulling it back to the belly and clenching it, fist heart down. Press the head up and look past the left fist. (image 2.52)

Pointers

○ This is the same as move 4e, just transposing right and left.

4j   Right Aligned Stance Driving Punch
yòu shùnbù bēngquán   右顺步崩拳

ACTION: Advance the right foot a long step and follow in the left foot a half-step, keeping most weight on the left leg. Rotate the left fist to tuck and press down, then pull it back to the belly, fist heart in. Punch the right fist forward to solar plexus height, elbow slightly bent, right shoulder slightly forward. Press the head up and look past the right fist. (image 2.53)

Pointers

- o This is the same as move 4f, just transposing right and left.

- Continue on alternating right and left sides, depending on the space available.

4k Turn Around for the Skill of Bridging kuà zìgōng huíshēn shì 跨字功回身势

Once you get to the end of your area and need to turn around, use *tiger carries*. The turn is done from the *aligned stance driving punch*, so begins slightly differently than usual.

- Starting from the <u>right</u> side punch:

ACTION 1: Hook-in the right foot in front of the left toes and shift onto the right leg, lifting the left foot by the right ankle and turning the body around one-eighty to face in the way you just came. Lower the right fist to the belly and unclench both hands, crossing them and lifting them, and then circling out to the sides, palms forward. Continue to circle the hands until they are back down to the sides, palms forward, fingers down. Press the head up and look forward. (images 2.54, 2.55)

ACTION 2: Take a long diagonal step with the left foot to the left front and follow in the right foot a half-step. Do a carrying action with both hands to the front to belly height, palms forward, with a fist width between them. Press the head up and look past the hands. (image 2.56)

- Right and left are the same, just transposing directions.

Pointers

- o Take a good sized hook-in step, turn the body quickly, and keep stable.

- o Complete the *tiger carries* with the hands at exactly the same time as the lead foot lands.

4l Closing Move of the Skill of Bridging kuàzìgōng shōushì 跨字功受势

- Continue back and forth until you get back to your starting point in an *aligned stance driving punch*, facing in the same direction that you did the *opening move*.

- From a <u>left</u> *aligned stance driving punch*:

ACTION 1: Withdraw the left foot to beside the right foot. Bend the left elbow to pull the left back to the belly, turning it to tuck in. Drill the right fist up and forward to nose height, turning the ulnar edge up. Look at the right fist. (image 2.57)

ACTION 2: Advance the left foot without moving the right foot, to take a *santi* stance. Perform a left split, splitting with the left hand and pulling the right hand back to the belly. (image 2.58)

2.57   2.58

- From a <u>right</u> *aligned stance driving punch*:

ACTION 1: Withdraw the right foot to beside the left foot, landing it and shifting onto the right leg. Unclench the right hand and pull it back to the belly, then clench it again and drill it up and forward to nose height, turning the ulnar edge up. Look at the right fist. (image 2.59)

2.59

ACTION 2: Advance the left foot without moving the right foot, to take a *santi* stance. Perform a left split. (see image 2.58 above)

- Then close the form the same as usual from left split, or *santishi*.

POWER GENERATION FOR THE SKILL OF BRIDGING

The skill of bridging sequence consists of a *withdrawing shoulder close,* a *step forward to bridge*, a *stamp and drill*, and an *aligned stance driving punch*.

Withdrawing shoulder close

The footwork is Xingyiquan's characteristic footwork, 'first retreat and then withdraw.' As the classics say, "To retreat, first retreat the rear foot, once you retreat, then you must withdraw [the lead foot]. To advance, first advance the lead foot, once you advance then you must follow in [the rear foot]." Since in Xingyiquan, most weight is on the rear leg, when the rear foot retreats the weight first shifts slightly forward, so that you use the lead foot to push back and the rear leg to extend back. The buttocks must settle down and the weight must shift back quickly. Be sure to pull in at the hips and close the knees.

The power of the hands is: stab the lead hand down towards the rear while threading the rear hand forward with an inner covering action, so that there is a twisting power between the hands. The lead shoulder first opens then closes. The shoulder closes when the lead hand stabs down, to empty the chest and tauten the upper back, pull in the abdomen and tuck in the torso.

This stance is low, sitting down to gather power in order to release it, like pressing down on a spring. Turn the body and pull the shoulder in as the hand stabs down, but be sure to press the head up.

Exhale when you release power, and relax as soon as you have done so. Whenever you release power, always immediately relax.

Step forward to bridge

The bridging step is to cover distance, and the follow-in step must be fast. The lead foot should land with a trampling power that acts as a brake.

When doing the slice up with the hand, the lead shoulder must extend forward so that the shoulder leads the elbow and the elbow leads the hand. The hand should be held in a hooked shape to be able to strike with a slicing up action.

When doing the pushing carry, put power to the root of the palm and tuck the elbow into the ribs, sitting down into the lumbar back, settling the shoulders, turning the waist so that the body is sideways, and extending the arm.

To release power into the bridge action: Step forward, landing with a trampling power; turn the waist and put the shoulder into the action with a twisting power; sit into the lumbar area, sit into the hips, settle the shoulders and drop the elbows with a settling power; slice the lead hand up and hook and pull back with a bracing power.

Coordinate the actions with an exhalation of breath. In this way the complete technique will be coordinated and have whole body power. It will be balanced and full. The emphasis is on the turn of the waist, the reach of the shoulder, and the sit into the hips.

Stamp and drill

The weight shifts slightly forward then back. This shifting is in order to coordinate the power, to make it fuller, integrated, and able to release more effectively.

The torso, shoulders, and elbows lead the movement of the hands. When the lead hand turns to tuck and press down, do this by rotating the shoulder to lead the elbow and hand. When the rear hand lowers, do this by taking the elbow back and down, rotating the forearm as it lowers.

The stomp is a raking action, not a lift and stamp. Roll the hips in and close the knee to bring the foot into the stomp.

Aligned stance driving punch

Keep the elbow tight to the ribs, turning the torso and reaching the shoulder forward, releasing the shoulder and settling the elbow to send the punch out.

Launch power equally into both the lead and the rear hands, to send one forward and one back. "Go out like a steel rasp, return like a grappling hook."

PRACTICAL APPLICATIONS FOR THE SKILL OF BRIDGING

Looking at the action of *retreat close the shoulders*, it is a defensive move. Retreat and duck out of the way, protecting the chest with the elbows, and the ribs with the arms. Tuck the waist and empty the chest to gather power for the strike. This defensive move places the body in a preparatory position for the counter-attack while awaiting an opportunity.

- If you advance when you close the shoulders, then you can do a shoulder strike. One hand protects the head while the other protects the groin. The hands and arms need to twist and roll in to protect you. When practising, do the actions large and open. When using it, keep the actions small and compact.

Bridging is a close range attack, so you must get the body in tight. During the lead hand slice, if you can get a grasp then pull, otherwise use the slice to knock away. The step in must charge into the opponent's groin area, the rear hand can then strike his belly, ribs, or hip area. If you get close enough then you can strike with your hip or shoulder.

- The key to bridging is the advancing footwork to get the body in. When you advance, advance everything. When you retreat, retreat everything. To use this properly, watch what the opponent is doing and take whatever opportunity presents. Using the technique courageously will guarantee success.

Stamp and drill together with *aligned stance driving punch* can be seen as a high fake combined with a low strike. They must be used together without hesitation. Use them to alternate from insubstantial to substantial – the drill is insubstantial and the driving punch is substantial. You can either advance or retreat, according to what is necessary. The drill can also be used as a defensive move or a full attack, combining with the following driving punch.

- When using techniques, don't try to think what technique is a counter to what technique, and exactly how it would work. You must be able to take whatever chance presents, make opportunities for yourself, fully use your own potential, and persevere until you win. If you want to reach a high level in combat, then during regular practice you must train hard and try out techniques with partners, gaining experience and examining the techniques.

THE POEM ABOUT THE SKILL OF BRIDGING

退步合肩要含胸，上下撩托跨步冲。拧要沉肩坐胯力，震脚钻拳紧连崩。

Empty your chest, retreat and close the shoulders,

Charge in with a bridging step, slicing up and carrying down.

The strength comes from turning the waist, settling the shoulders, and sitting into the hips,

Stomp the foot and drill the fist, followed tightly by a punch.

FIVE: THE SKILL OF SCOOPING 挑字功

INTRODUCTION TO SCOOP, *TIAO*

The classics say, "The strength of the scoop comes from the shoulders and legs, when the right hand scoops, the right foot opens fiercely, and the left leg braces strongly, so the shoulder is able to exert all the force. It is like the snake technique, but with the hand a bit higher." The Xinhua dictionary definition of scoop is, "to use a long and pointed weapon to stab and lift,"[36] and "to knock away or cause something to move." Scooping is both the application and the way of applying of power. The definition within the martial arts is "a palm or fist technique that exerts force upward and forward from below while the arm maintains a certain flexion." It is both a defensive and offensive technique. Scooping is the opposite of splitting, as split exerts force down and forward while scoop exerts force up and forward. So, while you press the head up to split, you sit the buttocks down to scoop.

The short sequence for the Skill Of Scooping is: *opening move, right step forward tiger carries, withdraw and close the shoulders, advance and scoop, withdraw and chop, advance and scoop, step forward eagle grasps.*

5a　**Opening Move (left *santishi*)**　qǐ shì　　　起势

As described in move 1a.

5b　**Right Step Forward, Tiger Carries**

yòu shàngbù hǔ tuō　　右上步虎托

As described in move 1b.

5c　**Withdraw, Close the Shoulders**[37]　chèbù héjiān　　撤步合肩

As described in move 4c.

5d　**Advance, Scoop**

　　jìnbù tiǎozhǎng　　　　进步挑掌

ACTION: Take a long step forward with the right foot and follow in a half-step with the left foot, keeping most weight on the rear leg, to take a *santi* stance. Turn the right hand and bring it from the left hip to in front of the belly, fingers up and palm forward, and keeping the elbow hugging the ribs. Then do a scooping strike upwards to nose height with the

2.60

---

[36] Translator's note: The best action to think of is stabbing a pitchfork into a bale of hay and lifting it onto a platform in one smooth motion.

[37] Translator's note: Called *retreat, close the shoulders* in move 4c. The rear foot retreats and the lead foot withdraws, so the name can go either way.

elbow bent and the power going through to the heel of the palm. Turn the left hand palm down and pull down and back to the belly. Sit down into the buttocks. Look past the right hand. (image 2.60)

Pointers

- o   Three actions must be completed simultaneously with integrated power: land the right foot, scoop the right arm, and pull back the left hand.

- o   When the right hand scoops up the elbow must first hug the ribs. Release and settle the shoulder, drop the elbow, and apply force to the heart of the palm.

5e   Withdraw, Chop   chèbù pīquán   撤步劈拳

ACTION: Withdraw the right foot a half-step to touch the ball down in front of the left foot. Shift back without moving the left foot. Slide the left hand along the top of the right arm to chop forward and down. Pull the right hand back and down to the belly. Complete the chop at chest height with the left shoulder reaching forward. Lean the torso slightly forward, press the head up and look at the left hand. (image 2.61)

Pointers

- o   Three actions must be completed simultaneously with integrated power: withdraw the right foot, pull back the right hand, and chop forward with the left hand.

- o   As the left hand chops, it should first slide along the right arm, so that it is a sliding grab. Tuck in the abdomen and empty the chest, turn the waist and reach the shoulder into the technique.

5f   Advance, Scoop   jìnbù tiǎozhǎng   进步挑掌

ACTION: Take a long step forward with the right foot and follow in a half-step with the left foot. Scoop the right hand forcefully up from the right hip to nose height. Keep the elbow bent, the fingers up and palm forward. Pull the left hand palm back to the belly. Sit down into the buttocks, press the head up, and look past the right hand. (images 2.62 and 2.62 front)

Pointers

- o Perform moves 5d, 5e, and 5f with no hesitation between them, increasing in strength.

- o Turn the waist and shoulders to the right and left to put force into the palms to the right and left.

5g   Step Forward, Eagle Grasps   shàngbù yīngzhuō   上步鹰捉

ACTION 1: First withdraw the right foot slightly and then advance it a half-step, following in with the left foot beside the right ankle without touching down. Clench the right hand and pull it back to the belly, and then drill it up by the sternum and forward to head height with the ulnar edge twisted up. Place the left fist tightly at the right elbow, fist heart up. Keep the left elbow tucked into the solar plexus so that the elbows are both tucked in. Look past the right fist. (image 2.63)

ACTION 2: Take a long step forward with the left foot and follow in a half-step with the right foot to take a sixty-forty *santi* stance. Slide the left fist along the right arm to drill up until the fists cross. Then unclench the hands, chop the left hand down,

palm forward, and pull the right hand back to the belly. Chop the left hand down to waist height with the arm slightly bent and palm down. Straighten the neck and press the head up. Look past the left hand. Flex the fingers slightly to form eagle claws. (image 2.64)

Pointers

- o Drill the right fist up as the right foot advances. Remember to withdraw the right foot before advancing it.

- o Chop the hands down as the left foot lands. Pay attention to pressing the head up, and to the height of the palm strikes. Do not hesitate during the actions.

5h   Retreat, Close the Shoulders

         tuìbù héjiān   退步合肩

ACTION: Retreat the right foot and shift onto the right leg. Withdraw the left foot to beside the right foot, touching the ball down. Flex the knees to squat down with the knees together, weight on the right leg. Turn the left hand palm up and bend the arm to circle it up and across in front of the face to do an elbow cover towards the right shoulder. Then turn the fingers down to stab past the right ribs to the right hip, palm in. Bring the right hand up and do an elbow cover to the left shoulder, palm turned up. Turn right and tuck the left shoulder towards the right shoulder, so that the left shoulder is forward. Tuck in the abdomen, empty the chest, press the head up, and look past the right hand. (image 2.65)

- Repeat moves 5d, 5e, 5f and 5g, that is, *advance scoop, withdraw chop, advance scoop, step forward eagle grasps*, performing them on the other side. Repeat both sides as long as your space and fitness allows.

5i   Turn Around for the Skill of Scooping tiǎo zìgōng huíshēnshì 挑字功回身势

- The *turn around* is *tiger carries* as described in move 1g. After turning, continue on with the *advance, scoop* and the rest of the sequence.

5l   Closing Move for the Skill of Scooping tiǎo zìgōng shōushì   挑字功收势

- Once you get back to where you started, sit into *santishi* and then close the form, as described in move 1h.

POWER GENERATION FOR THE SKILL OF SCOOPING

The power of the first three movements of the sequence is described in the section on the Skill Of Bridging.

Advance, scoop

Advance a long step forward and follow in quickly.

Before applying the scoop, fix the right upper arm tightly to the ribs, placing the elbow between the waist and belly and keeping the elbow bent a hundred degrees. Then flex the waist and settle the shoulder using the waist and abdomen to lift up, keeping the shoulder and elbow dropped. Release the shoulder to send it forward, and extend the arm to do a scooping hit forward.

Both the upward scoop and the downward pull are done on the same plane. Strike the belly with the hand that pulls back to aid the *qi* to settle to the *dantian*, and exhale to launch power.

Lengthen the spine to urge the shoulder forward. Settle the shoulders to send the elbow forward. Drop the elbow to urge the hand forward, finishing with an upward exertion of power into the scoop. Drop into the buttocks at the instant that you launch power.

Withdraw, chop

This exerts power forward and down. The lead hand should clench and pull down and back forcefully. Put equal force into the lead and rear hands. The rear hand should slide along the lead forearm, rubbing before pushing out.

Press the head forward, tuck in the abdomen and empty the chest. Settle the shoulder and drop the elbow, turn the waist and reach the shoulder, turning the shoulders into the action to do the chopping palm. Keep the elbow rolled in when chopping. Lean the torso slightly forward to create a downward pressure.

Step forward eagle grasps

During the half-step advance, drill both fists up simultaneously, one behind the other. Expand the body core, lengthen the spine, hug the elbows together in front of the chest, empty the chest, close the shoulders, and stretch the upper back.

During the step forward splitting action, tuck in the abdomen, flex the body core, and draw the elbows down forcefully. The torso should have a forward butting, pressing down power as the foot lands. In the final position, the head should have an upward butting power, the legs should have a scissoring power. The entire body must be integrated and show the clear spirit of the eagle.

PRACTICAL APPLICATIONS FOR THE SKILL OF SCOOPING

The use of the *eagle grasps* is the same as described in the eagle model, see Volume I, Chapter Ten.

The heart of the Skill Of Scooping is the scoop itself, which strikes upward and forward through the palm. It is intended to inflict heavy damage on your opponent, knocking him far away. Because the scoop exerts power up and forward, it you strike the opponent's chest you can easily break his root and send him away.

- Both of the main actions of the scoop – the scoop of the rear hand and the withdrawal of the lead hand – are circular actions along the same plane as the body. From the point of view of biomechanics, when the centre of gravity of every segment is in motion, the closer their line of action to the body's centre of gravity the more effective the action will be. From the point of view of combat effectiveness, this 'protects the centre and hits the centre.' To protect your own centre and strike your opponent's centre, use your footwork to trample into him, taking over his centre. The scoop strikes directly to your opponent's core, between the chest and abdomen, and your goal is to knock him away, knock him down, or heavily injure him.

The short sequence for the Skill Of Scooping consists of three palm techniques: advance scoop, withdraw chop, and advance scoop. You can use them as continuous attacks, each one faster and stronger than the previous one. The classics say, "Launch the first punch but hit with the second punch; success depends on the following punch coming quickly." You can use the strikes as a fake and following attack. You can also use one hand to block up, trap, hook, or draw in the opponent, to allow the next hand to get in. There are no set rules on to how to use the techniques – you need to assess the situation.

- When using the scoop you must turn the torso sideways to get in. This presents a smaller surface area to your opponent and gives you more reach as you turn the torso, extend the shoulder, and reach the arm, thus giving you a greater force.

- The classics say, "never send a hand out without purpose, never bring it back without purpose." When you bring the hand back after the strike, hook onto something, grab something, press something down – anything to prevent the opponent from launching a counter attack.

To apply the Skill Of Scooping you need to take advantage of the timing and placement, you need to be flexible, don't do it like it is set in stone.

THE POEM ABOUT THE SKILL OF SCOOPING

挑掌去意敌胸膛，坐臀长腰臂伸长。上挑下劈连环进，护中打中是主张。

Scooping palm is meant for the opponent's chest or groin.

Sit the buttocks down, fill up the kidney area, extend the arm to lengthen your reach.

Scoop up and chop down in one continuous advancing attack.

The main goal is to protect your centre and hit your opponent's centre.

SIX: THE SKILL OF BUTTING 顶字功

INTRODUCTION TO BUTT, *DING*

The classics say, "The strength of butting is in the head, so the most important thing is to straighten the neck and drop the shoulders. Combine this with a cover and punch." *Ding* means to support something on the head, to brace up, or to carry. It also means to go against the flow of something, butting up against something. As a technique in Xingyiquan it means to strike with the head, "the head strikes as the feet go in, it starts and ends in the centre. When the feet take over the central gate and take over the space, even a skilled player cannot defend against the attack."

The short sequence for training the Skill Of Butting is: *opening move, step forward tiger carries, advance double elbow covers, step forward head butt, pull and knee butt, step forward elbow butt, stroke and driving punch, step forward split.*[38]

6a   Opening Move (left *santishi*)   qǐ shì   起势

As described in move 1a.

6b   Right Step Forward, Tiger Carries   yòu shàngbù hǔtuō   右上步虎托

As described in move 1b.

6c   Advance, Double Elbow Covers   jìnbù shuāng yǎnzhǒu   进步双掩肘

ACTION: Advance the right foot a half-step and lift the left foot by the right ankle without touching down. Keep the legs together and stand firmly on the right leg. Clench the right hand and bend the right elbow to drill the right hand up to head height, then do an elbow cover leftwards, lowering the fist to the left ribs, fist heart in. Clench the left hand and bend the left elbow, drill the fist to head height, then do an elbow cover rightwards, lowering the fist to the right ribs, fist heart in. When the forearms cross in front of the chest the right arm is inside the left. Empty the chest, stretch the upper back and press the head up slightly. Look ahead. (images 2.66, 2.67, 2,68)

---

[38] Author's note: My reference text described a head butt, a straight push and a cover to punch in the short sequence. Since in martial arts, elbow and knee strikes are also called butt [*ding*], the Skill Of Butting should include elbow and knee strikes as well as head strikes, so I have added them.

Pointers

○ Coordinate the right foot advance with the outward circles and inward covers of the arms. The elbow covers must be done quickly.

○ When doing the elbow covers to left and right, transfer power from the waist to the shoulders, the shoulders to the elbows, and the elbows to the arms. Complete the actions without pausing.

6d   Step Forward, Head Butt   shàngbù tóudǐng   上步头顶

ACTION: Take a long step forward with the left foot and follow in a half-step with the right, putting most weight on the left leg. Keep the fists clenched and the forearms crossed and push / press them forward and down to belly height. Shift forward and lean the torso forward, tucking in the chin, pulling in the abdomen and emptying the chest in order to butt forward with the forehead. Settle the shoulders down, close the teeth, straighten the nape of the neck and look forward. (images 2.69 and 2.69 front)

Pointers

○ Butt with the head as the left foot lands, hitting at exactly the same time.

○ *Advance double elbow covers* and *step forward head butt* should be done as one move with no break between them.

6e   Pull and Knee Butt   lǚshǒu xīzhuàng   捋手膝撞

ACTION 1: Advance the left foot forward diagonally to the left and shift forward, bending the right leg and lifting the right heel. Unclench the hands and extend them to the forward left, fingers forward, left palm forward, right hand in front of the left elbow. Turn the left palm to face right and turn the right hand thumb down, palm also facing right. Both hands are chest height as if grabbing to pull. Look past the left hand. (image 2.70)

ACTION 2: Shift onto the left leg to stand on it with the knee slightly bent, leaning the torso slightly forward. Bend the right knee and shove forward with it to chest height. Clench the hands and pull back towards the right – pull the left fist back to in front of the chest, fist heart up, and pull the right fist back on the ride side, fist heart down. Look at the left fist and stand firmly on the left leg. (image 2.71)

Pointers

- o   Extend the hands forward as the lead foot advances. Grab and pull the hands back as the knee butts forward. Be sure to flex the supporting leg slightly and to grab the ground with the toes to stand firmly.

- o   Dodge the torso to the left so that the entire move is coordinated and the use of power is balanced throughout the body.

6f   Step Forward, Right Elbow Butt   shàngbù yòu dǐngzhǒu   上步右顶肘

ACTION: Take a long step straight forward with the right foot and follow in the left foot a half-step. Bring the right elbow into the right ribs, and then as the right foot lands, butt forward and up with the elbow bent. Bring the right fist to above the right shoulder with the fist heart in, so that the elbow butts up above shoulder height. Place the left hand behind the right elbow to support it, tucking the left elbow into the solar plexus. Shift partially onto the right leg. Look straight forward. (image 2.72)

Pointers

- o   The elbow strike must come as the lead foot lands, so that the whole body is coordinated. Be sure to shift slightly forward.

- o   Land the foot well forward and bring the rear foot in quickly. The stance should be long enough that the body is fairly low.

6g   Stroke and Driving Punch   lǔshǒu bēngquán   捋手崩拳

ACTION 1: Shift back and withdraw the right foot a half-step to touch the ball of the foot down in front of the left foot. Do not move the left foot yet. Extend the right hand forward then cover and press down, clench to grab, and pull back to the right side. Slide the left hand along the right arm to chop out to chest height, fingers up, palm forward. Put the left shoulder forward into the action, lean the torso slightly forward and lift the buttocks slightly. Look past the left hand. (image

2.73)

ACTION 2: Advance the right foot a long step and follow in the left foot a half-step,

keeping the weight mostly on the left leg. Punch the right fist forward to solar plexus height, fist eye up and fist surface angled forward slightly. Clench and pull the left hand back to the belly, fist heart in. Press the head up and look past the right fist. (image 2.74)

Pointers

- o Push the left hand forward as the right hand covers and pulls back, so that the whole action works as a unit.

- o The *Advance driving punch* must be fast. Drive the footwork forward for distance and punch quickly.

- o Chop the left hand down when the right foot withdraws for the pull back. Then advance the foot and punch at exactly the same time.

6h   Step Forward, Left Split   shàngbù zuǒ pīquán   上步左劈拳

ACTION 1: First withdraw the right foot slightly and pull the right fist back to the belly. Then advance the right foot a half-step and follow in the left foot, lifting it beside the right without touching down. Drill the right fist up by the sternum and forward to nose height. twisting the ulnar edge up. Press the head up and look forward. (image 2.75)

ACTION 2: Take a long step forward with the left foot and follow in the right foot a

half-step. Drill the left fist up by the sternum and out along to the right elbow. When the fists meet, unclench the hands and turn the palms down, splitting the left hand forward and down to chest height while pulling the right hand back to the belly. Press the head up and look forward. (image 2.76)

- • Carry on, repeating the same moves on the other side: *left advance double elbow covers, step forward head butt, pull and knee butt, step forward left elbow butt, stroke and driving punch.* The actions are the same, just switching right and left.

6i   Turn Around for the Skill of Butting dǐng zìgōng huíshēn shì 顶字功回身势

- The turn around is the same as *split turn around*. Whichever hand is forward, pull the lead hand back and hook-in the lead foot to turn around. Then advance with a drilling fist and step forward into a split. (See Volume I for details on *split turn around*.)

6l   Closing Move for the Skill of Butting dǐng zìgōng shōushì   顶字功收势

- Once you get back to where you started, and are sitting in left split, you may close the form. Close as is usual from *santishi*.

POWER GENERATION FOR THE SKILL OF BUTTING

Double elbow covers

The hands wrap around to bring the elbows in to cover, so the forearms have a sticky wrapping power. The forearms need to rotate, drawn by the waist and shoulders. The whole action is circular. When the right hand extends forward and the left elbow covers, the right shoulder should reach forward slightly. When the left hand reaches forward and the right elbow covers, the left shoulder should reach forward slightly. Empty the chest, tuck the elbows in tightly, and keep the action smooth. Relax the waist to be able to do the bodywork.

Head butt

Settle the shoulders as the arms cross and stab down. The arms have a bracing power forward and down.

As the head butts forwards, empty the chest and spread the upper back, bow from the waist and tuck in the abdomen, releasing power from the body core to transfer to the spine, linking through each segment of the body.

Tuck in the chin, straighten and tighten the nape of the neck, clench the teeth, and hit with the forehead. Coordinate the strike with an exhalation. Be sure to shift forward.

Knee butt

The knees strike either up or across. Both work well. When striking with the knee the body should lean about fifty degrees. Tuck in the abdomen, empty the chest, and use both hands to pull back to create an equal and opposite force for the knee strike. The body core is the fulcrum, so that the lower and upper limbs work together to release the integrated power of the whole body.

Elbow butt

Drive the footwork forward and shove with the body. Reach the shoulder forward and put power from the lower back upward, sitting the buttocks down. Shift forward and lean slightly into the action.

Keep the elbow tight to the ribs at first, then drive forward and up.

When releasing power, connect through the whole body.

Pull back and punch

This consists of a withdrawing step and covering chop followed by a step forward into a driving punch. The footwork is to first withdraw and then advance; withdraw only a little, then advance a good distance, remembering that the rear foot must then follow in. The hand technique has a hooking pull back, first with the right hand and then with the left.

The whole movement must link together without hesitation. When releasing power be sure to turn the waist and reach the shoulder. When withdrawing, press the head up and lift the torso slightly. When punching, drop the torso slightly to focus forward.

- The power in Xingyiquan movements can only be found by practice, and in practicing with a mind to fulfilling all the requirements of Xingyiquan in each body segment. On this foundation, when you release power you should focus on feeling and understanding the laws of physics. Transitional moves between each position must follow the structure of the body and follow the principles of movement. This focus helps you to find both the internal and the external aspects of each movement. Of course, it is vital to follow the principles of combat. If you leave the principles of combat then you are no longer doing martial arts. The martial arts are intrinsically combative.

PRACTICAL APPLICATIONS FOR THE SKILL OF BUTTING

The main techniques in the sequence of the skill of butting are the head butt, the knee butt, and the elbow butt. These are all close range techniques. The classics say, "use the hands and feet for long range, use the knees and elbows for short range." Xingyiquan emphasizes the 'seven fists' and the fourteen targets. The head is one of the 'seven fists' so the skill of butting emphasizes its training and application.

Head butt

To hit with the head the hands must open up the opponent's defense. "Stomp into his main door to steal his position," get the body in close. As lead foot lands the rear foot must drive to push into the head to hit the opponent's face or chest.

This technique only works when you are wholly committed to victory. Be sure to use both hands to control the opponent's hands to protect your head from possible attack. A head butt is like a kiss – you cannot do it if you are not close.

Knee butt

A knee strike can be used as a dodging counter attack to an opponent's straight attack. You grab his arm with both hands, pulling him along his line of attack and striking his chest or belly strongly with the knee. If you can get a grip, then grab, otherwise knock his arms aside.

Be sure to dodge the body to the side to make space, then you can step forward to hit with the knee.

You must hit hard and fast and get in tight to your opponent in order to be effective.

Elbow butt

Step forward elbow butt is actually an upward scooping elbow strike. You have to get close for this to work. You have to react to your opportunities in order to get in for an elbow strike, and this depends on your footwork and courage. You have to dare to step into your opponent's groin, taking his 'central gate,' getting close enough to shove with your whole body.

- Because this is a short range technique it puts you at risk. You must protect your head, and "use long and short together, use long to reinforce the short and use short to control the long."

Stroke and punch

This can be done together with the elbow butt to 'use long to reinforce the short' or it can be used on its own. It is a fast attack that protects the centre while attacking the centre, 'eating a fist and returning a fist.'

Withdraw and cover to split

This is essentially a defensive move, but it could also be done as a high fake before a low strike. Additionally it serves to gather power for the punch.

Punch directly into the opponent's heart, focussing a foot behind him.

- The butting techniques are all close range. This means that you have to get your whole body in close, so courage is vital to their effectiveness. You have to have a no holds barred spirit that oppresses your opponent, otherwise you are just 'discussing tactics on paper.' To use a technique you must master its principles, practise its power, and thoroughly examine what attacks it is effective against. You need to fully use your own abilities, be flexible and natural to be able to change with the situation, to "get the feeling when you see the view."

THE POEM ABOUT THE SKILL OF BUTTING

顶技三法头膝肘，全凭步法往里走。节短势险护己身，贴身打法强中手。

The three methods of butting are the head, knee, and elbow.

They all depend on the footwork getting you inside.

It is dangerous to use short segments, so you must protect yourself.

To use short range techniques you must take over and control the centre.

SEVEN: THE SKILL OF PASSING 云字功

INTRODUCTION TO PASS, *YUN*

Clouds [*yun*] pass by in the sky, turning and flowing, so the word passing [*yun*] is often used for smooth turning techniques. The technique pulls to the side with both hands, flowing like clouds. 'Cloud hands' in Taijiquan is a passing technique, as are flat brandishing techniques of weapons. The Skill Of Passing in Xingyiquan describes the spinning of the hands in front of the head, and also includes an upward block, a knocking draw, and a grabbing pull, all used as compact defense. If well used, pass is very effective. It can be combined with a reverse stance drill, combining defense with offense. It develops quick and agile hand and body techniques, quick footwork, and should show the continuity of passing clouds or flowing water.

Pass can be done with either large or small actions. The hands perform large, expansive movements for the large pass, one hand circling above the head while the other hand circles in front of the body. The hands perform a small circle in front of the face for the small pass, with a compact movement. Pass can be practised alone with advancing and retreating footwork. When combined with the drill, it must be done with advancing footwork.

The short sequence for training the Skill Of Passing contains *opening move, right step forward tiger carries, leftw pass, right pass,* and two *reverse stance drills.*

7a   Opening Move (left *santishi*)   qǐ shì   起势

As described in move 1a.

7b   Right Step Forward, Tiger Carries   yòu shàngbù hǔtuō   右上步虎托

As described in move 1b.

7c   Step Forward, Left Pass   shàngbù zuǒ yúnshì   上步左云势

ACTION 1: Advance the right foot a small step forward and then take a step forward with the left foot, bending the legs and shifting the weight to between the feet. Turn the left hand palm up and bend the elbow, lifting the elbow up so that the forearm blocks across above the head. Turn the right palm up and bring it by the sternum then extend out to the left front at nose height, keeping the elbow tucked in. Empty the chest and stretch the upper back. Look at the right hand. (image 2.77)

ACTION 2: Without moving the left foot, take a step forward with the right foot, turning it out as you land. Shift more weight onto the left leg. Circle the left hand above the head, back at the left to the left side of the body, then carry forward and up to shoulder height on the midline of the body with the elbow slightly bent and the palm up. At the same time, circle the right hand across to the right. When it arrives in front at the right, bend the elbow and turn the palm up, circling past in front of the face. When it circles to the left side, turn the palm out and thumb down with the thumb web open, finishing with the right hand at the right side of the head. Look past the left hand. (images 2.78 and 2.78 front)

2.77   2.78

Pointers

2.78
FRONT

- o Take small quick steps for the left and right stepping during *left pass*. The right foot must land turned out, across the line. Keep the centre of gravity low to move with stability.

- o The hands should circle at the same time. When one hand is above the head the other is in front of the body. The hands draw opposite circles. When they arrive in front of the body then the left hand carries and the right hand pulls back. This action should happen as the right foot steps forward.

- o The hands and feet must be coordinated, and the movement must be completed smoothly as one action.

7d   Reverse Stance Right Drill   àobù yòu zuānquán   拗步右钻拳

ACTION: Take a long step forward with the left foot and follow in a half-step with the right foot, keeping most weight on the left leg. Turn the left hand palm down and tuck it in, pulling down, left, and back while bending the arm and clenching the fist, and then circle it up to the left side of the head, fist heart out, fist eye down, elbow a bit higher than the shoulder. At the same time, clench and draw the right fist back slightly and lower it by the right waist, turning the fist heart up, and then drilling forward and up to nose height. Press the head up and look past the right fist. (image 2.79)

2.79

Pointers

- o The right drill must be completed as the right foot lands. The punch must have a focal point. Keep the body well balanced and use whole body power.

7e   Step Forward, Right Pass   shàngbù yòu yúnshì   上步右云势

ACTION 1: Advance the left foot a short step and then step the right foot forward, bending the knees and shifting between the legs with a bit more weight on the rear leg. Unclench the right hand and rotate it thumb inward, lifting the elbow to block up above the head with the forearm across, hand at the left side of the head, palm up. Unclench the left hand and rotate it thumb outward, bringing it by the sternum and extending it to the right front to nose height palm up, elbow tucked into the solar plexus. Empty the chest and stretch the upper back. Look at the left hand. (image 2.80)

2.80

ACTION 2: Step the left foot forward without moving the right foot, land with the foot turned out, bend the knees and keep most weight on the right leg. Circle the right hand back and right above the head. Then lower it down the right side to sternum height with the elbow slightly bent, palm up. Complete the action with a carry on the midline of the body, palm up at shoulder height. Circle the left hand, palm up, to the forward left, using the elbow as the pivot point. When it arrives at the forward left, bend the elbow and turn the palm out, thumb down, and stretch the thumb web open. Then pull the left hand down, left, and back, pulling it to the left side of the head, palm out, fingers forward. Look at the right hand. (image 2.81)

Pointers

- o Do not pause between actions 1 and 2. The hands should circle like carrying plates, using body action. Keep the waist relaxed, compress the torso slightly, keep the movement smooth and continuous, and coordinate the feet with the hands.

- o Focus on the hand techniques while circling. One closes off, blocks up, hoists and pulls while the other settles, brushes aside, and hooks.

7f   Reverse Stance Left Drill   àobù zuǒ zuānquán   拗步左钻拳

ACTION: Take a long step forward with the right foot and follow in a half-step with the left foot, keeping most weight on the left leg. Rotate the right hand thumb inward to tuck it in, palm down, and circle down, right, and back to brush aside and draw. Bend the elbow and clench the fist to pull back to above the right shoulder, fist heart out, fist eye down. Draw the left fist back a bit then lower it to the left waist, fist heart up. Once it arrives at the waist, drill forward and up to nose height, twisting the ulnar edge up. Press the head up and look past the left fist. (image 2.82)

- • Continue on, alternating left and right, the number of repetitions determined by the space and your fitness.

Pointers

- o Be sure to rotate the fist and arm before doing the drill.

- o Three actions must be completed at the same time: the right foot lands, the right hand draws back, and the left fist drills.

- o This move should be explosive.

7g   Turn Around for the Skill of Passing yún zìgōng huíshēnshì   云字功回身势

Turn around when you are in a *reverse stance drill*, turning into a *tiger carries*. See movement 1g for the description of the *tiger carries* turn.

- To turn from a *reverse stance left drill*, hook-in the right foot and turn around, advancing the left foot into *tiger carries.*

- To turn from a *reverse stance right drill*, hook-in the left foot and turn around, advancing the right foot for *tiger carries.*

The exact hand actions will differ slightly, you will need to bring the rear hand forward and drop the lead hand slightly to cross the hands. Note that you are turning from a reverse stance instead of an aligned stance, so the feeling will be a bit different.

- After you turn around, then continue on to repeat the passing sequence.

7h   Closing Move for the Skill of Passing   yún zìgōng shōushì 云字功收势

When you are back to the starting point, in a *reverse stance drill* facing in the same direction that you started from, you may close the form.

- From *reverse stance <u>left</u> drill*:

Withdraw the right foot and place it beside the left foot, feet parallel. Tuck the left fist to cover / press with the forearm across the body and lower the right fist to the waist. Drill the right fist up to nose height and pull the left fist back to the belly. Look at the right fist. (image 2.83)

2.83

- From *reverse stance <u>right</u> drill*:

Withdraw the left foot to beside the right foot. Circle the right fist right, down, and then drill forward and up. Unclench the left hand and circle it left and up, then right and down to cover and press down, pulling back to the belly. Look at the right fist (image 2.84)

2.84

- Advance the left foot without moving the right foot, to settle into a *santi* stance. Split the left hand forward and pull the right hand back to the belly to take a *santishi*. Then close as usual from *santishi*. See the description in movement 1h.

POWER GENERATION FOR THE SKILL OF PASSING

Pass

Analyzing the action of passing, the hands each draw a circle in front of the face in a nonstandard elipse. Using the left pass as example, the left hand rotates and lifts the forearm up, opening out the left shoulder. The right hand extends forward, closing in the right shoulder. You need to empty the chest and gather in the lower back, keeping the waist relaxed and lively to draw the arms into action, so that the hands guide, the waist urges, and the shoulders follow.

When the right hand circles in front, the right shoulder reaches forward. When the left hand circles in front, the left shoulder reaches forward. When the left hand has the carrying power, then the right hand has a drawing back power. The power comes from the body core. With the coordination of the footwork, the actions alternate left and right.

Reverse stance drill

The torso must first draw back before the drill. This gathers power by 'pre-loading back to launch forward.' If you will punch the right fist then the right shoulder should roll and draw to the right, compressing down, and the right upper arm should be tight to the ribs. In this way the lower back will urge the shoulder forward, the shoulder will urge the elbow, and the fist will twist and drill to the midline of the body. This makes the drilling punch solid and heavy, completed with whole body power.

- The completed drilling punch should be neither too short nor too long – "too bent lacks reach, too straight lacks strength" – an elbow angle of one hundred and twenty degrees is ideal.

In addition, when the left hand tucks in and presses down, then brushes aside to draw back, keep the arm relaxed and settled. Do not use brute force. Transfer power from the waist to the shoulder and from the shoulder to the elbow, which in turn draws the hand. The power should be heavy, sudden, shaking. The right hand drills forward and the left hand draws back, completely connected through the waist, using the power of the body core.

- During the short sequence of the *skill of passing*, during the pass the chest should be empty and the upper back stretched, the abdomen should be pulled in and the lower back compressed, and the torso should be lowered. During the drill, the lower back should first gather and then straighten and hump. The buttocks should first drop down slightly. Breathe out to release power, settling the breath to the *dantian* to increase the whole body power of the drill.

PRACTICAL APPLICATIONS FOR THE SKILL OF PASSING

Passing is essentially a defensive move, lifting the elbow and hand to protect the head. The rear hand comes through to protect your chest and ribs. You need to close in your chest and close in the rear shoulder to better protect your upper body's upper portion and midline.

The rear hand knocks aside as it circles, catching the opponent's arm and pulling it to the side and back as the lead hand comes through. It works whether you advance or retreat, but it works best with a retreating step. You need to coordinate the hand action with the footwork. To use it advancing, both hands need to continuously and quickly circle in front of the body to protect you. This serves also to confuse the opponent and create an opportunity to get in with another technique.

Reverse stance drill covers the opponent's arm and presses it down, using the power from your back to shake him and take him sideways so that the rear hand can come through with an uppercut to his chest or jaw. The key is to drive the footwork into the opponent to get a tight punch. Drill is a close range technique, so if you can't get in close then you won't be able to use its full potential as a strong hit.

- Talking about fighting is not fighting. Similarly, knowing techniques without having deep skills is useless. You need to get a feel for applications with a lot of thoughtful practice. As you gain practical experience and learn from others you will gradually improve. Remember that in actual combat the techniques are not set in cement. You have to react according to the situation and use techniques fluidly, according to your own natural abilities.

The Poem About The Skill Of Passing

云势两手绕身前，架拨捋带神意联。搂手钻打腰肩劲，快步进身拳上钻。

The hands circle in front of the body to pass.

Block up, knock away, pull and guide, connecting your spirit and mind.

Brush aside and drill using the power of your back and shoulders.

Quick footwork gets the body in close so that you can drill up.

EIGHT: THE SKILL OF GUIDING 领字功

Introduction To Guide, *Ling*

Guide means to catch or to accept an oncoming force and guide it along the same direction – to draw something along, accepting and taking it somewhere else – so the Skill Of Guiding is that of redirecting an attack off to the side. If the opponent strikes down the midline you defend with both hands, quickly grabbing and drawing him along, guiding him to the outside line. Take the force of the opponent and add a little along the same direction, so that he misses his target, 'guiding his attack to land in emptiness.' Once he is turned away from you, you are in a smooth position to counter attack at will. Guide can also be used as a direct grabbing attack, pulling your opponent forcefully to the side to put him off balance and throw him off stride.[39] Guide can be practised alone, as advance guide, retreat

---

[39] Author's note: Some classics write, "guide is the snake model," but looking at the technique and line of action of snake model, guide is quite different. Snake model is mainly a slice up, a scoop, or a low drag. Guide, on the other hand, follows the line of attack smoothly. Perhaps in some branches of Xingyiquan the Skill Of Guiding is similar to the snake model's technique, but as far as we are concerned they are not at all alike.

guide, aligned stance guide, reverse stance guide, and so on.

The short sequence for the Skill Of Guiding is: *opening move, right step forward tiger carries, left guide, left aligned stance cannon punch, turn around tiger carries, pivot triple palm strikes, advance left driving punch, right guide*, and so on.

8a   Opening Move (left *santishi*)   qǐ shì   起势

As described in move 1a.

8b   Right Step Forward, Tiger Carries   yòu shàngbù hǔtuō   右上步虎托

As described in move 1b.

8c   Step Forward, Left Guide   shàngbù zuǒ lǐngshì   上步左领势

ACTION 1: Advance the right foot a half-step and bring in the left foot by the right ankle without touching down. Stand firmly on the right leg with the knees bent and together. Cross the wrists with the left on the outside, left palm facing in and right palm facing out. Push and block up in front of the head, hands to nose height. Empty the chest, stretch the upper back, and drop the elbows. Look past the hands. (image 2.85)

ACTION 2: Step the left foot a long step forward and follow in a half-step with the right foot, shifting back a bit into a sixty-forty stance. Entwine the wrists around each other, rotating the right hand thumb outward and the left hand thumb inward, so that the hands draw a small circle at the right in front of the body. When the palms both face forward then clench the hands and pull down and back to the left with a guiding action. The left hand completes the move behind the body with the palm down, and the right hand pulls back below the left armpit, fist heart up. Press the head up and look forward. (images 2.86 and 2.86 front)

Pointers

- o Complete the upward crossed block as the right foot lands. Sit the torso down.

- o Complete the guiding back action as the left foot lands. Be sure to rotate and grab, and to draw a small circle.

8d   Left Aligned Stance Cannon Punch   zuǒ shùnbù pàoquán   左顺步炮拳

ACTION: Advance the left foot and follow in the right foot a half-step, keeping most weight on the right leg. Turn the right fist heart in and drill up toward the left temple. Bend the left elbow and bring the fist in to in front of the chest. As the left foot advances, punch the left fist forward to sternum height and draw the right fist across to the right temple, rotating the thumb in. Reach the left shoulder forward and settle the right elbow down. Press the head up and look past the left fist. (image 2.87)

Pointers

o   Complete the left punch as the left foot lands.

o   Turn the waist and extend the shoulder into the punch. Keep the right elbow down and rotate the thumb side of the fist in towards the palm [called internal rotation]. In this high position, this action will turn the fist heart out.

8e   Turn Around, Tiger Carries   huíshēn hǔtuō   回身虎托

ACTION 1: Hook-in step the left foot at the right toes and turn the body around one-eighty degrees to the right, sitting onto the left leg. When you have turned around, withdraw the right foot to just in front of the left. Bring the left fist to in front of the chest, and stab the right fist from under the right armpit behind the body out to sternum height, fist eye down. Keep the right arm slightly bent. Look at the right fist. (image 2.88)

ACTION 2: Advance the right foot a half-step and bring the left foot up by the right foot without touching down. Thread the left fist forward along under the right arm. When the fists cross, unclench the hands and lift them, crossed, then open out to the sides. Continue to circle them down to the sides, palms forward, fingers down. Press the head up and look forward. (images 2.89, 2.90)

ACTION 3: Step the left foot forward and follow the right foot in a half-step, keeping most weight on the right leg. Push the hands forward and down, palms forward at belly height, a fist width apart. Keep the arms slightly bent, empty the

chest, stretch the upper back, sit into the buttocks, and settle the shoulders. Look past the hands. (image 2.91)

Pointers

- o Hook-in the lead foot as the fist stabs out towards the rear.

- o Turn the body and step forward as the hands circle and come into the waist.

- o Push the hands forward and down as the foot lands.

8f   Pivot, Triple Palm Strikes   zhuànshēn sānzhǎng   转身三掌

ACTION 1: Hook-in the left foot towards the right toes and turn around one-eighty to the right to face back in the way which you came. Shift onto the left leg and, after you have pivoted, advance the right foot a half-step without moving the left foot. Rotate the right hand so the thumb is down and the little finger is up and bring it past the left side of the body, up, forward, and then down in a circular chop, hitting with the ulnar edge at sternum height with the arm slightly bent. Look at the right hand. (image 2.92)

ACTION 2: Step the left foot forward without moving the right foot. Bend the left arm and lift the hand, then circle it from the back up, forward and down with a circular chop, finishing at sternum height with the arm slightly bent. Pull the right hand back to the right side. Look at the left hand. (image 2.93)

ACTION 3: Shift back and withdraw the left foot a half-step to touch the ball down in front of the right foot. Do not move the right foot. Circle the right hand up and forward in a circling chop and cover with the palm down at sternum height. Pull the left hand back to the left side and clench it. Reach the right shoulder forward and lift the torso slightly. Look at the right hand. (image 2.94)

Pointers

- o The hook-in to pivot should be a large range movement, hooking to take a T stance.

○ Complete the inverted hand circular chop as the body turns. Complete the left circular chop as the left foot steps forward. Complete the right covering chop as the left foot withdraws.

○ These three palms – one inverted chop, one straight chop, and one covering chop – should be fully connected without a pause between them, completed as one action.

8g   Aligned Stance Left Driving Punch   shùnbù zuǒ bēngquán 顺步左崩拳

ACTION: Advance the left foot and follow in a half-step with the right foot. Clench the right hand and pull it back to the belly, fist heart in. Do a left driving punch forward to sternum height, arm slightly bent. Press the head up and look past the left fist. (image 2.95)

2.95

Pointers

○ Complete the left punch at exactly the same time that the left foot lands.

○ Do not pause between *pivot three palms* and *left driving punch*. They are connected and completed as one action.

8h   Right Guide   yòu lǐngshì   右领势

ACTION 1: Advance the left foot a half-step and follow in the right foot to beside the left without touching down, bending the left leg to stand firmly. Thread the right fist out under the left arm until the fists meet, then unclench them with the wrists crossed, left hand above the right, palms angled up. Drill and block up in front of the head with the hands at nose height. Empty the chest and stretch the upper back. Look past the hands. (image 2.96)

ACTION 2: Take a long step forward with the right foot and follow in the left foot a half-step. Keep the wrists crossed and rotate the left thumb outwards and the right thumb inwards. When both palms face forward, clench the hands. Pull, guiding down to the rear right until the right fist is behind the body, fist heart down, and the left fist is under the right armpit, fist heart up. Press the head up and look forward. (image 2.97)

2.96

2.97

Pointers:

○ The same as *left guide*, see pointers for move 8c.

8i   **Right Aligned Stance Cannon Punch** yòu shùnbù pàoquán   右顺步炮拳

ACTION: Tuck the left elbow in and drill up, fist heart in, to the right temple. Bend the right elbow and bring the fist to the chest. Advance the right foot and follow in the left foot a half-step. Punch with a *right cannon punch* as the right foot lands. The right fist punches to sternum height, fist eye up. The left fist rotates the thumb inward and moves to beside the left temple. Keep the left elbow down. Press the head up and look past the right fist. (image 2.98)

Pointers:

- o The same as *left aligned stance cannon punch*, see pointers for move 8d.

8j   **Turn Around, Tiger Carries**   huíshēn hǔtuō   回身虎托

The same as move 8e described above, just transposing left and right.

8k   **Pivot, Triple Palm Strikes**   zhuànshēn sānzhǎng   转身三掌

The same as move 8f described above, just transposing left and right.

8l **Aligned Stance Right Driving Punch** shùnbù yòu bēngquán   顺步右崩拳

The same as move 8g described above, just transposing left and right.

- • Since the sequence for the *skill of guiding* contains turning moves within it, it is practiced without a 'turn around' move.

8m   **Closing Move for the Skill of Guiding**   lǐng zìgōng shōushì   领字功收势

On getting back to the starting place, you will close from a *driving punch*.

- • From a <u>left</u> *aligned stance driving punch*:

ACTION 1: Without moving the feet, tuck in and pull the left fist back to the belly. (image 2.99)

ACTION 2: Bring the right foot back to the left, feet parallel. Unclench the hands and lift them to the sides, palms up, until they reach shoulder height. Look at the

right hand. (images 2.100, 2.101)

ACTION 3: Without moving the legs, bend the elbows to bring the hands together in front of the face at shoulder height, pointing to each other with the palms down. (image 2.102)

ACTION 4: Press the hands down and stand up. Bring the hands to hang at the sides, to stand at attention. (image 2.103)

- If you are in a <u>right</u> *aligned stance driving punch*:

ACTION 1: Retreat the right foot and then retreat the left foot behind the right, landing with the whole foot. Shift back with the weight between the legs and turn the right foot out slightly to take a crossed stance. Rotate the right fist heart up and pull it back to the belly. Punch the left fist forward to sternum height. Press the head up and look at the left fist. This is a *retreating driving punch*. (images 2.104, 2.105)

ACTION 2: Step the left foot forward without moving the right foot, to take a *santi* stance. Tuck in the left fist and pull it back to the belly. Press the head up and look forward. (image 2.106)

- Continue on to close the same as described in Actions 2, 3, and 4 above (see images 2.100, 2.101, 2.102, 2.103).

POWER GENERATION FOR THE SKILL OF GUIDING

When the hands cross and push/block up in front, you should empty the chest and stretch the upper back, putting an inflating energy, or bracing power, into the arms. As the hands grab and rotate, just before they guide back, they should pre-load forward and rightward, as they will be pulling back and to the left. In order to guide back, the hands should first draw a small circle forward. This helps to get a feel for the whole body power, and help to gather power.

- The waist needs to be relaxed and supple so that its natural elasticity leads the actions of the hands. When guiding, power transfers from the waist to shoulders, from the shoulders to the elbows, and from the elbows to the hands. When guiding to the left, the right shoulder is forward. When guiding to the right, the left shoulder is forward. In this way the shoulders have a hidden shove. Turn the waist to align the shoulders into the action, and lean the torso slightly.

- The lead foot should have a raking power as it lands and the head should butt forward, so that your entire intention is to charge forward. The hand that guides back should have a pulling power back and a settling power down.

Aligned stance cannon punch

Keep the elbow tightly hugging the ribs and punch to the midline. Turn the waist and extend into the shoulder to launch power. Tuck in the elbow to drill the fist up. Exhale to assist the power release by combing internal with external movement.

Pivot, triple palm strikes

Relax the shoulders during the hook-in step, turn around, and inverted circling chop. Transfer power from the shoulders to the elbows, and from the elbows to the hands. As the circling chop lowers it should have heavy power. As the arm circles, keep the elbow bent at a certain angle, then bend it and move forward, and then extend it as it reaches forward. This increases the force and speed of the circle. This is how to use both angular and linear velocity effectively. The angular velocity achieves a quick turn around, and the linear velocity gains a greater strength for the hit.

The inverted chop, straight chop, and covering chop are all achieved by transferring power from the waist to the shoulders, from the shoulders to the elbows to turn, and then to the hands as the elbows extend, so that the power reaches to the hands at the point of contact. Be sure to chop to the midline of the body.

Turn around tiger carries

Lift the elbow, close the shoulders and rotate the arms to do the stab to the rear, so that the whole body is connected without a weak point.

- If you want to use whole body power in every position and technique, you must first clearly understand the correct trajectory of the feet and hands, and absolutely understand the fixed positions, the coordination between the hands and feet, and the height of the stances. In addition, you must understand the power release – what is the order of the release? Where is the origin of the power? Where is the hitting surface? How do the hands and feet work together? How do you use the torso? You also need to understand the breathing coordination with the power launch. Once you are clear on the movements and how to do them, then you need to undergo a period of intense training. The classics say, "from familiarity grows skill, and from skill grows the true essence." During intense training you need to study and examine whether or not your movements are in accordance with the principles of physics. Do they fit the laws of physics? Do they fit the structure of the body? Of course, the most important thing is to fit the principles of combat. While you are concentrating on all this, you also must remember that the body should feel comfortable, smooth and unimpeded, clear minded, and carefree.

PRACTICAL APPLICATIONS FOR THE SKILL OF GUIDING

The Skill Of Guiding uses a crossed upper pushing block that can be a defense against a straight line punch. The block also prepares for the two handed grab and pull. When you step forward and turn the body then you can guide the attack back by pulling forcefully on the opponent's arm. Grab clothes or 'meat' depending on what's there.

- The optimal situation would be: I grab the opponent's right arm with both hands and guide it towards the rear on my right side. Or, if I grab his left arm then I guide it back on my left. This way I prevent him from counter attacking with his other arm as I pull. But in reality, where is an ideal situation awaiting us? You have to create your opportunity and take advantage of whatever opportunity might present itself, and use the technique as best you can. When using guiding as an independent technique you can retreat as you pull. Otherwise, try to step in with a cannon punch afterwards.

The *pivot triple palm strikes* are meant to deal with an attack from the rear. They must be done quickly, and immediately connected to a driving punch. If someone comes at you from the rear, you can turn around and defend with an inverted chop. Attack then with the second palm, striking to his face, and add the third chop to his face, immediately following up with a driving punch to his solar plexus. This combination prevents him from responding to your attack and he will lose the exchange.

- You can never expect to use any technique in a combat situation without altering it. You will need to change the exact movement from what you normally practise. But if you utilize the power that you have trained then you can change the techniques and make combinations as needed to control your opponent and win. The principle of combat is, "control your opponent and do not let him control you."

General Qi Jiguan said in his classic manual on the martial arts, "To win you must understand your enemy. Winning and losing is not determined by magic but by the will to win. Whoever has the strongest desire to win, will win. If the enemy has low skill but is talented at tactics then he should be considered skilled. The ancients say, 'The skilled man is brave. He believes in himself, so will win.'" I suggest that the reader should consider this carefully.

THE POEM ABOUT THE SKILL OF GUIDING

双手抓挌侧身领，暗藏肩撞炮拳攻。转身顾后连三掌，得机得势进步崩。

Grab with both hands and turn sideways to guide.

This hides a shoulder strike and a cannon punch attack.

Turn around to deal with the back with three continuous palms.

Take the opportunities offered to advance and punch.

THE EIGHT SKILLS CONNECTED FORM

八字功连还拳

INTRODUCTION TO THE EIGHT SKILLS CONNECTED FORM, BAZIGONG LIANHUAN QUAN

The Eight Skills Form is a form that connects the individual eight skills, and which is widespread and popular amongst traditional Xingyiquan practitioners. It includes all of the most important and representative techniques of each of the eight skills of spread, intercept, wrap, bridge, scoop, butt, pass, and guide. There are some additional techniques in the form, necessary to smooth out the transitions and maintian a good power flow, so the Eight Skills Form is quite rich in content.

The Eight Skills Form teaches you techniques outside the standard five elements and twelve animals. You use different body parts, directions, angles, power, techniques, and applications. This will give you a richer and better movement vocabulary in Xingyiquan and improve your combative ability.

You should learn the Eight Skills Form only after you have mastered the individual eight skills, then you can master the form fairly quickly. Of course, if you have a good foundation and are good at Xingyiquan forms, you could learn the form directly, but you will need to work very hard at it to get it properly

NAMES OF THE MOVEMENTS

1. Opening Move (left *santishi*)
2. Advance, Right Driving Punch, or Crushing Punch
3. Step Forward, Tiger Carries
4. Step Forward, Spread, Right Side
5. Step Forward Swinging Chop with Crossing Cut
6. Advance, Double Intercept on Left Side
7. Step forward, Double Intercept on Right Side
8. Push a Boat Downstream
9. Dodging Double Wrap
10. Step Forward, Double Shove
11. Withdraw, Close the Shoulders
12. Step Forward Left Bridge
13. Step Forward, Left Split
14. Step Forward, Right Eagle Grasps
15. Turn Around, Snake Coils its Body
16. Step Forward, Right Scoop
17. Withdraw, Left Chop

18.   Advance, Scoop

19.   Retreat, Elbow Cover

20.   Advance, Head Butt

21.   Pull and Knee Butt

22.   Step Forward, Elbow Butt

23.   Stroke and Driving Punch,   or Crushing Punch

24.   Pass, Pull and Drag

25.   Reverse Stance Left Drill and Hit

26.   Left Guide

27.   Step Forward, Left Cannon Punch, or Pounding Punch

28.   Turn Around, Tiger Carries

29.   Push the Shutter to Gaze at the Moon

30.   Closing Move

Description of the Movements

1.   Opening Move (left *santishi*)   qǐ shì   起势

ACTION 1: Stand to attention, facing forty-five degrees, ninety degrees, or directly facing the line on which you will travel. (image 2.107)

ACTION 2: Without moving the feet, gradually lift the hands at the sides to shoulder height, palms up and arms naturally bent. Look at the right hand. (image 2.108)

ACTION 3: Bend the elbows so that the hands point to each other in front of the face, palms down. Then press the hands down to the belly, bending the legs to sit with the knees together. Press the head up and tuck the chin in. Turn the head to look forward to the left, along the line which you will travel. (image 2.109)

2.107   2.108   2.109

ACTION 4: Clench the fists at the belly and turn the fist hearts up, keeping the elbows tight to the ribs. Drill the right fist up by the sternum then forward to nose height, twist the ulnar edge of the forearm up. Turn leftward to look in the direction that the form will take. Press the head up, and look at the right fist. (image 2.110)

ACTION 5: Advance the left foot without moving the right foot, settling into a *santi* stance, with more weight on the right leg. Bring the left fist up by the sternum and out to the right elbow, drilling forward by sliding along the right forearm, fist heart up. When the left fist arrives at the right fist, unclench both hands and  turn the palms down. Split the left hand forward and down with the arm slightly bent and the wrist cocked, fingers at shoulder height. Pull the right hand back to the belly, palm down. Press the head up, tuck in the chin, and look past the left hand. (image 2.111)

Pointers

   o   See pointers for details on *santishi* in Part One Chapter Two.

2.   Advance, Right Driving Punch, or Crushing Punch

   jìnbù yòu bēngquán   进步右崩拳

ACTION: Advance the left foot a long step and follow in the right foot a half-step, keeping most weight on the right leg. Turn the left fist to tuck and press down, then pull it back to the belly, fist heart in. Lift the right fist to sternum height then punch straight forward with the elbow slightly bent and the fist eye up. Reach the right shoulder slightly forward. Press the head up, tuck in the chin, and look past the right fist. (image 2.112)

Pointers

   o   The entire move must be well integrated, the right fist landing as the right foot comes in. The right foot should shovel in with a thump. Coordinate the power impulse with an expulsion of breath.

3.   Step Forward, Tiger Carries   shàngbù hǔtuō   上步虎托

ACTION 1: Advance the left foot a half-step and follow in the right foot beside the left ankle without touching down. Rotate both palms in and thread the left hand forward, under the right forearm. Once the wrists cross, circle the hands out to the sides, palms angled forward. Complete the circles by bringing the hands back to the waist, keeping the elbows snug to the ribs, palms forward, and fingers down. Press the head up and look forward. (images 2.113, 2.114)

ACTION 2: Take a long step to the forward right with the right foot and follow in a half-step with the left foot into a stance with most weight on the left leg. Do a carrying technique with the palms to belly height, pushing forward and down. The hands should be about ten centimetres apart, with the palms forward and the fingers down. Press the head up, settle the shoulders, tuck in the elbows, and look past the hands. (image 2.115)

2.113　　　2.114　　　2.115

Pointers

o Circle the hands while advancing the left foot.

o You must apply an integrated power by completing the carrying action of the hands as the right foot lands.

4.　　Step Forward, Spread, Right Side　　shàngbù yòu zhǎnshì　上步右展势

ACTION 1: Advance the right foot a half-step. Tuck the left hand down, first circling left, up, and forward, to to do a crossing cover in front of the body at chest height. Clench the right fist and bring it back to the belly. Look at the left hand. (image 2.116)

ACTION 2: Step the left foot forward a half-step, turning the foot out as it lands. Bring the right fist up past the sternum then drill forward and up along inside the left forearm to nose height. Press the left hand down towards the waist. Look forward. (image 2.117)

ACTION 3: Take a long step forward with the right foot, landing with the foot turned in. Bring the left foot a half-step in, turned parallel to the right foot, and sit down with more weight on the left leg, in a half horse stance. Bring the left forearm across to block above the head. Bend the right elbow and bring it back to

2.116　　　2.117　　　2.118

the armpit, rolling the fist over so that the fist eye is down and the fist heart faces back. Punch forward to sternum height with the right fist, completing the punch with the arm slightly bent and the fist eye down. Pull the left fist up and back to the left of the head, rotating the fist and bending the elbow with the fist eye down and the arm bracing out. Turn leftward, turning the waist and reaching forward with the shoulder. Press the head up, look past the right fist. (image 2.118)

Pointers

- o Complete the whole move without pausing, with full connected power.

- o Complete the right planting punch as the right foot lands. Put power into the right fist by turning the lower back and extending the right shoulder, turning the body sideways to hit. Brace back with the left elbow as the left fist pulls back. Lean slightly into the left side and grab the ground with the right foot. Be sure to connect the lower back, shoulders and elbows, and coordinate the hit with an expulsion of breath.

5.   Step Forward, Swinging Chop with Crossing Cut

shàngbù lūnpī héng zhé   上步抢劈横折

ACTION 1: Rise slightly and withdraw the right foot a half-step, then advance it a half-step. Lower the left hand by the left waist. Lower the right fist in front of the body, then circle it back, up, and finally forward in a swinging chop downwards. Finish with the right open palm vertical at chest height. Look at the right hand. (image 2.119)

ACTION 2: Step the left foot forward to touch down beside the right foot, turning the body a one-eighty degrees rightward by pivoting on the right foot. Rotate the left hand so the palm faces in, and bend the elbow to bring the forearm to block across in front of the body as it turns. Finish with the left hand at nose height in front of the right shoulder, palm down. Place the right palm under the left armpit. Look to the forward left. (image 2.120)

ACTION 3: Take a long step forward with the left foot and follow in a half-step with the right foot. Cut across tranversely with the full left arm, keeping the arm slightly bent. Brace back with the right hand with the arm slighly bent. The left hand is at neck height and the right hand is at shoulder height, both palms down. Look at the left hand. (image 2.121)

2.119   2.120   2.121

Pointers

- ○ The right swinging chop is connected to the right foot, so the waist must remain relaxed to transfer power to the arm through the shoulder. The power must remain settled.

- ○ The crossing cut of the left arm must get its power from the waist by containing the chest and closing the shoulders.

- ○ Three actions are done as one: the left arm cuts across, the left foot steps forward, and the right arm braces back. The arms must remain rounded. Open the chest, solidify the abdomen, and breathe out to launch power.

- ○ The two actions must be done as one, with no pause between them.

6.   Advance, Double Intercept on Left Side jìnbù zuǒ shuāng jié 进步左双截

ACTION 1: Withdraw the left foot a half-step and shift back onto the right leg without moving the right foot. Clench the left fist, bring it down, then drill it up in front of the right shoulder, fist heart in, elbow protecting the solar plexus. Clench the right fist, bend the elbow, and draw the fist to in front of the right shoulder at head height, fist eye facing back. Look forward. (image 2.122)

ACTION 2: Advance the left foot a long step to the forward left, following the right foot in a half-step. Turn the waist to pull the fists to the left, bending the elbows to intercept with the forearms across the body. Rotate the right fist heart to face in at mouth height and the left fist heart to face out at shoulder height. The right elbow is covering in front of the body. Press the head up, tuck in the jaw, and look forward. (image 2.123)

Pointers

- ○ Withdraw the left foot as the left fist drills upward. Be sure to turn the waist right and sit down into the torso to gather power.

- ○ Cut across with the fists and forearms as the left foot lands forward. Turn the waist and reach with the shoulders, rotate the arms and settle the elbows. The power comes from the lower back and is expressed in the elbows, forearms and fists. Be sure to keep the waist relaxed and lively.

7.   Step Forward, Double Intercept on Right Side

shàngbù yòu shuāngjié   上步右双截

ACTION 1: Advance the left foot a half-step and bring in the right foot without touching down. Slightly extend the arms and lower the fists in front. Bend the right elbow and drill the fist up past the sterum to in front of the left shoulder, fist heart in. Circle the left fist back and up, then bend the elbow and twist the fist heart out beside the left shoulder at ear height. Turn the body a bit to the left. Look to the forward right. (image 2.124)

ACTION 2: Advance the right foot a long step to the forward left, following the left foot in a half-step, keeping most weight on the left leg. Pull the fists to the right, bending the elbows to intercept with the forearms across the body by turning the waist rightward. Rotate the left fist heart to face in at mouth height and the right fist heart to face out at shoulder height. The left elbow is covering in front of the body. Press the head up, tuck in the jaw, and look past the left fist. (image 2.125)

Pointers

o   Complete the intercept as one action, keeping the movement connected.

o   Be sure to lead the movement of the shoulders from the body core, and to lead the movement of the elbows from the shoulders. The left and right action of the torso follows the principle of 'to go forward first pre-load back, to go left first pre-load right.'

8.   Push a Boat Downstream   shùn shuǐ tuī zhōu   顺水推舟

ACTION 1: Retreat the left foot a half-step then withdraw the right foot a half-step, keeping most weight on the left leg. Unclench the hands, extend the right hand forward, and turn both palms down. Do a pulling drag with both hands from the forward right – pulling left, down and back – with the right hand forward of the left. Complete the pull with the left hand by the left waist and the right hand in front of the belly. Solidify the abdomen and contain the chest, turning the torso slightly left. Press the head up and look forward. (image 2.126)

ACTION 2: Take a long step forward with the right foot and follow in a half-step with the left foot, keeping most weight on the left leg. Push forcefully forward with both hands, extending the arms with the palms facing forward. The right hand is in front at chest height and the left hand is just in front of the right

elbow. Press the head up, tuck in the chin, and look straight ahead. (image 2.127)

Pointers

- When the left foot retreats and the right foot withdraws, the feet must move quickly. Then when the right foot advances it must go for a good distance, and the left foot must follow in quickly.

- The cover, press, pull and drag should follow a full circle and move together with the backward weight shift. When the hands push forward they must move with the forward advance of the right foot. When issuing power the elbows must stay tucked in, and shoulders and elbows must setttle. Lengthen the waist, extend the arms, and exhale to issue power.

9.　　Dodging Double Wrap yáoshēn shuāng guǒ　　摇身双裹

ACTION 1: Shift the right foot a half-step to the forward right and bring in the left foot to beside the right. Extend the right hand forward, palm facing left, fingers up. Extend it at the right, then once it reaches forward, circle it horizontally leftward across to in front of the left shoulder. Lead to the right with the head. Bring the left hand back to the belly. Look at the right hand. (image 2.128)

ACTION 2: Step the left foot to the forward left and follow in the right foot to beside the right without touching down. Extend the left hand to the left, forward and up with the palm facing right and fingers up. After it reaches forward, circle it flat across to in front of the right shoulder, palm in. Lead to the left with the head and the body action. Look at the left hand. (image 2.129)

2.128　　　2.129

Pointers

- The circling action of the hands works together with the dodging action of the feet. Lead the action of the hands from the shoulders, and the action of the shoulders from the waist.

- Wrapping is a soft, continuous movement. Be sure to dodge the body sideways as the arms pass across. Dodge with the body and turn the head to the right as the hands wrap to the left, and vice versa.

10.　　Step Forward, Double Shove shàngbù shuāng zhuàng zhǎng　　上步双撞掌

ACTION: Take a long step forward with the right foot and follow in the left foot a half-step, keeping most weight back on the left leg. Roll the hands over in front of the chest to face the palms out, fingers pointing to each other, thumbs down, then shove forward forcefully. Shove straight forward with the arms slightly rounded and the palms out at chest height. Expand the upper back, contain the chest, and breathe out forcefully, settling the breath to the *dantian*. Press the head up, and look forward. (image 2.130)

Pointers

2.130

- o Complete the pushing shove as the right foot lands.

- o Contain the chest and open the upper back to put strength forward. Use the expulsion of breath to put power into the shove. Keep the arms rounded to brace forward.

11. **Withdraw, Close the Shoulders**   chèbù héjiān shì   撤步合肩势

ACTION: Retreat the left foot a half-step and withdraw the right foot inside the left foot, touching the ball of the foot down and shifting the weight to the left foot. Bend the knees and sit the torso down slightly. Turn the body leftward to bring the right shoulder in front. Circle the right hand past the chest, down, and stab down by the left hip, rotating the thumb outwards to turn the palm in. Pull the left hand back and lower it to by the left waist. Then bring the left hand up and forward, and wrap it towards the right shoulder, palm in. Both elbows are in front of the chest. Tuck in the abdomen and close the chest. Compress the body in and squat. Look past the right shoulder. (image 2.131)

2.131

Pointers

- o Coordinate the actions of the body, feet, and hands; retreat the rear foot, withdraw the lead foot, tuck the body, stab the right hand down, and wrap the left hand forward.

- o Try to shrink the torso as you squat down. Contain the chest and expand the upper back. This move stores power for the following strike.

12. **Step Forward, Left Bridge**   shàngbù zuǒ kuàshì   上步左跨势

ACTION 1: Step the right foot straight forward, landing with the foot turned outward. Don't move the left foot, and settle the weight between the feet. Turn the right hand so the thumb web is down and the palm forward and slice forward from the hip, up in a curving manner, clenching the fist as it arrives at head height. Lower the left hand and bring it back to beside the left waist, palm forward, fingers down. Look at the right hand. (image 2.132)

ACTION 2: Take a long step to the front with the left foot, landing with the foot turned slightly inward. Follow-in the right foot a bit, landing it turned

2.132

crossways, sitting down into a half horse stance. Extend the left arm to push forward at hip height, elbow slightly bent, palm forward, fingers down. Pull the right fist back to the right above the head with the fist eye down. Turn the torso leftward. Look past the left hand. (image 2.133)

Pointers

- Advance the right foot a half-step as the right hand slices up.

- Step the left foot forward as the left hand pushes out at the hip. Use the waist and shoulders, turning and settling. Be sure to coordinate upper and lower hands so that they act together.

13.   Step Forward, Left Split   shàngbù zuǒ pīquán   上步左劈拳

ACTION 1: Advance the left foot slightly and shift between the two feet. Turn the left hand and cut with the forearm to cover and press down at chest height, palm down. Lower the right hand by the right waist. Look past the left hand. (image 2.134)

ACTION 2: Step the right foot forward with the foot turned out. Clench the left fist and pull it back to the belly. Drill the right fist up to the sternum and forward to nose height with the ulnar edge turned up. Look past the right fist. (image 2.135)

ACTION 3: Take a step forward with the left foot and follow in a half-step with the right foot, settling into a *santi* stance. Bring the left fist by the sternum then out along the right forearm, then unclench it and split forward. Pull the right hand back to the belly, palm down. The split is done to shoulder height. Press the head up, tuck in the chin, and look past the left hand. (image 2.136)

Pointers

- These three actions are done as one movement – a stepping forward split. The actions should be done without pause and the hands and feet must be tightly coordinated.

- Split with the left hand as the left foot steps forward.

14. Step Forward, Right Eagle Grasp   shàngbù yòu yīngzhuō   上步右鹰捉

ACTION 1: First withdraw the left foot slightly and then advance it a half-step, following in with the right foot beside the left ankle. Clench the left hand and pull it back to the belly, and then drill it up by the sternum and forward to nose height with the ulnar edge twisted up. Place the right fist at the left elbow, fist heart up. Press the head up. Look past the left fist. (image 2.137)

ACTION 2: Take a long step forward with the right foot and follow in a half-step with the left foot, keeping the weight slightly back. Slide the right fist along the left arm to drill up to head height. Once the fists cross unclench the hands, chop the hands down, right hand finishing palm forward at waist height, and left hand pulling back to the belly, both palms down. Straighten the back and press the head up. Look past the right hand. (image 2.138)

Pointers

o   You may hook the fingers slightly into eagle claws, or you may use a normal palm shape.

o   Chop the right hand down as the right foot lands. Pay attention to pressing the head up, settling the elbows, sitting into the buttocks, and keeping a scissoring pressure between the legs.

15. Turn Around, Snake Coils its Body   huíshēn shé chánshēn   回身蛇缠身

ACTION 1: Stand up and pivot around a full one-eighty degrees on the feet to face around in the opposite direction. Turn the left hand thumb inward and lift the elbow to swing the left hand up, back and down to the left hip, arm slightly bent. Lift the right hand to the right of the head, keeping the arm slightly bent, thumb web forward, and palm up. Follow the movement of the left hand with the eyes. (image 2.139)

ACTION 2: Twist the body and sit down into a resting stance with the left foot forward. Stab the right hand down outside the left hip, palm out. Wrap the left hand in, threading up to the right shoulder, palm in. In the resting stance, the right heel is raised and the left foot is turned out, the thighs crosssed and

squeezing together. Look past the left hand. (image 2.140)

Pointers

- o   Rise up as the arms circle around.

- o   Stab the right hand down as you turn and sit into the resting stance. The whole movement must be done in one action with no pausing.

16.   **Step Forward, Right Scoop**   shàngbù yòu tiǎozhǎng   上步右挑掌

2.141

ACTION: Advance the left foot a half-step then take a long step forward with the right foot and follow in a half-step with the left foot. Turn the left hand palm down and pull down and back to the belly. Turn the right hand and bring it from front of the belly, fingers up and palm forward, to do a scooping strike upwards to chest height with the elbow bent. Settle the shoulders and elbows and press the head up. Look past the right hand. (image 2.141)

Pointers

- o   Complete the right arm scoop as the right foot lands. Before the right hand scoops up the elbow must first hug the ribs. Sit into the hips, lengthen the lower back, release and settle the shoulders, and drop the elbows.

17.   **Withdraw, Left Chop**   chèbù zuǒ pīquán   撤步左劈拳

ACTION: Withdraw the right foot a half-step to touch the ball down in front of the left foot. Shift back without moving the left foot. Slide the left hand along the top of the right arm to chop forward and down. Pull the right hand back and down to the belly. Complete the chop at chest height with the left shoulder reaching forward. Press the head up and look past the left hand. (image 2.142)

2.142

Pointers

- o   The hands must work together simultaneously with integrated power: pull back the right hand and chop forward with the left hand as you withdraw the right foot.

- o   Tuck in the abdomen and empty the chest, turn the waist, lean slightly into the movement, and reach the shoulder into the technique.

18.   **Advance, Right Scoop**   jìnbù yòu tiǎozhǎng   进步右挑掌

ACTION: Advance the right foot a long step forward and follow in a half-step with the left foot, keeping the weight back on the left leg. Scoop up the right hand from in front of the belly, fingers up and palm forward at shoulder height with the elbow bent. Pull the left palm back to the belly. Press the head up, tuck the jaw in, and look past the right hand. (image 2.143)

Pointers

- This is the same as move 16 described above.

- Moves 16, 17, and 18 are done continuously without pausing between them. Be sure to apply force forward and upward to each of the scoops.

19.   **Retreat, Elbow Cover**   tuìbù yǎnzhǒu   退步掩肘

ACTION 1: Retreat the left foot a half-step and shift the weight back, then withdraw the right foot a half-step. Clench the right hand and rotate the right elbow to do an elbow/forearm cover leftwards with the fist at nose height and the elbow below shoulder height. Keep the left fist at the belly. Look past the right fist. (image 2.144)

ACTION 2: Retreat the right foot a step, shift the weight back, and withdraw the left foot a half-step to in front of the right foot. Lower the right fist with a covering action down the left to the left ribs, fist heart in. Bring the left fist up and rightward, bending the left elbow to do an elbow cover rightwards. Turn rightward. Lower the left fist to the right waist, fist heart in. When the forearms cross in front of the chest the left arm is inside the right. Empty the chest and stretch the upper back. Look ahead. (image 2.145)

Pointers

- Coordinate the left foot retreat with the right elbow cover and the right foot retreat with the left elbow cover.

- Complete the two actions without pausing. Turn the body as the feet move. You need to turn sideways to do the elbow covers, so keep the waist lively and the shoulders settled.

20.   **Advance, Head Butt**   jìnbù tóudǐng   进步头顶

ACTION: Advance the left foot and follow in a half-step with the right, shifting the weight to a forward weighted sixty-forty stance. Brace the arms forward, the wrists crossed and the fists clenched at belly height, fist hearts down. Butt forward with the forehead, leaning the torso forward, tucking in the chin and putting the head slightly forward of the body. Stiffen the nape of the neck, clench the teeth, and look forward. (image 2.146)

Pointers

2.146

- o Butt with the head and brace with the arms as the left foot lands, hitting with hands, feet and head at exactly the same time.

- o Be sure to shift the weight forward to be able to hit with the head. Tuck in the abdomen and close the chest. When head butting, remember "to hit with the head you must use the feet, controlling the centre from beginning to ending; no one can defend against a foot charging through the front door."

21.   Pull and Knee Butt   lǔshǒu xīzhuàng   将手膝撞

ACTION: Advance the left foot a half-step forward diagonally to the left and shift forward. Shift onto the left leg and stand with the knee slightly bent, leaning the torso slightly forward. Unclench the hands and extend them to the forward left at shoulder height, left hand in front, right hand at the left elbow. Stretch open the thumb webs. Bend the right knee and shove forward and up with it to waist height. As the right knee strikes, clench the hands and pull back towards the right. Pull the left fist back to in front of the chest, fist heart up, left elbow at the solar plexus, and pull the right fist back on the ride side, fist heart down. Press the head forward and look past the left fist. (image 2.147)

2.147

Pointers

- o Grab and pull the hands back as the knee butts forward, exerting force both forward and back. Tuck in the belly, lift the knee, and rotate the waist to pull back. Dodge the torso to lean a bit to the left.

22.   Step Forward, Elbow Butt   shàngbù dǐngzhǒu   上步顶肘

ACTION: Take a long step straight forward with the right foot and follow in the left foot a half-step, shifting the weight forward to a forward weighted sixty-forty stance. Bring the right elbow into the right ribs, and then as the right foot lands, butt forward and up with the elbow bent. Bring the right fist to above the right shoulder with the fist heart in, so that the elbow butts up at shoulder height. Place the left hand behind the right elbow to support it. Reach the right shoulder forward. Press the head up and look straight forward. (image 2.148)

2.148

Pointers

- o Land the foot well forward, land firmly, and bring the rear foot in quickly. Be sure to shift slightly forward to be able to strike with the elbow.

23. **Stroke and Driving Punch, or Crushing Punch** lǔshǒu bēngquán 捋手崩拳

ACTION 1: Shift back and withdraw the right foot a half-step without moving the left foot. Unclench the right hand and extend it forward then cover and press down, clenching to grab and pull back to the right side. Slide the left hand along the right arm to chop out to chest height. Put the left shoulder forward into the action, tuck in the belly and empty the chest. Look past the left hand. (image 2.149)

ACTION 2: Advance the right foot a long step and follow in the left foot a half-step, keeping the weight mostly on the left leg. Punch the right fist forward to chest height. Clench and pull the left hand back to the belly. Press the head up, tuck in the chin, and look past the right fist. (image 2.150)

Pointers

- Chop the left hand down as the right hand pulls back, both when the right foot withdraws.

- Advance the right foot and punch the right fist at exactly the same time.

24. **Pass, Pull and Drag** yún shì lǔ daì 云势捋带

ACTION 1: Advance the right foot a half-step and follow in the left foot to beside the right foot without touching down. Unclench both hands and bend the right arm to lift the elbow above the head, close by the ear. Circle the right hand up and back at the right, and then forward, finishing at the forward right, palm up. Turn the left palm up and circle it past the chest, forward, and then left. When the left hand arrives at the left side, bend the elbow and bring it in front of the face then around to the forward right. At this time, the right hand is at the forward right with the palm up and the left hand is at the right elbow, palm forward, thumb down, and thumb web stretched open. Look past the right hand. (image 2.151)

ACTION 2: Take a long step forward with the left foot, foot turned out. Bend the legs and shift the weight between the feet. Drag the hands down, forward and up in a carrying position, the right palm angled up at nose height, arm slightly bent. The left hand finishes to the left of and above the head, palm out. Turn the waist, reach the right shoulder forward, and look past the right hand. (image

2.152)

Pointers

- The right hand passes and circles above the head while the left hand circles in front of the body. The hands are performing an opposing passing action, so they must coordinate together.

- The left foot steps forward as the hands carry up and then drag back to the left. Get power from the waist so that the movement is coordinated.

25.   Reverse Stance, Left Drilling Punch   àobù zuǒ zuāndǎ   拗步左钻打

2.153

ACTION: Take a long step forward with the right foot and follow in a half-step with the left foot. Turn the right hand palm down and tuck it in, bending the wrist, then bend the elbow and clench the fist, circling it up to the right side of the head. Clench and lower the left fist back to the left waist, then, keeping it tight to the ribs and rotating the ulnar edge in, drill forward and up to nose height. Press the head up, tuck in the chin, and look forward. (image 2.153)

Pointers

- Punch with the left fist as the right foot lands.

- Use the waist and shoulder to get power to the right wrist to hook and drag back. Use a shaking power from the waist, keeping the shoulders and elbows settled. Keep the waist, shoulders, and elbows relaxed before using power. Be sure to keep the elbow snug to the ribs during the drilling punch, to get power into it from the lower back.

26.   Left Guide   zuǒ lǐngshì   左领势

ACTION 1: Advance the right foot a half-step and follow in the left foot without touching down. Bring the right fist in to cross the wrists with the right inside the left, unclenching the hands with the left palm facing up and right palm facing forward. Draw a circle forward, up, and then rightward. When the hands arrrive at the forward right, externally rotate the right hand and internally rotate the left hand so that the palms are angled to the left. Reach the right hand forward to the right to nose height and the left to the right elbow. Look past the right hand. (image 2.154)

ACTION 2: Step the left foot a long step forward and follow in a half-step with the right foot. Clench both hands and pull down and back to the left with a guiding action. The left hand completes the move behind the body with the fist heart down, and the right hand pulls

2.154

2.155

back to the left ribs, fist heart up. Press the head up and look at the left hand. (image 2.155)

Pointers

○ Complete the guiding back action as the left foot lands. Press the head up as the hands pull down. Press the right shoulder forward as the hands pull back. In this way the body works as a unit, applying force in equal and opposite directions.

○ The hands do a grappling action as they circle, and then pull back. The intent is grabbing an opponent's arm and pulling it down to the left.

27.   Step Forward, Left Cannon Punch, or Pounding Punch

shàngbù zuǒ pàoquán   上步左炮拳

ACTION: Take a big step forward with the right foot and follow in the left foot a half-step. Drill the right fist forward and up. Bring the left hand in to the waist then hit out with a cannon punch – punch the left fist forward to sternum height, reaching the left shoulder forward. The right fist finishes at the right temple with the fist eye in and elbow down. Press the head up and look past the left fist. (image 2.156)

Pointers

○ Complete the left punch as the left foot lands. You must turn the waist and extend the shoulder into the punch.

28.   Turn Around, Tiger Carries   huíshēn hǔtuō   回身虎托

ACTION 1: Hook-in step the right foot at the left toes and turn the body around to the left, lifting the left foot at the right ankle without touching down. Cross the hands in front of the body and unclench them, palms out. Then lift them, open out to the sides, and continue to circle them down to either side, palms forward, fingers down. Tuck the elbows in snug to the ribs. Press the head up and look forward. (images 2.157, 2.158)

ACTION 2: Step the left foot forward and follow the right foot in a half-step, keeping most weight on the right leg. Push the hands forcefully forward and down, palms forward at belly height about a fist's width apart. Press the head up and sit into the buttocks. Look past the hands. (image 2.159)

Pointers

- ○ Hook-in the foot well to get around, and turn around quickly in one coordinated action

- ○ Push the hands forward and down as the left foot lands. To get power, sit into the hips, reach the shoulders, settle the elbows, squeeze the ribs, and breathe out.

29.   Push the Shutter to Gaze at the Moon   tuī chuāng wàng yuè   推窗望月

ACTION 1: Withdraw the left foot to touch down in front of the right foot, most weight on the right leg. Turn the left palm up and rotate the right ulnar edge up, palm rightward. Circle the hands in front of the belly forward, up, and then back. Bring the right hand down to beside the right waist, fingers up. Bring the left hand to in front of the right shoulder, palm down. Turn the torso slightly rightward and look at the left hand. (image 2.160)

ACTION 2: Advance the left foot and bend the knees to sit down into a half horse stance. Brace forward and up with the left arm rounded, palm forward and thumb down at head height, blocking up and across. Push forcefully forward to chest height with the right hand, palm forward and thumb up. Push the right hand forward past the left elbow. Press the head up, tuck in the chin, and look forward. (image 2.161)

Pointers

- ○ Coordinate the circling of the hands with the withdrawing step. Coordinate the pushing brace of the hands with the advancing step.

- ○ The hands must draw a circle and use a circular power. Use the body to get power to the hands. In the final position the torso should lean upwards slightly.

30.   Closing Move   shòu shì   收势

ACTION 1: Withdraw the left foot to in front of the right foot, touching the toes down. Clench the right hand and pull it back to the belly, then drill the right fist up by the sternum and forward to nose height, ulnar edge turned up. Turn the left hand over and clench it, covering and pressing down as it pulls back to the belly, clenching it. Look at the right hand. (image 2.162)

ACTION 2: Advance the left foot and shift the right foot slightly to sit into a *santi* stance. Drill the left fist out past the sternum to the right elbow then unclench the hands and split forward with the left hand while pulling the right hand back to the belly. Press the head up and look past the left hand. (image 2.163)

ACTION 3: Without moving the feet, clench the fists and pull them back to the belly. Press the head up and look forward (image 2.164)

ACTION 4: Shift forward and bring the right foot up to the left foot, keeping the knees bent. Unclench the hands and lift them at the sides, palms up, to shoulder height. Then bend the elbows to bring the hands to the front, palms down and fingers facing each other. Look forward. (images 2.165, 2.166, and 2.167)

ACTION 5: Press the hands down in front of the belly and stand up to attention, letting the hands hang down to the sides. Look forward. The form is now finished. (image 2.168)

Pointers

o   Bring the feet together as the hands rise together.

o   Stand to attention as the hands press down.

o   The closing movement must be continuous, steady, and stable, with full spirit and intent, and a serious mien.

ADVANCED PARTNER FORM

PROTECT THE BODY 安身炮

INTRODUCTION TO PROTECT THE BODY, *ANSHEN PAO*

Anshenpao, the Protect The Body partner form, is one of the outstanding classic partner forms of Xingyiquan, and as such is very popular and widespread. Different branches and localities of Xingyi show only small differences. It exemplifies the fighting characteristics and flavour of Xingyi, with its well-organized path, its smoothly flowing movements, its realistic attack and defense, and its practical applicability. The classics say that this form involves the whole of the Xingyi system.

The name 'protect the body' probably comes from its practical nature, since there are an abundance of self defense moves within the form. If you practise it often you can develop a smooth and natural fighting ability, or the ability to '*an shen*' – keep yourself safe.

Partners A and B each do twenty one attacking and defending actions, so that each has a total of forty two actions. Since partners A and B trade places, each learns and practises both attack and defense. All five element techniques are here, as are some animal models such as monkey, snake, and sparrow hawk. There are also some extra moves – such as *hook to the ear, steal a punch, sparrow hawk grabs a shoulder, lead along a sheep, intercept to right and left,* and *cut to the neck*. Split and drive occur the most often (*cut to the neck* counts as a split), partners A and B both use split nineteen times, and drive eight times. There is a good variety of split techniques such as *advance split, retreat split, dodging split, reverse stance split,* and *cut to the neck*.

You can see Xingyiquan's close range fighting and fast straight line attacking methods clearly in this form. The first and second thirds of the form show the main targets of attack: the head, neck, ribs, solar plexus and groin. These points are the weak points, as the classics say, "when going high, go for the throat, when going low, go for the groin, when going for the centre, go for the ribs." You can use a smaller force to greater effect when hitting these weak points. If you use greater force then you can incapacitate your opponent.

The protect the body partner form has the following characteristics:

- It takes care of everything at once – attack and defense are simultaneous. The defensive action is an attack, and an attack contains a defensive action. This is typical of Xingyi methods. For example, the advancing block and punch of the cannon punch, the split within the lead back, the driving punch that flows directly from the double intercept, and sparrow hawk grabs the shoulder.

- The techniques flow well and are practical. The short sequences of hand techniques are exceptional. The power is very smooth and tightly knit, the movements make sense, are practical, and in keeping with the principles of combat. There are some very nice sequences in the form, like *intercept and punch, hook to the ear and steal a punch, pull left knock right and punch, step forward slap and reverse pull, brush and shop, pull and cross kick to split,* and *monkey pulls the rope.* These applications can be taken out of the form and practised as individual sequences, alternating right and left, in practical sparring drills. When these short drills have been practised repeatedly until their use becomes a natural, instinctive reaction, then they can be used in a fight. Short combinations drills can improve your combat ability considerably.

- You freely advance and retreat, quickly and accurately. Both A and B show the characteristic Xingyi footwork: To advance, first advance the lead foot, then you must follow in with the rear foot. To retreat, first retreat the rear foot, then you must withdraw the lead foot."

- This footwork is quick and agile. When you advance, everything advances, and when you retreat, everything retreats. This keeps the body stable and well balanced. If you look at the footwork of both sides of the form, this characteristic is very clear. Both advance and retreat very naturally, advancing with a follow up step, and retreating with a withdrawing step, so that the whole body moves forward or backward.

- Attack and defense follow the rules of Xingyi, and the moves are well knit. All techniques show the characteristics and flavour of Xingyi. The lines of power, the path that the moves take, all follow the characteristic fighting principles of Xingyi. You protect the centre and attack the centre, almost always attacking the midline. The moves connect together so smoothly that attack and defense are tightly knit, which shows Xingyi's spirit of "chasing the wind and chasing the moon without slackening."

To sum up, the protect the body partner form is one of the most important forms in the Xingyi system. It has abundant content, tightly knit techniques, well-organized attack and defense, remarkable flavour, and is highly practical.

NAMES OF THE MOVEMENTS

1. A: Advance Right Driving Punch

    B: Retreat, Left Press Down, Right Driving Punch

2. A: Step Forward, Left Split

    B: Left Aligned Stance Cannon Punch

3. A: Dodging Right Split

    B: Dodging Right Split

4. A: Double Intercept to the Left

    B: Stationary Left Cut to the Neck

5. A: Double Intercept to the Right, Right Driving Punch

    B: Withdraw, Pull, Knock Aside and Hit

6. A: Monkey Pulls the Rope

    B: Retreat, Right Drill

7. A: Step Forward, Right Cannon Punch

    B: Retreat, Left Split

8. A: Step Forward, Right Hook to the Ear

    B: Withdraw, Left Drill

9. A: Advance and Steal a Hit

    B: Changeover Step, Slap to Knock Aside and Draw Out

10. A: Changeover Step Left Split

    B: Pull and Grab the Head

11. A: Step Forward, Snake

    B: Retreat, Left Cut to the Neck

12. A: Left and Right Cut to the Neck

    B: Right Drill, Left Driving Punch

13. A: Ape Pulls the Rope

    B: Retreat, Right Drill

14. A: Step Forward, Pull Back, Right Cut to the Neck

    B: Withdraw, Double Intercept to the Left

15. A: Left Cut to the Neck

    B: Double Intercept to the Right, Right Driving Punch

16. A: Pull Back, Crossing Kick, Step Forward, Right Split

    B: Retreat, Left Crosscut

17. A: Step Forward, Left Scoop Up, Right Split

    B: Grab the Shoulder with the Left Hand (Sparrow Hawk Grabs the Shoulder)

18. A: Brush Aside, Right Split

    B: Left Hooking Block, Right Cut to the Neck

19. A: Double Intercept to the Left

    B: Left Cut to the Neck

20. A: Double Intercept to the Right, Right Driving Punch

    B: Retreat, Left Press Down

21. A: Advance, Right Driving Punch

    B: Retreat, Left Press Down, Right Driving Punch

Description of the movements

Partner A is in the 'attacker' in dark uniform on the left, partner B is the 'counter-attacker' in the light uniform on the right. Partner A starts facing south, and partner B starts facing north. During the first section of the form, partner A will generally start and partner B will react. In general, but not always, partner A will attack with forward moving steps and partner B will defend with retreating steps.

In general, for each move the first action and image describe partner A's attack, with partner B not reacting. The second action and image describe partner B's defensive reaction with partner A not reacting. If necessary, a third action and image describe partner B's counter-attack with partner A not reacting.

Opening and *Santishi*   sāntǐshì   三体势

ACTION 1: Partners A and B stand about three to four steps away from each other, presenting their sides to each other. They stand properly to attention to show they are ready. (image 3.1)

Pointers

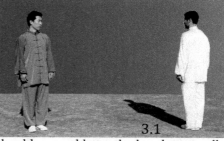
3.1

o Hold the head straight and tuck in the jaw. Press the head up, keep the lower back flat, settle the shoulders, and hang the hands naturally at the sides. Keep a calm expression, empty the mind of extraneous thoughts, settle the *qi* to the *dantian*, and focus on the task at hand. Prepare fully for the partner practice.

ACTION 2: Partners A and B move together, raising the hands to the sides to shoulder height, with the elbows bent. They then bring the hands together in front of the face, and press down to the belly. While doing this, they sink to a 120 degree bend in the knees. (image 3.2)

ACTION 3: Partners A and B both turn ninety degrees and twist the right fist up to the solar plexus, then drill it forward to nose height. (image 3.3)

3.2   3.3

ACTION 4: Partners A and B both step the left foot forward without moving the right foot. At this time, they unclench the left hand and bring it along the right forearm to split forward, pulling the right hand back to the belly. They look in the direction of the left hand, and settle into a *santishi*. (image 3.4)

Pointers

3.4

o Partners A and B must step forward into the *santishi* at exactly the same time and at the same speed – all movement occurs simultaneously. The on guard stance should be taken quickly and with power.

1. A: Advance Right Driving Punch   jìnbù yòu bēngquán   进步右崩拳

B: Retreat, Left Press Down, Right Driving Punch

tuìbù zuǒ àn yòu bēngquán   退步左按右崩拳

ACTION 1: Partner A advances the left foot forward and follows in the right foot to behind the left heel, keeping the weight on the right leg. Partner A slaps B's left hand down with the left hand and throws a driving punch towards B's solar plexus with the right fist. (image 3.5)

ACTION 2: Partner B retreats the right foot a half-step then withdraws the left foot a half- step, pressing the left palm down on A's right fist. Partner B controls and presses the arm down forward along the line of attack, making A miss the target. (image 3.6)

ACTION 3: Partner B advances the left foot a half-step and follows in the right foot a half- step, throwing a driving punch towards A's solar plexus. Partner B looks at A. (image 3.7)

Pointers

- When doing the driving punch, the forward hand should control the opponent by slapping his hand away or grabbing it. The punch should be fast and strong, driving towards the solar plexus. When stepping forward, thrust strongly from the rear foot and charge forward with the lead foot. The punch is timed with the landing of the foot, and should have one-inch power.

- Partner A should adjust the size of the step when he advances, according to how far away they are in the *santishi*. If they are far away then partner A should take a big step in, and if they are close then A should advance just a little. If they are too far away for one step to enter, then A may take a step forward with the right foot and then advance with the left. The step must bring partner A close enough to hit with the driving punch. When doing partner forms, it is important to get the spacing right – the punch should touch the partner.

o Partner B must retreat and withdraw the feet quickly, getting out of the way as A enters. In actual application B would hook and grab the punch, but in a partner form should just press down and keep it out of the way.

o Partners A and B need to coordinate the advancing and retreating so that they move smoothly together. They should not actually hit each other with force, but neither should they do empty and useless techniques. The cooperation should be tight, the techniques correct, the attack and defense appropriate, and the intentions true to life.[40]

2.   **A: Step Forward, Left Split**   shàngbù zuǒ pīquán   上步左劈拳

   B: Left Aligned Stance Cannon Punch   zuǒ shùnbù pàoquán   左顺步炮拳

ACTION 1: Partner A withdrawchs the right foot a half-step then withdraws the left foot. Partner A first brings back the right fist, then drills it up underneath B's right fist, and then unclenches the right hand and pulls B's hand down and back. Partner A prepares his left hand at the chest, looking at B's right fist. Partner A then advances the left foot a half-step and does a split towards B's face with the left hand. Partner A looks at B. (image 3.8)

ACTION 2: Partner B retreats the right foot and withdraws the left foot, bringing the right fist inside A's left arm to drill up, hooking up to the right ear, and moving the left fist up to the chest. Partner B advances the left foot a half-step and turns the left fist eye up, punching to A's solar plexus with the punching arm slightly bent. Partner B looks at A. (image 3.9)

Pointers

o To apply split, first drill the rear hand up to deflect, and then turn and unclench it, circling and coiling around the attacking limb to hook and pull. The foot should move in quickly and the lead hand strike the opponent's face. When doing a partner form, the hooking hand should not grab, just be aware of the possibility. When striking to B's face, A should have a point of focus, to avoid accidentally hitting B if B defends poorly.

---

[40] Editor's note: Always attack to the required height so that the defensive response is realistic. Here, for example, if parter B punches too low, then partner A's counter would not make sense.

o The *aligned stance cannon punch* is also called *sparrow hawk enters the woods*. When using it, the right fist drills up and deflects the attack. The body needs to tuck in as the fist rises, then the left foot must step forward quickly and the body turn to present the side, aiming to enter the opponent's groin area. The left punch is fierce and extended with good body action. When doing a partner form B should aim at A's solar plexus, but with a controlled focus. Also, B should not take too big a step forward, but keep a certain distance.

3. **A: Dodging Right Split**   yáoshēn yòu pīquán   摇身右劈拳

   B: Dodging Right Split   yáoshēn yòu pīquán   摇身右劈拳

ACTION 1: Partner A first withdraws the left foot, then takes a circling hook-out step to the right – the foot circles forward a half-step with the foot turned slightly out. Partner A drills the left hand up underneath B's left fist to knock it away, then pull down. A looks at the left hand. Partner A then steps the right foot forward and chops B's face with the right hand, looking at B. (image 3.10)

ACTION 2: Partner B retreats the right foot a half-step and brings the left fist back. Partner B then withdraws the left foot, then circles it forward a half-step to the right with the foot turned out. B drills the left hand up and turns it to hit A's right hand to knock it away to the left, looking at the left hand. Partner B then steps the right foot forward and chops A's face with the right hand. (image 3.11)

Pointers

o Partner A should first withdraw the left foot, and then circle it to advance. Pay attention to the body technique and body shape to first move back then advance. The body should move with the foot, dodging slightly as the foot circles – the backwards countermovement prepares for a smooth forward movement.

o Partner B should first retreat the right foot, withdraw the left foot, and then immediately circle the left foot to advance. The retreat and withdrawal is a dodging action to readjust positioning in order to follow up with an advance and attack.

o When A and B strike to the face they should stop the hand just before it reaches the face, to avoid unwanted accidents.

4.   A: Double Intercept to the Left   zuǒ shuāng jiéshǒu   左双截手

B: Stationary Left Cut to the Neck   yuánbù yòu qiēbō   原步右切脖

ACTION 1: Partner A shifts back mostly onto the left leg. A clenches both hands and bends both elbows to place the forearms vertical – the right fist in front with the fist heart facing in, and left fist behind with the fist heart facing out. Partner A connects both forearms on the inside of B's right arm, to intercept horizontally to the left. Partner A's fists are at nose height, and he looks at B. (image 3.12)

ACTION 2: Partner B, without moving the feet, turns the left palm up and slices towards the right side of A's neck with the palm edge, arm slightly bent. Partner B pulls the right hand back to the belly and looks at A. (image 3.13)

Pointers

o   The double intercept is a technique that uses both forearms to knock an attack aside horizontally. The right forearm rotates palm towards thumb so that the ulnar bone side is the point of contact, either on the forearm or the upper arm of the opponent. The power comes from the lower back and waist, which draw the shoulders and elbows across. The lower back should be relaxed and the buttocks should settle down.

o   The cut to the neck is a horizontal strike that goes for the carotid artery. In a partner form you should focus the hit and not use hard power or really hit, to avoid unwanted accidents.

5.   A: Double Intercept to the Right, Right Driving Punch

yòu shuāngjié yòu bēngquán   右双截右崩拳

B: Withdraw, Pull, Knock Aside and Hit   chèbù lā bō dǎ   撤步拉拨打

ACTION 1: Partner A withdraws the right foot a half-step and intercepts to the right with both fists – the left arm forward and the right fist behind – knocking B's left forearm towards the right. Partner A looks at B. (image 3.14)

ACTION 2: Partner A advances the right foot a half-step and drives a right punch towards B's solar plexus. The fist eye is up and the arm slightly bent. Partner A pulls the left fist back to the side of the waist and looks at B. (image 3.15)

ACTION 3: Partner B retreats the left foot a half-step and withdraws the right foot, shifting back. B turns the right palm to face right and stretches open the web of the palm, extending to slide along the inside of A's forearm. (image 3.16)

ACTION 4: Partner B extends the left fist, with the elbow bent, up inside A's fist and knocks it away to the left while pressing it down, bringing the fist back towards the left waist. Partner B advances the right foot a half-step and drives a right punch towards A's solar plexus. (image 3.17)

Pointers

- The double intercept / driving punch combination that repeats in this form is a particularly useful technique. It is compact, flows smoothly and is readily used. When actually using it, be sure to advance for the punch to hit harder. When doing it in the partner form, use the intercept technique to get the feel for the waist power. Defend yourself with just as much force as necessary, and do the driving punch with a focal point.

- Partner B should do the pull, knock aside, and hit in one continuous coordinated action, quickly and smoothly, hands and feet working together. Partners A and B must cooperate closely to coordinate appropriate speed, timing, and distance.

6. **A: Monkey Pulls the Rope**　　hóu dáo shéng　　　　猴捯绳

   B: Retreat, Right Drill　　tuìbù yòu zuānquán　　退步右钻拳

ACTION 1: Partner A withdraws the right foot a half-step and shifts back to the left leg. Partner A unclenches both hands with the palms down. Partner A places the right hand on B's right forearm and draws it down and back. Partner A does the same action with the left hand, timed slightly after the right hand, so that both hands are controlling B's arm. (image 3.18)

ACTION 2: Partner A advances the right foot a half-step and strikes towards B's face with the right palm, looking at B. (image 3.19)

ACTION 3: Partner B retreats the left foot and withdraws the right foot a half-step, shifting back. Partner B brings back the right fist then drills it out along the outside of A's right hand towards the nose. Partner B looks at the right fist. (image 3.20)

Pointers

○ *Monkey pulls the rope* should be done with both hands moving continuously and quickly, with no pause at all [like a monkey pulling hand over hand on a rope]. In the partner form, do not really grab and pull – just slap. When A advances the right palm he should stop as he approaches B's face.

○ Partner B must retreat the left foot quickly then withdraw the right foot immediately. Partner B should drill the fist up as the foot withdraws, with fully integrated power.

7.   A: Step Forward, Right Cannon Punch   shàngbù yòu pàoquán   上步右炮拳

   B: Retreat, Left Split   tuìbù zuǒ pīquán   退步左劈拳

ACTION 1: Partner A takes a big step forward with the left foot and follows in a half-step with the right foot, clenching both hands. Partner A extends the left fist under B's right forearm, then bends the elbow and drills the fist up and forward. Partner A first brings the right fist in, then punches hard towards B's solar plexus. The fist surface is the contact point, the fist eye is up, the arm is slightly bent, the torso leans slightly into the punch, and the eyes look at B. (image 3.21)

ACTION 2: Partner B retreats the right foot back and withdraws the left foot a half-step, shifting back and bringing the right fist back beside the waist. Partner B lifts the left hand in front of the left shoulder and chops forward and down to take A's fist down. Partner B looks at the left hand. (image 3.22)

Pointers

o   When actually using the cannon punch, the step must be fast and the body must charge forward. One hand slices up and turns to deflect while the other hand protects the centre with the elbow. The punch comes from the turn of the body, driving down the centre line to the opponent's solar plexus. It must be fierce and penetrating.

o   In the partner form, A must be careful with his partner when doing the cannon punch. He must not hit the solar plexus, but he can hit the large muscled area on the chest. To avoid unwanted injury A may first step forward with the deflection, wait until B has retreated, and then punch,

o   When B does the retreat step he turns his body sideways to avoid A's attacking force. Partner B should cover with the left elbow and chop down with the palm so that A's punch does not connect. This is the way to break the cannon punch.

o   In the partner form the partners need to cooperate with their footwork to get the timing and spacing right.

8.   A: Step Forward, Right Hook to the Ear   shàngbù yòu guàn'ěr   上步右贯耳

   B: Withdraw, Left Drill   chèbù zuǒ zuānquán   撤步左钻拳

ACTION 1: Partner A steps the right foot forward to the outside of B's left foot, then follows in with the left foot. Partner A unclenches the left hand and extends it to B's wrist with the palm down to cover, press down, grab and pull, drawing B's hand down to the left, looking at the left hand. Partner A brings the right fist back, rotates the palm away from the thumb, then swings it right and forward in an arc with the fist eye inward, to punch B's ears with the knuckle edge of the fist. Partner A looks at his right fist. (image 3.23)

ACTION 2: Partner B retreats the right foot to the right and withdraws the left foot a half- step, shifting back and drilling the left fist up along the inside of A's right forearm. This is a slight crosscut to the left. Partner B looks at his left fist. (image

3.24)

Pointers

- The actual application is a grab and pull to draw the opponent's hand down. In a partner form, one should just slap down. Also, when striking the ear, one should stop short of the ear. One should not use the full force of the back to swing the arm forcefully to hit the ear.

- Partner B needs to do the retreat and withdraw footwork quickly and shift the weight back quickly. Partner B's upward drill should have a bit of crossing power in it.

- The partners need to work out a mutual understanding to coordinate the advancing and retreating techniques.

9. A: Advance and Steal a Hit   jìnbù tōu dǎ   进步偷打

B: Changeover Step, Slap, Check, Punch   huànbù pāi bō dǎ   换步拍拨打

ACTION 1: Partner A advances the right foot a half-step and extends the left hand to slap B's left fist. Partner A unclenches the right hand, bringing it back to the chest in preparation for the hit. Partner A looks at the left hand. (image 3.25)

ACTION 2: Partner A strikes out at B's face with the right hand, palm facing forward, bringing the left hand back to the chest, and looking at the right hand. (image 3.26)

ACTION 3: Partner B withdraws the left foot to inside the right foot and lands it, shifting weight to the left foot and lifting the right hand with the palm facing left to slap A's right forearm towards the left. Partner B looks at the right hand. (image 3.27)

ACTION 4: Partner B bends the left arm and slides it up inside A's arm, extending it and hooking it back to brush aside to the left. Partner B looks at the left hand. Partner B advances the right foot without moving the left foot and slaps A's face with the back of the right hand, bracing out with the left hand to develop more power. Partner B braces both arms, contains the chest and opens the upper back. Partner B looks at A. (image 3.28)

Pointers

o Partner A's stolen hit is the right hand chopping the opponent's face while the left hand deals with the opponent's left hand. The left hand has a covering, pressing down, pulling back and down power, and the right hand pounces out in an arcing move. The hands move forward and back in one integrated action. The right hand should strike out exactly as the right foot steps forward. When doing a partner form the striking hand needs to have a focal point. Partner A should also just slap B's hand down to the right instead of grabbing and pulling back, so that B can continue on with the next action.

o Partner B should withdraw the left foot and slap across with the right hand to the left at the same time. After B withdraws the left foot he must shift immediately to the left foot. Partner B should advance the right foot and do the backhand strike with the right hand while bracing out with the left hand, all at the same time, with fully integrated power. B must not use full power to hit A's face, the strike must have a focal point.

10. A: Changeover Step, Left Split   huànbù zuǒpī   换步左劈

   B: Pull and Grab the Head   lǔshǒu zhuā tóu   捋手抓头

ACTION 1: Partner A withdraws the right foot to inside the left foot and shifts to the right leg, while bringing the right hand back to the belly, clenching it, then drilling it up along the outside of B's right arm. This breaks B's backhand strike. Partner A prepares the left hand at the chest and looks at the right fist. (image 3.29)

ACTION 2: Partner A advances the left foot while unclenching the right hand and turning the palm down to grab and pull B's right forearm. Partner A chops towards B's face with the left palm and pulls the right hand down to the belly. Partner A looks at B. (image 3.30)

ACTION 3: Partner B retreats the left foot and withdraws the right foot a half-step, bending the right arm. Partner B swings the right arm up to the right and circles it to bring it in front of the chest to break A's left split. Partner B brings the left hand forward and right to grab and pull A's left arm. Partner B looks at A's left hand. (image 3.31)

ACTION 4: Partner B advances the right foot a half- step and pulls the left hand back to the belly, striking A's head with the right hand with the palm facing forward. Partner B looks at his right hand. (image 3.32)

Pointers

o   Partner A should withdraw the right foot and drill the right fist at the same time, moving quickly. The drilling fist must contain a bracing forward power. Partner A should step the left foot forward, chop with the left hand and pull back with the right hand all at the same time. In a partner form the pulling hand should not grab and hold on, but just indicate the intent. The changeover step must be done quickly.

o   Partner B should coordinate the two hands – one forward and one back, one up and one down – moving simultaneously. In a partner form one should not actually grab. The footwork and hand techniques must be coordinated and move together.

11. A: Step Forward, Snake   shàngbù shéxíng   上步蛇形

   B: Retreat, Left Cut to the Neck   tuìbù zuǒ qiēbō   退步左切脖

ACTION 1: Partner A first withdraws the left foot a half-step, bringing back the left hand to drill up inside B's right forearm. Partner A unclenches the left hand and turns it to grab B's right wrist, pulling it back to the head and preparing the right hand at the belly. Partner A looks at B's right hand. (image 3.33)

ACTION 2: Partner A steps the right foot into B's groin and follows in a half-step with the left foot, dropping the stance a bit. While doing this, A forcefully slices up into B's groin with the backhand, continuing to pull up and back with the left hand. Partner A looks at B. (image 3.34)

ACTION 3: Partner B retreats the left foot a half-step, retreats the right foot a big step to the rear, and withdraws the left foot another half-step. Partner B rotates the right hand palm away from the thumb so the palm faces right, fingers down, and slides it along the outside of A's right arm, hooking it back to the right hip. Partner B turns the left palm up and strikes to A's neck. Partner B looks at A. (image 3.35)

Pointers

- o The main technique of the snake tehcnique is the slice to the groin. The application is that the upper hand pulls back to open up the opponent while the lower hand slices up with a straight arm as the footwork moves in. The footwork should take over the opponents groin area as if you were going to do a shoulder strike. The key lies in entering the footwork to get the body as close as possible, so the footwork needs to be agile and quick. In a partner form you do not grab and hold on, and you must be sure to focus the groin strike to not to hit your partner's groin. This stance is relatively low.

○ Partner B must retreat quickly and shift well back. The right hand needs to be accurate with the hook and deflection. When B retreats the right foot to the rear the body must turn sideways so that A's groin slice misses its target. When B slices to the neck he should use a twisting power in the body. Be sure to have a focal point, and stop before hitting your partner's neck.

12. A: Left and Right Cut to the Neck   zuǒ yòu qiēbō   左右切脖

**   B: Right Drill, Left Driving Punch**   yòu zuān zuǒ bēngquán   右钻左崩拳

ACTION 1: Partner A shifts back without moving the feet, shifting almost completely back to the left leg. Partner A bends the right elbow and hooks back by the right ear to defend against B's neck cut. While doing this, A turns the left palm up and cuts horizontally to B's neck. Partner A looks at B. (image 3.36)

ACTION 2: Partner B drills the right fist up along the inside of A's left arm to knock it horizontally to the right. (image 3.37)

ACTION 3: Partner A turns the right palm up and cuts horizontally to B's neck. Partner A looks at B. (image 3.38)

ACTION 4: Partner B brings the left hand back to the left waist and unclenches the right hand, bringing it along the inside of A's right arm to slap to the left. Partner B advances the left foot a half- step without moving the right foot, and turns the body rightward, forming a half horse stance. Partner B does a left driving punch to A's right ribs, fist eye up, and brings the right hand back to the belly. Partner B looks at the left fist. (image 3.39)

Pointers

- o Partner A should do two continuous cuts to the neck. When doing the cuts, the arms should stay slightly bent and the power should come from the turning of the waist and shoulders. The palms swing forward, cutting diagonally down. The elbows should stay settled. The cuts should have a forward subduing power. In a partner form you should not hit with power, just place the palms at the side of the partner's neck.

- o Partner B needs to do two continuous deflections with the right hand, to the right and left. When slapping leftward, he should slide leftward and back along A's right arm. The left foot advance and left driving punch are simultaneous, and the body should twist rightward to increase the power of the punch. In a partner form the punch should be focused near the ribs. Be sure to sit down into the punch.

13. A: Ape Pulls the Rope   yuánhóu dáo shéng   猿猴捯绳

 B: Retreat, Right Drill   tuìbù zuānquán   退步钻拳

ACTION 1: Partner A withdraws the right foot back a bit and turns the right palm down to slide along the top of B's arm, pulling it down and back to in front of the chest. Partner A also turns the left palm down and slides it along the top of B's left arm, pulling it down. Partner A looks at B. (image 3.40)

ACTION 2: Partner A advances the right foot a half- step and follows in a bit with the left foot, striking to B's face with the right hand, palm forward, fingers up. Partner A looks at B. (image 3.41)

ACTION 3: Partner B retreats the left foot to the rear and withdraws the right foot a half-step, drilling the right fist along the outside of A's right forearm to deflect A's right strike. Partner B brings the left fist back to the belly and looks at A. (image 3.42)

Pointers

  o   Points to consider are the same as in move 6.

14. A: Step Forward, Pull Back, Right Cut to the Neck

shàngbù lǔshǒu yòu qiēbō   上步捋手右切脖

B: Withdraw, Double Intercept to the Left

chèbù zuǒ shuāng jiéshǒu   撤步左双截手

ACTION 1: Partner A advances the right foot a half-step and drills the left fist up along the inside of B's right arm. Partner A unclenches the left hand and turns it palm down to hook onto and pull B's hand down to the left. Partner A steps the left foot forward and turns the right palm up to cut forcefully towards B's neck, the arm slightly bent. (image 3.43)

ACTION 2: Partner B retreats the left foot to the rear and withdraws the right foot a half-step, shifting back. Partner B clenches both fists, bends and drops the elbows to place the forearms vertically. The right fist is forward with the fist heart turned in, and the left fist is behind with the fist heart turned out. Partner B does a horizontal intercept to the left with both fists on A's right forearm, fists at nose height. Partner B looks at A's right hand. (image 3.44)

3.43   3.44

Pointers

  o   When A does the drill and grab he should not actually grab during a partner form, but should just knock the hand aside to allow his partner to continue with the next action. The step forward is timed with the neck cut, and be sure to focus the strike. When actually using this strike, the foot should step forward behind the opponent's foot so that he cannot retreat and get away. In a partner form you need to wait until the partner has retreated, then step forward.

  o   Partner B should retreat quickly and with a big step. After retreating, he should quickly withdraw the other foot. The intercepting action should also have forward leading power.

15.   **A: Left Cut to the Neck**   zuǒ qiēbó   左切脖

B: Double Intercept to the Right, Right Driving Punch

yòu shuāngjié yòu bēngquán   右双截右崩拳

ACTION 1: Partner A does not move the feet yet, and turns the left palm up to cut towards B's neck with the palm edge. Partner A looks at B. (image 3.45)

ACTION 2: Partner B, after intercepting to the left, quickly turns rightward and withdraws the right foot slightly, turning both fists to intercept A's left forearm to the right. Partner B's left fist is forward with the fist heart turned in. (image 3.46)

ACTION 3: Partner B lowers the right fist lowers to the right waist. Partner B advances the right foot a half-step and punches to A's solar plexus with the right fist, pulling the left fist back to the belly. Partner B looks at A. (image 3.47)

Pointers

○ Partner A should do the two neck cuts continuously without hesitation.

○ Partner B should do the two intercepting actions continuously, being sure to defend strongly. After taking A across to the right, B should quickly do the driving punch.

○ The partners should cooperate closely so that the actions appear and feel realistic.

16.   **A: Pull Back, Crossing Kick, Step Forward, Right Split**

lǚshǒu héngtī shàngbù yòu pī   捋手横踢上步右劈

B: Retreat, Left Crosscut   tuìbù zuǒ héngquán   退步左横拳

ACTION 1: Partner A shifts back to the right leg and slides the left hand outside B's right arm to pull down and to the right. Partner A rotates the right palm away from the thumb in front of the chest to grab B's right wrist. Partner A grabs and pulls with both hands down to the right, pressing the head up and looking at B. (image 3.48)

ACTION 2: Partner A turns the right foot out and does a crossing kick to B's knee, keeping the grip on B's arm. (image 3.49)

ACTION 3: Partner A lands the right foot forward and steps the left foot forward, chopping the right hand to B's face, palm forward. (image 3.50)

ACTION 4: Partner B retreats the left foot a half-step then retreats the right foot a step, to avoid A's kick. Partner B then withdraws the left foot a half-step and drills the right fist up along the outside of A's right forearm, crossing it to the right, fist centre up. Partner B pulls the left fist back to the belly, shifts most weight to the left leg and looks at A. (image 3.51)

Pointers

o   When A uses both hands to draw B's right wrist and shifts back, this is called "lead the sheep while going along." Drawing someone in along the line of their stance causes them to lose balance forward. In a partner form one should not grab and pull, but just defend and then attack.

o   The target for the crossing kick is the opponent's knee. When actually using this technique, first pull back then kick, still holding on, so that the opponent cannot step away. In a partner form you should make sure your partner has stepped away before kicking. You must time this carefully and cooperate tightly to avoid injury. B must retreat quickly, shift back quickly, and coordinate well with A.[41]

17. A: Step Forward, Left Scoop Up, Right Split

shàngbù zuǒ tiǎo yòu pī　　　　　　　上步左挑右劈

B: Grab the Shoulder with the Left Hand　zuǒ shǒu zhuā jiān　左手抓肩

ACTION 1: Partner A advances the left foot a half-step and follows up with the right foot, clenching the left fist with the fist heart up and scooping up under B's right arm. Partner A then unclenches the left hand and turns the palm out to pull B's right arm towards the left. Partner A chops to B's face with the right hand, looking at B. (image 3.52)

ACTION 2: Partner B retreats the right foot a half-step and withdraws the left foot. Partner B turns the left thumb down and the fingers up, stretching the thumb to forefinger web widely. Partner B shifts slightly to the right and turns to forcefully brace on A's right shoulder. Partner B looks at his left hand. (image 3.53)

Pointers

- When doing a partner form A should not grab the arm after doing the scoop up. Do not move the feet yet when scooping up. Advance the left foot a half-step and follow in with the right foot when doing the chop.

- Partner B should first retreat then brace on A's shoulder, to prevent A's arm from landing the chop. This move is traditionally called "sparrow hawk grabs the shoulder."

18. A: Brush Aside, Right Split　　　lōushǒu yòu pī　　搂手右劈

B: Left Hooking Block, Right Cut to the Neck

zuǒ guà yòu qiēbō　　　　　　　左挂右切脖

---

[41] Editor's note: Partner A can help B get away by pushing partner B's arm forward. If partner B stiffens his arm, this push will send him back. The cooperation is hardly noticeable to an audience if done smoothly.

ACTION 1: Partner A withdraws the left foot then the right foot slightly and turns the left palm to face right, fingers up, to push B's left hand to the right. Partner A turns the right palm down and hooks the right wrist onto B's left elbow to brush it out to the right. Partner A looks at B. (image 3.54)

ACTION 2: Partner A advances the right foot a half-step and turns the right palm forward to slap towards B's face. Partner A looks at B. (image 3.55)

ACTION 3: Partner B retreats the right foot a half-step and withdraws the left foot, bending the left elbow. Partner B turns and lifts the left hand inside A's right arm to hook it back towards his left ear. B turns the right palm up and cuts towards A's neck. Partner B looks at A. (image 3.56)

Pointers

o Partner A coordinates three actions together: the right foot withdraws slightly, the left hand knocks aside to the right, and the right hand brushes down and out. The brush aside should use a cold, heavy, shaking power.

o Partner B coordinates two actions together: the right foot advances and the right hand slaps forward. He should settle the elbow and wrist for the strike.

o Partner B should first retreat the right foot. He should withdraw the left foot when hooking the left hand. He should turn the body and extend the shoulder to chop the neck. In a partner form all strikes should have fixed focal points to avoid unwanted injury.

19. A: Double Intercept to the Left   zuǒ shuāng jiéshǒu   左双截手

   B: Left Cut to the Neck   zuǒ qiēbó   左切脖

ACTION 1: Partner A clenches both fists and bends the elbows to put the forearms vertical. He uses both arms inside B's right arm to intercept horizontally to the left. The right fist is forward with the fist heart in and the left fist is back with the fist heart out. The feet do not move, and A looks at B's right hand. (image 3.57)

ACTION 2: Partner B does not move the feet, and turns the left palm up to chop towards A's neck, bringing the right hand back to the belly. The left arm is slightly bent. Partner B looks at A. (image 3.58, partner A already doing the double intercept)

Pointers

o   The intercept and cut are the same as done previously in move 4.

20.   A: Double Intercept to the Right, Right Driving Punch

    yòu shuāng jiéshǒu yòu bēngquán   右双截手右崩拳

    B: Retreat, Left Press Down   tuìbù zuǒ àn   退步左按

ACTION 1: Partner A withdraws the right foot back slightly and hits across to the right with the left forearm forward and the right fist back, inside B's left forearm, intercepting across to the right, looking at B (see image 3.58). Partner A advances the right foot a half-step and launches a driving punch with the right fist towards B's solar plexus. The fist eye is up and the arm slightly bent. A pulls the left fist back to the side while punching. Partner A looks at B. (image 3.59)

ACTION 2: Partner B retreats the right foot and withdraws the left foot to just in front of the fight foot. Partner B turns the left palm down and crossways and presses down on A's right fist. B brings the right hand back to the belly and looks at A's right fist. (image 3.60)

Pointers

- o The intercept and driving punch are the same as done previously in move 5.

- o Partner B must retreat and withdraw quickly. The palm press must be timed just right to catch the oncoming fist.

21. A: Advance, Right Driving Punch   jìnbù yòu bēngquán   进步右崩拳

   B: Retreat, Left Press Down, Right Driving Punch

   tuìbù zuǒ àn yòu bēngquán   退步左按右崩拳

This move is the same as move 1, but partners A and B have just traded places. The white uniform is now partner A and the dark uniform is now partner B. (image 3.61)

- • The first twenty moves are the first section of the form. From move 21 on is the second section. The form repeats going back, and partners A and B trade sides in the second section. Both partners learn both sides, taking turns being the initiator and the defender. This makes the form more interesting and involves learning and mastering more techniques.

- • On getting to the end of a section, you could also change places and repeat the same side. To do this you need to stop and change places at the end of the section so that you return to the starting point.

22. Closing Move   shōu shì   收势

ACTION 1:[42] Partners A and B both retreat the right foot back a big step and shift back, putting most weight on the right leg. (image 3.62)

They then withdraw the left foot to touch the toes down in front of the right foot. Partners A and B both bring the right fist back to the belly, then drill it up past the solar plexus to nose height, the ulnar side twisted up. They

---

[42] Editor's note: Prior to closing, partner, B can signal the desire to stop by pressing down and controlling a bit longer in movement 20, and not punching. Similarly, partner A can press and control in movement 2, when he has just become side B.

press their heads up and look at their right fists. The left fist stays in front of the belly. (image 3.63)

3.63

ACTION 2: Partners A and B both advance the left foot a half-step without moving the right foot, to sit into a *santi* stance. Both unclench the hands and do a left split, pulling the right hand back to the belly. Both press the head up and look at the left hand. (image 3.64)

ACTION 3: Partners A and B both withdraw the left foot to place the feet together. Both pull the left hand back to the belly and clench it, standing steadily with the legs slightly bent. Both then lift the palms up beside the body to shoulder height, then bend the elbows to bring the hands together in

3.64

front of the face, then press with palms down in front of the belly. Both stand up and allow the hands to hang naturally at the sides. Both look forward, and the closing of the form is completed. (images 3.65, 3.66)

3.65

Pointers

3.66

- o Partners A and B do the closing together, moving in unison. When both partners retreat the right foot a big step this should be as big as possible. Be sure to keep balance when moving back, and keep the whole movement together.

FIVE ELEMENT BROADSWORD

五行刀

INTRODUCTION TO FIVE ELEMENT BROADSWORD, *WUXING DAO*

The five element techniques of the broadsword are the culmination of the work of previous generations of Xingyi masters who refined, practiced, and synthesized broadsword methods from many martial styles. They developed the broadsword techniques based on the movements, footwork, body work, and power generation of Xingyi's five element empty hand techniques and the methodology of the five elements – metal, water, wood, fire, and earth.

The characteristics of the five element broadsword techniques are: the techniques are simple, power expression is emphasized, and the movements are aggressive, quick, well anchored, and highly applicable. Following the principle of simplicity and effectiveness, there are no flowery or extraneous movements. Emphasis is on deep trained skill and on the power of the body. By principle, broadsword methods fully integrate with body methods. The techniques show a intimidating air, advance and retreat quickly, move abruptly and stop firmly, all fully integrated as one, to manifest the characteristics and flavour of the system of Xingyiquan.

The techniques of the five element broadsword take their name from the five element fist techniques of split, drive (crush, thrust), drill, pound (cannon), and crosscut, and are called broadsword chop, broadsword drill, broadsword thrust, broadsword slash, and broadsword crosscut.[43] Each broadsword element is practised in a short combination that is centered around the attacking technique. For example, the broadsword chop combination contains left and right *hook and chop,* high and low *block and chop, coil around the head and chop,* and *wrap the head and chop.* The 'soul' of the broadsword chop combination is the chop. That is to say, chop is the main technique – the other techniques in each combination set up for the chop. The combinations of the other elements have a similar structure –

---

[43] Translator's note: In Chinese the terms are exactly the same. This works in Chinese, but I have changed the words for weapons techniques to make more sense in English.

a primary technique set up by short combinations.

Xingyi's five element broadsword form is widespread, though there is great variety within the form due to differences in styles and teachers. The five element techniques are much less known. This is because the individual techniques are very effective for fighting, so were not taught openly in most Xingyi systems. The five element techniques that I introduce here is a new set that I have created by combining what I learned from many elder masters, what I have studied from books, what I learned from other branches of Xingyi, and what I have developed through my years of training. It keeps the essence and methods of the traditional five element techniques, with some deletions and changes that serve to emphasize the broadsword's flavour and characteristics of simplicity and applicability.

You should have a solid foundation in the empty hand five elements and five element form before learning broadsword techniques. All weapons practice should be based on a solid foundation of fist skills. That means that if your empty hand skills are not solid you shouldn't try to learn weapons yet.

The Xingyi classics say, "Ten thousand techniques start from *santishi*." *Santishi* is the source of all Xingyi techniques, so you must practise the *santishi* post standing. You get a feel for the requirements, power, intent, and spirit of Xingyi within the post standing. Xingyi weapons are no different You should do post standing in the opening posture with each weapon. This is vital, and after much training you will discover the importance for yourself.

The five element broadsword techniques place great importance on whole body power and connection to the broadsword, so how you hold the hilt is emphasized and the requirements are strict. Only if you hold the broadsword properly can you transmit your body power to the broadsword and move with fluidity. The grip on the hilt must adjust according to the technique, and is called by different names such as pincer grip, hooking grip, or full grip. Broadsword chop uses a full grip, broadsword thrust uses a spiral grip, broadsword drill uses a twisted spiral grip, broadsword slash and broadsword crosscut use a firm full grip. When the broadsword is moving the grip must be supple, and when using power the grip must be firm.

In addition, the left hand must coordinate its actions with the right hand. Within the five element broadsword techniques, the left hand quite often assists by supporting the right wrist, to offset any weakness in the right wrist. In actual use the left hand can hold the hilt as well to add even more power. Xingyi weapons are extentions of the power of the body, you need to apply the power of the whole body through the weapons in each technique.

FIVE ELEMENT BROADSWORD TECHNIQUES

On Guard   yùbèishì   预备势

The *on guard* position of the broadsword serves the same purpose as *santishi*, so you need to stand a great deal and focus on the requirements and rules to set your position into the ideal shape. During post standing you should pay attention to the feeling in both hands, feel the position of the broadsword in front of the body, and focus on making the body smooth with the broadsword, with your power transmitting to the broadsword. You need to do post standing for a long time to achieve this feeling. The movements are *Stand at attention hold the broadsword;*

Transfer the hilt over the head; Retreat and chop.

ACTION 1: Stand to attention facing forty-five degrees to the line in which you will go. Place the right hand at the side. Cradle the guard in the left hand with the tip pointing up, the blade spine snug to the left arm, and the blade edge facing forward. Press the head up and look forward. (image 1.1)

ACTION 2: Lift the hands by the sides to above and in front of the head. Transfer the hilt to the right hand, releasing the left hand and placing it at the right wrist. Look to the left – the line in which you will go. (image 1.2)

ACTION 3: Retreat the right foot and shift back into a *santi* stance with the weight sixty to seventy percent on the back leg. Chop both hands forward and down from above the head to bring the blade edge angled forward with the tip at nose height. The right hand holds the hilt, pulling back to about a forearm distance from the belly. Close the elbows towards each other, release the shoulders and settle the elbows, so that the broadsword lines up on the midline of the body. Close the chest and stretch the upper back taut. Press your head up and look past the broadsword tip. (image 1.3)

1.1   1.2   1.3

Pointers

- *On guard* is used to start all broadsword combinations and forms, the same as *santishi* is used to commence hand technique practice.

- When setting up for practice, you can start facing the line of practice or at forty-five or ninety degrees to the line. It doesn't matter, choose whichever direction you prefer.

- When lifting the arms be sure to maintain a certain bend in them. When transferring the hilt, use a pincer grip – gripping mainly with the thumb, index, and middle fingers, and only lightly with the ring and little fingers. This hold enables the tip to point down and the blade spine to come around past the left shoulder, across the back to the right shoulder, keeping the blade spine snug to the back and the tip down as it travels. Keep your wrist and grip supple.

- Chop the broadsword forward as you retreat the right foot and sit back. Do not launch power when chopping, but keep the *qi* full and spirit focused. Once in the final position, pay attention to aligning the three tips: the tip of the feet, the tip of the nose, and the tip of the broadsword. They should be aligned on the same plane on the midline of the body to keep a tight defensive position.

PRACTICAL APPLICATION FOR ON GUARD

This is the same as *santishi* – it is the position taken when facing an opponent. Once you take your position the broadsword is on your midline with its tip, your nose, and your feet lined up, covering the high, mid, and low lines. This position defends your midline while it is prepared to attack. The proper frame of mind for combat is a firm *qi* and a mind at peace, so gather your spirit and still your *qi*.

BROADSWORD CHOP

INTRODUCTION TO BROADSWORD CHOP, *PI DAO*

Chop is the technique that most manifests the character of the broadsword. Looking at the shape of a broadsword, its spirit comes out in a chop. The classics say, "the broadsword chops and the straight sword pierces, the spear stabs and the staff strikes." You must practise chop with the ferocity and unyielding spirit of a tiger. Chop is a technique that comes forward and down from above. To use this action you must first set up the conditions for it to work, that is, the broadsword must be raised. The footwork for chop is: left stance, right stance, advance, and retreat. The key techniques for chop are: *Hook left and right and chop; High and low block across and chop; Swinging chop; Coil the head and chop; Wrap the head and chop.*

1a Right Stance Chop   yòubù pīdāo   右步劈刀

Start from *on guard*. Continue with *Left withdraw, right lifting draw; Left advance, pushing pierce; Right step forward, coil the head and chop.*

ACTION 1: Without moving the right foot, shift back mostly onto the right leg and withdraw the left foot a half-step, touching down. Rotate the right hand, bend the elbow, and lift the hilt at the right of the head. Place the left hand on the right wrist, keeping the left elbow in front of the chest. Turn the blade edge up, with the tip pointing forward and down to sternum height. Close the shoulders, compress the torso, turn slightly rightward. Look past the broadsword tip. (image 1.4)

ACTION 2: Advance the left foot and shift forward. Keep the left hand at the right wrist and push forward with both hands with the blade edge forward and tip angled down. Extend the arms, maintaining a certain flexion, and finish with the broadsword tip at between belly and chest height. Look at the broadsword tip. (image 1.5)

ACTION 3: Advance the left foot and bring the right foot in to the ankle. Take a loose grip and lift the hilt above the head to bring the broadsword to the left shoulder and around the back to the right shoulder with the tip down and the blade edge out, so that the blade spine is snug to your back. (images 1.6a and b)

Take a long step forward with the right foot and follow in the left foot a half-step to sit into a *santi* stance. Extend the arms forward to chop forcefully forward and down, and finally pull the right hand back towards the belly. Keep the left hand at the right wrist throughout. Finish with the tip at shoulder height. Press your head up and look past the broadsword tip. (images 1.6 and 1.6 from the front)

Pointers

- o Coordinate the right foot's withdrawal with the rotation and lifting of the broadsword.

- o Coordinate the left foot's advance with the pushing pierce.

- o The rear foot must step forward quickly and for a good distance, must land firmly, and must land as the broadsword chops.

- o Chopping is an integrated power, and must be practised as one movement, with all actions within it connected quickly.

1b Left Stance Chop   zuǒbù pīdāo   左步劈刀

Right withdraw, left lifting draw; Right advance, pushing pierce; Left step forward, wrap the head and chop.

ACTION 1: Withdraw the right foot a half-step and shift back without moving the left foot. Rotate the right hand to turn the blade edge out and lift it up to the left side of the head. Keep the left hand on the right wrist. Finish with the tip angled forward and down to sternum height. Keep the right elbow in front of the chest and lift the left elbow. Look past the broadsword tip. (image 1.7)

ACTION 2: Advance the right foot a half-step and shift forward, following in with the left foot to beside the right ankle. Hold the hilt with a spiral grip and push forward with both hands with the blade edge up and the tip forward and down. Keep the left hand on the right wrist. Finish with the tip between belly and chest height. Look past the broadsword tip. (image 1.8)

ACTION 3: Take a long step forward with the left foot and follow in a half-step with the right foot to take a *santi* stance. Hold the hilt with a hanging grip and lift it to the right above the head with the tip down and the blade edge out. Bring the blade spine around the right shoulder, past the upper back to the left shoulder. Adjust the right hand to a spiral grip and bring it over the head, extending the arm to chop forward and down, then pull it back just in front of the belly. Finish with the tip at sternum height, edge down. Keep the left hand at the right wrist throughout. Press your head up, look past the tip. (image 1.9)

Pointers

- o All pointers are the same as the *right stance chop*, just reversing right and left. Note that 'wrap' goes around the head in the opposite direction as 'coil.'

- • Continue on with right and left chop, restricted only by the size of your training space.

1c Chop Turn Around

pīdāo zhuànshēn   劈刀转身

Using the _left stance chop_ (left foot forward) as example. *Left hook-in step, turn around and present the broadsword; Right advance, pushing pierce; Left step forward, wrap head and chop.*

ACTION 1: Advance the left foot a half-step with the foot hooked in and shift forward onto the left leg. Turn around 180 degrees rightward to face back in the direction from which you came. Bring

in the right foot by the left foot, touching the toes down. Keep the left hand on the right wrist. Push forward and up at the right side, circling the tip up and back so that it points back in the direction from which you came. Finish with the blade edge up and the blade spine above the right shoulder. Sit down slightly. Look past the broadsword tip. (image 1.10)

ACTION 2: Advance the right foot a half-step and follow in the left foot. Keeping the left hand on the right wrist, extend the arms not quite fully to push with both hands to the lower front. Finish with the tip between belly and chest height, the blade edge forward. Look past the broadsword tip. (image 1.11)

ACTION 3: This movement is the same as that described in action 3 of movement 1b, just in the opposite direction. (see image 1.9)

- The action of *turn around* is the same whether on the right or left side, just transpose the right and left actions. To turn around the other way, step the right foot hooked in and turn around 180 degrees leftward.

Pointers

- o The turn around should be smoothly connected without hesitation. Hook-in and turn around quickly, taking care to first bring the tip up and to circle it back as you turn. The movement should be gentle and the broadsword should wrap around the body snugly. Close the chest and tuck in the abdomen, compressing the torso slightly.

- o After turning, push the broadsword as the foot advances. Chop as the foot steps forward, the same as described above in movement 1b.

1d Chop Closing Move   pīdāo shōushì   劈刀收势

On arriving back at the starting point, do a *turn around* to face the original direction. *Return and cut across; Wrap the head and change hands; Hold the broadsword in the left hand and flash the palm; Stand at attention holding the broadsword.*

ACTION 1: If the <u>left</u> foot is forward, then withdraw the right foot a bit and shift to the right leg, hooking in the left foot on the spot. Cut flat across with the blade edge facing right at chest height. Extend the left arm to the left to brace out, palm out. Keep both arms slightly bent. Turn rightward and look at the broadsword tip. (image 1.12)

ACTION 2: Shift to the left leg without moving the feet. Rotate the right hand so the palm is up, then back, loosening the grip on the hilt to take the broadsword up over the head and leftward. Circle the broadsword, first placing the blade spine outside the right shoulder, then taking it across the back to the left shoulder in a *wrap the head* movement. Extend the right hand forward to meet the left hand and place the hilt in the left palm. Turn the body leftward. Look at the left hand. (image 1.13)

ACTION 3: Shift back to the right leg and straighten it, bringing the left foot in beside it to stand to attention. Turn the left palm up so that the thumb, ring finger and little finger cradle the guard, and the index and middle fingers wrap around it. Swing the right hand down, right, and then up to above the head, palm up. Hold the broadsword in the left hand with the blade spine snug to the arm and circle it up, rightward, and then down to the left hip. Follow the right hand with the eyes, then snap the head to the left when the right hand flashes, to look to the left. (image 1.14)

ACTION 4: Without moving the feet, let the left hand hang naturally at the side, still holding the broadsword with the blade edge forward and tip up. Bring the right hand down at the right side to stand to attention. Press the head up and look forward. (image 1.15)

-

- If the <u>right</u> foot is forward then in action one retreat the right foot behind the left foot and shift onto the right leg. Cut flat across to the right and back. The rest of the closing is the same as described.

Pointers

- Be sure to move both hands simultaneously during *turn around and cut across,* opening out to brace to right and left. Bring the foot in and flash the palm simultaneously.

- When wrapping the head and changing hands, be sure to adjust your grip on the hilt. Keep the broadsword spine snug to the body, *wrap around the head* must be tight. Be sure to shift the body left and right during the movement.

- The whole movement must be coordinated, fully concentrated, and dignified.

PROBLEMS OFTEN MET IN BROADSWORD CHOP

PROBLEM 1: During *withdraw, lifting draw* the student does not keep the broadsword on the midline of the body, taking it either too far to the right or to the left.

CORRECTIONS: Draw a small circle with the tip, keeping the left hand on the right wrist, so that the tip first circles down from above, and then withdraw and do the lifting draw. In this way it is easier to maintain the tip on the midline.

PROBLEM 2: During *withdraw, lifting draw* the student draws too large a circle with the broadsword tip.

CORRECTIONS: The cause of this error usually is that the student is taking too tight a hold on the hilt. When in movement, the right wrist needs to be able to rotate freely, so the grip should adjust to allow this. Remind the student to first rotate and extend the arm and then raise the elbow to draw the broadsword back.

PROBLEM 3: During *step forward, chop* the broadsword wobbles or sways.

CORRECTIONS: The student should first practise slowly and speed up only when the action is under control. Be sure to first extend both arms forward and then chop down. Pull in the abdomen and press the head up when pulling back, holding the hilt firmly. The hands must use a closing power and the elbows should come in snug to the ribs to keep the blade stable. First find the correct power during slow movement, then gradually speed up.

PROBLEM 4: During *wrap and coil the head* the student does not keep the broadsword spine on the upper back, so that the broadsword technique is not accurate.

CORRECTIONS: The cause of this error usually is that the student is gripping the hilt too tightly and the wrist is too stiff. The student should use a hanging grip so that the tip is able to point down and the broadsword spine is able to come in to the back and shoulders. These actions must be practised over and over, looking for the feeling slowly and gradually.

POWER GENERATION FOR BROADSWORD CHOP

Left withdraw, right lifting draw. Use the power of the waist to draw the arms, which in turn make the broadsword tip draw a circle downward. The torso should compact and settle down, and then rise. The hand lifts the broadsword hilt so that the blade protects the body.

Advance, push. The footwork follows the broadsword. When you push the broadsword forward, use both hand to push forcefully, reaching with the torso and extending the arms. There should be a feeling of pushing and of piercing, with an additional feeling of blocking or knocking aside. This is the hidden meaning within the movement.

Step forward, chop. This must use the fully integrated power of the body. In the final position the broadsword must have a point of focus and must be stable. It must not wobble.

- Broadsword chop is not just a chop forward and down. It must also contain a pulling back, or sawing, action. In this way, it chops, hacks, and slices. Press the head up to lengthen the body. Herein lies the essence of the broadsword. This is one of the most distinctive characteristics of Xingyi broadsword.

Advance, pushing pierce. When pushing, close the chest and stretch the upper back taut, putting a closing-in power into the arms. Advance accurately and firmly with the broadsword. Straighten the back and open the chest when lifting the broadsword above the head. When advancing to chop, withdraw the abdomen and close the chest, and use both hands to chop down. Press your head up forcefully. When pulling the hands back towards the belly, use the power from the lower back, lengthening the torso. Use the power from the whole body and transmit it to the body of the broadsword – the broadsword is an extension of the body

- Grip technique for the chop: adjust the grip on the hilt according to the needs of the techniques.

- *Withdraw, lifting draw*: the hand turns in and out, and uses a spiral grip.

- *Coil the head* and *wrap the head*: use a hanging grip.

- *Chop*: press your head up and use a full grip and settle the wrist.

- When training on your own you may develop strength and power by using a heavy weapon. The weight of a heavy broadsword is up to you, but you must be able to swing it around and to do the techniques correctly. If it is too heavy then you won't be able to do the moves properly. When using a heavy broadsword you should do the moves more slowly, but you must not change any of the technique. This training will improve your body strength and coordination, arm and wrist strength, and help you feel how to use the left hand to assist the right hand.

PRACTICAL APPLICATIONS FOR BROADSWORD CHOP

Looking at the structure of the chop combination, it entails three separate actions: a *withdraw lifting draw,* an *advance pushing pierce,* and a *step forward chop and stab.*

Withdraw, lifting draw is a defensive posture and technique. If, for example, the opponent stabs to your chest with a weapon, you quickly retreat your rear foot a half- step and withdraw your lead foot a half-step. While stepping, rotate your right hand to circle the broadsword tip down to bring the blade edge forward with the tip pointing forward and down to block his weapon with the broadsword body. Then you can follow the line that his weapon stabs to lift and draw back so that it misses its mark.

Advance, pushing pierce can be either an attack or a block. Advance and stab forward with the blade edge forward in a pushing action, following the line of the opponent's weapon to strike his hand and make him lose his hold. You could also stab his belly. You must keep the tip of your broadsword pointing forward on the midline at all times to protect your centre.

Step forward chop and stab attacks by bringing the broadsword around the head. The coiling or wrapping protects your head and chest, in a quick action that both defends and prepares for the following attack. You then step in quickly and as far as you can to get close to the opponent while chopping forward and down. The chop must be aggressive and strong.

- The broadsword is a short weapon so you need to get in close. This means that you must be intimidating, you must have quick footwork, and the actions must be direct. You must dare to attack with no thought of losing, driving straight forward to take down anyone in your way.

- The main power of chop is the forward and downward action, so the main action is chopping the opponent's head, shoulder, and/or chest. You must use the power of your whole body and apply it through the body of the broadsword, so that your chop is unstoppable. When chopping, you can grip with both hands to get maximum strength. Do not forget to pull backwards as you chop, to add a sawing, slicing action, which increases the damage to your opponent.

- Breathe out when chopping. You may make a sound to augment your strength and give the impression of a tiger leaping from the mountains.

THE POEM ABOUT BROADSWORD CHOP

劈刀气势猛如虎，遇敌不怵气宜鼓。缠头裹脑冲进去，劈刺头顶收腰腹。

The broadsword chop is as fierce as a tiger,

The *qi* is aroused to meet the opponent without fear.

Coil and wrap around the head and charge forward,

Chop and slice, pressing the head up and settling the body core.

BROADSWORD DRILL

INTRODUCTION TO BROADSWORD DRILL, *ZUAN DAO*

Broadsword drill is based on the empty hand drill technique of Xingyi. One of the characteristics of Xingyiquan is that almost all Xingyi weapon techniques share the name of a five element or twelve animal model technique. The definition of 'drill' in the martial arts is a forward twisting strike that can go either high or low, and the strike is no different with the broadsword.

Among traditional Xingyi styles there is a broadsword drill that pushes forward with the blade edge forward, tip to the right and blade body flat. Even though the hand holding the hilt turns as if doing an empty hand drill, this is really a broadsword push. When we are holding a broadsword we must bring out the techniques of the broadsword – this sort of technique should not be called a drill, since the broadsword itself is not doing a drilling action. There is also another technique whereby the broadsword is held in both hands, circled in front of the body, and then stabbed forward and up with the blade edge down. This is a straight stab to the head, there is no rotation in the stab – once again, not truly a drill with the broadsword, but similar to the broadsword thrust. I feel that a proper broadsword drill should rotate the blade while stabbing, either upwards or downwards.

The combination for drill is *right stance low drill, left stance high drill, turn around drill*, and *closing move*.

2a Right Stance Low Drill   yòubù xiā zuāndāo   右步下钻刀

Start from *on guard*. Continue with *left advance, lifting draw; Right step forward, inverted grip low stab*.

ACTION 1: Advance the left foot a half-step and follow in the right foot beside the left ankle.[44] Keep the knees together and squat slightly on the left leg. Draw a semi-circle in a counter-clockwise direction, finishing with the right hand rotated palm out, the ulnar edge of the right arm up, the right elbow raised to ear height, and arm bent. The blade edge is turned up and angled forward with the tip forward and down between chest and belly height. Keep the left hand at the right wrist throughout the action. Look past the broadsword tip. (image 1.16)

ACTION 2: Take a long step forward with the right foot and follow in a half-step with the left foot, keeping most weight on the left leg. Extend the right arm with the hand in an inverted grip, reaching the right shoulder forward to stab the broadsword tip to belly height, blade edge up. Swing the left palm up to above the head at the left side of the body. The right wrist is at chest height and the broadsword body is angled down. Look past the tip. (image 1.17)

1.16   1.17

Pointers

- o   As the left foot advances the broadsword knocks down and draws back. These actions must be coordinated with the footwork.

- o   The inverted grip stab must land as the right foot lands.

2b Left Stance High Drill   yòubù shàng zuāndāo   右步上钻刀

Right advance, wrap and draw; Left step forward, inverted grip stab.

ACTION 1: Advance the right foot a half-step and follow in the left foot to the right ankle. Place the left hand on the right wrist. Circle the blade to the left, up, and then circle right and draw it back, keeping the tip forward throughout. Finish with

---

[44] Translator's note: Holding the foot at the ankle develops strength, flexibility, and balance. Another way to step is to touch down the foot as shown in the photo. Either way is correct, so I have translated the text as is throughout the book, even when it differs from the photos.

the right arm bent, the right elbow up, and the torso turned right. Once the right hand has drawn back to the right shoulder, bring it down to the right waist, rotating it palm up to turn the blade edge up. Keep the broadsword tip forward, now at solar plexus height. Keep the left hand at the right wrist throughout the action. Look forward past the tip. (images 1.18 and 1.19)

ACTION 2: Take a long step forward with the left foot and follow in a half-step with the right foot, keeping most weight back on the right leg. Circle the left palm across the chest and up to brace / block up above the head with the palm up. Bring the right hand in to the chest, keeping the tip forward and the blade edge up. Extend the right arm while rotating it palm up so that the blade spirals as it stabs forward. Complete the stab with the right hand at chest height and the tip at nose height. Turn the waist, reach the shoulder forward, and press the head up. Look past the tip. (image 1.20 and from the front)

Pointers

- o Complete the wrapping draw back as the right foot lands. Complete the lower spiraling stab as the left foot lands.

- o Complete all the actions as one movement with no hesitation.

- Connect to *right stance lower drill*, and continue. The number of repetitions is restricted only by the size of your training space.

2c Drill Turn Around　　　　　zuāndāo zhuànshēn　钻刀转身

With the *right stance upper drill* as example. *Turn and chop; Withdraw, lifting draw; Right advance, inverted grip low stab.*

ACTION 1: Step the left foot forward, landing hooked in. Do not move the right foot yet. Bring the left hand down to the right wrist. Turn the body around to face in the direction from which you came. Bring the broadsword up and around in a swinging chop. Keep the left hand at the right wrist to put power into the broadsword from both hands. Pivot the right foot onto the straight line and advance it slightly, shifting forward slightly towards the right leg. Chop the broadsword blade to waist height. Look past the tip. (image 1.21)

1.21

ACTION 2: Shift back to the left leg and withdraw the right foot a half-step to in front of the left foot. Draw the blade back and up without pausing from the chop. Lift the right elbow above the shoulder, bending the arm and rotating the right wrist to bring the ulnar edge up, palm out, hilt at nose height. This brings the blade edge to face forward with the tip angled down at chest/belly height. Turn the body slightly rightward. Keep the left hand at the right wrist throughout, and finish with the left elbow in front of the chest. Look past the tip. (image 1.22)

ACTION 3: Advance the right foot and follow in the left foot a half-step. Extend the right arm with an inverted grip to stab the broadsword forward with the tip at belly height, blade edge up. Reach the right shoulder forward. Brace the left hand up above the head at the left side. The hilt is at chest height, so the blade is angled down. Look past the tip. (image 1.23)

1.22

1.23

Pointers

- o   The turn around must be quick. To achieve this, take a considerable hook-in with the right foot. The chop must be forceful, transferring power from the body core to the shoulders, from the shoulders to the elbows, from the elbows to the hands, and from the hands to the broadsword. Do not fully extend the right arm. Use both hands for the chop, turning first, then chopping.

- o   Continue into *withdraw and draw back* immediately from *chop* with no pause. Shift the weight quickly but with good balance. During the turn around, the weight shifts first to the right leg, and then back to the left leg for the withdrawing step.

- o   After completing *withdraw and draw back* you must immediately go into *right advance inverted grip low stab*. The two are really one complete movement. Remember always that the end of one move is the beginning of the next move – the power for the following move is gained from the set up in the preceding move. This is a basic principle; always pay attention to getting a smooth and sound power flow.

- If starting from *left stance drill*, step the left foot hooked-in, place the left hand on the right wrist, and rotate inward to turn the blade edge up. From then on the action of *turn around* is the same.

2d Drill Closing Move   zuāndāo shōushì   钻刀收势

If starting from *right low drill*, first do *right retreat, left swinging chop.*

ACTION 1: Slide the left hand to the right wrist. Circle the broadsword so that the tip goes forward, down, and then left, past the left side of the body, lifting the hilt up in front of and above the head. Shift back to the left leg and retreat the right foot, touching down for stability. (image 1.24)

ACTION 2: Retreat the right foot and shift back to the right leg to take a *santi* stance. Swing the broadsword forward and down to chop with the tip at chest height. Pull the hands in towards the belly – keep the left hand on the right wrist. Press your head up and look past the tip. (image 1.25)

- The rest of *closing move* is the same as described above in *chop closing move*. *Turn and right cut; Wrap the head and change hands; Hold the broadsword and flash the palm; Stand at attention holding the broadsword.*

If starting from *left inverted grip high drill* first do *withdraw, right swinging chop.*

ACTION 1: Retreat the right foot a half-step then withdraw the left foot a half-step, so that you are still in a *santi* stance. Lower the left hand to the right wrist. Brandish the broadsword so that the tip goes down and back, swinging past the right side of the body. (image 1.26)

ACTION 2: Swing the broadsword up, then chop forward and down until the tip is at chest height, then pull the hands back towards the belly. Press your head up and look past the broadsword tip. (images 1.27, 1.28)

- Continue on to close as described in *chop closing move*.

Pointers

    o To properly perform the left or right *swinging chop* the broadsword must pass by the side of the body, so the right hand's grip must adjust. When the tip circles downward the body should turn slightly so that the body leads the shoulders. At this time, lift the right wrist slightly. When the tip moves back, send the right hand forward slightly, extending it forward to assist the momentum of the broadsword so that it smoothly chops forward and down. The tip draws a large circle while the right hand draws a small circle. Try to get a kinesthetic awareness of the hand.

    o Complete the chop as the right foot lands behind. Points to consider are the same as those of chop.

PROBLEMS OFTEN MET IN BROADSWORD DRILL

PROBLEM 1: During *right inverted low stab* the student does not control the tip, stabbing too low with not enough forward motion.

CORRECTIONS: The cause of this error is usually that the student has not straightened the wrist, or that his wrist is not strong enough. The student should do wrist strengthening exercises. If he lacks wrist strength, he can bring the thumb under to support the hilt. The student should also focus on the stabbing action to knee height.

PROBLEM 2: The student makes too large a circle with the tip during *right advance lower block and draw*.

CORRECTIONS: The student should extend the arm and turn the wrist, rotating the palm away from the thumb, to lift up. The grip must be supple and the wrist must be lively so that the tip does not draw more than a thirty centimetre circle.

PROBLEM 3: During *right drill* the student stops between the actions for too long a time, losing the power transfer in the body.

CORRECTIONS: Emphasize that right drill is one complete movement. It is taught as two actions for the convenience of learning. Once learned, it must be completed as a single move.

PROBLEM 4: The student uses only the arm to perform *right advance wrap and draw,* so that the movement is not coordinated with the body action.

CORRECTIONS: The broadsword uses the same principle as all Xingyi movements: pre-load back to go forward, pre-load right to go left. The body and both arms are used to give power to the broadsword. During practice the student must focus on the body action, slowly gaining the kinesthetic awareness.

PROBLEM 5: The student does not rotate the wrist enough during the drill. Also, when stabbing, the student uses only the arm and doesn't get power from the body.

CORRECTIONS: Whether stabbing low or high, there must be a twisting action. Drill is a twisting action. If you stab without any rotation, then it is a thrust, not a drill. To launch power into the drill you must turn the waist, reach the shoulder forward, and extend the arm. Pay attention also to assisting the power launch with the left hand. When stabbing the broadsword forward, the left assists by pushing back to balance the power.

POWER GENERATION FOR BROADSWORD DRILL

Right stance low drill: You may step forward or retreat. The right palm must rotate away from the thumb when lowering the blade to block, because the lower block uses the power of the wrist. When lifting and drawing back the blade, use the power of the torso and arm. These actions and transfers of power must co-ordinate smoothly.

Step forward inverted grip low stab: Step forward and turn the waist, sending the right shoulder forward. Settle and release the shoulder to transfer power to the arm and into the stab. The left hand assists the power launch by bracing back. Settle the torso down slightly to increase the strength of the low stab.

Right advance wrap and draw: Pay attention to the body work. Draw the broadsword back by drawing the arm from the waist. First draw back and then rotate the right hand so that the blade wraps. Use the power of the body core and shoulder, first open and then close. Turn the waist and settle the shoulder to gather power.

- Drill is an inverted grip, twisting stab. In a standard stab the blade edge is down, while in an inverted grip stab the blade edge is up. During the low drill, reach the right shoulder forward and brace the left hand back as you stab. During the high drill, keep the right elbow in front of the chest and send the broadsword forward from the lower back and shoulder. Be sure to keep a certain bend in the arm.

- When circling to block, use the power of the wrist. When lifting and drawing back, use the power of the shoulder and elbow. When stabbing forward, whether high or low, use the power from the lower back and shoulder. The whole body must be connected with no gaps in power.

PRACTICAL APPLICATIONS FOR BROADSWORD DRILL

- The different structure and actions of *left stance drill* and *right stance drill* show two different attacking moves. *Right stance drill* is an inverted grip stab, striking low to the opponent's knee or belly. *Left stance drill* is in reverse stance with the broadsword twisted to stab up, striking high to the opponent's head or chest.

Left advance low block and draw is a defensive move. 'Block' is a blocking action right or left with the tip down and the blade edge out. 'Draw' is a withdrawing action to the side and back with the tip forward and the blade edge out. Drawing back on the left side is a left draw, and drawing back on the right side is a right draw. The point of contact is the proximal third of the broadsword body, gradually shifting forward as the blade moves back. The full move of draw is a defensive action that includes the block – block and draw work together. The tip draws a counter-clockwise semi-circle in front of the body to catch a weapon stabbing towards the chest, knocking it down to the right so that it misses. Then draw the weapon back, keeping the blade in contact with the opponent's weapon to move in on him. The draw back is also a means of gathering power for the stab. You can advance or retreat, depending on the situation. The footwork needs to be quick and well connected so that you can change from one to the other smoothly.

Right step forward, inverted grip low stab stabs to the opponent's leading knee or thigh, or belly. Keep in line with the opponent's attack and enter into any space that presents itself. A single handed stab is quick, a double handed stab is strong. The key is to advance along the line of the stance, and to have quick footwork. Also, do not be content with one strike – if you miss then immediately flip the wrist to chop the opponent's head or body. Continue to attack with a flurry of moves. 'When learning practise set stances, when using there is no set technique.' You must move into any opportunity that you see, changing with the situation.

Left high drill first blocks high with the spine of the blade, then slides along the opponent's weapon to draw it back, then turns to stab the opponent's head. When blocking up use the strength of the wrist, when drawing back use the strength of the body, when stabbing forward use the turn of the waist and extension of the shoulder to send power into the blade. The circling action of the blade is the defensive move, controlling the opponent's weapon. The draw back wraps and presses onto his weapon, controlling it so that he cannot make good his escape. Then if he tries to take his weapon away you can follow it to stab. Quickly stab his head or chest. This twisting stab is called 'snake coiling its body,' or 'snake spits its tongue.'

Drill turn around is a means to get turned around to chop someone coming at you from behind. You must extend the arm and chop forcefully. If you can reach his opponent then chop his body, if you can only reach his weapon then chop his weapon. This is both an attacking and a defensive move, and is immediately followed by an advancing inverted grip stab. You must withdraw the foot quickly when turning. You must lift and draw accurately and quickly. You must step forward and stab quickly and forcefully.

- When training broadsword drill you must pay attention to the line that the whole broadsword takes, especially the circles drawn by the tip and the action taken by the hilt. You may make large circles at first. Once the actions are comfortable you should make the circles smaller, as this is more practical. It is often said, "large movements are not as good as small movements, large circles are not as good as small circles." Emphasize quick action – "no technique cannot be dealt with, only speed cannot be dealt with." This is a question of taking the short road or going the long way around. A small circle takes the short road – the hand, blade, and body are quick. If this is based on quick footwork then they will be effective. Entering into the opponent depends on the footwork getting in.

THE POEM ABOUT BROADSWORD DRILL

钻刀如蛇见缝钻，动作敏捷势势连。绞带上提下刺膝，进步上钻找鼻尖。

Broadsword drill is like a snake seeing a crevice and drilling into it.

The actions are quick and nimble and connect one after the other.

Coil around and draw to lift then stab to the knee,

Advance and drill up to find the nose.

BROADSWORD THRUST

INTRODUCTION TO BROADSWORD THRUST, *BENG DAO*

Broadsword thrust is based on the five element empty hand technique of driving punch, or crushing fist, and is a forward stab. In broadsword terminology, a thrust is a straight stabbing action with the tip, the arm and blade making a straight line, the power of the body reaching the tip of the broadsword.[45]

The key techniques for thrust are: *left stance thrust, right stance thrust, retreating thrust.* Within the combinations are: *left high hook and thrust, right high hook and thrust, left and right sticking draw and thrust,* and *chop and press and thrust.* There is also a distinction between a single handed thrust and a double handed thrust.

METHOD ONE: DRAW BACK AND THRUST

3a   Right Stance Thrust   yòubù bēngdāo   右步崩刀

Start from *on guard.* Continue with *Left advance, right draw; Right stance thrust.*

ACTION 1: Advance the left foot and follow in the right foot to the left ankle. Lift the right hand to shoulder height, keeping the tip extended forward, the blade horizontal. Rotate the right hand so that the blade edge is up, and turn the body right, pulling the arm back and keeping it bent. Keep the left hand on the right wrist throughout. Look forward. (image 1.29)

ACTION 2: Rotate the right palm towards the thumb and bring it down to between the waist and chest with the palm out. This turns the blade over, the edge once again up.

1.29

---

[45] Author's note: In normal wushu terminology, *zha* is a thrust and *beng* is a snap. In Xingyi terminology, the broadsword thrust is called *beng dao* because is based on the driving punch – *beng quan.*

ACTION 3: Take a long step forward with the right foot and follow in a half-step with the left foot to land behind the right foot with most weight on the left leg. The legs are bent, the left knee behind the right knee, just to the side. Extend the right arm to thrust forcefully forward to chest height, rotating the arm as it moves forward so that the blade edge turns down. The tip points forward at chest height. Keep the right arm slightly bent and transfer power to the tip of the broadsword. Keep the left hand at the right wrist throughout. Press your head up and look past the tip. (image 1.30)

Pointers

- ○ Complete the rightward draw as the left foot advances.

- ○ The draw and the thrust must connect smoothly in one action. It must be quick and well anchored.

- ○ The stab must be completed as the right foot lands.

3b Left Stance Thrust   zuǒbù bēngdāo   左步崩刀

Right advance, left draw; Left step forward, thrust.

ACTION 1: Advance the right foot a half-step and follow in the left foot to the right ankle. Pull and draw the right hand back to the left, rotating to turn the blade edge up. Tuck in the right elbow in front of the left shoulder, keeping the blade horizontal with the tip pointing forward. Turn the waist left, tucking in slightly and closing in the chest. Keep the left hand on the right wrist. Look past the tip. (image 1.31)

ACTION 2: Take a long step forward with the left foot and follow in the right foot to behind the left foot, keeping most weight on the right leg. Rotate the right wrist and bring it in to the left chest to turn the blade edge down, tip still pointing forward at chest height. Take the hilt with the left hand behind the right, then thrust forward forcefully with both hands as the left foot lands (or, for back foot timed, as the right foot comes in). Keep the arms slightly bent, release the shoulders and settle the elbows. The hands complete the thrust at chest height. Look past the broadsword tip. (image 1.32 and from the front)

Pointers

- Draw the broadsword back as the right foot advances. Keep the body well anchored, do not rise or fall. Turn the waist to the left and close the right shoulder towards the left to draw the broadsword leftward. Tuck the right elbow in and rotate the palm towards the thumb. Keep the movement gentle, using the body power.

- Thrust the broadsword forward as the left foot steps forward. Transfer power from the body core to the broadsword. Use both hands to get a stronger thrust, so that the thrust is strong and aggressive, the power reaching to the tip. Breathe out to launch power.

METHOD TWO: HOOK UP AND THRUST

3c Right Stance Thrust   yòubù bēngdāo   右步崩刀

Start from *on guard*. Continue with *Left advance, hook up; Right step forward, thrust.*

ACTION 1: Advance the left foot a half-step and follow in the right foot to the left ankle. Settle the right wrist and take a firm grip to bring the broadsword tip up, the blade vertical with the edge forward, to hook back with the spine. Bring the right arm in to the right side just above the waist to hook back with the broadsword spine to in front of the shoulder. Keep the left hand on the right wrist. Look forward. (image 1.33)

ACTION 2: Take a long step forward with the right foot and follow in the left foot to just behind the right foot, keeping most weight on the left leg. Lift the right hand to the chest and take a spiral grip to bring the tip down to the front to point straight forward. Keep the left hand on the right wrist. Extend both hands out forcefully to thrust forward to just short of straight arms, sending the power to the broadsword tip. The broadsword tip is at chest height. Look past the tip. (image 1.34)

3d Left Stance Thrust   zuǒbù bēngdāo   左步崩刀

Right advance, hook up; Right step forward, thrust.

ACTION 1: Advance the right foot a half-step and follow in the left foot to the right ankle. Cock the right wrist and settle the arm down in front of the body so that the broadsword blade hooks back to vertical with the tip up and the edge forward, the spine in front of the right shoulder. Bend both legs to sit slightly, tuck in the abdomen and empty the chest. Keep the left hand at the right wrist. Look forward. (image 1.35)

ACTION 2: Take a long step forward with the left foot and follow in the right foot to just behind the left foot, keeping most weight on the right leg. Lift the right hand to the chest and take a spiral grip to bring the tip down in the front to point straight forward. Keep the left hand on the right wrist. Extend both hands out forcefully to thrust forward to just short of straight arms, sending the power to the broadsword tip. The tip is at chest height. Press your head up and look past the tip. (image 1.36)

1.35   1.36

Pointers

- o Complete the hook up and back as the leading foot lands forward.

- o Complete the broadsword thrust as the rear foot steps forward.

- o *Left stance thrust* and *right stance thrust* are both complete actions. Do not pause midway through them.

3e Thrust Turn Around   bēngdāo zhuànshēn   崩刀转身

If in <u>*left* stance thrust</u>, hook the left foot in and turn around to the right. If in <u>*right* stance thrust</u>, step the left foot forward, landing with it hooked in and turn around to the right. *Left hook-in step turn around, crossing cut; Right crossways kick; Left empty stance chop.*

ACTION 1: Step the left foot forward and land with it hooked in, turning the body around to the right to face back in the way from which you came. Pull the right hand back to the left waist, rotating the palm away from the thumb to turn the blade edge out. Then turn the body right and cut across to the right in a flat cut at chest height. Stop when the blade cuts across to the right, bracing out with the left hand at the left, palm facing left. Look for ward. (images 1.37, 1.38)

1.37

ACTION 2: Lift the right knee with the foot turned out, then kick forward and up with a crossways kick to shoulder height. Bend the left leg slightly for stability. Look forward. (image 1.39)

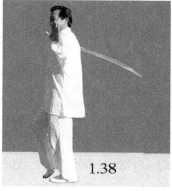

ACTION 3: Land the right foot forward, still turned crossways, and bring the left foot in to squat down, lifting the left heel, with most weight on the left leg. Turn the body right to sit into a resting stance. Rotate the right palm towards the thumb to bring the hilt above the right side of the head with the tip down and the blade edge away from the body, the spine nestled on the right shoulder. Bring it around the upper back to the left shoulder, keeping close all the time. Bring the left hand in to the right wrist or to hold the hilt and chop forward and down forcefully with both hands. The tip is forward, the blade edge down at knee height, the power in the distal third of the blade. Look forward past the tip. (image 1.40)

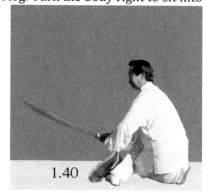

- Continue on with *left stance thrust*, advancing the leading foot first.

Pointers

- The *turn around* for broadsword thrust is similar to the *crushing fist turn around – leopard cat turns over whilst climbing a tree.* It must be done smoothly as one move.

- To get turned around with the crossing cut, the left foot must hook-in considerably. It should hook-in to in front of and outside the right foot. First pull the broadsword in to the left side of the body, and then use the turn of the body to put power into the horizontal cut. This is what makes it a strong technique. Be sure to stand steadily on the left leg and gain more power by bracing the left hand out.

- The crossways kick is a heel kick. Tuck in the right hip and extend the knee. Stand firmly on the left leg.

3f   Thrust Closing Move   bēngdāo shōushì   崩刀收势

If the <u>left</u> foot is forward then retreat the right foot a half-step and turn while cutting across.

If the <u>right</u> foot is forward then retreat the right foot and turn while cutting across.

The rest of *closing move* is the same as described in *chop closing move.*

Problems Often Met In Broadsword Thrust

Problem 1: The student lets the blade wobble when thrusting, or thrusts with no point of focus.

Corrections: This is usually because the wrist is too relaxed and the hold is slack. If the right wrist is not strong enough, press the left hand firmly on it to help out. Settle and release both shoulders and close the elbows in towards each other to send the broadsword tip forwards, letting the forearms follow it. Transfer power from the body core to the shoulders, and from the shoulder to the elbows. Start the move slowly and then speed up, and launch power at the final point of focus. Focus on launching power with accuracy.

Problem 2: During *advance draw the broadsword* left and right, the student takes the right hand too far across to the left or right. The broadsword hilt should not be taken further to the side than half an arm length away from either shoulder.

Corrections: The student must focus on correct application of the draw. Draw is an action that draws back at the side with the tip pointing forward and the blade edge facing away from the body. A left draw takes the blade to the left side, and a right draw takes the blade to the right side. The student must be sure to take the blade from the front towards the rear, and to pull the hilt back just to beside the right or left shoulder, keeping the tip pointing forward at all times.

Problem 3: When combining the thrust with the hook up, the student does not do a clean thrust, but does an action more resembling a chop.

Corrections: This is because, after the hook, the student brings the tip down while starting the stab. After the hook he must first bring the tip down to point forward, and then extend the arm to stab. The teacher must watch out for this and correct it immediately. Before the stab, bring the right hand up to the chest, snug to the body – this places the blade horizontal. Then extend the arm to thrust forward, sending the broadsword hilt and tip out in a straight line.

Problem 4: The student does not thrust with integrated power, he does not connect the thrust with the step forward. This is a common error.

Corrections: Explain and correct repeatedly, and have the student practise over and over. At first start with small steps, and fairly slowly, paying much attention to the getting the right feeling. Then gradually increase speed and distance.

Power Generation For Broadsword Thrust

Draw back in the first method should be gentle, using the waist to draw the shoulder, the shoulder to draw the elbow, and the elbow to draw the hand. When the hand lifts, the chest should be emptied, the upper back stretched taut, the abdomen tucked in, and the weight settled down. This body technique is a slight pre-loading back to gain power for the forward thrust. The body then lengthens when the hand rotates to wrap and press down with the broadsword.

Right draw back: Pay attention to the grip on the hilt. First take a full grip. Then take a spiral grip as you lift the broadsword and draw it back. Then press the hilt down when you rotate the hand to wrap and press down.

Hook: When you knock upwards and hook back, empty the chest, settle the shoulders and sit into the lower back. Take a tight, full grip on the hilt and cock the wrist down. Place the left hand on the right wrist to support it, or you can even hold the hilt with the left hand to get more power.

Thrust: Be sure to keep the blade horizontal, and to keep the tip pointing forward from beginning to end of the action. Empty the chest, stretch the upper back taut, release the shoulders, settle the elbows, turn the waist and reach the shoulder into the stab. Your strength should transfer right through to the tip of the broadsword, so be sure to stab straight and not let the blade wobble. Step quickly and for distance, charging forward with the leading foot and pushing off the rear foot. Release the shoulder and extend the arm, putting a closing power between the arms. Breathe out when launching power, settling the *qi* to the *dantian.* Your power launch must be aggressive, and you must show confidence.

Resting stance chop: Trample the ground when you land the right foot. Do not forget to pull the broadsword back after chopping, to slice in and be ready for a stab. Turn the waist, tuck in the abdomen, and press the head up to gain power in the resting stance. Trample and drop into the stance to chop quickly but with stability. To do this, turn the waist to the right and press the legs together. The stance is low and the power is smooth; the power is integrated and the mind is focused.

- In terms of practical application, there are two types of thrust – a draw back and thrust, and a hook up and thrust. In terms of power application, there are also two types; the connection with the footwork is either front foot timed or back foot timed. That is, stab when the front foot lands or stab when the back foot lands. This variation in power launch also occurs in the driving punch.

- Broadsword thrust should show a strong forward stab. The technique must be accurate, the footwork must be quick, the power must be integrated, the spirit must be strong, the body should look like a swimming dragon. Pay attention to the body action and the power, drawing back to pre-load for the forward thrust.

PRACTICAL APPLICATIONS FOR BROADSWORD THRUST

Looking at the structure of the thrust combinations, thrust is a reactive strike. The main technique is a strong stab to the chest, belly, or other sensitive areas. The forward charging drive is similar to the driving punch of the five elements.

Advance draw and *advance hook up* are both defensive moves. If a short weapon is stabbing towards your chest, draw it back as you step in, so that the weapon is taken off line. If a long weapon is coming in with a chop to the head or a stab to the chest, hook up strongly, connecting with the distal third of the broadsword to catch the weapon and take it off line.

Step forward thrust continues directly from the defensive move. Whether from the draw or the hook up, switch immediately to the stab, getting in close without haste. The stab must be stable, accurate, and aggressive. Do not get sloppy. The stab will only work if the draw or hook has taken the opponent's weapon slightly off line. You need to finish the defensive move so that you can slide along the opponent's weapon to stab his chest or belly. You can also slide along a long weapon to slice his arm or hand.

- In using the footwork you can retreat the leading foot and then advance, or you can step aside a little and then advance. Use whatever footwork is needed. The main thing is, because you have a short weapon, when you advance you must get in close to the opponent – your footwork must be quick and agile. Courage is the key word – you must dare to attack and have a strong will to win.

- The main technique of thrusting is the straight line stab to the chest or belly, but you must be attentive to any adjustments made by your opponent. If you miss your target or your opponent blocks your stab you must be able to change your technique immediately.

- You should also be able to use a variety of deceitful tactics such as 'pretending you don't know how to fight' or 'feinting first then attacking.' In general, you need more than skill, you need to further develop, practise, and deepen your combative knowledge and experience.

THE POEM ABOUT BROADSWORD THRUST

崩刀身法似游龙，左右挂带护我中。刀进身进全凭步，粘顺其械扎其胸。

The body action of the broadsword thrust is like a swimming dragon,

Hooking or drawing to right and left to protect the midline.

Getting the broadsword and the body in depends on the footwork,

Stick to and follow the opponent's weapon to stab his chest.

BROADSWORD SLASH

INTRODUCTION TO BROADSWORD SLASH, *PAO DAO*

Broadsword slash is based on cannon punch, or pounding fist, of the five element techniques. The main technique is an oblique upward slice to right or left. The slice technique is an upward slicing action with the blade edge facing up, the power in the distal third of the blade. A normal slice is done with the forearm rotated and the broadsword at the right side of the body. An inverted grip slice is done with the palm rotated away from the thumb and the broadsword at the left side of the body. Slash is the opposite of chop. A chop is done with the blade edge down, and comes forward and down from above. A slash is done with the blade edge up, and comes forward and up from below. Traditionally the Xingyi slash is practised as just a slice. I have added a diagonal hack to bring out the attacking nature of the broadsword and give an additional technique. The slash and hack techniques work well together, and the combination practice is more realistic.

The key techniques for slash are: *left stance slash* and *right stance slash*. The *left stance slash* combination is: *Right retreat, right draw; Left advance, slice; Right step forward, diagonal hack*. The *right stance slash* combination is: *Left retreat, left draw; Right advance, inverted grip slice; Left step forward, diagonal hack*.

4a   Left Stance Slash　　　　　zuǒbù pàodāo　　　　左步炮刀

Start from *on guard*. Continue with *Right retreat, right draw; Left advance, slice;*

Step forward, hack.

ACTION 1: Retreat the right foot a half-step and then withdraw the left foot a step, shifting back with most weight on the right leg. Bend the right leg and touch down the left foot in front of the right foot. Turn the right palm away from the body to rotate the blade edge diagonally upwards. Bring the right hand up and back at the right side to draw the blade back to the right side of the head. The hand is at eyebrow height and the blade level with the edge up and the tip pointing forward. Keep the left hand on the right wrist throughout. Turn the body right, flex the waist and contain the chest. Look forward past the tip. (image 1.41)

1.41

ACTION 2: Take a long step to the forward left with the left foot and follow in a half- step with the right foot, keeping most weight on the right leg. Circle the blade back and down at the right side, turning right and keeping the left hand on the right wrist. Continue to circle the blade, rotating the right palm towards the thumb to slice upwards to the forward left, blade edge up and tip pointing to the forward left. Finish with the right arm slightly bent, the hand at eyebrow height and broadsword tip at shoulder height. Swing the left arm up to block with the arm bent, palm up above the head at the left. Turn the waist, and reach the right shoulder forward slightly. Follow the broadsword tip with the eyes, looking just past the tip throughout the action. (image 1.42)

ACTION 3: Advance the left foot a half-step and bring the right foot past the left ankle then step it out to the forward right. Follow in the left foot a half-step, keeping most weight on the left leg. Relax the hold on the hilt to lower the tip and draw a circle with the blade at the right side, using the right hand as the pivot point of the circle. Once the circle is completed to the front, rotate the right palm away from the thumb and take a full grip, then extend the arm forward and up. Finally, hack forward and down at an angle. Bring the left hand in to the wrist when circling, and keep it there. Pull the hilt down and back at the right side, at the waist. The blade edge is down, the tip at chest height, pointing in the direction that the action is moving. Put power to the blade body, press your head up, and look past the tip. (image 1.43)

1.42

1.43

Pointers

- o Slash is one continuous movement. Combine the three actions together smoothly.

- o Complete the upward slice and backward draw with the right retreat and left withdraw of the feet, so that feet and hands work together.

- o Advance the left foot and slice the blade in the same diagonal direction, landing both at the same time with integrated power.

- o During *step forward hack,* the right foot should first come in to the left foot and then step out. Circle the blade as the right foot comes in, lifting the blade. Hack down as the right foot steps forward.

4b Right Stance Slash   yòubù pàodāo   右步炮刀

Left retreat, draw; Right advance, inverted grip slice; Step forward, hack.

ACTION 1: Retreat the left foot a half-step then withdraw the right foot a half-step, shifting back to the left leg. Bring both hands together up and back to the left side at eyebrow height. Rotate the right palm to face towards the body. Hold the blade edge up with the tip pointing to the forward right. Tuck in the right elbow in front of the chest as the left foot retreats. Turn leftward and draw the blade back to the left. Look past the tip. (image 1.44)

ACTION 2: Take a spiral grip, turn the body leftward and rotate the right hand to circle left and down to circle the blade at the left side of the body. Advance the right foot to the forward right and follow in the left foot a half-step, keeping most weight on the left leg. Continue to circle the broadsword, turning the body rightward and rotating the right palm away from the thumb, to slice up to the forward right. Finish with the blade edge up and tip pointing diagonally forward at shoulder height, the right arm slightly bent and the hand at eyebrow height at the forward right side. Send the right shoulder forward into the slice. Watch the movement of the blade tip throughout. (images 1.45, 1.46 and 1.46 from the front)

1.44

1.45

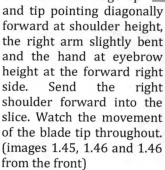

1.46

1.46

FRONT

ACTION 3. Advance the right foot a half-step, bring the left foot past the right ankle, then take a long step with the left foot out to the forward left. Follow in the right foot a half-step, keeping most weight on the right leg. Relax the hold of the right hand and circle the broadsword tip down, using the hand as the pivot point of the circle, so that the blade hooks down in a circular action outside the left arm. Use the spine of the blade to hook. Once the blade circles to above the head, take a firm grip and extend the arms to swing the blade forward and down to hack diagonally. Keep the left hand on the right wrist throughout. Finish by pulling the hilt in to the left waist, blade edge down and tip at chest height, tip slightly angled to the straight line. Send power to the body of the blade. Turn the waist slightly left, press the head up, and look past the tip. (image 1.47)

1.47

Pointers

- o The movement of broadsword during the left and right slashes are basically the same, but since you hold the broadsword in the right hand your actions are quite different. The methods and power applications differ.

- o In *left stance draw* the right hand must first send the blade tip forward at the right side. Then retreat, turn the waist, close the shoulders, flex the arms, and tuck in the elbows. And finally draw the blade back to the left, using the power from the body core to integrate the blade with the body.

- o Complete the inverted grip slice as the right foot advances.

- o *Step forward, hack*: to cut strongly down to the front is a chop, to cut strongly down to an angle is a hack.

4c Slash Turn Around   pàodāo zhuànshēn   炮刀转身

From the *right* stance angled hack. *Right hook-in step turn around; withdraw, right draw; left advance slice.*

ACTION 1: Step the right foot to hook-in in front of the left toes and shift onto the right leg, turning around to the left to face back in the way from which you came. Keep the hands at the right waist, the left hand still on the right wrist. Press your head up and look past the tip. (image 1.48)

ACTION 2: Withdraw the left foot to touch down beside the right foot, staying on the right leg. Extend the arms to slice up with both hands to the left front, broadsword tip forward and blade edge up. After withdrawing the foot, draw the blade back to the right side of the head, turning the body slightly right. Look forward past the tip. (image 1.49)

1.48

1.49

ACTION 3: Step the left foot to the forward left and follow in a half-step with the right foot, keeping most weight on the right leg. Keep the left hand on the right wrist and circle the broadsword back and down on the right side, turning the body right. Keep the broadsword moving and slice it up to the forward left, rotating the right hand to bring the blade edge up. The tip points to the forward left at shoulder height and the hilt is at eyebrow height. Keep the right arm slightly bent, turn the waist, and reach the right shoulder forward slightly. Follow the broadsword with the eyes, looking always past the tip. (image 1.50)

1.50

- Continue on with *right advance, angled hack*.

- If you start *turn around* from *left advance, angled hack*, then hook-in the left foot and turn around. Then continue with *right withdraw, left draw*, and so on, just transpose the right and left actions.

Pointers

  o You must hook-in and turn around quickly, so need to hook the foot considerably to get around. Do not take a big step, but hook-in well, so that the turn around is stable.

  o When turning, the broadsword stays at the side and comes around with the body, it does not move by itself. Wait until you are facing around in the other direction, before extending the arms forward and lifting the blade. Then when you withdraw the foot draw the blade back. Be sure to keep this order so that the movement is agile and quick, coordinated and gentle.

4d Slash Closing Move   pàodāo shōushì   炮刀收势

On arriving back at the starting point, do another *turn around*. If in a *left angled hack*, then do *left withdraw, right hook down; Left advance, swinging chop*.

ACTION 1: Without moving the right foot, shift onto the right leg and bend it to stand firmly, withdrawing the left foot to in front of the right foot. Extend the arms forward, rotate the right hand, and loosen the grip to circle around the wrist, hooking the broadsword tip down and bringing the broadsword spine on the right side of the body. Keep the left hand on the right wrist throughout. Look forward. (image 1.51)

ACTION 2: Advance the left foot a half-step forward without moving the right foot, to settle into a *santi* stance. Use the momentum of the broadsword to swing up and then chop forward and down. The position and use of power is the same as the normal chop. (image 1.52)

1.51

- The rest of the closing move is the same as that of the broadsword chop *closing move: Wrap the head and change hands; Hold the broadsword and flash the palm; Stand at attention holding the broadsword.*

If the right foot is forward then do *Right withdraw, left hook; Right retreat, swinging chop.*

ACTION 3: Withdraw the right foot to the left foot without touching down, shifting onto the left leg. Extend the arms forward and rotate the right hand to turn the blade edge up. Then circle the blade with the right wrist at the pivot point of the circle so that the tip is down, then hooks back to the left side of the body. Keep the left hand on the right wrist throughout and look forward. (image 1.53)

ACTION 4: Shift back and retreat the right foot without moving the left foot, shifting most weight onto the right leg in a *santi* stance. Swing the blade up then forward and down to chop. The final position is the same as a normal *chop*. (image 1.54)

- The rest of the movement is the same as the *chop closing move*.

Pointers

- o Hook the blade down as the foot withdraws. The hook technique uses the broadsword spine as point of contact. The wrist must be supple and the movement must be quick. Be sure to keep the broadsword snug to the side of the body, whether hooking to left or right.

- o The chop in *closing move* may be done gently and slowly, as long as the hands and feet still arrive together. Keep the spirit full and use internal power, keeping the body fully connected to the weapon.

Problems Often Met In Broadsword Slash

PROBLEM 1: During *retreat and draw*, the student doesn't draw an adequate circle with the right hand, so just pulls the broadsword straight back. This is not the proper technique for the draw.

CORRECTIONS: The definition of draw is to pull back from the front at the side, keeping the weapon horizontal. The right hand must first rotate to that the blade edge is angled up. Prior to drawing back, the blade must first reach forward. Then retreat the foot, turn the waist, and draw the blade back. The movement should be gentle and coordinated, not hard and strong.

PROBLEM 2: The student has no point of focus in *advance and slice*, often sending the blade too high.

CORRECTIONS: The slice should strike and be focused straight forward. Once the blade moves past the body then it should be slicing forward. Once the blade has reached shoulder height then the hand and arms should stop rising, and the power should come from the shoulder and waist. Take a firm grip on the hilt and pay particular attention to controlling the position of the shoulder and elbow.

PROBLEM 3: The student is inaccurate in the placement of the *step forward angled hack*, or steps the rear foot through without passing by the other foot, or steps forward to the wrong place.

CORRECTIONS: The rear foot must come in to the other foot first, this is the characteristic stepping pattern of Xingyi – shin rubbing stepping. Then step out to forty-five degrees. If the feet are placed correctly, take a perpendicular line from the midpoint of the line between them. The hack is then done diagonally at a forty-five degree angle.

Power Generation For Broadsword Slash

Withdraw and draw: First rotate the right palm away from the thumb, then lift the broadsword and draw it back. Use the waist to bring the shoulder back, which brings the elbow back, which brings the hand holding the broadsword back, so that power transfers from the body to the broadsword.

Slice: The right hand draws a small circle to make the broadsword draw a large circle. Rotate the right palm towards the thumb as it slices up, taking a spiral grip. Put power to the midsection of the blade. Turn the waist and reach the shoulder forward.

- In Xingyi, the techniques of chop and hack both have a characteristic action – a pull back at the end. In the first action of swinging up, extend the arms, lengthen the torso and expand the abdomen. When chopping or hacking down, settle the shoulders and elbows and pull the arms, contain the chest, tuck in the abdomen, and press the head up.

BREATHING CYCLE FOR BROADSWORD SLASH

Once you are comfortable with the actions, you should improve your deep skill by co- ordinating breathing with the actions. The actions guide the breathing and the breathing synchronizes with the actions. In this way you can find the power in the movements and find the whole body power.

- Inhale as you withdraw the foot and draw the broadsword back to gather power.

- Exhale as you advance and slice, launching power.

- Use a short quick inhalation as you step forward and hook down or swing up before the hack. Then exhale quickly as you step forward and hack. Settle the *qi* to the *dantian*.

- Use a long and gentle inhalation during the closing, as it is a gentle move. Settle the *qi* to the *dantian* and connect the whole body together.

PRACTICAL APPLICATIONS FOR BROADSWORD SLASH

- Looking at the structure of the slash combination, it contains a draw, a slice, a hook, and a hack. This gives a short, practical combination similar to a sparring combination. The combination is very practical while showing the flavour of Xingyi and the characteristics of the five element techniques.

Withdraw and draw defends against a stab to the head, chest, or abdomen. Retreat or withdraw a step to dodge out of the way, and reach the body of the blade forward to meet the opponent's weapon. Then follow its direction and draw it back so that it misses its target. Whether or not you succeed depends on mastering the crucial moment; 'you can't be late, and you can't be early.' You have to wait until the opponent's weapon is within your space. This is easy to say but hard to do. You need to practise this and gradually get used to it and master the timing. Practice with a partner feeding techniques, to get a feel for the timing. Then you can gradually develop the ability to defend yourself with the technique.

Step forward slice goes in along the line of the opponent's stance to slice to the belly or chest, or to go on the line of his weapon, slicing up to his wrist or forearm, or to his leg. The key to getting in is to take a long, quick step. When going smoothly along the line of his stance you can move his weapon out of the way as you get in. The classics say, "Short can be made long with quick entering footwork." Your footwork must be quick and you must dare to use it to get the body in close.

Step forward hook and hack starts with a defensive action against a stab to your chest or belly made as the opponent, for example, dodges to the side and comes into the opening made when you completed a slice up. You quickly hook the tip down to catch his weapon with your blade spine, then quickly enter, using both hands to lift your broadsword, then hack down, using the full force of your back and shoulders. A double grip makes the hack much stronger. The classics say, "a single handed hold is supple and used in normal situations. A double handed hold is strong and should be used for fighting." If the opponent blocks the hack then you put the strength of your whole body into the blade and hack whatever you can catch – his body or his weapon.

- Slash is a powerful technique so you should show a strong and confident attitude like a leopard cat. You should charge straight in with the belief that you can't be blocked or stopped. You should always train with this attitude.

THE POEM ABOUT BROADSWORD SLASH

炮刀气势如猫豹，撤步后带进步撩。上步挂劈势要勇，手脚齐到方为妙。

The broadsword slash has the spirit of a leopard cat,

Withdraw and draw back, then advance and slice.

Step forward to hook and hack ferociously,

The secret lies in the hands and feet arriving as one.

BROADSWORD CROSSCUT

INTRODUCTION TO BROADSWORD CROSSCUT, *HENG DAO*

Broadsword crosscut is a horizontal cutting action from left to right, and right to left. The footwork is the same as the empty hand crosscut, following a zigzag line. Of course, the technique differs with a weapon, so you need to start again at the beginning. The weapon must become one with the body. You must learn how to fully utilise the character of each weapon with each technique – each weapon has its own characteristics due to its structure and use, and each original technique of the five elements or twelve animals has its characteristic power.

Broadsword crosscut contains two techniques: a brandishing check and a crossing cut. The brandishing check is a mix between two techniques. It has the large movement of a brandish,[46] but the blade is not absolutely horizontal, so it is not a pure brandish. There is a checking technique in this movement, but it is larger than a pure check. The crossing cut is a crossing hack with the blade horizontal.

The key techniques for crosscut are: *left stance crosscut, right stance crosscut, step forward crosscut, retreat crosscut,* and *turning crosscut.*

5a   Right Stance Crosscut   yòubù héngdāo   右步横刀

Start from *on guard.* Continue with *Left advance, right brandishing check; Right step forward, crossing cut.*

ACTION 1: Advance the left foot a half-step and follow in the right foot to the left ankle. Keep the knees together and bend the left leg slightly to stand firmly. Bring the hands from the belly forwards and up to the chest, about a forearm length away from the body, until the broadsword tip is at head height. Brandish the broadsword to circle the tip forward and right, then back, and then around to the left. Once the tip is in front of the left shoulder, turn the right palm down so that the blade edge is forward. During the brandish the right hand rotates outwardly

---

[46] Translator's note: a brandish is a large, flat circling block, usually overhead. A check is short, hard knock to the side.

then inwardly. Turn the body left. Keep the left hand on the right wrist throughout. Follow the broadsword tip with the eyes. Finish looking forward. (image 1.55)

ACTION 2: Take a long step to the forward right with the right foot and follow in a half-step with the left foot, keeping most weight on the left leg to sit into a *santi* stance. Using a spiral grip, palm down, cut diagonally across to the forward right with the blade flat. Keep a 120 degrees bend in the right arm and keep it at shoulder height. Turn the body rightward slightly. The tip finishes the cut angled

to the forward right at shoulder height. Keep the left hand on the right wrist throughout. Press your head up and look at the broadsword tip. (image 1.56)

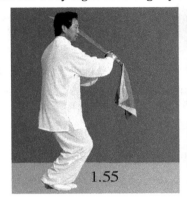 

Pointers

o   Brandish the broadsword as you advance the left foot. Draw a conical shape with the hilt and tip – the hilt as the point and the tip as the large circle.

o   Take a considerable step forward with the right foot and follow in the left foot quickly, timing the footwork with the horizontal cut.

o   The crosscut is one movement, do not pause midway through the action.

5b   Left Stance Crosscut   zuǒbù héngdāo   左步横刀

Right advance, left brandishing check; Left step forward, left crossing cut.

ACTION 1: Advance the right foot a half-step and follow in the left foot to the right ankle. Keep the knees and thighs together and bend the right leg to stand firmly. Lower the broadsword to chest height and circle the tip left and back. When the right hand is in front of the face, brandish the broadsword around to the right to in front of the right shoulder. At this time the right palm is up. When brandishing the broadsword, the tip circles higher than the head and the right hand draws a small horizontal circle in front of the chest. When the tip arrives in front of the right

shoulder, bring it down to shoulder height and place the blade flat with the edge facing forward. During the action, first turn the body left and then right. Keep the left hand on the right wrist throughout. Press the head up. Watch the broadsword tip throughout the action. (image 1.57)

ACTION 2: Take a long step to the forward left with the left foot and follow in a half- step with the right foot, keeping most weight on the right leg. Take a spiral grip on the hilt with the palm up and cut across horizontally, taking the blade forward and diagonally left. The blade edge faces left, the

right arm stays slightly bent, the hand is at shoulder height and the tip is slightly higher than the shoulders. Turn the body slightly to the left and reach the right shoulder forward slightly. The tip finishes pointing at the same angle as the left foot. Keep the left hand on the right wrist

throughout. Press your head up and look past the tip. (image 1.58 and from the front)

Pointers

○ Complete the brandishing check as the right foot advances.

○ The broadsword must arrive at the same time as the foot in the crossing cut, using the power of the whole body.

5c Crosscut Turn Around   héngdāo zhuànshēn   横刀转身

From *right* stance crosscut. Right hook-in step, turn around, left brandishing check; Left advance, crosscut.

ACTION 1: Hook-in the right foot to the outside of the left foot and shift onto the right leg, turning around to the left to face in the way from which you came. Lift the left foot by the right ankle. Lift the hilt to nose height, rotating the palm away from the thumb and lowering the tip to waist height with the blade angled forward and down, the blade edge out. Once you are turned around, lower the hilt to chest height and brandish the tip up, left, back, and then right. Keep the right wrist lively, rotating as the blade circles to finish with the palm up in a spiral grip. Keep the left hand on the right wrist throughout. When the broadsword circles to the right shoulder the blade edge is forward. Watch the blade as it moves and then look forward. (image 1.59)

ACTION 2: Take a long step to the forward left with the left foot and follow in a half-step with the right foot, keeping most weight on the right leg. Cut across forward and left forcefully with both hands. (image 1.60)

- If from *left stance crosscut* the action of *turn around* is the same, just transpose right and left.

Pointers

- o The action and requirements of the crossing cut are the same as described above.

- o The turn around should be smooth, stable and quick, done as one movement.

- o The leading foot must hook-in well, landing outside the rear foot. This gets the body turned around easily and sets up for the next step. The more the foot is hooked-in the easier it is to push off for the next step.

- o When hooking-in to turn around, as the hilt is raised and the blade lowered, contain the chest and abdomen. Crouch the body down slightly to protect it.

5d Crosscut Closing Move   héngdāo shōushì   横刀收势

The closing is the same as *broadsword slash closing move.*

If in *right stance crosscut,* then step the right foot back with *right retreat left hook down* before the *left advance chop.*

If in *left stance crosscut,* then move the left foot with *left withdraw, right hook down* before the *left advance, chop.*

The rest of the closing is the same as usual.

PROBLEMS OFTEN MET IN BROADSWORD CROSSCUT

PROBLEM 1: The student hangs on too hard when trying to brandish the broadsword so that it can't move smoothly.

CORRECTIONS: The grip must adjust and the wrist must be relaxed. Hold firmly to check, then loosen the grip to brandish.

PROBLEM 2: The student brandishes the broadsword completely over the head.

CORRECTIONS: The student should keep the right hand about a foot in front of the chest. When the hand makes a small circle in front of the chest, the tip makes a large circle above. So the broadsword tip draws a circle in front of the body, like a vertical cone. This is an effective defensive move, while swinging wildly over the head is not.

PROBLEM 3: The student does the crossing cut with a straight arm.

CORRECTIONS: If the arm is straight then the body's power cannot transfer through it and the strength will be weak. The student must pay attention to maintaining a certain flexion in the arm throughout the move. To connect the broadsword to the body, the optimum elbow angle is 135-150 degrees.

PROBLEM 4: When the student cuts forcefully he creates considerable momentum, so he cannot control the force or direction of the blade. This is a common error.

CORRECTIONS: First use both arms to brandish the blade, then, to cut across, wait until the blade is almost to the final point and bring the arms in slightly. This connects the blade more to the body, gives it power and keeps it under control. This is the sawing, slicing power of Xingyi broadsword.

POWER GENERATION FOR BROADSWORD CROSSCUT

The *brandishing check* works together with the advancing footwork. First use the broadsword spine to check to the side and then circle with the brandishing action. The right wrist must move easily, rotating throughout the action. The wrist draws a small circle so that the broadsword tip draws a large circle in front of the body. The broadsword forms a cone, that is, as the hilt lowers the tip rises. When launching power, launch from the body core to transfer to the shoulder, elbow, hand, and broadsword. This movement should be gentle and coordinated, using the body.

The crossing cut should be prepared for with a pre-loading action. Gather power to the right before launching to the left, and vice versa. This gives more power transfer from the body to the broadsword. Just before launching power, take a firm grip on the hilt. Keep the right arm bent and use the left hand to assist. Co-ordinate this with the breath, breathing out to get more power. Put the power of the whole body into the body of the broadsword and focus forward.

- The power launch of crosscut is not simply a cut across to the side. It should contain a sawing, slicing power as well. Turn the body and sit into the buttocks to make a slicing action so that the strike is more damaging. This is one of the main characteristics of Xingyi broadsword.

- The power of the turn around must fully utilize the spinning of the body, so swing the broadsword around without stopping. The power should go through all segments of the body out to the broadsword tip. Be careful to control the direction and angle of the crosscut after this.

BREATHING CYCLE FOR BROADSWORD CROSSCUT

- Inhale as you advance the leading foot with the brandishing check, to gather power.

- Exhale as you step forward with the crossing cut, launching power.

- Hold the breath briefly as you turn quickly around.

Use a long inhalation and exhalation during the closing, as it is a gentle move.

PRACTICAL APPLICATIONS FOR BROADSWORD CROSSCUT

- The core technique for broadsword crosscut is the crossing cut to either side. This can also be called a horizontal hack. Crosscut can attack high, middle or low – high is to the head, middle is to the chest, and low is to the waist. It is said, 'broadsword crosscut has the spirit of a raging elephant.' You want to bring out the direct charging spirit of an angry elephant. Its strength has no equal, there is nothing that can stop it. If you train like this, then when you want to use the technique you should be able to do the same.

Advance brandishing check is a combination of brandish and check. Check is a short knock to the side, using the fore-section of the broadsword spine to knock the opponent's weapon offline. Brandish is a horizontal turning, usually used to connect movements smoothly and gather power for the following movement. Brandishing check first checks, and then brandishes, to prepare for the following cut. If the opponent stabs towards your head or chest, once the weapon enters your space, that is, once he is within reach of your blade tip, knock his weapon aside with the end of your blade so that he misses you. Then stick to his weapon and draw it back borrowing his power to advance a half-step.

Step forward crossing cut is an attack meant to kill, and is the heart of the broadsword crosscut combination. The check has taken the opponent's weapon aside, and the brandish has gathered your power. You can now charge in with a horizontal cut, combining your hands with your leading foot, your *qi* with your will, and your strength with your *qi.* Spot your opponent and launch power forcefully into the cut. As usual, this move depends on quick and long footwork. As the classics say, "stepping slowly means losing, stepping quickly means winning." The power of the crosscut comes from the turn and pause in rhythm of the waist – first cutting and then slicing. If you use the crosscut effectively, really using the power of your whole body, then I think that there is no way the opponent can deal with you.

Crosscut turn around takes care of an opponent behind you, so you must get around quickly. Lift the hilt to bring the broadsword body around your head, protecting your head and upper body, then immediately step forward and cut across. The saying "left is coil the head, right is wrap the head' means that they are the same technique, just done differently in the different directions because the broadsword is held in the right hand.

- You must use the crosscut according to the situation, do not try to use it as if the technique is set in stone. Think about the situation between yourself and your opponent. If you feel he is stronger, then use strategy. If you feel he is weaker, then attack strongly.

THE POEM ABOUT BROADSWORD CROSSCUT

横刀气势如怒象，左右上步横冲撞。腰肩带手刀拨云，横折锉刺找敌项。

Broadsword crosscut has the spirit of a raging elephant.

Step in with a charging, ramming power, cutting left and right.

Check and brandish, sending the power from the back and shoulders to the hand and blade.

Cut across with a short sawing slice to seek out the opponent's neck.

FIVE ELEMENTS LINKED BROADSWORD FORM

INTRODUCTION TO THE FIVE ELEMENTS LINKED (FIVE PHASES CONNECTED) BROADSWORD, *WUXING LIANHUAN DAO*

The Five Elements Linked Broadsword form is a short form that combines the foundation of the five element techniques with additional broadsword techniques. It is quite widespread and popular among traditional Xingyi practitioners.

Looking at the structure of the form, it contains all the five elements plus a few new moves such as *wheel around lift knee and chop, cross step hook down swinging chop, lift knee high stab,* and *leopard cat climbs a tree.* So, although short, it is rich in content. It is tightly and logically structured with smooth power transfer, good practicality, aggressive power moves, and strong attitude. The form has a clear rhythm, and each short combination links together quickly and smoothly. The hands and feet work smoothly together, the power combines gentle and hard, and the whole form is complete and full. The attitude is confident and solid as a mountain.

Performed well, the form can fully show the flavour and characteristics of Xingyi weapon play. If you want to perform it well, though, you must have a good foundation in the broadsword five element techniques. Once you are comfortable with the actions, power, and use of the techniques then it is easy to learn the form. Where Xingyi broadsword differs from most other broadsword methods is in the body power – the use of the fully integrated power that connects the body integrally with the broadsword. If you have not mastered the five element techniques then it is most difficult to master the form.

NAMES OF THE MOVEMENTS

1. Opening Move
2. Chop: Right Step Forward, Chop
3. Thrust: Step Forward, Hook Up, Stab Forward
4. Drill: Withdraw, Inverted Grip Low Stab
5. Chop: Step Forward, Hook Down, Swinging Chop
6. Drill: Lift Knee, Inverted Grip High Stab
7. Turn Around and Hide the Broadsword
8. Thrust: Step Forward, Hook Up, Stab Forward
9. Chop: Wheel Around, Lift Knee and Chop
10. Slash: Step Forward, Right Slice, Swinging Hack
11. Crosscut: Right Step Forward, Brandishing Check, Crossing Cut
12. Crosscut: Left Step Forward, Brandishing Check, Crossing Cut
13. Drill: Right Step Forward, Outer Block and Draw Back, Inverted Grip Low Stab
14. Drill: Left Step Forward, Wind Around and Draw Back, High Stab
15. Leopard Cat Climbs a Tree: Step Forward, Heel Kick, Resting Stance Chop
16. Thrust: Step Forward Wrap and Draw Back, Stab
17. Leopard Cat Turns Over Whilst Climbing a Tree: Turn Around, Crossing Cut, Heel Kick, Resting Stance Chop

    (The following moves are repetition back in the returning direction)
18. Thrust
19. Thrust
20. Drill

21.   Chop

22.   Drill

23.   Turn Around and Hide the Broadsword

24.   Thrust

25.   Chop

26.   Slash

27.   Crosscut

28.   Crosscut

29.   Drill

30.   Drill

31.   Leopard Cat Climbs a Tree

32.   Thrust

33.   Leopard Cat Turns Over Whilst Climbing a Tree
      (Closing combination)

34.   Thrust

35.   Closing Move

Description of the Movements

1.   Opening Move   qǐ shì   起势

The whole action is the same as setting into *ready stance*. The movements are *Stand at attention holding the broadsword; Transfer the hilt over the head; Retreat and chop.*

ACTION 1: Stand at attention facing straight ahead or forty-five degrees to the line of the form. Let the right arm hang at the side, and nestle the broadsword guard in the left hand. The broadsword tip points up, the spine nestles into the left arm, the edge is forward. Press your head up and look forward. (image 1.61)

ACTION 2: Raise the hands at the sides until they arrive in front of and above the head. Bring the hilt to the right hand and release the left hand, placing it on the right wrist. Look at the right hand as it comes up, then look to the left. (images 1.62, 1.63)

1.61   1.62   1.63

ACTION 3: Retreat the right foot and shift back, bending the right leg and keeping the left leg a bit more straight, to sit into a *santi* stance. Chop forward and down, the blade edge facing forward and down, the tip pointing forward at nose height. Pull the right hand in towards the belly, about a forearm length away. Keep both arms slightly bent, close the elbows towards each other, release the shoulders and settle the elbows, contain the chest and stretch the upper back taut. Keep the blade on the body's midline. Keep the left hand at the right wrist throughout. Press your head up and look past the tip. (image 1.64)

Pointers

- Keep the arms naturally bent when lifting them. Turn a bit to the left when transferring the hilt to the right hand, and take the hilt with a pincer grip.

- Complete the chop as the left foot retreats and you shift back. Do not launch power for the chop, do a full, focused, slow move.

2. Chop   pīdāo   劈刀

Withdraw, lifting draw back; Advance, push away; Right step forward, coil around the head and chop.

ACTION 1: Withdraw the left foot a half-step without moving the right foot. Shift back onto the right leg and lift the left heel, touching the toes to the ground. Rotate the right palm away from the thumb and lift it at the right side to in front of and to the right of the head, also lifting the elbow. Keep the left hand at the right wrist and bring the elbow in front of the chest. The broadsword tip points forward throughout, and first circles left and down in front of the belly, then rotates and draws back as it is lifted. In the final position blade edge is up and the tip angles down to the front at chest height. Contain the chest, tuck in the abdomen, turn a bit to the right, and look past the tip. (image 1.65)

ACTION 2: Advance the left foot and shift forward without moving the right foot. Extend both arms, the left hand still at the right wrist, to push the blade edge forward, the tip staying angled down at chest/belly height. Keep the arms slightly bent. Look past the broadsword tip. (image 1.66)

ACTION 3: Take a long step forward with the right foot and follow in the left foot a half-step to take a *santi* stance. Loosen the hold of the right hand and bring it up over head at the left so that the broadsword tip points down, the blade edge is out, and the spine is on the left shoulder. Bring the blade around to the right shoulder, passing snugly along the upper back, then extend both arms to chop forcefully forward and down. Pull the right hand back towards the belly. keeping the tip at chest height. Keep the left hand on the right wrist. Press your head up and look past the blade tip. (images 1.67, 1.68)

Pointers

o   Rotate and draw back the broadsword as you withdraw the left foot. When you advance and push the blade, follow the blade with the footwork. When you step the right foot forward the footwork must be fast and for distance, and land as the blade chops.

o   The movement must be completed without stopping, especially actions 2 and 3. The actions must be quick and connected. Broadsword chop must also contain a sawing, or inward slicing, power.

3.   Thrust   bēngdāo   崩刀

Left step forward, hook up; Right step forward, stab forward.

ACTION 1: Step the left foot forward and follow in the right foot to the left ankle. Take a full grip with the right hand and cock the wrist down, pulling the hilt down to the right belly. The broadsword tip hooks up in front of the right shoulder with the blade edge forward. Keep the left hand at the right wrist. Both hands are at waist height. Look forward. (image 1.69)

ACTION 2: Take a long step forward with the right foot and follow in the left foot to just behind the right foot, most weight on the left leg. Lift the right hand to chest height and change to a spiral grip to bring the tip down to point straight forward. Extend both arms forcefully forward, keeping them slightly bent, to stab forward to chest height. Send the power out to the broadsword tip. Reach the right shoulder forward

slightly. Keep the left hand on the right wrist throughout. Look past the tip. (image 1.70)

Pointers

- o Complete the hook up as the left foot lands. Be sure to bring the broadsword spine towards the right shoulder.

- o Complete the stab as the right foot lands. Do not let the blade wobble. Keep the whole movement continuous and coordinated.

4. Drill   zuāndāo   钻刀

Left retreat, lifting draw back; Right advance, inverted grip low stab.

ACTION 1: Retreat the left foot and shift back towards the left leg, withdrawing the right foot a half-step and touching the toes down. Rotate the right palm away from the thumb, to circle the tip left and down. Then lift and draw the blade back, lifting the right elbow to draw the blade edge up with the tip angled down to chest height. Turn slightly to the right. Keep the left hand on the right wrist throughout. Look past the tip. (image 1.71)

ACTION 2: Advance the right foot and follow in the left foot a half-step, keeping most weight on the left leg. Using a spiral grip with the hand inverted, stab forward and down to finish with the tip at knee height and the blade edge up. Swing the left hand up to the left to brace out, arm bent, above the head. Look past the broadsword tip. (image 1.72)

1.71   1.72

Pointers

- o Complete the rotation, lifting, and drawing back the blade as the left foot retreats. Lift the blade by using the weight shift, withdrawing the right foot, and lifting the elbow. Use the turn of the body to draw the blade back.

- o Complete the low stab as the right foot steps forward – foot and broadsword tip landing simultaneously. Turn the waist, reach the right shoulder forward and brace the left hand up and back to assist the power launch.

5. Chop   pīdāo   劈刀

Left step forward, left hook down; Step forward, swinging chop.

ACTION 1: Step the left foot forward in front of the right leg, landing hooked out. Don't move the right foot, but lift the heel and bend both legs in a crossover stance. Take a full grip on the hilt with the right hand and lift the bent wrist slightly to circle the broadsword tip down, left and back. This hooks with the broadsword spine. Turn the body left, circle the blade at the left side then lift it. Stab the left hand down under the right armpit. Look at the tip. (image 1.73)

ACTION 2: Take a long step to the forward right with the right foot and follow in a half-step with the left foot to sit into a *santi* stance. Rotate the right palm away from the thumb to turn the blade edge up, then swing the right hand up, forward, and down to waist height to chop with the broadsword tip at chest height. Circle the left hand down, left, and up to brace out at the left side of the head. Look past the tip. (image 1.74)

Pointers

- Hook the broadsword down as the left foot does the cross-step. Turn the body to the left and close the shoulders. As the broadsword hooks to the lower left, stab the left hand under the right armpit, so that the two arms perform complimentary opposite actions.

- The right foot must step forward quickly and for distance, and the left foot must follow in immediately. The swinging chop must have balance in all directions – up and down, forward and back.

6. Drill   zuāndāo   钻刀

Lift knee, inverted grip high push.

ACTION: Advance the right foot a half-step and shift to the right leg. Bend the right leg slightly for stability and lift the left knee. Bend the right arm and do an elbow cover, rotating the right palm towards the thumb to turn the palm up. This draws a semi-circle with the broadsword to the left, up, and then right. The blade is flat, the edge forward and tip pointing to the right. Press down slightly with the blade. Lower the left hand to the right wrist. As the left knee lifts, push forward and up with the horizontal blade to nose height. Keep the right arm slightly bent. Look past the blade. (image 1.75)

Pointers

o The lift knee and the broadsword push must be coordinated, integrating the upper and lower actions. Be sure to rotate the right hand and bend the arm, so that the blade body draws a horizontal circle to block. Tuck in the abdomen and contain the chest. Then push forward.

o This is a traditional alternate method of doing broadsword drill.

7. Turn Around and Hide the Broadsword   huíshēn cángdāo   回身藏刀

ACTION: Rotate the right foot on the spot to turn around 180 degrees to the left. Bend the right knee and land the left foot to sit into a *santi* stance. Lift the hilt past the head with a pincer grip with the blade edge down and the blade body on the right shoulder. Wrap the blade past the upper back to the left shoulder. Keep the left hand at the right wrist. Take a full grip and bring the blade forward, down and then pull back at the right side, keeping the blade on the thigh with the tip forward. Push the left hand forward to shoulder height. Look past the left hand. (image 1.76)

1.76

Pointers

o Turn around, land the foot, chop and pull back all as one coordinated movement. Turn around quickly, paying attention to the angle.

o The turn around may also be completed as a <u>chop</u>, keeping the blade in front. Pull the blade back just in front of the belly, place the left hand on the right wrist, and press the head up more.

8. Thrust   bēngdāo   崩刀

Left advance, hook up; Right step forward, stab.

ACTION 1: Advance the left foot a step and follow in the right foot to the left ankle. Bend the left leg and press the knees together. Send the blade forward then take a full grip and cock the wrist to pull the hilt back to the right side, which brings the tip up, hooking the blade back to the right shoulder with the blade edge forward. Keep the left hand on the right wrist. Look forward. (image 1.77)

ACTION 2: Take a long step forward with the right foot and follow in the left foot to behind the right, in the same short stance as a driving punch. Keep the left hand on the right wrist, lower the broadsword tip to point forward, then stab forcefully forward at chest height.

1.77

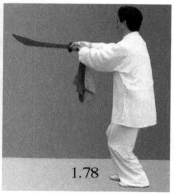

1.78

Look past the tip. (image 1.78)

9. Chop   pīdāo   劈刀

Hook-in and wheel around. Lift knee, chop.

ACTION 1: Advance the right foot a half-step, landing hooked-in and shifting to the right leg, to turn the body around to the left 180 degrees to face in the way in which you came. Take a hanging grip with the right hand, rotate the palm towards the thumb and lift the hilt so that the blade edge is to the left. Turn the left palm out and swing it up past the face to the upper left of the head. Look towards the left hand. (image 1.79)

ACTION 2: Stand firmly on the right leg, keeping the knee bent, and lift the left knee. Circle the left hand forward and down, then back and up to the upper left of the head with the palm out and the arm bracing outward. Use a spiral grip with the right hand and circle it up, forward, then down to waist height, arm bent, so that the blade does a swinging chop and the tip finishes at chest height. Reach the torso forward slightly. Send the power to the distal third of the broadsword blade and look past the tip. (image 1.80)

1.79   1.80

Pointers

- o Hook-in the right foot before turning around. The more you hook-in the easier it is to turn.

- o The three actions – wheel around, lift the knee, and chop – are one movement. Co-ordinate the hands to assist each other. When launching power, turn the waist and send the shoulder forward, tuck in the abdomen and contain the chest. Reach the torso forward slightly. Use a firm grip on the hilt.

10. Slash   pàodāo   炮刀

Left step forward, carry and draw; Right step forward, inverted slice; Left step forward, hack across the wrist.

ACTION 1: Land the left foot forward, hooked-out. Rotate the right palm towards the thumb to bring the blade edge up, and lift it to draw across towards the left at eyebrow height, tip pointing to the forward right. Turn the body slightly to the left. Keep the left hand on the right wrist. Look past the tip. (image 1.81)

1.81

ACTION 2: Step the right foot forward diagonally to the right without moving the left foot and shift forward. Using a spiral grip, circle the right hand left, down, and then forward again to complete an inverted grip slice. The right palm is rotated away from the thumb at head height with the arm bent, the blade edge up, and the tip pointing forward. Send the power to the distal third of the blade. Keep the left hand at the right wrist. Look past the tip. (image 1.82)

ACTION 3: Shift forward without moving the right foot. Bring the left foot in to the right ankle then step it out to the forward left. Follow in the right foot and shift the weight equally between the legs. Circle the blade vertically with the wrist as the pivot point, so that the tip goes down, left, back, and then up and forward to chop in a wrist cutting action. Keep the left hand at the right wrist. Keep the broadsword moving, and extend the right arm with a full grip to hack down, pulling the blade back to the left side. Finish with the tip at chest height. Press your head up and look past the tip. (images 1.83, 1.84)

Pointers

- o The right hand must complete the lift and draw as the left foot lands hooked- out. Turn the waist, close the shoulders, and cover with the elbow to draw the hand and thus the broadsword to the left. The movement is gentle. Keep the legs slightly bent and sit the torso slightly down.

- o The inverted grip slice must be completed as the right foot lands. The blade must stay close to the body as it circles in the slicing action. Transfer power from the waist to the shoulder, from the shoulder to the arm, and from the arm to the blade.

- o In the wrist cutting action the right wrist draws a small circle, so the wrist must be supple. When hacking down, first extend the arm and lengthen the back. Then contain the chest, tuck in the abdomen, settle the shoulders and elbows, and pull in. Be sure to press the head up.

11. Crosscut   héngdāo   橫刀

Left advance, right brandishing check; Right step forward, crossing cut.

ACTION 1: Advance the left foot a half-step and follow in the right foot to the left ankle. With the left hand supporting the right wrist, extend the arms forward and up to bring the broadsword tip forward and check to the right. Then brandish in a circle back, and finally come around to the left in front of the body, tip forward. To do this, the right wrist first rotates palm towards the thumb and then palm away from the thumb to bring the palm down in front of the left shoulder. Turn the body to the left. Follow the tip with the eyes during the movement. (image 1.85)

ACTION 2: Take a long step to the forward right with the right foot and follow in a half- step with the left foot, keeping most weight on the left leg. Take a spiral grip and turn the waist to the right to cut the blade horizontally across to the right, keeping the right elbow bent at about 120 degrees. Bring the hand and broadsword tip across at shoulder height in line with and pointing in the same direction as the right foot. Look past the tip. (image 1.86)

Pointers

- o   Coordinate the brandishing check with the step of the left foot. First check to the side and then brandish around. Adjust the grip so that as the right hand draws a small circle the broadsword draws a large circle in front of the body. Be sure to move the blade by the movement of the body and arms, not just the wrist. The action is gentle and coordinated.

- o   When cutting across, you need to add a short sawing in power to the crossing cut by turning the waist and sitting the buttocks at the end of the movement. Exhale to put more power into the strike, transferring the power of the whole body into the blade.

12. Crosscut   héngdāo   横刀

Right advance, left brandishing check; Left step forward, crossing cut.

ACTION 1: Advance the right foot a half-step and follow in the left foot to the right ankle. With the left hand supporting the right wrist, lower them slightly to chest height, then draw a small circle to the left, back, then forward, so that the broadsword tip draws a large circle right, forward, left, back, and then again to the right. Rotate the right palm up in front of the right shoulder, the blade angled up at head height. When the tip arrives at the right shoulder then lower it to shoulder height, blade edge forward. Follow the tip with the eyes during the movement. (image 1.87)

ACTION 2: Take a long step to the forward left with the left foot and follow in a half-step with the right foot, keeping most weight on the left leg. Take a spiral grip and turn the waist to the left to cut the blade horizontally across to the left,

pointing in the same direction as the left foot. Finish the cut with the right palm up, the blade edge to the left, and the tip at nose height. Keep the left hand on the right wrist. Look past the tip. (image 1.88)

Pointers

- Points to consider are the same as those for move 11, *right crosscut*.

13. Drill   zuāndāo   钻刀

Left advance, right outer block and draw back; Right step forward, inverted grip stab down.

ACTION 1: Advance the left foot a half-step and follow in the right foot to the left ankle. Lower the right elbow slightly to first block to the right with the blade spine. Then rotate the right palm away from the thumb and flex the right wrist to bring the broadsword tip left and down. Then lift the right elbow and bend the elbow, pulling the hand back to draw the blade back, edge up and tip forward at chest height. Keep the left hand at the right wrist throughout. Look past the tip. (image 1.89)

ACTION 2: Take a long step forward with the right foot and follow in a half-step with the left foot. Extend the right arm to stab forward in an inverted grip, blade edge still up and tip pointing forward. Finish with the elbow slightly bent, the blade tip at chest height. You may keep the left hand on the right wrist or swing it up by the head at the left side. Look past the tip. (image 1.90)

Pointers

- As the left foot advances the blade needs to complete three actions: block with the spine to the right, block across and down to the right, and then lift and draw back. The broadsword's action must be continuous, smooth, and quick.

- The stab is completed as the right foot steps forward. Extend the right wrist and keep a firm grip. You may press the thumb under the hilt to help keep the tip up. The stab is downward with the blade angled down, the exact height of the tip is determined by the placement of the hand.

- o The two actions must be closely connected to use the power transfer within the torso.

14. Drill   zuāndāo   钻刀

Right advance, entangle and draw back; Left step forward, inverted grip stab up.

ACTION 1: Advance the right foot a half-step and follow in the left foot to the right ankle. Draw a clockwise trapping circle with the blade tip, first lowering it, then taking it left, up, and finally right, drawing it back at the right side and lowering it to the waist. Rotate the blade edge up with the tip forward at chest height. Keep the left hand at the right wrist. Look past the tip. (image 1.91)

ACTION 2: Take a long step forward with the left foot and follow in a half-step with the right foot, keeping most weight on the right leg. Slice the left hand across in front of the body to block up at the upper left, palm up above the head. Extend the right arm forward to stab up with the blade edge up. Finish with the right hand at chest height and the broadsword tip at nose height. Turn the waist and reach the right shoulder forward. Press the head up and look past the broadsword tip. (image 1.92)

Pointers

- o Entangle and draw back as the right foot advances, completing all movement at once. Be sure to use the waist so that the power of the body transfers to the arm and thus to the blade. Complete the trapping action before drawing back.

- o Land the stab as the left foot lands. Lengthen the lower back, release the shoulder forward, and extend the arm. Swing up the left hand to assist the power launch of the stab.

15. Leopard Cat Climbs aTree   límāo shàngshù   狸猫上树

Advance, wrist cut, separate broadsword, heel kick; Resting stance chop.

ACTION 1: Lower the left hand to the right wrist. Use a pincer grip to lower and pull the broadsword tip back outside the right arm. Then circle it in a vertical circle up and forward, rotating to that the blade edge is down. Advance the left foot a half-step. Swing the blade down and back. Swing the left hand down and to the left. Lift the right knee and kick to chest height with the foot turned out across. Bend the left leg to stand firmly. Look past the kicking leg. (image 1.93)

ACTION 2: Land the right foot forward, hooked out, and follow in the left foot slightly to sit into a resting stance. Lift the right hand over the head and bring the left hand in to meet the right wrist. As the right foot lands, chop forward and down with the blade, then pull the hands back toward the belly, the blade at waist height. Press your head up and look past the tip. (images 1.94, 1.95)

Pointers

- o Complete the whole movement as one smooth continuation – but make sure that the actions are correct and the techniques clear.

- o Keep the right wrist supple to be able to swing, hook, and circle the broadsword down and out to the right.

- o Chop down as the right foot lands, turning the waist and closing the hips.

16. Thrust   bēngdāo   崩刀

Right advance, wrap and draw back; Left step forward, stab.

ACTION 1: Advance the right foot a half-step and follow in the left foot to the right ankle. Extend the broadsword forward then rotate the blade edge up and pull it back to the right shoulder, keeping the tip forward. Turn to the right and pull back until the right hand is in front of the right chest. Keep the left hand on the right wrist. Look past the tip. (image 1.96)

ACTION 2: Take a long step forward with the left foot and follow in the right foot to behind the left foot, most weight on the right leg, in the normal stance for a driving punch. Rotate the right hand and extend it forcefully to stab the blade forward, turning the edge down. The blade is level with the tip forward at chest height. Send the power forward to

the tip. Keep the left hand on the right wrist. Look past the tip. (image 1.97)

Pointers

- o Wrap and draw the blade as the right foot advances. This is a gentle action. Use the waist, shoulder, and arm to draw the blade around and back, and be sure to rotate the right hand.

- o Stab forward as the left foot lands, using integrated power. Take a long step and land firmly. Stab strongly into the blade.

17. Leopard Cat Turns Over Whilst Climbing a Tree

límāo dào shàng shù   狸猫倒上树

Hook-in turn around, crossing cut; Right heel kick; Resting stance chop.

ACTION 1: Step the left foot forward, land hooked-in, and turn fully around to the right. Rotate the right palm down and pull the blade back to the left side with the edge out. Open out both hands to either side, cutting flat across to the right with the blade at chest height and bracing the left hand out to the left. Look forward. (images 1.98, 1.99)

 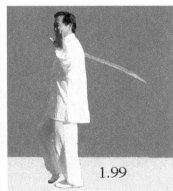

ACTION 2: Lift the right knee and then do a crossways heel hick forward and up to shoulder height. Stand firmly on the left leg. Look forward. (image 1.100)

ACTION 3: Land the right foot forward, pushing it down crossways, and bring in the left foot to sit into a resting stance. Change the right hand to a spiral grip, rotate it. and lift the hilt above the head so that the broadsword tip drops at the right shoulder. Bring the left hand in to the right wrist. Chop forward and down, bringing the hands down to hip height with the broadsword tip at waist height. Press the head up slightly. Look past the tip. (image 1.101)

Pointers

- o Hook-in considerably to be able to turn around smoothly. Cut the blade around to the back while turning. Turn quickly and cut with power.

o   The other points to consider are the same as for move 15.

18. Thrust   bēngdāo   崩刀

Right advance, wrap and draw back; Left step forward, stab.

ACTION 1: Advance the right foot a half-step and follow in the left foot to the right ankle. Extend the broadsword forward then rotate the blade edge up and pull it back to the right shoulder, keeping the tip forward. Turn to the right and pull back until the right hand is in front of the right chest. Keep the left hand on the right wrist. Look past the tip. (see image 1.96, and reverse the direction)

ACTION 2: Take a long step forward with the left foot and follow in the right foot to behind the left foot, most weight on the right leg, in the standard stance for a driving punch. Rotate the right hand and extend it forcefully to stab the blade forward, turning the edge down. The blade is level, with the tip forward at chest height. Send power forward to the broadsword tip. Keep the left hand on the right wrist. Look past the tip. (see image 1.97, and reverse the direction)

Pointers

o   This is the same as move 16, but going in the other direction.

•   The following sequence of moves, 19 through 33, is the same as the first section, move 3 through 17, repeated in the other direction. Perform the *turn around* again when you get back to the starting place, another *step forward thrust* in the original direction, and then close the form.

19. Thrust   See move 3.

20. Drill   See move 4. (images 1.102 and 1.103)

21. **Chop**   See move 5. (image 1.104)

1.104

22. **Drill**   See move 6.

23. **Turn Around and Hide the Broadsword**   See move 7.

24. **Thrust**   See move 8.

25. **Chop**   See move 9.

26. **Slash**   See move 10. (images 1.105, 1.106)

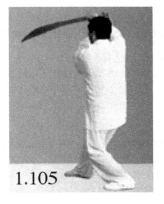

1.105   1.106

27. **Crosscut**   See move 11. (image 1.107)

28. **Crosscut**   See move 12. (image 1.108)

1.107   1.108

29. Drill   See move 13.

30. Drill   See move 14. (image 1.109)

1.109

31. Leopard Cat Climbs a Tree   See move 15.

32. Thrust   See move 16.

33. Leopard Cat Turns Over Whilst Climbing a Tree   See move 17.

34. Thrust   See move 16.

35. Closing Move   shōu shì   收势

Return and cut across. Wrap the head and change hands; Hold the broadsword in the left hand and flash the palm; Stand at attention holding the broadsword.

ACTION 1: Retreat the right foot a bit and shift to the right leg, hooking in the left foot slightly on the spot. Cut flat across with the blade edge facing right at chest height. Extend the left arm to the left to brace out, palm out. Keep both arms slightly bent. Turn rightward, brace out with both arms, and look at the broadsword tip. (image 1.110)

ACTION 2: Shift to the left leg without moving the feet. Rotate the right hand so the palm is up, then lift it over the head at the right, loosening the hold to place the broadsword spine outside the right shoulder on the back. Circle the right hand to the left, taking the blade across the back to the left shoulder in a *wrap the head* movement. Extend the right hand forward to meet the left hand and place the hilt in the left palm. Turn the body leftward. Look at the left hand. (image 1.111)

1.110

1.111

ACTION 3: Shift back to the right leg and straighten it, bringing the left foot in beside it to stand to attention. Turn the left palm up so that the thumb, ring, and little fingers cradle the guard, and the index and middle fingers wrap around the hilt. Swing the right hand down, right, and then up to above the head, palm up. Hold the broadsword in the left hand with the blade spine snug to the arm and circle it up, rightward, and then down to the left hip. Follow the right hand with the eyes, then snap the head to the left when the right hand flashes, to look to the left. (image 1.112)

ACTION 4: Without moving the feet, straighten the left hand naturally at the side, still holding the broadsword with the blade edge forward and tip up. Bring the right hand down to the right side and stand to attention. Press the head up and look forward. (image 1.113)

1.112   1.113

Pointers

o   Brace out with both hands simultaneously during the turn around and cut across.

o   Bring the foot in and flash the palm simultaneously.

o   When wrapping the head be sure to adjust your grip on the hilt. Keep the broadsword spine snug to the body – the wrap must be tight. Be sure to shift the body left and right during the movement.

o   The whole movement must be well coordinated, fully focused, and dignified.

FIVE ELEMENT SWORD 五行剑

INTRODUCTION TO FIVE ELEMENT SWORD, *WUXING JIAN*

Previous generations of Xingyi masters developed the five element sword techniques. They examined a multitude of sword techniques in many styles, deleted what they felt was superfluous, selected the best, the most practical and those which would best represent the flavour and character of Xingyiquan. They created five sword techniques, which they named after the five elemental fist techniques of Xingyiquan. The names of the techniques are sword chop, sword drill, sword thrust, sword slash, and sword crosscut – the same as the five element fists.[47]

The traditional five element sword techniques are simple and practical with no extraneous movements, and emphasize deep skill. The footwork, body actions, power applications, and five element theory of Xingyi empty hand are combined with techniques that are characteristic of the sword. Each of the five short combinations is practised on its own, and contain both a left and a right-sided technique.

The five element sword techniques are not commonly practised in traditional circles. There are three possible reasons for this. One: teachers felt they were too valuable to teach openly, so they lost transmission. Two: few teachers knew them. Three: students did not like to learn and practise them because they seemed too simple and plain. The sword's five element form is, however, very popular and widespread. The form is built on the five techniques, but people do not realize that real deep skill comes from training the individual techniques.

Each weapon has its own character, techniques and uses. The sword is considered the master of the short weapons, or the king of all weapons. The shape of the sword determines how it is used. The sword is a short weapon with a relatively

---

[47] Author's note: In this book I have kept the traditional names but have included modern terminology for clarity. For example, *beng* is the word used in Xingyi weapons terminology for a straight thrust, as it is like *beng* [crushing or driving punch]. In standard weapons terminology *beng* is a snap up, while *ci* [pierce] is the standard terminology for a straight thrust with a sword. Similarly, what we call *pao jian* [sword slash] is normally called a *liao* [slice up]; and what we call *heng jian* [sword crosscut] is normally called a *pingzhe* [flat cut]. Translator's note: The names are slightly different in English for clarity. I have kept the names different from the modern terms, though, and in keeping with the Xingyi feeling.

light, straight, double-edged blade that tapers to a sharp tip. This blade makes it an agile weapon that allows you to adapt techniques quickly. In addition to the character of the sword itself, you must respect the nature of the Xingyi sword. The manner in which we use the sword in Xingyi – the footwork, bodywork, power, and application – is quite different from most other styles. The Xingyi sword techniques are highly practical and at all times show the flavour and characteristics of empty hand Xingyi. It is said in martial arts that the weapon is an extension of the arm, and in Xingyi this is certainly true – the weapons are fully integrated with the body. The movements are weighty and well anchored, the techniques are practical, and the power is integrated. Xingyi sword can be classified as a 'static sword.' That is, each completed position is held, each and every position can be seen clearly, and a clear distinction is made between action and stillness. The positions are well anchored and firm, it is suffused with power, defense and attack can be seen clearly, there is interplay between gentle and hard, and the bearing is resolute. The five sword techniques must be built on the foundation of the five element hand techniques. Without this foundation, you cannot master the sword techniques.

FIVE ELEMENT SWORD TECHNIQUES

On Guard   yùbèishì   预备势

The *on guard* position is the opening of any Xingyi weapon form or practice session, equivalent to the empty hand left *santishi*. For the sword, this means to stand in *santi* stance with the sword ready in the right hand. *On guard* is the beginning of any practice session or fight, so it is important to collect the mind. It must be done as post standing to develop the correct habits for holding the sword and prepare the way for the other techniques.

The actions are: *Left hand holds the sword behind; Transfer the sword over the head; Left santi stance, chop.*

ACTION 1: Stand to attention, press the head up, and look forward. Place the right hand at the side with the hand in sword fingers shape (thumb tucked onto bent little finger and ring finger, other fingers straight). Hold the hilt upside down with the left hand, with the thumb, ring and little fingers on the guard and the index and middle fingers extended along the hilt. The arms are naturally extended at the sides and the sword is vertical, the tip up and the flat of the blade snug to the left arm. Face forward or in the direction in which you will practise. (image 2.1)

ACTION 2: Lift the hands by the sides to above and in front of the head. Transfer the hilt to the right hand. Release the left hand and form the sword fingers shape. Unless otherwise stated, the left hand will remain in sword fingers shape throughout all the movements from now on. Look forward. (images 2.2, 2.3)

ACTION 3: Retreat the right foot and shift back towards the right leg to sit into a left *santi* stance. Chop forward and down from above the head to bring the tip angled forward at nose height. The right hand holds the hilt, pulling back to about a foot distance from the belly. Keep the right arm slightly bent, release the shoulders and settle the elbows. Line up the blade on the midline of the body with the blade standing. [48] Keep the left hand at the right wrist throughout. Press the head up and look past the sword tip. (image 2.4)

Pointers

o When you lift the sword to the side in the left hand it must not wobble. The flat of the blade must be pressed to the forearm so that it is lifted behind the arm.

o Be careful to make a clean and firm hand transfer above the head.

o Chop forward and down as the weight shifts back, pressing the head up at the same time.

o Perform the actions smoothly connected. Show an attitude of combat preparedness even though there is no power launch, Keep focused and show vitality and well-anchored power. Settle the *qi* to the *dantian.* Do not perform the movement quickly or with overt force.

o You should practise the final position as a post standing exercise. Pay particular attention to lining up the blade along the midline of the body, with the three tips aligned – tip of the feet, tip of the nose, and tip of the sword.

SWORD CHOP

INTRODUCTION TO SWORD CHOP, *PI JIAN*

Sword chop is similar to the empty hand split and uses the same type of integrated body power. Sword chop uses a standing blade to chop forward and down. The

[48] Translator's note: A 'standing' blade is the edges 'standing' vertically. If the sword were horizontal, the edges would align up and down. A 'flat' blade is the edges lying flat. If the sword were horizontal, the edges would align side to side. A sword strike may be 'flat,' 'standing,' or angled, independent of the angle to which the tip points. For example, a horizontal pierce may use either a standing or a flat blade.

power must reach the blade of the sword.

The traditional techniques of sword chop include: *hook and chop, swinging chop, straight chop,* and *angled chop.* Footwork includes: *right stance chop, left stance chop, advance chop, retreat chop.* There are also a *left and right swinging chop* and a *left and right hook up and down to chop.* The main traditional technique is the *left and right hook up and chop,* and the *left and right hook down swinging chop.* The other techniques are mainly slight differences in footwork or order of combining the moves.

METHOD ONE: HOOK DOWN AND CHOP

1a   Right Stance Chop   yòubù pījiàn   右步劈剑

Start from *on guard.* Continue with *Left advance, right hook down; Right step forward, chop.*

ACTION 1: Advance the left foot a half-step and follow in the right foot to the left ankle. Keep the knees together and stand firmly on the bent left leg. Lift the right hand to the shoulder, rotating the palm towards the thumb so the sword tip draws a vertical circle at the right of the body, first pointing down, then back. Lift the right hand slightly to nose height as you finish the circle, lifting the sword tip. Turn the body slightly to the right. Keep the left hand at the right wrist throughout. Follow the sword tip with the eyes then look forward. (image 2.5)

ACTION 2: Take a long step forward with the right foot and follow in a half-step with the left foot, keeping most weight on the left leg to sit into a sixty/forty *santi* stance. Take a full grip with the right hand to chop forward and down with a standing blade. Pull the right hand in to about a foot away from the belly, so that the sword tip finishes at shoulder height. Keep the left hand at the right wrist throughout. You may also take the hilt with the left hand during the chop to do a stronger, double handed chop. Lengthen the lower back, press the head up, and settle the shoulders and elbows. Look forward. (image 2.6, and from the front)

Pointers

o   Complete the hook down at the right side as the left foot advances. Keep the blade close to the body. Keep the wrist loose and rotate the palm towards the thumb to accomplish this.

o Complete the swinging chop as the right foot steps forward. The whole body must be connected through to the sword blade, so the sword and foot must arrive simultaneously.

o The hook and chop is one combined movement, and must be done without hesitation so that the hook sets up the chop.

o The chop must arrive accurately with a point of focus. Every chop must be clean and sharp. Using a double-handed grasp can give more control. Do not get carried away and use so much force that the sword blade wobbles.

1b Left Stance Chop   zuǒbù pījiàn   左步劈剑

Right advance, left hook down; Left step forward, chop.

ACTION 1: Advance the right foot a half-step and follow in the left foot to the right ankle. Lift the right hand to in front of the face, then rotate the palm away from the thumb so that the palm faces right and the thumb is down. This brings the sword tip down and back to circle and hook at the left of the body. Bend the right elbow and lift it to shoulder height, dropping the right hand to chest height. Keep the left hand at the right wrist throughout. Turn slightly to the left. Look at the sword tip. (image 2.7)

ACTION 2: Take a long step forward with the left foot and follow in the right foot a half-step, keeping most weight on the right leg in a sixty/forty stance. Take a firm grip with the right hand and bring the sword up and forward, extending the arm to chop forward and down. Then pull the hilt back   to about thirty centimetres from the belly, bringing the sword tip to   shoulder height. Keep both arms slightly bent. Keep the left hand at the right wrist throughout or take the hilt with the left hand to do a stronger double- handed chop. Release the shoulders and settle the elbows. Sink the *qi* to the *dantian*. Press the head up. Lengthen the torso slightly. Look past the sword tip. (image 2.8)

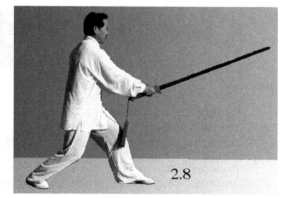

2.7

2.8

Pointers

o The points to consider are the same as *right stance chop*, the only difference being which foot is forward.

• Continue on with *right chop* and *left chop*, restricted only by the size of your training space.

METHOD TWO: HOOK UP AND CHOP

1c Right Stance Chop   yòubù pījiàn   右步劈剑

Start from *on guard. Left advance, scooping hook up; Right step forward, chop.*

ACTION 1: Advance the left foot a half-step and follow in the right foot to the left ankle. Extend the right arm forward slightly to lower the sword tip to chest height. Then take a full grip and sit the right wrist down, bending the arm and bringing the hand to the right side of the chest, tucking the elbows in snugly to the ribs, to scoop up and hook back with the sword tip. Keep the left hand at the right wrist or grasp the hilt on the other side, palms facing each other, right hand above the left. The right hand and sword hilt are vertical in front of the chest. Draw the right shoulder back slightly, angle the torso slightly, and bend the left leg. Look forward. (image 2.9)

ACTION 2: Take a long step forward with the right foot and follow in a half- step with the left foot, keeping most weight on the left leg. Grip the hilt with both hands and extend the arms to chop forward and down, then pull in to about thirty centimetres from the belly. The sword tip completes the chop at shoulder height. Sit into the buttocks, tuck in the abdomen, lengthen the back, press the head up, and look past the sword tip. Your power should reach the sword blade. (images 2.10, 2.11)

Pointers

- Complete the scooping hook as the lead foot advances a half-step. Complete the chop as the rear foot steps through and lands. The sword arrives as the feet arrive, so that hands, feet, and sword work as one.

- Although these actions are described separately they are one movement and must be done continuously. The hook up must be quick and the chop must be strong.

1d Left Stance Chop   zuǒbù pījiàn   左步劈剑

Right advance, scooping hook up; Left step forward, chop.

ACTION 1: Advance the right foot a half-step and follow in the left foot to the right ankle. Take the hilt in both hands and extend both arms slightly to lower the sword tip to solar plexus height. Then take a full grip, cock the wrists down, and bend the arms, pulling back to in front of the left chest with the elbows snug to the ribs to scoop the tip up and hook back. The sword finishes with the blade vertical in front of the left chest. Pull the left shoulder back a bit and angle the torso slightly, bending the right leg. Look forward. (image 2.12)

ACTION 2: Take a long step forward with the left foot and follow in the right foot a half- step, keeping most weight on the right leg. Extend both arms with both hands holding the hilt to chop forward, then pull both hands down and back to about thirty centimetres in front of the belly. Finish the chop with the tip at shoulder height, sending the power to the sword blade. Sit into the buttocks, tuck in the belly, lengthen the back, press the head up, and look past the sword tip. (images 2.13, 2.14)

Pointers

- o   Points to consider are the same as *right stance chop.*

- •   Continue on to repeat, limited only by the space available.

1e Chop Turn Around   pījiàn zhuànshēn   劈剑转身

Using the *left stance chop* as example. *Left hook-in step, lift; Right step forward, chop.*

ACTION 1: Hook-in the left foot to in front of and just outside the right foot. Shift onto the left leg and lift the right foot at the left ankle. Rotate the right hand and lift it above the head, lifting the hilt with the sword tip angled down. Support the right wrist with the left hand. Look past the sword tip. (image 2.15)

ACTION 2: Turn the body around 180 degrees to the right to face back in the way from which you came. Step the right foot forward and follow in a half-step with the left foot, with most weight still on the left leg, forming a sixty/forty *santi* stance. Lower the right hand

to do a swinging chop forward, then pull it back in front of the belly. The sword tip finishes at shoulder height. Keep the left hand at the right wrist. Press the head up. Look past the sword. (images 2.16, 2.17)

2.16   2.17

- The basic action of *turn around* is the same whether on the right or left side, just transpose the right and left stepping. To turn around the other way, step the right foot hooked in and turn around 180 degrees leftward. With the <u>right</u> foot hook-in step, to turn around to the left, rotate the right palm <u>towards</u> the thumb. Use a hanging grip to keep the sword blade close to the body.

- Note that with the left foot hook-in step, to turn around to the right, the right palm rotates <u>away</u> from the thumb as it lifts the sword. Use a pincer grip to keep the sword blade close to the body.

Pointers

o   Lift the sword as the foot hooks in.

o   Be sure not to knock yourself with the sword blade.

o   Chop with the sword as you turn around and step forward. This movement should be fast and strong.

1f   Chop Closing Move   pījiàn shōushì   劈剑收势

On arriving back at the starting point, do a *turn around* to face the starting direction. Once you are in *left stance chop* then do *closing move: Right retreat, draw the sword; Stand at attention and transfer the sword; Left hand holds the sword behind.*

ACTION 1: Retreat the right foot a half-step and shift to the right leg, extending the left leg and turning the foot in. Lift the right hand and pull it back to in front of the right shoulder, palm in, so that the sword blade is horizontal at shoulder height with a standing blade. Bend the left arm and turn the palm out, placing the hand on the guard with the thumb down. Turn the body ninety degrees to the right. Look past the sword tip. (image 2.18)

2.18

ACTION 2: Grasp the guard with the left hand upside down with the thumb, ring, and little fingers cradling the guard. Align the index and middle fingers along the hilt so that the blade is flat on the left forearm. Lift the left hand and extend it, circling to the left to lower at the left side so that the sword is vertical at the left side. Circle the right hand down, left, and then up to above the head at the right, palm up and arm bent to

brace. Withdraw the left foot and stand up with the feet together. At first follow the right hand with the eyes, then turn the head to look left when the right hand flashes above the head. (image 2.19)

ACTION 3: Do not move the feet. Swing the right hand down to the side and open to a normal palm shape. Turn the head to look forward. Do not move the left hand. At this point you are at attention, and the practice is completed. (image 2.20)

Pointers

o The footwork and sword work must be well coordinated: pull the right hand back to draw the sword back with the blade horizontal, retreat the right foot, and shift back.

o The left hand must take the sword hilt accurately and immediately snug the flat of the blade to the forearm. Extend the index and middle fingers along the hilt to press and control it. Circle the hands coordinated together and with the withdrawal of the left foot. Pay attention to the actions and spirit of the eyes.

o After you have completed *closing move* you should still show full spirit. Settle the *qi* and calm the mind.

PROBLEMS OFTEN MET IN SWORD CHOP

PROBLEM 1: The student holds the hilt too tightly during the hook down so that the wrist is stiff and the sword cannot move smoothly, making the whole movement uncoordinated.

CORRECTIONS: First of all, you must explain the different ways of gripping the hilt. Then you must explain how each gripping technique combines with each sword technique. For the hook down, the right palm must rotate towards the thumb and then hook down, using force on the hook down. When turning, the grip must be relaxed so that the sword can circle quickly and stay close to the body.

PROBLEM 2: During the chop the student loses control due to the momentum of the sword. The blade is unstable, not coordinated with the body, or even wobbles.

CORRECTIONS: The student should start out not putting too much force into the chop, and gradually increase the force as he gains control. He should also start out slowly and gradually increase the speed as he gets used to it.

PROBLEM 3: During the hook up and chop, the student lifts the hilt up too high to do the scooping hook upwards, lifting above the shoulder. This makes the blade touch the body, which should never be done with a sword.

CORRECTIONS: Explain to the student that this action is made up of two techniques – a scoop and a hook up. He must first sit the wrist down to scoop and then pull the arm back to hook up. In this way the sword is first brought vertical and then pulled back. He also must be careful to place both hands in front of the chest so that the blade is not pulled back into his body.

POWER GENERATION FOR SWORD CHOP

Right hook down and chop: the right hand needs to take a relaxed grip and rotate the palm towards the thumb with a supple wrist to complete an effective hook down. The hand and hilt complete a small circle while the sword blade completes a large circle. When bringing the blade up you should lengthen the body core, lift the shoulder and draw the elbow. When chopping forward you should first extend both arms forward, and then move down and pull back in. Tuck in the abdomen, contain the chest, sit into the lower back, press the head up, release the shoulders, and settle the elbows to give full body power to the chop.

- Chop is not a simple chop down. It does a sawing, inward slicing, action to complete the movement, pulling and gathering towards the body. This is a characteristic of Xingyi's sword chop. This method lengthens the line of action of the blade and increases the power of the chop.

- When chopping, respect the theories of Xingyi's power application: "use a firm grip to strike" and "launch power after the halfway point." That is to say, when launching power to chop, take a full, firm grip on the hilt. The sword circles into the chop, so wait until it has completed half of the circle, then augment its momentum with your power launch. In the first half of the circle, keep your grip and wrist relaxed. As the sword blade arrives over the head then firm up and launch power forward to chop down.

- The technique scoop is applied with the sword tip, while hook is applied with the sword blade. The *scooping hook* in the chop combination unites these two techniques. First scoop then hook, but all in one continuum. When scooping, extend the arm and cock the wrist down. When hooking, bend the arm and pull in. When scooping/hooking to the left be sure to pull the hilt in to the left chest. When scooping/hooking to the right be sure to pull the hilt in to the right chest. Contain the chest, bend the lower back, contract the belly, and compress the torso to gather power.

- To chop you must draw a circle with the hands, first up, then forward, then down, and then back in towards the body. Lengthen the torso as you raise the hands. Extend the arms as you reach the hands forward. Settle the elbows as you lower the hands. Tuck in the belly and press the head up as you pull the hands in. In this way you use the whole body throughout the strike. The sword blade does not simply chop down, but saws or slices in towards the body at the end of the action.

Turn around: Gather power as you hook-in and lift the sword. Launch power as you turn around and chop. Transfer power from the lower back to the shoulders, from the shoulders to the arms, and from the arms to the blade. The right hand draws a circle above the head, so the hand moves the hilt, transferring the action and power to the blade. As the hand arrives at the upper front, it rotates to turn the blade to standing in preparation for the forward chop.

BREATHING CYCLE FOR SWORD CHOP

- Inhale as you advance and hook, whether hooking up or down.

- Exhale as you step forward and chop. Settle the *qi* to the *dantian*.

Use long and deep breathing when practising slowly. Use a long inhalation and a short, sharp exhalation when practising quickly.

PRACTICAL APPLICATIONS FOR SWORD CHOP

- The sword is a relatively short and light weapon, so this needs to be taken into account when applying its techniques. The blade is narrow and thin with a sharp tip and two sharp edges, so its movements are light and agile. Because of its structure you should avoid clashing directly with an opponent's weapon. Techniques should be done firmly and gently – never with overt force, but not weak, either. You need deft power with a confident attitude to play the sword.

Chop: This is a chop down from above, and so is an attack. The target is the opponent's head, hand or arm, or body. You can turn a defense into an attack by directly chopping down on an opponent's straight oncoming weapon. To chop an opponent's weapon you must first step aside so that the sword chops down a bit at an angle, crossing with the weapon. As soon as you make contact with the weapon, advance to pierce, scoop or slice up. Do not be content with one strike, but always continue with successive attacks without giving the opponent any breathing space. If you can seriously hurt him then he will lose the capacity to fight.

Hook down and chop: Looking at this movement, the hook down to left or right is a defensive move, defending yourself from a straight stab towards or below your centre. You cannot use the thin, light and short blade to directly block, so the hook is a technique that follows along the line of action to deflect from your midline. You must retreat or dodge to the side while hooking down. Then you advance to chop, moving in with the body and sword simultaneously. Chop to the head, body, or arm. You can chop either with a one handed grip or a two handed grip. Ordinarily the one handed grip is used as it is agile, but the two handed grip is much stronger and is used for real combat.

Hook up and chop: This primarily defends against a high stab. First scoop, then hook. When you scoop up, don't go past your head. When you hook back don't go past your shoulder. This technique will defend against a straight stab from almost any weapon. You need to step a bit to the left when hooking on the right side, to dodge the attack. Touch the opponent's weapon with the scooping action, then slide along it with the hooking action to deflect it and draw it into the empty space. The immediately follow up, sliding along his weapon to chop his hand or body. This attack depends on getting in quickly with the feet, body, and hands. Getting in close with ferocity lengthens the range of the sword.

- The chop can also be combined with other techniques. For example, you can first chop onto the opponent's weapon and immediately follow up with a step in pierce to his chest. Or you can first chop down then and then snap the wrist up to cut his hand or arm. Or you can follow the chop with a step in crossing cut, or with a slice up, to slice the opponent's chest, head, hands or arm. You must be able to follow up the chop smoothly with many techniques to take advantage of whatever opportunity presents. 'When the technique changes in the heart, the method comes out in the hands.'

- When you do the hook up or hook down you should be ready to advance or retreat as needed, but you will usually retreat. You need to react to whether or not the opponent gets into your zone of defense. To have the appropriate reaction time you need to recognize 'old and young.' 'Old' is when the opponent gets too deeply into your zone, and 'young' is when he doesn't get in enough. In an 'old' situation, you haven't defended on time. In a 'young' situation the opponent can change easily. So this is the window of opportunity that you need to master. You must react when the opponent's weapon gets thirty centimetres into your zone of defense. As soon as the opponent's weapon has entered your zone you must stick your sword to his weapon. As his weapon advances you follow his force to draw him off target. If he retreats then you can go along with this and advance, stabbing his arm or body. When using the hook you must pay attention to the opponent's balance; if he hasn't entered deeply into the attack then you must not attempt an attack, but prepare to defend against a second or third attacking technique. Use agile stepping and tight defensive measures to protect yourself. Of course, 'saying is not doing.' As Sunzi said: "There are no fixed moves in the opponent's weapon, just as there is no fixed shape in water. You must change with the opponent to gain victory."

THE POEM ABOUT SWORD CHOP

劈剑技法最平长，左右上下挂劈忙。上步抢劈随身走，劈中带刺内中藏。

The most common technique of the sword is the chop.

Hook left or right, up or down, and follow up with a chop.

Step in with a swinging chop to follow the opponent.

There is a hidden draw and sawing slice in the chop.

SWORD DRILL

INTRODUCTION TO SWORD DRILL, *ZUAN JIAN*

Sword drill gets its name from the empty hand drill of the five elements. When drill is done as a hand technique the fist rotates as it moves forward and up. When done as a sword technique, drill uses a twisted grip. The right hand rotates to turn the under edge of the blade as the blade pierces forward, to complete a drilling action. The rotation turns the under edge of the blade up for the high drill or forward for the low drill. For the <u>low</u> pierce the right palm is rotated away from the thumb so that the under edge of the blade is angled forward and the sword tip points forward and down, usually in a right, or aligned, stance. For the <u>high</u> pierce the palm is rotated towards the thumb to turn the under edge of the blade up and the tip forward and up, usually in a left, or reverse, stance.

The combination for drill is *right stance drill, left stance drill, turn around drill,* and *closing move.* The right low drill combination contains an entangle with a lift. The left high drill combination contains a wrap with a draw. The low pierce is to the knee, while the high pierce is to the head.

2a Right Stance Drill   yòubù zuānjiàn   右步钻剑

Start from *on guard*. Continue with *left advance, entangle and lift; Right step forward, low pierce.*

ACTION 1: Advance the left foot a half-step and follow in the right foot by the left ankle. Rotate the right palm away from the thumb to bring the under edge of the blade forward. Lift the right elbow to lift the blade with the arm bent, and draw the hand up and back to in front of the right shoulder. Keep the left hand at the right wrist, following along with the action of the right hand. This action will make the sword tip circle counterclockwise left, down, right, and up, finishing angled forward and down at belly height. At this point, turn the body a bit to the right. The left elbow is in front of the chest. Look at the sword tip. (image 2.21)

ACTION 2: Take a long step forward with the right foot and follow in a half-step with the left foot to take a *santi* stance. Thrust the right hand in an inverted grip forward and down to chest height as the right foot lands, to pierce with the sword tip to front at knee height. Reach the right shoulder forward and almost fully extend the arm. The thumb / forefinger web of the right hand is forward and down. Swing the left hand up to the left of the head to brace out with the arm, keeping it rounded. Look past the sword tip. (image 2.22)

Pointers

- ○ Complete the circling entanglement with the blade as the left foot advances.

- ○ Complete the low pierce as the right foot steps forward. The power must reach to the sword tip. Be sure to rotate the right hand into an inverted grip so that the under edge of the blade is turned forward. The right hand must control the sword blade so that the tip pierces forward and down. You may brace the thumb against the guard to prevent the sword tip from dropping.

2b Left Stance Drill   zuǒbù zuānjiàn   左步钻剑

Right advance, entangle and draw; Left step forward, twisted pierce to the throat.

ACTION 1: Advance the right foot a half-step and follow in the left foot to the right ankle. Bend the right leg and keep the knees together. Bring the left hand to the right wrist. Circle the right hand to make the sword tip circle left and then up to the right. When the tip arrives up, bend the right arm and draw the hand back to beside the right shoulder and turn the body a bit to the right. (image 2.23)

Then rotate the right palm towards the thumb and bring it down to the waist, palm up, turning the under edge of the blade up. Keep the sword level and pointing forward at all times during these actions. Bend the waist and settle the chest, turning slightly right. Look past the sword tip.

ACTION 2: Take a long step forward with the left foot and follow in a half-step with the right foot. Use a spiral grip and extend the right hand in front of the chest to pierce forward with the palm heart up. The under edge of the blade will be on top, the tip at head height, the arm slightly bent, and the right hand at chest height. Swing the left hand up to the left side, above the head, arm rounded to brace out. Reach the right shoulder forward slightly. Press the head up. Look past the sword tip. (image 2.24)

 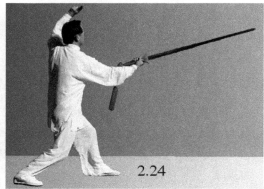

Pointers

- o Complete the entangling circle and draw back with the blade as the right foot advances.

- o Complete the pierce as the left foot steps forward. Both feet and hands must work together to balance the power.

- Connect to *right stance drill*, and repeat right and left until you run out of space.

2c Drill Turn Around

zuānjiàn zhuànshēn   钻剑转身

Using the *left stance drill* as example. *Turn and crossing cut; Right withdraw, entangle and lift; Right advance, low pierce.*

ACTION 1: Hook-in the left foot on the spot to turn around 180 degrees to the right to face back in the way from which you came. Hook-out the right foot so that it points straight, and shift onto the right leg to take a bow stance. Lower the left hand to the right wrist and rotate the right palm away from the thumb so that the palm faces down and the blade is horizontal and flat. Brandish the sword as the body turns, to cut horizontally back at chest height. Bring the right hand to the right front. Swing the left hand horizontally to shoulder height at the left. Look forward after you have turned around. (image 2.25)

ACTION 2: Shift back to the left leg, bending it, and withdraw the right foot a half-step, touching the toes down. Draw the blade in a flat circle up, left and down. Keep the left hand on the right wrist. First rotate the right palm towards the thumb to turn the palm up, then circle the hand while rotating the palm away from the thumb so that the blade tip points down. Bend the right arm and lift the elbow, bringing the hand in front of and above the right shoulder so that the blade is angled down and forward, and the tip at waist height. Look past the tip. (image 2.26)

ACTION 3: Step the right foot straight forward and advance the left foot a half-step. Extend the right arm forcefully forward and down, palm facing right at chest height, to pierce the blade tip to knee height. Swing the left hand up above the head at the left, bracing out with the arm rounded. Look past the tip. (image 2.27)

Pointers

- Complete the turn as one move.

- Complete the hook-in step and horizontal cut with force. Transfer power from your waist to your arm to the body of the blade, cutting flat around to the rear. Be sure to shift onto the right leg when you hook-in and turn around, and reach with the torso and the arm to cut. Pretend you are cutting an opponent behind you.

- The pointers for *withdraw and lift*, and *advance and pierce down* are the same as above. The only difference is that the right palm first needs to rotate towards the thumb and circle. Once the sword tip is pointing down to the left, then rotate the right palm away from the thumb. The right hand draws a small circle to make the sword tip draw a large circle. The movement must be coordinated, tightly knit, and be connected throughout the whole body.

2d Drill Closing Move   zuānjiàn shòushì   钻剑收势

If starting from *left* drill.

ACTION: Retreat the left foot a half-step and shift to the right leg, bending the right

leg and extending the left leg. Pull the
right hand back to the right shoulder,
rotating the palm away from the thumb to
face forward, to draw the sword straight
back. The sword blade is at shoulder
height, the blade standing. Open the left
hand and then take the guard in the hand,
palm facing forward. Look at the sword tip.
(image 2.28)

If starting from _right_ drill.

ACTION: Retreat the right foot behind the left and shift to the right leg, bending the
right leg and extending the left leg. (image 2.29)

- The rest of _closing move_ is the same as sword _chop closing move_.

Pointers

    o   Whether the left or right foot is forward, the <u>right</u> foot moves back and the
<u>right</u> hand pulls the sword back. When the left foot is forward the hand
must rotate as it pulls back, so be sure to keep the blade flat. Be firm and
stable when taking the hilt in the left hand. Lift the left elbow so that the flat
of the blade is pressed along the outside of the forearm.

    o   The entire movement must be connected and well anchored, and must be
focused to the end. The upper and lower actions must be coordinated. Be
sure to show clarity in the eyes.

PROBLEMS OFTEN MET IN SWORD DRILL

PROBLEM 1: During the _left advance entangle and lift_ action of _right drill_, the student
draws too large a circle with the sword tip as he does the counterclockwise
circle with the blade. This results in the blade moving stiffly with poor
coordination, as well as being an ineffective technique.

CORRECTIONS: The main reason for moving stiffly or with poor coordination is
that the student is holding the hilt too tightly, which makes the wrist very stiff.
The student must learn to loosen up the wrist, and adjust to use the grip

appropriate to each movement and technique. For example, piercing needs a spiral grip, chopping needs a full grip, lifting needs a pincer grip, cutting needs a full grip, and slicing needs a spiral grip.

PROBLEM 2: The student drops the tip during the *step forward inverted grip low pierce* of *right drill*. The tip hangs, with not enough forward piercing action.

CORRECTIONS: The student must understand that this is a pierce to the knee, not the foot, so the tip must pierce forward and down, not just down. The student may not have enough wrist strength to pierce when the wrist is rotated in this way. He should reach the wrist forward and grip the butt end of the hilt firmly with the ring and little fingers. This will help him to control the direction of the sword tip. If this grip does not solve the problem, he may slide the thumb onto the guard to lift the front end of the hilt and grip firmly with the other fingers.

PROBLEM 3: The student has no power in the *low pierce*.

CORRECTIONS: Poor feeling for the *low pierce* causes this to be an awkward action. The student must practise quick and long stepping. When launching power, he should turn the waist, reach the shoulder forward and extend the arm. He must focus on applying power in a sequential and integrated way. First advance one foot, then prepare power in the waist and turn, reach the shoulder forward, extend the arm, so that when the other foot lands the sword tip arrives. If he pierces in this way then the sword will have power.

PROBLEM 4: During the *right advance entangle and draw back* action of *left drill* the student makes too big a circle with the right hand, and separates the actions of entangling and drawing.

CORRECTIONS: The student must first understand the action. The technique entangle uses the fore section and tip of the blade, while that of draw uses the midsection of the blade. He must first entangle and then draw, but the entangling action contains a draw, and draw is the continuation of the entangle. So these two techniques must be done as one action. The method of correction is to repeat this technique over and over to get a feel for it.

PROBLEM 5: During the *left step forward twisted pierce to the throat* of *left drill*, the student lets the blade wobble, and the tip has no point of focus. Another error is to not twist the blade over sufficiently, so that the under edge is not on top.

CORRECTIONS: The tip will never pierce effectively if the blade wobbles. Firstly, the student must step firmly. When he extends the right arm he should keep a slight bend in the elbow, reach the shoulder forward, and roll the elbow in, so that the hand can rotate more easily. He must rotate the hand fully so that the under edge of the blade is on top. When practising this technique, the student must concentrate on leading the tip forward, following it with the arm, and using the power of the whole body to urge it forward. He must seek out the meaning of the words lead, follow, and urge.

POWER GENERATION FOR SWORD DRILL

Advance, entangle and lift: The left foot advances and the sword lifts and draws back, so you must first rotate the palm away from the thumb to circle the sword left and down to entangle. Then lift the elbow and pull the right shoulder back to lift and draw the sword. The body of the blade should feel like it is sticking to an opponent's weapon and drawing it back. The movement must be weighty and well anchored, and the mind must be focused. The body sits down slightly at this time.

Step forward, low pierce: Turn the waist, reach the shoulder forward, and extend the arm to pierce down. The left hand must swing to the upper rear left to give an equal and opposite force to balance the action of the right hand and give more power to the blade that is piercing to the lower front right. This balances the diagonal power line so that the body and weapon are as one. The posture is rounded, the power is full, the movement is smooth, and the strength is integrated.

Advance, wrap and draw: Keep the bodywork gentle and rounded. Transfer power from the waist to the shoulder, from the shoulder to the elbow, from the elbow to the hand, and from the hand to the blade. When drawing the sword back be sure to turn the under edge of the blade up. When lowering the hand to the waist, rotate the palm towards the thumb gradually as it lowers. Contain the chest and store power in the lower back, so that the move has a hidden technique of wrapping and pressing down. Keep the sword tip pointing forward at all times throughout the action.

Step forward, twisted pierce to the throat: Rotate the blade as it pierces forward, so that it finishes with the blade standing and the under edge up. Keep the waist relaxed and turn, reaching the shoulder and elbow forward in a settled way. Just as the sword pierces, urge forward from the lower back to the shoulder, shoulder to elbow, elbow to hand, and hand to sword, sequentially and consecutively to transer the power of the whole body into the tip of the blade.

BREATHING CYCLE FOR SWORD DRILL

- Inhale as you entangle and lift, or entangle and draw.

- Exhale as you step forward or advance and pierce.

Breathe slowly, deeply, and evenly when practising slowly, still breathing out for the piercing actions.

PRACTICAL APPLICATIONS FOR SWORD DRILL

- The main targets of drill are the throat and the knee. The high drill can target the head, face, neck, throat or chest. The low drill can target the belly, knee, thigh, or shank. The right drill withdraws, entangles and lifts, then advances to pierce the knee. The left drill advances, entangles and draws, then steps forward to pierce the throat.

Right drill entangles, lifts, then pierces down. The entangling action is defensive, used when the opponent stabs a bit below your centre. You may retreat, advance, or dodge, whatever is appropriate, so your footwork must be quick and agile. If the opponent comes in strongly you should retreat your rear foot then withdraw your lead foot. Connect the front half of your blade to the opponent's weapon and deflect it to the right and down, encircling it as you move. Connect your blade to use the lift and draw to stick and draw the opponent's weapon back to take him off target. Then you can advance and pierce to the knee or thigh. As it says in the classics, "Move like a running rabbit with your body like the wind; eyes are bright, hands are fast, body and feet are light."

Pay attention whether you advance, retreat, or withdraw that you are using the footwork to keep out of the way of the opponent's attack, and using the sword to gently lead his weapon. Never use a sword to strike or block directly against another weapon. The blade of a sword is easily damaged by hard contact with another weapon. This is what the classics mean when they say: "skill is in dodging, control to the angle."

Left drill advances, entangles, draws back, and then steps forward to pierce up. The entangle, draw, twist and press down takes care of the defensive needs, and the pierce to the throat is the attack. The sword tip circles leftward and upward to knock aside a stab to the upper body. At the same time stick the sword blade to his weapon and use his force to draw him in, then twist your arm and rotate your wrist to wrap up and press his weapon down. As he tries to get away, step forward quickly to pierce to his head or chest. When you are dodging out of the way be sure to press his weapon down, pressing it forward.

Turn around is a method of dealing with an attack from behind. When you cut horizontally as you turn, you can slice the opponent's chest or head if he has come within your space. You must turn and slice quickly. If the opponent has not come in close then you at least hinder his attack with your cut. Once you have turned then you can use whatever technique is appropriate to attack. For either of these situations to work you must be sure to cut around directly behind you as you turn, and control the momentum of the sword, keeping control of the focus and direction. If you swing too wide then you will leave a gap for the opponent to enter.

- Whether or not the drill can be applied effectively depends on the person. You must continuously examine the technique and practise with a partner in order to progress.

THE POEM ABOUT SWORD DRILL

钻剑技法快中求，巧闪旁扼步法游。绞剑上提下刺膝，缠带裹压反刺喉。

The techniques of sword drill are quick and seek out the midline,

Stepping as if swimming, dodge and control off to theside.

Entangle with the sword to lift up and pierce down to the knee,

Coil and draw, wrap and press, and pierce with an inverted blade to the throat.

SWORD THRUST

INTRODUCTION TO SWORD THRUST, *BENG JIAN*

Sword thrust is based on the empty hand technique of driving punch, or crushing fist, which is a relatively level straight punch with the right or left fist. So as long as the blade edge is standing and the tip pierces straight forward, the technique is considered a thrust. In sword terminology this is normally called a pierce, but in Xingyi, all weapons techniques are named after the empty hand technique that they resemble.[49]

Sword thrust uses the same integrated power as the crushing punch, sending the power of the whole body out to the tip of the sword. The main technique during the thrust practice is the straight pierce itself. Within the combinations are hook, check, entangle, and draw. There is also a distinction between single handed thrust and double handed thrust – the single handed being quick and agile, and the double handed being strong and aggressive.

There are variations in the way the sword thrust is done in different regions and between different teachers, but all use a straight piercing action. I will describe two variations. One is *hook, check, thrust,* the other is *entangle, draw, thrust.*

METHOD ONE: HOOK, CHECK, THRUST

3a Right Hook, Check, Thrust   yòu guà bō bēngjiàn   右挂拨崩剑

Start from *on guard. Left advance, right hook, check; Right step forward, pierce.*

ACTION 1: Advance the left foot a half-step and follow in the right foot to by the left ankle. Bend the legs, keeping the knees together. Open the left hand and grasp the hilt behind the right hand. Cock both wrists and bend the arms, pulling the hilt back beside the right waist so that the sword tip draws a circle up and back to finish pointing up with the blade vertical at the right side. Do not allow the blade to touch the body – keep it about twenty centimetres away. Settle the chest and tuck in the belly, tuck the elbows in to the ribs, turn the torso slightly to the right. Look forward. (image 2.30)

ACTION 2: Bring the hands, still both on the hilt, up to the solar plexus, which brings the sword tip down to chest height. The tip now points forward with the blade horizontal and standing. Take a long step forward with the right foot and follow in the left foot to behind the right foot, into the same short stance used for the crushing punch. The weight is on the right leg, the legs are slightly bent. Forcefully thrust forward with both hands, almost fully extending the arms, to pierce forward at chest height, sending the power to the sword tip. Press the head up and look forward. (image 2.31)

2.30   2.31

---

[49] Translator's note: I have translated *beng* as thrust, rather than using something like 'crushing sword.' In this way the term is different from the usual word, pierce [*ci*], but still makes sense in English and gives the feeling of the technique. In the book, for clarity, the full technique is called sword thrust, while the stabbing action alone is called pierce.

3b Left Hook, Check, Thrust   zuǒ guà bō bēngjiàn   左挂拨崩剑

Right advance, right hook, check; Left step forward, pierce.

ACTION 1: Advance the right foot a half-step and follow in the left foot without touching down. Bend the arms and cock the wrists to bring the hands in to the left side of the waist, tucking the elbows to the ribs. This circles the sword tip forward, up, and then back to hook up and check with the tip up and the blade vertical in front of the body. Settle the shoulders down, contain the chest, tuck in the belly, press the head up, and look forward. Place the sword blade about twenty centimetres in front of the left shoulder. (image 2.32)

ACTION 2: Take a long step forward with the left foot and follow in the right foot to just behind the left foot, in the same stance as used in the crushing punch. Lift both hands to the chest to bring the sword tip forward and down to chest height. As the left foot lands, thrust forward forcefully with both hands to pierce forward at chest height. Keep the arms slightly bent, release tension in the shoulders, settle the elbows, and send your power to the sword tip. Press the head up and look past the sword tip. (images 2.33 and 2.33 from the front)

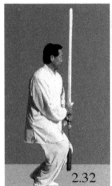 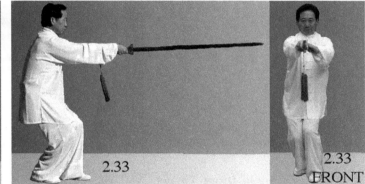

Pointers

- Cock the wrists to hook up and check as the foot advances, whether left or right.

- Thrust forward as you take the long step forward. Make the step long and quick, and land as the sword completes the pierce. Send power out to the sword tip.

- There are two actions but they must be done as one movement without a break. The forward step must be quick and go for distance. The landing must be stable, and the follow-in step must be quick.

- Use a full grip for the hook up and a spiral grip for the pierce.

METHOD TWO: ENTANGLE, DRAW, THRUST

3c Right Entangle, Draw, Thrust   yòu jiǎo dài bēngjiàn   右绞带崩剑

Start from *on guard. Left advance, entangle and draw to the right; Right step forward, pierce.*

ACTION 1: Advance the left foot a half-step and follow in the right foot to the right ankle. Bend both legs and keep the knees together, standing firmly on the left leg. Place the left hand at the right wrist. Rotate the right palm away from the thumb and lift it, then draw it back on the right side to in front of the right shoulder, drawing a counter-clockwise circle with the sword tip. Draw the sword back on the right side, tucking the left elbow in at the solar plexus. Turn the torso slightly to the right. The sword tip has drawn a small circle in front, keeping the blade horizontal. Look past the sword tip. (image 2.34)

ACTION 2: Take a long step forward with the right foot and follow in a long half-step with the left foot to about a foot length behind the right foot, putting most weight on the left leg. Extend the arms forward to pierce with a standing blade. You may grasp the hilt in both hands or keep the left hand at the right wrist. Keep the arms slightly bent and the blade horizontal at chest height. Reach the right shoulder forward slightly and send power to the sword tip. Press the head up and look past the sword tip. (image 2.35)

3d   Left Entangle, Draw, Thrust   zuǒ jiǎo dài bēngjiàn   左绞带崩剑

Right advance, entangle and draw to the left; Left step forward, pierce.

ACTION 1: Advance the right foot a half-step and follow in the left foot to beside the right without touching down. Place the left hand on the right wrist. Draw a clockwise circle at the front with the sword tip, then draw it back to the left. Rotate the right palm towards the thumb and draw it back to in front of the left shoulder, palm up and elbow tucked in to protect the heart. Turn the torso slightly to the left. Keep the blade horizontal. Look past the sword tip. (image 2.36)

ACTION 2: Take a long step forward with the left foot and follow in with the right foot. Extend the right hand forward to pierce the sword straight to chest height. Keep the right arm slightly bent. Either support the butt with the left palm or place it on the right wrist. Press the head up and look past the sword tip. (image 2.37)

Pointers

- ○ The footwork of the second method is the same as that of the first – bring the rear foot through to step forward into the pierce. The only difference is that method one uses a hook up and method two uses an entangling action with the sword. The hook moves directly back while the entangle circles back, so they are different uses and power applications.

- ○ Complete the entangling draw to the side as the foot advances. Draw back to the right when the left foot advances, and draw back to the left when the right foot advances.

- ○ As the foot steps through to pierce, complete the action of the foot with the sword, both arriving at the same time.

- ○ Complete the actions as one movement, do not hesitate between them.

3e Thrust Turn Around   bēngjiàn zhuànshēn   崩剑转身

Continue the thrust combination until you run out of space. If the <u>right</u> foot is in front then step the <u>left</u> foot forward with a hook-in step. If the <u>left</u> foot is forward then hook it in on the spot. *Left hook-in, turn around, horizontal cut; Right crossing heel kick; Resting stance, chop.*

ACTION 1: Hook-in the left foot outside the right toes and shift onto the left leg. Bend the left leg slightly and grip the ground with the toes to stand firmly, and lift the right foot by the left ankle. Bring the sword back to in front of the left chest, rotating the right palm down to place the blade flat with the edges to left and right. Turn the body around 180 degrees to face back in the way from which you came. Bring the right hand around with the body turn, so that the sword cuts horizontally across from left to right in front of the body, finishing at the right side at shoulder height. Open the left hand out horizontally to brace out to the left at shoulder height. Keep the arms slightly bent. Look forward. (image 2.38)

ACTION 2: Lift the right knee and dorsi-flex the right ankle, turning the foot out. Kick forcefully forward and up to waist height. Stand firmly on the left leg. Look forward. (image 2.39)

ACTION 3: Land the right foot forward, keeping it hooked out, and follow in the left foot a half-step. Squat on the left leg with the heel up and slightly extend the right leg, to sit into a resting stance with the weight mostly on the left leg. Lift the right hand above the head while rotating it palm towards the thumb to hang the hilt. This causes the sword to brandish down and then up above the head. Bring the left hand in above the head to settle onto the right wrist. Once the right foot has landed, chop forward and down with the sword until the blade is horizontal at waist height. The right hand finishes in front of and above the right knee. The left shoulder is forward of the right shoulder, so that the torso is turned about forty-five degrees. Press the head up. Look past the sword tip. (image 2.40)

2.39

2.40

- Continue on with *advance, hook and thrust.*

Pointers

o Turn around in one movement without pausing. Stop for an instant in the resting stance, showing stability in the stance.

o *Sword thrust turn around* is the same general move as the empty hand turn around *leopard cat turns over whilst climbing a tree.* It consists of a hook-in step with a wrist turn, a turn around with a horizontal cut, a crossing kick, and a resting stance with a chop. There is only a turn around to the right, not to the left. Be sure to turn around quickly. Be sure, also, to keep the head up and back straight. The left hook-in step must be well hooked and placed outside the right foot, so that the body can get turned around and the kick can be done comfortably.

o Swing the left hand out horizontally as the sword cuts across, to assist power transfer to the right hand.

o Tuck in the belly when lifting the right foot, and tuck in the hip when kicking. Do not throw the hip forward into the kick. Kick at least to waist height, but it is best to kick to shoulder height. Kick as soon as the sword tip has passed the midline in its cut. You must not kick too early or too late – kick just as the sword passes.

o The *resting stance chop* is also called *dragon model chop.* You may half-sit in a scissor stance if need be. When you land from the right kick, be sure to advance the foot as much as possible to stomp forward and down. Complete the chop down as you land into the resting stance. Press the head up as the sword chops down. Gain stability by pressing the legs tightly together and tucking the arms into the ribs. Release tension in the shoulders, press the head up, and chop down the midline.

3f   Thrust Closing Move   bēngjiàn shòushì   崩剑收势

Continue back to your starting place and turn around, then close. It doesn't matter which foot is forward. *Right retreat, hold the sword; Stand at attention and transfer the sword; Hold the sword behind in the left hand.*

ACTION: Retreat the right foot behind the left and shift back to the right leg without moving the left foot, to sit into a *santi* stance. Bend the right arm and bring the right hand in front of the right shoulder to pull the sword directly back. Open the left hand with the thumb down and palm out, bending the arm to place the hand on the guard. Hold the blade horizontal in front of the body at shoulder height with the blade standing. Turn the body a bit to the right and look past the sword tip. (image 2.41)

- The rest of the closing is the same as that of *sword chop closing move.*

PROBLEMS OFTEN MET IN SWORD THRUST

PROBLEM 1: The student hits himself with the blade when hooking up.

> CORRECTIONS: Remind the student that touching yourself with the blade of the sword is a grave error in swordplay, as the double edged blade can cut. The student should use a firm grip when cocking the wrist and bringing in the arm forcefully. He must focus on bringing the blade vertical; once the blade is vertical then he should bend the elbow and bring the arm in, keeping the hand in a tight full grip on the hilt to control any movement of the blade. The elbows must be brought tightly in to the ribs, as this also helps to keep the blade away from the body. The hilt should be about twenty centimetres away from the body, and the blade about thirty centimetres away from the shoulder.

PROBLEM 2: Three common errors in *entangle and draw back* are: the student draws too big a circle with the sword tip; he is too stiff when drawing back; he does not smoothly connect the entangling and the drawing back actions.

> CORRECTIONS: The entangle must be done with a supple wrist, using mostly the wrist for the action, so that the sword tip draws a circle about thirty centimetres in diameter. The draw back must be done with the waist drawing the arm back, then bending the arm to draw the sword back. Done in this way it cannot be stiff. Although entrap and draw are two different actions, they must be linked smoothly together. First entangle and then draw, but the entangling action contains a draw, and the drawing action contains an entangle. It really is one action with two parts.

PROBLEM 3: Three common errors in pierce are: the student overextends the arms to pierce; the sword tip wobbles with no point of focus; the sword does not arrive at the same time as the stepping forward foot lands.

CORRECTIONS: The student should keep about a 160 degrees bend in the elbow on the final pierce. In this way the power of the whole body can transfer through the arm, and it is also easier to change the technique for defense. The cause of the tip wobbling is usually that the sword and arm are not aligned, the arm and body are not united, the footwork is unstable and the body disunited. The student must grip the hilt firmly and extend the wrist, release tension in the shoulders and sink the elbows, tuck the elbows in to the ribs, contain the chest, stretch the upper back open, press the head up and lengthen the spine, and settle the *qi* to the *dantian.* He should first practise slowly to find all the requirements and then practise more quickly to find the power.

POWER GENERATION FOR SWORD THRUST

Hook and check: The lead foot lands as the hands grip the hilt to bring the sword up and back – hook up is the main technique and check is the secondary technique. That is, when hooking up, there is a hidden power that knocks aside to left or right. When the left foot advances the sword has a slight checking power to the right, and when the right foot advances the sword has a slight checking power to the left. This should not be too large or too obvious a movement. Sit the wrists to bring the blade upright, and bend the arms to bring the blade back to hook. Turn the waist slightly to right or left to take the blade slightly to the side for the hidden check. You may grasp with the hands together or with them spread on the hilt, the right on top and the left underneath. Be careful to stop the blade about twenty centimetres from the body – a sword blade must never hit the body.

Entangle and draw: When the sword 'entangles' in front of the face, whether clockwise or counter-clockwise, both the tip and the hilt should form vertical circles. The central portion is the balance point as the hilt and tip circle. The central balance point stays at all times on the midline of the body as the tip forms a larger circle and the hilt a smaller one. When drawing to the left or right, draw the sword from the waist and arms. Use the strength of the wrists to make stirring circles, and use the strength of the body for the draw back. Sit the body down slightly when drawing back, to gather power.

Pierce: The pierce must be completed exactly as the forward stepping foot lands. The hands must first lift to bring the tip of the sword forward. At this time bend the waist, contain the chest and bring in the arms to gather power. Extend the wrists to pierce. To pierce, send the sword tip forward, drive from the feet into the body, lengthen the back and settle the shoulders. Urge the hands forward from the elbows, and the elbows from the shoulders, breathing out and settling the *qi* to the *dantian* so that the power reaches to the sword tip, causing the blade to quiver. Lower the hands slightly and lengthen the back when piercing the sword tip forward. Lower the sword with a gathering power. Press the head up with the final pierce. The classics say, "Compress the body when rising and lengthen the body when landing." You need to find the real meaning behind this by feeling it inside. The pierce must be forceful, and the power launch done with an exhalation and sinking of the *qi* to the *dantian.* The power of the whole body is integrated and shows Xingyi sword's powerful flavour and unflinching demeanor.

Turn around: Cut horizontally around behind you, turning right, using the waist to turn around. Transfer power from the waist to the shoulder, from the shoulder to the arm, and from the arm to the sword, to draw a 370 degree circle with the sword tip. The point of focus of the cut is directly behind the body, so you should wait until the blade gets to the left side of the body before applying force. Then, once the blade has crossed the midline, don't use any more force – let momentum cut across to the right. Control the sword's direction to prepare for the following move.

Breathing Cycle For Sword Thrust

- Inhale as you advance whether doing a hook or an entangle and draw.

- Exhale as you step forward and pierce, exhaling to launch power. Use a short and powerful exhalation, and settle the *qi* to the *dantian*.

Practical Applications For Sword Thrust

- The key element of sword thrust is the straight forward pierce. Its goal is to stab the opponent's chest, but of course you can stab the head or any other part. You should pierce to an area that can cause serious harm, to a key place that at least takes away his ability to fight. Of course, you pierce to an open area; tactics do not always allow you to choose your ideal target.

First method: The defensive move is *hook up and check*, which also sets up the attack. If the opponent stabs to your head or chest you can withdraw your lead foot and knock away his weapon so that it misses its target, and then advance to pierce his chest. If his weapon does not come in close you can hold your position, shifting back to prepare to attack. Similarly, you can adjust to the right or left as needed. You can also withdraw then advance, or withdraw and step forward, switching feet. You can also do exactly as in the practice, first advancing the lead foot and then stepping the other foot through. As long as your footwork is skillful, fast, and nimble you can adapt your technique to the situation. Effective defense also depends on the close coordination between your body and the sword, and the tight connection between the techniques. When attacking, your footwork must be quick and your attitude must be intimidating.

Second method: The defensive move is *entangle and draw back* to left or right. The use of this technique is to encircle and entrap a weapon coming towards you, then stick to it and draw it back out of the way, causing it to miss your body. Then you can advance and pierce to the opponent's chest. Adjust your footwork according to the situation. If the opponent stabs to your chest you can withdraw your lead foot or you can advance it a half-step. If the opponent comes in very strongly you can retreat your rear foot, also withdrawing your lead foot to get out of the way. Encircle his weapon with the front or middle section of your sword blade, then keep your blade stuck to his weapon and draw it back so that it misses your body. Then as he tries to take his weapon away, follow with a step forward and pierce to his chest. This movement must be quick and aggressive, and your intention must be to penetrate right through.

- Use one hand or two on the hilt to pierce. Two handed is stronger.

Sword thrust turn around horizontal cut is a method of dealing with an attack from behind. The horizontal cut can either cut the opponent or swing across to knock away the opponent's weapon. When thinking of connecting with the opponent's weapon, cut the tip across at waist height. When thinking of cutting the opponent, cut across with the hilt at shoulder height. If the opponent continues to come in, kick him with your right foot, then immediately advance and chop with a double handed hold. The chopping action also contains a sawing, or inward slicing action. Chop his weapon or body, whatever you can get.

- Just practising the techniques isn't enough to become skilled at using them. You must practise with a partner to develop the timing, strength, and speed needed for combat. Of course, skilled technique is important for combat, but just as important are well timed reactions, good judgment, the ability to adapt, and on overall feel for correct timing, spacing, and distance. You also need to develop combative awareness to develop and improve your courage and fighting ability.

THE POEM ABOUT SWORD THRUST

崩剑技法气势雄，步进身进向前冲。左右上挂须坐腕，摇身绞带刺其胸。

The bearing of the sword thrust is dauntless,

The footwork enters, the body enters, charging forward.

To hook up to left and right you must cock and press down the wrist,

Dodge the body, entangle and draw, pierce his chest.

SWORD SLASH

INTRODUCTION TO SWORD SLASH, *PAO JIAN*

Xingyi's sword slash is a slice on either side. The definition of slice is to use the under edge of the blade and slice up from below. A direct slice uses a normal grip and an inverted slice uses an inverted grip. Slice usually circles by one side of the body then continues forward and up. The wushu regulations define slice as: with a standing blade, slice forward and up from below, putting power to the forward section of the blade. A direct slice has the palm rotated towards the thumb, the palm up, and circles closely past the body before slicing out. An inverted slice is the same action, but with the palm rotated away from the thumb. Xingyi's left stance slash is a direct slice and right stance slash is an inverted slice. The footwork is the same as the empty hand pounding punch. The slicing action to left and right look similar to the pounding punch [*pao quan*], which is why this technique is called *pao jian*, here translated as slash. Xingyi's slash is not exactly like most slicing techniques – it contains a sculling and sawing action as well.

The key techniques for slash are: *advance, block up and draw* and *step forward slice.* Block up and draw is a combination of a block up and a draw back. Block up uses a standing blade that moves across to block up with the blade higher than the head, power reaching the body of the blade, palm in or out, depending on which side you are blocking. Draw back uses a standing blade or a flat blade and withdraws at the side, either straight back or back and up, the power reaching the body of the blade.

4a   Right Stance Slash   yòubù pàojiàn   右步炮剑

Start from *on guard*. Continue with *left advance, left block up and draw; Right step forward, inverted slice.*

ACTION 1: Advance the left foot a half-step and follow in the right foot to beside the ankle. Place the left hand at the right wrist. Slice up to block up, then draw the sword back at the left side, rotating the right palm towards the thumb and bending the right elbow. The right hand, and thus the sword hilt, finishes near the left ear. The sword blade is standing, the tip slightly lower than the hilt and pointing directly forward. Use a full grip on the hilt. Turn the body a bit to the left, contain the chest and tuck in the belly. Look past the sword tip. (image 2.42)

ACTION 2: Take a long step diagonally forward and right with the right foot and follow in a half step with the left foot to take a *santi* stance. Bring the right hand left, down, and then right, diagonally forward, extending the arm to slice up. Keep the sword close to the left side then slice diagonally forward, rotating the right palm away from the thumb so that the palm turns out. Extend the right wrist and use a spiral grip on the hilt. Keep the right arm slightly bent and lift the elbow, finishing with the hand and sword hilt about ear height, the sword tip about chest height. Sit the body slightly down. Keep the left hand at the right wrist throughout. Put power to the forward section of the sword blade. Press the head up. Follow the movement of the sword with the eyes, then look forward past the tip. (image 2.43 and from the front)

Pointers

- o Complete the slicing block up on the left side as the left foot advances. Complete the inverted slice as the right foot steps forward. Complete all techniques as the leading foot lands.

- o The right stance slash is one move; do not stop on *advance and block up,* but continue directly through to the *step forward slice.*

4b Left Stance Slash   zuǒbù pàojiàn   左步炮剑

Right advance, right block up and draw; Left step forward, direct slice.

ACTION 1: Advance the right foot a half-step straight forward and follow in the left foot to beside the right ankle. Angle the sword tip to the left then swing it down, left, then right to block up. Do not stop here, but pull the hand back on the right side to the right ear. Keep the left hand on the right wrist throughout. The sword tip is angled towards the forward left, slightly lower than the hilt. Turn the body slightly to the right and look past the sword tip. (image 2.44)

ACTION 2: Take a long step to the forward left with the left foot and follow in a half-step with the right foot. Circle the sword back on the right side, around down to the waist. At this point release the left hand from the right wrist and swing it down then up past the chest to the forward left to above the left side of the head. Rotate the right palm towards the thumb to turn the palm up and slice diagonally to the forward left. Keep the right arm slightly bent, the hilt just above shoulder height, the sword tip angled to about chest height. Turn the body slightly left and reach the right shoulder forward. Press the head up. Follow the movement of the left hand at first, then look past the sword tip. (image 2.45)

Pointers

- o *Block up and draw back* must be completed as the lead foot advances a half-step. The *direct slice* must be completed as the stepping forward foot lands.

- o The body must be fully integrated with the sword, slashing right and left with complete power.

- To continue on to *right stance slash* from *left stance slash*, first advance the left foot a half-step and follow in the right foot without touching down. Replace the left hand on the right wrist. Lower the sword tip and then circle it to the forward right, then up to block up, pulling it back by the left of the head. The rest of the action is the same as described above.

4c Slash Turn Around   pàojiàn zhuànshēn   炮剑转身

From the <u>right</u> *stance slash. Right hook-in step, hook; Left step forward, direct slice.*

ACTION 1: Hook-in the right foot in front of the left toes and shift onto the right leg. Lift the left foot by the right ankle and turn around 225 degrees to the left to face back in the way from which you came. Place the left hand on the right wrist. Pivot around the right wrist to circle the sword tip down, left, up, and then forward. Look at the sword tip. (image 2.46)

ACTION 2: Take a long step to the forward left with the left foot and follow in a half- step with the right foot. Circle the left hand from the right side down, then diagonally up to the forward left. Rotate the right palm towards the thumb and slice the sword snug at the right side of the body, then forward and up. The left hand finishes above the left side of the head. The sword slice is the same as the direct slice described above. Follow tthe

left hand with the eyes, then look forward past the sword tip. (image 2.47)

From the *left stance slash. Left hook-in step, wrist cut; Turn around, right step forward, inverted slice.*

ACTION 1: Hook-in the left foot in front of the right toes and shift onto the left leg, lifting the right foot at the left ankle. Lower the left hand to the right wrist. Using the right wrist as pivot point, circle the sword tip down and back, keeping close to the right side of the body. Then circle the sword up and forward. Use a pincer grip. Look at the sword tip. (image 2.48)

ACTION 2: Turn the body 180 degrees to the right to face back in the way from which you came. Take a long step to the forward right with the right foot and follow in a half- step with the left foot. Bring the sword blade closely past the left side of the body to slice forward. (image 2.49)

Pointers

- Complete a wrist cutting action during the hook-in step. Keep your wrist supple and use a pincer grip. Hook-in the foot considerably.

- Turn around, step forward, and slice up all as one integrated action, without a pause.

- Be sure not to lower the head or bend the waist when turning around. Keep the spine upright and straight and press the head up. Turn around quickly, step forward for distance, and slice aggressively.

4d Slash Closing Move   pàojiàn shōushì   炮剑收势

On arriving back at the starting point, do *turn around* to face the original direction. It doesn't matter which foot is forward, just step the right foot back and shift back to the right leg. Pull the sword straight back until the right hand is in front of the right shoulder, palm rotated out with the blade flat. Turn the left palm out and take the hilt with an inverted grip. Look at the sword tip.

- The rest of *closing move* is the same as *sword chop closing move*.

PROBLEMS OFTEN MET IN SWORD SLASH

PROBLEM 1: During the slice up to either side the student is inaccurate in direction, with no point of focus or poorly timed power launch. The blade wobbles. This is a common error for beginners.

CORRECTIONS: Firstly, the slice should be done so that the tip points in the same direction as the leading foot. That is, to a forty-five degree angle, as the combination advances in a zigzag pattern. The student must keep the head upright and look in the direction of the sword. If the eyes are looking in the correct direction then the sword will go there – the eyes follow the sword but they also lead it. The main reason for a lack of focus, poor power launch, and wobbly blade is that the body and weapon are not working as an integrated unit. The student must do some post standing in the final slash position until the requirements are drilled into the body. Then he should practise slowly, and add speed only when ready.

PROBLEM 2: When going into the block and draw on either side, the student doesn't control the sword tip. That is, he misses the first action of the movement.

CORRECTIONS: Start out from the final move of slash then do the block and draw to each side. Pay particular attention to the sword tip, first circling down then to the left or right to block up, and then drawing back. The sword tip must point in the direction of the right or left slice.

PROBLEM 3: The student holds the hilt too tightly while trying to bring the slice through, so that the blade cannot stay close to the body.

CORRECTIONS: While slicing, use a spiral grip and keep the wrist supple, remembering to rotate the forearm and to keep a bend in the arm. The student should concentrate on the hilt when doing the slice, controlling the sword from the hilt. The power reaches to the middle section of the blade. The sword must stay close to either side of the body.

POWER GENERATION FOR SWORD SLASH

- To find the proper power you must respect the following principle: the completion of each move is the origin of the following move. Every action is a preparatory gathering of power for the action that follows.

Draw back: The blade comes across and blocks up. When it gets in front of the head then pull it back. You must use the body for this – draw the hand back with the waist. The right hand draws a small elliptical circle to make the sword tip draw a large one. Rotate the right palm towards the thumb when blocking up and drawing back to the rear left. Rotate the right palm away from the thumb when blocking up and drawing back to the rear right. Adjust the grip on the hilt as needed while moving the sword.

Inverted grip slice: The height to which you slice must have a point of focus, you cannot randomly slice up. The sword must pass closely by the left side of the body and then slice up to the front. Gather power in the body and then launch – perform a countermovement to load back prior to moving forward, and to load right prior to moving left. Take the sword diagonally to the rear left to gather power for the slice diagonally to the forward right. This makes the power flow smoothly and gives a strong slice. First gather power in the lower back then lengthen it. First close the shoulders then open them. Send power to the middle portion of the blade.

Direct grip slice: The sword needs to pass closely by the right side of the body before slicing forward. The right hand rotates towards the thumb while slicing, taking the hilt with a spiral grip. First draw the hilt forward, making sure not to strike the ground with the sword tip. Reach the right shoulder forward and use the left hand to assist in launching power. When launching power, sit the torso down slightly.

- You can also slash with a double handed grip. The single handed grip allows for agile movement, but the double handed grip is stronger.

- In the final instant of launching power, pull the shoulder back slightly using the body core to create a short 'one inch power' to perform a backward sawing, slicing action in the sword blade. This is a unique characteristic of Xingyi sword. This kind of fine detail cannot be achieved without the instruction of a skilled teacher and considerable, careful and attentive practice.

- The path of movement of the slice follows the hand and wrist, but the origin is at the shoulder. The power of the slice follows the shoulder and elbow, but the origin is at the waist. The position of the hilt is due to the agility of the hand and fingers, but the origin is at the wrist.

When brandishing the sword or cutting the wrist, the hand and wrist must rotate as the sword moves, turning gradually and smoothly. The wrist and grip must adjust easily. The grip must change to a full grip when launching power, respecting the principle of hitting with a firm grasp. This is common to all weapons.

BREATHING CYCLE FOR SWORD SLASH

- Inhale as you advance, block and draw on either side.

- Exhale as you step forward and slice.

This is the general coordination of breathing with the techniques done at normal speed. You may also take a long breath in and a short breath out to assist the power launch.

PRACTICAL APPLICATIONS FOR SWORD SLASH

- The main attack of the slash combination is the slice. This can be a slice to deflect the opponent's weapon, a slice to his hand, arm, or leg, or, combined with a step, a move in to slice his torso. The slice can be used to attack or defend. As a defense, it knocks the opponent's weapon, and as an attack it slices directly to the body.

But, should the opponent come at you chopping down strongly with a long weapon such as a staff or spear, the slice is not going to be an effective defense. The oncoming weapon is heavy and long while the sword is light, sharp and thin, and thus can't be used to directly hit something. In this case you should follow the principle; "Avoid hard force, enter into the smallest crack and the sword will see blood red." That is to say, the sword should slice dierectly to the target in one strike, avoiding touching the opponent's weapon.

- The footwork for slash uses the lead foot to enter or retreat according to the situation. If the opponent comes in strongly then you should retreat. If the opponent keeps his distance then you should enter. When entering, you can either enter directly or advance a bit to the side, again, according to the situation. You can slice when you advance, retreat, or step to either side. You can also step the rear foot through to get the body in even closer as you slice. In this case, you must drive in strongly, confidently, and quickly.

Right stance slash combines *advance left block up, draw back* with *step forward inverted slice*. Looking at its form and technique, the right hand circles and blocks to knock aside an opponent's weapon, this action both defending and preparing the way for your attack. While blocking up you draw back to the left, sticking to the opponent's weapon and leading it back so that it is drawn off target. While you are drawing back to the left this also puts you into the position for stepping forward with the inverted slice. If you can get in close then slice to his body, if not, then slice his hand or arm. The key lies in being courageous and quick. *Left stance slash* uses the same principle, just using a direct slice instead of an inverted slice.

- Practise sword slash with large movements, but apply it with small movements. Smaller movements are quicker. They say that the only technique that has no counter is speed. Train with large movements to find the power. That is to say, once you have the correct power, then any technique that slices up and forward from below, using the under edge of the blade to slice up, is a slash. You can slide along the opponent's weapon to cut his hand, cut his arm, cut into his belly, or dig into his chest. Once you can use the moves freely then it is like ignoring the opponent in front of you – the highest level of skill in combat.

Slash can be used as a separate technique or combined with others. It combines well with chop, drill, and thrust. If you have just completed a chop, then you can rotate the right palm away from the thumb to bring the under edge of the blade forward and up to slice. After slicing up you can quickly circle the wrist to chop forward. If you tried and missed with an inverted grip low pierce (drill) then you can quickly advance with a rising slice. If the opponent stabs at your lower body you can hook down and back and then slide along his weapon to slice his hand and into his groin or whatever. As it says in the art of war; "There are no fixed tactics, just as water has no fixed form. The secret is to adapt to the enemy and wrest victory."

THE POEM ABOUT SWORD SLASH

炮剑技法正反撩，斜身拗步劲透梢。架带身转随步走，撩在肩肘劲在腰。

The sword slash is either a direct or an inverted slice.

Angle the body and use a reverse stance for penetrating power to the tip.

Block up and draw back, turning the body and following the footwork.

Slice from the shoulder and elbow, getting power from the body core.

SWORD CROSSCUT

INTRODUCTION TO SWORD CROSSCUT, *HENG JIAN*

Sword crosscut is a type of horizontal cutting, plastering technique across to left and right. The wushu competition regulations define 'cut' as a horizontal cut with a flat blade to left or right between head and shoulder height, with the power reaching the body of the blade and the arm straight. 'Plaster' is defined as to draw a flat blade back from the front in a circular action to right or left between chest and abdomen height with the power reaching the body of the blade. Xingyi's crosscut combines these two techniques – it cuts transversely across and draws back with a plastering action. This makes the technique more devastating and increases the integration of the sword blade with the whole body. The transverse cut is done more with the hand and arm, while the plastering is done more with the waist and torso. Combining the two brings out the characteristics and flavour of Xingyi.

The key techniques for crosscut are: *Advance check and hook to left and right* and *Step forward crossing cut to left and right*. The actions and footwork are similar to the empty hand crossing fist, advancing in a zigzag pattern.

5a Right Stance Crosscut   yòubù héngjiàn   右步横剑

Start from *on guard. Left advance, right block and hook; Step forward, crossing cut.*

ACTION 1: Advance the left foot a half-step and follow in the right foot to the left ankle. Place the left hand at the right wrist. With the right hand, bring the hilt across in front of the body to block across to the right with the sword tip, hooking back, and then circle across to the left in front of the face. The hands draw a small circle in front of the body. Once the right hand has circled to the left side, rotate it to turn the palm down, change it to a spiral grip to place the sword blade flat, the edges to right and left. Follow the sword movement with the eyes, watching the sword tip. (image 2.50)

ACTION 2: Take a long step forward with the right foot to the forward front and follow in a half-step with the left foot, putting most weight on the right leg to take a *santi* stance. Grip the hilt in firmly and bring the sword across the body from the left to the right in a flat cutting action, using the whole arm, until the tip points to the forward right. Then bend the right arm to pull back with a plastering action, keeping the palm down. The hand is slightly lower than the shoulder and the sword tip is slightly higher than the shoulder. Keep the left hand on the right wrist throughout. Press the head up and look past the sword tip. You may pull the right hand back as far as the right side to increase the final sideways sawing power, but be sure to press the head up. (image 2.51)

2.50   2.51

Pointers

- ○ Complete the sword's circle in front of the body as the left foot advances. Pay attention to the positioning of the sword tip and hilt.

- ○ Complete the transverse cut as the right foot steps forward, using fully integrated power between the feet and the hands.

5b Left Stance Crosscut   zuǒbù héngjiàn   左步横剑

Right advance, left block and hook; Step forward, left crossing cut.

ACTION 1: Advance the right foot a half-step and follow in the left foot to the right ankle. Circle the sword tip to the front, then block to the left, and then hook back. Finally rotate the right palm up and take the sword past the face to the right. Keep the left hand on the right wrist throughout. The hands draw a small circle in front of the body at the forward right, the arms finishing bent in front of the chest. Follow the movement of the sword tip with the eyes. (image 2.52)

ACTION 2: Take a long step to the forward left with the left foot and follow in the right foot a half-step to take a *santi* stance. Take the hilt in a full grip and turn the palm up. Cut across from right to left with the blade flat and the arm extended. When the blade arrives at the forward left, bend the right arm and tuck the elbow into the solar plexus and lift the left hand to above the head at the left. The sword tip is slightly higher than the shoulder. Send the power to the fore section of the blade. Press the head up and settle the *qi* to the *dantian*. Follow the movement of the sword tip, then look past it. (image 2.53 and from the front)

Pointers

- o Coordinate the left and right block and hook with the half-step advance of the lead foot. Block to the right when the left foot advances. Block to the left when the right foot advances.

- o Coordinate the crossing cut with the forward step. Cut to the right when the right foot steps forward. Cut to the left when the left foot steps forward.

- o Each crosscut is one complete movement. Do not pause in the middle of the action. Keep the whole movement integrated.

- • Continue on repeating right and left crosscut until you run out of space.

5c Crosscut Turn Around   héngjiàn zhuànshēn   横剑转身

Turn around is essentially the same no matter which foot is forward. The leading foot will do a hook-in step to turn the body around. From <u>*left stance crosscut*</u>. *Left hook-in step, turn around, left block and hook; Right step forward, crossing cut.*

ACTION 1: Hook-in the left foot in front of the right toes and shift to the left leg, lifting the right foot at the left ankle and pressing the knees together. Hook-in a considerable angle to turn around 270 degrees to face back in the way from which you came. Press the left hand on the right wrist and bring the sword around with the body as it turns right, so that it cuts across from left to right, then hooks back, circling in front of the face and across to the left. The right palm rotates away from the thumb to turn the palm down, to cut with the blade flat across to the left. Follow the movement of the sword with the eyes. (image 2.54)

ACTION 2: Take a long step to the forward right with the right foot and follow in a half-step with the left foot. Cut the sword across from left to right in an arcing horizontal cut, the tip angled to the forward right, extending the right arm with the elbow slightly bent. Hold the hilt with a full grip, palm down. Finish the cut with the hand slightly lower and the tip slightly higher than the shoulder. Keep the left hand on the right wrist throughout. Press the head up and look past the tip. (image 2.55)

- From *right stance crosscut, turn around* is the same, just transpose right and left.

Pointers

- o Be sure to first hook the foot in then turn the body around. Take a good hook-in step. The foot must hook-in at the outside of the rear foot, pointing to the toes. Do not step too far away from the rear foot, as this will make the weight shift too extreme, causing instability. Coordinate the cut around of the sword with the rotation of the body. Press the head up to keep the body upright, and be sure to shift the weight. Be careful to not look down or bend at the waist.

- o The checking hook must be smooth, rounded, gentle, and well connected to the preceding move. Use the body to do the technique.

- o Complete the crossing cut as the foot steps forward, as one integrated movement. Use the action of the body turning to put power into the sword. Transfer power from the lower back to the shoulder, from the shoulder to the arm, and from the arm to the hand and thus to the sword. The crossing cut conceals a sawing, slicing in power.

5d Crosscut Closing Move   héngjiàn shōushì   横剑收势

No matter which foot is forward, the closing is essentially the same. From *right stance crosscut*, do *right retreat chop*.

ACTION: Retreat the right foot and shift back to the right leg to take a *santi* stance. Rotate the right palm away from the thumb to circle the sword tip forward, down, to the left side, to the right side, then up and forward to chop down in front. Keep the left hand on the right wrist throughout. (images 2.56, 2.57)

If from _left_ stance crosscut the first action is slightly different to get into _santi_ stance.

ACTION: Retreat the right foot a half-step then withdraw the left foot to in front of the right foot. Rotate the right hand to circle the sword tip forward, down, and to the right side, then up and forward to chop down. Advance the left foot a small step without moving the right foot, to sit into a _sant i_ stance. (image 2.58, transitional)

- Complete _closing move_ the same as described in _sword chop closing move_.

Pointers

    o   Complete the downward hook, upward circle, and forward chop by the time you complete the backward weight shift. Vary the grip to keep the action smooth as you do the internal or external rotation.

    o   Keep the spirit full while completing _closing move._ Keep the movements clean and accurate. Be sure to take the hilt cleanly with the left hand and to press the flat of the blade on the forearm.

PROBLEMS OFTEN MET IN SWORD CROSSCUT

PROBLEM 1: The student lifts his hand too high during the block and hook, so that the sword circles more like a brandish over the head.

CORRECTIONS: Explain the application of the move to help students understand the movement; this helps them to do a blocking and hooking action. The right hand should stay in front of the body, above the waist but below the shoulder, with the pivot point staying around the chest.

PROBLEM 2: The student holds the hilt too firmly during the block and hook so that his body is stiff and the sword's circle is uncoordinated.

CORRECTIONS: The student should grip the hilt firmly during the block to the right or left, but should loosen up during the circling action. In this way the wrist is supple, the action of the sword is fluid, and the power of the body can transfer to the sword. The student should work on the principle of setting up the left or right movement with a right or left countermovement, keeping the body relaxed. The only way to get the coordination is to practise repeatedly, and to apply some thought to the training – skill grows from thought.

PROBLEM 3: When doing the crossing cut, the student extends the arm too straight so that the sword is unstable or goes in the wrong direction.

CORRECTIONS: Remind the student to always keep a certain flexion in the arms, as this helps to launch power. The arm must keep a certain angle to maintain a good distance from the body so that you can use the full power of the waist and shoulder. The proper balance has spring. If the student is unstable when hitting the final posture, this is usually because he is trying to go too fast and using too much strength, so loses control. The incorrect direction is also often a case of too much momentum causing him to lose control over the blade. The student should first practise the action with a slow, quick, slow pattern. First gather power in the waist and shoulder with a slow action. Then extend the arm into the crossing cut with a quick action. Then sit the lower back, settle the shoulder, drop the elbow, and settle the buttocks with a controlling, stopping action so that the whole body is integrated with the sword – upper and lower, inner and outer. The sword tip should point in the direction that the lead foot points.

POWER GENERATION FOR SWORD CROSSCUT

Block and hook: The sword tip should draw a complete circle. The hands draw a small circle in front of the chest while the sword draws an elliptical circle with the top larger than the bottom. Draw a large circle when training, but a small circle if using the technique. Be sure to use the power from the body, transferring from the waist through to the hand, and from the hand to the sword. Use the principle of countermovement to get smooth power from the body – pre-load right to move left, pre-load left to move right. The movement should be coordinated and gentle, connected through the whole body, and with full spirit. Find the power and the technique by practising a large circle. Then find the application and speed by practising a small circle.

Right crosscut uses a spiral grip with the palm down, while *left crosscut* uses a full grip with the palm up. The final power launch comes after the halfway point. Wait until the sword tip has passed the midline, then accelerate. When launching power, coordinate the power of the torso and waist with the hand, transferring from the waist to the shoulder, shoulder to hand, and hand to sword.

- Power transfer uses the principle that each move is the preparation for the following move. The completion of a move always gathers power for the launching of the following move. You must put a lot of thought into your training to find this feeling.

- Crosscut contains a hidden pull back. In the last instant of the crossing cut, turn the waist to increase the reserve power in the sword body. This pulling power is integrally connected to the crossing cut – a continuation of the cut. To

increase the pulling power, prepare ahead of time, during the cutting action –
extend the right arm forward while cutting, sit the lower back and settle the
shoulder, drop the elbow and pull. Keep your intent forward, press the head up.
Pulling back during a crossing cut is a unique characteristic of Xingyi sword. It
is a distinct type of power and technique – hidden and hard to judge. It is a very
dangerous and effective technique, so is usually kept secret, not lightly taught.

- You may practise crosscut with a double handed grip. The single handed grip is
  agile, and good for performance. The double handed hold is strong, and good
  for combat. You can alter the final placement of the hands, pulling to the left
  and right in front, or pulling fully back to either side of the waist. Pulling
  further back makes the sawing, or inward slicing action, larger. You can do this
  with the double handed hold as well.

- The most important points about Xingyi sword are: move the sword and the
  body as one – the sword is an extension of the arm; emphasize the dignified
  bearing and integrated power; the techniques are simple and practical.

BREATHING CYCLE FOR SWORD CROSSCUT

- Inhale as you advance the lead foot a half-step, circling the sword in the
  checking hook. Breathe fully and evenly.

- Exhale as you step forward with the crossing cut. Exhale quickly.

Use natural, comfortable breathing during slow and easy practice.

PRACTICAL APPLICATIONS FOR SWORD CROSSCUT

- The main technique of the crosscut is the crossing cut with the under edge of
  the blade, targeting the neck. The neck is a weak link of the body, and vital, so
  you can gain considerable effect with little force.

Advance, block and hook is a defensive technique. In actual combat you can
advance, retreat, or dodge to the side. If the opponent stabs towards your central
area with a long or short weapon you follow along to whichever side is smoothest
to block to right or left and hook back. The block takes him off target, and the hook
draws his weapon further towards the rear. The masters of old could use this
technique to take the weapon right out of the hands of the opponent. Of course,
this sort of skill is not the work of a day.

Step forward crossing cut is the attack that follows your deflection. Step in quickly
to get the body close, turn over the wrist to cut across the neck with the under
edge of the blade. In combat, you don't aim too carefully when cutting across –
cutting the head, neck, chest, abdomen, hand or arm will all work.

- One important point in applying the crosscut is that it must be applied in
  combination with other techniques. Take whatever opportunity presents to
  continue the attack, chopping, piercing or slicing up until you completely
  vanquish the opponent. Don't give your opponent any breathing space. If the
  opponent stabs with a long weapon you can do the crossing cut along his
  weapon to slice his hand and arm.

- The Xingyi sword is used mostly to counter attack. 'If the enemy does not move
  then I don't move. If the enemy moves slightly then I attack first. As the second

person starts the first person has already arrived." You must develop your confidence, you must not be shy in a fight. If you are shy then you are afraid and will certainly lose in a fight. You must develop a confident winning attitude. Of course, confidence comes from competence. If you have not developed the skills then confidence is just blind and you will most likely lose the fight. Thoroughly mastered skills come from long hours of daily intelligent training and frequent practical training.

THE POEM ABOUT SWORD CROSSCUT

横剑技法取敌项，临敌不惧胆要壮。左右格挂顺势折，沉肘坐腰劲内藏。

Sword crosscut goes for the opponent's neck,

You cannot be afraid to you get close, you must be courageous.

Block and hook to right or left then go smoothly to cut,

Your power is hidden inside when you settle the elbows and sit the spine.

FIVE ELEMENTS LINKED SWORD FORM

INTRODUCTION TO THE FIVE ELEMENTS LINKED (FIVE PHASES CONNECTED) SWORD, *WUXING LIANHUAN JIAN*

The Five Elements Linked Sword is a short form that combines the sword's five element techniques with the basic structure of the five element hand form. It is quite widespread and popular among traditional Xingyi practitioners. The form varies by region and by branch of Xingyi, so there are quite a few Xingyi sword five element linked forms. Not all show the true characteristics of Xingyi. The form should show Xingyi footwork and power and the flavour and characteristics of Xingyi. The form is based on Xingyi principles, so if it doesn't have the flavour of Xingyi then it has lost the intrinsic nature that makes it Xingyi sword.

The form presented in this book has sixteen movements that contain all five of the five element techniques. The movements are repeated out and back. It contains the techniques chop, pierce, cut, slice up, scull, entangle, hook, draw, lift, and check. The overall characteristics of the form are: the techniques are tightly connected, simple and practical; the power is integrated; stillness and movement alternate clearly; the rhythm is distinct; the form has a complete and full feeling; form and spirit are one; and hard and gentle blend together.

NAMES OF THE MOVEMENTS

1. Opening Move
2. Thrust: Advance, Draw and Pierce
3. Thrust: Hook Up, Right Stance Pierce Forward
4. Drill: Entangle and Lift, Right Stance Pierce Down
5. Chop: Hook Down, Right Stance Swinging Chop
6. Thrust: Lift Knee, Entangle, Flat Pierce

7.   Turn Around Hide the Sword: Turn Around and Chop

8.   Thrust: Step Forward, Hook Up, Right Stance Pierce

9.   Chop: Wheel Around, Lift Knee and Chop

10.   Slash: Step Forward, Right Stance Slice Up

11.   Crosscut: Left Stance Crossing Cut

12.   Crosscut: Right Stance Crossing Cut

13.   Drill: Entangle, Draw Back, Left Stance Twisted Pierce

14.   Pierce Behind: Cross-over Step, Turning Pierce Behind

15.   Reaching Pierce: Step Forward, Reaching Pierce Forward

16.   Chop: Hook Left, Right Stance Chop

17.   Leopard Cat Turns Over Whilst Climbing a Tree: Turn Around, Crossing Cut, Heel Kick, Resting Stance Chop

      (The following moves are repetition back in the returning direction)

18.   Thrust

19.   Thrust

20.   Drill

21.   Chop

22.   Thrust

23.   Turn Around and Hide the Sword

24.   Thrust

25.   Chop

26.   Slash

27.   Crosscut

28.   Crosscut

29.   Drill

30.   Pierce Behind

31.   Reaching Pierce

32.   Chop

33.   Leopard Cat Turns Over Whilst Climbing a Tree

      (The following moves are the closing combination)

34.   Thrust

35.   Closing Move

Description of the Movements

1. Opening Move   qǐ shì   起势

The movement is the same as setting into *ready stance*. The actions are *Stand at attention holding the sword in the left hand; Transfer the hilt to the right hand; Right retreat and chop.*

ACTION 1: Stand at attention facing ninety degrees to the line of the form. Let the arms hang at the side. Nestle the sword guard in the left hand in an upside down hold. The sword tip points up, the flat of the blade nestles on the left forearm. Look straight forward. (image 2.59)

ACTION 2: Raise the hands at the sides until they arrive at shoulder height. Turn the torso ninety degrees to the left. Bring the right hand across to meet the left hand and change the hilt to the right hand. Release the left hand, taking the sword fingers shape. The left hand will remain in sword fingers shape throughout the form unless otherwise stated. Look forward. (image 2.60)

ACTION 3: Retreat the right foot and shift back, bending the right leg to sit into a *santi* stance. Circle the sword tip up, then chop forward and down, the blade standing, the tip pointing forward at nose height. Pull the right hand in towards the belly, about a f orearm length away. Keep the left hand at the righ t wrist throughout. Press the head up and look past the tip. (images 2.61, 2.62)

Pointers

o   The left hand must hold the sword steady, not letting the blade wobble. The right hand must then take the sword accurately.

o   Complete the sword chop as the right foot retreats. The power must be well anchored and weighty, the spirit full, with concentrated focus.

2.   Thrust   bēngjiàn   崩剑

Left advance, right draw; Right follow-in step, forward pierce.

ACTION 1: Advance the left foot a half-step without moving the right foot, shifting weight forward between the feet. Rotate the right palm away from the thumb and lift it, pulling the sword back on the right side of the body. Draw a small circle with the sword tip, keeping the tip pointing forward at all times. The right hand finishes a bit lower than shoulder height, the blade horizontal. Place the left hand at the right wrist. Turn the body slightly right and look past the sword tip. (image 2.63)

ACTION 2: Follow-in the right foot a half-step to land with a thump in the *crushing punch* stance. Rotate the right hand slightly to turn the blade to a standing blade and then pierce forward forcefully to chest height, sending power to the sword tip. Keep the right arm slightly bent and keep the left hand at the right wrist. Tuck in the jaw, press the head up, and look forward past the sword tip. (image 2.64)

2.63

2.64

Pointers

o   Complete the draw back as the left foot advances. Complete the pierce as the right foot lands with a shoveling thump.

3.   Thrust   bēngjiàn   崩剑

Left advance, hook up; Right step forward, pierce forward.

ACTION 1: Advance the left foot a half-step and follow in the right foot to the left ankle. Take a full grip with the right hand and cock the wrist down, bending the arm to pull the hilt down to the right belly. The tip points up and hooks back in front of the right side of the body. Keep the blade about twenty centimetres from the body. Keep the left hand at the right wrist. Tuck in the elbows, contain the chest and tuck in the belly. Look forward. (image 2.65)

ACTION 2: Take a long step forward with the right foot and follow in the left foot to just behind the right foot, most weight on the left leg as with the *crushing punch* stance. Lift the right hand to chest height and use a spiral grip to bring the tip down to point straight forward. Extend the right hand forcefully forward to pierce to chest height, sending power out to the sword tip. Keep the left hand on the right wrist throughout. Press the head up, look past the sword tip. (image 2.66)

2.65

2.66

Pointers

o Complete each sword technique as each foot lands. Complete the hook back as the left foot advances. Complete the pierce as the right foot steps forward.

o When hooking, take a firm grip and cock the wrist to hook up and pull back with the blade. Pull back and hook as one action, bending the elbow to gather power. Then extend the arm to pierce. Connect the hook and pierce smoothly, so that the whole movement is quick.

4. Drill   zuānjiàn   钻剑

Left retreat, entangle and lift; Right step forward, pierce down.

ACTION 1: Retreat the left foot and shift back towards the left leg, withdrawing the right foot a half-step and touching the toes down. Rotate the right palm away from the thumb and circle it right and down, then lift it to in front of the right shoulder, circling the sword tip down from the front, to entangle then draw back. The sword tip is angled down to chest height. Turn slightly to the right. Keep the left hand on the right wrist throughout. Look past the tip. (image 2.67)

ACTION 2: Advance the right foot a long step and follow in the left foot a half-step, keeping most weight on the left leg in a *santi* stance. Pierce forward and down with the hand inverted (thumb web is forward and down) at chest height, the sword tip at knee height. Almost fully extend the right arm and reach the right shoulder forward. Swing the left hand up to the left to brace out, arm bent, above the head. Look past the sword tip. (image 2.68)

Pointers

o Circle and lift the sword as the left foot retreats, in a fully coordinated movement. Rotate the right hand to entangle with the sword, then lift the elbow to lift and draw with the sword. Use the body core to draw the shoulder, the shoulder to draw the elbow, the elbow to draw the hand, and the hand to draw the sword.

o Complete the pierce down as the right foot lands forward. Turn the waist, reach with the shoulder, and extend the arm to pierce forward. Swing the left arm up to apply an equal and opposite force that balances and integrates the movement's power.

5. Chop pījiàn 劈剑

Left step forward, left hook down; Right step forward, swinging chop.

ACTION 1: Step the left foot forward in front of the right leg, landing hooked out. Don't move the right foot, but lift the heel and bend both legs to sit into an evenly weighted cross-over stance. Take a full grip on the hilt with the right hand and bring the sword tip down and back to the left rear of the body. Bring the left hand down to the right elbow. Turn the body left. Look at the sword tip. (image 2.69)

ACTION 2: Take a long step to the forward right with the right foot and follow in a half-step with the left foot to sit into a *santi* stance. Rotate the right palm away from the thumb and lift it above the head to circle the sword tip back and up. Then take a full grip on the hilt and chop forward and down to waist height with a standing blade. Circle the left hand back and up to above the left side of the head. Look past the sword tip. (image 2.70)

Pointers

o Hook the sword down to the left as the left foot lands forward in the cross-over step. Circle and chop the sword and brace back with the left hand as the right foot lands forward. The chop needs equal and opposite forces acting upwards and downwards, forward and back. Start and complete the movement as a coordinated whole, and swing the arm with force, sending the power out to the leading edge of the blade.

o The entire movement is one coordinated action, with no pause midway. Take a long step forward, and take a quick follow-in step. The chop must have a point of focus. The final action of the chop is a sawing pull back. Settle the shoulder and elbow to pull the sword back.

6. Thrust bēngjiàn 崩剑

Right advance, entangle; Lift knee, flat pierce.

ACTION 1: Advance the right foot a half-step and shift the weight between the feet without moving the left foot. Lower the left hand to the right wrist. Use a spiral grip with the right hand to bring the sword tip right, down, and then left and up, completing a full circle. Then bend the arms and bring them together in front of the chest, the right hand rotated palm up, the blade flat, and the tip at chest height. Look past the sword tip. (image 2.71)

ACTION 2: Bend the right leg slightly for stability, shift to the right leg, and lift the left knee. Extend the arms forward to pierce with the flat blade, tip to shoulder height. Open the left hand and support the right hand with it. Press the head up, release tension in the shoulders, settle the *qi* to the *dantian*, and send the power out to the sword tip. Look past the sword tip. (image 2.72)

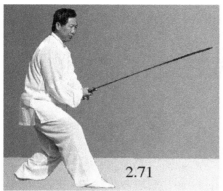

Pointers

o   Complete the entangling action as the right foot advances. Complete the piercing action as the left knee lifts.

o   The tip draws a clockwise circle about twenty centimetres in radius during the entangling action. The right wrist needs to be loose so that the movement is round and gentle, and the power reaches the tip of the sword.

o   Shift forward as you settle the hands and bend the elbows and lift, putting the power out to the sword tip.

7.   Turn Around and Hide the Sword   huíshēn cángjiàn   回身藏剑

Turn around, swinging chop; Left hook, chop and pull.

ACTION 1: Land the left foot behind and turn around 180 degrees to the left, rotating on both feet. Rotate the right palm towards the thumb and lift the elbow above the head. Once turned, shift forward to the left leg and chop the sword forward and down. Place the left hand, back in sword fingers shape, on the right wrist and extend both arms slightly. The sword tip is at chest height. Look past the sword tip. (image 2.73 transitional)

ACTION 2: After chopping down, pivot around the right wrist to bring the sword tip down, back past the left side of the body, then up and forward to chop down. Keep the left hand at the right wrist. Shift back to a *santi* stance on the right leg. Press the

hilt down and pull back and down at the right side of the body, bringing the standing blade close to the right thigh with the tip pointing forward and up. Extend the left arm out at chest height. Look forward. (image 2.74)

Pointers

- o The movement is completed without hesitation. Be sure to shift the weight forward and back along with the movement of the sword.

- o The sword chops twice: a chop, a hook, and then another chop without a pause in between. Shift to the left leg during the first swinging chop, then shift back to the right leg during the second chop and pull.

8. Thrust   bēngjiàn   崩剑

Left advance, hook up; Right step forward, pierce.

ACTION 1: Advance the left foot a half-step and follow in the right foot to the left ankle. Extend the right arm to send the blade forward then take a full grip and cock the wrist down to bring the tip up. Then bring the right arm back, the hand in front of the belly, to bring the sword tip back to hook up about a foot away from the body, tip up. Keep the left hand on the right wrist throughout. Look forward. (image 2.75)

ACTION 2: Take a step forward with the right foot and follow in the left foot to behind the right, in the same short stance as *crushing punch*. Lift the sword hilt to in front of the chest to lower the tip to point straight forward, then pierce

forcefully forward at chest height. The arms are almost straight. Keep the left hand on the right wrist throughout. Tuck in the jaw and press the head up. Look past the sword tip. (image 2.76)

 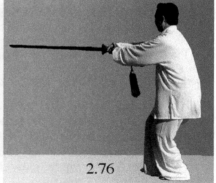

2.75   2.76

Pointers

- o Move 8 is the same as move 2.

9. Chop   pījiàn   劈剑

Right hook-in and wheel around; Left lift knee, chop.

ACTION 1: Advance the right foot a half-step, landing hooked-in and shifting to the right leg, so that the body turns around to the left 180 degrees to face in the way in which you came. Turn the left foot to point forward. Rotate the right palm away from the thumb and lift the elbow so that the blade under edge is up. Circle the left hand up past the face to above the head while turning, then continue to circle forward and down to level with the left shoulder. Look past the left hand. (image 2.77)

ACTION 2: Stand steadily on the right leg, keeping the knee bent and lifting the left knee with the foot tucked in at the crotch. Circle the left hand down and back, then up to the upper left of the head to brace out with the arm. Use a full grip with the right hand and circle it from the back, up, forward, then down to chop at waist height. Finish with the arm bent and sword tip at chest height. Reach the right shoulder forward and reach the torso forward slightly. Send the power to the distal third of the blade. Look past the tip. (image 2.78)

Pointers   2.77   2.78

- o The more you hook the foot in, the smoother the turn around will be. Do not step the hooking foot too far away, as this will destabilize the turn.

- o Three actions link without a pause: wheel around, lift the knee, and chop.

- o Be sure to coordinate the hands in opposite actions to assist the power – the one forward and down and the other back and up. When launching power into the chop, turn the waist, extend the shoulder, reach the torso, swing the arm and lift the knee. The power transfer must be smooth.

10. Slash   pàojiàn   炮剑

Left step forward, crossing draw; Right step forward, inverted slice.

ACTION 1: Land the left foot forward and right, hooked-out. Bend the legs and shift between them equally. Rotate the right palm towards the thumb and bend and lift the elbow to bring the sword's under edge up. Lift the blade to draw across towards the left at eyebrow height, right hand at eyebrow height and sword tip pointing to the forward right. Turn the body slightly to the left. Keep the left hand inside the right wrist throughout. Look past the tip. (image 2.79)

ACTION 2: Take a long step forward with the right foot diagonally to the right and follow-in the left foot to take a *santi* stance. Using a spiral grip, circle the right hand to circle the sword tip up then back and down, staying close

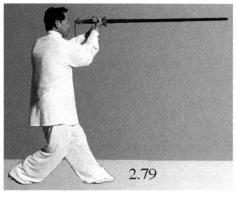

2.79   2.80

by the left side. Then continue forward and up to complete an inverted grip slice with the under edge of the blade up. The right palm is rotated away from the thumb above the shoulders with the arm bent, and the sword tip points forward at chest height. Send the power to the body of the blade. Keep the left hand at the right wrist. Look past the sword tip. (image 2.80)

Pointers

- o Rotate the right hand to lift the sword and draw back as the left foot steps forward. Turn the waist to draw the sword back, closing the shoulders and bending the elbow to take the sword across to the left. Use the power of the body core and keep the movement gentle and coordinated.

- o Complete the inverted slice as the right foot steps forward, arriving exactly at the same time. Keep the sword blade close to the body as it circles, and be sure to turn the wrist, keeping it supple. Transfer power from body core to shoulder, from shoulder to elbow, from elbow to hand, and from hand to sword.

11. Crosscut   héngjiàn   横剑

Right advance, left brandishing entangle; Left step forward, crossing cut.

ACTION 1: Advance the left foot a half-step and follow in the right foot to the left ankle. With the left hand supporting the right wrist, extend the arms forward and up to bring the sword tip flat, encircling across from right to left, pointing forward. Then brandish in a circle back, passing by the face to circle to the right. To do this, the right hand rotates palm towards the thumb to bring the palm up and the sword tip across. Bend the arms in front of the chest. Follow the tip with the eyes during the movement. (image 2.81)

ACTION 2: Take a long step to the forward left with the left foot and follow in a half- step with the right foot. Take a full grip with the palm up and, with the right arm bent at about 120 degrees, cut the blade horizontally across to the left. When the sword arrives at the left side, bend the right arm and tuck the elbow towards the solar plexus. The sword tip is just above shoulder height, the power in the forward portion. Circle the left hand to above the left side of the head. Press the head up, settle the *qi* to the *dantian*. Look past the sword tip. (image 2.82)

 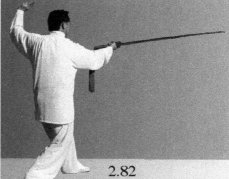

2.81   2.82

Pointers

- o Circle the sword as the right foot advances, keeping the movement gentle. Draw the hand from the body core, and thus to the sword. Turn the wrist and adjust the grip as needed.

- o Complete the leftward crossing cut as the left foot lands. Launch power with fully integrated strength.

12. Crosscut   héngjiàn   横剑

Left advance, right brandishing entangle; Right step forward, crossing cut.

ACTION 1: Advance the left foot a half-step and follow in the right foot to the right ankle. With the left hand supporting the right wrist, lower them slightly to chest height, then swing them to the right, so that the sword tip circles from the front left to the front right, and then circles back in front of the face to the left. Rotate the right palm down to turn the blade flat. Close the shoulders towards the left. Follow the sword tip with the eyes during the movement. (image 2.83)

ACTION 2: Take a long step to the forward right with the right foot and follow in a half-step with the left foot, keeping most weight on the left leg. Take a full grip, turn the palm down, and almost fully extend the arm to cut to the right. Cut with the blade flat and the tip angled to the forward right at nose height. Keep the left hand on the right wrist. Press the head up. Look past the sword tip. (image 2.84)

Pointers

- o Left and right crosscut are similar actions, but because they go in different directions the rotation is slightly different. The right palm rotates up for the left crosscut and down for the right crosscut.

13. Drill   zuānjiàn   钻剑

Right advance, entangle and draw back; Left step forward, twisted pierce.

ACTION 1: Advance the right foot a half-step and follow in the left foot to the right ankle. Keep the left hand at the right wrist. Lower the sword tip and circle it left then up, and then again to the right and pull to draw back. Once the hands are outside the right shoulder, bend the elbows to lower the hands to the right waist, rotating the right hand palm up so that the under edge of the blade is up and the tip points forward. Turn the body to the right, tuck in the belly and contain the chest, compressing the torso. Look past the tip. (image 2.85 transitional)

ACTION 2: Take a long step forward with the left foot and follow in a half-step with the right foot, keeping most weight on the right leg. Using a spiral grip, extend the right arm in front of the chest to pierce forward in an inverted grip, the under edge of the blade up and tip pointing forward. Finish with the arm slightly bent, the right shoulder extended and released, the elbow tucked in, and the blade tip at eyebrow height. Send power

2.86

to the sword tip. Swing the left hand forward and up by the head to brace out to the left side. Press the head up. Look past the sword tip. (image 2.86)

Pointers

- o   Circle and draw the sword to complete the action as the right foot advances. Transfer movement from the body core to the shoulder, from the shoulder to the elbow, from the elbow to the hands and from the hands to the sword. Keep the body action gentle and rounded, and keep the sword technique tight and well knit.

- o   Pierce with the sword as the left foot lands forward, sword and foot arriving simultaneously. As you first entangle, then draw back, and then twist and roll down, contain the chest and gather power in the lower back, turning the body as you move. When you then turn the blade over and pierce forward, turn the waist, reach the shoulder forward, and extend the arm. Extend the right shoulder forward and bring the left shoulder back, swinging the left hand up to assist the power launch.

14. Pierce Behind   huí cì   回刺

Cross-over step, turning pierce behind.

ACTION: Shift forward without moving the left foot, and step the right foot across in front of the left foot, landing turned out. Bend the right leg and lift the left heel, turning the body to the right so that the legs are crossed, most weight on the right leg. Lower the left hand to support the right wrist. Tuck the right elbow in and extend the wrist, circling the sword tip down behind, pivoting around the wrist. The sword is now outside the right arm, pointing down behind the body. Look at the sword tip. Extend the right arm, almost straight, to the lower rear to pierce the sword tip to knee height with a standing blade. Extend the left hand forward to the upper left. Look at the sword tip. (images 2.87, 2.88)

2.87

Pointers

- o Complete the whole action without hesitation.

- o Adjust your grip on the hilt. First tuck in the elbow and extend the wrist. The left hand may push on the hilt to assist in pushing the sword tip down behind. Use a firm spiral grip for the pierce.

- o Extend the left hand up to the front as the sword pierces down behind, perfectly timed together.

15. Reaching Pierce   tàn cì   探刺

Step forward, reach the body and pierce forward.

ACTION: Take a long step forward with the left foot and follow in the right foot a half-step, shifting forward to a *santi* stance. Rotate the right palm away from the thumb and extend the wrist, taking a firm grip on the hilt to cause the sword tip to rise, coming in towards the right side of the head to point forward. Turn the body left and turn the palm to face out, then extend the arm to pierce forward with a standing horizontal blade above head height. Place the left hand on the right wrist. Reach forward slightly with the torso. Keep the right arm snug to the right ear. Look past the sword tip. (image 2.89)

Pointers

- o Pierce forward from above the head as the left foot lands. First sit the sword hilt up before piercing.

16. Chop   pījiàn   劈剑

Left advance, hook; Right step forward, chop.

ACTION 1: Advance the left foot a half-step and follow in the right foot lifted at the ankle. Lower the sword and hook back, passing closely by the left side of the body, then circle up to above and behind the head. Use a supple grip on the hilt, so that as the right hand draws a small circle the sword draws a large circle. Keep the left hand on the right wrist. Follow the sword with the eyes, then look forward. (image 2.90)

ACTION 2: Take a long step forward with the right foot and follow in the left foot a half-step, keeping most weight on the left leg. Chop the sword forward and down, then pull the right hand in to about a foot away from the abdomen. The sword tip is at shoulder height, the blade standing. Keep the left hand on the right wrist throughout.
Press the head up and look forward. (image 2.91)

Pointers

    o Hook back as the left foot advances, and chop as the right foot steps forward. The sword always acts in conjunction with the stepping. Complete the actions as one movement.

    o First chop forward and down, then pull back, as one movement. When pulling back, settle the shoulders and elbows, keep the elbows tucked to the ribs, press the head up, and sit into the buttocks. The chop must have a point of focus.

17. Leopard Cat Turns Over Whilst Climbing a Tree

límāo dào shàng shù   狸猫倒上树

Turn around, crossing cut; Right heel kick; Resting stance chop.

ACTION 1: Step the left foot forward, landing hooked-in, and turn around 180 degrees to the right to face back in the direction from which you came. Shift onto the left leg. Keep the left hand on the right wrist, rotate the right palm down, and place the blade flat in front of the chest. As the body turns, open out both hands to either side, cutting flat across to the right with the blade at chest height and bracing the left hand out to the left. Look forward. (images 2.92)

ACTION 2: Bend the left leg slightly to stand firmly. Lift the right knee and then do a crossways heel hick forward and up to shoulder height. Look

forward past the kick. (image 2.93)

ACTION 3: Land the right foot forward, still crossways, and bring in the left foot a half-step, sitting down into a resting stance. Most weight is on the left leg, the left heel is raised, and the right leg is a bit straighter than the left. Rotate the right palm towards the thumb and lift the hand above the head and bring the left hand in to the right wrist. As the body drops, chop forward and down, finishing with the blade standing, the tip between waist and knee height. Press the head up. Look past the sword tip. (image 2.94)

2.94

Pointers

- o   The turn must be completed smoothly in one move. Turn quickly, swing the arm forcefully to cut across with power. Kick with force. Sit and chop with stability.

- o   To do the crossing kick, tuck in the right hip. To land, drive forward to stomp forward and down.

- o   You must sit into the resting stance with stability. Chop down as the body lowers. Don't use too much force, but use a hidden power.

- •   The following moves, 18 through 33, are a repetition of the first section, moves 2 thorugh 17, back in the returning direction.

18.	**Thrust**	See move 2.
19.	**Thrust**	See move 3.
20.	**Drill**	See move 4.
21.	**Chop**	See move 5.
22.	**Thrust**	See move 6. (image 2.95 with standing blade)

2.95

23.	**Turn Around and Hide the Sword**	See move 7.
24.	**Thrust**	See move 8.

| 25. | **Chop** | See move 9. (image 2.96) |
| 26. | **Slash** | See move 10. |

27.   **Crosscut** See move 11. (images 2.97, 2.98)

28.	**Crosscut**	See move 12.
29.	**Drill**	See move 13.
30.	**Pierce Behind**	See move 14.
31.	**Reaching Pierce**	See move 15.
32.	**Chop**	See move 16.
33.	**Leopard Cat Turns Over Whilst Climbing a Tree**	See move 17.
34.	**Thrust**	See move 2, back in the original direction.
35.	**Closing Move**	shōu shì 收势

Starting from *thrust. Retreat and pull the sword; Stand and change hands; Stand at attention and hold the sword.*

ACTION 1: Retreat the right foot and shift back to the right leg, extending the left leg and hooking in the left foot on the spot. Pull the right hand back to in front of the right shoulder with a standing blade placed horizontally at shoulder height. Rotate the left palm away from the thumb to turn the palm out with the thumb down, and cradle the guard. Turn ninety degrees to the right. Look past the sword tip. (image 2.99)

ACTION 2: Withdraw the left foot in beside the right foot so that the feet are parallel. Hold the hilt with the left hand – thumb, little finger and ring finger cradling the guard, and index and middle finger along the hilt to keep the flat of the blade snug to the forearm. Circle the left hand up and left, then down to the left side. With the right hand in sword fingers shape, circle it down, right, then up to the right side above the head. Follow the movement of the right hand with the eyes, then look to the left. (image 2.100)

ACTION 3: Without moving the feet, bring the right hand down to the right side to stand to attention. Look forward. (image 2.101)

Pointers

o   The hand transfer must be smooth and accurate, taking the sword firmly in the left hand.

o   Complete the hand actions as the feet come to attention.

o   The movement must be well anchored and have full spirit. The *qi* must be settled and the attitude at peace.

FIVE ELEMENT SPEAR 五行枪

INTRODUCTION TO FIVE ELEMENT SPEAR, *WUXING QIANG*

The style of Xingyi is famous for its spear, Bagua for its sabre, Taiji for its sword, and Shaolin for its staff. In Xingyi, practising spear improves empty hand skills, and empty hand skills are the foundation of spear skills. The creator of Xinyi Liuhequan, Ji Longfeng, excelled at the spear. "He could hit a target from a galloping horse, when he raised his spear no one could escape. He was called the spear spirit." He applied the principles of the spear to empty hand techniques when he created Xinyi Liuhequan, and spear practice retained its place of importance as *xin-yi* developed into *xing-yi quan*.

Previous generations of Xingyi masters examined many spear techniques and selected the most practical and strongest – those which most showed the flavour and characteristics of Xingyiquan. Xingyi spear emphasizes power and trained skill, and uses no flowery movements. It is simple and practical, and especially emphasizes spear and body moving as one with a full, integrated power and intimidating air. The power of the whole body connects through to the tip of the spear, so that the spear is truly an extension of the body. The five element techniques of the spear are the same as those of the five fists – chop, drill, thrust, slash, and crosscut. Although the moves are named simply spear chop, spear drill, spear thrust, spear slash, and spear crosscut, there are at least two moves contained in each short combination.[50]

The spear demands a high degree of deep skill and coordination. The spear is the king of the weapons. They say 'a year for the fist, a month for the staff, but day by day for the spear.' That is, it takes a year to master empty hand skills with hard training. With this foundation, a month is sufficient to learn staff. But the spear must be practised daily, year in and year out. There are no shortcuts in learning the spear, only hard practice. If you are not willing to work hard then you won't master the spear.

If you want your spear technique to be familiar and refined then you must practise the techniques, the forms, and partner spear 'shaft sliding.' You must understand the application of all the techniques. If you think of the application and imagine an

---

[50] Author's note: In the descriptions I use both the traditional and the modern names for each technique to make it easier to learn and teach.

opponent, you will learn the techniques quicker. You should also study spear theory, learn from the experience of past masters, and study spear applications to improve your ability with the spear.

There are three lengths of spear – long, medium, and short. The long spear is about four meters, the medium spear about three meters, and the short spear about two meters. The long spear develops strength, the short spear develops agility, and the medium spear develops both strength and agility. Not many people practise the long spear, mostly because it is awkward to carry and store. Most Xingyi players like to use something between the medium and short spears – about 2.5 meters.

In choosing the wood for a spear shaft, you need a good quality white waxwood. It should be supple and smooth skinned with no knots or kinks. The base should be the size of your own thumb and forefinger held in a circle. A short spear can be a bit thinner, and a long spear a bit thicker. The circumference of the tip should be the natural thickness of the wood as it has grown. You should not shave down the wood as this reduces its natural suppleness and can lead to breakage.

A spear is comprised of three parts, the wooden shaft, the metal head, and the horsehair tassel. The spear shaft is divided into thirds – the third of the shaft at the tip is the fore-section, the third of the shaft at the base is the aft-section, and the third in the middle is the midsection. During spear practice, the hands often slide up and down the shaft to best carry out the different techniques. The very end of the spearhead is called the tip, and the other end of the shaft is called the base or butt.

FIVE ELEMENT SPEAR TECHNIQUES

On Guard   yùbèishì   预备势

On guard position is the opening of any Xingyi weapon form or practice session, and is the ready position for many techniques. *On guard* is the *santi* stance with both hands holding the spear, ready to do any technique. *On guard* is the foundation for spear training, so you need to do post standing, similar to *santishi* post standing, in this position to establish the correct posture in the body and prepare the way for further spear study.

The actions are: *Stand the spear; Left bow stance send out the spear; Left on guard position.*

ACTION 1: Stand at attention with the right hand holding the spear vertical at the right side with the base on the ground. Let the left hand hang naturally, press the head up, and look forward. (image 3.1)

ACTION 2: Turn ninety degrees to the left to face the way in which the stance will face. Step the left foot forward and bend the knee while straightening the right leg, shifting forward into a bow stance. Lift the spear horizontally with the right hand, pointing the tip forward [to the side, in the new direction], extending the right arm with the spear shaft at chest height. Bring the left hand to the right armpit with the palm up to support the shaft. Look past the spear tip. (images 3.2)

3.1

ACTION 3: Shift back, extending the left leg more and bending the right leg to shift back into a *santi* stance. Extend the left arm to send the spear out and slide the right hand back to the base, pulling the base to the right waist. Keep the left arm almost straight, and hold the shaft with the palm down. Keep the spear

on the midline of the body, the shaft almost horizontal, but the tip at chest height. (image 3.3 and from the front)

Pointers

- ○ Complete the three actions smoothly as one move.

- ○ When moving into the bow stance and sending the spear forward, be sure to send the tip directly forward without wobbling around. Slide the right hand smoothly, maintaining contact with the shaft.

- ○ Complete the placement of the spear as you sit into the *santi* stance. This is the final posture of the ready stance.

- ○ This is the spear's equivalent to the *santishi*, and the posture is adjusted to suit the spear. In the empty hand *santishi*, the trunk is angled forty-five degrees to the front. With the spear, however, the trunk should turn more, about sixty to seventy degrees. The rear foot is also turned out more — about seventy degrees. The spear shaft must be held snug to the trunk, with the right hand holding the base at waist height on the right side. The left hand is in front, pointing the spear in the correct direction. Three points serve to stabilize the spear – the lead hand, the rear hand, and the waist – so that the spear and body are joined as one. Practice post standing in this posture. Post standing might seem like a waste of time, but it builds a strong foundation for future mastery of the techniques and proper performance of the movements. Post standing sets the basic posture into the ideal shape so that movements can become correct. During post standing you should seek kinesthetic awareness, get a feel for the power lines, and master the requirements of the spear.

SPEAR CHOP

INTRODUCTION TO SPEAR CHOP, *PI QIANG*

The chop is the most basic of the spear techniques. The definition of a spear chop in the wushu dictionary is 'holding the spear in both hands, strike downward from above with power and speed, sending power to the tip.' In the competition regulations it is 'holding the spear in both hands, chop down from above, sending power to the fore-section.' This is simply for the actual chop. In Xingyi, spear chop is practised as a number of combinations that contain hook, scoop, swinging chop, and stab. The spear chop combinations contain both defensive and attacking techniques. The movements are simple but very practical, taking care of defense and attack in one move.

There are five different footwork or stances: step forward, retreat, roundabout steps, left stance, and right stance. Any technique that brings the spear down in a chopping action from above is considered a chop. There are three different hand methods: left handed, right handed, and changeover. There is also a chop with the base.

METHOD ONE: CHECK, HOOK, AND CHOP

1a Right Stance Chop   yòubù pīqiāng   右步劈枪

Start from *on guard*. Continue with *Advance, right checking hook; Right step forward, chop.*

ACTION 1: Advance the left foot a half-step and follow in the right foot to the left ankle without touching down. Bend the left elbow slightly and rotate the palm to face in, to turn the shaft counterclockwise, lifting the tip above head height. At the right waist, rotate the right palm away from the thumb. These actions cause the fore-section of the spear to check to the right. Look past the spear tip. (image 3.4)

ACTION 2: Take a long step forward with the right foot and follow in the left foot a half-step. Rotate the left palm towards the thumb and tuck in the left elbow so that the thumb to forefinger web presses down. Chop the spear forward and down forcefully with the left hand, the spear tip finishing at waist height. Keep the right hand at the waist and assist the left hand with a small turning and lifting action. Press the head up and look past the spear tip. (image 3.5 and from the front)

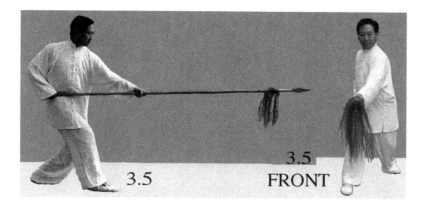

1b Left Stance Chop

zuǒbù pīqiāng   左步劈枪

Advance, left hooking check; Left step forward, chop.

ACTION 1: Advance the right foot a half-step and follow in the left foot to the right ankle without touching down. Place the left hand near the aft-section of the shaft

and rotate the palm towards the thumb while bending the elbow, so that the palm turns in – lifting and turning the spear tip above head height. Bend the left elbow so that the left hand is in front of the left shoulder. Keep the right hand at the waist and assist the left hand with a turning action. These actions cause the fore-section of the shaft to check to the left and hook back as the feet advance. Look forward. (image 3.6)

ACTION 2: Take a long step forward with the left foot and follow in a half-step with the right foot to tale a *santi* stance. Rotate the left palm away from the thumb to press down with the thumb/forefinger web, and extend the arm forward and down forcefully to chop the spear tip down to waist height. Hold the base with the

right hand at the waist. Send the power to the fore-section of the spear. Press the head up and look forward. (image 3.7 and from the front)

Pointers

- o Complete the check and hook with the advance step. Complete the chop with the step forward. The feet, hands, and spear must all arrive at the same time.

- o The spear points straight forward when it chops. To assist the action, when advancing, step the lead foot about fifteen degrees to the side. This helps to keep the spear on the midline.

- o Always send the left shoulder forward into the spear chop, whether in right stance or left stance.

- • Continue on with right and left chop as space permits.

METHOD TWO: CHOP AND STAB

1c Right Stance Chop and Stab yòubù pīzhā qiāng 右步劈扎枪

Start from *on guard. Left advance, scoop; Right step forward, chop; Stab.*

ACTION 1: Advance the left foot a half-step and follow in the right foot without touching down. Lower the spear tip to knee height, then, as the left foot lands, bend the left elbow and pull the spear back. Push the base forward and down slightly with the right hand. These actions cause the spear tip to scoop up above the head. Look forward. (image 3.8)

ACTION 2: Step the right foot a long step forward and follow in the left foot a half-step. Push the left hand forward and down on the shaft, and pull the right hand back to the right waist on the base. This causes the fore-section of the spear to chop strongly down, the tip arriving at waist height, the power in the fore-section. Press the head up and look past the spear tip. (image 3.9)

ACTION 3: Without moving the feet, push the base forcefully forward with the right hand to send the spear forward. Loosen the left hand to guide the shaft. Accelerate the right hand as it approaches the left hand to send power forward to the spear tip so that it quivers. The shaft is horizontal at chest height. Shift the weight forward. The right hand is nestled in the left hand. Look past the spear tip. (image 3.10)

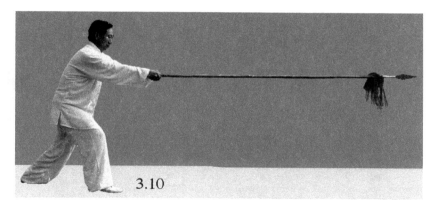

1d Left Stance Chop and Stab   zuǒbù pīzhā qiāng   左步劈扎枪

Right advance, scoop; Left step forward, chop: Stab.

ACTION 1: Lower the spear tip to knee height. Advance the right foot a half-step and follow in the left foot to beside the right ankle without touching down. Loosen the left hand and pull the right hand with the spear base back to the right side, pressing down slightly. Slide the left hand forward and bend the elbow. These actions cause the spear to scoop up, the tip finishing above the head. Look forward. (image 3.11)

ACTION 2: Take a long step forward with the left foot and follow in a half-step with the right foot. Push the left hand forward and down and pull the right hand slightly upwards, using both hands to chop the spear tip forcefully forward and down. Send the power to the spear tip, at waist height. Press the head up and look forward. (image 3.12)

ACTION 3: Without moving the feet, extend the right arm forcefully to send the spear forward. Loosen the left hand to allow the spear to slide through. As the right hand approaches the left hand, abruptly accelerate to send the power to the spear tip, causing it to quiver. The spear is level at chest height. Shift the weight slightly forward. Nestle the right hand in the left hand. Press the head up and look forward. (image 3.13)

3.13

Pointers

   o Although described as three actions, this is one unbroken movement. Complete the scoop up as the lead foot advances. Complete the chop as the rear foot steps through. Follow closely and quickly with a forceful stab.

   • Continue on to repeat right and left, limited only by the space available.

1e Chop Turn Around   pīqiāng zhuànshēn   劈枪转身

Using the _left stance chop_ or _stab_ as example. _Left step forward, lift and punt; Turn around, retreat, chop._

ACTION 1: Advance the left foot hooked in without moving the right foot, straightening the legs to stand up. (From _left stance stab_ hook the left foot in on the spot.) Rotate the right palm away from the thumb and lift it to turn and bring the spear base above the head at the right side with the palm up and the arm rounded. Loosen the left hand and slide it forward, rotating the palm away from the thumb to face out and bending the arm. This brings the spear tip in an arc to the left and down to in front of the body, the tip at knee height. Look past the spear tip. (image 3.14)

3.14

ACTION 2: Turn around 180 degrees to the right to face back behind, pivoting both feet on the spot. Shift back and retreat the right foot, then settle the body down and shift back some more to sit mostly on the right leg, in a _santi_ stance. Swing the spear forward and down from above the head to chop forcefully. Pull the right hand, holding the base, to the right waist. Finish with the left hand in

3.15

front of the body, the spear tip at waist height. Press the head up and look past the spear tip. (image 3.15)

From _right_ stance chop step the left foot forward hooked in. Do the _lift and punt_ then _turn and retreat_, the same as described above.

Pointers

- o Hook in, turn around, and retreat smoothly – link the steps together closely.

- o Rotate the hands to do the punting and lifting action. Turn the right palm away from the thumb and the left palm towards the thumb. This action of '_yin_ and _yang_ mutually rotate' goes through the whole body.

- o Complete the chop as the retreating foot lands. Settle the trunk down slightly. The spear must have a focal point in the chop, and the tip must not hit the ground.

1f   Chop Closing Move   pīqiāng shōushì   劈枪收势

On arriving back at the starting point, do a _turn around_ to face the original direction. Once you are in _left stance chop_ or _stab_ then do _closing move: Right retreat, snap the spear; Close the feet and put the spear at attention; Stand at attention with the spear._

ACTION 1: Retreat the right foot a half-step then withdraw the left foot a half-step and shift back mostly to the right leg. Pull the spear base back to the right side between the hip and waist. Slide the left hand forward and tighten the grip abruptly to snap the spear up. The spear tip should quiver up and down. The spear tip is at head height. Look forward. (image 3.16)

3.16

ACTION 2: Turn and shift to the right leg. Hold the spear shaft in the left hand and bring the shaft to vertical at the right of the right shoulder. Slide the right hand, supporting the shaft at the right of the body. Look at the left hand. (image 3.17)

ACTION 3: Bring the left foot in beside the right foot and stand up to attention. Release the left hand and lower it across the body to the left side, then lift it at the side, and then bend the elbow to press down in front of the body, finishing with the arm vertical at the left side. Follow the movement of the left hand with the eyes, and once the left hand has pressed down, look forward. Keep the right hand holding the spear. The

3.17

3.18

closing is now completed. (image 3.18)

- If the <u>right</u> foot is forward then retreat the right foot behind the left and shift back, withdrawing the left foot slightly.

Pointers

- o Each of the five elemental techniques uses the same closing move.

- o The power must reach the tip of the spear in *retreat and snap the spear.* The tip must quiver up and down.

- o The closing move must be done continuously and be well coordinated between the upper and lower segments. It must be stable. The eyes and spirit must be bright and focused to the completion of the movement.

POWER GENERATION FOR SPEAR CHOP

Chop: the hands work together as a unit on the shaft of the spear. The left hand uses a downward and forward pushing and pressing power while the right hand grips tightly with a backward pulling and slightly lifting power. Be sure to use the waist, torso and shoulders to move the hands. The actual hand movements are slight, relatively hidden. The chop must have a focal point at waist height. As the left hand arrives at the focal point it must stop sharply. At this time tighten its grip with an upward pulling power and press the spear base down with the right hand. The spear momentum is stopped abruptly, and a snap is developed, the power reaching to the tip, which is the chopping power.

- The power in the hands comes from the body core, the shoulders, and the arms. The trunk compresses then lengthens while the chest closes then opens and the shoulders close then open. Turn the waist, reach with the shoulders, extend the arms, sit into the hips, and press the head up to create a whole body coordinated power.

- The classics say, "Chop depends on sitting the knee." Sitting the knee means that the front leg must maintain a certain flexion. Because the spear chops down with considerable force the lead knee must absorb more force than usual. To lengthen the time of power application the knee bends with a springing action. This springing flexion is what 'sitting' means – it is not just a static sitting or flexion of the knee. Pushing into the lead foot creates it. The momentum of the body will cause the knee to flex with a springing action.

Check and hook: Both hands must twist simultaneously. When checking and hooking to the right, close the left shoulder a bit to the right by using the waist. Hook up by twisting and bending the arms, check by using the right or left turn of the trunk. The power of the check is in the body core, while the power of the hook is in the hands.

Scoop: The power comes from the shoulders, shoulder girdle and arms. Release and settle the shoulders, put a sharp checking action into the shoulder girdle, and move the arms in a turning action. Keep the hands firm on the spear so that the power of the body transfers through to the spear fore-section or tip to complete the scoop. Do not use too large an action when practising the scoop on its own. When practising the scoop with the chop you may use a bigger action to gather more power for the chop.

Turn around: *Lift and punt* is a low defensive action. The hands work in opposite directions, rotating in opposite directions. The right hand rotates and pulls as it lifts the spear, using a bracing out power. The left hand uses a carrying power. Transfer power from the body core to the arms. During the *retreat and chop* action, slide the left hand. Turn around, retreat, turn the waist, and reach the shoulder, to send power through to the fore-section of the spear.

Closing: During the retreat and snap action pull and snap the right hand quickly, pressing down at the last instant. Brace the right arm and keep the body solid. Slide the left hand then abruptly tighten the grip to stop the spear. The left arm also has a bracing power, so that it moves as one with the body. The hands must coordinate these two actions together, and with the retreating footwork.

BREATHING CYCLE FOR SPEAR CHOP

- Inhale during defensive actions.

- Exhale as you step forward and chop. Settle the *qi* to the *dantian*.

PRACTICAL APPLICATIONS FOR SPEAR CHOP

Each of the upward actions is an effective defense that also serves to place the spear tip in position for the downward chop. Chop should always be followed up with a stab – the spear has a straight sharp tip, so the stab is its most effective technique.

Checking hook and chop and *upward scoop* are defensive actions, knocking the opponent's weapon either aside or up. With a scoop you can knock the opponent's weapon up or knock his lead hand or arm. With a check and hook you can lead his weapon back as you knock it aside. If the opponent is chopping towards you, use a checking hook to take him off target then slide along his weapon's shaft to chop, sliding directly along to his lead hand or arm. If he retreats, then stab his chest.

With either technique, use the fore-section of your spear shaft to contact halfway along the opponent's long weapon as he stabs towards you. You then must chop instantly, moving smoothly into the chop, and then stab to his chest.

Chop can be used either as an attack or a defense. You can use the chop directly, knocking the opponent's weapon out of his hands to create an attacking opportunity. You can attack by chopping the opponent's arm or body. You can defend by chopping his weapon. The classics say, "use the clockwise trap for inside, use the counterclockwise trap for outside, use the lift for low attacks, and use the seize for high attacks. Only the chop can be used for either right or left." You can see that the chop is a very practical and strong technique.

- The footwork must be agile to use chop. Step to either side when defending so that the opponent has difficulty taking his aim. Stepping to the side also sets up your spear to cross his weapon. The spear must be at a certain angle to the opponent's weapon to be used to block or knock aside effectively. Step straight in to attack, sending the spear tip directly to the target.

- The head, chest, belly, hips, knees, and feet and the lead hand are the targets of the spear. They are the seven spots that the spear 'sees.' Attack quickly, fiercely, and accurately, and don't take any pity on the opponent.

THE POEM ABOUT SPEAR CHOP

劈枪技法最平常，劈开敌械扎胸膛。左右挂挑枪上起，劈手劈械把敌伤。

The most common technique of the spear is a chop.

Chop aside the opponent's weapon and stab to his chest.

Lift the spear to hook or scoop his weapon to the side,

Chop the opponent's hand or weapon to injure him.

SPEAR DRILL

INTRODUCTION TO SPEAR DRILL, *ZUAN QIANG*

The spear drill takes its name from the empty hand drilling punch of the five element fists. The drilling punch is a punch up and forward from below, so as long as you are doing this type of technique, then you are within the category of drilling. So what sort of technique should a spear drill be? Different sources answer this question differently. Some classics say that the spear drill is a low outer trap to left or right combined with a step forward and stab to the head. The Shang style Xingyi book says that the spear drill is a back step with an inverted hand stab to the top of the head. Some books say it is an outer trap, inner trap, and then high stab to the head. Others say that it is a block to left or right, then step forward to stab to the head. Each source has its own way of looking at the technique, and each has reason.

After many years of practice and thought on spear drill, and analysis of the five element techniques of the spear, I feel that spear drill combination should have a stab to the head – coming from below to attack high – but should also have an inverted hand low stab. The low stab uses a lift and punt to defend and then advances with an inverted hand stab to the knee or foot. "Lift and punt to control below" is an important traditional technique, and its inclusion here ensures it will be practised. If the opponent blocks the low attack, then you can cover and press down, and then stab his face. This keeps the traditional view of spear drill as a stab to the head, while also adding a low stab to the knee or foot into the spear's repertoire. Including both upper and lower stabs in the drill combination enriches spear drill practice.

The spear drill combinations include *Lift and punt, stab to the knee; Cover and press, stab to the face; Spear drill turn around;* and *Spear drill closing move.*

2a Right Stance Drill: Lift, Punt and Low Stab   yòubù zuānqiāng   右步钻枪

Start from *on guard*. Continue with *Advance, lift, punt; Step forward, stab to knee.*

ACTION 1: Advance the left foot a half-step and follow in the right foot to the left ankle without touching down. Lift the spear base to above the right of the head, rotating the right palm away from the thumb to turn the palm up, and bracing out with the arm bent. Let the shaft slide through the left hand to bring the hand forward and rotate the palm towards the thumb to turn the palm angled forward.

Bend the left arm and hold the shaft tightly with the left hand at waist height, pushing the hand forward slightly. This makes the spear tip circle left, down, and right, finishing at knee height. Follow the movement of the spear tip with the eyes. (image 3.19)

ACTION 2: Step the right foot forward and follow in the left foot a half-step to take a sixty/forty stance. Hold the base tightly with the right hand and thrust it forward and down. Let the shaft slide through the left hand, keeping the left hand extended to aim. Push the right hand forward and down until it meets the left hand. The hands will be a bit higher than the shoulders and the spear tip will be at knee height. Send the power to the spear tip. Look at the spear tip. (image 3.20 and from the front)

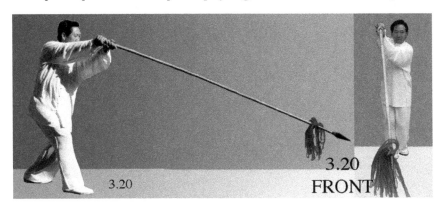

Pointers

- o Coordinate the action of the hands to do the lifting scull as the left foot advances.

- o Complete the stab as the right foot lands. To do the inverted grip low stab close the chest, open the upper back, and bring the shoulders in together.

- o Although you learn the techniques as two actions, they should be done continuously as one move.

2b Left Stance Drill: Cover, Press and Stab zuǒbù zuānqiāng   左步钻枪

Advance, cover and press; Step forward, stab up.

ACTION 1: Advance the right foot a half-step and follow in the left foot to by the right ankle without touching down. Bend the elbows and set down slightly. Pull the spear base back with the right hand, lowering the hand to the right waist. Rotate the right palm towards the thumb to turn the palm up. Slide the shaft through the left hand, rotating the left palm away from the thumb to turn the palm down. Bend the left elbow and press down with the thumb/forefinger web. The spear tip circles left, up, and then right with the shaft remaining level at waist height. Look at the spear tip. (image 3.21)

ACTION 2: Step the left foot forward and follow in the right foot a half-step. Lift the left hand slightly to aim the spear to head height and release slightly to allow the spear to slide through. Push the spear forcefully with the right hand, accelerating until the right hand arrives at the left hand. Open the left hand to support the right hand. The spear stabs to head height while the hands are at chest height. Send power out to the spear tip so that it quivers. Look past the tip. (image 3.22 and from the front)

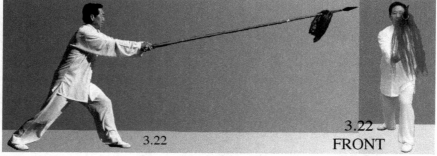

Pointers

- o Complete the circle and press down with the hands as the right foot advances, coordinating everything together. Remember to open and close the body.

- o Stab forward as the left foot steps. The whole movement should be completed as one action, without pause.

- • Connect to *right stance drill*, and continue. The number of repetitions is limited only by the size of your training space.

2c Drill Turn Around   zuānqiāng zhuànshēn   钻枪转身

Using the <u>*left*</u> *stance upper drill* as example. *Hook-in lift, scull; Turn around, retreat and chop.*

ACTION 1: Hook-in the left foot on the spot and shift to the left leg, standing up. Rotate the right hand and pull the spear while lifting and rotating. Lift the base above the head. Slide the spear through the left hand to bring the left hand forward on the shaft. The spear tip is forward, pointing down at knee height. Look at the spear tip. (image 3.23)

ACTION 2: Turn around 180 degrees to the right to face back in the way from which you came. Retreat the right foot and shift back mostly onto the right leg. Pull the spear base forward and down to the right side with the right hand. Bring the left hand up and forward, then chop down with the shaft, so that the spear tip has drawn a circle up, then forward and down. The spear finishes horizontal at waist height. Send the power to the fore-section of the spear shaft. Press the head up and look past the spear tip. (image 3.24)

Pointers

- o Lift the spear as the left foot hooks in, chop the spear as the right foot retreats. Complete both moves without hesitation.

2d Drill Closing Move   zuānqiāng shōushì   钻枪收势

- The *closing move* is the same as described above in *chop closing move*.

POWER GENERATION FOR SPEAR DRILL

Lift: The hands must alternate between *yin* and *yang*. That is, as the right palm rotates away from the thumb, the left palm rotates towards the thumb, working together and gaining power from the body. Transfer the power of the body to both shoulders, both arms, and through them to the fore-section of the spear shaft. The right hand combines pulling, bracing, and rotating while the left hand combines bracing and presenting. The power of the body, together with the flexibility of the shaft, makes the spear tip quiver.

Step forward low stab: The right hand starts out above the head and stabs down with an inverted grip, so this naturally is not as strong as a straight thrust. To put as much power as possible to the inverted grip, raise the elbow, close the shoulders together, send the arms forward, and reach forward slightly with the torso, opening the upper back and closing the chest, while tucking in the lower back. Stab down quickly and pull the spear back quickly.

Advance cover and press: This technique emphasizes body technique. Shift the body back slightly as the right hand pulls the spear base back. Shift the body forward as the hands rotate to trap, closing the shoulders and chest and pressing the head up. Put all of the body's power to the spear's fore-section as the right hand sets the base at the waist and the left hand presses down the shaft. Skilled spear technique can only be achieved when the spear becomes one with the body.

Stab up: The key to the high stab is the left hand – it is used like the sight of a rifle to determine the direction and placement of the tip. The left hand must control the spear shaft, not allowing any swaying at all. The right hand puts the force into the stab, the left hand aims the spear. When the spear stabs, turn the waist, release the shoulders forward, and extend the arms.

Turn around: The turning move is expansive and in a high stance. Then settle down into the retreat and chop, collecting the body together. Press the head up. Breathe out to give more power. Be sure to set the base of the spear firmly to gain power for the chop. Remember to bring the shaft past the halfway point before accelerating the power, and to have a focal point.

PRACTICAL APPLICATIONS SPEAR DRILL

Lift and punt is a defensive move, what is called 'lift and punt to remove something underneath.' If an opponent comes at you with a low stab, just as he is fully extended but not quite in contact, that is, just before his right hand reaches his left hand, lift your right hand above your head and snap your spear head down in a semi-circle. Your spear shaft will hit his and knock it off target.

Inverted grip low stab is a stab to the lead leg, knee or foot. This is not a strong stab since it uses an inverted grip, so it must be fast. Whether or not you hit your target, you must also pull it back quickly because your inverted grip is relatively easily knocked out of your hands should the opponent have time to knock your spear.

Advance press down contains a stir, a knock away, a trap and a press down, all of which protect the central or lower areas of your body. If your opponent stabs at you from out of reach you can knock his spear with your tip and then slide along his spear with a stirring action to trap and press down. Snap the spear at the end to knock his spear down. Then stab to his face.

Always wait for the crucial moment before defending. The crucial moment is just as the opponent has committed to the attack but not yet reached the target. You must react neither early nor late. If you react too early the opponent can easily change his technique. If you react too late you will get hit. This is a question of training the timing and recognition of the crucial moment. The crucial moment is something that many masters know but don't teach. As they say, 'rather teach ten techniques than the skill of timing.' Mastery of a technique is really a question of knowing the timing and how to gain the crucial moment.

You need instruction and practice with sliding spears together. General Qi Jiguang described this in his book: "Face each other with two spears, one chops and the other presses, trapping with a large or small circle. Lining up the spears counts as one repetition. After 10,000 repetitions without losing contact, each lining up perfectly, then skill is perfected." This precious theory should be pondered until understanding comes, be repeated until the technique comes, and be practised until the application comes.

THE POEM ABOUT SPEAR DRILL

钻枪习练过万遍，提撸防下阴阳转。上步反手扎膝脚，绞拨盖压扎其面。

The spear drill must be practised more than ten thousand times.

Lift and punt to protect below, alternating *yin* and *yang*.

Step forward and invert the grip to stab the opponent's knee or foot,

Stir, knock, cover and press to stab his face.

SPEAR THRUST

INTRODUCTION TO SPEAR THRUST, *BENG QIANG*

What is traditionally called *'bengqiang'* in Xingyi is the spear technique of outer trap, inner trap, and stab. The final stab is similar to the *'beng'* driving punch of the five elements – a half step advance with a straight attack.[51]

Traditionally the spear thrust is done with a half step advance and following step. I have added a cover step, a back step, and a circling step to make the footwork more agile, train the connection between the spear and body more effectively, and make the spear technique more applicable.

Spear thrust includes *stationary thrust, back-cross step thrust, cross-over step thrust, roundabout step thrust, turn around thrust,* and *closing move.*

3a Stationary Thrust　　　　yuánbù bēngqiāng　　原步崩枪

Start from *on guard* (image 3.25). *Stationary outer trap; Stationary inner trap; Stationary stab.*

ACTION 1: Without moving the feet, rotate the left palm towards the thumb to circle the palm up while rotating the right palm away from the thumb at the side. Work the hands together so that the spear tip circles up, left, and down in a counter clockwise half-circle about thirty centimetres in diameter. Look past the spear tip. (image 3.26)

3.25

ACTION 2: Close the left arm a bit forwards and rotate to press down with the thumb/ forefinger web. Rotate the right palm towards the thumb. Work the hands together so that the spear tip circles clockwise down, left, and up, and then right and down. Send power out to the spear tip. Look past the

3.26

---

[51] Author's note: In most styles, *'beng qiang'* is defined as an upwards or sideways snap of the fore-section, with the power shaking the tip. Only in Xingyi is the thrust technique called a *'beng.'* So when in Xingyi you perform a normal, snapping *'beng qiang,'* it is called a *'bibeng qiang,'* or, 'the other *beng'* to differentiate the two.

spear tip. (image 3.27)

ACTION 3: Shift forward, pushing into the right leg and bending the left leg to shift about sixty percent of the weight forward on the left leg. Allow the shaft to slide through the left hand, using it to aim forward. Send the spear out forcefully with the right

hand, accelerating into the stab. Cup the right hand in the left hand. Send power to the tip of the spear so that it quivers. Almost fully straighten the arms, and hold the spear horizontal at chest height. Look past the spear tip. (image 3.28)

Pointers

○ The hands must rotate at the same time to turn the spear. The spear must be held tight to the body while trapping inward and outward. The spear tip must draw two half circles.

○ When stabbing, the spear must go in a straight line and the power must go out to the tip. It must be sent out like an arrow, and be brought back in a straight line.

3b Back-cross Step Thrust   bēibù bēngqiāng   背步崩枪

Back-cross step outer trap; Step forward inner trap; Stab.

ACTION 1: After stabbing, pull the spear back in a straight line to the right side of the body with the right hand, letting the spear slide through the left hand. Without moving the left foot, step the right foot forward behind the left foot and shift into a cross step. Rotate the hands to circle the spear up, left and then down to complete an outer trap. Look forward. (image 3.29)

ACTION 2: Step the left foot forward and shift mostly onto the right leg. Rotate both hands to circle the spear tip down, left, up, and then right and down to complete an inner trap. (image 3.30)

ACTION 3: Without moving the feet, shift forward, straightening the right leg and bending the left leg with most weight on the left leg.[52] Stab forward forcefully with the spear, sliding it through the left hand. Finish with the spear tip at chest height and the shaft level. Send power to the spear tip so that it quivers. Support the right hand in the left hand. Keep the arms slightly bent. Look past the spear tip. (image 3.31)

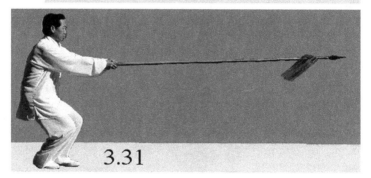

Pointers

- Complete the outer trap while the right foot steps through behind the left leg.

- Complete the inner trap while the left foot is stepping forward.

- Be sure to transfer your power through to the spear tip so that it quivers.

3c Cross-over Step Thrust   gàibù bēngqiāng   盖步崩枪

Right cross-over step, outer trap; Left step forward, inner trap; Stab.

ACTION 1: Without moving the left foot, step the right foot forward in front of the left foot, turning the foot out to land with a hooked out foot. Shift weight forward

---

[52] Translator's note: The stab may be done shifting into a forward stance or bringing the right foot forward to a closed stance. Either way is correct. I have translated the text as is throughout, even when the author has done the alternate stance in the photo.

between the feet to take a cross step with the legs slightly bent. Rotate the left palm towards the thumb to turn the palm up. Rotate the right hand at the waist, palm away from thumb. Rotate both hands simultaneously to cause the spear tip to draw a counter clockwise half-circle up, left, and down. Keep the spear shaft tight to the belly. Look past the spear tip. (image 3.32)

ACTION 2: Step the left foot forward without moving the right foot, keeping most weight on the right leg. Rotate and press down on the shaft with the thumb/forefinger web of the left hand. Rotate the right palm towards

the thumb, so that both hands work together to draw a clockwise circle down, left, up, right and down with the spear tip. Keep the spear shaft tight to the belly. Send the power to the spear tip. Press the head up and look past the spear tip. (image 3.33)

ACTION 3: Without moving the feet, shift the weight forward by pushing the right leg straight and bending the left leg to take a sixty/forty stance weighted to the left leg. Push the spear straight forward forcefully with the right hand, letting it slide through the left hand. Stab to chest height with tthe spear shaft level. Open the left hand to support the right hand. Keep the arms almost straight. Send power to the spear tip so that it quivers. Look past the spear tip. (image 3.34)

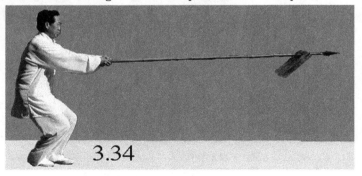

Pointers

- o   Complete the outer trap as the right foot does the cross-over step.

- o   Complete the inner trap as the left foot steps forward.

3d Roundabout Step Thrust   ràobù bēngqiāng   绕步崩枪

Left roundabout step, outer trap; Right step forward inner trap; Stab.

ACTION 1: Pull the spear base back to the right side with the right hand, letting the shaft slide through the left hand. This forms a ready stance. Advance the left foot with a circular step, landing to the forward right with the foot hooked out. Rotate the left hand palm towards the thumb to complete an outer trap with the spear tip. Rotate the right palm away from the thumb, keeping the spear shaft tight to the waist. The spear tip draws a counter clockwise half-circle up, left and down. Look past the spear tip. (image 3.35)

ACTION 2: Step the right foot forward without moving the left foot, shifting most weight to the left leg. Rotate both hands to complete a clockwise inner trap with the spear. (image 3.36)

ACTION 3: Shift forward towards the right leg, extending the left leg almost straight and bending the right leg to take a right bow stance. Slide the spear through the left hand, releasing just enough to let it slide while aiming. Holding the spear base in the right hand, push forward forcefully, finishing with the right arm almost straight. Slide the left hand back until it snugs onto the right hand. Stab the spear straight forward at chest height with the shaft level. Press the head up and send the power to the spear tip. Look forward. (image 3.37)

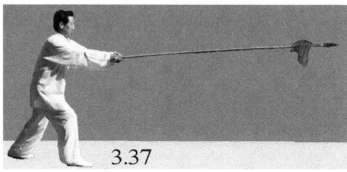

Pointers

- o Use a circular pathway to complete the roundabout step. Use both hands to complete the outer trap.

- o Complete the inner trap as the right foot steps forward. Complete the stab as the body shifts forward.

- o Do three clear movements – outer trap, inner trap, and stab – but complete them without hesitation.

- Do another stationary thrust by bringing the left foot forward while pulling the spear base back to the waist to take a ready stance. Then continue on.

3e Thrust Turn Around   bēngqiāng zhuànshēn   崩枪转身

When you run out of space, if the <u>left</u> foot is forward, hook-in in front of the right foot. If the <u>right</u> foot is forward, then step the left foot through to hook-in in front of the right foot. *Hook-in step, lift and punt; Turn around, heel kick; Rotate, spear chop.*

ACTION 1: Hook-in the left foot and stand up. Lift the spear base with the right hand as you rotate the palm away from the thumb. As the right hand arrives above the head, the palm should face out. Slide the spear in the left hand to bring the hand closer to the right hand. As the right hand arrives above the head, rotate the left palm towards the thumb and bend the arm. This makes the spear shaft snap towards the left side. The tip should be slanted downward to knee height. Look at the spear tip. (image 3.38)

ACTION 2: Turn around to the 180 degrees to the right, shifting to the left leg and bending it. You are now facing back in the way from which you came. Bend the right knee and lift it with the foot turned out, then kick with the heel at least to waist height, keeping the foot turned. Do not move the hands or the spear. Look ahead of the kicking foot. (image 3.39)

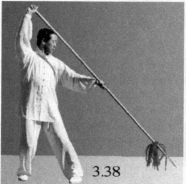 

ACTION 3: Quickly land the right foot forward and down with the foot still turned out. Rotate the body rightward and land with the legs crossed, dropping down and bending the legs in a scissors stance. Bring the spear base forward, down, and then pull back with the right hand to the side of the waist. Bring the left hand down and back then slide it up the spear shaft, and then chop forward and down from above. Tighten the left hand as it arrives, pressing down with the thumb/forefinger web,

palm down. The spear is level, just below the waist. Send power to the fore-section of the spear. Press the head up and look forward. (images 3.40 transitional and 3.40)

- Continue on, stepping the left foot forward to move into *outer trap, inner trap, and stab.*

Pointers

- o *Turn around* is one move and should be completed without hesitation. Hook- in well to get the body turned around. Turn around quickly and kick as high as you can. Land firmly. Coordinate the action of the hands and spear with that of the feet and body.

- o *Lift and punt* uses a rotation of the hands. To chop, first slide the left hand and then tighten it to put force into the chop. Be sure to lower the body to chop.

3f Thrust Closing Move   bēngqiāng shōushì   崩枪收势

Closing move is always the same. See the description in *spear chop*. First complete a stab, then retreat the right foot a half-step and withdraw the left foot slightly, shifting back. Pull the spear back and snap it up. The tip should quiver up and down. This will place you in a ready stance. From there, continue on to finish as usual.

POWER GENERATION FOR SPEAR THRUST

Thrust is the most characteristic and fundamental technique of the spear, as it combines outer trap, inner trap, and stab. It is done with various footwork patterns – stationary, back-cross step, cross-over step, and roundabout step. The primary technique is the stab, but first you must circle. This structure of the spear determines this defensive circling. The spear must first control and cross an oncoming weapon before it can stab. Thus, inner trap and outer trap are the most fundamental of spear techniques, and the most important skills. This fundamental combination is traditionally called 'circle spear' or 'circle spear mother technique.'

There are four main principles to the outer trap, inner trap.

- First, outer trap and inner trap draw two half circles to left and right, completing a full circle. The aft-section of the spear shaft must be held tight to the belly, it must not leave the body.

- Second, the hands must alternate *yin* and *yang*, rotating together in opposite directions. As the left hand turns out the right hand turns in, when the left hand closes in the right hand turns out. This is called 'twist the spear, twist the pole.'

- Third, the radius of the circle should be thirty centimetres. When learning, the spear tip may move in a large circle, but not over head height or under hip height.

- Fourth, the power of the circles comes from the body, transferring directly from the body to the spear. The spear is flexible, so the tip circles from the power transfer. Hold the spear with the left hand neither too loosely nor too tightly. If the left hand is too tight the technique is stiff, and if it is too loose the technique is flaccid. Keep the wrist supple and the grip just right, firm but supple. The right hand should hold firmly with a supple wrist.

To do the outer trap, turn the left hand out, draw back and open the left shoulder, settling it down. The belly should have a very slight power pressing forward, turning rightward. To do the inner trap the left hand rotates in and presses forward and down with the thumb/forefinger web, closing the left shoulder and turning the body slightly rightward. In this way the power of the body core transfers to the spear shaft, giving it more power than just the arms. The spear flexes as the body's power reaches it, completing the circle.

To stab, the spear should shoot out like an arrow and come back like pulling in a line. The spear absolutely must go in and out in a straight line. The power must reach the tip, making it quiver.

The left hand controls the direction and height of the spear tip, sending it accurately to its target. Stab quickly and bring the spear back quickly. When stabbing, release the left hand's grip enough to slide the spear through, using the left hand to aim.

The right hand sends the spear forward, accelerating gradually, releasing power sharply. As the right hand arrives near the left hand, apply one inch power to complete the stab. Turn the hips and waist, close the shoulders, extend the arms and send the hands out to transfer power to the spear tip.

The spear shaft and arms form one straight line. The spear must stab accurately with a focal point. The tip must not wobble.

The bodywork and waist action must be coordinated with the footwork. The footwork must be agile. The bodywork should work together with the footwork to combine with the spear.

Turn around is made up of three actions: *hook-in step and lift, turn heel kick,* and *rotate chop.* When the right hand lifts and pulls the spear, the spear tip should draw a circle left and down while being pulled back. The right hand must rotate and put a bracing power into the spear while the left hand stabilizes the spear with a carrying power. The turn and kick is the same as the thrusting punch turn and kick, and uses the same trampling power on landing. When rotating and chopping, rotate the waist, settle in the belly, reach the left shoulder forward, tuck in the left elbow, and put the body's power into the chop. Press up into the head while sitting down.

PRACTICAL APPLICATIONS FOR SPEAR THRUST

The essence of spear techniques, and the most representative, is the outer trap, inner trap and stab combination, normally called 'middle level spear,' which in Xingyi is called *spear thrust.*

Outer trap and inner trap are used to defend against a straight attack from another long weapon. If a long weapon is coming towards your left side – your 'outside' – use the outer trap. If a long weapon is coming towards your right side – your 'inside' – use the inner trap.

Because of the spear's shape, the stab is the most important of all spear techniques, and all other techniques are based on setting up for this technique. The spear stabs out quickly in a straight line with its sharp tip. If it reaches its target it can inflict serious damage or death. Its main targets are high, middle, and low – the head, chest, and abdomen. Other effective targets are the opponent's leading hand or arm. The opponent's leading hand and arm are close, so easily reached; you just need to extend your arm to get them with the spear. So if you are good with a spear you should go for your opponent's lead hand first. Once the opponent's lead hand is injured he will lose his grip and drop his weapon, and then you can attack at will.

Using different footwork – back-cross step, cross-over step, roundabout step, advance, retreat, and shifting to right and left – has two purposes. One is to keep moving so that the opponent cannot fix on you. The other is to use footwork to get your spear shaft to cross your opponent's weapon. Your spear can be used for defense much more effectively once it crosses your opponent's weapon. You attack to the centre, getting inside, and defend by crossing, to take your opponent offline.

The spear's 'middle stab' is the spear's strongest attack and the hardest to defend against. There are many descriptions of this in the classics. "The spear is the king of the centre." "The spear stabs out in a straight line." "The spear goes out like an arrow and comes back like (pulling) a rope." These are all attempts to describe the directness, speed, and ferocity of the spear stab. You must take care to keep your spear aligned straight with your opponent's weapon when stabbing, as his position is very hard to defend. There is another way to use the stab, and that is as a direct counter attack. As the opponent stabs towards you, stab back without any defensive action, just sitting back to get your body out of the way. Once the opponent fully extends the spear without hitting the target, he will pull it back. You then follow his spear back to stab. This is called 'eating a spear and returning a spear,' also known as 'don't defend or block, just use one strike.' And, once your opponent goes on the defensive, you can follow up with continuous multiple stabs – high, middle and low – without giving any breathing space. This is called 'responding to an attack with ten.'

For the spear you need to remember: 'cross weapons to defend, straight line to attack.'

As well as practising the outer trap, inner trap, and stab combination, you should be able to stab directly from the outer trap or just the inner trap. You should always, however, start the outer trap action when doing the drawing back action after a stab. And you should always start to stab forward as you do an inner trap. These actions set up the habits that will enable you to take advantage of situations with the spear. This is what the classics mean by "going out is a circle, coming back is also a circle, there is a straight line within the circle, and there is a circle within the straight line, the original spirit of the spear is in the circle." Circling the spear is its defensive technique, and is the means to the end, which is to attack. The best attacking technique of the spear is the stab.

You must practise the basics diligently if you hope to ever be able to use the spear in a fighting situation. Just training the techniques and forms is not enough, you must do partner 'shaft sliding' training. You need to master the techniques on your own. Partner training is to gain feeling and the ability to slide and stab, finding the distancing, timing, and ability to attack. It is hard to find a partner who understands the 'shaft sliding' practise, they are 'as scarce as phoenix feathers and unicorn horns.' Most people now just practise forms.

THE POEM ABOUT SPEAR THRUST

崩枪技法强中强，拦拿圆中找其枪。背盖绕步随身走，中平一点是枪王。

Spear thrust's strength lies in attacking the midline.

Use the circles of the outer trap and inner trap to control the opponent's weapon.

The footwork follows the body work – back-cross step, crossover step, and roundabout step.

One touch with the middle level stab shows why the spear is the king of weapons.

SPEAR SLASH

INTRODUCTION TO SPEAR SLASH, *PAO QIANG*

The spear slash uses the footwork and the same directional power of the empty hand pounding fist. With both hands on the spear, it strikes diagonally forward with an action that combines blocking, slicing, dragging, and scooping. There is also a traditional technique that blocks with the base, switching the hand grip and applying power similar to the pounding fist, stepping in a diagonal pattern. This technique is good because it uses the base and puts the circular movement of the spear to good use. The first method is more practical since it sets the tip up for a stab. The two methods show the technique and flavour of the pounding technique. You should practise both to develop your abilities more fully.

The first slash method includes *right back-cross step inner coil; left advance outer coil; step forward block up and push with a sculling slice up; retreat pound with the base; hook with the base; wheel and trap,* and *step in and stab.* The second slash method includes *right stance slash, left stance slash,* a continuation to *right stance slash,* and *slash turn around.*

METHOD ONE: COIL, SLASH, POUND, TRAP, STAB

4a Right Back-cross Step, Inner Coil   yòu bēibù lǐchán qiāng   右背步里缠枪

Start from *on guard. Back-cross step inner coil; Left advance outer coil; Step forward, high block and push with a sculling slice up; Retreat, pound with the base; Hook with the base, sheel and inner trap; Step in and stab.*

ACTION 1: Shift forward without stepping the left foot, stepping the right foot behind the left to advance in a back-cross step. The legs are crossed with the weight between them. The right hand always grips the spear base. Slide the left hand forward along the spear shaft and lower the tip, keeping the shaft tight to the body, to circle the tip down to the left. Turn the waist slightly left. Look at the spear tip. (image 3.41)

ACTION 2: Step the left foot forward without moving the right foot. Continue to circle the spear

3.41

with the left hand, moving the tip up and right. Finish with the left

thumb/forefinger web down, pressing the spear tip at waist height. The right hand, on the spear base, draws opposite circles to the left hand, keeping the shaft on the body. Look at the spear tip. (image 3.42)

Pointers

- Complete the right back-cross step as the spear tip circles down to the left. Complete the left step forward as the spear tip circles in. The spear should not stop between circles, so the stepping needs to be quick.

- The left hand controls the height of the spear tip, which should not go above the shoulders or below the hips. Transfer power from the waist to the spear, keeping the power gentle and connected.

4b   Left Advance, Outer Coil   zuǒ jìnbù wàichán qiāng   左进步外缠枪

ACTION: Advance the left foot a half-step and follow in the right foot to beside the left ankle, bending the left leg slightly to stand firmly. Control the spear tip with the left hand to draw it up, left, and then down with an outward coiling action. Keep the right hand at the right waist, then move in the opposite direction as the left hand and keep the shaft tight to the body. Draw a circle with the spear tip, no higher than the shoulders and no lower than the knees. Look at the spear tip. (image 3.43)

Pointers

- Step the left foot forward as the spear tip draws a circle up to the left.

- Slide the left hand forward along the shaft. Press the right hand firmly to keep the shaft tight to the body.

- *Right back-cross inner coil* connects immediately to *left advance outer coil*. The spear tip should draw two circles in two opposite directions in front of the body.

4c   Step Forward, High Block and Push with a Sculling Slice Up

shàngbù jiàtuī huōliāo   上步架推擤撩

ACTION: Take a long step to the forward right with the right foot and follow in a half-step with the left foot, to take a sixty/forty stance with the weight back. Bring the right hand from the waist to brace out above the head with the arm almost straight, rotating the palm to face out. Rotate the left palm towards the thumb slightly and bring the spear tip from the lower left to the upper right to slice up with the palm facing obliquely to the right front. Bend the left arm and push diagonally forward and right, finishing at chest height. The spear tip is pointing to the forward right at waist height with the power in the fore-section. Look past the spear tip. (images 3.44 and 3.44 from the front)

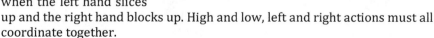

Pointers

- o Step the right foot a long step forward, landing when the left hand slices up and the right hand blocks up. High and low, left and right actions must all coordinate together.

- o This move is connected directly to *left advance outer coil*, without a pause.

4d Retreat, Pound with the Base   tuìbù zábà   退步砸把

ACTION: Retreat the left foot a half-step and shift back, withdrawing the right foot a half-step to sit mostly onto the left leg. Slide the left hand up the spear shaft and tighten it at the one third mark. Pull the left hand to the left waist with the palm turned out. Slide the right hand to about fifty centimetres from the spear base and press down with the thumb/forefinger web so that the spear base covers and presses forward and down. Pound the spear base down at waist height. Turn the body left and tuck in the right shoulder. Press the head up. Look past the spear base. (image 3.45)

Pointers

- o Retreat and withdraw the feet quickly. First slide the left hand along the spear. Then slide the right hand and pound down with the base. The covering pound must be done forcefully.

- o The hand slide must be coordinated, and the movement quick. The length of shaft extended to pound should be the length of your own arm.

4e Hook with the Base, Wheel and Inner Trap

guàbà fānshēn náqiāng   挂把翻身拿枪

ACTION 1: Hold the shaft with the right hand and bend the arm to hook the base up and back. As the base arrives above the head, slide the right hand back to the base. Push forward with the left hand. Shift back to the left leg. Look forward. (image 3.46)

ACTION 2: Wheel the body 180 degrees to the right, landing with the right foot hooked out, then stepping the left foot forward. Most weight is on the right leg.

Pull the spear base back to the right waist with the right hand, drawing a small circle. Slide the left hand back along the shaft to a placement conducive to the trapping action. Circle the spear tip left, up, and then right, finishing at waist height. Look past the spear tip. (image 3.47, left foot not yet landed)

3.46

Pointers

- The right hand first completes the backward hook. It slides back to the base after it gets to shoulder height. When the right hand is at the base it should always be completely at the end. If it does not make it fully back during the wheeling action, it must be placed at the end by the time you do the trapping action.

3.47

- You may jump when you do the body wheel. The inner trap should be done quickly with a forceful snap.

4f Step in and Stab   gēnbù zhāqiāng   跟步扎枪

ACTION: Do a follow-in step with the right foot to bring it up behind the left foot, keeping the weight back on the right foot similar to the stepping pattern of the driving punch footwork. Loosen the left hand to allow the spear to slide through it, and use it to aim. Push forcefully forward with the right hand until it meets the left hand and stops with the left hand supporting it. The spear must remain level with the tip at chest height. The arms are straight, the head up. Look past the spear tip. (image 3.48)

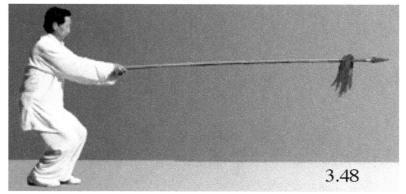

3.48

Pointers

- Send the spear out as the right foot lands. Send power to the tip so that it quivers.

o   Connect *hook and wheel* immediately to *step in and stab.*

4g Right Back-cross Step Inner Coil   yòu bēibù lǐchán qiāng   右背步里缠枪

ACTION 1: Advance the left foot a half-step without moving the right foot, keeping

most weight on the right leg in the same stance as *on guard*. Release the left hand enough to slide the spear shaft through, and pull the spear back with the right hand to the right side. Keep the spear shaft snug to the body. Look past the spear tip. (image 3.49)

ACTION 2: Shift forward and step the right foot behind the left foot, shifting onto the left leg without moving the left foot, to take a back-cross stance with the legs bent. Slide the left hand forward along the shaft a bit without moving the right hand. Use the waist and left hand to circle the spear tip down and to the left. Look at the spear tip. (image 3.50)

ACTION 3: Step the left foot forward without moving the right foot. Continue to circle the spear up and right until the left thumb/forefinger web presses down, holding the spear at waist height. Circle the right hand in a small circle in opposite direction to the left hand, keeping the spear shaft tight to the body. Look past the spear tip. (image 3.51)

Pointers

o   Actions 4a through 4f are the full combination, then action 4g starts a repetition of the combination. The combination should be done without a break in movement. The spear technique must be clear and completed. Never allow any technique to become messy just because you are trying to make the movement continuous.

METHOD TWO: RIGHT AND LEFT SLASH

4h Right Stance Slash   yòubù pàoqiāng   右步炮枪

Start from *on guard*. Continue with *Left advance, outer coil; Right step forward, scull and slice up.*

ACTION 1: Advance the left foot a half-step and follow-in with the right foot to beside the left ankle. Pull the spear base back with the right hand and slide the left hand forward along the shaft. Lift the left hand, bringing it to the rear left, circling the spear tip up, left, and then back. Follow this action with the right hand, pushing forward. Look at the spear tip. (image 3.52)

ACTION 2: Take a long step diagonally forward with the right foot and follow in the left foot a half-step. Lift the right hand up from the waist to above and to the right of the head, rotated palm up and with the arm rounded to brace. Push the left hand forcefully to the forward right as the right foot lands, palm facing in that direction. The spear tip circles from below, diagonally forward, the spear tip finishing at waist height. Send power to the fore-section so that it quivers. The left arm is almost straight, the left hand at chest height. Look past the spear tip. (image 3.53)

Pointers

- o Coil the spear as the left foot advances. Make a large circle with the spear.

- o As the right foot steps forward, lift the base with the right hand and slide the left hand on the shaft to scull and slice. The spear must arrive as the foot arrives.

4i Left Stance Slash   zuǒbù pàoqiāng   左步炮枪

Right advance, slice and changeover the hands; Left step forward, sculling slice.

ACTION 1: Advance the right foot a half-step and follow in the left foot to beside the right ankle. Swing the left hand to the left to circle the spear tip from the forward left up and back to the right. When the spear tip is up and the spear base is above the head, switch the position of the hands on the shaft. Lower the left hand, sliding it along the shaft to the base. Slide the right hand along the shaft to the midsection. Pull the spear back to the rear right with the right hand. Watch the spear as it moves. (image 3.54)

ACTION 2: Take a long step to the forward left with the left foot and follow in the right foot a half-step, keeping most weight on the right leg. Lift the left hand, holding the spear base, to above and to the side of the head, rotating it palm out. With the right palm facing the left front, push it forcefully to the forward left. The spear tip finishes at waist height. Almost fully extend the right arm, the hand at chest height, and send power to the fore-section of the spear. Press the head up.

Look past the spear tip. (image 3.55)

Pointers

○ Circle the spear up as the right foot advances. Switch positions quickly and smoothly, in a well coordinated way. The hands should switch over as the spear is lifted, when it is above the head. Keep the palms facing each other as they change over.

○ Lift the spear base with the left hand and slide the right hand to push the shaft as the left foot steps forward. The spear must arrive as the foot lands.

4j   Right Stance Slash   yòubù pàoqiāng   右步炮枪

Left advance, slice and changeover the hands; Right step forward, sculling slice.

ACTION 1: Advance the left foot a half-step and follow in the right foot to beside the left ankle. Swing the right hand to the right to circle the spear tip to the forward right. Lower the left hand to the left waist. Push the spear base forward with the left hand and slice up with the right hand to circle the spear tip up. When the spear tip is above the head, switch the position of the hands on the shaft. Lower the right hand, sliding it along the shaft to the base. As the spear circles down, slide the left hand along the shaft to the midsection. Watch the spear as it moves, and

watch the hands as they switch over. (image 3.56)

ACTION 2: Take a long step to the forward right with the right foot and follow in the left foot a half-step. Lift the right hand, holding the spear base, to block above and to the side of the head, rotating it palm out with the arm bent. With the left palm facing the right front, push it forcefully to the forward right, palm forward and

arm bent. The spear tip completes a scull and slice, finishing at waist height. Send power to the fore- section of the spear. Look past the spear tip. (image 3.57)

Pointers

- o Advance the half-step and switchover the hands in front of the head at the same time. Make the switch quickly.

- o When alternating left and right slash, first swing the spear into position, then push to the direction, whether right or left. Complete the slice up as the lead foot lands.

- Continue on with left and right slash, as space permits.

4k Slash Turn Around   pàoqiāng zhuànshēn 炮枪转身

From the _right_ stance slash. _Right hook-in step, slice, change over the hands; Left step forward, sculling slice._ If the _left_ foot is forward, do the same thing, just reversing right and left.

ACTION 1: Hook-in the right foot to the outside of the left foot and shift onto the right leg to turn around 270 degrees to the left. Lift the left foot to the right ankle, bending both legs and keeping them together. You have now turned around to face back. Bring the spear around as you turn, circling the tip left and up. Switch hands when the spear tip is up and the base is in front. Slide the left hand along the shaft back to the base and slide the right hand up to the middle. Continue to circle the spear tip to the right and down, bringing it down at the right side of the body. Watch the movement of the spear, and watch the hands as they switch over. (image 3.58)

ACTION 2: Take a long step forward with the left foot and follow in a half-step with the right foot. Gripping the spear base with the left hand, rotate it palm away from thumb and lift it above the head. Rotate the right palm towards the thumb so that the palm faces diagonally to the forward left and push it forcefully forward. Send power to the fore-section of the spear shaft, causing it to quiver. The spear tip finishes at waist height. Look past the tip. (image 3.59)

3.58 3.59

Pointers

- o   Turn around quickly. To do this, hook-in the foot considerably. Be sure to bring the spear around with the body, then slice up and switch hands after the turn.

- o   The action is the same as a normal slash, with the same points to remember.

4l   Slash Closing Move   pàoqiāng shōushì   炮枪收势

On arriving back at the starting point, do a *turn around* to face the original direction. If you are doing the first method, go until you are have the right foot forward in the stabbing posture, then close the same as from spear chop. If you are doing the second method, turn and go until you are in *right stance slash*. Then do *left step forward inner trap, right follow step stab*. The rest of the closing move is the same as usual: *Right follow in step, stab; Right retreat, snap the spear; Close the feet and put the spear at attention; Stand at attention with the spear.*

ACTION: Shift forward without moving the right foot, and take a step forward with the left foot, keeping most weight on the right leg. Rotate the right palm towards the thumb and control the spear with the left hand so that the tip circles left, up, and right to do an inner trap. Rotate the left palm away from the thumb so that the palm is down, pressing down with the thumb/forefinger web. The spear shaft is horizontal with the tip at waist height. Press the head up and look past the spear tip. (image 3.60)

3.60

POWER GENERATION FOR SPEAR SLASH

Sculling slice: Spear slash applies the structure of the empty hand cannon, or pounding punch, to the characteristics of the spear. The posture and character of the pounding punch work well applied to the sculling slice technique of the spear. The main technique of the spear slash combination is the sculling slice, which applies power to the fore-section of the spear. The power application must be smooth and forceful and coordinated with an exhalation to increase strength. The upper hand first lifts and pulls to above the head, then braces out. When the lower hand launches power to push forward strongly the arm must stay tight to the body so that the power comes from the body. The lower back uses a straightening power. Use full body power, connecting fully into the spear.

Coiling: This is a circular technique, taking the tip around to the inside or outside, also called left or right coiling. A clockwise coil is an inner coil, and a counter clockwise coil is an outer coil. To do the coil the spear shaft must stay connected to the body, otherwise the movement of the body will not control it. The arms move from the body, the left hand circling the spear, transferring the power completely to the tip. The inner coil is the same power as the inner trapping press, and the outer coil is the same power as a scooping hook. You must feel as if you are controlling an opponent's weapon, circling and sticking to it. You should feel as if you cannot be made to lose contact with his weapon. Be sure to use the hands in opposite directions, acting as 'yin' and 'yang.' The circle should keep the spear tip no higher than the head and no lower than the knees.

Pound with the base: The power of the whole body presses down into the base of the spear. Be sure to slide the hands quickly to get into position. Tuck in the belly and contain the chest when pounding down. When retreating the foot, first retreat the rear foot then withdraw the lead foot. Make sure you turn your body to pound.

- The overall principle of the body technique is to pre-load in the opposite direction to gain power for the weapon technique. You should examine this principle in each and every technique. Once you can apply it then your bodywork will be correct and you can be fully connected and strong.

PRACTICAL APPLICATIONS FOR SPEAR SLASH

Block up and slice: The main technique of slash is the upper block with a slice. An upper block normally blocks up over the head, but because the spear slash's upper block is angled, it does more than this. The action of blocking across and up with the base brings the tip through to slice up. The slice up brings the tip forward and up from below. This can also be called a scull and scoop. <u>Scull</u> is a power used to bring the spear through from the rear. <u>Scoop</u> is any technique that strikes up and forward with the fore-section of the shaft. So this technique blocks up to protect the head, but the action contains a low attack. Attack and defense are completely integrated.

Scull and slice: If someone comes at you using a sweeping action with a long weapon, you lift the base of your weapon to protect your midline and head and push your spear through with the other hand to attack his leg, groin, or stomach. Combined with a charging step, this technique protects and attacks at the same time – one of the characteristics of Xingyi. You must step in quickly and attack forcefully with full intent and spirit. Try to completely uproot your opponent.

Coil: The main idea is to coil around an incoming long weapon to control it. You must stick to his weapon, not allowing him to pull it away. This is not as simple as is sounds – this skill takes years to develop. You need to practise coiling with a partner. You need to develop the same sensitivity as Taiji push hands so that you can stick with the shaft of your spear. Once you can stick to and control another weapon then you can create opportunities to get in with a stab. While coiling, get the fore-section of your spear on the mid-section of your partner's spear. Coiling is just the means to the end, which is the stab. Inner (clockwise) coiling, contains a hidden inner trap and press down. Outer (counter clockwise) coiling, contains a hidden scoop and hook.

Pound the base: This technique uses a long weapon as if is a short one, using a short technique to control the attack of a long weapon. Retreat and withdraw to dodge the attack and strike the oncoming weapon or your opponent's body with the base of the spear. If the opponent pulls his weapon back to try to stab your head, then bring the butt with your right hand to slide the base of your spear along to hook and knock his weapon away to the right. Quickly wheel your body and do an inner trap with your spear, then step in and stab to his heart. These are the theoretical applications of the technique, to give you an idea of how it could be used. Of course you need to respond freely in a real situation.

THE POEM ABOUT SPEAR SLASH

炮枪技法气势雄，架撩擂挑劲要冲。里外缠绞粘敌械，砸把翻拿扎其胸。

The spear slash is a fierce technique.

Block up and slice, scull and scoop while charging in.

Coil in or out to stick to the opponent's weapon.

Pound the base of the spear, wheel, trap and stab his chest.

SPEAR CROSSCUT

INTRODUCTION TO SPEAR CROSSCUT, *HENG QIANG*

The spear crosscut takes its name from the empty hand crosscut technique. This is the traditional name, and what everyone calls it from habit. Crosscut is a technique that moves horizontally from side to side. It always moves flatly from left to right, or from right to left, as opposed to moving vertically or straight forward. It is a method of training to utilize a sideways strike with the spear.[53] It uses a full body, evenly balanced power that starts from the body core and utilizes the flexibility of the spear to reach and snap the fore-section of the shaft. The sudden stop at the end of the movement causes the spear to quiver. You need to practise crosscut with attention to detail over a long time to get a feel for the technique and to learn how to transfer power out to the spear tip.

The techniques in spear crosscut are *Left stance crosscut* and *Right stance crosscut*. Left stance crosscut contains a *Right advance encircle* and *Left step forward crossing snap*, while *Right stance crosscut* contains a *Left stance encircle* and a *Right stance crossing snap*.

5a   Right Stance Crosscut   yòubù héngqiāng   右步横枪

Start from *on guard. Left stance encircle; Right stance crossing snap.*

ACTION 1: Advance the left foot a half-step and follow in the right foot to the left ankle. Lift the right hand to the chest and extend the left hand forward. The palms face each other. Draw a counter clockwise circle with the spear tip. The spear tip should not go above the head or below the waist. The right hand makes the spear base draw a small circle in front of the chest. Look past the spear tip. (image 3.61)

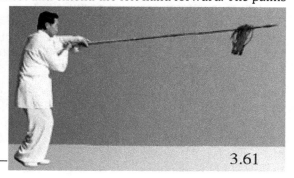

3.61

---

[53] Translator's note: In Xingyi this sideways snapping action is traditionally named the same as the empty hand crosscut that is resembles – *heng*. This snap is normally called a 'sideways *beng*' in other styles.

ACTION 2: Take a long step to the forward right with the right foot and follow in a half-step with the left foot, keeping most weight on the left leg. Pull the right hand across to the right, stopping in front of the right shoulder with the arm bent to ninety degrees. While doing this, rotate the right palm away from the thumb so that the palm faces out. Slide the left  hand along the shaft and push it horizontally to the right, abruptly stopping so that the fore-section snaps to the right. Keep the left arm slightly bent. The spear shaft is almost horizontal, with the tip slightly higher than the shoulders. Turn the body slightly to the right. Look past the spear tip. (image 3.62)

Pointers

- Circle with the spear while advancing the left foot. Be sure to send the spear forward. Both hands must be in front of the body.

- Snap the spear when the right foot steps forward. Coordinate the upper and lower movements so that the power impulse is all together. Transfer power to the spear tip. Be sure to control the hand's slide along the shaft.

- The actions must be completed as one movement. The encircling action is gentle, while the snapping action is strong.

5b Left Stance Crosscut   zuǒbù héngqiāng   左步横枪

Right advance, encircle; Left stance crossing snap.

ACTION 1: Advance the right foot a half-step and follow in the left foot to beside the right ankle. Send the spear forward, keeping the right hand on the base and sliding the left hand along the shaft. Turn the body a bit to the left. Circle the spear tip down, left, and then up and right in a clockwise circle. The right hand should draw a small circle in front of the body, under the left armpit. The spear tip circles between head height and waist height. Follow the action of the spear tip with the eyes. (image 3.63)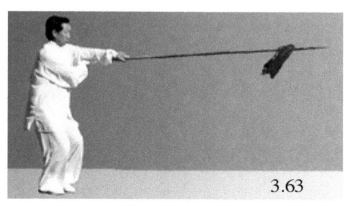

ACTION 2: Take a long step to the forward left with the left foot and follow in a half- step with the right foot, keeping the weight evenly balanced with both legs bent. Pull the spear base back from beneath the left armpit towards the right

shoulder, rotating the right palm away from the thumb so that the palm faces out. Pull the elbow back at shoulder height. Slide the left hand along the spear shaft and bring it across to the left, abruptly stopping it and gripping firmly, making the spear quiver. The spear should be horizontal with the tip slightly above the shoulder. Turn the body slightly to the right. Look past the spear tip. (image 3.64 and from the front)

Pointers

- o The hands must work together to draw the circle with the spear. The right hand draws a small circle while the spear tip draws a large circle. The hands operate in opposite directions, and snap forcefully at the end.

- o Do not stop midway through the movement.

5c Crosscut Turn Around   héngqiāng zhuànshēn   横枪转身

Starting from a *Left stance crosscut. Left hook-in turn around and sweep; Right advance and encircle; Left step forward and crossing snap.*

ACTION 1: Hook-in the left foot towards the right foot, turning the body around 180 degrees to the right to face back in the way from which you came. Advance the right foot a half-step without moving the left foot, keeping most weight on the left leg. Lower the right hand to the waist and slide the left hand a bit forward along the spear shaft, turning the palm forward. Bring the spear around as the body turns sweeping it horizontally around to point forward at shoulder height. Follow the movement of the spear with the eyes, looking past the spear tip at the end of the action. (image 3.65)

- • The rest of the turn continues on the same as usual for *left stance crosscut.*

Pointers

- o Hook-in the left foot well and turn around quickly. Sweep the spear using the power from the body core. Make sure to move the body and spear as one, launching power from the waist.

From a *right stance crosscut,* do *Left hook-in lift and scull; Right retreat and chop; Crosscut.*

ACTION 1: Step the left foot forward, landing it hooked-in in front of the right foot and shifting onto the left leg. Lift the right hand above the head, turning it palm away from thumb so that the palm faces out. Lower the left hand and swing it a bit to the right so that the spear tip circles left, down and then right. The spear tip is at ankle height. Look at the spear tip. (image 3.66)

ACTION 2: Turn the body around 180 degrees to face back in the way from which you came. Retreat the right foot and shift back so that a bit more weight is on the right leg. Bring the spear through so that the tip moves back, up and then forward to chop down. Pull the right hand back to the waist and extend the left arm. The spear is near horizontal at chest height. Look past the spear tip. (image 3.67)

3.66   3.67

- The rest of the turn continues on with *crosscut.*

Pointers

  o Lift the spear base to cut down as the left foot hooks in. Be sure to rotate both hands.

  o Wheel the body around as the right foot retreats so that the full power goes to the spear chop.

5d Crosscut Closing Move   héngqiāng shōushì   橫枪收势

Continue on and turn when you are back where you started. From a *right stance crosscut,* do *Left step forward inner trap; Follow-in stab; Retreat snap up.* Then complete the closing as described in *spear chop.*

ACTION 1: Step the left foot forward without moving the right foot, keeping the weight on

3.68

the right leg. Press the spear base down at the right waist, rotating both hands to do an inward trap. The spear shaft should be relatively level with the tip at waist height. Look past the spear tip. (image 3.68)

ACTION 2: Shift forward and follow in the right foot a half-step to behind the left foot. Push the spear base forward forcefully with the right hand, allowing the spear to slide through the left hand, using it as a guide. The spear is level and moves straight forward to chest height, the power reaching the tip. Look past the spear tip. (image 3.69)

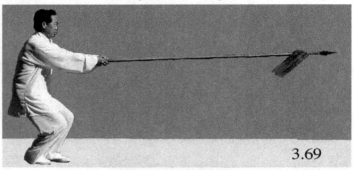

3.69

ACTION 3: Retreat the right foot a half-step and shift back to the right leg without moving the left foot. Pull the right hand back to beside the waist and slide the left hand up the spear shaft. Use both hands to snap the spear up so that the tip quivers at head height. Look past the spear tip. (image 3.70)

3.70

- The rest of the closing is the same as described in *spear chop*.

Pointers

- o Rotate the hands to perform the inner trap as the left foot steps forward. Stab as the right foot steps up. The spear must arrive as the foot lands.

- o Snap the spear up as the foot retreats. The left hand must slide and then grip strongly, and the timing must be perfect in order to send the power to the tip of the spear.

POWER GENERATION FOR SPEAR CROSSCUT

- Spear crosscut is made up two techniques – circling and sideways snap. Circling means to circle the spear tip in front of the body. The snap is a sudden acceleration and braking action coming from within the circle, to snap the spear tip to the side. Use the momentum of the spear tip to snap it to either side.

Circle: The action should be soft and fully rounded. Close the shoulders and chest in slightly, and gather power in the lower back area. Use the left hand in front as the pivot point and draw a small circle with the right hand in front of the chest. The spear tip will thus draw a large circle as the hands use power in opposite directions. That is, as the right hand goes down the left hand goes up, and as the right hand goes left the left hand goes right. The power in the hands is entirely due to the action of the waist and shoulders. The left hand should have a light grip, neither too tight nor too loose. If it grips too tightly then the action will be stiff. If it grips too loosely then the action will be weak. Work to find the principle of loading within the body to create power in the opposite direction.

Snap: The left arm drives across to the left or pushes across to the right. The right hand pulls back and braces out. Both hands rotate in opposite directions. At the point of power application, turn the body slightly right, straighten the lower back slightly, spread the chest and open the shoulders, and put a bracing and pulling power in the hands. The left hand braces forward while the right hand pulls back. Use power in the shoulders and arms, but that power is transferred from the lower back to the shoulders and from the shoulders to the arms. In this way the power will transfer through to the spear. Breathe out to gain more power, and send all your power to the fore-section of the spear. The left hand is the key in controlling the snap. Coordinate the upper and lower, forward and back, inner and outer elements of the movement so that the backward and forward movement of the arms and the pulling and bracing action of the hands results in a strong snap of the spear shaft.

Turn around: This is a crossing sweep that uses the power from the waist as the body turns. You need to sit down into the buttocks and rotate the waist. Shift back to help the power release, and rotate both hands. Move the spear as one with the body.

- When doing the crosscut, the left hand's slide and the arm's flexion adjust. The slide and degree of flexion determines how far you take the spear across to either side and how large the circle is. This is coordinated with the right hand's placement and amount of pull. And all this is coordinated with the body's action. Respect the principle of 'every single posture and action of all parts of the body must assist actively in the power launch.' The body must be comfortable and natural at all times. In addition, and most importantly, the structure and action must conform to the principles of defense and attack. So when you are training for the feeling of the spear, you must most of all find 'complete power.' That is – how do you gather the power of the entire body and send it to the end of the spear?

PRACTICAL APPLICATIONS FOR SPEAR CROSSCUT

- The crosscut is a snap that cuts to the side from within circling. Circling is not simply a fully rounded and even circle of the spear tip. The circle is actually a partial circle that is constantly adjusting the extent of its curve to control an opponent. The circle is one of the most important of spear techniques. They say that it is the 'primary basic' of all spear techniques.

Circle: The application of the circle is mostly to defend. As one classic[54] says most clearly,

> "To use a spear, the key lies in circling. With a circle you can defend to right and left, up and down. It is as if you have a shield three feet in front of you. Also, used to attack, who can defend against it? Go out with a circle and you will win. Come back with a

---

[54] Wu Shu, "Record of hand techniques"

circle and you can turn defeat into success."

Circling can be done clockwise (called inner circling) and counter clockwise (called outer circling). If an opponent comes on your right side, this is your inside, so you use an inner circle to protect against him. If an opponent comes on your left side, this is your outside, so you use an outer circle to defend.

If the opponent stabs to your head then lift your left hand slightly to cross the fore-section of your spear with the midsection of his spear. If he stabs to your waist, lift your right hand to your left armpit and rise slightly so that you can easily cross your spear with his, once again crossing the fore-section of your spear with the midsection of his. Crossing the shank of the spear is the main principle of defense. Your spear tip comes closer to the opponent, so that you have a quick and direct route and have the advantage over him. Crossing at the midsection of his spear puts him at a disadvantage, as it is difficult for him to pull his spear back or adjust the line of action. This is the main defensive principle of 'using the front to control the middle.' It uses the technique of the circle to trap. The circle has the inner trap and outer trap techniques contained within it.

Snap: The snap attacks mainly the opponent's head, neck, or chest, though of course his lead hand or arm is also a prime target. You could also knock his weapon out of the way. If the opponent attacks with a short weapon, once the blade touches your spear then a well timed and well placed snap will knock it out of his hands.

Used as an attack, crosscut strikes the opponent's head, body or hands. Used as a defense it knocks the opponent's weapon away. This is also really an attack. Attack and defense are done together and can quickly change from one to the other. Once you have knocked the opponent's weapon then you should quickly snap to his body. This is really one action.

- Your footwork must be agile. You must be able to advance, retreat, and dodge to the side. You must take control of the distance between you and the opponent. The distance that you want is the distance that is optimal for the spear. That is, it is not the distance sought when you are fighting empty handed – 'hit as if you are giving a kiss.' That is too close for a spear. The distance you want is one that will kiss the opponent with your spear tip – that is, you want to be at a distance that the spear will be on him when it is extended.

- The essence of the spear lies in mastering the circle. You must train hard and long so that it becomes 'more natural than natural,' 'more perfect than perfect.' Only then can you be considered a true spear player.

THE POEM ABOUT SPEAR CROSSCUT

横枪技法是圈崩，圈枪久练德其精。横崩两膀腰身力，勤学苦练日日功。

The technique of the crosscut combines a circle and a snap.

You must train the circle long and hard to master its essence.

Use the strength of the body and shoulders to snap.

Study diligently and train hard day after day to gain skill.

FIVE ELEMENTS LINKED SPEAR FORM

INTRODUCTION TO THE FIVE ELEMENTS LINKED (FIVE PHASES CONNECTED) SPEAR, *WUXING LIANHUAN QIANG*

The Five Elements Linked Spear form is a short traditional form that combines the foundation of the five element techniques of the spear. Forms that share this name vary by region and by branch of Xingyi. The common thread is that the form must show the flavour and characteristics of Xingyi spear. The characteristics of Xingyi spear are: the techniques must be refined, they are succinct and practical, the power is hard and strong, the spirit is imposing, all moves can be directly applied, and the body and weapon must move as one.

The overall characteristics of the form are: the movements connect smoothly, the power is unimpeded, the actions connect well, the attitude is fierce, the power is hard, the spear technique is clean, the intent and spirit are focused. The footwork is based on the *santi* stance. The power is whole body power that transfers to the spear, the body and spear acting as one.

The Xingyi world respects the spear immensely. Training the spear is a vital part of Xingyi training. This is why they say, 'Taiji sword, Bagua sabre, Xingyi spear, and Shaolin staff.' Every Xingyi player should practise the spear often to learn how to become one with it, and improve power in Xingyi. As they say, 'the deeper your spear skills, the deeper your fist skills.' Training the Xingyi spear improves your overall body skills and deepens your fist skills, strengthens your body and improves your self defense ability.

NAMES OF THE MOVEMENTS

1. Opening Move (On Guard)
2. Thrust (Stationary Outer Trap, Inner Trap, Stab)
3. Thrust (Back Cross Step, Outer Trap, Inner Trap, Stab)
4. Thrust (Roundabout Step, Outer Trap, Inner Trap, Stab)
5. Chop (Step Forward, Swinging Chop)
6. Slash (Coil, Step Forward, Block, Slice, Sculling Scoop)
7. White Crane Flashes its Wings (Retreat, Circle, Poke, Wheel, Cover and Stab)
8. Chop (Step Forward, Scoop the Base, Chop, Stab)
9. Drill (Lift, Punt, Right Stance Inverted Grip Low Stab)
10. Drill (Step Forward Covering Inner Trap, Left Stance High Stab)
11. Thrust (Back Step, Entangle, Inner Trap and Stab)
12. Crosscut (Right Step Forward, Circle, Right Stance Crossing Snap)
13. Crosscut (Left Step Forward, Circle, Left Stance Crossing Snap)
14. Spear Thrust Turn Around (Turn Around, Heel Kick, Twist the Body, Swinging Chop)

    (The following moves are repetition back in the returning direction)

15.   Thrust (Step Forward, Outer Trap, Inner Trap, Stab)

16.   Thrust

17.   Thrust

18.   Chop

19.   Slash

20.   White Crane Flashes its Wings

21.   Chop

22.   Drill

23.   Drill

24.   Thrust

25.   Crosscut

26.   Crosscut

27.   Thrust Turn Around

      (The following moves are the closing combination.)

28.   Thrust

29.   Closing Move

Description of the Movements

1.   Opening Move   qǐ shì   起势

This is the same as setting into *ready stance*. The movements are *Stand at attention with the spear; Left aligned spear; Left santi stance hold the spear.*

ACTION 1: Stand to attention with the right hand holding the spear vertical at the right side with the base on the ground. Hold the spear with the thumb and index finger circling the shaft, the arm naturally straight with the spear shaft snug to the right shoulder. Let the left hand hang naturally with the palm on the left thigh. Press the head up and look straight ahead. (image 3.71)

ACTION 2: Turn the body ninety degrees to the left to face the direction in which the form will go. Step the left foot forward and straighten the right leg, bending the left leg to sit into a left bow stance. Extend the spear out flat with the right hand, the spear tip pointing forward. Extend the right arm so that the spear shaft is at chest height. Place the left hand under the right armpit with the palm up to support the spear shaft. Look past the spear tip. (image 3.72)

3.71

3.72

ACTION 3: Shift back so that most weight is on the right leg, bending the legs to take a *santi* stance. Extend the left hand forward, holding the spear shaft. Release the right hand to slide the spear through, bringing it back to the base. Hold the spear base at the right side of the waist. Keep the left arm almost straight with the elbow tucked in, palm down, pressing firmly on the shaft. The spear is on the midline of the body, level, with the tip at chest height. Press the head up and look past the spear tip. (image 3.73)

3.73

Pointers

- The opening move must be stable and smoothly connected without any breaks.

- Place the legs, body, hands, and spear into the *santi* stance as one. Do not allow any portion of the body or spear to finish separately.

2. Thrust   bēngqiāng   崩枪

Stationary outer trap; Stationary inner trap; Stationary stab.

ACTION 1: Without moving the feet, rotate the left palm up and the right palm down. This makes the spear tip draw a half-circle up, left, and down. Keep the shaft snug to the abdomen. Press the head up and look at the spear tip. (image 3.74)

3.74

ACTION 2: Rotate the left palm down to press down with the thumb/forefinger web. Rotate the right palm in, keeping it at the waist. Use the power of the waist combined with the flexibility of the spear shaft to draw a half-circle the spear tip up, right, and down. Keep the shaft snug to the abdomen. Press the head up and look past the spear tip. (image 3.75)

3.75

ACTION 3: Bend the left leg slightly and extend the right leg slightly, shifting forward into a slightly forward stance. Release the left hand to direct the spear shaft through it and extend the right hand quickly and forcefully forward. When the right hand arrives at the left hand, settle it into the left hand. The right arm is almost fully extended. The spear is level with the tip stabbing to chest height. The body is turned to face forward. Press the head up and look at the spear tip. (image 3.76)

3.76

Pointers

- These three actions must be smoothly and integrally connected.

- Send power to the spear tip for the stab. The tip should quiver.

- Use the body to do the outer and inner traps. First shift back slightly, then shift forward. The body turns slightly right to do the out trap, then turns slightly left for the inner trap. Keep the spear shaft snug to the abdomen so that the body's actions transfer to it.

3.   Thrust   bēngqiāng   崩枪

Cross-over step, outer trap; Step forward inner trap; Stab.

ACTION 1: Do not move the left foot, and step the right foot across in front of it with the foot turned out. This forms a cross-step with the legs bent and weight between them. Pull the spear base back to the right waist, sliding the shaft through the left hand. Do the outer trap action. Look past the spear tip. (image 3.77)

3.77

ACTION 2:. Step the left foot forward without moving the right foot, shifting mostly onto the right leg. Rotate the hands to do an inner trap action. (image 3.78)

ACTION 3: Shift forward and stab, sliding the shaft through the left hand. (image 3.79)

Pointers

○ Complete the outer trap as the right foot steps across.

○ Complete the inner trap as the left foot steps forward.

4. Thrust　　　　　　bēngqiāng　　　崩枪

Roundabout step, outer trap; Step forward inner trap; Stab.

ACTION 1: Advance the left foot diagonally to the right with the foot turned out. Do not move the right foot but shift weight forward between the feet. Pull the right hand back to the right side, sliding the shaft through the left hand. Complete the outer trap as the left foot steps. Look at the spear tip. (image 3.80)

ACTION 2: Step the right foot in front of the left foot. Land with the foot hooked in slightly and turn the body slightly left so that the stance is facing straight forward. Do the inner trap at the same time. Look at the spear tip. (image 3.81)

ACTION 3: Shift forward a bit towards the right leg. Push the right hand forward forcefully, sliding the spear through the left hand to stab forward. Support the right hand in the left when it arrives. The spear shaft is level with the tip at chest height. Send power to the spear tip. Look past the spear tip. (image 3.82)

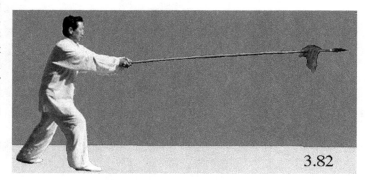

3.82

Pointers

- o Pay attention to the direction and angle of the stepping. The feet step in a roundabout way, drawing a curved line. The stepping must be agile and quick and coordinated well with the spear traps.

- o As you step, the left hand must control the direction in which the spear points – to the front. The spear must not wobble. The spear tip must point accurately to its forward target during the outer trap, inner trap, and stab.

5. Chop   pīqiāng   劈枪

Advance and vertical circle; Step forward with a swinging chop.

ACTION 1: Advance the right foot a half-step and bring the left foot in to the right ankle. Pull the spear base back with the right hand then lift it up above the head at the right side with the arm almost fully extended. Slide the left hand forward along the spear, reaching it down to the front, pointing the spear tip down. Circle the spear tip back at the left side of the body. Lift the body slightly. Watch the spear tip as it moves. (image 3.83)

3.83

ACTION 2: Take a long step forward with the left foot and follow in the right foot a half-step, sitting between the legs. Circle the left hand back then lift it, and then chop the spear down to the front. The right hand brings the spear base forward, then down, then pulls back to the right side. Finish with the spear shaft level, the tip at waist height. The left arm is almost straight. Press the head up and look past the spear tip. (images 3.84 and 3.85)

3.84

3.85

Pointers

- o The swinging chop is a continuous move, and must be practised as such. The final chop must be completed as the left foot lands.

- o The left hand slides along the spear. Slide forward as you bring the spear tip down. Slide back as you bring the spear through to chop. Tighten the grip at exactly the right time and in the optimal position to send power to chop strongly with the spear's fore-section.

6. Slash   pàoqiāng   炮枪

Advance and coil; Step forward, block, slice, sculling scoop.

ACTION 1: Advance the left foot a half-step and follow in the right foot to beside the left ankle. Slide the left hand forward along the spear and circle the spear tip up, left, then down. Move the right hand in the opposite direction, bringing the spear base up. Keep the spear shaft snug to the body. The spear tip should circle no higher than the eyebrows and no lower than the knees. Watch the tip as it moves. (image 3.86)

ACTION 2: Take a long step diagonally to the forward right with the right foot and follow in the left foot a half-step to take a *santi* stance. Bring the right hand forward and then lift it up, rotating the palm to face out – brace out above the head with the arm rounded. Rotate the left palm towards the thumb so that the spear tip circles diagonally forward and to the right, to slice up with the left palm angled to the forward right. Push the spear shaft forward forcefully with the left hand, keeping the arm slightly bent. Finish with the left hand at chest height and the spear tip at waist height. Send the power to the fore-section of the spear. Look past the spear tip. (image 3.87)

3.86

3.87

Pointers

o   Coil the spear with the left hand as the left foot advances. Be sure to slide the left hand fluidly along the shaft. The coiling action should be large and smooth, and use bodywork. Draw the body with the arm and lead the arm with the body, moving the spear along.

o   The slash must be completed all at once – the right foot lands forward, the right hand lifts to block and the left hand pushes with a sculling scoop. The feet and hands must arrive together. The left hand must have a focal point. Using the power from the body core, slide the hand until the right moment then tighten the grip to strike.

7.   White Crane Flashes its Wings   báihé liàngchì   白鹤亮翅

Retreat, circle and poke; Wheel and block; Cover and stab.

ACTION 1: Retreat the left foot and withdraw the right foot, touching down and shifting onto the left leg. Bend the left leg to squat down and turn left to bring the right shoulder on line with the front. Slide the left hand along the shaft and bring it left, up, and then down to in front of the right shoulder with the palm pressing down. Bring the right hand down and then push under the left armpit. The right hand under the left armpit makes the spear tip poke with a dotting action, moving in a circular motion from the forward lower right, up, and then forward and down. The spear shaft is level with the tip around chest height or lower. Look at the spear tip. (image 3.88)

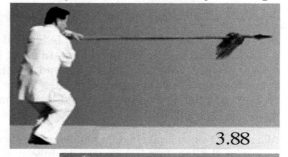

3.88

ACTION 2: Lift the right knee and push off the left leg, turning rightward and landing on the right foot, foot turned out. Then land the left foot forward and sit into a half-horse stance with most weight on the right leg. Rotate the right palm away from the thumb and pull it up in front of the right shoulder, palm out. Slide the left hand along the spear shaft and control the tip with the left hand to circle the spear tip up, left, and then down. The spear tip is at waist height. Look past the spear tip. (image 3.89 transitional)

3.89

ACTION 3: Keep the hands in motion without moving the feet. Bring the spear base down to the right waist and rotate the right palm up.

3.90

Circle the spear with the left hand to bring the tip left, up, then down, to complete a cover and inner trap. Keep the left arm bent and press down with the palm. Press the head up and look past the spear tip. (image 3.90)

ACTION 4: Bring the right foot up behind the left foot. Push the spear base forward forcefully with the right hand, controlling the shaft by sliding it through the left hand to stab forward. Support the right hand with the left when it arrives beside the left. Stab with the spear shaft level at chest height, sending power forward to make the tip quiver. Look past the spear tip. (image 3.91)

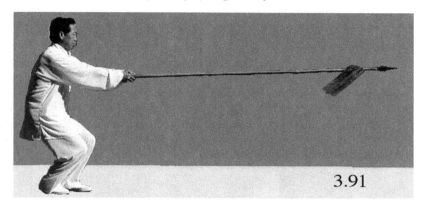

Pointers

- o Take a considerable retreating step and withdraw the other foot quickly to do the 'dotting' action. The footwork must be coordinated with the hand action moving the spear. Be sure to circle the spear tip – it draws quite a large circle while the hands move in a small circle. Turn the body left when the spear tip pokes down. The movement is soft and the strike does not use a lot of strength – just a touch is enough.

- o During the jumping wheel both hands rotate and both arms open so that the spear tip circles. In this way, the shaft blocks up with quite a large movement. All elements of this move must be completed together.

- o Complete the covering inner trap as the feet land. Stab forward with a shift in weight.

8. Chop   pīqiāng   劈枪

Step forward, scoop the base: Step forward, chop; Stab.

ACTION 1: Advance the left foot a half-step and follow in the right foot to the left ankle. Pull the spear base back with the right hand, sliding the left hand forward along the shaft. Extend the left arm forward to reach the spear tip forward, keeping the shaft on the body. Look past the spear tip. (image 3.92)

ACTION 2: Step the right foot forward and advance the left foot a half-step, shifting forward towards the right leg. Slide the left hand forward along the spear shaft and

scoop up the tip, then hook it down to the rear, the left hand finishing at the left hip, palm out. Slide the right hand along the shaft until about fifty centimetres of shaft is showing, and bring it forward and up to scoop up. The right hand is at chest height with the thumb/forefinger web up. The spear base is at head height. Keep the shaft snug to the left hip. Look past the spear base. (image 3.93)

ACTION 3: Withdraw the right foot and place it in front of the left foot. Shift onto the right leg and step the left foot forward without stepping the right foot, to settle into a *santi* stance. First lower the right hand to hook back with the spear base beside the right leg. Then slide the right hand along to grasp the base and pull it to the right waist. Lift the left hand to above the head then swing the spear forward and down. The spear tip comes up, forward, then down in a swinging chop until the shaft is level at waist height. Send power to the fore-section of the spear. Look past the spear tip. (images 3.94, 3.95)

ACTION 4: Shift forward to the left leg. Send the spear forward forcefully with the right hand to stab. Slide the spear through the left hand, lifting the hand slightly to guide the spear tip to chest height. The right arm is almost straight, the hands connected. The spear shaft is level at chest height, power in the tip. Look past the spear tip. (image 3.96)

Pointers

- Scoop the base up as the right foot steps forward. The hands must slide along the shaft quickly and smoothly. Use the body to scoop into the spear base. Keep the right hand tight to the body with the elbow tucked in and the shoulder settled to put power into the elbow. Settle the left shoulder back and down.

- *Step forward and chop* connects immediately to *withdraw and hook down* without hesitation. The whole body must be coordinated. The chop must be strong, and land as the foot lands. The hands work together to chop – the left hand pushes while the right hand pulls.

- Turn the waist, release the shoulders, and extend the arms to stab. The stab must be strong and quick, and the power must be in the tip.

9. Drill   zuānqiāng   钻枪

Lift and punt; Right stance inverted grip low stab.

ACTION 1: Advance the left foot a half-step and follow in the right foot to the left ankle. Pull the spear base back to the chest, then lift it above the head at the right side, rotating the right palm up and bracing out with the arm. Slide the left hand forward along the shaft. When the right hand lifts, rotate the left palm towards the thumb to turn the palm forward, so that the spear tip draws a half-circle left, down, and then right, pointing to knee height. Tuck in the left elbow. Look at the spear tip. (image 3.97)

3.97

ACTION 2: Step the right foot forward and follow in a half-step with the left foot to take a *santi* stance. Keep the left arm extended to aim the spear to the lower left. Push forward and down with the right hand inverted. Slide the spear shaft through the left hand. Lift the left hand slightly and stab with the right until it meets the left. The right hand and spear base are at shoulder height, the arms are almost straight, and the spear tip is twenty to thirty centimetres above the ground. Lean forward slightly and look at the spear tip. (image 3.98)

3.98

Pointers

- Lift the spear base as the left foot advances. Stab the spear down as the right foot steps forward. The spear should always arrive as the foot lands, so that hands and feet work together in an action that is fully connected through the whole body.

- Rotate the right palm away from the thumb as you lift to block. Rotate the left palm towards the thumb as you slide it forward along the shaft to pull and check. The inverted grip stab is not as strong as the regular grip stab, so you must send the power to the tip and control the action cleanly.

10.	**Drill**	zuānqiāng	钻枪

Step forward covering inner trap; Left stance high stab.

ACTION 1: Step the left foot forward without moving the right foot, keeping most weight on the right leg. Pull the spear base back to the right waist, rotating the right hand to press down. Slide the left hand forward along the shaft, circling and rotating it to press palm down, so that the spear tip draws a circle left and up, then right and down – do an inner trap. The spear shaft remains level with the tip at waist height. Look at the spear tip. (image 3.99)

ACTION 2: Shift slightly forward without moving the feet. Push the spear base forcefully forward with the right hand, sliding the shaft through the left hand. Angle the tip to stab up to nose height with the hands together at chest height. Send power to the tip so that it quivers. Press the head up and look past the spear tip. (image 3.100)

Pointers

- Complete the inner trap as the left foot steps forward. Press the trunk slightly forward as you do the inner trap. Press the head up. The hands must rotate simultaneously in opposite directions. Press down with the left hand.

- Send power to the spear tip when you stab. Accelerate the right hand as it pushes the spear forward, reaching peak acceleration at the end of the stab.

11.	**Thrust**	bēngqiāng	崩枪

Back-cross step, entangle; Inner trap; Back-cross step, entangle; Inner trap; Stab.

ACTION 1: Cross the right foot back behind the left foot and shift forward onto the left leg without moving the left foot. The legs are bent and crossed. Pull the spear base back to the right side, sliding the shaft through the left hand, keeping the left arm almost straight. Circle the spear tip down, left, then up. The tip should circle no higher than the head and no lower than the knees. The right and left hands work in opposite circles, keeping the spear shaft snug to the trunk throughout the action. Look at the spear tip. (image 3.101)

ACTION 2: Step the left foot forward and continue to circle the spear with the hands so that the tip goes up, right, and then down. Keep the shaft on the torso throughout. The hands do not slide on the spear. Look at the spear tip. (image 3.102)

3.101

3.102

ACTION 3: Cross the right foot back behind the left foot. Continue to circle the spear tip left, then up, keeping the spear shaft snug to the trunk throughout. The right hand circles at the right side of the body as the spear circles. Watch the spear tip. (image 3.103)

ACTION 4: Step the left foot forward without moving the right foot. Rotate the right hand and bring the spear base in to the right waist. Continue to circle the spear with the left hand so that the tip goes right and then down – a covering inner trap. The spear is level with the tip at waist height. (image 3.104)

ACTION 5: Shift forward towards the left leg without moving the feet. Stab the spear forward level to chest height with the right hand, sliding the shaft through the left hand. Look past the spear tip. (image 3.105)

3.104

3.105

Pointers

- o The back-cross step coil is repeated twice in an unbroken movement. The stepping should be small and quick.

- o The spear coil is a soft movement, with full, nicely rounded circles. The hands work together. Be sure to keep the spear shaft snug to the trunk of the body, using it as the pivot point. The circling of the hands uses the action of the body. Coordinated with the footwork, the whole body works in an integrated whole, strong but soft, containing a certain hardness within.

12. Crosscut   héngqiāng   横枪

Right step forward, circle; Right stance crossing snap.

ACTION 1: Advance the left foot a half-step and follow in the right foot to the left ankle. Pull the right hand back to in front of the chest and slide the left hand forward along the spear shaft. Turn the right palm up, rotating the spear, and draw a small circle with the base to the left and down. Control the spear shaft with the left hand, using it as the pivot point, so that the spear tip draws one circle right and up. Look past the spear tip. (image 3.106)

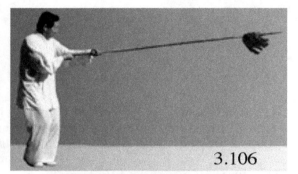

3.106

ACTION 2: Take a long step to the forward right with the right foot and follow in the left foot a half-step, keeping most weight on the left leg. Slide the left hand forward along the spear shaft and push it towards the forward right with the palm facing right. Then tighten the grip and stop abruptly. Rotate the right palm away from the thumb and pull back to the right strongly, palm turning out. Bend the right arm and pull the spear base back to in front of the right shoulder. Send power to the fore-section of the spear so that the spear tip snaps toward the right. The spear is level at about shoulder height. Look past the spear tip. (image 3.107)

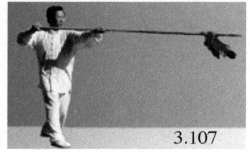

3.107

Pointers

- o The movement must be continuous without a break. Neither the footwork nor the handwork should hesitate, and they must integrate fully together.

- o The circle is counter-clockwise, and the tip should circle between head and knee height. Contain the chest during the circling so that the body gathers energy. Pull back and rotate to snap the spear, launching power with the whole body connected through to the hands. The key is the controlling action of the left hand. You must practise this carefully to find how to do it.

13. Crosscut   héngqiāng   横枪

Left step forward, circle; Left stance crossing snap.

ACTION 1: Advance the left foot a short step forward without moving the right foot, shifting evenly between the feet. Loosen the left grip to allow the spear to slide and rotate within it. Send the right hand forward in front of the chest. Work with both hands to circle the spear tip clockwise, the right hand drawing a small circle. Rotate the hands in opposite directions, rotating the left palm away from the thumb so that the palm faces down, and the right palm towards the thumb so that the palm faces up. Bring the right hand under the left armpit. Look past the spear tip. (image 3.108)

ACTION 2: Step the left foot forward and follow in the right foot a half-step, keeping most weight on the right leg. Pull the right hand back to in front of the right shoulder, rotating it palm away from thumb so that the palm faces out. Bend the right arm to hold the spear base in front of the right shoulder. Slide the left hand forward along the shaft and rotate it palm away from thumb so that the palm faces back, then snap the left arm to the left, sharply stopping the spear. This stops the tip in the midst of its circle, abruptly accelerating and snapping left with an oscillation. The spear tip is at shoulder height. Turn the body a bit to the right. Look past the spear tip. (image 3.109)

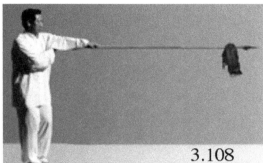

3.108

3.109

Pointers

  o   The circling is soft, gathering power in the hands and body.

  o   The snap is sudden and sharp. The hands rotate – the right hand pulls back while the left hand stops the spear. Coordinate the spear snap with a snap from the waist, timing the slide and stop of the left hand.

14.   Spear Thrust Turn Around   bēngqiāng huíshēn   崩枪回身

Turn around, heel kick; Twist the body, swinging chop.

ACTION 1: Hook-in the left foot towards the right foot. Bend the legs and shift onto the left leg. Rotate the right palm away from the thumb and lift it above the head with the palm facing out. Slide the left hand forward along the shaft and bring the hand down and a bit towards the right. This circles the spear tip left, down, and right to point down at knee height. Look at the spear tip. (image 3.110)

ACTION 2: Turn a full 180 degrees, holding the spear motionless. Lift the right knee then do a heel kick forward to waist height with the foot turned

3.110

out. Look forward. (image 3.111)

ACTION 3: Land with a trampling action forward and down, keeping the foot turned out. Follow in the left foot slightly, turn the body to the right, cross the legs into a scissors stance, and sit down. Bring the spear base forward, down, and then pull back to the right waist. Lift the left hand, then bring it forward and down to chop forcefully. Tighten the grip and press down with the thumb/forefinger web. The spear chops level with the tip at about waist height, power in the fore-section.

3.111

Press the head up and look forward. (image 3.112)

Pointers

3.112

o The turn around should be smooth, well balanced, quick, and stable without hesitation in the movement.

o Hook-in the left foot as you lift the spear. Turn around and kick quickly and strongly, but keep balanced. Land, turn the body, and chop the spear all at the same time.

o The chop is low and well rooted. Control the slide of the left hand along the shaft and stop it under control with focus so that the spear does not hit the ground.

• The following moves, 15 through 27, are a repetition of the first section, moves 2 through 14, back in the returning direction.

15. Thrust   bēngqiāng   崩枪

Step forward, outer trap; Inner trap; Stab.

ACTION: Step the left foot forward without moving the right foot. Pull the right hand back to the right waist and perform the outer trap, inner trap and stab the same as described in movement 2. (outer trap image 3.113) (See also images 3.74, 3.75, 3.76)

3.113

16.	**Thrust**	See move 3.
17.	**Thrust**	See move 4.
18.	**Chop**	See move 5
19.	**Slash**	See move 6.
20.	**White Crane Flashes its Wings**	See move 7.
21.	**Chop**	See move 8.
22.	**Drill**	See move 9.
23.	**Drill**	See move 10. (image 3.114)

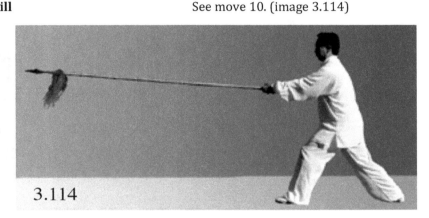

3.114

24.	**Thrust**	See move 11.
25.	**Crosscut**	See move 12.
26.	**Crosscut**	See move 13.
27.	**Thrust Turn Around**	See move 14.
28.	**Thrust**	See moves 2 and 15. This is now facing in the original direction.

29. **Closing Move** shōu shì 收势

Starting from *thrust. Snap up the spear; Stand the spear to attention; Stand to attention.*

ACTION 1: Shift back towards the right leg without moving the feet. Pull the right hand back to the right side and slide the left hand forward along the spear shaft. Stop the left hand abruptly to snap the spear tip upward, sending power to the fore-section of the shaft. The spear tip should be no higher than the head. Press the head up and look past the spear tip. (image 3.115)

3.115

ACTION 2: Stand up, bringing the left foot in beside the right foot and turning ninety degrees to face front. Bring the left hand to the side to stand the spear vertically beside the right shoulder. Slide the right hand along the shaft and bring the hand to the waist to put the spear base on the ground. Look at the left hand. (image 3.116)

ACTION 3: Release the left hand and circle it down and to the left, then up to shoulder height. Look at the left hand. (image 3.117)

ACTION 4: Bend the elbow and press down in front of the face. Then let the left hand hang naturally at the side. Turn the head to look straight ahead. Stand to attention, and the form is completed. (image 3.118)

Pointers

o   The eyes must remain bright and attentive throughout the closing move. The spirit and feeling must remain full. The facial expression must remain dignified through to the final completion of the form.

FIVE ELEMENT STAFF 五行棍

INTRODUCTION TO FIVE ELEMENT STAFF, *WUXING GUN*

As with the sabre, sword, and spear, the names of the staff techniques are taken from the five element hand techniques. Xingyi masters of old selected the most straightforward and practical staff techniques and blended them with the characteristics of Xingyi. In this way we have a set of five elemental techniques that fit the theories and methods of Xingyi.

The five element staff techniques are simple and easy to learn. All Xingyi staff techniques are clear, powerful, full of spirit, and show obvious applications. Just like the five fist techniques, the emphasis is placed on full power, body core power, and improving deep skills. Power is applied with the body, leading from the lower back and waist with a fully integrated strength. There are no dazzling or entertaining moves.

The five staff techniques are more than just five different techniques, but are five different ways of applying power. Although the movements appear simple, they have rich techniques hidden within. The combinations for the five element techniques actually involve over ten techniques, and include: chop, cover, scoop, hook, poke, slice, block up, brandish, sweep, and check. Each of the five element combinations includes at least two techniques. For example, the chop combination includes a hook up and chop, a hook down and chop, and hook right or left and chop. The drill combination has a hook and a scoop. The thrust combination includes an outer trap, a press down, and a poke. The slash combination includes entangle, cover, block up, and slice. The crosscut combination includes a brandish, a check and a crosscut strike. Each technique must be clear and distinct, and you must clearly understand the movement, power use, and application of each. If you do, it will help you to learn and master the techniques quickly.

Although the five element technique combinations are not widely practised, the Five Elements Staff form is popular. The form differs in different regions, but only in small ways. The five element techniques that I present here combine the traditional techniques with what I have learned from different masters and my own training and teaching experiences over the years. I have of course kept the traditional characteristics. I have included the standard names for the staff techniques in addition to the old names, as name standardization makes it easier to spread and popularize.

The length of the staff in Xingyi should be slightly longer than the height of the player. An overly long staff is awkward, while a shorter staff lacks power. The thickness at the base is that of the circle made by the player's thumb and index finger. The tip will then be the natural circumference of the staff. You must not shave it down, as this destroys its natural suppleness and risks breakage. When choosing a staff, pick the best quality white wax wood that you can – clean and shiny with as few kinks and knots as possible, and with good spring.

The narrow end is called the tip, the thick end is called the base or butt. The shaft is divided into three parts to better explain the actions. The third at the tip is called the fore-section, the third at the base is called the aft-section, and the third in the middle is called the midsection.

FIVE ELEMENT STAFF TECHNIQUES

On Guard   yùbèishì   预备势

Before training the staff techniques you must first do post standing, similar to when you learned the five element hand techniques. *On guard* position is similar to *santishi,* and similarly serves as a foundation for all techniques to come. All techniques come from this posture, so it must be perfected.

On guard standing develops an understanding of the position and sets the proper feeling of each part of the body and its relation to the staff – the placement, direction, angles, and height. While post standing you find the power in each part of the body, and the proper requirements of the posture. This sets the posture so that the movements can become regulation and the techniques will be correct. This is the foundation for all of the five element techniques. You must not only do post standing in the *on guard* position, but in every single basic posture. In this way you will find the posture, requirements, and power for every technique. Post standing takes time but it is time well spent. Setting the postures well will speed up your mastery of the movements.

The actions of *on guard* are: *Stand with the staff; Raise the staff in both hands; Left advance and chop.*

ACTION 1: Stand to attention with the feet together, angled forty-five degrees to the line that the form will take. Hold the staff vertically at the right side with the base on the ground. Extend the right arm and hold the midsection of the shaft with the thumb/forefinger web. Extend the left arm at the left side. Press the head up slightly and look forward. (image 4.1)

ACTION 2: Grip with the right hand and raise the staff vertically. Bring the left hand to the right armpit and grasp the staff about ten centimetres from the base. Turn the head to look to the left. (image 4.2)

ACTION 3: Turn to the left and step the left foot forward, following in the right step slightly to take a *santi* stance – the weight sixty percent on the rear leg. Grip the staff with both hands and chop down and forward. Pull the left hand back to the left, midway between the waist and hip socket. Push the right hand out to chest height. Extend the right shoulder forward, keep the right arm slightly bent with the elbow rolled inward, and press down on the staff with the thumb/forefinger web. The tip of the staff is at nose height. Press the head up and look past the tip. (image 4.3)

Pointers

- o Focus your mind during *stand with the staff*.

- o During *raise the staff in both hands,* when the head turns to the left, tuck the jaw in and show spirit in the eyes. Raise the right hand and take the staff in the left hand slowly. Start an intention of turning the body to the left.

- o Complete the chop when the left foot lands. Before stepping the left foot forward, turn the body to the left and sit down. Put power to the staff tip. The distance between the hands should be the length of the player's forearm. The chop must have a focal point, and that is when the right hand stops its action. Turn the waist, reach the shoulder forward, and breathe out to launch power.

STAFF CHOP

INTRODUCTION TO STAFF CHOP, *PI GUN*

Chop is a strike that moves forward and down. The wushu regulations definition of chop is "the staff chops down from above with power and speed. Power is applied with the tip of the staff." The Xingyi staff chop should be strong, focusing the power of the whole body into the tip of the staff. Xingyi particularly emphasizes that weapons are extensions of the body. This means that the power of the whole body must transfer to the weapon so that the weapon and body become one.

Because the chop comes down from above, it must first be placed in the optimal position for this – this includes the position of the staff and the placement of the body for power application. The tip must be above horizontal, aligned on the circle of the strike, with the optimal placement being above the head. You must pay particular attention to getting a feel for this during practice.

There are two methods for staff chop. The chop is set up with a hook up or a hook down. The techniques involved are: *hook up to left or right and chop, hook down to left or right and chop, swinging chop, covering chop with the butt, reverse grip chop, wheeling around chop.*

METHOD ONE: HOOK UP AND CHOP

1a Left Stance Chop   yòubù pīgùn   右步劈棍

Start from *on guard*. Continue with *Right step forward, hook up; Left step forward, chop.*

ACTION 1: Shift forward without moving the left foot. Then step the right foot forward a long step, landing firmly with the knee bent, and bring the left foot up to the right ankle, keeping the thighs together. With the right hand, first lower the staff tip to waist height, then pull it to hook up and back. The right arm pulls to the chest, the right hand to in front of the right shoulder. Push forward with the left hand to waist height. Tuck in the abdomen and move the right shoulder back slightly. Look forward. (image 4.4)

ACTION 2: Take a long step forward with the left foot and follow in a half-step with the right foot to sit into a *santi* stance. Hold the staff firmly with the right hand and chop forcefully down directly to the front, the tip at chest height. With the left hand pull back to the side, sticking tightly to the body at a height between the waist and hip crease. Reach the right shoulder forward, keep the right arm slightly bent with the elbow tucked in, and press down with the thumb/forefinger web just below chest height. Press the head up and look past the staff tip. (image 4.5)

Pointers

- o The combination is made up of a hook up and a chop down – these actions must connect without hesitation to develop the power transfer. Step forward for distance, and follow in the rear foot quickly.

- o Lower the staff tip as the weight shifts forward, then raise the tip to hook up as the right foot steps forward.

- o Complete the chop as the left foot lands. The staff must always arrive simultaneously with the foot, so that the movement is fully connected from top to bottom.

- • Continue on, repeating as space permits.

1b   Turn Around for Hook Up and Chop

shàngguà pīgùn zhuànshēn   上挂劈棍转身

Right hook-in, lift the staff; Turn around, retreat, chop.

ACTION 1: Take a step forward with the right foot, hooking it in. Lift the base of the staff above the head with the left hand, rotating the left palm away from the thumb to turn it out away from the body. Slide the right hand forward along the shaft and turn the palm forward. The staff is angled in front of the body with the tip just below knee height. Look at the fore-section of the staff. (image 4.6)

ACTION 2: Turn around 180 degrees to the left to face back in the way from which you came. Shift onto the right leg and retreat the left leg behind. Then shift back to a *santi* stance weighted to the left leg – putting a trampling power forward and down into the right foot. Use both hands to bring the staff up, forward, then down in a swinging chop, finishing with the staff tip at chest height. Pull the left hand back to stick tightly to the body between the hips and waist. Press the head up, tuck the jaw in, and look past the staff tip. (image 4.7)

Pointers

- o Do not hesitate between the hook-in turn and the sit back and chop. The power must continue between the actions to develop the power transfer.

- o Land the retreating left foot, grab with the right foot, and chop with the staff all at the same time. Use the turning of the waist and tucking in of the abdomen to send power to the staff

- Continue on with *right advance hook up, left step forward chop*. Repeat as space and energy permit.

METHOD TWO: HOOK DOWN AND CHOP

1c   Hook Down to the Right, Covering Chop

yòu xiàguà gàipī gùn   右下挂盖劈棍

Start from *on guard. Left advance, hook down to the right; Right step forward, covering chop.*

ACTION 1: Advance the left foot a half-step and follow in the right foot to the left ankle. Raise the base of the staff with the left hand, pushing forward and up in front of the left shoulder. Hold the right hand at mid-shaft and circle down and back so that the tip circles down and back to the right, then swings up. Turn to the right. Press the

head up and follow the staff tip with the eyes. (image 4.8)

ACTION 2: Take a long step forward with the right foot and follow in the left foot a half-step to sit into a *santi* stance.

Push and pull the staff base with the left hand, finishing with the hand under the right armpit, palm up. With the right hand, bring the staff up above the head then forward and down in a covering chop.[55] The right hand finishes with the palm down on top of the staff. The staff finishes level, the tip slightly below shoulder height. Press the head up and look past the tip. (image 4.9)

Pointers

- Hook the staff tip down as the leading foot advances.

- Complete the chop as the right foot steps forward.

1d   Hook Down to the Left, Reverse Grip Chop

zuǒ xiàguà fǎnpīgùn   左下挂反劈棍

Left retreat, hook down to the left; Right advance, reverse grip chop.

ACTION 1: Retreat the left foot a half step and withdraw the right foot back to in front of the left foot. Control the staff with the right hand to bring the tip down and back at the left side, then to swing up. Turn the body leftward. Keep the left hand at the armpit, coordinating with the action of the right hand. Follow the movement of the staff tip with the eyes. (image 4.10)

ACTION 2: Take a long step forward and follow in the left foot a half-step to sit into a *santi* stance. Swing the staff up, forward, and then down with the right hand, finishing with the palm in a reverse grip – palm up and hand under the staff. The staff tip is at shoulder height. Follow the action of the staff with the left hand, sliding it back to the butt, pulling it back tight to the body at the left side. Focus power to the staff fore-section. Press the head up and look past the staff tip. (image 4.11)

---

[55] Editor's note: Bend the right arm as you circle the staff at the side. The staff stays outside the right arm all the way around the circle, just tucks under the arm at the final strike.

Pointers

- The retreating and withdrawing steps must work together to enable the staff tip to hook around on the left side. Be sure to turn the body to the left.

- The staff must complete its chop as the right foot advances.

- The two actions must be completed as one with no hesitation between them.

1e   Hook Down to the Right, Reverse Stance, Covering Chop

yòu xiàguà àobù gàipīgùn   右下挂拗步盖劈棍

Right advance, hook down to the right; Left step forward, covering chop.

ACTION 1: Advance the right foot a half-step and follow in the left foot to the right ankle. Control the staff with the right hand to circle the tip down and back at the right side. Coordinate with the left hand, lifting up and pushing forward to above the head. Turn the body right. Look at the staff tip. (image 4.12)

ACTION 2: Take a long step forward with the left foot and follow in a half-step with the right foot to sit into a *santi* stance. Continue to circle the staff with both hands, the right hand pulling the tip back, up, then forward and down, finishing with a strong covering chop. The left hand finishes pulled into the right armpit, palm up at the base end of the staff. The staff is level at shoulder height. Look past the staff tip. (image 4.13)

Pointers

- Hook down as the right foot advances. Be sure to turn the body to the right.

- Complete the covering chop as the left foot steps forward. The staff must arrive as the foot lands.

1f   Hook Down to the Left, Reverse Grip Chop

zuǒ xiàguà àobù fǎnpīgùn   左下挂拗步反劈棍

Left advance, hook down to the left; Right step forward, reverse grip chop.

ACTION 1: Advance the left foot a half-step and follow in the right foot to the left ankle. Control the staff tip with the right hand to circle it down at the left. Turn the body to the left. Keep the left hand at the right armpit to help coordinate the action of the staff. Follow the staff tip with the eyes. (image 4.14)

ACTION 2: Take a long step forward with the right foot and follow in the left foot a half-step. Continue to circle the staff with the right hand, to go back, up, and then forward and down with a reverse grip chop. The right hand is palm up, with the forearm under the staff. Keep a grip on the base of the staff with the left hand, and pull it back to the left side, finishing with the palm down tight to the body. The staff tip is at shoulder height. Press the head up and look past the staff tip. (image 4.15)

Pointers

- o   The hook down and chop is one action; there cannot be any hesitation midway through. This pertains whether you're doing a covering chop or a reverse grip chop, and whether you're moving into an aligned stance or a reverse stance.

- o   Hook forward and down as you step forward, fully coordinated.

- •   Continue to repeat the actions. When you are doing the reverse grip chop, you can change the footwork, sometimes retreating, sometimes advancing. When you are doing the covering chop you can change the stance, sometimes an aligned stance, sometimes a reverse stance. You should be able to do the techniques in a variety of ways.

1g   Turn Around for the Hook Down and Chop

xiàguà pīgùn zhuànshēn   下挂劈棍转身

Using the *reverse stance covering chop* with the <u>left</u> foot forward as example. *Left hook-in, turn around, hook down to the right; Right step forward, covering chop.*

ACTION 1: Hook-in the left foot in front of the right foot and shift to the left leg. Lift the right foot and turn around 180 degrees to the right to face back. Bring the right hand around to circle the staff tip up, forward, and then to hook down at the right side. Lift the left hand to lift the staff base and push forward a bit. Follow the staff tip with the eyes. (image 4.16)

ACTION 2: Step the right foot forward and follow in the left foot a half-step. With the right hand, bring the staff tip up, forward, and then down to chop at chest height. Pull the staff base back under the right armpit with the left hand. Press the head up and look past the staff tip. (image 4.17

If the <u>right</u> foot is forward in a *reverse grip chop*:

ACTION: Step the left foot forward, hooking in as it lands. Shift onto the left leg and turn around 180 degrees to the right. The rest of the turn around is the same as described above.

Pointers

- o To complete the hook-in and turn, hook-in a considerable amount and turn quickly.

- o When doing the turn around and hook down, coordinate the action of the hands.

- o Complete the covering chop as the right foot lands. Launch power with a firm grip and a strong strike.

1h Chop Closing Move   pīgùn shōushì   劈棍收势

On arriving back at the starting point, do a *turn around* to face the original direction. The *closing move* is: *Right retreat, raise the staff in both hands; Stand at attention with the staff.* If the <u>right</u> foot is forward in a *reverse grip chop* or a *covering chop*, then you need to first retreat the right foot and withdraw the left foot. The description is from a <u>*left* stance covering chop</u>.

ACTION 1: Retreat the right foot a half-step and withdraw the left foot beside the right foot. Turn the body forty-five degrees to the right. Straighten the legs and stand to attention. With the right hand on the shaft, pull it back to the right side of the body then raise it up above the head. With the left hand on the staff base, push it under the right armpit. The staff is now standing vertically. Press the head up and turn it to look straight to the left. (image 4.18)

ACTION 2: Keep standing at attention. Lower the right hand to bring the staff butt to the ground so that the staff stands at the right side. Let go with the left hand and bring it to the left side. Turn the head to look straight ahead. (image 4.19)

Pointers

- o Be sure to remain focused throughout the closing move. Do not let your attention dissipate.

- o Stand up straight when standing to attention with the staff. Show good spirit, do not relax yet.

- o When retreating or withdrawing the foot and shifting back, the right hand is bringing the staff tip through with a slicing action that hooks back. This is the hidden technique within the move.

POWER GENERATION FOR STAFF CHOP

Hook up: The hands must work together. Bend the right arm and pull back towards the chest. Extend the left arm and push forward. One pulling and one pushing, one bending and one extending – both arms do the hook up. Of course, the action of the arms comes from the shoulders, and that of the shoulders comes from the lower back. The torso should contract during the hook up, tucking the abdomen and closing the chest.

Chop: The chop must have a focal point and stop at chest height. Momentum must not carry it further down than that. It must chop down so quickly that the staff makes a whooshing sound. And it must stop so abruptly and accurately that the staff tip quivers. Turn the waist, reach the shoulder forward and use both arms – push with the right and pull with the left. At the instant of striking the hands' grip must tighten and stop the staff. The left hand stops tight to the body, between the waist and hips. The right arm should finish with a 150 degree bend in the elbow. The principle is that a firm grip is needed to strike. When chopping, lengthen the body slightly, press the head up, and tuck in the jaw. Send the power of the whole body forward into the chop. The whole body must be connected with no slackness in it. Coordinate the strike with an exhalation.

Hook down: The body should turn slightly in the direction of the hook down – whether to right or to left – so that the body leads the action of the hands. Turn the body to move the arms, and transfer from the hands to the staff. Keep the staff close to the body whenever moving it. Movement should be soft but without any slackness in the body.

- • Be sure to slide the right hand along the shaft. Slide the hand down as you hook the staff down. The hook down is intended to knock aside the opponent's weapon with the fore-section of the staff – the right hand hooks down and the left hand pushes forward slightly. When the right hand is moving down it should slide forwards a bit to give more strength to the hooking action.

- Each hook down should draw a full circle to either side of the body. The initial action of circling down from the front is the actual 'hook down,' and this action should be gentle. The continuation – circling towards the rear – contains a drawing action, and a gathering of power for the chop. Circling upwards above the head is 'traveling,' and this should accelerate. The rest of the circle – down from above – is the chop. This is the final goal of the rest of the circle, and it should be fast and strong. The chop follows the principle of launching full power after the midpoint of the movement.

Turn around: The hands rotate during the turning lift. The left hand blocks up with the staff as the right hand pushes outwards. When wheeling the body around with the retreating step, turn the waist to gather power for the strong chop. Tuck in the abdomen, swing the arms, and press the head up.

BREATHING CYCLE FOR STAFF CHOP

In order to have whole body integrated power, in addition to moving the hands and feet together, making the body and weapon as one, sending power smoothly through to the focal point, and showing strong spirit, you need to coordinate your breathing with the movements. Only when the breath works exactly with the movements can you fully utilize your power.

- Inhale as you do the hook up or hook down.

- Exhale as you chop.

In general, breathe in during actions that are non forceful or gathering power, and breathe out during the forceful actions. Breathing out helps you to use *qi* to launch power, and you must settle the *qi* to the *dantian*.

PRACTICAL APPLICATIONS FOR STAFF CHOP

Hook up and chop: The hook up defends against a mid to high strike, and includes a slicing action. Use the fore-section of your staff to hook and scoop the mid-section of the opponent's long weapon – once it is knocked away you can enter with your chop. Use the hook to protect yourself so that you can get in with the chop. So the circle of the hook up should not be too large a movement, as that would slow you down and give the opponent an opportunity to get in. The action should be small, just knocking aside and entering, using your speed to your full advantage. Chop strongly to whatever you can reach – body or weapon. The key is to enter in as close as possible and to fully utilize the whole body power of Xingyi.

Hook down and chop: The hook down defends against a low stab down the midline. You hook down to knock away the opponent's weapon then quickly move in with a covering chop or reverse grip chop to his head. The hook down can draw back, or it can check away. When you do the hook down, contact the mid-section of the opponent's weapon with your fore-section – as soon as you make contact, stick to his weapon and draw it back. Then you can follow the line of action to chop.

- Your footwork must adjust to the situation. Whether you are hooking up or down you can enter or retreat. If the opponent comes in strongly you can retreat as you hook. But you must advance or step forward when you chop. Your feet, body, and staff must charge forward all at once. Chop to your opponent's head, body, arms or weapon.

- Chop can be used as a defensive action as well as the main attack. Used to defend, you can chop directly to the opponent's weapon. If you hit the tip of his weapon with full power he is likely to lose his grip. You can then follow up with a variety of techniques. Chop can either hit or break down, and can combine and alternate the two, taking care of attack and defense. It is a very practical technique that fully shows the flavour and character Xingyi staff.

THE POEM ABOUT STAFF CHOP

劈棍气势要勇猛，上挂前劈步要冲。左右下挂侧身走，劈械劈身紧连崩。

The staff chop must be fierce.

The footwork must charge in to do the hook up and chop forward.

Move in with the body turned to effectively hook down to left or right.

Chop to a weapon or a body, and follow up immediately with a poke.

STAFF DRILL

INTRODUCTION TO STAFF DRILL, *ZUAN GUN*

The definition of drilling fist in Xingyi is any punch that hits forward and upward. Staff drill is named from the drilling punch, so staff drill is a scoop that moves forward and up. The definition of a staff scoop in the wushu regulations is "with both hands holding the staff, either end of the staff is scooped forward and up from below. The action must be fast and the power must reach to the effective end." The scoop is a very practical technique. The staff drill combination uses both the tip and the butt to scoop. It is said that the staff has two heads, and the drill combination uses this characteristic fully.

Staff drill includes any technique that strikes forward and up with a slicing action, whether with the tip or butt, whether advancing or retreating, whether into an aligned stance or a reverse stance. All are within the range of staff drill.

The staff drill combinations include: *Left stance drill, right stance drill, aligned stance drill, reverse stance drill, advancing drill,* and *retreating drill.* The actions include *hook up and scoop, hook down and scoop,* and *hook up and scoop with the butt.*

METHOD ONE: HOOK DOWN AND SCOOP

2a   Reverse Stance Drill   àobù zuāngùn   拗步钻棍

Start from *on guard. Right step forward, hook down to the right; Left step forward, sculling scoop.*

ACTION 1: Shift forward without moving the left foot. Take a step forward with the right foot. Slide the right hand forward along the shaft and hook the staff tip down past the right leg towards the rear. [First rotate the right palm away from the thumb, then hook with the arm rotated.] Hold the base with the left hand and raise it at the left front of the head. Turn to the right. Press the head forward and look at the staff tip. (image 4.20)

ACTION 2: Take a long step forward with the left foot and follow in the right foot a half-step to sit into a *santi* stance. Bring the right hand forward and up to do a sculling scoop with the staff tip. Rotate the right palm towards the thumb as the staff comes through so that it finishes with the palm up. Pull the base back with the left hand, pressing down at the left side, tight to the body. The staff tip is at head height. The right hand supports under the shaft with the elbow tucked in. Reach the right shoulder forward. Sit down into the stance. The left palm faces down. Press the head up and look past the staff tip. (image 4.21)

Pointers

- o Complete the hooking down action as the right foot steps forward.

- o Complete the sculling scoop forward and up as the left foot lands.

- o The reverse stance drill is one continuous technique. Do not hesitate midway through the actions

- Continue on, repeating the actions.

METHOD TWO: HOOK UP SCULLING SCOOP

2b Right Aligned Stance Drill   yòu shùnbù zuāngùn   右顺步钻棍

Start from *on guard. Left advance, hook up; Right step forward, scoop.*

ACTION 1: Advance the left foot a half-step and follow in the right foot to the left ankle. Slide the right hand along the shaft and bring the staff tip up and then back. Raise the right arm above the head, then lower it behind the body. Turn to the right and reach the left shoulder forward. Push the staff base forward in front of the chest with the left hand. Look forward. (image 4.22)

ACTION 2: Take a long step forward with the right foot and follow in the left foot a half-step. Keep most weight on the left leg. Slide the left hand forward along the

shaft and bring the base of the staff up and then hook back. Circle the right hand down at the right side to bring the staff tip forward and up, higher than the head. Rotate the right palm towards the thumb to turn the palm up as the staff scoops up. Tuck in the right elbow with the forearm under the staff. Pull the staff butt back to the left side, turning the left palm down. Turn the waist and reach the right shoulder forward. The staff is along the midline. Look past the staff tip. (image 4.23)

Pointers

- ○ Complete the hook back as the left foot advances.

- ○ Complete the sculling scoop as the right foot steps forward. The staff tip must finish the scoop as the right foot lands – upper and lower actions must work together.

- ○ Keep moving through the two actions; use the full movement to gain power.

2c Left Aligned Stance Scoop with the Butt   zuǒ shùnbù tiǎobà 左顺步挑把

Right advance, hook up; Left step forward, scoop with the butt.

ACTION 1: Advance the right foot a half-step and follow in the left foot to the right ankle. Pull the staff tip up and then back on the right side with the right hand, sliding it forward along the shaft to hook up. Continue on to lower the right hand to in front of the right shoulder. Slide the left hand along the shaft to about thirty to fifty centimetres from the butt and bring it to the left side. Look forward. (image 4.24)

ACTION 2: Take a long step forward with the left foot and follow in the right foot a half-step. Pull the staff down to the right waist with the right hand, putting it tight to the body. Scoop the staff butt up and forward to nose height with the left hand. Reach the left shoulder forward and bend the left arm under the staff, keeping the elbow tucked down. The left thumb/forefinger web is in front of the chest. Look past the staff butt. (image 4.25)

Pointers

- ○ Complete the hook up with the right hand as the right foot advances.

- ○ Complete the scoop up with the left hand as the left foot steps forward.

- o Three actions must be coordinated for the movement to work: scoop the left hand up, step the left foot forward, and pull the right hand back.

- o [Editor's note: make sure to slide the hands each time as you alternate left and right, so that the striking end sticks out.]

2d Right Aligned Stance Drill yòu shùnbù zuāngùn 右顺步钻棍

Left advance, hook up with the butt; Right step forward, scoop.

ACTION 1: Advance the left foot a half-step and follow in the right foot to the left ankle. Hook the staff butt up and then back with the left hand, reaching the left shoulder forward. Keep the right hand at the right waist. Follow the movement of the staff butt with the eyes, then look forward. (image 4.26)

ACTION 2: This is the same as described above in 2b, action 2.

Pointers

- o Complete the hook up with the butt as the left foot advances.

- o Be sure to draw a full circle with the staff as it completes the hooking action.

- Repeat this combination as long as energy and space permit.

2e Drill Turn Around zuāngùn zhuànshēn 钻棍转身

The drill combination uses the same turn around no matter which stance or footwork combination you are doing. You will always end up in a *reverse stance drill* after turning. You will hook-in the right foot and turn around leftward to turn, so the first step needs to adjust to accomplish this. If the <u>left</u> foot is in front then step the right foot forward, hooked in. If the <u>right</u> foot is in front, then hook-in on the spot.

Right hook-in step, hook down; Turn around, left step forward, sculling scoop.

ACTION 1: Hook the right foot in, and shift onto the right leg. Lift the left foot at the right ankle. Turn around 180 degrees to the left to face back in the opposite direction. Bring the right hand to the left, down, and then right so that the staff tip circles in a full hooking down action by the right thigh. The circle is full, but the tip should not hit the ground. Lift the staff base in front of the left shoulder to the left side of the head with the left hand. Look past the staff tip. (image 4.27)

ACTION 2: Take a long step forward with the left foot and follow in the right foot a half-step, keeping most weight on the right leg. Do a sculling scoop forward and up with the right hand controlling the staff tip, finishing with the tip at head height. Pull the staff butt with the left hand back to the left side, turning the palm down and keeping it tight to the body. Rotate the right palm towards the thumb and tuck the forearm under the staff. Reach the right

shoulder forward slightly. Press the
head up. Follow the action of the staff
with the eyes. (image 4.28)

Pointers

- o Complete the hook up with the
  staff as the right foot does the
  hook-in step.

- o Complete the scoop as the left
  foot steps forward. The points to
  consider and power are the same
  as the normal *reverse stance drill*.

2f Drill Closing Move   *zuāngùn shōushì*   钻棍收势

The staff's action in the *closing move* is always the same, no matter which foot is
forward. *Right retreat, raise the staff in both hands; Stand to attention with the staff.*

ACTION 1: If the <u>right</u> foot is forward it retreats behind the left foot. If the <u>left</u> foot
is forward, the right foot retreats a half-step. Then the left foot withdraws to meet
the right foot. Once the feet are together, stand to attention. Turn the body forty-
five degrees to the right. Pull the staff to the right
side with the right hand and raise it vertically
above the head, almost fully extending the right
arm. Push the left hand to under the right armpit
to bring the staff base to the side. Look to the left.
(image 4.29)

ACTION 2: Without moving the feet, lower the
right hand to place the butt of the staff on the
ground and stand it vertically at the right side of
the body. Bring the left hand to hang at the left
side. Press the head up and turn it to look straight
forward. The closing is now complete. (image 4.30)

Pointers

- o Points to consider are the same as the closing for *staff chop closing move*.

POWER GENERATION FOR STAFF DRILL

Opening: The first *right aligned stance drill*, coming from the ready stance,
completes two upward hooks – one on the right side and one on the left. Both are
completed while the left foot advances a half-step. When doing the hook up, the
hands should slide along the shaft. This action should be quick but concealed. The
mid-section of the shaft should always stay close to the body. The body action
must use the principle of power loading during the drill – load back to go forward,
load right to go left.

Reverse stance drill: The staff shaft must stay close to the right side of the body as it
hooks back and down. The body must turn to the right as the right foot steps
forward to accomplish this. The movement develops a smoothly flowing power by
having one part move up as the other moves down, and one part move forward as

the other moves backward. When the right hand hooks down the palm should rotate away from the thumb so that the palm faces back. The hand should also slide forward along the shaft. These actions increase the power of the hook down.

Sculling scoop: Transfer power from the waist to the shoulders – turn the waist and reach the shoulders into the movement. Lengthen the spine and sit into the buttocks to gain power from the body. Rotate the right palm towards the thumb and tuck the elbow in with the arm bent – in the usual drilling fist action. Add to this the pull back and press down of the left hand plus the driving forward from the rear leg, and the whole body has a power that charges forward. In this way the drill gains power from the whole body so that it hits strongly and cannot be defended against.

- The footwork for the staff drill must be quick, long, and fierce. The staff drill must have a focal point. The hands must slide to the appropriate places on the shaft. The hands must also rotate to apply power in the correct way. First practise slowly to get a feel for this, paying a lot of attention to the fine details.

Slicing up: The power must transfer from the waist to the shoulders, the shoulders to the hands, and the hands to the staff. The staff must stay tight to the body. The right hand should rotate palm towards thumb and the elbow should tuck in. The left hand should pull back and press down. The hands work together with their actions. At the instant of impact, sit down into the buttocks. Breathe out to connect the inner power with the outer actions, so that the body's power reaches to the fore-section of the staff.

- The hands must slide smoothly and quickly along the shaft. They slide as the staff is moving, as the steps are being taken, to get into the optimal position for the strike at the optimal time. Sliding the hands makes the technique work better and allows for better application of power.

- When the left hand does the scoop up with the butt, the elbow must stay snug to the ribs so that the staff stays close to the body.

PRACTICAL APPLICATIONS FOR STAFF DRILL

The drill is basically a scoop forward and up from below. The objective is to strike the opponent's weapon or body. If you are close enough, hit the body, if not, hit the weapon.

Left stance drill and *right stance drill*: These techniques both use a hooking back action before the strike, whether with the butt or the tip. First hook away a high strike from the opponent's weapon. If the right hand is forward then it hooks back on the right side. If the left hand is forward then it hooks back on the left side. When hooking back the hands must draw a full circle so that the staff makes contact with the opponent's weapon and then hooks it back. At this point you must step quickly forward and use the other end of the staff to do the slicing strike. The keys to the drill are daring to get in very close to the opponent and mastering the exact timing.

Reverse stance drill: This technique first hooks down then comes through with a sculling scoop up. The hook down defends against a low strike. Your staff tip just needs to touch the opponent's weapon to cause it to go off target. Then you stick to his weapon and follow the line of the shaft forward and up to strike his hand, arm, or body. The key lies in stepping in quickly and fearlessly with a strong technique.

On the first touch, the defensive action of drill must create the circumstances that make it possible to get in with the other end of the staff. This applies to the positioning and the timing.

If you have done a chop, then you can follow up with a scoop. Chop to the head then scoop to the groin so that your opponent has to defend high and low and may be thrown off. When he backs up you should follow up with a thrust to ensure victory. There are no fixed combinations, you need to adjust as opportunities present.

THE POEM ABOUT STAFF DRILL

棍法挂挑谓之钻，两臂拧旋腰催肩。挂开敌械进身挑，快步向前冲中间。

Drill with the staff is a hook and a scoop.

The arms twist and turn, and the body core sends the shoulder forward.

Hook away the enemy's weapon and enter to scoop,

Step in quickly to charge into his midline.

STAFF THRUST

INTRODUCTION TO STAFF THRUST, *BENG GUN*

The name 'thrust' comes from the five element fist techniques. Usually this staff technique is called 'poke.' In the wushu regulations, a poke is "to strike forward, back, or to the side in a straight line with the tip or the butt of the staff. Power is applied to the striking end." The main technique of the staff thrust is to forcefully poke straight forward with the tip or butt, and the thrust combination also includes an outer trap and a covering press down. In the martial world it is said that one would rather take a hit than a poke. A lot of power can be directed through the end of a staff due to its small surface area, so it can cause a lot of damage.

The thrust combinations include: *left stance thrust, right stance thrust, advance thrust,* and *retreat thrust.* Connecting moves include: *inner trap and press down, covering press down,* and *chop and pound.* There are also thrusts to front and back, left and right. The thrust combination is centered on the poke.

3a Right Stance Thrust   yòubù bēnggùn   右步崩棍

Start from *on guard. Left advance, inner trap to press; Right step forward, poke.*

ACTION 1: Advance the left foot a half-step and follow in the right foot to the left ankle. Circle the staff with the right hand so that the tip draws a full thirty centimetres circle in front of the body – down, right, and then up and left. Bend the right arm and draw it back a bit, tucking the elbow in towards the solar plexus, and pressing down on the staff. Keep the staff tight to the left side of the body with the left hand, also rotating. The staff tip finishes at chest height. Press the head up and look past the staff tip. (image 4.31)

ACTION 2: Take a long step forward with the right foot and follow in the left foot a half-step, keeping most weight back on the left leg. With the left hand, lift the staff base at the left ribs so that the shaft is horizontal, pointing straight forward. Poke the staff forcefully straight forward at chest height with both hands. Almost fully straighten the right arm, and keep the forearm tight to the shaft. Keep the left arm bent, the upper arm tight to the ribs, and the left hand in front of the chest. The striking surface is the tip of the staff. Press the head up and look past the staff tip. (image 4.32)

Pointers

- ○ Complete the inner trap as the left foot advances.

- ○ Complete the poke as the right foot steps forward.

3b Left Stance Poke with the Butt　　　yòubù chuōbà　　　右步戳把

Right advance, cover and press with the butt; Left step forward, poke with the butt.

ACTION 1: Advance the right foot a half-step and follow in the left foot to the right ankle. Pull the staff butt back with the left hand, keep the right arm almost straight, sliding the shaft through the right hand. Then, gripping the staff, circle the right hand down then pull it back to the right armpit, palm up. Slide the shaft through the left hand, stopping at the middle, and circle the butt up, forward, then down – to complete a covering press down. Reach the left shoulder forward. Turn the body ninety degrees to the right. The left palm is down, the thumb/forefinger web to the right, and the hand is pressing down in front of the left side of the chest. The right hand is behind the right ribs. The staff shaft is horizontal at chest height. Press the head up and look past the staff butt. (image 4.33)

ACTION 2: Take a long step forward with the left foot and follow in the right foot a half-step, keeping sixty percent of the weight on the right leg. Firmly grasp the staff with both hands and thrust forward with the staff butt at chest height. The left palm faces right and the right palm faces left. Almost fully extend the left arm and keep the right hand in front of the chest. The staff tip finishes on the right upper arm,

under the shoulder. Press the head up and look past the staff butt. (image 4.34)

Pointers

o   Complete the covering press down as the right foot advances.

o   Complete the forward thrust as the left foot steps forward.

3c Right Stance Thrust   yòubù bēnggùn   右步崩棍

Left advance, hook with the butt, inner trap and press down; Right step forward, poke.

ACTION 1: Advance the left foot a half-step and follow in the right foot to the left ankle. Bring the staff butt down and hook back with the left hand, and as the hand arrives at the rear left, slide it back along the shaft. Bring the staff tip up, forward, then down with the right hand to do a pounding, covering press down. Turn the body to the left, tuck in the abdomen and contain the chest. Draw the right hand

back slightly towards the chest. The right thumb/ forefinger web presses down on the staff, the right elbow tucks into the solar plexus. The left hand holds the staff base behind the left ribs. The staff shaft is horizontal at chest height. Follow the action of the left hand with the eyes as it hooks, then watch the right hand as it presses down. (image 4.35)

ACTION 2: This is the same as described above in movement 3a, action 2. (see image 4.32)

Pointers

o   Three actions are completed as one: advance the left foot, hook up the staff butt with the left hand, and pound / press down the staff tip forward with the right hand.

o   The points to consider for *right stance poke* are the same as movement 3a.

3d Thrust Turn Around   bēnggùn huíshēn   崩棍回身

Starting from _right_ stance thrust: _Left hook-in step, wheel around, hook down to the right; Right heel kick; Resting stance covering chop._

ACTION 1: Hook-out the right foot on the spot and step the left foot forward, landing with it hooked in, in front of the right toes. Shift to the left leg and turn the body 180 degrees around to the right to face back behind. Scoop the staff tip up with the right hand, then, coming around with the body turn, hook forward and down to the right rear of the body. Lift the staff base up with the left hand, pushing forward slightly. Twist the waist a bit to the right. Look at the staff tip. (image 4.36)

ACTION 2: Stand firmly on the left leg and lift the right knee, then do a crossing heel kick forward and up to waist height. Look past the right foot. (image 4.37)

ACTION 3: Land the right foot forward, keeping it hooked out. Follow in the left foot a half-step, bend both legs, lift the left heel, and sit into a crossed leg stance (the dragon model stance). Bring the right hand forward and down to do a covering chop with the staff. Pull the left hand back to under the right armpit, so that the staff finishes horizontal at chest height. Press the head up and look past the staff tip. (image 4.38)

Pointers

o The turn around is one complete movement. Do not hesitate in the middle, but complete it in one go.

o Complete the scoop up with the staff tip as the right foot hooks out. Complete the hook down with the staff tip as the left foot hooks in and the body turns around. Spread the lower back when doing the scoop up. Tuck in the abdomen when doing the hook down.

o Kick as high as you can. Lift your leg to kick at the proper time and place – after the staff has hooked down to the right side.

o You do not need to hit hard for the resting stance covering chop. Just do a coordinated movement and be sure that everything lands at once. Complete the chop as the right foot lands. Be sure to tuck in the abdomen and contain the chest.

3e Thrust Closing Move   bēnggùn shōushì   崩棍收势

Practise until you get back to your opening place, turn around, and then you may close. *Close the feet, raise the staff in both hands; Stand to attention with the staff.* From a *left* stance thrust:

ACTION 1: Retreat the right foot a half-step and shift back. Withdraw the left foot to beside the right foot, turn the body ninety degrees to the right, and stand up. Raise the staff in the right hand so that the tip points straight up. Slide the left hand along towards the base and push it out under the right ribs. Look to the left. (image 4.39)

ACTION 2: Lower the right hand so that the staff comes directly down to stand vertically at the right side, placing the butt on the ground. Release the left hand and let it hang at the left side. Look straight ahead. (image 4.40)

- From a *right* stance thrust, first retreat the right foot behind the left foot, then withdraw the left foot to beside the right. The rest of the actions are the same.

POWER GENERATION FOR STAFF THRUST

Right stance thrust: Prior to the poke, the inner trap combines two powers: pressing down and drawing back. The inner trap itself is a circular, coiling power that uses the movement of the body – tucking the abdomen and containing the chest – to press down. The right hand should slide forward along the shaft as you circle, and slide back towards the base as you draw back.

- *Poke with the tip*: The body and staff must move as one to poke forcefully forward. The step must go for distance and speed, as it is the step that takes the staff forward and gives distance to the strike. When poking, settle the shoulders down and close the elbows, so that the hands have a closing power between them. The actual strike is a 'one inch power' strike, and the footwork must have a charging power. Be very careful that the staff tip does not waver – it must poke straight forward. Gather all the power in your body and direct it to the tip of the staff.

Left stance poke with the butt: First slide the right hand forward along the shaft. The body must load in the opposite direction before striking, so that it leads the arms, which in turn move the staff, causing the staff to circle and hook down. The hands must work together – one pulls while the other pushes, one lifts while the other presses down – and this is accomplished by using the power from the body. The hands need to slide easily and comfortably along the shaft.

- When poking with the butt, there is only thirty to fifty centimetres of base sticking out, so you must use your footwork to the fullest. The footwork must charge forward for as much distance as possible. Adding a good step forward to the shaft of the staff give you about 1.5 meters. The key to a good thrust is in the charging footwork.

Turn around: The action of hooking with the butt with the left hand: The staff must first circle, drawn by the body, so the body must load in the opposite direction. As the hands do the trapping/ pressing down with the tip and covering/pressing down with the base, the waist must twist and the shoulders must reach. There is not just a pressing down power, but also a power drawing back. This gathers power for a strong thrust forward. Contain the chest and tuck in the abdomen, settling the body down slightly. Then, to thrust forward, lengthen the back and extend the arms. Always try to use the power of the body, not just the arms, to try to make the weapon one with the body.

PRACTICAL APPLICATIONS FOR STAFF THRUST

Poke: Poke is the main technique of the staff – the tip or the butt drives forward in a straight line. The small surface area applies a great deal of pressure. A well directed poke will always do considerable damage. The staff has two 'heads,' and the staff thrust uses both. To set up for the poke, a trapping action similar to that of the spear is used. The inner trap and the encoiling press down are the defensive actions that break the opponent's attack and control his weapon. Then you advance to get close, and poke directly forward to the chest or abdomen.

Inner trap, press down and poke: If the opponent stabs to your chest you use the right hand to do an inner trap and press down with the staff tip to take his weapon off target. Press down with the fore-section of your staff so that he has trouble pulling his weapon away or changing his attack. Then quickly move in and poke to his chest. The inner trap and press down must have a sticking, drawing power.

Encircle, press down and poke with the butt: If the opponent attacks your left side or turns and does a technique to the rear, you hook down or scoop up with tip. You need to slide your hands quickly on the shaft so that the right hand can hook or scoop with the tip. Then the left hand can pound and press down the butt, or scoop up to check away. Coordinate the defense with the footwork, either retreating or dodging. The poke, however, must be done with strong forward moving footwork, to direct the power strongly forward.

Staff thrust turn around: This is also called *leopard cat turns over whilst climbing a tree*. It is just a hook down, a kick, and a cover. If the opponent stabs towards you from behind, you step the left foot forward to get out of the way, hooking the foot in to get turned around. Use the staff tip to hook down, knocking his weapon away. If he is close, you can kick him, then immediately strike his head with the fore-section of the staff. Can you really use this technique? That depends on the situation – if everything is right then it would work, but this will rarely happen.

- The staff thrust is often linked with the chop. After you have chopped the staff is perfectly lined up for a thrust forward. This is a fierce and very practical attack.

THE POEM ABOUT STAFF THRUST

崩棍技法是戳击，戳时身械要合一。拿压盖把侧身走，对准心窝疾如急。

The technique of the thrust is to hit with a poke.

To poke, the body needs to unite with the weapon.

You must move in with the body sideways to trap, press down, or cover with the butt.

Aim accurately at the solar plexus and be quicker than quick.

STAFF SLASH

INTRODUCTION TO STAFF SLASH, *PAO GUN*

The staff slash is similar to the empty hand pounding punch – moving forward diagonally into a reverse stance as the staff blocks and slices up. There are a number of branch and regional variations, but they almost all hold the push, block up, slice and scull in common. The exact connecting movements and power use may differ. Each region performs according to their understanding as passed on from masters in their region, and all are correct for their style. Here I present two combinations that I think are the most practical, allow the smoothest power flow, and best show the flavour and characteristics of Xingyi.

Slash combinations include *left slash, right slash,* and *slash turn around.* The first slash method includes *left advance entangling press down, step forward slicing block up and sculling slice with the butt, advance entangle and press down with the butt, step forward scoop to block up and sculling slice.* The second slash method includes *advance and change the grip, step forward and sculling slice.*

METHOD ONE: ALTERNATING ENDS

4a Right Stance Slash   yòubù pàogùn   右步炮棍

Start from *on guard. Left advance entangling press down; Step forward, slicing block up and sculling slice with the butt.*

ACTION 1: Advance the left foot a half-step and follow in the right foot to the left ankle. Keep the legs together and squat slightly. Circle the staff tip with the right hand to the left, down, then right and up, then left to cover and press down. The tip draws a full counterclockwise circle. Slide the right hand forward along the shaft and press down with the thumb/forefinger web on top of the shaft. The staff is horizontal at waist height, and points diagonally to the forward right. Hold the base with the left hand and rotate it at the left waist. Press the head up and look past the staff tip. (image 4.41)

ACTION 2: Take a long step diagonally to the forward right with the right foot and follow in a half-step with the left foot, keeping most weight on the left leg. Slide the right hand forward along the shaft and slice up the staff tip. Keep the right arm bent, raised above the head at the right side, thumb/forefinger web back. Slide the left hand forward along the shaft to show more staff base. Push the left hand to the forward right so that the staff base does a sculling upward slice to the front and up. The butt

4.41   4.42

stops at waist height so that the shaft completes a blocking up action in front of the body. Look past the staff butt. (image 4.42)

Pointers

- o   Complete the entangling press with the staff tip as the left foot advances.

- o   Complete the sculling slice with the staff butt as the right foot steps forward.

- o   [Editor's note: the left hand pushes strongly, like punching.]

- o   The two actions should be done without hesitation between them. Keep the body action soft, but with intended power, during the entangling press down. Launch power into the step forward sculling slice up. Take a long step forward and strike fiercely.

4b   Left Stance Slash   zuǒbù pàogùn   左步炮棍

Start from *on guard. Right advance, entangle and press down with the butt; Left step forward, scoop to block up and sculling slice.*

ACTION 1: Advance the right foot a half-step and follow in the left foot to the right ankle. Squat down slightly, keeping the legs together. Controlling the staff with the right hand, bring it down to the right side of the ribs. With the left hand circle the staff base down, left, then up and right so that it entangles then presses down. The staff butt should draw a full clockwise circle and finish pointing to the forward left. Finish with the left elbow bent above shaft height, and the thumb/ forefinger web facing right. The staff shaft is level at waist height. Press the head up and look past the staff butt. (image 4.43)

ACTION 2: Take a long diagonal step to the forward left with the left foot and follow in the right foot a half-step, keeping most weight on the right leg. Slice up the staff base with the left hand, sliding the hand back to the butt and raising it up above and to the left of the head with the thumb/forefinger web down and the arm bent. Slide the right hand back on the shaft and do a sculling slice to the forward left with the staff tip.[56] The tip finishes at waist height. The right arm is slightly bent, the palm facing forward, and the shoulder reaching forward. Look past the staff tip. (image 4.44)

---

[56] Editor's note: be sure to move the shaft closely past the body, do not let it swing out.

Pointers

- o Complete *entangle and press down* with the staff butt as the right foot advances.

- o Complete both tip and butt actions as the left foot steps forward. The tip does a sculling slice up and the butt does a hooking back upper block.

- • Continue on, repeating the actions to left and right as space permits.

METHOD TWO: CHANGING GRIP SLASH

4c Right Stance Slash   yòubù pàogùn   右步炮棍

Start from *on guard*. Continue with *Left advance, change the grip; Right step forward, scull and slice.*

ACTION 1: Advance the left foot a half-step and follow in the right foot to the left ankle. Loosen the grasp of the right hand and shoot the staff butt forward from the left hand, controlling it with the right hand. This makes the staff tip go forward and lift up above the head. When the tip arrives above the head, the right hand has slid along to the butt to grasp it. Slide the left hand up and back to the left along the shaft, controlling its action and finally grasping it as the tip arrives at the rear lower left. The right hand is now holding the butt in front of the left shoulder while the staff tip is about ten centimetres from the ground behind the body at the left side. Twist the body left. Follow the action of the staff tip with the eyes then look forward. (image 4.45)

ACTION 2: Take a long step diagonally to the forward right with the right foot and follow in the left foot a half-step, keeping most weight on the left leg. Grasp the staff butt in the right hand and bring it from the left side to lift and pull forward and up on the right side to above the head. Keep the arm slightly bent. Push the shaft forward with the left hand, palm up, finishing with the staff tip at waist height. Reach the left shoulder forward. Press the head up and look past the staff tip. (image 4.46)

Pointers

- o Change the hand grip as the left foot advances. The changeover is a smooth, gentle action and must be well coordinated. Pay attention to controlling the staff tip's line of action and the direction in which it points.

- o Complete the sculling slice up as the right foot steps forward.

- o [Editor's note: this is more a slice than a push, note that the left hand is palm up.]

- o The two actions must be done as one, with no hesitation between them.

4d Left Stance Slash   zuǒbù pàogùn   左步炮棍

Right advance, slice and change the grip; Left step forward, sculling slice.

ACTION 1: Advance the right foot a half-step and follow in the left foot to the right ankle. Swing the staff tip to the forward left with the left hand, sliding the shaft through it. Push the staff base forward with the right hand so that the staff tip goes forward and up. When the staff tip arrives above the head, slide the left hand down the shaft to the base and slide the right hand up the shaft. Lower the right hand to the rear right to behind the body on the right side. Hold the staff base with the left hand in front of the right shoulder. The staff tip is about ten centimetres from the ground. Turn the body a bit to the right. Follow the action of the staff tip with the eyes, then look forward. (image 4.47)

ACTION 2: Take a long step diagonally to the forward left with the left foot and follow in a half-step with the right foot, keeping most weight on the left leg. Grip the staff base with the left hand and lift and pull it to above the head at the forward left. The arm is slightly bent to brace out. Push the staff shaft forcefully to the forward left with the right hand. The palm faces forward at chest height. The combined actions make the staff tip do a sculling slice up forward to waist height. Reach the right shoulder forward. Press the head up and look past the staff tip. (image 4.48)

Pointers

- o Points to consider are the same as 4b, *left stance slash.*

- • Continue on, alternating *right* and *left stance slash.*

4e Slash Turn Around for Method One   pàogùn huíshēn   炮棍回身

From the *left* stance slash. *Left hook-in step, turn around, entangling press down; Right step forward, sculling slice.*

ACTION 1: Hook-in the left foot in front of the right toes and shift to the left leg. Lift the right foot and turn around 270 degrees to the right. With the right hand, swing the staff tip around to the right as the body turns, and, after turning, draw a counterclockwise circle then press down. Lower the left hand to the left waist. The staff tip is at waist height. Look past the staff tip. (image 4.49)

ACTION 2: Continue on with *right stance slash.*

- From the *right stance slash,* hook-in the right foot in front of the left toes and do the encircling press down with the left hand. Then continue on with *left stance slash.*

Slash Turn Around for Method Two

From the *left stance slash. Left hook-in step, turn around, change the grip; Right step forward, sculling slice.*

ACTION 1: The footwork is the same as described above, just slide the hands to change the grip as usual for method two.

Pointers

o The hook-in needs to be well placed and well turned so that the body can turn around quickly.

o Press the head up and keep the body upright – don't look down, as this tends to make the body lean over.

o Don't hesitate between the turn around and the following slash.

o Editor's note: Keep the shaft on the body as you turn and press down. Step, bring the shaft to the body and turn, then circle and press.

4f   Slash Closing Move   pàogùn shōushì   炮棍收势

If the left foot is forward, then withdraw the right foot further back. If the right foot is forward then retreat it behind the left foot. Then bring the left foot back to beside the right foot. The rest is the same as described in 1h, *staff chop closing move: raise the staff in both hands, stand at attention with the staff.*

POWER GENERATION FOR STAFF SLASH

FIRST METHOD

Use the power of the torso and waist to draw the counterclockwise circle of the encircling press down, so that the power transfers from the lower back to the arms, and the hands work in opposite directions. The fore-section of the staff should have coiling plus drawing actions. When encircling and coiling, reach the staff forward slightly. While the right hand draws a large circle in the front, the left hand draws a small circle in the rear. When pressing down and drawing, compress the body and draw back slightly. Tuck in the abdomen, contain the chest, and use the whole body as a unit.

The clockwise circle of the staff butt during the coiling press down should stay between shoulder and waist heights. Transfer power from the lower back to the shoulders, from the shoulders to the arms, and from the arms to the staff. Do not simply use the forearms. Keep the staff shaft snug to the body so that the body and staff move as one. The left hand draws a large circle in the front while the right hand draws a small circle behind.

SECOND METHOD

The hands must changeover quickly and smoothly. First slice up the staff base, then hook it back, and then change the hands. The right hand slices the staff tip up and then hooks it back. The hand change must be smooth and slide along the shaft easily, keeping it under control even during the switchover. Everything must be smooth – the body action, the power transfer, and the movement of the staff.

Left and right slash: Turn the waist and reach the leading shoulder forward, tucking in the leading elbow. The leading arm must strike with a focal point. The upper arm of the leading arm must stay close to the ribs with the elbow tucked in to push the staff with a quick, powerful, and focused sculling slice. The rear hand must brace out above the head. When launching power, lengthen the back and reach the shoulder forward to send power out to the fore-section of the staff. Exhale to assist the power launch and to put the power of the whole body into the strike.

The power of the staff slash comes from the feet, centers in the lower back/waist, is expressed through the shoulders, and applies through the arms to reach the staff shaft. As the staff tip comes through from the rear that is the *scull*. As it comes up from below that is the *slice up*. The leading hand has a lifting, pulling, bracing power. The rear hand has a pushing, sculling, slicing power. You have to practise over and over to get a feel for the power. Start out slowly to find the power, then gradually add speed and strength.

PRACTICAL APPLICATIONS FOR STAFF SLASH

Encircle and press down: The encircling press down uses the tip or the base of the staff to wrap around and press down the opponent's weapon. The action circles inward and sticks to the opponent's weapon to prevent him from withdrawing it.

Scoop up and hook back: This is one action with two phases. The scoop works forward and up, while the hook works to the rear. Scoop to knock the opponent's weapon forward and up. Then hook to control it, pulling it back.

Sculling slice up: Whichever end of the staff is below slices forward and up, and this is the main attack of the staff slash technique. The target is the leading hand, arm, leg or knee of the opponent. Or, if you can get in close, his groin.

One important characteristic of the staff is that it has two 'heads' – you put either the tip or the butt to good use.

- It is interesting to analyse the application of a technique by looking at its structure and movement. But to actually use the weapon is another thing. You must be able to react to the actual situation and do what is necessary; nothing works 'by the book.' It is of utmost importance that you develop and train courage, the winning instinct, and your tactical sense.

THE POEM ABOUT STAFF SLASH

左右撬撩是炮棍，绞压挑架不停顿。技法劲力腰肩找，前冲后蹬脚下问。

The staff slash is a sculling slice up to either side.

Entangle and press down, slice up and block up without hesitation.

Look for the technique and power in the waist and shoulders.

Look to the feet to charge forward, pushing off strongly.

STAFF CROSSCUT

INTRODUCTION TO STAFF CROSSCUT, *HENG GUN*

Xingyi staff crosscut has its own unique characteristics and flavour, sharing characteristics with, but yet not quite the same as other staff techniques. Staff crosscut is basically a horizontal crossing strike to either side. This is classified as a sideways strike in staff terminology. The wushu regulations defines a sideways strike as "the tip or the butt of the staff strikes sideways, to either right or left, hitting with the striking end." But the Xingyi crosscut is not performed exactly the same as a normal sideways strike. The striking surface of a sideways strike is the end of the staff, while that of the Xingyi crosscut is the entire fore-section. The crosscut also holds similarities with a horizontal swing. The definition of a horizontal swing is, "the tip is swung in a half circle to either side at a height above the chest and is then accelerated, and strikes with the fore-section." But the horizontal swing is usually done with both hands holding the butt and swinging the staff for a full circle or more. The Xingyi crosscut holds the staff with the hands separated as usual on the shaft and completes only one circle to strike. It also holds similarities and differences to the flat action of a brandish. Brandish usually goes fully over the head, while the crosscut does not.

The crosscut combination includes *right stance crosscut, left stance crosscut, crosscut turn around,* and *closing move.*

5a Right Stance Crosscut   yòubù hénggùn   右步横棍

Start from *on guard. Left advance, checking brandish to the right; Right step forward right crosscut.*

ACTION 1: Advance the left foot a half-step and follow in the right foot to the left ankle. Move the staff with the right hand to check to the right with the fore-section, continuing on to circle to the rear, then circle above the head to arrive in front of the left shoulder. The right forearm finishes on top of the shaft with the right palm turned to face forward. Hold the base in the left hand and draw a small circle in front of the body, assisting the right hand by moving in the opposite direction. The left hand finishes under the right armpit with the palm turned up. Turn the body to the left and look at the staff tip. (image 4.50)

ACTION 2: Take a long step to the forward right with the right foot and follow in a half-step with the left foot, staying back on the left leg in a *santi* stance. Swing the staff to the right with the right hand, so that the tip passes horizontally in front of the body from the left to the right, stopping at a forty-five degree angle at the front right. Rotate the right palm to face right. Keep the left hand at the right armpit to keep the staff base snug to the right ribs. The staff tip is just above shoulder height. Press the head up, tuck the jaw in, and look past the staff tip. (image 4.51)[57]

Pointers

o Coordinate the swinging of the staff as the left foot advances. Complete the sideways strike as the right foot hands. Complete the two actions without a pause midway.

5b Left Stance Crosscut   zuǒbù hénggùn   左步横棍

Right advance, check to the left; Left step forward crosscut.

ACTION 1: Advance the right foot a half-step and follow in the left foot to the right ankle. With the right hand, check with the staff to the left, then continue on, so that the staff tip circles forward, left, back, and over the head to the right side, in front of the right shoulder. Extend the right arm and rotate the palm towards the thumb so that the palm faces forward. Hold the staff base in the left hand and draw a small circle in front of the body in the opposite direction to coordinate with the action of the right hand. Bring the left hand to in front of the shoulders, rotating the palm away from the thumb to turn the palm down. Watch the staff tip as it starts to circle, then look forward once the tip is behind the head. (image 4.52)

---

[57] Editor's note: Get the left hand in to the body soon, to bring the staff tight to the body before the strike. The staff does not slap or hit the body.

ACTION 2: Take a long step to the forward left with the left foot and follow in the right foot a half-step, keeping the weight mostly back on the right leg. Swing the staff with both hands so that the tip comes across in front of the body from the

right to the left in a horizontal strike. Hold the base in the left hand and pull it in to in front of the left shoulder, tucking the elbow down. Bend the right arm slightly and stop it at the forward left. Both palms face left. The staff tip is just higher than the shoulders. Turn the waist to the left and reach the right shoulder forward. Press the head up, tuck the jaw in, and look past the staff tip. (image 4.53)

Pointers

- Be sure to pull the left hand into place.

- Swing the staff as the right foot advances. Strike as the left foot lands.

5c Crosscut Turn Around   hénggùn huíshēn   横棍回身

Starting from a *left stance crosscut. Left hook-in turn around, checking brandish; Right step forward crosscut.*

ACTION 1: Hook-in the left foot towards the right toes and shift onto the left leg, lifting the right foot to the left ankle. Turn around to the right to face back. Bring the staff tip around with the right hand, following the turning of the body to check to the right. Then continue to circle the staff so that it goes right, back, around over the head, and out to the left to in front of the left shoulder. Rotate the right palm away from the thumb. Tuck the left hand in to the right armpit with the palm up. Look at the staff tip. (image 4.54)

ACTION 2: Complete the right crosscut, described in movement 5a.

- If turning from *right stance crosscut*, hook-in the right foot, turn around, and move into a *left stance crosscut*. The only difference in the actions is the direction of the turn.

Pointers

- Points to consider in the staff's actions during the turn around are the same as for the advancing crosscut. You just need to pay attention to getting a good hook-in step and turning around quickly.

5d Crosscut Closing Move   hénggùn shōushì   横棍收势

The closing move is always the same. Turn around when you arrive back where you started. If you are in a *left stance crosscut,* retreat the right foot a half-step and bring the left foot in. If you are in a *right stance crosscut*, retreat the right foot to behind the left foot, then bring the left foot to beside it. Then raise the staff and stand to attention as described in movement 1h, *staff chop closing*.

POWER GENERATION FOR STAFF CROSSCUT

Checking brandish: First check to the side, then brandish over the head. Use the power of the body to check. Circle the hands in opposite directions to brandish. As the right hand does a large circle, the left hand does a small circle in the opposite direction. Turn the body to move the arms, which in turn move the staff. Remember the principle of counter movements to gather and release power – pre-load left to go right, pre-load right to go left.

Crosscut: The crossing strike must have a focal point. Use the strength of the waist turn to strike with the fore-section of the staff. Gradually accelerate during the brandish. The staff tip should move fast enough to whoosh, and stop sharply enough to vibrate.

You must first gather power then launch. Gather gradually and launch immediately. Follow the principle of 'go past the midpoint, firm up the grip and launch power' when doing the checking brandish. This means that you wait to accelerate until you get just past the midpoint of the circle. During the first half of the circle you need to gather power to prepare for the acceleration in the latter half. Gather power within the body – this is very important. If you do not do a preparatory gathering in the first half of the circle, then 'launch power at the midpoint' is just idle talk. Also remember to firm up the grip before launching power – you can't strike anything with a loose hold on your weapon.

All Xingyi staff techniques emphasize using the body and weapon moving as one, so the primary power comes from the lower back and torso. For the crosscut, you need to add a twist in the waist and a sit into the hip so that there is a pulling back and settling power in addition to the power striking directly to the side.

- You may adjust the placement of the right hand during the crosscut – slide forward and backward slightly along the shaft. The left hand may allow about fifteen centimetres of the base to show or may hold at the very end. Minor adjustments allow the staff to move more freely and smoothly, making the power application stronger.

PRACTICAL APPLICATIONS FOR STAFF CROSSCUT

Crosscut: Crosscut is a swinging strike across to the side, the main target being the opponent's head. The most effective target is the head, but anywhere on the torso is also effective. A strong crosscut can also break the opponent's weapon or knock it out of his hands. This sets you up for a following attack.

Right stance crosscut: If the opponent does a high stab towards your midline you check your staff tip across to the right with your right hand to knock his weapon offline. Then you quickly move in along the line and do a crossing strike to the right with the fore-section of your staff striking his head.

Left stance crosscut: If the opponent does a high stab towards your midline you check your staff tip across to the left with your right hand to knock his weapon offline. Then you use the leftward momentum to swing the staff around and do a crossing strike to his head, arm, body, or whatever you can get.

- When you check to the right or left you may step forward or back, whatever is necessary. When you strike you should step forward. Of course, though, you have to do whatever works for the situation.

- During practice you should swing the staff in a large circle to get a feel for the power, add to the momentum, and develop whole body power. When using the technique, though, the action should be small. The classics say that a large movement is never as effective as a small movement. The smaller the amplitude, the fiercer the technique, and the faster. Speed is the way to control and beat the opponent. As the classics say, "you can defend against everything but speed."

THE POEM ABOUT STAFF CROSSCUT

横棍劲力气势雄，左右云拨任意行。过中固把身发劲，上步横棍似旋风。

The staff crosscut is fierce.

Brandish to right and left to go where you will.

Wait until the halfway point, then firm up your grip and shoot power from the body.

Step forward and swing the staff like a tornado.

FIVE ELEMENTS LINKED STAFF FORM

INTRODUCTION TO THE FIVE ELEMENTS LINKED (FIVE PHASES CONNECTED) STAFF, *WUXING LIANHUAN GUN*

The Five Elements Linked Staff form is a widespread and popular form. It uses the pattern, movements, and characteristics of the five element fist form, but with the staff techniques. The form is short and sweet – once up and back – with postures that flow smoothly from one to the other. The techniques are simple and practical, the power is full, and the spirit is fierce. The main techniques are chop, drill, and crosscut, with the supplementary techniques of hook, scoop, block, check, and swing. The structure and performance style of this form shows very clearly the characteristics and flavour of Xingyi staff.

The rhythm of the form is as follows: The opening move is slow and steady. Moves two, three, and four hit strongly, linking together with smooth footwork. Be careful to make the footwork – both advance and retreat – clear. The fifth move emphasizes body technique, and should start gently and finish strongly. Use body technique to gently set it up, then finish with a power launch. Moves six, seven, eight and nine should connect together without hesitation. This combination should be fast and fierce, like 'chasing the wind and the moon without relief.' The moves all advance – charging forward as if nothing could stop them. The tenth move, the turn around, should be stable and firm. The landing should go to a low stance, and should not be rushed. The spirit and focus must remain full and connected throughout the closing movement.

NAMES OF THE MOVEMENTS

1.   Opening Move (On guard)

2.   Chop: Hook up and Chop

3.   Chop: Hook down and Covering Chop

4.   Chop: Hook down and Reverse Grip Chop

5.   White Crane Flashes its Wings: Close the Feet and Block

6.   Crosscut: Right stance Crosscut

7.   Crosscut: Left Stance Crosscut

8.   Drill: Reverse Stance Drill

9.   Chop: Hook up and Chop

10.   Leopard Cat Turns Over Whilst Climbing a Tree: Turn Around with a Hook Down, Heel Kick, and Resting Stance Chop

       (The following moves are a repetition of the first section, coming back in the returning direction)

11.   Chop

12.   Chop

13.   Chop

14.   White Crane Flashes its Wings

15.   Crosscut

16.   Crosscut

17.   Drill

18.   Chop

19.   Leopard Cat Turns Over Whilst Climbing a Tree

       (The following moves are the closing combination.)

20.   Chop

21.   Closing Move

Description of the Movements

1.   Opening Move   qǐ shì   起势

Stand with the staff; Raise the staff in both hands; Left advance and chop.

ACTION 1: Stand with the feet together and the legs straight, facing in a forty-five degree angle to the line of the form. Stand the staff vertically with the butt on the ground at the right side of the body. Hold the staff midsection in the right hand with the thumb/forefinger web up as the arm hangs naturally straight. Let the left arm hang straight at the left side. Press the head up and look forward. (image 4.55)

ACTION 2: Raise the staff straight up with the right hand. Bring the left hand to the right armpit and

grasp the staff about ten centimetres from the base. Turn the head left and look to the forward left. (image 4.56)

ACTION 3: Step the left foot to the forward left and turn a bit to the left, sitting into a *santi* stance. Chop forward and down by pulling the left hand back tight to the

4.57

body between the left waist and hip. and extending the right arm forward. Keep the right arm slightly bent and tuck in the elbow, the right hand at chest height. The staff tip is at shoulder height. Press the head up and look past the staff. (image 4.57)

Pointers

- ○ Turn the head left as you raise the staff.

- ○ Complete the chop as the left foot lands.

2. Chop   pīgùn   劈棍

Right step forward, hook up; Left step forward and chop.

ACTION 1: Take a long step forward with the right foot and land firmly with the knee bent. Follow in the left foot to the right ankle. Controlling the staff with the right hand, bring the staff tip down to waist height, then bend the elbow and lift the hand back to above the right shoulder to hook up with the staff. Push the staff base forward with the left hand, the hand finishing at waist height. Tuck in the abdomen and contain the chest. Bring the right shoulder back. Look forward. (image 4.58)

ACTION 2: Take a long step forward with the left foot and follow in a half-step with the right foot, settling into a *santi* stance. Controlling the staff with the right hand, chop the staff tip forcefully down the midline to chest height. Pull the left hand back tight to the body between waist and hip crease height. Reach the right shoulder forward, keep the arm bent and the elbow tucked in, and press the thumb/ forefinger web down on the staff. Press the head up and look past the staff tip. (image 4.59)

4.58

4.59

Pointers

- ○ Unite the hook up with the chop down, using the hook up to prepare for the chop down without any hesitation. Take long steps and follow in quickly.

- ○ Complete the hook up with the staff as the right foot steps forward. Complete the chop down as the left foot steps forward. The staff must arrive at the same time as the feet so that upper and lower work together.

3. Chop   pīgùn   劈棍

Left advance, hook down to the right; Right step forward, covering chop.

ACTION 1: Advance the left foot a half-step and follow in the right foot to the left ankle. Lift the staff base with the left hand, pushing it forward in front of the left shoulder. Pull the right hand back to hook down and back on the right side with the staff tip, then continue to swing it upwards. Turn the body to the right. Follow the staff tip with the eyes. (image 4.60)

ACTION 2: Take a long step forward with the right foot and follow in the left foot a half-step. Pull the left hand down to the right armpit with the palm up underneath the staff, so that the staff base is snug to the right ribs. With the right hand, bring the staff tip forward and down with a covering chop. The right arm in on top of the staff, palm down. The staff shaft is horizontal, the tip just below shoulder height. Press the head up and look forward. (image 4.61)

Pointers

- ○ Complete the hook down as the left foot advances.

- ○ Complete the covering chop as the right foot steps forward.

4. Chop   pīgùn   劈棍

Left retreat, hook down to the left; Right advance, reverse grip chop.

ACTION 1: Retreat the left foot a half-step and withdraw the right foot to just in front of the left foot. Circle the staff tip with the right hand down, back, and then up on the left side of the body. Turn the body to the left. Help the action with the left hand, keeping it at the right armpit. Follow the action of the staff tip with the eyes, turning the head to look back on the left side. (image 4.62)

ACTION 2: Advance the right foot a long step and follow in the left foot a half-step, keeping most weight back on the left leg. Circle the staff tip with the right hand up on the left side, then forward and down. The right hand finishes in a reverse grip, forearm under the staff with the palm up. The staff tip finishes at shoulder height. Hold the staff base in the left hand and pull it back to the left side, between hip and waist height. Focus power to the fore-section of the shaft. press the head up and look past the staff tip. (image 4.63)

Pointers

o   Complete the hook down to the left as the feet retreat and withdraw.

o   Complete the covering chop as the right foot advances.

o   Complete both actions as one, without a break in between. Lead the body with the staff during the hook down, then lead the staff with the body during the chop.

5.   White Crane Flashes its Wings   báihé liàngchì   白鹤亮翅

Left retreat, entangle; Feet together, block to the left.

ACTION 1: Shift forward to the right leg and retreat the left foot a half-step. Circle the staff tip with the right hand – up, left, and then down – drawing a circle of forty centimetres diameter. Keep the left hand in front of the abdomen and help with the encircling action. Look past the staff tip. (image 4.64)

ACTION 2: Shift back to the left leg and withdraw the right foot to beside the left foot, settling it on the ground with a thump. Both legs are bent. Rotate the right palm towards the thumb and block to the left side in front of the body with the staff tip. The right hand finishes about twenty cm in front of the left chest. Pull the staff base back with the left hand, placing it snugly on the left side. Turn the body left so that the right shoulder is directly forward. Look to the forward right. (image 4.65 and from behind)

Pointers

- o Complete the encircling action as the left foot retreats. Use the power of the body and waist, and keep the movement gentle.

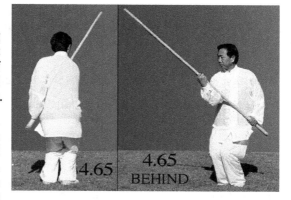

- o The right foot should stomp with a sound when it withdraws, but it should not lift and stamp. Complete the block with both hands as the foot lands. The power launch should be fierce and the block should have a focal point.

6. Crosscut   hénggùn   横棍

Right checking brandish; Right step forward crossing cut.

ACTION 1: Shift onto the left leg without moving the feet. Swing the right hand to the right and turn the body right so that the staff tip moves forward then checks to the right. Do not stop at all, but continue to circle the staff back up over the head to brandish in a complete circle over to the left side. the right hand is in front of the left shoulder, palm rotated away from the thumb. Hold the staff base in the left hand and draw a smaller circle in the opposite direction in front of the body, bringing the base finally in to under the right armpit with the palm up under the shaft. Turn the body to the left. Look to the forward right. (image 4.66)

ACTION 2: Take a long step to the forward right with the right foot and follow in a half-step with the left foot, keeping most weight on the left leg. Swing the staff forcefully to the right with the right hand so that the tip strikes with a crossing hit to the forward right, stopping at a forty-five degree angle to the right front. Rotate the right palm away from the thumb to turn the palm to the right. Keep the left hand under the right armpit to keep the staff base snug to the right ribs. The staff tip is at shoulder height. Press the head up, tuck the jaw in, and look past the staff tip. (image 4.67)

Pointers

- o The staff draws a conical shape during the check, and then cuts across horizontally for the crossing strike. Gather power in the body during the check to pre-load for the strike in the opposite direction.

- Complete the crosscut as the right foot advances. Exhale to assist in getting power. Unite the staff and body as one, and send power to the staff tip.

7. Crosscut   hénggùn   橫棍

Right advance, left checking brandish; Left step forward crossing cut.

ACTION 1: Advance the right foot a half-step and follow in the left foot to the right ankle. Check the staff to the left with the right hand so that the staff tip moves across to the left in front of the body, and then circles back and around over the head. The right hand finishes palm up in front of the right shoulder with the arm extended. With the left hand, draw a smaller circle in the opposite direction with the staff base. Finish with the left hand in front of the right shoulder, the palm rotated away from the thumb with the palm down. Press the head up and look forward. (image 4.68)

ACTION 2: Take a long step to the forward left with the left foot and follow in the right foot a half-step, keeping most weight back on the right leg. Swing the staff with both hands so that the tip comes across the front to the left to strike sideways. Bend the right arm slightly and stop it at the forward left. The staff tip is at shoulder height. Hold the staff base in the left hand with the arm bent, pulling to in front of the left shoulder, elbow tucked down and back, palm facing left. Turn the body to the left and reach the right shoulder forward. Press the head up, tuck the jaw in, and look past the staff tip. (image 4.69)

Pointers

- Check the staff to the left as the right foot advances.

- Complete the swinging crosscut to the left as the left foot steps forward. Use both hands to strike, turn the waist and put the shoulders into the action. Hit with whole body power, uniting the staff and body as one.

8. Drill (Reverse Stance Drill)   zuāngùn   钻棍

Right step forward, hook down; Left step forward, sculling scoop.

ACTION 1: Shift forward onto the left leg without moving the foot. Step the right foot forward. Slide the right hand a bit forward along the shaft and rotate the palm away from the thumb, taking the staff tip down outside the right leg to hook back to the rear right. Twist the body to the right. Lift the staff base up in front of the left shoulder with the left hand. Look at the staff tip. (image 4.70)

ACTION 2: Take a long step forward with the left foot and follow in the right foot a half-step, keeping most weight back on the right leg. Rotate the right palm towards the thumb so that the palm faces forward, and scull the staff tip forward then scoop up to nose height. The forearm is under the shaft, palm facing up. Lift the left hand then press it down beside the left side. Tuck the left elbow in close to the ribs. Straighten the back, settle the shoulders, and press the head up. Look forward. (image 4.71)

Pointers

- o Hook the staff back as the right foot steps across to balance the action – forward and up with backward and down.

- o Scoop the staff up as the left foot steps forward. Be sure to slide the right hand along the shaft and to rotate it palm towards thumb. You must first lift the left hand and then press down. These hand actions must coordinate to put power into the staff.

9. Chop   pīgùn   劈棍

Right step forward, hook up; Left step forward, chop.

ACTION 1: Shift forward and step the right foot forward. Pull the right hand back to in front of the right shoulder so that the staff tip hooks up and back. Push the staff base forward with the left hand to waist height. Bring the right shoulder back. Look forward. (image 4.72)

ACTION 2: Take a long step forward with the left foot and follow in a half-step with the right foot. Extend the right arm forcefully straight forward to chop down with the staff, the tip at chest height. Pull the left hand back snug to the body between waist and hip height. Reach the right shoulder forward. Almost fully extend the right arm, but tuck the elbow in. Press the head up and look past the staff tip. (image 4.73)

4.73

Pointers

o All the points to consider
   are the same as move 2.

10. Leopard Cat Turns Over Whilst Climbing a Tree   huíshēn   回身

Turn around hooking down; Right heel kick; Resting stance, covering chop.

ACTION 1: Hook-in the left foot to the outside of the right toes. Shift onto the left leg and turn the body around 180 degrees to the right to face back along the line of the form Pivot the right foot to face straight as well. Scoop up the staff tip with the right hand and bring it around as the body turns. Then hook down and back at the right side. Lift the staff butt with the left hand above the left shoulder. Twist the body around to the right. Follow the staff tip with the eyes then look forward. (image 4.74)

ACTION 2: Stand firmly on the left leg, lift the right knee, and kick forward and up with the foot turned out at chest height. Look past the kick. (image 4.75)

4.74

4.75

ACTION 3: Land the right foot forward, still turned out. Follow in the left foot and lift the heel to squat down into a resting stance – Xingyi's dragon stance. Continue to circle the staff with the right hand, bringing the tip up behind, then forward and down in a covering chop. Pull the left hand in to the right armpit, palm up, to settle the staff base at the right ribs. The staff is near horizontal with the tip at chest height. Press the head up and look forward. (image 4.76)

4.76

Pointers

o Hook-in the foot considerably so that the turn around is easily done.

o Time the kick so that the staff first hooks smoothly down outside the right leg.

○ Complete the drop into resting stance and the staff chop together.

○ Complete all three actions as one without hesitation between them.

- The following moves, 11 through 19, are a repetition of the first section, moves 2 through 10, going back in the returning direction.

11.	**Chop**	See move 2.
12.	**Covering Chop**	See move 3.
13.	**Reverse Grip Chop**	See move 4. (image 4.77)
14.	**White Crane Flashes its Wings**	See move 5. (image 4.78)

15.   Right Stance Crosscut

See move 6. (image 4.79)

16.   Left Stance Crosscut

See move 7.

17.   Drill

See move 8. (image 4.80)

18.   **Chop**   See move 9.

19.   **Leopard Cat Turns Over Whilst Climbing a Tree**   See move 10.

20.   **Chop**   This is the same as move 2. This is now going in the original direction.

21. Closing Move   shōu shì   收势

Starting from *thrust. Right retreat, raise the staff in both hands; Stand to attention with the staff.*

ACTION 1: Retreat the right foot a half-step and withdraw the left foot to beside the right foot. Turn the body forty-five degrees and stand up straight. Pull the staff back to the right side, then raise the staff in the right hand straight up at the right side. Push the base of the staff with the left hand under the right armpit so that the staff is vertical. Press the head up and look to the left side. (image 4.81)

ACTION 2: Release the left hand and bring it to the left side. Lower the right hand, still holding the staff, to place the staff vertically on the ground at the right side. Turn the head to look straight forward. (image 4.82)

Pointers

- o   Straighten the back when holding the staff up, and show good spirit. Do not slack off when almost done. Keep focus and concentration to the very end of the form.

TEACHING XINGYIQUAN

BREATHING FOR POWER

All Xingyi techniques are done as integrated movements. The hands initiate and land the technique; the legs stride forward with a thrust backward; the power gathers then launches; and the breath flows in then out. Breathing in Xingyi is 'positional breathing,' in which the techniques incorporate the breathing. The classic texts say; "to attain adequate power you must first attain complete breath," and "techniques have form and the strength of the breath has no form. Techniques must gain strength from the breath." You must focus on synchronizing breathing and movements. This type of breathing improves the body's ability to take a hit, helps apply power, and increases the speed of explosive power.

Each technique uses a full breathing cycle.

- Inhale to store power with a long deep breath, exhale to launch power with a short powerful breath. "Inhale long and exhale short" is a characteristic of the synchronized breath and action of Xingyi. This makes the power integrated and the strength full.

- When breathing out, do not simply exhale all of the breath that you inhaled. Instead, as you deliver force, exhale a portion of your breath then suddenly stop, tightening the *dantian* area of your abdomen to brace your whole body, delivering a whole body power.

- The general rule is: inhale when the limbs are circling and when the body technique is folding or closing in; exhale when the limbs are extending or applying power and when the body is turning or opening up. More simply: inhale when the lead hand and foot move and exhale when the rear foot and fist come through to apply power. Contain the breath, that is, breathe neither in nor out when readying.

- Breathe naturally during non-forceful movements.

Positional breathing technique is the main method used during the obvious power stage of 'training spirit to change energy and change sinews.' This is also the main method used to gain whole body power. You must also understand that you use exhalation to assist the action of delivering power; you are not "exhaling power." In other words, you need to breathe out in order to deliver a powerful hit, but the breath is not the power itself (obviously, you can breathe out without delivering power).

Breathing is greatly affected by the speed of movement. It is easy to regulate breathing while moving slowly, but more difficult when moving quickly. When training Xingyi the movements should not be done too quickly; they should <u>not</u> 'flow like the current of a river' as do the movements of Longfist. Xingyi uses a rhythmic alternation of action and stillness that emphasizes whole body power. To develop the whole body power it is essential to work on the proper co-ordination of breath and power.

At the beginning a student should breathe naturally without much thought to breathing. You should pay attention to learning the proper movements and gaining a basic command of the requirements of the movements. You should not try too hard to coordinate breathing with actions. The first thing to do is learn the movements, master the lines, directions, angles and synchronization of all the body segments, and to work on integrated power. Breathe naturally, just keeping breathing smooth with the actions. Once the actions have been grasped then you may start to pay more attention to using breath together with the movement.

Xingyi uses reverse abdominal breathing, which is the natural way to put power into a movement. Raise the diaphragm and bring in the abdomen as you inhale, lower the diaphragm and round the abdomen as you exhale. This keeps power in the *dantian* area and allows you to launch power to wherever it is needed.

The general principle to apply to breathing is: control your body with your mind; control your breath with your body. But, once you've reached a high level, then "you can use your *qi* anytime, following your inclination; hit hard or enter hard without impediment."

A DISCUSSION OF POWER

Both teacher and player need to understand the difference between power and strength, or force. The power (*jin*) spoken of in martial arts is far removed from the strength (*li*) spoken of in daily life. Strength (*li*) refers to the amount of strength or force a person has. This includes the physical ability or fitness and the strength of contraction of the muscles. Power (*jin*) in martial arts refers to a combination of repeatedly trained skills added to the muscular force trained in these skills. Power is integrated body strength created by the intentional coordination of muscular contraction plus the orderly synchronization called for to perform specific skills. For this reason, each specific power needs to be trained for each specific skill. Power is developed gradually with repeated practice of proper technique.[58]

TEACHING PROGRESSIONS

1. First teach post standing in each position to teach students the proper hand and body placement, shapes, and angles. This reinforces their self-awareness so that the correct position becomes habitual sooner than if they only practised moving techniques. Post standing teaches the amount of flex in the legs, the position of the feet and knees, the angles of the body, the exact flex of the arms and the forward

[58] Editor's note: Simply put, power is strength that has been harnessed and trained until actions can be done in a relaxed and smooth way with the same force output.

press of the hands. The students first need to find the correct outer appearance, then train the intent, energy and power and put that into the stance. This will speed up mastery of the technique. The teacher must explain the most essential points and make sure every body segment is in the correct position. Correct the students when they are post standing. If mistakes are corrected in a timely fashion the students will form correct habits.

2. Have students practise stationary alternation of the hand techniques without moving their feet. Do not have them apply power for this practice, but concentrate on the line of action, proper height and angles of the hands and arms, and focus on the requirements and movement standards.

3. Have the students perform the full movement slowly. Keep the movement slow and stop for a while in every set position, for every single movement. This training method helps to fine-tune the movement, helps master the lines and movement patterns of each body segment, and gradually develops a conditioned reflex, serving to make the movement more coordinated. This is simply a training method however, and once the movement has been mastered it should be sped up and trained at regular speed.

4. In group practice, have the students do the movements in unison on command. On the count of one take the half-step advance and do the first hand actions. On the count of two step forward and hit. Carry on the practice according to the size of the training area.

To use *standard drill* as an example, on 'one' advance the lead foot a half-step, lift the rear foot and press down the lead hand. On 'two' step the rear foot through, follow in with the other foot, drill the rear hand forward and up and pull the lead hand back to the belly.

SAMPLE TEACHING PROGRESSION OVER THREE YEARS

1. Post standing (in the old days, this would last the full three years before going on to anything else).

2. Part training (first for split, then more quickly for the other four).

3. Slow and soft whole training (first for split, then more quickly for the other four).

4. Body technique within the techniques.

5. Pounding post standing.

6. Five elements connected form.

7. Partner forms.

8. Applications.

TEACHING PROGRESSION WITHIN THE FIVE PHASES

DRILL: Drill should be learned after split. Many teachers teach drive after split because of the five element controlling order 'metal controlling wood' but I teach drill after split, using the creation order 'metal creates water.' Drill uses the same footwork as split, so teaching it after split reinforces the most basic footwork of Xingyi.

DRIVE: When teaching drive, the *back leg hit drive* should be learned first, then the *lead leg hit drive,* then the variation *reverse stance (alternating) drive.* There are many different ways of doing drive but they all involve the basic idea that the arm extends into a straight punch. The various punches look quite similar, but their intent will differ – some hook and hit, some press and hit, some block out and hit, some drop the wrist and hit. Some do a punch for each step, some do a punch for two steps, and some do two punches for each step. If the basic power of the straight punch has not been found, the variations will not be well done.

TEACHING SUGGESTIONS[59]

- All five of the basic techniques have different positions and power applications, and different requirements for body position, hand form and stance. So you must always start out with post standing for each to form an initial model of the position. This helps the student gain a basic understanding of the structure and action.

- The teacher must correct mistakes as soon as they occur, and point out the key elements of the technique. Correct the students individually and as a group. Some errors are almost universal, and some are idiosyncratic. As the classics say, "it is easy to learn but very difficult to change," so it is particularly important to form correct form at the beginning. If a mistake becomes a habit it will be more difficult to change later.

- The above being said, allow time for the student to examine his or her own movement. Do not constantly correct or correct fine details beyond the level of the student. In the old days, the teacher would show something three times, then it was up to you to find the technique yourself – "if you find it yourself you won't forget it."[60]

- Explain and demonstrate the universal principles of Xingyi behind each action, so the students can understand and apply the principles and learn to self correct.

- Demonstrate often to give the students a firm impression of the actions. Demonstrate not only the proper movements as you wish students to perform them, but also lively action with power and rhythm to give students an image of what they seek to achieve.

- When the students are learning they should start out slowly and speed up only when they are comfortable with the action.

- Do not explain too much about rhythm and power at first. Wait until the students are ready to absorb new or advanced information. When a comfort

---

[59] Editor's note: I have collected these teaching suggestions from throughout the original book and placed them all together to avoid repetition and make sure they are noticed. I have also added a few notes taken during teaching sessions, not written in the book. I have not put words into the author's mouth, but I have taken them from his mouth and written them down (with his permission).

[60] Editor's note: My Chen Taijiquan teacher Huan Dahai used to say this, but the author agreed that he had also heard it from his teachers.

level is reached at a certain level, you can explain more detailed action, power and coordination.

- Use 'part and whole' method for both teaching and training. This establishes a solid understanding of the movement. This method is explained in detail in the following pages.

- Explain and demonstrate the line of power and the expression of both soft and hard power in each action so the student understands the efficiency of the proper movements and has an idea of whole body power for each action.

- Explain and demonstrate fighting and self-defense applications so that students can easily see where a wrong action would not work, and can imagine what they might be doing.

- Once the students have placed the feet and hands essentially in the right place, emphasize the action of the more central segments – shoulders, hips, elbows, and knees. Power and smooth lines come from moving from the centre of the body.

- Beginners must study and practise the basics diligently to master the requirements. They must wholeheartedly work on the finer points of the movements. They must work gradually and in an orderly way, never trying to rush the learning process. Repeated practice will bring gradual improvement. Although the movements are not complex, mastering their essence is not the work of a day.

SAMPLE CLASS ORGANIZATION

1. Post standing.

2. Warm-up.

3. Five minutes of soft techniques.

4. Main class: steady and hard (techniques, forms, applications).

5. Gradual cool down with soft techniques.

6. Cool down relaxing movements.

PART AND WHOLE METHOD TEACHING

Techniques should be taught using the 'part and whole' method to help students learn and get a good grasp of the actions and specific requirements of each technique. This methodology has quite good results and helps students learn quickly. Note, however, that the part method should not be continued too long because all actions in Xingyi form an integrated whole.[61]

---

[61] Editor's note: In stepping, for example, the body action is not done. Doing straight-line stepping as a practice is good for learning the drive off the back leg and the raking power of the lead foot, but does not use the body power of, for example, split or drill. Too much stepping alone may lead to students not understanding the difference between the

PART METHOD: (EXAMPLE) STRAIGHT-LINE ADVANCING FOOTWORK

ACTION 1: Stand in the *santi* stance with the left foot leading. Clench the right fist and place the fist heart on the belly. Grasp the right wrist with the left hand. Tuck the elbows lightly in at the ribs. Hold the head up and look forward. (image: legs only 1)

ACTION 2: Advance the left foot a half-step and follow in with the right to beside the left ankle without touching down (beginners may touch the toes down). Stand firmly on the left leg with the right foot about an inch off the ground and the knees flexed and together. The body should not come up. Stance height should remain the same as the *santi* stance. Press up the head and look forward. (image: legs only 2)

ACTION 3: Take a big step forward with the right foot and follow in a half-step with the left to take a *santi* stance with the right foot leading and the left behind. The hands remain on the belly. Press the head up and look forward. (image: legs only 3)

LEGS ONLY   1   2   3

- Carry on with right and left steps.

Pointers for Part Method Footwork Practice

o   Do not take too big a step forward with the first half-step advance; the back foot should be able to step without great effort. Do not lift the toes up too much when stepping. Lift the foot naturally and keep in mind that you are using the toes to reach forward and grab. This should prevent you from lifting the foot up too high and flipping the sole of the foot upwards. The progression for landing the foot is: first land the heel, then immediately place the whole foot and grab with the toes.

o   Press the knees together when you follow the right foot in beside the left. The right foot should stop at the inside of the left ankle. Pick up the foot quickly and stop with stability. The sole of the raised foot should be level and about an inch off the ground.

o   When you stride the right foot forward into the final stance, you should reach out, keeping in mind that the right foot is striking forward. Fully

---

techniques. Both stepping and hand technique part training are useful, however, as a warm-up even for advanced practitioners.

utilize the backward thrust from the left foot – the lead foot charges and the rear foot thrusts. As the right foot lands it should have a forward and downward trampling power. Once you are comfortable with the action of the stepping you can increase the trampling power and pay more attention to the kinesthetic awareness in the knees [the feeling of compressing like a spring, and getting the spring rebound back for the drive forward, and the sharp braking power of the lead knee, neither holding it stiff nor really bending].

- o The left foot follows in again to take a *santi* stance but the stance length is slightly shorter than a post standing *santishi*. Pay attention to using the lower back to bring the hip up, keeping the hip joint rolled inward, using the hip to bring the knee in, and using the knee to bring the foot in. The follow-in step should be quick.

- o You should train the footwork a lot to develop a correct and dependable movement pattern.

PART METHOD: (EXAMPLE) HANDWORK FOR SPLIT

Separate hand technique practice is a fixed stance practice. Stand with the feet shoulder width apart and parallel, with the left hand in front and the right hand at the belly. Put the left shoulder forward, so that the hands are in a similar position to *santishi*. (image: arms only 1)

ACTION 1: Clench the left hand and pull the fist in to the belly, then bring it up past the solar plexus to drill forward and up to nose height, twisting the ulnar edge and fist heart up. (image: arms only 2)

ACTION 2: Drill the right fist out to the left elbow and along above the left forearm. As it approaches the left hand rotate both inwardly and unclench the hands. Chop the right hand forward and down to chest height, and pull the left hand back to the belly. Put the right shoulder into the split. Press the head up and look forward. (image: arms only 3)

ARMS ONLY   1   2   3

- • Carry on alternating left and right until you get a good grasp of the line and the requirements of the hand technique. This develops the correct pattern that should carry over when the footwork is added.

WHOLE METHOD

Once the student has gained a basic command of and becomes comfortable with the movements of the feet and hands separately he is ready for whole movement training.

The foot and hand actions can be put together and practised following a count from the teacher. The command must be cleanly followed, especially in group situations. The command should be given slowly at first then sped up once the students are comfortable with the movements.

During this process the teacher should continually work to improve the students' understanding of and body awareness towards Xingyiquan's basic requirements.

USE OF IMAGERY TO TEACH XINGYIQUAN

A teacher needs to demonstrate the correct movement so that the student can imitate the action. But in order for the student to learn more quickly, the teacher needs to explain how to use power, the nature of the specific power, and the coordination between body segments. Otherwise, the student will simply copy the apparent action and not get the full idea, with less than ideal results. The use of power is especially difficult to understand and difficult to teach. Imagery is a good method to use when the student is learning the movements, before he is used to them, before he understands the requirements, and before he understands how to get and use power. At this time the student can use imagination to direct his actions. Using this method enables the student to get a grasp of the power in each movement within a relatively short time.

It is important that the teacher uses the appropriate method, and it is also important that the students are enthusiastic and involved. If the students are mentally engaged in a practice session then they get a grasp on the actions more quickly and have better quality of movement. The method is to borrow some image when explaining movements, usually an action or example that is met with or seen everyday, something the student can personally know from experience. It needs to be something that further illustrates the power of Xingyiquan, which can deepen the understanding of a movement from a variety of angles. When the students are practising, they have a clear example or an image of an action imprinted in their minds, so that they can get the feeling themselves and find the action from their own experience. The things that one learns through imagery leave a deeper imprint, are understood more quickly, and remembered more surely. Using imagery can get twice the results with half the effort.

A FEW EXAMPLES OF IMAGERY:

CANNON: Introduce the image of how the cannon punch hits out, "It explodes like an artillery cannon, the cannon ball is launched suddenly, and it has the most violent nature." How can one reflect this violent nature? How can one perform this whole body power, then add in the driving footwork, and get the upper and lower segments to work together? How can one pre-load then launch the punch to hit out quickly with stability and ferocity? When doing slow motion practice you should try to feel the connections between the segments, but when fighting there is no separation between the first to start and the last to arrive. "Once one thing moves there is nothing that does not move," "the eyes arrive, the spirit arrives, and the hands arrive." Often, students can get the basic movement, but cannot get the power of the back and shoulders.

- Give the students this image – pretend the lead fist is a heavy rock. When you launch your power, forcefully push the rock forward, the farther the better. Do this action in a fixed stance position at first to learn it, and then add the footwork.

CROSSCUT: Crosscut is like wringing a rope. The fists and arms must have three types of power – twist, roll in, and drill. The legs should have a scissoring power between them. How can this type of power be put into action? How do you need to do it to be exactly the right kind of power?

- Give the students this image – pretend you are wringing a towel to dry, one arm twists outwardly and one twists inwardly. The leading hand twists and extends outward, while the rear hand twists inward and pulls back, tightening the towel.

This example gives them the idea of twisting the arms, one outwardly and one inwardly, one up and one down, helping each other out. You need to add that when the leading hand hits with the crosscut it should have a drilling power, as if it is an awl boring a hole, driving forward. It should have a pressure forward and a spiraling strength.

- To learn the scissoring power of the legs, pretend you are standing on ice. Rotate the hip joints to prevent your legs from sliding out.

- To learn the bodywork, pretend you are squeezing a rubber ball. Pull back with the leading hip and push forward with the rear hip, compressing the body core.

- The legs as they step are just like scissors cutting – the shins rub against each other as they pass.

You can add up the images of wringing the towel to feel the twisting power of the arms, the awl to feel the drilling power, standing on ice and cutting with scissors to feel the scissoring power of the legs and body. In this way, the various powers of the crosscut can be understood and the students can more quickly come to grips with the technique.

TIGER POUNCE [similar to a double split]: When teaching the tiger pounce, four statements can explain the action well:

"The hands drill as they rise,

The hands turn over as they drop.

The hands and feet land together.

The lower back lengthens and the shoulders extend."

The first three are relatively easy to understand and do, but the last is neither easy to understand nor do. What exactly is lengthening? What exactly is extending? When do you lengthen and extend? The actions of lengthening the lower back and extending the shoulders are key to launching this splitting power. If these questions are not resolved clearly it will be difficult to get power into the tiger pounce. You should emphasize the actions of lengthening the lower back and extending the shoulders. First explain the line of action, then, once the students have mastered the line of action, add the image.

- Give the students this image: pretend you are holding a large rock at your belly. As you drill up, raise the rock to your chest, and then forcefully push the rock forward with both hands. Use power from your belly as you do the turning over action, use your lower back to press forward and up (bring the shoulders back slightly, open the chest, press the head up) – be sure to do the actions at the same time. At the instant that you push forward, release the shoulders, close the chest, and tuck the belly. This action is what extends the shoulders forward.

Performing the action like this fits with both biomechanical and combat principles. Only when it is done this way does it fit with martial theory of using the body's core area to launch power, give a fierce whole body power, and use internal power.

NOTE:

- o The power of Xingyiquan has this characteristic – if a student can get a feel for the power of one or two techniques then it is relatively easy to get power for the others.

- o The use of images must be appropriate and apt, so that the teacher can explain clearly and the students can understand the power of the action. If the power of an action is complicated, then it should be explained from a number of angles.

- o You should choose actions or images often seen in daily life. Transform the strange to the commonplace, the complicated to the simple, and the imaginary to the concrete.

There is also a natural progression in the use of this method.

- In the early stages of learning you should emphasize correct static positions and final positions after action.

- In the intermediate stages of learning you can use imagery to speed up the mastery of power use, using the mind to lead, solidify, and put more detail into the movements themselves.

- After the power of the techniques has been gradually mastered you have to practise more – repeat and repeat to solidify the action, so that the action becomes an established pattern and the use of power becomes deeply ingrained. Once the movements become well established then you don't need to use an image when practising. You can think of the combat application, imagining the attachment and power flow to the opponent's body. In this way you can gradually develop from imitation of an action to being the likeness of the action.

Only with long term, unceasing, and thoughtful repetition can we improve our fundamental skill. Any teaching method is an aid to the student, but in the end, it is up to the student to learn.

TEACHING AND TRAINING SUGGESTIONS FOR WEAPONS

TEACHING SUGGESTIONS FOR WEAPONS[62]

POST STANDING

Students must do post standing on both sides of each posture. This enables them to master the exact position, height, and direction of the weapon tip, the blade or shaft angle, the hand positions, the feeling of the hold on the weapon, the elbow position and the structure of every part of the body. This improves the kinesthetic awareness and sets the correct model into the body.

The spear is a difficult weapon, so student absolutely must stand in *santishi* with it. Getting comfortable with the correct position with spear sets the foundation for all applications of power and all changes in techniques. The shoulders must be settled and released. The hands must work together with the lead hand bracing forward and the rear hand pulling back. The spear must always be aligned with the midline of the body so that the 'three points line up' – the tips of the foot, nose, and spear. The qi must be settled, the spirit must be at peace, and the mind must be focused.

FIXED STANCE PRACTICE

The students can practise any technique in a fixed stance. This means standing on the spot and repeating a move without stepping. This allows them to find the overall line of action, get used to the changes that the hand has to do on the grip, find the lines of power in the body, and get the details of the direction and height that the weapon points and which blade edge is where. Once they have basically mastered all of this, then they can combine it with the footwork.

SLOW PRACTICE

In a class, have the students learn and practise the movements slowly so that they can pay careful attention to all the details of each movement, getting the coordination between the hands and feet, finding the correct line of the weapon, finding the correct hand adjustments on the weapons, and seeking out the body action to coordinate with the weapon. Be strict about them following the model for each movement; do not allow them to become casual. Even when they know the movements, make sure that they practise slowly for the first 10 to 20 minutes of a class, and then allow them to practise at normal speed. You may have them practise together on command so that you control the speed.

GROUP DRILLING

To watch the students, keep them together, and avoid accidents with weapons, the teacher can have them perform the movements together on command. Line them up with good spacing between them. Call the actions as broken up in the descriptions in the book to make sure that all students move at the same time. The interval between commands depends on the ability of the students to keep up. Leave time in between moves for beginners, then leave less time when the

---

[62] Editor's note: I have gathered these teaching and training suggestions from throughout the original book and placed them together to save space and avoid repetition.

students can link the moves together better.

- Do not ever call too quickly. A characteristic of Xingyi is that you need time to gather power before each move. But do not call too slowly, either, as this will destroy the completeness of the movements.

Example one. Call 'one' and the students perform action 1 of broadsword thrust: left advance right broadsword draw; call 'two' and the students perform action 2: right step forward broadsword thrust. Call 'two' quickly and strongly, so that the students respond with a fast, strong action.

Example two. Call 'one' and the students perform action 1 of sword slash: advance block up and draw back. Call 'two' and the students perform action 2: step forward sword slice. For sword slash turn around, call 'one' and the students perform hook-in chop. Call 'two' and the students perform turn around step forward and slice.

WHOLE – PART – WHOLE TEACHING

When teaching the weapons, the teacher should first show the entire movement at the correct speed to give the students an impression of the proper model that they will follow. The best way to get an idea of the action at first is to carefully watch the teacher's demonstration. Watching a correct action creates a model in the head. So the teacher must show the movements correctly and do them with proper power, speed, and spirit to create the proper model.

Once the technique has been shown at normal power and speed, then 'part teaching' should be done. Break down the movement into its components for teaching purposes, and explain the practical and power applications. Show each movement slowly, pointing out the key points so that the students can understand the outline and get a feel in slow motion of the line of action and correct postures. With weapons, you must focus on placement and path of movement of the grip and tip of a weapon, the direction of the blade or shaft actions, and of the changes in grip. This must be in concert with the body work, arms, elbows, and shoulders. Have the students follow along as you do each component, explaining clearly. After three or four times they should be able to basically do the move. Then you may do the whole move with them, and they should practise the whole move.

Always first let the students get a rough idea of the movements and then gradually explain in more detail. Add more detail after the students have learned the basic moves – gradually adding in body action, power flow, and the smaller, detailed actions. Once the students have practised some more, then add further detail – breathing co-ordination and technique, and practical applications of all the moves. The student must then practise over and over for a long time to become comfortable, skilled, and consistent.

EXAMPLES OF TEACHING PROGRESSIONS

SWORD THRUST

The final stab position should be practised as a post standing exercise. Then have the students practise fixed stance hook and check, paying particular attention to the action of the wrist, the line of movement of the sword blade, and the placement of the blade after the hooking action. The correct movement and placement must become second nature. Then add the footwork. Pay attention to the whole body, but particularly the angle and placement of the arm and the height of the sword.

The same principle applies the second method of the sword thrust – first teach fixed stance circles with the sword, paying particular attention to the wrist and arm movement and how they control the size of the blade's circle. The students should practise circling in both directions, paying particular attention to adjusting the grip and the rotation of the hand until this becomes comfortable. Once the circling is comfortable, then add the draw back.

SWORD OR BROADSWORD CROSSCUT

Have the students practise fixed stance block and hook. Pay particular attention to adjusting the grip of the right hand and its placement in front of the body. Make the distinction between the block and the hook – the sword first blocks and then hooks, using the fore-section of the upper edge of the sword blade or spine of the broadsword blade.

SPEAR CHOP

The core of the spear chop combination is the actual chop. The students should practise the chop action separately in a fixed stance to get a feel for the action of the chop – how to use the hands together, the line of movement of the spear tip, the final position, and so on through all the details. The students should start out slowly then speed up, and start out without power then add power as the action becomes comfortable. The student should strive to make the movement correct and to find the feeling for each part of the body. The most important thing to learn first is the kinesthetic awareness.

Once the basic chop is correct, then the student should practise the full movements – check and chop, and scoop, chop and stab – again starting out with fixed stance techniques, then moving. The student must clarify the techniques – check, hook, and scoop. What are the similarities and what are the differences?

SPEAR THRUST

The main techniques of the spear thrust – outer trap, inner trap, and stab – are the most basic and important of all the techniques of the spear. If you can't do them properly then you are not a spear player. This is the key spear technique for any style, and it must be practised diligently. The spear classic says,

"If you want to be a spear player then you must practise the circle long and hard. It must become more familiar than familiar, more refined than refined."

At first the student should practise the movement slowly, making large circles with the spear tip to learn the movement of the hands. The student should first practise in fixed stance. The spear must be stable and the positions must be correct, the line taken by the spear tip must be correct. The most important aspect in early learning is to make everything correct. During slow movement the student has time to find the correct body positioning, use of power and coordination, and to discover how to send power to the tip of the spear. Only after the techniques are correct should speed and power be added. The circle drawn by the spear tip should gradually decrease down to the size of a saucer – about 30 cm. Stepping may now be added as well – back-cross step, crossover step, and roundabout step.

- While this method of gradual additive learning – post standing, fixed stance training, slow practice, part practice, and moving on command – seems to advance slowly, the movements are learned more clearly and correctly. Once the basic movements are properly learned then the pieces can be put together with more success in the long run. The goal is whole body integration with the weapon, so the full movements should be put together fairly soon.

SMALL GROUP PRACTICE

You may put the students into groups and assign a certain time limit, a certain number of repetitions of a move, or a certain goal for them to achieve. When students practise together in groups they may help each other out, watching and correcting each other. This helps them advance together.

Have the students perform in front of each other frequently. In particular, have the students who have learned a bit better and mastered the moves a bit quicker perform in front of the others.

GIVE TIMELY AND POSITIVE CORRECTIONS

The teacher must constantly correct the positions and actions of the students. Corrections must be made as soon as possible, to catch the mistakes before they become habitual. Timely corrections will ensure better results.

- Whether the students are practising in small groups or on their own, correct mistakes in a timely way when you see them.

- When the students are practising, the teacher should use praise while correcting their errors. This encourages the students to try harder, rather than discouraging them. If there is nothing to praise in the actual technique, then praise their effort and give encouragement to those who are trying hard.

ADJUST TEACHING METHOD TO STUDENT AGE

Do not ask older students to do full power movements. Place more emphasis on developing the co-ordination of mind with movement, and of breathing with movement. Emphasize regulation of qi and development of the spirit.

With young students, do more demonstration and have them copy you more. Explain the movements and their requirements repeatedly and do more repetitions. You must also must try to keep the class interesting and to avoid overtiredness.

EXPLAIN APPLICATIONS

You should always explain the combative application when showing new moves, so that the students understand the techniques fully. This gives them more of a goal in their study and training, and makes it easier to learn and train as well.

Example: the idea of sword drill is to drill into the smallest crack, following the line of the opponent's weapon. It is either a reverse grip low pierce to the knee or a twisted high pierce to the head. Four techniques are done within the sword drill practice – entwine, lift, draw, and pierce. Entwine, lift, and draw are the assisting techniques for the pierce, which is the main technique. Entwine uses the sword tip to draw a vertical circle either in a clockwise or counterclockwise direction, sending the power to the front end of the blade. Lift is to use the lift the blade in an arc up to the right or left side, close to the body, finishing at shoulder height with the tip angled slightly down. When lifting to the left side, you must first externally rotate the arm to turn the palm up, and then lift at the left side. Draw uses the whole of the blade, either flat or vertical blade edges, to carry the opponent's weapon directly back or up and back. When doing right stance drill, you must first entwine, and then lift, but the lifting action must be part of the entwining action. Entwining and lifting are the defensive actions that prepare the way for the low pierce, which is the goal.

TRAINING SUGGESTIONS FOR WEAPONS

ATTITUDE TO TRAINING

When learning weapons you must first have a good foundation in the empty hand techniques. All of Xingyi's weapon techniques are based on footwork, body work, and power application of the empty hand techniques. If you perform a weapon without bringing out the footwork, body work and power of Xingyiquan, or without bringing out the flavour and characteristics of Xingyiquan, then you are not performing a Xingyi weapon. Also you should first know the standard techniques. Only do any alternate methods once you are comfortable with the standard method. You must be honest in the assessment of your skill level.

Once you have mastered the basic actions, then you need to practise over and over. That is the only way to develop real skill and power. You should not content yourself with learning the movements, but should work hard to develop power. During practice, gradually add intent, imagining what you are doing to an opponent. You should hit hard and fast with no mercy, as if pushing a mountain into the sea. If you use this type of intent and attitude in practice then you will progress quicker and further. The type of intent and attitude with which you practise determines the type of skill that you will develop.

Learning is just a stage, a process. The main thing is the training; you want to train until you can do the movements, until you understand the techniques, until you forge the deep skill, until you have developed a strong body and mind.

LEARNING FROM BOOKS

If you are using a book as study aid, you should look at the movements stance by stance, breaking them down clearly. First study the photographs or diagrams to get the general idea. Pay particular attention to the feet – is it the right or the left – is it advancing or retreating? Then look at the position and line of action of the hands and weapon – from where to where. Once you are clear on the diagrams then try out the movements yourself. Then read the accompanying text. Once you are pretty sure that you are doing the movements correctly then read the pointers and section on power application. Then you can practise to improve your mastery of the techniques, gradually getting a feel for the requirements and power. As you get more comfortable with the movements then you will gradually improve and have your own feelings and understanding of them,

POST STANDING

When learning weapons, always start out with post standing in the on guard position, and learn each and every part of it correctly. First you must understand the 'four methods and three structures.' The four methods are the hand technique, footwork, body technique, and weapon technique. The three structures are the hand shapes, stances, and body structure.

You must practise post standing with each technique to fix the model position into your body. For example, the final position of each technique of broadsword chop: withdraw lifting draw, advance pushing stab, and chop.

When doing post standing, be sure to have the proper structure, smoothly aligned strength, full power, and fully concentrated mind. You want to train your body to the model stance to guarantee that it will take an unerring stance when in the midst of quick action. Post standing is a means to an end; the end is to perform the movements.

SLOW TO FAST PROGRESSION

When learning weapons you must not try to go fast right away. The movements are simple and easy to learn, but they need to be practised over and over to find the right power to be able to use them properly. You must not be content with just being able to do the moves; you must train hard and persevere to get a feel for the moves and combinations in order to become really skilled.

First practise any new movement slowly and softly to seek out the correct coordination, power flow and technique. Once you have mastered the basic movements in slow motion, then you should speed up gradually, paying attention to the power flow and technique. This phase takes a long time but it is the phase that builds real skill and develops power. During this phase you should also try to better understand the applications and train the spirit.

Once you have achieved the required speed then you must practise repeatedly. The only way to master the techniques is through repeated practice – this is the path to deep skill. Once you are comfortable with the movement then increase the speed further, being careful that the movement and techniques do not become sloppy. Seek out the natural rhythm in fast movements – this is how they will become practical, which is the goal.

Even when you know the movements well, train a combination of fast and slow – mainly fast, but also slow. Seek out the details of the techniques in slow movement, and seek out the power of the techniques in fast movement. Take this time to work on finding the power of each move. First gather then launch, the gathering period is drawn out, and the launching period is short – like the drawing of a bow is slow and the shooting of the arrow is quick.

AWARENESS OF THE WEAPON

When learning a movement, first try to do the large actions and then the small and more detailed ones. First learn the outer actions, and then the inner feelings. You must do the movements to feel and develop awareness – feel the position of your body, the line of movement and speed of the actions, the feeling of the hands on the hilt or shaft, and the feeling of using power through the weapon.

You must focus especially on placement and path of movement of the hilt, tip, and blade edge of a broadsword or sword, and the butt, shaft, and tip of the staff or spear, and the different holds used. The manner in which the hand holds the hilt is of vital importance, so you must learn to use each method appropriately. Your grip directly affects your ability to correctly transfer power to the blade. Each grip is a vital component of the technique, and the ability to perform and to apply power in each technique is directly related to the grip. The overall principle is that your grip must be versatile and your wrist must be supple. You must be able to slide freely along the shaft of the staff and spear, and to stop automatically in the correct place for each technique.

You must master the movements, be able to use whole body power, have agile and adjustable footwork, and practise often with a partner before you can say you can use a weapon.

EXAMPLES OF TRAINING PROGRESSIONS

SPEAR CROSSCUT

First of all, practise fixed stance circling and snapping. Stand in a comfortable stance and alternate circling and snapping in both directions. Draw a relatively large circle with the spear tip, keeping a smooth line. Work on coordinating the body and hands and on finding out how to transfer through from the body to the spear tip.

First work on the actions slowly. You can find the coordination better by working slowly. Find the cooperation between the hands. Find how to gather power and release. Find the smooth lines of the action. Start out with large circles and gradually shrink them. Start out gently and gradually put more and more power into the movement. Gradually speed up.

Once you are comfortable with the action then add the stepping. If you build up each skill gradually then you will be able to coordinate the entire action sooner than if you tried to do everything at once. A teacher's instruction is important, but your own diligent training is more important.

STAFF CHOP

First do fixed stance chop. Stand in *santi* stance with the left foot forward in a good ready stance and perform a simple chop. Keep the action gentle and slow to carefully feel the route of the chopping action. Pay attention to the hooking action of the right hand and the pushing and pulling action of the left hand. You should be looking for the power transfer from the body to the shoulders, and to the hands, and thus to the staff.

Once the movement is correct, gradually speed up and add more force. Be sure to have a focal point to the chop – do not lose control just because you are striking harder. The staff should make a whooshing sound as you swing it, and should vibrate when you stop it.

The next phase is to add the stepping. Go back to slow and gentle movement and add the retreat, forward, and follow in steps. Gradually speed up, paying attention to correct requirements and power application. Always learn actions slowing and gently, then add speed and power.

IMAGINATION

As you repeatedly practise and think about the actions, you should study the outer actions and seek the inner meanings. You need to find the application for each and every action before you can really understand them. Only with thorough understanding can you hope to show the true meaning of the actions and gain even deeper understanding and gain deeper performance levels.

During repetitive training you must be sure that you understand the combative use of each technique. Once you have the foundation of full understanding and hard training, you should imagine an opponent in front of you, and imagine what you are doing with the techniques.

As the masters said "Practise as if there is someone in front of you." Imagine the attack and defense use of the techniques to develop the practical knowledge and instincts for combat with the weapon. If you train with this intent then you will progress quicker.

HEAVY WEAPONS

You may use a heavier weapon to improve your strength and deep skill. Chose a weight that you can control but cannot flash around. You must be able to do all the moves properly. The training effect is lost if it is so heavy that you cannot handle it.

Move slower with a heavier weapon, and do not change the movement requirements or techniques. Strengthen the arms, wrists, and body, and then gradually speed up. A heavy weapon also helps you to find the real meaning behind the left hand – placing it at the right wrist, and how to use it in coordination to gain power.

A TRAINING SESSION

Once you have basically mastered the movements then you should use 'three periods training' during a session of practice.

The first period is: Start out slowly and softly, diligently feeling the details of each movement, looking for all the requirements of the move and the application, feeling the path of each segment of the body, the placement and positioning of every part of the body, the body action and the power of the weapons. This is the time that you can fine-tune the actions. Do this for about 10 to 20 minutes.

The second period is: Increase your speed and put full power into the moves. Do not lose the correctness and techniques. Do not get sloppy or hasty. This is the period where you gain skills and develop power. Do this for about 30 minutes.

The third period is: Slow down the movements. Regulate the qi and gradually bring your heart rate and breathing back to normal. Do this for about 10 minutes.

PERSERVERENCE

You must not be content with learning and being able to do the moves. You must repeat them over and over to develop deep skill. The classics say, "skill comes from ripeness, essence comes from skill," and "to gain the true essence of techniques, deep skill comes from perseverance."

Deep skill is not achieved in an instant; do not expect to reach your goal in one step. You must train and ponder for many years to fully develop deep skills. "Live to old age, learn to old age, train to old age."

There is no limit to mastery, hard training will bring real deep skill. You must have this attitude towards each and every movement. You must constantly polish and improve yourself, keep trying to make progress. The way to mastery is perseverance and training.

XINGYIQUAN THEORY

A DISCUSSION OF THE FIVE ELEMENTS IN XINGYIQUAN

UNDERSTANDING THE RELATIONSHIP BETWEEN THE FIVE ELEMENT TECHNIQUES AND THE FIVE INTERNAL ORGANS

How the five elements relate to the internal organs

The five elemental techniques of Xingyiquan are traditionally called metal, wood, water, fire and earth. Is it scientific and logical to name them in this way? The theory of the five elements sums up the martial techniques; it uses the mutual creation and mutual control cycles of the five elements to direct martial techniques. This shows the close connection between martial arts and ancient Chinese philosophical thought. From today's scientific point of view, it is a little sweeping and crude to interpret everything according to the five elements theory, but this ancient methodology and worldview is still able to guide us and deepen our understanding of Xingyyiquan.

The theory of the five elements made traditional Chinese medical theory more comprehensive and more rational. The five elements are used to explain the interplay of mutual harmony and harm between the five internal organs. Their connections are described in terms of physiological functions and pathological changes, which explain the connection of the body to the outside environment[63] and guide diagnosis and treatment.

The relationships between the five elements and the five internal organs are:

- Metal relates to the Lung.[64] The Lung rules *qi*[65] and manages respiration. It rules the exterior of the body, which means the skin and body hair. It rules descending and liquefying. The Lung moves and adjusts the water channels. It opens to the nose.

---

[63] Editor's note: The external correspondences are: metal – dryness, wood – wind, water – cold, fire – heat, and earth – damp. This is one step beyond where martial techniques are likely to relate to the five elements.

[64] Translator's note: Chinese medical theory does not see the five internal organs – Heart, Liver, Spleen, Lung, and Kidney – as the anatomical organs as understood in Western medical theory. The Chinese terms are the energetic functions of the organ, which include the physical organ and its associated organs, sensory organs, channels, tissues, and emotions. It is standard to write them with a capital letter to indicate the Chinese meaning, and in small letters to indicate the Western meaning.

[65] Translator's note: both the natural air '*qi*' and the '*qi*' of the body.

- Wood relates to the Liver. The Liver rules flowing and spreading of *qi* and blood, and governs the storage of blood. The Liver governs the tendons and is manifest in the nails. It opens to the eyes.

- Water relates to the Kidney. The Kidney stores the essence, and rules the body's development and reproduction. It governs fluids, the grasping of *qi*, governs the bones, produces marrow, and goes through to the brain. It manifests in the hair. It opens to the ears.

- Fire relates to the Heart. The Heart rules the blood and vessels. It is manifest in the face. It governs the spirit and the will. It opens to the tongue.

- Earth relates to the Spleen. The Spleen rules transformation and transportation [of raw materials of food and liquids for production of *qi* and blood]. It governs the muscles, flesh, the four limbs, and blood. It manifests in the lips. It opens to the mouth.

How the five techniques relate to the five internal organs through *qi*

Each of the internal organs governs something specific according to the traditional Chinese medical system, but I feel that [for the martial artist] something else is more important – the five visceral *qi*. Chinese medical theory says that the *qi* of each of the five internal organs has a close connection to the activity of the spirit and will. The relationship of exterior and interior each influences and assists the other:

- The Lung contains the corporeal soul, the Liver contains the ethereal soul, the Kidney contains the will, the Heart contains the spirit, and the Spleen contains the cognitive mind.

Whether or not the five internal organs are functioning properly, whether they are strong or weak, directly affects the activity of these five aspects of consciousness or senses. And the opposite is also true – changes in the corporeal soul, the ethereal soul, the will, the spirit, and the cognitive mind can also influence the normal functioning of the five internal organs. The internal – the five internal organs – is the foundation, the root. The external – the five senses – is what is apparent, the outward manifestation. The Chinese medical system says that the outward manifestation and the root affect each other, but that the root is the ruler.

Sun Lutang stated the relationship between the five techniques, five elements, and five internal organs and their *qi* in his Study of Xingyiquan:

> "Train the five fists externally to develop the five internal organs internally.
>
> Split is like an axe. It correlates to metal and the Lung. When split's power is smooth then the Lung's *qi* is harmonious; when its power is awkward then the Lung's qi is perverse.[66]
>
> Drill is like lightning. It correlates to water and the Kidney. When drill's power is smooth then the Kidney's *qi* is sufficient.

---

[66] Translator's note: 'perverse' means that the *qi* flows in the opposite direction to normal. Smooth Lung *qi* flows upward, so perverse flow is downward.

Drive is like an arrow. It correlates to wood and the Liver. When drive's power is smooth then the Liver's *qi* flows smoothly. When its power is contrary then the Liver's *qi* is damaged.

Cannon is like explosives. It correlates to fire and the Heart. When cannon's *qi* is harmonious then the Heart is carefree. When its *qi* is contrary then the Heart is clouded.[67]

Crosscut is like a cannonball. It correlates to the earth and the Spleen. When it is round then its nature is solid. When crosscut's *qi* is smooth then the Liver and stomach are harmonious. When it is contrary then the Spleen is empty and the stomach weak, and then all five internal organs lose their ability to work harmoniously together.[68]

When the techniques are smooth then the internal five elements are harmonious and *qi* flows smoothly within the channels. When the techniques are awkward then the *qi* becomes blocked."

Techniques being 'smooth' or 'awkward' refers to whether or not the movements are coordinated, and how this relates to whether the *qi* flow of the internal organs is unimpeded, blocked or perverse, which in turn affects the health of the organs. When a technique is 'smooth' then the movement is coordinated and the power flows well, and that is good for the internal organs. This is obvious. The opposite is also true – when a technique is poorly done, the movement is uncoordinated and the power is stiff and awkward, and this is not good for the internal organs. But should one say that the techniques harm the internal organs so specifically as in the following phrases?

"When the technique of split is awkward then the Lung's *qi* is perverse.

When the technique of drive is awkward then this harms the Liver.

When the technique of drill is awkward then it creates a crossing strength which makes the Kidney empty and the *qi* perverse.

When the technique of cannon is awkward then the limbs hang flaccidly, the Heart's *qi* is perverse, and all the channels are blocked.

When the technique of crosscut is awkward then the *qi* is overexerted and the strength is harsh, harming the Spleen."

This harm to the internal organs is a bit exaggerated, and puts undue emphasis on the damage that the techniques can do to the internal organs. You should simply say that if the techniques are not smooth and coordinated then this does not help the regulation of the internal organs, and that is enough. Looking at it from

---

[67] Translator's note: In both the physical and emotional sense.

[68] Editor's note: Just as crosscut is a pivotal technique, the Spleen and stomach are pivotal organs. When they are healthy then all other organs benefit. When they are weak then all other organs eventually suffer.

another angle, the old masters were emphasizing to their students that it was important to train the five techniques until they became correct and had smooth power flow. Only when the techniques are correct and the power flow is smooth can you achieve the goal of regulating the internal organs. This serves to emphasize the importance of the basic techniques and foundation postures.

How the five techniques relate to the internal organs through their nature

There is another way of matching the five techniques to the five internal organs. The outer appearance can relate to the outer manifestation of the organs. The classics often say:

> "The Lung moves like the sound of thunder.
>
> The Liver moves like a flying arrow.
>
> The Kidney moves as fast as the wind.
>
> The Heart moves like a blazing fire.
>
> The Spleen moves in strong attacking force."

This is a type of connection that one can hold in the mind when doing the actions.

How the five techniques relate to the internal organs through the meridian system

The five techniques are also related to the five internal organs by means of the meridian system, or the energy lines throughout the body. The meridians and collaterals are the pathways that circulate to interconnect the organs and internal organs, and connect them with the extremities of the body. They connect the interior and exterior of the body, the surface and the deep, the upper part and lower parts of the body, circulate the *qi* and the blood, and nourish the body. There is nowhere the meridian system does not reach, nowhere that is not connected. The term meridian system is a collective term for the meridian channels and the collateral vessels. The meridian channels are the trunks that travel longitudinally, the collateral vessels are the branches that wrap around the body. There are twelve meridians directly related to the various internal organs, as well as several extraordinary vessels.

The connection between the meridians and the internal organs is roughly thus:[69]

The Lung meridian (the hand greater *yin*) originates in the lung area and, after running down internally to the large intestine, then back up to the throat, emerges to the surface at the *Zhongfu* acupoint [Lu1; the lateral aspect of the chest, then along the medial aspect of the upper arm], through *Chize* [Lu5], *Kongzui* [Lu6], *Liuque* [Lu7], and *Yuji* [Lu10] to *Shaoshang* [Lu11; the radial side tip of the thumb].

---

[69] Editor's note: This is a very rough description of the meridians. I have added clarification, and did not always indicate where is my voice and where is the authors. I also plotted the points on the photos as best I could in the position relating to each internal organ. There are many books available that go into the meridians in much more detail. Please note that 1) I drew points that are inside the body just to give an idea of the lines, and 2) I drew only on the side most visible in the photos – the meridians are bilateral.

Lung

The Heart meridian (the hand lesser *yin*) originates in the heart, emerges to the surface through the *Jiquan* acupoint [Ht1; in the armpit], and the external branch runs out the midline of the inner arm, elbow and forearm through *Shaohai* [Ht3], *Lingdao* [Ht4], *Shenmen* [Ht7], and *Shaofu* [Ht8] to *Shaochong* [Ht9; the inside tip of the little finger].

The Kidney meridian (the foot lesser *yin*) originates in the *Yongquan* acupoint [Ki1] on the sole of the foot, emerges to the surface through the *Rangu* [Ki2; at the arch of the foot], and ascends the medial side of the leg through *Taixi* [Ki3], *Zhaohai* [Ki6], *Yingu* [Ki10], penetrates the body at the base of the spine, and continues up the body to the *Shufu* [Ki27].

Heart

The Liver meridian (the foot terminal *yin*) originates in the *Dadun* acupoint [Liv1] on top of the big toe, and emerges to the surface through the *Xingjian* [Liv2], *Taichong* [Liv3], ascends the medial side of the leg through *Zhongdu* [Liv6], *Xiguan* [Liv7], *Ququan* [Liv8], *Wuli* [Liv10; penetrates the body in the lower abdomen, continues up] *Zhangmen* [Liv13], and connects to the Liver and gall bladder at *Qimen* [Liv14].

The Spleen meridian (the foot great *yin*) originates in the *Yinbai* acupoint [Sp1] on the medial side of the big toe, circulates through the *Gongsun* [Sp4], *Shangqiu* [Sp5], *Sanyinjiao* [Sp6], and up to through the medial aspect of the shank, knee and thigh through *Yinlingquan* [Sp9], *Xuehai* [Sp10], *Jimen* [Sp11], enters the abdominal cavity and moves up inside the body, emerging at *Xiongxiang* [Sp19], to *Dabao* [Sp21].

Kidney

Liver

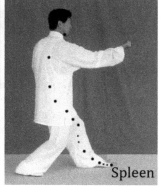

Spleen

DEVELOPING THE RELATIONSHIP BETWEEN THE FIVE TECHNIQUES AND THE FIVE INTERNAL ORGANS

Everyone risks falling ill at some point in their lives, martial artists included. Martial artists must strengthen their bodies to nurture their health and prevent illness. In ancient times, martial artists already knew quite well that the body is the vehicle for trained deep martial skill [gong]. There is a direct relationship between the level of deep skill and the strength or weakness of the body, both internal and external. There is no way that high level martial skill can be put to good use if it is not based on a healthy solid body. Before firearms, the main purpose for martial arts training was combat. An unknown martial artist could advance socially once he became skilled through hard training. On gaining a reputation, one needed to maintain it in order to earn a living as a bodyguard, security guard, or teacher. But once a master became famous he would meet many challengers; "a person fears becoming famous, a pig fears getting fat." A martial artist would have to condition his body regularly to remain combat fit and successful, because if he lost a fight all his years of hard work would come to nothing. For this reason martial artists put great store in a healthy and strong body. The Chinese medical system gave a readymade body of theory and practical experience in diagnosis and treatment to nurture health. Xingyi masters took the theory concerning the internal organs into their martial system, as well as absorbing some Daoist cultivation methods. Old Xingyiquan classics say:

> "Strengthen your root internally, strengthen your body externally.
> The internal is the way to nourish health, the external is the way
> to move.
>
> If you have the internal but not the external then you cannot
> succeed at martial arts, if you have the external but not the
> internal then you cannot succeed at deep trained skill.
>
> The five internal elements must be united, the five external
> elements must flow smoothly."

Both medical theory and Daoist cultivation techniques emphasize that training must include both the internal and the external. This is why Xingyi masters drew a correlation between the five internal organs and the five techniques in Xingyiquan.

The inter-relationship of mutual creation and control of the five techniques [A] is explained by the five elements [B]. The interrelations of the physiological functions and conditions of the five internal organs [C] are also explained through the interrelationship of the five elements [B]. So, with the reasoning "if A=B and B=C, then A=C," the five techniques were related with the five internal organs. There is a certain analytic logic at work here.

The power of each of the five techniques combines to form the whole system – each different power complements the others, so each is necessary to the system. The five internal organs are also an integrated unit. Each organ is necessary to the body. Chinese medical theory believes that if any one organ is unbalanced or develops a problem then this can affect all the other organs and the whole system. Each organ is a vital part of life, something that the whole cannot do without. As described above, each has its own qi and each type of qi interacts with and blends with the others. The internal organs are connected by their qi, a different qi for each connection between them, and the whole this forms an integrated and interacting unit. The *qi* of the five internal organs have a tight connection with the vitality of the person. These five kinds of vitality and expression are the outer manifestation of the fullness of the internal organs, that is, the manifestation of the *qi* of each internal organ. Nurturing the internal organs through training the techniques promotes the health of the whole system.

Using the meridian connections of the five techniques to strengthen the internal organs

The ability to connect the five techniques and the five internal organs came about after the Xingyi masters built up a certain level of skill. They directed their thoughts to move their *qi* to further build a strong and healthy body. That is, they led their internal environment with their external movements, with an internal training method of connecting movements with the internal organs. Of course, at the beginning stages of training obvious power there is no way to make this kind of connection, or to kinesthetically feel the hidden meaning of internal training. This kind of training can be used only after one attains the hidden power stage of training, after one has developed a kinesthetic awareness and a feeling of *qi*.

The five elemental techniques and the five internal organs can, under the direction of the mind, be connected through the pathways of the meridians.

- Seek to feel the body and *qi,* under the conditions of a quiet heart and spirit, a relaxed mind and body, slow and steady breathing, and slow practice. This feeling of *qi* comes naturally when the body is healthy and the skill is deeply trained, while one is doing relaxed and soft movements.

- Once the feeling of *qi* is achieved, move the *qi* along the meridians to the five internal organs by using the movements of the five techniques. Lead the *qi* with the techniques by using the mind to lead the internal *qi* along the meridians to reach the internal organs.

- Over a long period of time one can gradually develop a thoroughfare for the *qi* to circulate through the meridians. This thoroughfare becomes more open and clear the more it is used, so that eventually the five elemental techniques are connected to the five internal organs.

The higher the level of practice and the deeper the achieved skill, the more coordinated the functions of the internal organs can become with the actions. This causes the actions of the internal organs to adjust to the needs of the physical actions, which in turn enables the internal organs to support the actions. This develops a strong and healthy body and creates a good environment for the further development of martial skills.

- If you want to treat illness or to rehabilitate from injury, then that is another emphasis in training. Pick one or two techniques that apply to your specific condition to use as supplemental therapy. The emphasis in the mind differs, and is more specific to strengthening the ailing organ.

Using the *qi* of the internal organs to strengthen the organs and the power of the five techniques

As shown above, the relationship between the five techniques and the five internal organs is one of *qi*. The five techniques are five internal powers and five external movements. The five internal organs are five internal *qi* and five external vitalities.

When training the five techniques, you train the five powers to experience and show the five vitalities. In this way you can connect with the five internal organs and regulate their *qi,* feel the responses of the internal organs' *qi* and feel the connection between the five techniques and the five internal organs.

- Perform the techniques as a *qigong* practice: calm the heart and collect your thoughts, relax the whole body, do the movements slowly, breathe deeply and long, and keep the power full.

- This enables you to experientially feel the connections [not in the imagination, but in reality]. Seek out the different vitalities of each technique, and feel the *qi* of each organ connecting. After a long time you will certainly feel something.

This type of training of course, can only be done once the five techniques are extremely well mastered, coordinated, and integrated into the body and brain. The mind no longer needs to pay full attention to the performance of the techniques and can fully concentrate on the essence and connection of the techniques to the internal organs. One uses the external to lead the internal, uses the mind to lead the *qi,* and connects the action to the *qi.* This builds a healthy and strong body, which in turn improves combat effectiveness.

The connection between the five techniques and the five internal organs may be explained to beginners to show that this viewpoint and this way of training exists, but a teacher should not explain the exact relationship and training method too early. Someone who has not reached the appropriate level of skill and understanding of Chinese medical theory and meridian theory cannot understand the training yet. The connection between the five techniques and the five internal organs is a bond that is gradually built up after a long period of training martial movements under the direction of the mind.

A DISCUSSION OF THE SIX MODELS FOR THE BODY IN XINGYIQUAN

Traditional Xingyiquan theory describes six models that the body must copy: chicken legs, dragon torso, bear shoulder girdle, eagle claw, 'tiger leopard head,' and thunder sound. The six models should inform all actions and postures of Xingyiquan.[70] Various opinions have been expressed on these within the Xinyi-quan and Xingyiquan worlds.[71] Sun Lutang, in his Study of Xingyiquan, was the first to discuss the 'four likenesses.' He said "Chicken legs have the shape of standing on one leg. Dragon torso is the form of having three folds. Bear shoulders is the power of standing upright. 'Tiger holds the head' is the form of the hands embracing like a tiger leaving its den." The book Explanation of Xingyiquan that

---

[70] Author's note: Or the four likenesses. Some texts speak of four likenesses of the body: 'chicken legs, dragon trunk, bear shoulders, and tiger leopard head.'

[71] Author's note: The old masters passed on their knowledge orally, so there were few written records, and the poems and materials passed on by the old masters are all drawn from the oral teachings by previous generations. There are many different accents and dialects in the different regions of China, so when the written word was put down, often there is a word that is pronounced the same but is written with a different character. There have also been errors made in copying texts.

followed also held this view, and most subsequent authors developed this same idea.

But the six models for the body should be understood to describe the overall picture, not individual techniques. We should analyze the six models as a whole, as they describe the character of Xingyiquan movements using the characteristics of animals. The six models are descriptive images for the hands, eyes, bodywork, legs, spirit, *qi*, strength, and deep achieved skill of Xingyiquan. They describe the requirements to help people find the feeling and achieve the spirit for themselves. This method is customarily used in Chinese martial arts as it is a traditional mode of thinking for the Chinese. For example, in Baguazhang they say 'dragon steps, monkey likeness, tiger sits, eagle wheels,' and in Taijiquan 'one body makes five bows.' These are images that help us understand and remember more deeply. Using this imagery during practice can help you analyse, imagine, reproduce and finally teach yourself through experience, more quickly understanding the requirements of the movements and the characteristics of the skills.

CHICKEN LEGS

Chicken legs means that the footwork of Xingiquan is fast and stable, moving suddenly and stopping steadily. Of course, describing the footwork only as chicken legs is not enough, so there is also the phrase "the skill of striking." The description of chicken legs also reminds you to try to set the legs solidly into the ground.

DRAGON TORSO

Dragon torso refers to bodywork. We can understand the 'three folds' of the dragon's body because, although a dragon is an imaginary magical animal, everyone has seen the performance of a dragon dance. The dragon's body is light and long, it flexes and extends, it can bend and move freely at will. Xingyiquan elders took the metaphor of the dragon's free body movements to describe how freely the human body should move. This is brilliant and apt imagery. Bodywork is the technique of moving the trunk, which includes the 'swallowing and spitting' of the chest, the twisting and turning of the waist, and the opening up and closing in of the chest and back.

BEAR SHOULDERS

Bear shoulders describes how the shoulder girdle area is released and settled. The shoulder girdle includes the shoulders and upper arms, the deltoid area, and the shoulder blades. When this area is released and settled like a bear then movement can be agile and power can be launched. If you look at a bear, its forelegs and shoulders are always very loose. Xingyiquan requires that the shoulders be relaxed, so describing this as bear shoulders is very apt. The classics also say: "bear shoulders is the power of holding the neck upright." This 'power of holding the neck upright' refers to the neck of the bear. Holding the neck upright helps you to release the shoulder girdle, and relaxing the shoulders helps you to hold the neck upright.

EAGLE CLAW

Eagle claw describes the hand shape and hand techniques of Xingyiquan. The hand shape of Xingyiquan is: the five fingers slightly bent and curving in, the palm curving in and the web of the palm spread. Although the hand shape is not held exactly in an 'eagle claw,' it does have the spirit of the grasping of the eagle claw at all times. "Don't try to imitate, but to borrow the right meaning." The meaning is quite broad and is just a model, and includes the power and the application. Freely imitate the whole range of meaning of eagle claw to deepen your understanding of the requirements and characteristics of Xingyiquan and better show it's flavour.

TIGER LEOPARD HEAD OR TIGER HOLD HEAD

The term 'tiger leopard head' 虎豹头 is written as 'tiger holds head' 虎抱头 in some texts. There are a variety of opinions over what the tiger leopard head means. Most respect the opinion of the classics, "tiger leopard head means the two hands embracing like a fierce tiger coming out of its den," or "tiger hold head refers to how the tiger protects its head with its front legs when it comes out of its den." It has also been explained as "the hands in front hold the position of protecting the neck." I think that this sort of explanation is incorrect, and clearly not what the elders originally meant. It is incorrect to see 'tiger leopard head' or 'tiger hold head' as specific techniques. Within the six models for Xingyiquan, the tiger leopard head is an image that refers to the spirit and mien of the head and eyes. 'Tiger leopard head' is the head of a tiger or a leopard, and 'tiger hold head' is the tiger holding up its head. You should have the same spirit showing in your eyes as a tiger or leopard, your stare should shoot at an opponent, making him too fearful to face you. Showing the spirit of a tiger or leopard causes an opponent to lose confidence and lose to you.

THUNDER SOUND

Thunder sound refers to the sound that you make when you emit power, which is a deep sound like thunder. You use your sound to assist your action, getting more spirit and power. Just as the sound of thunder rolls on, your power is not broken. A lightning flash is followed by a thunderclap, so swift that it is too late to cover the ears. The practice of using sound when launching power has fallen into disuse in Xingyiquan. Although the thunder sound is little used during practice, it should be used appropriately in fighting to put fear into your opponent. It puts more *qi* into your strength, increases your hitting power, and increases your ability to take hits. Thunder sound describes both your sound and your mien.

SUMMATION

The six models for the body use the imagery of animals to explain principles that apply to the whole body. Chicken, dragon, bear, eagle, tiger, and thunder explain the handwork, eye movement, body action and footwork of Xingyiquan. This is an overall concept, not a specific technical description – you should follow the six models in every stance and every action, in the hands, eyes, body, footwork, essence, spirit, *qi*, strength, and skill.

Xingyiquan imitates shape to some extent, but more important is the intent and the spirit. "Do not seek to imitate, but seek to find the essence." Xingyiquan is not an imitative style, it is a style that emphasizes intent. Moreover, within the range of imitation one should use the hands, eyes, body and footwork, the essence and spirit, the *qi* and the strength as an integrated whole to show the martial intent and the imposing nature of Xingyiquan.

A DISCUSSION OF THE THREE LEVELS OF XINGYIQUAN

CLEAR, HIDDEN, AND TRANSFORMED POWER

The three levels of Xingyi were first written up by Sun Lutang, who said, "Xingyiquan has three levels of theory, three stages of deep skill, and three types of training." Sun referred to Guo Yunsheng's talk on Xingyiquan to introduce, define and explain these three levels, but actually they represented his own ideas. They were the culmination of Sun's many years of research and collection of materials, study of theory, his own thought on Xingyiquan, and his knowledge of Daoist internal training theories. Indeed, the stages were not created by martial artists, but were borrowed from Daoist thought and training methods – Daoist thought, spirit, theory, and training methods have long influenced and permeated Xingyiquan theory and methods. They have become a part of the Xingyiquan system, which further developed and improved its theoretical foundation.

As to the three levels of deep skill, the first is to change the bones, the second is to changes the tendons, and the third is to wash the marrow. Sun Lutang said, "Master Da Mo passed on two classics, the tendon changing and the marrow washing. Study them to strengthen your body. This should be the first goal of the beginning student. In the later Song dynasty, Yue Wumu expanded on the two classics by developing the three classics; bone changing, tendon changing, and marrow washing. The three classics were incorporated into martial arts theory." Although Sun Lutang quoted Yue Fei and Guo Yunsheng, this is not historically verifiable. Probably Sun Lutang developed them himself and used the names of Yue Fei and Guo Yunsheng to authenticate his ideas. The theory behind these three levels of theory, three stages of deep training, and three methods of training made Xingyiquan's training more systematic and linked it to ancient culture.

The three training methods, clear, hidden, and transformed power were not clearly defined by previous generations of masters and are difficult for a modern beginner to understand. The three levels of theory are meant to describe three layers and types of training power. The three stages of deep skill are three stages of training. Each one has a specific goal and uses specific methods.

Xingyiquan's theory of clear, hidden, and transformed power has been applied by other martial arts styles. They are not only three types of training and three types of power, but also describe how someone advances and changes gradually from a low level to a high level of skill. During this process each stage is not clearly separated from the other, but there is a gradual accumulation of changes. Once someone reaches a certain level this creates the conditions to pass to the next level.

The following table breaks down the three levels of theory, three stages of skill, and three types of training to a chart. This is presented to give a basis for analysis. Some categories explain the overall picture, some categories give a partial analysis, and some just emphasize a certain aspect. Please use the chart to help you understand and get a feel for the requirements and characteristics of the three stages.

CATEGORIES	LEVEL ONE	LEVEL TWO	LEVEL THREE
stage	beginner	intermediate	advanced
principle of the level	train essence to transform *qi*	train *qi* to transform spirit	train spirit to return to emptiness
power application	clear, obvious	hidden	transformed
compared to school	primary and high school	university	specialist, teacher
relative to theory	most difficult work stage	necessary road to become skilled	highest stage of martial study
relative to changing the body	change bones	change tendons	wash marrow
relative to martial and Daoist skill	martial skill	Daoist skill	martial and Daoist combined
function and goal	train to build foundation, strengthen the body	train to expand the membranes, to develop the tendons	train to cleanse the inside to emptiness, lighten the body
training the body	train the muscles and willpower	discipline the spirit	combine heaven and man
characteristic power	whole body power	internal power	soft and dissolving
goal of power in attack	explode	penetrate	adhere
basics and internal training mix	emphasis on basics and applications	emphasis on applications and internal power	applications secondary
what is changing	change power	change the physical makeup	emphasis on internal power, change the energy's makeup
what is being disciplined	muscles	mind	spirit

what capability is being developed	train to become self capable	train to become instinctive	train to have concealed potential
training of internal and external	use the external to develop the internal	use the internal to develop the external	no division between internal and external
emphasis in each stage	train shape and structure	train intent	train spirit
motor control of the brain	extensive	differentiated	natural
intentional control of the mind	fully intentional	low control	natural
speed used	fast	slow	fast and slow intermingle
three internal combinations	strength and *qi*	*qi* and mind	mind and spirit
what to strength to remove	remove brute strength	remove hard strength	power is smooth and flowing
type of power	hard and forceful	soft and smooth	hard and soft together
movement requirements	strictly in accordance to rules	in accordance to rules	naturally will fit patterns
positions	expansive	compact	round and full
power to train	train whole body power, seek hardness	train relaxed power, seek softness	train agility, seek high skill
speed to train	seek integration in speed	seek lengthening in slowness	fast and slow blend naturally
attitude	body upright and *qi* strong	take care of all directions	spirit rounded and lively
qualities manifested in movements	rise and fall as a unit	power rounded, mind farseeing	spirit and mind fully connected
use	have shape and image	have name, have shape, but leave no trace	no shape, no image, no sound

control of power	can release whole body power	can accept and control	can use naturally
combative use	emphasize attack	emphasize control	emphasize diffusion
foot landing	has sound	no sound	hear the sound of thunder although there is no sound
power applied from	hands	elbows	body core
coordination of *qi* in the *dantian* during power release	settle *qi* to *dantian*	gather *qi* in *dantian*	move *qi* in *dantian*
big heavenly circuit and *dantian*	strengthen *dantian*	train whole heavenly circuit	move through whole heavenly circuit
qi and mind connection	urge the strength with the *qi*	lead the *qi* with the mind	no mind, no *qi*
use of *qi*	use strength to lead *qi*	use *qi* to nourish the spirit	use spirit to control *qi*
the *dantian* being trained	lower *dantian*	middle *dantian*	upper *dantian*
breathing	control breath, shows form outside	controlled breath, shows form inside	embryo breath, shows no form
length of breath	inhale long, exhale short; short and powerful	inhale and exhale long; controlled and soft, lead short to draw long	long and short as needed; gentle, level, deep, long
breathing requirements	controlled	coordinated	natural

XINGYIQUAN VOCABULARY

PINYIN ORDER

SECTION ONE: BASIC PARTS OF THE BODY

bǎng	膀	upper arm and shoulder, deltoid area
bēi or bī	臂	upper arm, or whole arm
bèi	背	upper and mid back
bō	脖	neck
chǐ gǔ	尺骨	ulnar bone; little finger side of forearm
dà tuǐ	大腿	thigh
ěr	耳	ear
fèi	肺	lungs; Lung when referring to the Chinese meaning
fù	腹	abdomen, belly
gān	肝	liver; Liver when referring to the Chinese meaning
gēn	跟	heel
hǔ kǒu	虎口	thumb to forefinger web, called the 'tiger's mouth'
jiān	肩	shoulder, also called jiān bǎng 肩膀
jiǎo	脚	foot
jiǎo gēn	脚跟	heel of the foot
jǐng	颈	nape of neck
kuà	胯	hip joint
lèi	肋	ribs
pí	脾	spleen; Spleen when referring to the Chinese meaning
qián bì	前臂	forearm, also pronounced qián bēi
quán	拳	fist
quán bèi	拳背	the back of the fist

quán fēng	拳峰	knuckle edge of the fist
quán lún	拳轮	the base of the fist
quán miàn	拳面	face of the fist, the normal punching surface
quán xīn	拳心	heart of the fist, into which the fingers curl
quán yǎn	拳眼	eye of the fist, formed by thumb and index finger
shèn	肾	kidney; Kidney when referring to the Chinese meaning
shǒu	手	hand
shǒu wàn	手腕	wrist
shǒu zhǐ	手指	fingers
tóu	头	head
tuǐ	腿	leg
xī	膝	knee, often pronounced qī
xiǎo tuǐ	小腿	lower leg, shank
xīn	心	heart; Heart when referring to the Chinese meaning
xīn wōr	心窝	pit of the stomach, solar plexus
xiōng	胸	chest
yāo	腰	lower back, small of the back, waist, lumbar area
zhǎng	掌	palm
zhǎng xīn	掌心	centre of the palm
zhǒu	肘	elbow

SECTION TWO: XINGYI TERMINOLOGY

àn	按	press down
àn jìn	暗劲	hidden power
ào bù	拗步	stance with the opposite hand and foot forward, commonly called a reverse stance. In Xingyi, this is usually done in *santi* stance.
bā lì	扒力	raking power
bā zì bù	八字步	character eight stance, feet close to and angled towards each other, not touching
bā zì gōng	八字功	eight skills of Xingyiquan
bǎi bù	摆步	hook-out step
bān	搬	remove, move something
bàn mǎ bù	半马步	half horse stance
bào	抱	hold in the crook of the arm, usually with both arms, looking like an embrace
bēng quán	崩拳	drive, crushing punch; a straight punch

		done with a driving power, one of the five mother fists of Xingyi
bīng bù	并步	stand upright with feet together
bō	拨	knock aside
cǎi	踩	step on, trample
chǎn shǒu	缠手	coil the hand around something, hooking
chāo	抄	hoist, bend the elbow to lift up with the forearm
chè bù	撤步	withdraw, step the rear foot back or bring the lead foot back to the rear foot
chén qì	沉气	settle or sink the *qi* down
chēng	撑	brace out with one or both hands
chōu	抽	draw out
cuī	催	urge, hurry, press
cùn jìn	寸劲	one inch power
cuò	挫	check, a short powerful block or strike
cuō dì	蹉地	land with a rubbing action, stamp with impetus forward and down
dǎ	打	hit
dài	带	draw, drag towards the rear
dàn	弹	a ball, pellet; a bomb
dān tián	丹田	*dantian*, in martial arts usually means the lower part of the torso; area within the pelvic girdle
dáo	捯	pull hand over hand
dìng bù	定步	a fixed stance, not moving the feet
dūn	蹲	squat, sit on haunches
fā jìn	发劲	launch power, shoot force, initiate a hit
fā lì	发力	launch power, shoot force, initiate a hit
fú hǔ zhuāng	伏虎桩	subdue the tiger post standing
fǔ zhǎng	俯掌	facing down palm
gài	盖	cover, a controlling move downwards
gāng jìn	刚劲	hard power
gé	格	block across
gēn bù	跟步	a follow-in step, the rear foot moving up towards the lead foot
gōng bù	弓步	bow stance
guà	挂	hooking block or trap
guàn	贯	inside hook punch
guǒ	裹	wrap around, enclose in the arms

guǒ jìn	裹劲	a wrapping power
héng	横	a horizontal, crossways or transverse movement or placement.
héng quán	横拳	crosscut, crossing fist, one of the five mother fists of Xingyi
huà jìn	化劲	transformed power
hún yuán	浑元	primordial, or mixed essence, refers to the time when the heaven and earth began.
hún yuán zhuāng	浑元桩	primordial post standing
huǒ	火	fire, one of the five elemental elements
huó bù	活步	moving stance
jī xíng bù	鸡形步	chicken stepping, raising the non-supporting foot by the supporting foot
jiàng lóng zhuāng	降龙桩	descend the dragon post standing
jiǎo	绞	wind around, entangle
jié	截	intercept, cut across
jīn	金	metal, one of the five elements
jìn	进	enter, advance: step the front foot a half-step forward or the back foot forward
kāi bù	开步	open parallel stance, shoulder width
kē	磕	knock, bump
kòu	扣	tuck in, concave shape
kòu bù	扣步	hook-in step
lā	拉	pull
lán	拦	circular block, trap
liāo quán	撩拳	slice up with a relatively straight arm
liàn gōng	练功	train skill; work hard to enhance health, develop fitness, develop martial arts internal and external skills.
lǐng	领	lead along
lōu	搂	brush aside
luò	落	to land, to lower
mǎ bù	马步	horse stance
mài bù	迈步	stride, a large step
míng jìn	明劲	obvious power, hard power
mù	木	wood, one of the five elements
ná	拿	trap, hold
níng jìn	拧劲	twisting power
pāi	拍	slap or control with open palm

pào quán	炮拳	cannon punch, pounding fist, simultaneous block and punch, one of the five mother fists of Xingyiquan
pī quán	劈拳	split, chop down, one of the five mother fists of Xingyi
pū	扑	pounce
qǐ	起	initiate an action, rise
qì	气	vital energy, breath; both energy and matter that carries vital energy
qiē	切	cut, slice
sān cái zhuāng	三才桩	'three attributes' standing, also referred to as *santi* post standing
sān tǐ	三体	the 60/40 to 70/30 weighted stance when the arms are in positions other than *santishi*
sān tǐ shì	三体势	three body stance, the stance itself rather than the post standing training
sān tǐ shì zhuāng	三体势桩	three body post standing
shàng bù	上步	step forward
shuǐ	水	water, one of the five elements
shùn	顺	smooth, going along with the natural path
shùn bù	顺步	aligned stance. In Xingyi, this is usually a *santi* stance with the same hand and foot forward
sōng	松	relax and extend, release the tension
suō shēn	缩身	contract, draw in or draw back in the body
tā wàn	塌腕	sit the wrist, sink the wrist
tán	弹	to shoot (as with a catapult); spring; springy, elastic
tī	踢	kick
tiǎo	挑	scoop
tiǎo jìn	挑劲	slicing up power with the arm quite solid and the wrist cocked
tǔ	土	earth, one of the five elements
tuì bù	退步	retreat: step the back foot a half-step back or step the front foot back
tuō	托	carry, hit with the palm fingers usually down
wǔ xíng lián huán	五行连环	the short name for the five elemental fists connected form
wǔ xíng lián huán quán	五行连环拳	the most basic Xingyi form, five

		elemental fists connected form
wǔ xíng quán	五行拳	Xingyi's five basic techniques, five training methods to develop five types of power generation
wǔ xíng xiāng kè	五行相克	the controlling order of the five elements
wǔ xíng xiāng shēng	五行相生	the creating order of the five elements
xiē bù	歇步	resting stance, legs crossed and sitting
xīn	心	heart, the emotional mind
xīn yì liù hé quán	心意六合拳	Xinyi Liuhequan, the style from which Xingyiquan grew
xīn yì quán	心意拳	Xinyiquan, 'heart and intent' style, also referred to as Xinyi Liuhequan
xíng	形	form, shape, structure; external structure and action
xíng yì lián quán	形意连拳	a basic Xingyi form combining the five elemental fists
xíng yì mǔ quán	形意母拳	the five fundamental techniques of Xingyi
xíng yì quán	形意拳	Xingyiquan, 'external shape combined with internal intent' style
yā	压	press down, control
yǎn zhǒu	掩肘	a hooking cover, usually rolling in, with an elbow
yǎng zhǎng	仰掌	facing up palm
yáo shēn	摇身	shaking the body, is often used to mean a technique of dodging with the footwork
yì	意	will, the intentional mind
yì quán	意拳	Yiquan, also called Dachengquan, a style developed from Xingyiquan
zá quán	砸拳	a pounding strike with the fist
zá zhuāng	砸桩	pounding post standing
zhāi	摘	pluck
zhàn zhuāng	站桩	post standing
zhèn jiǎo	震脚	stomp, a heavy stamp
zhuā	抓	grab
zhuàn shēn	转身	turn around
zhuāng gōng	桩功	the training of post standing
zhuàng	撞	shove, barge into, ram
zǐ wǔ zhuāng	子午桩	meridian line post standing, also referred to as *santi* post standing

| zuān quán | 钻拳 | drill, one of the five mother fists of Xingyi |

SECTION THREE: XINGYI MOVEMENT NAMES

bā zì gōng	八字功	Eight Skills
bái hè liàng chì	白鹤亮翅	White Crane Flashes Its Wings
bái shé bō cǎo	白蛇拨草	White Snake Slithers through the Grass
bái shé chǎn shēn	白蛇缠身	White Snake Coils its Body
bái shé tù xìn	白蛇吐信	White Snake Spits its Tongue
bái yuán xiàn guǒ	白猿献果	White Ape Presents Fruit
bēng quán	崩拳	Crushing Fist, Driving Punch
dài	带	Draw
dān mǎ xíng	单马形	Single Horse
dān zhǎn chì	单展翅	Stretch Out One Wing
dīng bù xià chā zhǎng	丁步下插掌	T Stance Stab Down
dǐng shì	顶势	Butt
dǐng zhǒu	顶肘	Elbow Butt
dǐng zì gōng	顶字功	Butting Skill
fān shēn pào	翻身炮	Wheel Around and Pound
fēng bǎi hē yè	风摆荷叶	Wind Sways the Lotus Leaves
gǔn shǒu	滚手	Trundle
guǒ shǒu	裹手	Wrap
guǒ zì gōng	裹字功	Wrapping Skill
hé jiān shì	合肩势	Close the Shoulders
hēi hǔ chū dòng	黑虎出洞	Black Tiger Leaves its Den
hēi xióng chū dòng	黑熊出洞	Black Bear Leaves its Den
héng dēng	横蹬	Crossways Heel Kick
héng jiāng fān làng	横江翻浪	Cross the River by Overturning the Waves
héng quán	横拳	Crosscut, Crossing Fist
hóu dūn	猴蹲	Monkey Sits on its Haunches
hóu xíng	猴形	Monkey Model
hǔ bào	虎抱	Tiger Embraces
hǔ chēng	虎撑	Tiger Braces
hǔ jié	虎截	Tiger Intercepts
hǔ lán	虎拦	Tiger Traps
hǔ pū	虎扑	Tiger Pounces
hǔ tuō	虎托	Tiger Carries
hǔ xíng	虎形	Tiger Model

jī xíng	鸡形	Chicken Model
jī xíng sì bǎ dòng zuò	鸡形四把动作	Four Techniques Of Chicken
jié shì	截势	Intercept
jié shǒu	截手	Interception
jié zì gōng	截字功	Intercepting Skill
jīn jī bào xiǎo	金鸡报晓	Golden Rooster Heralds the Dawn
jīn jī dēng jiǎo	金鸡蹬脚	Golden Rooster Thrusts a Foot
jīn jī dǒu líng	金鸡抖翎	Golden Rooster Shakes its Feathers
jīn jī dú lì	金鸡独立	Golden Rooster Stands on One Leg
jīn jī shàng jià	金鸡上架	Golden Rooster Blocks Up
jīn jī shí mǐ	金鸡食米	Golden Rooster Pecks a Grain of Rice
jīn jī tà xuě	金鸡踏雪	Golden Rooster Treads on Snow
jīn jī zhǎn chì	金鸡展翅	Golden Rooster Spreads its Wings
jīn jī zhuó shuǐ	金鸡啄水	Golden Rooster Drinks Water
kuà hǔ	跨虎	Sit Astride the Tiger
kuà shì	跨势	Bridge
kuà zì gōng	跨字功	Bridging Skill
lā bō dǎ	拉拨打	Pull, Knock Aside and Hit
lǎn lóng wò dào	懒龙卧道	Lazy Dragon Lies in the Road
lǎo xióng zhuàng bǎng	老熊撞膀	Old Bear Shoves from its Shoulder
lēi quán	勒拳	Restrain
liāo yīn zhǎng	撩阴掌	Slice to the Groin
lǐng shì	领势	Guide
lǐng zì gōng	领字功	Guiding Skill
lóng hǔ xiāng jiāo	龙虎相交	Dragon and Tiger Play Together
lóng xíng	龙形	Dragon Model
lōu shǒu gài pī	搂手盖劈	Brush Aside, Cover and Chop
lǔ dài	捋带	Stroking Draw
lǔ shǒu	捋手	Stroke or Pull
lǔ shǒu guàn ér	捋手贯耳	Stroke, Hook to Ear
lǔ shǒu xī zhuàng	捋手膝撞	Pull and Knee Butt
lūn pī héng zhé	抡劈横折	Swinging Chop with Crossing Cut
mǎ xíng	马形	Horse Model
māo xǐ liǎn	猫洗脸	Cat Washes its Face
měng hǔ tiào jiàn	猛虎跳涧	Fierce Tiger Jumps over the Ravine
pào quán	炮拳	Cannon Punch, Pounding Fist
pī quán	劈拳	Split, Splitting Fist
qǐ shì	起势	Opening Move

qiē bō	切脖	Cut to the Neck
sān pán luò dì	三盘落地	Three Basins on the Ground
sān zhǎng	三掌	Triple Palm Strike
shé chán shēn	蛇缠身	Snake Coils its Body
shé xíng	蛇形	Snake Model
shōu shì	收势	Closing Move
shuāng guǒ	双裹	Double Wrap
shuāng jié	双截	Double Intercept
shuāng mǎ xíng	双马形	Double Horse
shuāng zhǎn chì	双展翅	Spread Both Wings
shuāng zhuàng zhǎng	双撞掌	Double Shove
shùn shǒu qiān yáng	顺手牵羊	Lead a sheep along
shùn shuǐ tuī zhōu	顺水推舟	Push a Boat Downstream
sì jiǎo hóu xíng	四角猴形	Monkey To Four Corners
tà bù lóng xíng	踏步龙形	Stomping Dragon Model
tà zhǎng	踏掌	Tamp
tāi xíng	鸟台形	Wedge-tailed Hawk Model
tiǎo lǔ	挑捋	Scoop and Pull
tiǎo zhǎng	挑掌	Scoop
tiǎo zì gōng	挑字功	Scooping Skill
tōu dǎ	偷打	Sneak in a Hit
tóu dǐng	头顶	Head Butt
tuī chuāng wàng yuè	推窗望月	Push the Shutter to Gaze at the Moon
tuī shǒu	推手	Push
tuó xíng	鼍形	Alligator Model
wū lóng dào shuǐ	乌龙倒水	Black Dragon Pours Water
wū lóng fān jiāng	乌龙翻江	Black Dragon Overturns the Waves
xià bēng quán	下崩拳	Low Crushing Punch
xióng xíng	熊形	Bear Model
yǎn zhǒu	掩肘	Elbow Cover
yàn zǐ chāo shuǐ	燕子抄水	Swallow Skims the Water
yàn zǐ zhǎn chì	燕子展翅	Swallow Spreads its Wings
yàn zǐ zuān tiān	燕子钻天	Swallow Pierces the Sky
yào xíng	鹞形	Sparrow Hawk Model
yào zǐ fān shēn	鹞子翻身	Sparrow Hawk Wheels Over
yào zǐ rù lín	鹞子入林	Sparrow Hawk Enters the Woods
yào zǐ shù shēn	鹞子束身	Sparrow Hawk Folds its Wings
yào zǐ zhǎn chì	鹞子展翅	Sparrow Hawk Spreads its Wings

yào zǐ zhuā jiān	鹞子抓肩	Sparrow Hawk Grasps a Shoulder
yào zǐ zhuō què	鹞子捉雀	Sparrow Hawk Grasps a Sparrow
yào zǐ zuān tiān	鹞子钻天	Sparrow Hawk Pierces the Sky
yīng xíng	鹰形	Eagle Model
yīng xióng hé liàn	鹰熊合练	Eagle and Bear Combined
yīng zhuō	鹰捉	Eagle Grasps
yuán hóu dào shéng	猿猴捯绳	Monkey Pulls at its Leash
yuán hóu dēng zhī	猿猴蹬枝	Ape Kicks a Branch
yuán hóu guà yìn	白猿挂印	Monkey Scratches its Mark
yuán hóu pá gān	猿猴爬竿	Monkey Scrambles up a Pole
yuán hóu zhāi táo	猿猴摘桃	Ape Plucks a Peach
yuán hóu zhuì zhī	猿猴坠枝	Ape Drops off a Branch
yuè bù lóng xíng	跃步龙形	Leaping Dragon
yún shì	云势	Pass
yún zì gōng	云字功	Passing Skill
zāi dǎ	栽打	Plant a Hit
zhǎn shì	展势	Spread
zhǎn zì gōng	展字功	Spreading Skill
zhé lóng chū xiàn	蛰龙出现	Hibernating Dragon Shows Itself
zhèn jiǎo	震脚	Stamp
zhí tàng hóu xíng	直趟猴形	Straight Line Monkey Model
zhuàng zhǎng	撞掌	Shove
zuān dǎ	钻打	Drilling Hit
zuān quán	钻拳	Drill, Drilling Fist
zuǒ lǐng yòu zāi	左领右栽	Lead left and Stick in right

SECTION FOUR: TERMS THAT FURTHER DEFINE THE MOVEMENT TO MAKE UP THE FULL NAME

ào bù	拗步	Reverse Stance
chē bù	撤步	Withdraw
fān shēn	翻身	Wheel Around
huàn bù	换步	Switchover Step
huí shēn	回身	Step Around, Turn Around
jìn bù	进步	Advance
shàng bù	上步	Step Forward
shuāng	双	Double
shuāng shǒu	双手	Two-handed
shùn bù	顺步	Aligned Stance

tuì bù	退步	Retreat
yáo shēn	摇身	Dodge
yòu	右	Right
yuán bù, yuán dì	原地, 原步	Fixed Step, Stationary
zhèn jiǎo	震脚	Stamp
zhuàn shēn	转身	Turn Around
zuǒ	左	Left

SECTION FIVE: PARTS OF WEAPONS

bà	把	base, the thick end of a long weapon. the hilt of a short weapon
bà duàn	把段	aft-section of blade or shaft, third nearest the grip or butt
bēi blade	背	blade spine, the non-sharp edge of a broadsword
bǐng	柄	guard of the grip of a short weapon
gǎn	杆	shaft, the wooden section of staff or spear
jiān, jiānr	尖	tip of sharp weapon
lì rèn	立刃	standing blade: blade edges up and down relative to the hand
pán	盘	guard of the grip of a short weapon
píng rèn hand	平刃	flat blade: blade edges side to side relative to the
qián duàn	前段	fore-section of blade or shaft (the third nearest the tip)
qiāng tóu	枪头	spear head
qiāng yīng	枪缨	spear tassel
rèn, rènr	刃	blade edge, the sharp edge
shàng rèn	上	upper edge: top edge (the thumb side) of blade
shēn	身	blade body, the whole blade
xià rèn	下刃	under edge: bottom edge (finger side) of blade
zhōng duàn	中段	midsection of blade or shaft, middle third

SECTION SIX: WEAPONS TERMS

bǎ	把	grip, hold, grasp a weapon
bēng	崩	snap, also for crossing snap. thrust, stab as one of the five

elements.

bō	拨	check, knock to the side
bō yún	拨云	checking brandish, first check to the side with the tip, then swing over the head
cáng dāo	藏刀	hide a broadsword; draw a broadsword behind
chán tóu	缠头	coil (a broadsword around) the head (from left shoulder to right shoulder)
chuō	戳	poke; stab with a blunt weapon, with the tip or butt
cì	刺	pierce, stab with a thin blade
cuò	错	rub
dài	带	draw back
dāo	刀	broadsword, sabre: curved single edged blade
diǎn	点	poke in, point; an action like dotting in calligraphy
diāo bǎ,	刁把,	grip, hanging (on the grip of a short weapon): to let the tip drop
fǎn cì	反刺	reverse pierce, hand or weapon turned over
fǎn pī	反劈	reverse grip chop, hand or weapon turned over
gài bù	盖步	cross-over stance, foot steps across in front
gài pī	盖劈	covering chop, chop folding a staff in on the arm
gé	格	block across
guà	挂	hook, trap with weapon, hook bladed weapons using the spine, or upper edge
gùn	棍	staff
guǒ nǎo	裹脑	wrap (a broadsword around) the head (from right shoulder to left shoulder)
héng	横	crosscut
huō	㧗	scull; a low drag on the side, from the rear
huō liāo	㧗撩	sculling slice: start with a low drag from the rear, coming forward with a high slice
huō tiǎo	㧗挑	sculling scoop: start with a low drag from the rear, coming forward with a scoop up (elbow bent)
jiàn	剑	sword, straight blade double edged sword
jiàn zhǐ zhǎng	剑指掌	sword fingers palm; index and middle fingers straight, other fingers bent and pressed with the thumb
jiǎo	绞	entangle, stir with a blade or shaft tip, hand draws a

		small circle to make the tip draw a large circle
kǎn	砍	hack, a short hard chop
lán	拦	trap, outer (counterclockwise circle and press)
lán ná zhā	拦拿扎	outer trap, inner trap, stab: spear technique
lì jiàn	立剑	standing blade of sword: edges vertical relative to the hand
liāo	撩	slice, slice up, arm relatively straight
lū	撸	punt, a low block with a long weapon, almost stirring action
luó bǎ	螺把	grip, spiral (on the grip of a short weapon)
mǎn bǎ	满把	grip, full (on the grip of a short weapon): grip with all fingers and full palm contact
ná	拿	trap, inner (clockwise circle and press)
pào	炮	slash
pī	劈	chop, strike vertically down
píng cì	平刺	level pierce
píng jiàn	平剑	flat blade of sword: edges horizontal relative to the strike
qián bǎ	钳把	grip, pincer (on the grip of a short weapon): hold mainly with the thumb, index, and middle fingers, and only lightly with the ring and little fingers.
qiāng	枪	spear
quān qiāng	圈枪	encircle with spear, full circles
sǎo	扫	sweep, a large, low circle
shàng guà	上挂	hook up
sōng wò	松握	grip, relaxed, can let shaft slide through
tí	提	lift
tiǎo	挑	scoop; bring a weapon up with the wrist cocked and/or elbow bent
tiǎo bà	挑把	scoop with the butt
tuī	推	push with flat of the blade or shaft of a long weapon
xià guà	下挂	hook down to trap with spine of weapon
xiāo	削	slice, usually down diagonally
yā	压	press down
yún	云	brandish horizontally, usually over the head

zhā	扎	stab, used for spear and broadsword
zhǎn	斩	cut
zuān	钻	drill

SECTION SEVEN: XINGYI PEOPLE REFERRED TO IN THE BOOK

Cao Jiwu (1622-1722) 曹继武. Apprenticed in Xinyi Liuhequan with Ji Longfeng.

Che Yizhai (1883-1914) 车毅斋. Apprenticed in Xingyiquan with Li Luoneng. Also known as Che Yonghong 车永宏.

Dai Longbang (c. 1713-1802) 戴龙帮. Apprenticed in Xinyi Liuhequan with Cao Jiwu.

Di Guoyong (1948-) 邸国勇. Apprenticed in Shaolinquan and Xingyiquan with Zhao Zhong.

Guo Yunshen (late Qing dynasty) 郭云深. Apprenticed in Xingyiquan with Li Luoneng. Famous for his driving punch. Also known as Guo Yusheng 郭峪生.

Hao En'guang (late Qing dynasty) 郝恩光. Apprenticed in Xingyiquan with Li Cunyi.

Ji Longfeng (1602-1680) 姬龙峰. Thought to have created Xinyi Liuhequan. Also known as Ji Longfeng 姬龙风 and Ji Jike 姬际可.

Li Cunyi (1847-1921) 李存义. Apprenticed in Xingyiquan with Liu Qilan.

Li Luoneng (c. 1808-1890) 李洛能. Apprenticed in Xinyi Liuhequan with Dai Longbang. Thought to have created Xingyiquan. Proper name Li Feiyu 李飞羽.

Liu Huafu (dates unknown) 刘华甫. Apprenticed in Xingyiquan with Shang Yunxiang.

Liu Qilan (late Qing dynasty) 刘奇兰. Apprenticed in Xingyiquan with Li Luoneng.

Shang Yunxiang (1863-1937) 尚云祥. Apprenticed in Xingyiquan with Li Zhihe and Li Cunyi.

Yue Fei (1103-1142) 岳飞. A famous general and hero of the Song dynasty. Legendary creator of Xingyiquan.

Zhao Zhong (1912-1978) 赵忠. Apprenticed in Xingyiquan with Liu Huafu.

ENGLISH ORDER

SECTION EIGHT: BASIC PARTS OF THE BODY

abdomen, belly	fù	腹
arm, upper or whole arm	bēi or bì	臂
back of the fist	quán bèi	拳背
base of the fist	quán lún	拳轮

chest	xiōng	胸
deltoid area, upper arm and shoulder	bǎng	膀
ear	ěr	耳
elbow	zhǒu	肘
fingers	shǒu zhǐ	手指
fist	quán	拳
fist eye, formed by thumb and index finger	quán yǎn	拳眼
foot	jiǎo	脚
forearm	qián bì, or qián bēi	前臂
hand	shǒu	手
head	tóu	头
heart	xīn	心
heart of the fist, into which the fingers curl	quán xīn	拳心
heel	gēn, jiǎo gēn	跟，脚跟
hip joint	kuà	胯
kidney	shèn	肾
knee	xī, often pronounced qī	膝
knuckles	quán miàn	拳面
knuckle edge	quán fēng	拳峰
leg	tuǐ	腿
liver	gān	肝
lungs	fèi	肺
nape of neck	jǐng	颈
neck	bō	脖
palm	zhǎng	掌
palm centre	zhǎng xīn	掌心
ribs	lèi	肋
shank, lower leg	xiǎo tuǐ	小腿
shoulder	jiān, also called jiān bǎng	肩，肩膀
small of the back, waist, lumbar area	yāo	腰
solar plexus, pit of the stomach	xīn wōr	心窝
spleen	pí	脾
thigh	dà tuǐ	大腿
thumb to forefinger web, the 'tiger's mouth'	hǔ kǒu	虎口
ulnar bone; little finger side of forearm	chǐ gǔ	尺骨
upper back	bèi	背
wrist	shǒu wàn	手腕

SECTION NINE: XINGYI TERMINOLOGY

advance, enter: step the front foot forward	jìn bù	进步
aligned stance, same hand and foot forward	shùn bù	顺步
block across	gé	格
bow stance	gōng bù	弓步
brace out	chēng	撑
brush aside	lōu	搂
cannon punch, pounding fist	pào quán	炮拳
carry; to hit or break	tuō	托
character eight stance	bā zì bù	八字步
check	cuò	挫
chicken stepping,	jī xíng bù	鸡形步
circular block, trap	lán	拦
clear or obvious power, hard power	míng jìn	明劲
coil the hand	chǎn shǒu	缠手
contract, draw in or draw back	suō shēn	缩身
controlling order of the five elements	wǔ xíng xiāng kè	五行相克
cover; a controlling move downwards	gài	盖
crosscut, crossing fist	héng quán	横拳
crossways or transverse movement or placement	héng	横
cut, slice	qiē	切
dantian, usually means the lower *dantian*	dān tián	丹田
draw out	chōu	抽
draw, drag towards the rear	dài	带
drill, drilling fist	zuān quán	钻拳
drive, crushing fist	bēng quán	崩拳
earth, one of the five elements	tǔ	土
elbow cover	yǎn zhǒu	掩肘
embrace, cradle, hold in the crook of the arms	bào	抱
entangle, wind around	jiǎo	绞
fire, one of the five elemental elements	huǒ	火
five basic techniques of Xingyiquan	wǔ xíng quán	五行拳
five elemental fists connected form	wǔ xíng lián huán (quán)	五行连环（拳）
fixed stance	dìng bù	定步
follow, smooth	shùn	顺
follow-in step	gēn bù	跟步
form, the external structure	xíng	形
generating order of the five elements	wǔ xíng xiāng shēng	五行相生

grab	zhuā	抓
half horse stance	bàn mǎ bù	半马步
hard power	gāng jìn	刚劲
heart, the emotional mind	xīn	心
hidden power	àn jìn	暗劲
hit	dǎ	打
hoist	chāo	抄
hook-in step	kòu bù	扣步
hooking block	guà	挂
hook-out step	bǎi bù	摆步
horse stance	mǎ bù	马步
inside hook punch	guàn	贯
intercept, cut across	jié	截
kick	tī	踢
knock aside	bō	拨
knock, bump	kē	磕
land, lower	luò	落
launch power. release, strength or energy	fā jìn, fā lì	发劲，发力
lead along	lǐng	领
lower the dragon post standing	jiàng lóng zhuāng	降龙桩
meridian post standing	zǐ wǔ zhuāng	子午桩
metal, one of the five elements	jīn	金
mother fists	xíng yì mǔ quán	形意母拳
moving stance	huó bù	活步
one inch power	cùn jìn	寸劲
open parallel stance, shoulder width	kāi bù	开步
palm down	fǔ zhǎng	俯掌
palm up	yǎng zhǎng	仰掌
pluck	zhāi	摘
post standing	zhàn zhuāng	站桩
post standing training	zhuāng gōng	桩功
pounce	pū	扑
pounding post training	zá zhuāng	砸桩
pounding strike with the fist	zá quán	砸拳
press down	àn	按
press down, control	yā	压
primordial post standing	hún yuán zhuāng	浑元桩
primordial, or mixed essence	hún yuán	浑元

pull	lā	拉
pull hand over hand	dáo	捯
raking power	bā lì	扒力
relax and extend, release the tension	sōng	松
remove, move something	bān	搬
resting stance, legs crossed and sitting	xiē bù	歇步
retreat	tuì bù	退步
reverse stance	ào bù	拗步
rise; initiate an action	qǐ	起
scoop	tiǎo	挑
settle the *qi* down	chén qì	沉气
shaking the body, dodging	yáo shēn	摇身
shoot (as with a catapult); springy, elastic	tán	弹
shove, barge into	zhuàng	撞
sink the wrist	tā wàn	塌腕
slap or control with an open palm	pāi	拍
slice up with a relatively straight arm	liāo	撩
split, chop down	pī quán	劈拳
squat	dūn	蹲
stamp with impetus forward and down	cuō dì	蹉地
stand with feet together	bīng bù	并步
step forward	shàng bù	上步
stomp; a heavy stamp	zhèn jiǎo	震脚
stride; a large step	mài bù	迈步
subdue the tiger post standing	fú hǔ zhuāng	伏虎桩
three attributes standing	sān cái zhuāng	三才桩
three bodies or trinity stance	sān tǐ shì	三体式
three bodies or trinity post standing	sān tǐ shì zhuāng	三体势桩
train skill	liàn gōng	练功
trample, step on	cǎi	踩
transformed power	huà jìn	化劲
trap, hold	ná	拿
tuck in, concave shape	kòu	扣
turn around	zhuàn shēn	转身
twisting power	níng jìn	拧劲
urge, hurry, press	cuī	催
vital energy, breath, life force; air	qì	气
water, one of the five elements	shuǐ	水

will, intent, the intentional mind	yì	意
withdraw	chè bù	撤步
wood, one of the five elements	mù	木
wrap around, enclose in the arms	guǒ	裹
wrapping power	guǒ jìn	裹劲
Xingyiquan, 'form combined with intent' style	xíng yì quán	形意拳
Xinyi Liuhe Quan	xīn yì liù hé quán	心意六合拳
Yiquan, also called Dachengquan	yì quán	意拳

SECTION TEN: XINGYI MOVEMENT NAMES

Alligator Model	tuó xíng	鼍形
Ape Drops off a Branch	yuán hóu zhuì zhī	猿猴坠枝
Ape Kicks a Branch	yuán hóu dēng zhī	猿猴蹬枝
Ape Plucks a Peach	yuán hóu zhāi táo	猿猴摘桃
Bear Model	xióng xíng	熊形
Black Bear Leaves its Den	hēi xióng chū dòng	黑熊出洞
Black Dragon Overturns the Waves	wū lóng fān jiāng	乌龙翻江
Black Dragon Pours Water	wū lóng dào shuǐ	乌龙倒水
Black Tiger Leaves its Den	hēi hǔ chū dòng	黑虎出洞
Bridge	kuà shì	跨势
Bridging Skill	kuà zì gōng	跨字功
Brush Aside, Cover and Chop	lōu shǒu gài pī	搂手盖劈
Butt	dǐng shì	顶势
Butting Skill	dǐng zì gōng	顶字功
Cannon Punch, Pounding Fist	pào quán	炮拳
Cat Washes its Face	māo xǐ liǎn	猫洗脸
Chicken Model	jī xíng	鸡形
Close the Shoulders	hé jiān shì	合肩势
Closing Move	shōu shì	收势
Cross the River by Overturning the Waves	héng jiāng fān làng	横江翻浪
Crosscut, Crossing Fist	héng quán	横拳
Crossways Heel Kick	héng dēng	横蹬
Crushing Fist, Driving Punch	bēng quán	崩拳
Cut to the Neck	qiē bó	切脖
Double Horse	shuāng mǎ xíng	双马形
Double Intercept	shuāng jié	双截
Double Wrap	shuāng guǒ	双裹
Double Shove	shuāng zhuàng zhǎng	双撞掌

Dragon and Tiger Play Together	lóng hǔ xiāng jiāo	龙虎相交
Dragon Model	lóng xíng	龙形
Draw	dài	带
Drill, Drilling Fist	zuān quán	钻拳
Drilling Hit	zuān dǎ	钻打
Driving Punch, Crushing Fist	bēng quán	崩拳
Eagle and Bear Combined	yīng xióng hé liàn	鹰熊合练
Eagle Model	yīng xíng	鹰形
Eagle Grasps	yīng zhuō	鹰捉
Eight Skills	bā zì gōng	八字功
Elbow Butt	dǐng zhǒu	顶肘
Elbow Cover	yǎn zhǒu	掩肘
Fierce Tiger Jumps over the Ravine	měng hǔ tiào jiàn	猛虎跳涧
Wheel Around and Pound	fān shēn pào	翻身炮
Four Techniques Of Chicken	jī xíng sì bǎ dòng zuò	鸡形四把动作
Golden Rooster Blocks Up	jīn jī shàng jià	金鸡上架
Golden Rooster Drinks Water	jīn jī zhuó shuǐ	金鸡啄水
Golden Rooster Heralds the Dawn	jīn jī bào xiǎo	金鸡报晓
Golden Rooster Pecks a Grain of Rice	jīn jī shí mǐ	金鸡食米
Golden Rooster Shakes its Feathers	jīn jī dǒu líng	金鸡抖翎
Golden Rooster Spreads its Wings	jīn jī zhǎn chì	金鸡展翅
Golden Rooster Stands on One Leg	jīn jī dú lì	金鸡独立
Golden Rooster Thrusts a Foot	jīn jī dēng jiǎo	金鸡蹬脚
Golden Rooster Treads on Snow	jīn jī tà xuě	金鸡踏雪
Guide	lǐng shì	领势
Guiding Skill	lǐng zì gōng	领字功
Head Butt	tóu dǐng	头顶
Hibernating Dragon Shows Itself	zhé lóng chū xiàn	蛰龙出现
Horse Model	mǎ xíng	马形
Intercept	jié shì	截势
Intercepting Skill	jié zì gōng	截字功
Interception	jié shǒu	截手
Lazy Dragon Lies in the Road	lǎn lóng wò dào	懒龙卧道
Lead a Sheep Along	shùn shǒu qiān yáng	顺手牵羊
Lead left and Stick in right	zuǒ lǐng yòu zāi	左领右栽
Leaping Dragon	yuè bù lóng xíng	跃步龙形
Low Crushing Punch	xià bēng quán	下崩拳
Monkey To Four Corners	sì jiǎo hóu xíng	四角猴形

Monkey Model	hóu xíng	猴形
Monkey Pulls at its Leash	yuán hóu dào shéng	猿猴捯绳
Monkey Scrambles up a Pole	yuán hóu pá gān	猿猴爬竿
Monkey Scratches its Mark	yuán hóu guà yìn	白猿挂印
Monkey Sits on its Haunches	hóu dūn	猴蹲
Old Bear Shoves from its Shoulder	lǎo xióng zhuàng bǎng	老熊撞膀
Opening Move	qǐ shì	起势
Pass	yún shì	云势
Passing Skill	yún zì gōng	云字功
Plant a Hit	zāi dǎ	栽打
Pounding Fist, Cannon Punch	pào quán	炮拳
Pull and Knee Butt	lǔ shǒu xī zhuàng	捋手膝撞
Pull, Knock Aside and Hit	lā bō dǎ	拉拨打
Push a Boat Downstream	shùn shuǐ tuī zhōu	顺水推舟
Push the Shutter to Gaze at the Moon	tuī chuāng wàng yuè	推窗望月
Push	tuī shǒu	推手
Restrain	lēi quán	勒拳
Scoop and Pull	tiǎo lǔ	挑捋
Scoop	tiǎo zhǎng	挑掌
Scooping Skill	tiǎo zì gōng	挑字功
Shove	zhuàng zhǎng	撞掌
Single Horse	dān mǎ xíng	单马形
Sit Astride the Tiger	kuà hǔ	跨虎
Slice to the Groin	liāo yīn zhǎng	撩阴掌
Snake Coils its Body	shé chán shēn	蛇缠身
Snake Model	shé xíng	蛇形
Sneak in a Hit	tōu dǎ	偷打
Sparrow Hawk Enters the Woods	yào zǐ rù lín	鹞子入林
Sparrow Hawk Folds its Wings	yào zǐ shù shēn	鹞子束身
Sparrow Hawk Model	yào xíng	鹞形
Sparrow Hawk Grasps a Shoulder	yào zǐ zhuā jiān	鹞子抓肩
Sparrow Hawk Grasps a Sparrow	yào zǐ zhuō què	鹞子捉雀
Sparrow Hawk Pierces the Sky	yào zǐ zuān tiān	鹞子钻天
Sparrow Hawk Spreads its Wings	yào zǐ zhǎn chì	鹞子展翅
Sparrow Hawk Wheels Over	yào zǐ fān shēn	鹞子翻身
Split, Splitting Fist	pī quán	劈拳
Spread Both Wings	shuāng zhǎn chì	双展翅
Spread	zhǎn shì	展势

Spreading Skill	zhǎn zì gōng	展字功
Stamp	zhèn jiǎo	震脚
Stomping Dragon Model	tà bù lóng xíng	踏步龙形
Straight Line Monkey Model	zhí tàng hóu xíng	直趟猴形
Stretch Out One Wing	dān zhǎn chì	单展翅
Stroke or Pull	lǔ shǒu	捋手
Stroke, Hook to Ear	lǔ shǒu guàn ér	捋手贯耳
Stroking Draw	lǔ dài	捋带
Swallow Pierces the Sky	yàn zǐ zuān tiān	燕子钻天
Swallow Skims the Water	yàn zǐ chāo shuǐ	燕子抄水
Swallow Spreads its Wings	yàn zǐ zhǎn chì	燕子展翅
Swinging Chop with Crossing Cut	lūn pī héng zhé	抡劈横折
T Stance Stab Down	dīng bù xià chā zhǎng	丁步下插掌
Tamp	tà zhǎng	踏掌
Three Basins on the Ground	sān pán luò dì	三盘落地
Tiger Braces	hǔ chēng	虎撑
Tiger Carries	hǔ tuō	虎托
Tiger Embraces	hǔ bào	虎抱
Tiger Model	hǔ xíng	虎形
Tiger Intercepts	hǔ jié	虎截
Tiger Pounces	hǔ pū	虎扑
Tiger Traps	hǔ lán	虎拦
Triple Palm Strike	sān zhǎng	三掌
Trundle	gǔn shǒu	滚手
Wedge-tailed Hawk Model	tāi xíng	鸟台形
White Ape Presents Fruit	bái yuán xiàn guǒ	白猿献果
White Crane Flashes Its Wings	bái hè liàng chì	白鹤亮翅
White Snake Coils its Body	bái shé chǎn shēn	白蛇缠身
White Snake Slithers through the Grass	bái shé bō cǎo	白蛇拨草
White Snake Spits its Tongue	bái shé tù xìn	白蛇吐信
Wind Sways the Lotus Leaves	fēng bǎi hē yè	风摆荷叶
Wrap	guǒ shǒu	裹手
Wrapping Skill	guǒ zì gōng	裹字功

SECTION ELEVEN: TERMS THAT FURTHER DEFINE THE MOVEMENT TO MAKE UP THE FULL NAME

Advance	jìn bù	进步
Aligned Stance	shùn bù	顺步

Dodge	yáo shēn	摇身
Double	shuāng	双
Fixed Step, Stationary	yuán bù	原步
	yuán dì	原地
Left	zuǒ	左
Retreat	tuì bù	退步
Reverse Stance	ào bù	拗步
Right	yòu	右
Stamp	zhèn jiǎo	震脚
Step Around, Turn Around	huí shēn	回身
Step Forward	shàng bù	上步
Switchover Step	huàn bù	换步
Turn Around	zhuàn shēn	转身
Two-handed	shuāng shǒu	双手
Wheel Around	fān shēn	翻身
Withdraw	chē bù	撤步

SECTION TWELVE: PARTS OF WEAPONS

Aft-section of blade or shaft	bà duàn	把段
Base, butt of a long weapon	bà	把
Blade body, the whole blade	shēn	身
Blade edge	rèn, rènr	刃
Blade spine	bēi	背
Fore-section of blade or shaft	qián duàn	前段
Flat blade	píng rèn	平刃
Guard of the grip of a short weapon	bǐng or pán	柄，盘
Hilt of a short weapon	bà	把
Midsection of blade or shaft, middle third	zhōng duàn	中段
Shaft	gǎn	杆
Spear tassel	qiāng yīng	枪缨
Spear head	qiāng tóu	枪头
Standing blade	lì rèn	立刃
Tip of sharp weapon	jiān, jiānr	尖
Under edge of blade	xià rèn	下刃
Upper edge	shàng rèn	上刃

SECTION THIRTEEN: WEAPONS TERMINOLOGY

| Block across | gé | 格 |
| Brandish horizontally, usually over the head | yún | 云 |

Broadsword, sabre	dāo	刀
Check	bō	拨
Checking brandish	bō yún	拨云
Chop	pī	劈
Coil the head	chán tóu	缠头
Covering chop	gài pī	盖劈
Crosscut	héng	横
Cross-over stance	gài bù	盖步
Cut	zhǎn	斩
Draw back	dài	带
Drill	zuān	钻
Encircle with spear	quān qiāng	圈枪
Entangle	jiǎo	绞
Flat blade of sword	píng jiàn	平剑
Full grip	mǎn bǎ	满把
Grip, hold	bǎ	把
Hack	kǎn	砍
Hanging Grip	diāo bǎ	刁把,
Hde a broadsword	cáng dāo	藏刀
Hook down to trap with spine	xià guà	下挂
Hook, trap with weapon	guà	挂
Hook up	shàng guà	上挂
Inner trap	ná	拿
Level pierce	píng cì	平刺
Lift	tī	提
Outer trap	lán	拦
Outer trap, inner trap, stab	lán ná zhā	拦拿扎
Pierce	cì	刺
Pincer grip	qián bǎ	钳把
Poke in	diǎn	点
Poke	chuō	戳
Press down	yā	压
Punt	lū	撸
Push with flat of the blade or shaft of a long weapon	tuī	推
Relaxed grip	sōng wò	松握
Reverse pierce, hand or weapon turned over	fǎn cì	反刺
Reverse grip chop, hand or weapon turned over	fǎn pī	反劈
Rub	cuò	错

Scoop	tiǎo	挑
Scoop with the butt	tiǎo bà	挑把
SculL	huō	攉
Sculling scoop	huō tiǎo	攉挑
Sculling slice	huō liāo	攉撩
Slash	pào	炮
Slice	liāo	撩
Slice, usually down diagonally	xiāo	削
Snap, also for crossing snap	bēng	崩
Spiral grip	luó bǎ	螺把
Staff	gùn	棍
Spear	qiāng	枪
Stab	zhā	扎
Standing blade	lì jiàn	立剑
Stir	jiǎo	绞
Sword	jiàn	剑
Sweep	sǎo	扫
Sword fingers palm	jiàn zhǐ zhǎng	剑指掌
Thrust	bēng	崩
Wrap (a broadsword around) the head)	guǒ nǎo	裹脑

PRONUNCIATION OF PINYIN, THE CHINESE NATIONAL PHONETIC ALPHABET (WITH INTERNATIONAL PHONETIC ALPHABET EQUIVALENTS)

INITIALS (words can start with these consonants, or have a glide or vowel initial)

PINYIN	IPA	ROUGH PRONUNCIATION GUIDE
p	p^h	Like English pet with a considerable puff of air.
b	p	Similar to the *pinyin* "p" but without the puff of air (unvoiced, neither English pet nor bet).
t	t^h	Like English tag with a considerable puff of air.
d	t	Similar to the *pinyin* "t" but with no puff of air (unvoiced, not dog).
k	k^h	Like English kill with a considerable puff of air.
g	k	Similar to the *pinyin* "k" but with no puff of air (unvoiced, not English get).
c	ts^h	Like exaggerating English cats.
z	ts	Like the *pinyin* "c" but without the puff of air (unvoiced).
ch	$tʂ^h$	Somewhat similar to English chat with a puff of air, but with the tip of the tongue rolled back.
zh	tʂ	Like the *pinyin* "ch" but with no puff of air (unvoiced).
q	$tþ^h$	Somewhat similar to English chat with a puff of air, but with the front of the tongue raised and the tip on the lower teeth.
j	tþ	Like the *pinyin* "q" but without the puff of air (unvoiced).
m	m	Like English met.
n	n	Like English net.
f	f	Similar to English fat, but with the teeth just touching lightly behind the lower lip.
s	s	Similar to English set.
sh	ʂ	Somewhat similar to English show, but with the same tongue placement as the *pinyin* "ch" and "zh."
x	þ	Somewhat similar to English shine but with the same tongue placement as the *pinyin* "q" and "j."

h	χ	Raise the back of the tongue and let the breath come through the obstructed passage without vibrating the vocal cords.
l	l	Like English l̲et.
r	ɻ	Like the *pinyin* "sh" but with voicing.

FINALS

n	n	Like English pin̲.
ng	ŋ	Like English si̲n̲g̲.

VOWELS

a	A a ɛ	Usually close to English fa̲ther (not pa̲t). Like ye̲t when written "-ian" or "yan."
e	ɣ e ɛ ə	Usually similar to English pe̲t, can tend towards a mid vowel.
i	i ɭ ɪ	Usually similar to English be̲e. Similar to we̲t when written "ui." After c, z, s, ch, zh, sh, and r it is similar to si̲r.
o	o u	Usually close to English ro̲ll. Similar to co̲w when written "ao," and o̲w̲e̲ when in "ou."
u	u y	Usually similar t English o bo̲ot. After the *pinyin* "x", "q", and "j" and in the vowel groups starting with these consonants, it is pronounced "ü".
ü	y	Similar to French ü̲. It is written after "n" or "l," because these are the only positions where both "u" and "ü" are possible
y	i	A glide, partially like an English 'y', tending towards i.
w	u	A glide, partially like an English 'w', tending towards u.

INITIAL CONSONANTS

place of articulation	manner of articulation						
	Unaspirated Stops	Aspirated Stops	Unaspirated Affricates	Aspirated Affricates	Nasals	Fricatives	Voiced Continuants
bilabials	b	p			m		
labio-dentals						f	
dental-alveolars	d	t	z	c	n	s	l
retroflexes			zh	ch		sh	r
palatals			j	q		x	
velars	g	k				h	

TONES IN PINYIN			
NUMBER	PINYIN	NAME	RANGE
1	ˉ	high level	55
2	´	high rising	35
3	ˇ	dipping	214
4	`	high falling	51
none	° or blank	neutral	in context

With tone sandhi, tones may change according to the preceding or following tone.

The tone marking is put over the main vowel when there are two vowels written together (usually involving the pronunciation of y or w).

ABOUT THE TRANSLATOR

Andrea Falk has practised external and internal Chinese martial arts since 1972, and has concentrated on internal styles since 1981. She met Di Guoyong in 2001 and has trained with him since then.

She moved from her hometown of Victoria to hone her skills in Vancouver, Beijing, and Shanghai – to receive a Bachelor of Arts majoring in Chinese, a Bachelor of Physical Education and later a Master of Physical Education with an emphasis on coaching science from the University of British Columbia. She trained in wushu full time from 1980 to 1983 at the Beijing Physical Culture Institute, earning an advanced studies diploma in wushu under the tutelage of professor Xia Bohua, and teaching from others. There she learned the basics of Yang and Chen style Taijiquan, Baguazhang, Xingyiquan, Chaquan, Tongbeiquan, and modern Wushu (long fist and weapons). After spending the summers of 1984 and 1986 at the Institute, she started learning purely traditionally, visiting China on extended trips as often as possible. She has trained Chen style Taijiquan and Jiang Rongqiao's Baguazhang as an inside apprentice of Huan Dahai and fellow apprentice of Cai Yuhua and Cheng Jiefeng in Shanghai; Xingyiquan and Baguazhang with Di Guoyong in Beijing; Baguazhang with Li Baohua in Beijing; and Baguazhang weapons with Lu Yan in Beijing. When not in China or traveling to teach, she is usually in Québec city or at a cottage in the Laurentian hills, Canada.

Andrea has worked teaching and translating since 1983. She founded the wushu centre in Montreal in 1984, in Victoria in 1992, and has been based again in Quebec since 2003. She has taught Chen Taijiquan, Baguazhang, and Xingyiquan around North America and Europe, but especially in Canada and England. For years Andrea translated materials for her own students, and in 2000 set up tgl books to try to bring the best Chinese martial arts books to a wider audience.

tgl books

trois gros lapins traversent le chemin

ISBN 978-1-989468-24-1

CPSIA information can be obtained
at www.ICGtesting.com
Printed in the USA
LVHW060031280122
709447LV00005B/119